THE BEGINNING OF HUMAN LIFE

THE BEGINNING OF HUMAN LIFE

Edited by

FRITZ K. BELLER AND ROBERT F. WEIR

Department of Obstetrics and Gynecology, The University of Iowa, U.S.A.

Kluwer Academic Publishers

Dordrecht / Boston / London

Library of Congress Cataloging-in-Publication Data

The Beginning of human life / edited by Fritz K. Beller, Robert F. Weir.
p. cm.
Includes index.
ISBN 0-7923-2165-0 (acid-free paper)
1. Human reproductive technology--Moral and ethical aspects--Congresses. 2. Unborn children (Law)--Congresses. 3. Fetal tissues--Research--United States--Congresses. 4. Pregnant women--Legal status, laws, etc.--Congresses. 5. Infants (Newborn)--Diseases--Treatment--Moral and ethical aspects--Congresses.
I. Beller, Fritz K. II. Weir, Robert F., 1943- .
RG133.5.B44 1993
179'.7--dc20 93-2827

ISBN 0-7923-2165-0

Published by Kluwer Academic Publishers,
P.O. Box 17, 3300 AA Dordrecht, The Netherlands.

Kluwer Academic Publishers incorporates
the publishing programmes of
D. Reidel, Martinus Nijhoff, Dr W. Junk and MTP Press.

Sold and distributed in the U.S.A. and Canada
by Kluwer Academic Publishers,
101 Philip Drive, Norwell, MA 02061, U.S.A.

In all other countries, sold and distributed
by Kluwer Academic Publishers Group,
P.O. Box 322, 3300 AH Dordrecht, The Netherlands.

Printed on acid-free paper

Printed in the Netherlands

Table of Contents

Part III. Contraception and Abortion

Part IV. Fetal Research and Fetal Tissue

Part V. Medical, Ethical, and Legal Aspects of Maternal/Fetal Relationships

Part VI. Rights and Obligations Related to the Beginning of Individual Human Lives

Preface

Progress in biomedical science and clinical medicine has in recent years provided great opportunities for the enhancement of human conception, the prevention and treatment of disease in fetuses and neonates, and the prolongation of young human lives. At the same time obstetricians and pediatricians, medical scientists, biomedical ethicists, health law attorneys, nurses, and numerous other concerned persons around the globe have been confronted with increasingly difficult ethical and legal issues connected with the advances of medical technology.

These developments have called for an international discussion of the medical, ethical, and legal problems that confront physicians, medical researchers, infertile couples, pregnant women, and parents of premature or disabled infants. In addition, the unprecedented technological developments in obstetrical, perinatal, and neonatal medicine in recent years have indicated a need for an international forum for interdisciplinary dialogue regarding the definition of early human life, the neurological development of early human life, the value of early human life, the obligations for its protection and prolongation, and the limits to these obligations.

On November 4–7, 1990, the University of Iowa held an International Symposium on the Beginning of Human Life to address some of these concerns. The symposium organizing committee consisted of Fritz K. Beller, M.D., and Robert F. Weir, Ph.D., both from the University of Iowa, and Hans-Martin Sass, Ph.D., from Georgetown University. The symposium organizers, working with generous funding from the Schering Company in Germany and the Ford Foundation in the United States, decided on the issues that were to be addressed and then proceeded to enlist the best speakers on the topics from a number of countries.

The result was a symposium that included 24 speakers of international standing (in medicine, ethics, or law) from five countries, 34 moderators and panelists from ten countries, members of several religions traditions (Hinduism, Judaism, Christianity, and Islam), and an international audience for the meeting in Iowa City. Fortunately, most of the speakers and panelists were in our "first choice" category, Unfortunately, some persons invited as speakers could

F.K. Beller and R.F. Weir (eds.), The Beginning of Human Life, ix–xiii.

not come, thus omitting a few philosophical and religious perspectives that would have made the symposium even more comprehensive.

The format for the symposium emphasized the importance of interdisciplinary exchange. Each symposium session had two parts. During the first part, three to four invited speakers addressed the session theme by presenting state-of-the-art medical information, analyzing ethical aspects of the issue under discussion, or interpreting legal implications of the issue in several countries. The second part of each session consisted of an international panel of four to five professionals who made short presentations on the session theme from the perspectives of their various disciplines and countries of residence.

Most of the major papers presented at the symposium are contained, in revised form, in this book. Some of the better papers by panelists are included as well. The result is not a proceedings volume from the symposium, but a collection of revised papers that represents, in our judgment, the strongest contributions made to the symposium. We regret that not all the papers presented at the symposium could be published in this volume, but limitations of space and resources compelled us finally to exclude even some of the papers we originally projected for the book. For the same reason, we have not included any of the discussion from the audience that occurred during the symposium.

The book is organized in six parts. Part I, entitled "General Perspectives," provides an overview of some of the issues and themes that are discussed more specifically later in the book. The first three papers, in particular, offer interpretations of a range of issues in obstetrics, perinatology, and neonatology from the perspectives of medicine, ethics, and law. Fritz Beller and Gail Zlatnik begin the book with a wide-ranging discussion of the status of the human fetus, neuromaturation during gestation, viability, personhood, and related matters of concern regarding medical aspects of the beginning of individual human lives. Robert Veatch uses the ongoing definition-of-death debate as a way of presenting alternative interpretations of the beginning of individual human lives, focusing on the questions of when and why some human lives have "full moral standing." Bernard Dickens then discusses the legal status of the human fetus and the human preembryo in vitro, as this legal status has been interpreted in the English Common Law tradition in Britain, Canada, and the United States.

The last two papers in Part I concern questions related to the neuromaturation of the fetus. Rodrigo Kuljis provides current medical data regarding the development of the human brain during gestation. Hans-Martin Sass builds on that medical data by proposing the development of a Uniform Determination of Life Protection Act that would protect individual human life from the point of fetal brain development, a point he calls "brain life" and dates from day 70 of gestation.

Part II contains three papers on assisted reproductive technologies. In the first paper Ricardo Asch provides a description of the various assisted reproductive technologies that are currently being used in countries having advanced technological medicine. In the second paper Tristram Engelthardt contrasts the Roman Catholic and "cosmopolitan" views of assisted human reproduction, then argues for a secular ethic of toleration regarding reproductive sexuality. In the third paper Karen Rothenberg examines the legal problems presented by gestational surrogacy and argues that the use of assisted reproductive technologies to combat the problem of infertility should not be expanded to include surrogate mothers.

Part III, which focuses on the related issues of contraception and abortion, begins with two papers by physicians. Luigi Mastroianni presents medical information on the continuum of procreation, the alternatives currently available for contraception, and contraceptive methods under development. Allan Rosenfield and Hillary Kunins then discuss abortion from the perspective of public health, concluding that medical problems related to abortion continue to be a major public health concern in many parts of the world even though the worldwide trend in abortion laws is toward liberalization. From a philosophical perspective, Helga Kuhse and Peter Singer argue that the conventional dichotomy between the morality of contraception and the morality of abortion is open to challenge, that new reproductive technologies raise questions about the moral significance of fertilization, and that fetuses do not have a right to life. Rebecca Cook followed with an international legal interpretation of contraception and abortion policies, an analysis of the way abortion laws have been used to oppress women, and call for countries to protect prenatal life only in ways that are consistent with women's rights to nondiscrimination.

The papers in Part IV address the related problem of fetal research and fetal tissue transplantation, especially as these scientific and medical interventions have been handled in the United States in recent years. All of the authors are Americans, and all of the papers (in contrast to other parts of this volume) address the particularities of the American society and the American government. Kenneth Ryan begins with a discussion of some of the medical aspects of using human fetal tissue for research and therapy, and provides some insights on the deliberations of the Human Fetal Tissue Transplantation Research Panel convened in 1988 by the National Institutes of Health. John Fletcher agrees with Ryan's analysis and charges that the U.S. Government has restricted and suppressed research on preembryos, embryos, and fetuses for almost 20 years, to the detriment of research scientists and patients with neurological and other disorders who might benefit from fetal tissue transplants. John Robertson then argues that research on preimplantation embryos is ethical in most circumstances, generally legal in the United States, and increasingly desirable for the purpose of preimplantation genetic diagnosis.

Papers from two panelists conclude this section. Mary Mahowald discusses fetal tissue transplantation from a feminist perspective, warning that fetuses not be considered apart from pregnant women. Susan Johnson analyzes fetal tissue transplantation research from the perspective of an American institutional review board, emphasizing the importance of donor consent to the research, the assessment of risks to the donor, and the protection of the recipient of fetal tissue.

Part V contains papers on the medical, ethical, and legal aspects of maternal/fetal relationships. Carl Weiner provides a description of current technologies for fetal diagnosis, as well as medical and surgical alternatives for fetal therapy, and emphasizes the unprecedented achievements of primary care fetal medicine as a recent multidisciplinary field. Frank Chervenak and Laurence McCullough address the problem of court-ordered cesarean delivery and argue that in the specific case of well-documented, complete placenta previa, a physician has a moral obligation not to accept refusal of cesarean delivery – and may be justified in seeking a court order to override a pregnant woman's refusal.

The remaining authors in this section (two philosophers, an attorney/ethicist, and four physicians) have serious reservations about using the courts to resolve maternal/fetal conflicts, but they do not address the specific example put forth by Chervenak and McCullough. Bonnie Steinbock argues that the problem of pregnant drug addicts should be handled by funding educational programs for pregnant women, adequate prenatal care, and drug treatment programs targeted for pregnant women with cocaine addiction – not by increasing the number of fetal abuse laws and prosecutions. Mary Anne Warren agrees, concluding that coercive "pregnancy policing" policies (including prebirth seizures and postbirth sanctions) are medically counterproductive, destructive, and unjust. Lawrence Nelson also agrees, and argues that court orders compelling pregnant women to change their behavior or to undergo medical treatment for the sake of their fetuses are unduly restrictive of personal freedom, a freedom that women should not lose because of pregnancy. The final paper in this part, authored by Mark Evans and three medical colleagues, raises serious questions about the experimental procedure of fetal therapy and concludes that when the rights of a pregnant woman and a fetus are in conflict, the rights of the woman carry more weight.

Part VI provides an extension into pediatrics of the discussion of rights and obligations related to the beginning of individual human lives. Neil Campbell begins this part with a wide-ranging discussion of medical problems confronted by neonatologists, including problems related to extreme prematurity, severe disability, and overly aggressive medical treatment. Robert Truog follows with a medical perspective on the issue of transplanting organs from anencephalic infants and suggests that there may be an ethical and legal way of handling this difficult problem. Robert Weir then addresses questions related to the personhood of neonates, the applicability of the best-interests standard to decisions not to sustain some neonates' lives, the issue of technological feeding, and the cost of life-sustaining treatment for neonates and other young children.

This part concludes with two papers on the issue of selective nontreatment decisions, one from the perspective of a philosopher and the other written by an attorney. Loretta Kopelman examines the concept of medical futility and indicates how this concept can and should be used in the context of neonatal medicine. Elizabeth Schmidt, impressed by the medical and ethical uncertainty on some neonatal cases, maintains that the legal system, too, it fraught with uncertainty as it tries to grapple with some of these difficult cases involving young human lives.

We hope that you find these symposium papers interesting, helpful, and challenging. The exemplary editorial work on the papers has been done by Gail Zlatnik in Iowa City. The publication of the papers have been made possible by financial assistance from Schering AG.

Iowa City, Iowa R.F.W.
June, 1992 F.K.B.

PART ONE

General Perspectives

FRITZ K. BELLER AND GAIL P. ZLATNIK

Medical Aspects of the Beginning of Individual Lives

The topic of the beginning of human life was of rather minor concern to gynecologists as recently as thirty years ago. And the practice of abortion, at that time, was virtually off-limits to members of a profession guided by the Oath of Hippocrates. What developments have made it imperative now, in the 1990s, to discuss the biology of the beginning of human life and its ethical implications?

The question is easily answered. It was not the introduction of the birth control pill by Pincus and Rock in 1960, a cornerstone of equal opportunity for women, nor was it the liberalization of abortion laws in many countries around the world. The change in interest was brought about by the new assisted reproductive technologies. A discussion of the beginning of life has become inevitable in order to deal with the medical and ethical dimensions of manipulating and even creating human life in the test tube.

The following reflections on the medical implications of the beginning of human life will, it is hoped, suggest the complexity and multiplicity of these dimensions.

CONCEPTION, FERTILIZATION, IMPLANTATION, AND PERSONHOOD

Historically, the term "conception" has often been used synonymously with "fertilization." The Catholic church is the largest and most significant of many groups that maintain categorically that personal human life begins with conception or, more precisely, with fertilization of the egg by a sperm through the zona pellucida. The actual period of time required for the process of fertilization is very brief, yet at its conclusion a new, unique, and unitary human being is believed to have been created. This belief is also an integral part of some abortion laws.

Genetic and physiologic facts do not appear to support this belief, however, since translation of DNA does not occur before 24 to 48 hours after fertilization. Fertilization is therefore a progressive development and not a fixed point.

F.K. Beller and R.F. Weir (eds.), The Beginning of Human Life, 3–17.

Suarez has recently indicated that the terms "conception" and "fertilization" are not identical: "Every fertilization is a conception, but not every conception is a fertilization. The life of the great majority of the human mammals begins with a fertilization, but the life of some human mammals begins otherwise, namely, with the separation of a totipotent part of an embryo."[1]

Implantation, like fertilization, is not a fixed point but rather a development over time. It begins approximately six to eight days after fertilization and ends, by convention, two weeks later; four weeks have elapsed since the first day of the last menstrual period (LMP) and two weeks since fertilization.

The belief that pregnancy begins with implantation rather than with fertilization does have considerable scientific support. First, until implantation occurs, it is not clear which cells will develop into the trophoblast/placenta and which into the embryo, since both exhibit identical DNA content. Second, until implantation human procreation is associated with an excessive biologic loss. It is estimated that, for a variety of reasons, approximately 50–70 percent of fertilized eggs do not implant. And, finally, up to the point of implantation the zygote is capable of dividing to produce two to four individuals. The opposite process has also been observed: twins can recombine into one individual, a true chimera.[2] These observations about multiplying and recombination provided the basis for the concept of individualization favored by some embryologists and recently supported by the Catholic priest Norman M. Ford in his book *When Did I Begin?*[3]

The case for considering implantation to be the beginning of human life can also be supported from the maternal standpoint: the pregnant woman exhibits signs of pregnancy only after implantation has occurred.

The laws of Austria, New Zealand, Germany, and the Netherlands state explicitly that pregnancy begins with implantation. Nevertheless, as FIGO stated in 1980, "The basic difference between the definitions of the beginning of pregnancy is a scientific question, and the beginning of life has moral and religious implications and cannot be answered scientifically."[4]

Human Life

Both the placenta and the embryo must be considered "human life," but the distinct differences between them allow us to consider the embryo as a "human *in being*"[5] and the placenta as "organic human life," development of which may result in a molar pregnancy or a malignant tumor, the choriocarcinoma. If it is thus clear that the zygote (or, for example, kidney tissue) is organic human life, and the newborn is a human being, then additional terminology seems to be needed to clarify what we mean by "human life."

Only approximately 30 percent of developing embryos achieve implantation. Because of this high rate of loss of pregnancy, and the uncertainty as to whether the zygote will eventually become a human being, the concept of "potentiality" has been introduced and widely discussed in the ethical literature. A zygote can be considered to have a variety of mutually exclusive potentials: It can implant and eventually become a mature human being; it may be prevented from developing; or, it can be aborted or even become a subject for human research.[6] The concept of potentiality thus permits a distinction to be made between the zygote and organic human life. The transition to the concept of personhood is less easily made.

The fetus is not a "person," at least not within the language of the Fourteenth Amendment of the U.S. Constitution and *Roe v. Wade*.[7] Indeed, few would maintain otherwise. The term "person" entails "consentience, which is paradigmatically or essentially a matter of the capacity for directed and flexible sensitivity toward the environment."[8] Similarly, Veatch defines "person" to include "the capacity to be consentient, to think, to feel and to become aware of other people."[9] The stage of consentience is reached only after months of newborn life, and the term "person" is therefore not helpful in discussing the beginning of human life. Nevertheless, according to Ann MacLaren, many religious groups use the term "personal life" or "personality," among them the Baptist Union, the Church of England Children's Society, and the Board of Bishops of the Church of Wales.[10]

Scientifically, the data support implantation, rather than fertilization, as the beginning of pregnancy and of the "human in being."[6] The introduction of notions of "personality" in a religious or moral sense seem to afford little clarification.

Contraception

The terms "contraception," "birth control," and "family planning" are poorly defined, and there is little agreement as to their meaning. Some use these terms only if pregnancy is prevented by interaction with gametes. Others include the prevention of implantation, which for still others constitutes early abortion.

The new term "contragestion" is a contraction of "contra gestation." As proposed by Baulieu,[11] Cook,[12] and many others, it includes not only implantation but early abortion. Contragestive drugs and devices exert their basic effect by preventing the morula and blastocyst stages from developing sufficiently to implant in the uterine wall. Cook defines "contraception" as both "the prevention of conception" and "the prevention of implantation of a fertilized ovum."[13] Her definition for "contragestion" includes these methods that act against gestation, including those that induce preembryonic or early embryonic loss. She continues, "The point at which contraception becomes abortion is not clearly defined." Indeed, further definition is urgently needed. Newer methods will enzymatically destroy the fertilized egg, and this process will for many people have a dimension other than simply the prevention of implantation.

In fact, it is precisely the multiple actions of most methods of birth control that complicate terminology. For example, the "birth-control pill" prevents implantation when breakthrough ovulation occurs. The IUD – which for philosophers serves as an example of implantation inhibition – acts by other means also, among them interference with sperm migration. The "morning-after pill" prevents implantation by changing the endometrium; menstrual evacuation does so by destroying the endometrium; and the antiprogesterones deactivate a component significant for procreation. The use of each of these is dependent upon the time of ovulation and unprotected intercourse.

The possibility that the antiprogesterone pill might reduce the need for surgical abortion is in itself an ethical point worth consideration. Tietze et al. demonstrated many years ago that the lowest mortality and morbidity of birth-control methods can be achieved if a less-effective contraceptive is backed up by early abortion.[14] It is to be expected that with the new anti-progesterones at hand mortality can be reduced even further.

Abortion

The fundamental principle of justice that similar cases be treated similarly requires that all women – not just French women – have access to both the antiprogesterone pill and the scientific progress represented by its development.[14] The extremely low side effects of this drug make it highly unethical to withhold it from the public. In fact, to do so means sacrificing lives for a moral principle that is not shared by the majority and is therefore unacceptable by any ethical standard. Accepting a higher death toll than necessary suggests that the means justifies the end. Do the so-called pro-life proponents feel that they have the right to expose to serious risk those people who do not share their convictions? The concern expressed by Lisa Cahill – that since the abortion pill makes abortion technically easier, it may make abortion more acceptable – is not a valid objection even if it proves to be true.[15] Glasgow has indicated that RU 486 is *mis*interpreted as a method of "no guilt, no planning (and no responsibility)."[16] The problem with Cahill's slippery-slope argument is that different people have different standards, not only for the slope itself, but also for where it begins. The present policy of the U.S. health agencies, government, and pharmaceutical industry is difficult to support and unethical.

In the early 1970s, abortion laws were liberalized in nearly all western countries. Abortion became permissible either upon request or upon broadly conceived indications. However, the gestational time limit varied from 8 weeks LMP to as late as 28 weeks LMP, as in two U.S. states (Florida and South Carolina). The laws of some states and countries refer to the last menstrual period, others begin to count with conception, and a smaller number with implantation (Netherlands, Germany). Some state laws give numbers without reference to LMP, PC (post conception), or PI (post implantation), thus permitting biologic variations of up to four weeks.[17]

The termination of a pregnancy, whether spontaneously or by induction, may be referred to as an "abortion" up until 22 weeks PC or 24 weeks LMP, according to the American College of Obstetricians and Gynecologists. The World Health Organization has not specifically defined abortion, but uses the term as most textbooks do. However, most U.S. states limit abortion to 12 weeks LMP. It is assumed that up to 12 weeks, termination can be performed by suction curette, a rather uncomplicated technique, but thereafter the fetus must be expelled or, if you will, delivered.

In some laws in the U.S. and abroad, the twenty-fourth week LMP or the twenty-second week PC is the cut-off point for any type of abortion. At 24 weeks LMP the fetus has reached an average weight of 600 grams. In the early 1970s, when abortion was legally defined, no fetus had survived the 600-gram limit outside the uterus, with or without artificial support. Hence the length of gestation has historically served as the expression of fetal weight, which in turn is the determinant of fetal survival.

The length of gestation, however, includes a number of variables with statistical variations: Any time limit after the first day of the last menstruation is derived from the biological rule that the menstrual cycle lasts 28 days as a mean, with a variation of 21 to 34 days. Since the second part of the cycle is in most instances stable, the time of ovulation is determined by subtracting 14 days from the first day of the next expected menstrual period; ovulation is assumed on the fourteenth day in a 28-day cycle. In a 34-day cycle, ovulation is assumed on day 20. If the cycle is shorter than 28 days, ovulation is assumed to have occurred earlier. The basic reality, however, is that not even the patient knows when ovulation has been delayed. The mathematical determination of ovulation is always retrospective. Only a basal body temperature chart – rarely available – can verify in a practical way the actual time of ovulation. The resultant uncertainty may support the patient's impression that minor psychologic irritations have produced an unnoticed delayed ovulation resulting in pregnancy.

Delayed ovulation also changes the estimated time of gestation. A 26-week pregnancy can thereby be reduced to a 24-week pregnancy that can be aborted legally. Fetal weight of 600 g is a mean with a large standard variation. Since the 1970s fetuses much smaller than 600 g have survived, and it has therefore been suggested that the WHO definition be corrected to appropriately earlier weeks of gestation.[18]

VIABILITY

The limit of 24 weeks – 600–700 g – is meant to indicate that the fetus has reached a stage at which it has a reasonable chance to survive outside the uterus. The chance of survival, which at present is of the magnitude of 30 percent either with or without external help, is termed "viability." This concept plays an important role in the law of the United States. It differs from being "alive." The latter refers to present qualities, the former to expectations.[19]

In the ethical sense, the fetus has reached a stage of development which requires interest in its own right. However, viability is not well defined, as indicated by the fact that three U.S. states – Iowa, Indiana, and Georgia – use three different definitions. In *Roe v. Wade* the U.S. Supreme Court specifically mentioned the use of ultrasonography to determine viability.[7] However, this technique itself entails several statistical variants. There is no viability test available, and presumably there will never be one, which makes the recent *Webster* ruling of the U.S. Supreme Court questionable.[20] As Hunter has pointed out, "Despite what the court has wished, viability cannot be seen as a clear line."[21] Given the range of variables, it is not a line at all, but a vague and broad gray zone.

Another aspect of the *Webster* decision is puzzling: in it the Court used a time limit of 22 weeks PC. Does that mean the Court has discarded the concept of a second trimester ending at 27 weeks? To do so would be appropriate, since by that time the fetus weighs approximately 1000 g, which gives it a survival chance in a neonatal care unit of almost 100 percent.

The concept of viability entails a yes-or-no or, better, a life-or-death definition, since we cannot speak of 20, 50, or 80 percent viability. The American judicial system may be faced with an interesting legal problem in determining whether those states that extend the abortion limit up to 28 weeks or have no abortion law at all are still protected by *Roe v. Wade*. One may question the validity of using biological facts in litigation.

Eugenic or Fetal Indications for Abortion

If *Roe v. Wade* is overturned, abortion legislation would revert to being the concern solely of the various states. Consider the fact that at present only twenty U.S. states and eight foreign countries have provisions in their laws for termination of pregnancy for fetal indications.[17] It is to be feared that state legislatures may fail to incorporate provisions dealing with fetal malformation, as has happened already in Louisiana and Guam. Failure to provide for fetal indications (be they genetic or of other origin) would result in a serious obstacle for the new field of fetal medicine: If termination of pregnancy cannot be an element of prenatal diagnosis and advice, can one possibly search for fetal abnormality? Conversely, without detection of fetal abnormality, no diagnosis will be made, and no treatment offered. The point can be made that our society does not consider mental retardation a discriminating factor that should be used determining medical treatment of adults or children.[22]

The identification of severe malformation means the death certificate for the fetal patient in more than 90 percent of cases; this fact identifies an ethical dilemma. Fortunately, the list of fetal malformations accessible to treatment is increasing. Nevertheless, to diagnose fetal abnormality of severe magnitude without providing for termination of pregnancy seems to be ethically unacceptable. Responsibility for providing a list of fetal malformations incompatible with life could devolve upon the national organizations of obstetricians and gynecologists and of pediatricians; such a list could provide indications for termination at any time during gestation.

It is rather interesting that in the *Webster* decision Justice O'Connor used the term "undue burden" in departing from the trimester framework.[23] This is almost exactly the same wording used in German law to explain the extension of the time limits in the abortion law from 12 to 24 weeks for fetal indications. That is, the termination of pregnancy is not punishable by law if the malformation of the fetus is so grave that it is an "undue burden" for the mother to continue the pregnancy. It is noteworthy that such a stipulation relies not upon a fetal indication, but upon reasoning derived from the maternal interest.

Maternal endangerment would seem to be an obvious indication for termination of pregnancy. However, it is at present mentioned in the laws of only fifteen U.S. states and seventeen countries.[17] Most states have no time limit for this indication, which seems reasonable. It is surprising, in fact, that some jurisdictions do impose limits: 24 weeks in Hong Kong, 26 weeks in the states of Colorado and Washington, and, until recently, 28 weeks in the United Kingdom. One would assume that the maternal life could be threatened by disease or other circumstances at any time during pregnancy. Of course, it is in some instances very difficult to agree on a given threat, because for rare diseases data are sometimes not available, or because disease outcomes have changed through modern treatment. The opinion of the obstetrical profession has historically been that in doubtful cases, the abortion should not be performed. This position has changed with recognition of the autonomy of the patient.

Feticide

In several states in the U.S. and elsewhere, termination of pregnancy is allowed beyond 24 weeks LMP. However, the larger the fetus the greater the chance it will be born alive, if conventional methods for termination, such as instillation of urea, acridine, or prostaglandins, are used. With these instillation techniques, it is expected that the fetus will be killed by the induction of contractions. The birth of a live newborn who has been subjected to abortion is a nightmare, most especially if the infant is malformed. Yet, whatever the ethicist may argue, under present law the failure to support this newborn baby is considered manslaughter or even murder.

The opinion of Singer and Kuhse regarding the lack of sanctity of human life is well known, and it seems relevant here.[24] Robertson phrases it differently: "Respecting the early embryo as a symbol or reminder of our membership in the human community is a matter of choice, not moral duty."[25] Techniques exist for mercy killing of animals, and in the U.S. a large national movement is concerned with the nonpainful death of food animals. Yet similar concern has not been directed toward fetuses, as Singer pointed out, although the methodology is now available: an air embolism can be introduced via cordocentesis, resulting in instantaneous death. This process, termed "feticide" in the context of reduction feticide, has not been so designated in other contexts. It may be time to define the terminology and elicit the consequences.

Assisted Reproductive Technologies

It is historical fact that Patrick Steptoe and Robert Edwards funded the research that resulted in IVF with an illegal abortion clinic. Today IVF is an accepted technique in nearly all cultures. The document issued by the Vatican's Congregation for the Doctrine of the Faith in which the Catholic church indicated its disapproval of assisted reproductive techniques has had the same effect on infertile couples as had *Humanae Vitae* on people using birth control: very little.

The storage and freezing of preembryos presents potential problems: A preembryo can be maintained in the frozen state beyond the lifetime of the genetic parents. Theoretically, a frozen preembryo might even fulfill certain criteria for indefinite eternal life. This possibility raises serious concern regarding the responsibility of the persons involved. Its misuse has already been demonstrated by William Shockley's advocacy of sperm banks for geniuses only.

Different countries have found different approaches to the dilemmas of embryo research. The extremes range from the statement made by the British Medical Research Council and the Royal College of Obstetricians and Gynecologists, brought recently into law, to the German law whereby *any* research on human embryos is punishable as a criminal offense. The spectrum of research projects reaches from improvement of assisted techniques for reproduction to improvement of contraceptive and abortifacient techniques.

Gene therapy at present is a reflection of research. Somatic cell repair may be more acceptable then somatic cell enhancement. Germline repair, and certainly enhancement, may ultimately serve as points of no return because the changes they create are reproducible in the offspring.[26]

Techniques for recombining DNA as constituents of chromosomes can serve to encode genetic data, allowing for a high-resolution genetic map of the genome. These techniques enable the identification of nearly three thousand specific genes and the potential for prevention of disease before its manifestation. However, the basic obstacle today to use of genetic mapping is concern for record-keeping confidentiality. The establishment of a genetic map without the security necessary to prevent its misuse seems to be ethically problematic.

To be sure, the misuse of genetic engineering in an eugenic sense, to create a superrace, is of concern. It takes no stretch of credulity to assume that if Adolf Hitler had had the requisite methodology at his disposal, he would have used it. The so-called *Lebensborn* was an attempt at genetic engineering, but one with insufficient means. We may need a ban by WHO similar to that on biological warfare, and it seems wise to anticipate the need for such a ban rather than try to create an adequate sanction after the fact. That is, such a ban might be more easily obtained when there is no actual need for it.

THE ANENCEPHALICS' STORY

In 1986 Chervenak et al. discussed the ethical concerns surrounding the termination of pregnancy after 24 weeks for fetal malformation. Such terminations, they proposed, are tenable only when both of two conditions exist: the fetus is afflicted with a condition that is incompatible with postnatal survival; and the fetus has total loss of cognitive functions.[27] The letters to the editors consequent to publication of their guidelines demonstrated a wide variety of opinions, indicating that some writers anticipated, and feared, a slippery slope of decision making.

In 1979 at a large referral center in Germany an increasing number of anencephalics were observed in diagnoses made after the twenty-fourth week of gestation. German law at that time allowed termination of pregnancy for fetal indications up to 24 weeks LMP only. For pragmatic reasons it was proposed in 1980 that anencephalics be considered not to be alive, since they lack a forebrain.[28] This proposal would permit termination of pregnancy at any time, even after 24 weeks; the proposal was accepted without discussion, and the leading commentary used for reference in courts of law described the anencephalic as a nonliving entity.[29] As a result, in Germany anencephalic fetuses could be terminated after 24 weeks' gestation.

In 1987 successful kidney transplants to children and adults from anencephalics of 32 to 36 weeks' gestation was reported from the same referral center. It was demonstrated that transplantation of both kidneys *en bloc* would also serve adults.[30] In this research the anencephalic was considered to be "not alive," as established in 1980; the nature of this malformation is that the forebrain has not been and cannot be achieved, and the fetus has no potential to become a human being. Nevertheless, care was taken that the anencephalics could be included within the framework of brainstem death.

An emotional outburst ensued. Organ transplantation succeeded, for less significant reasons, where the original position paper had failed, in providing the stimulus and opportunity for public discussion.[31] The eventual result, however, was not thoughtful discussion, but revocation of the legal commentary.

In the aftermath of this controversy, it must be recognized that there are countless numbers of small children who need organs, and many of them will die before a transplant becomes available. The argument that infant transplantation is too costly is not founded in fact. One can make the point that an organ transplant in a child serves society better than a similar transplant in a sixty-year-old; a baby has the potential to reimburse society for the cost of this procedure during his or her lifetime.[32]

Fetal Cell Transplantation

Tristram Engelhardt has said, "If fetuses are not persons in the strictest sense, it is difficult to understand why women may seek abortions for any reason but researchers may not engage in fetal experimentation with the altruistic goal of producing knowledge and well-being."[33]

Engelhardt's statement suggests to a certain degree why progress with fetal cell transplantation seems to be slow. Another factor may be the fact that the data on effectiveness are not fully established in neurologic problems like Parkinson's and Alzheimer's diseases. However, knowledge or success would allow us to evaluate the ethical benefits of this procedure.

McCullough has summarized the possibilities in fetal research: (1) experimentation on the fetus in utero; (2) experimentation on the fetus in utero in anticipation of abortion; (3) experimentation on the aborted fetus; and (4) experimentation with tissues removed from the aborted fetus.[34]

Some of these possibilities, such as the utilization of fetal tissue in vaccine production, have not attracted great interest. Of the others, experimentation in utero, although at present associated with a very high risk, may ethically be the least-complex possibility, since the fetus itself may benefit. Such experimentation might by considered a noninnovative treatment rather than fetal research, as indicated by Fletcher.[35]

Experimentation on the fetus in utero in anticipation of abortion and experimentation on the aborted fetus are associated with many unclarified issues, as, for instance, the ethics of experimentation when the fetus is alive, and the question of anesthesia. Concern may also be directed to the possibility that intra- or extrauterine life may be prolonged for the sake of the procedure.

The main problem relative to experimentation with tissue removed from the aborted fetus seems to be the separation between fetal tissue transplantation and abortion. If abortion is felt to be wrong, the use of fetal tissue may be considered to be wrong also. However, acceptance of abortion as a method of birth control does not necessarily mean acceptance of fetal cell transplantation. Acceptance of abortion for birth control has occurred in most of the Pacific Rim nations, but technology has not become uniformly available there to test the acceptability of using fetal tissues. In Japan the concept of brain death has not found popular acceptance, and although the technology is available there, transplantation is rarely used.

There is no question that the women to be aborted should have the right to decide on the disposition of fetal organs. That a woman subjected to an illegal abortion would lose this right is irrelevant. The argument that every human being, old or young, can be considered as a living organ bank in the light of modern transplantation technology serves the press better than it does the ethicist.

Maternal-Fetal Conflicts

New technology has focused interest on the conflicts between fetal and maternal rights. The ethical considerations regarding the mother are related to her autonomy and bodily integrity. The rights of the fetus, especially the fetus beyond viability and of near-term gestation, are recognized as well. Problems may arise when, for example, the pregnant women does not cooperate in medical care designed for the benefit of the fetus, or she creates a potentially hazardous environment for the fetus.

The problem of the status of the fetus may become more pertinent when pregnancy is to be terminated in its interest. Such terminations seem to mean that the fetus's right to life supersedes the woman's right to be autonomous. Chervenak's concept of "viability in utero" (rather than ex utero) will be discussed in the future because it implies a basis for treating the fetus as a patient.[36] The interest of the fetus may require that the integrity of the mother be compromised. Court decisions and position papers from the Committee on Ethics of the American College of Obstetricians and Gynecologists already exist on this subject.[37]

Evans et al. phrased their discussion of feto-maternal conflicts in terms of three "generations" of issues.[38] The first generation was that of judicial sanctions to force women to undergo cesarean sections against their will for the presumed benefit (however defined) of their viable fetuses. The second generation brought attention to attempts to coerce substance-abusing mothers to abstain by incarcerating them. Finally, the third generation deals with efforts at treatment in utero and correction of certain birth defects. The position of Ruth Macklin is that attempts to limit the liberty of pregnant women cannot be ethically justified.[39]

Although the U.S. Supreme Court has repeatedly refused to rule on whether human life begins at conception, recent court actions in the U.S. would seem to indicate that the court sees in the fetus a human being who needs protection. Such a view marks a deviation from previous abortion laws. Resolution of the issue might result if a time in pregnancy were set after which human life would be protected by law. Such a legal step would make abortion laws meaningless.

However, such a law would not necessarily provide guidelines for the mother who appears to disregard the well-being of her fetus. Should the time arrive when mothers are held responsible for behaviors that affect their unborn babies, in order to "prevent" certain fetal problems, the physician may be held responsible for supervising the patient. Such a supervisory role, for which there is no provision in the Oath of Hippocrates, would place physicians with the legal authorities as police officers of health.

Similar concerns about the practice of medicine arise with relation to "wrongful life." A few courts have recognized a "wrongful life" suit on behalf of the infant, and the majority of courts allow "wrongful birth" suits on behalf of the infant's parents.[40] However, it has not been established, and it would be nearly impossible to do so, whether the failure to diagnose a fetal malformation using modern techniques (for example, ultrasound) constitutes negligence. If knowledge of the defect would have led the woman to obtain an abortion, must the state allow the parents to bring a claim for wrongful birth? But what *is* a "severe malformation"? To date no court has addressed that question, nor do the diagnostic facilities exist at present to make such diagnoses generally available. If physicians are held responsible for not diagnosing any given malformation, as the prelude to ending a "wrongful life," the practice of obstetrics enters yet another unexplored area of responsibility.

The Premature and Disabled Newborn

Robert Weir and James Bale summarized the present problems regarding the disabled newborn nicely when they stated that "more conservative thinkers tend to argue that all newborns are actual persons. More liberal thinkers tend to argue that all newborns are nonpersons."[41] In a different usage of the concept of potentiality, admittedly vague and undefined in the case of the preembryo, Weir and Bale support the idea that the newborn has the potential to become a person. It seems feasible that a group of physicians could evaluate this potential in a given premature or disabled newborn. Then, according to Bale and Weir, "the newborn as a potential person has a prima facie claim to the moral benefits of personhood, including the right not to have its life terminated." Nonselectivity of treatment would become subject to the same standards as nonselectivity of treatment for any person – child, adult, or dying elderly.

Neuromaturation

In 1975 Baruch Brody formulated what is now called the symmetry concept: If the death of a human being requires the death of the brain, then the beginning of human life shall correspond with the beginning of the life of the brain.[42] Or, if the death of the brainstem is required for the definition of death, the functioning of the brainstem signifies brain life. This concept has been adopted by physicians, among them Goldenring.[43]

Studies of the anencephalic fetus have established that this fetus cannot develop a forebrain: if the neural tube has not fused by day 31 PC, it cannot do so later. Beller equated the fusion of the neural tube with the beginning of the connection between center and periphery, and called that fusion the beginning of brain life.[45] H. M. Sass came to the same conclusion from a different line of thinking.[45] However, it has since become evident that a certain number of neurons are needed to form such a functional connection.[46] Sass makes the symmetry dependent on the formation of a sufficient number of synapses, around day 70 PC.

Even if the seventieth day is the chosen boundary, there is ample reserve in this period of embryonic organogenesis to determine definitively that no functional connection that is more than vegetative exists between centrum and periphery. The fetus is absolutely incapable of experiencing pain or any other sensation. It is passive and behaviorless. Vegetative functions and reflexes only are present. One may argue that this state of vegetative life is different from that of a dying adult, who dies from the upper brain levels downward until the brainstem has died. In any event the film *The Silent Scream* misleads, and purposefully; all of the depicted fetal reactions are reflexive and not organized by cognition.

Downie has objected to an association between brainstem death and brainstem life.[47] If brainstem death were taken to be the definition of death, he argues, the symmetry might hold. However, if death is the permanent cessation of functioning organs as a whole, and brainstem death is only the criterion for assessing this cessation, then the symmetry does not hold. Indeed, a number of philosophers have objected to using the cessation of brainstem function is measurable, whereas cortical death is not. Brainstem function is however not related to forebrain function, which determines human personhood.

Truog and Fletcher recently proposed a new definition of death, also derived from thoughts on the anencephalic. Their criterion for whole-brain death is that there must be sufficient loss of brain function such that somatic death is imminent. They recognize that even when brainstem activity ceases, at least some degree of coordinated neurological functioning is maintained.[48] Death is therefore a progressive development, reaching a point of no return. Their ideas complement those of Hans Jonas, who objects to the 1968 Harvard definition of death because by its very nature death has an unknown component.[49]

The problem regarding the beginning of brain life is that of insufficient knowledge: we do not know how many functioning neurons are needed. The new definition of death offered by Truog and Fletcher can be brought into symmetry with the beginning of brain life: the beginning of brainstem life can be considered to occur when there are a sufficient number of neurons developed to imply that brainstem function and thus brain life is imminent.[50]

Ann MacLaren has stated that "different cultures have different views about life after death; it is clear that they will also have different views about life before birth."[10] We observe with increasing frequency the attempt of minorities to force their moral attitudes into law, thereby overpowering other minorities or even majorities. Clifford Grobstein's question is important: "In a pluralistic community, what are the purposes to be served by public policy as against group or personal morality? Should any particular morality be made the basis of public policy?"[5] It should not. To allow private morality to dominate public policy would shake the foundation of our society: Liberty is based on tolerance. We must respect the various opinions of different lifestyles in our pluralistic society, but we should also prevent the domination of any single one over the others.

Jose Barzelatto, who was for many years the World Health Organization Representative for Scientific Affairs of Reproduction, has stated: "The world is becoming pluralistic in a very real sense, and recognition and respect for this pluralism may be the prerequisite for the maintenance of peace and even the survival of mankind."[51]

References

1. Suarez A. Hydatidiform moles and teratomas confirm the human identity of the preimplantation embryo. J Med Ethics 1990; 15: 627–653.
2. Hellegers A. Fetal development. Theological Studies 1970; 31: 5–9.
3. Ford N M. When did I begin Conception of the human individual in history, philosophy and science. Cambridge: Cambridge Univ Press, 1988.
4. Quoted in Cook, R. Abortion laws and policies. Int J Gynecol Obstet 1989: Suppl 3: 61–87.
5. Grobstein C. Science and the newborn. New York: Basic Books, 1988.
6. Buckle S T. Arguing from potential. Bioethics 1988; 2: 225–229.
7. Roe v. Wade: 410 U.S. 113, 138, 1973.
8. Grobstein C. The moral uses of "spare" embryos. Hastings Center Rep 1982; 12: 6–10.
9. Veatch R M. Whole-brain, neocortical and higher brain related concepts. In R M Zaner, (ed). Death: Beyond whole-brain criteria. Dordrecht: Kluwer Academ Publ, 1988.
10. MacLaren, A. Keynote address. In: Bankowsky Z, Barzellatto J, Capron, A M, (eds). Ethics and human values in family planning. Geneva: CIMS 1989: 7–15.
11. Baulieu E M. Contragestion and other clinical applications of RU 486, an antiprogesterone at the receptor. Science 1989; 245: 1351.
12. Cook R. Antiprogestin drugs: Medical and legal issues. Fam Plann Perspect 1989; 21: 267–272.
13. Tietze C H, Bongaartes J, Schaerer B. Mortality associated with the control of fertility. Fam Plann Perspect 1976; 8: 6–14.
14. Reproductive health and mifepristone [editorial]. Lancet 1990; 336: 1480.
15. Cahill L S. Abortion pill RU 486: Ethics, rhetoric and social practice. Hastings Center Rep 1981; 17: 5–8.
16. Glasgow R D. 1986 Chemical warfare on the unborn. The Pro-Life year in review. Washington DC: National Right to Life Committee, Inc, 1987.
17. Beller F K, De Prosse C H A. The confusion of trimester and viability and the consequences for the abortion law. J Reprod Med 1992; 37: 537–40.
18. Beller F K. Interruption of pregnancy after the 24th week of gestation. In: Ludwig H, Thomasen K T, eds. Gynecology and obstetrics. Berlin: Springer Publ, 1986: 257–259.
19. McCullough P. The fetus as transplant donor. Chichester: Wiley, 1987: 7.
20. Webster v. Reproductive Health Services, 109 S. Ct. 3040 (1989).
21. Hunter N. Time limits on abortion. In: Cohen and Taub, eds. Reproductive laws for the 1990s. Clifton NJ: Humana Press, 1989.
22. Johnson R S, Elkins T E. Ethical issues in prenatal diagnosis. Clin Obstet Gynecol 1988; 31: 408.

23. O'Connor, Justice Sandra Day: Concurring opinion in Webster, p. 8134.
24. Kuhse H, Singer P. Should the baby live? Oxford: Oxford Univ Press, 1985.
25. Robertson J A. In the beginning: The legal status of early embryos. Virg Law Rev Assoc 1990; 76: 447, 448.
26. Young E W D. Alpha and Omega. Ethics at the frontiers of life and death. Reading PA: Addison Wesley, 1988.
27. Chervenak F A, McFarley M A, Walters L et al. When is termination of pregnancy during the third trimester morally justifiable? NEJM 1984; 310: 501–504.
28. Beller F K, Quakernack K. Fragen Zur Bioethik: Terminierung der Schwangerschaft im II. und III. Trimenon aus eugenischer Indikation. Geburtshilfe Frauenheilkd 1980; 40: 142–145.
29. Jähnke B. Leipziger Kommentar 10. Aufl. Berlin: DeGryter, 1983.
30. Holzgreve W, Beller F K, Bucholz B. et al. Kidney transplantation from anencephalic donors. NEJM 1987; 316: 1069–1070.
31. Beller F K, Reeve J. Brain life and brain death. The anencephalic as an explanatory example. J Med Philos 1989; 14: 5–23.
32. Medical Task Force on Anencephaly. The infant with anencephaly. Neth J Med 1990; 322: 699–674.
33. Engelhardt H T, Jr. The foundations of bioethics. New York: Oxford Univ Press, 1986.
34. McCullough P. The foetus as transplant donor. Chichester: Wiley, 1987.
35. Fletcher J C. Ethical considerations in and beyond experimental fetal therapy. Sem Perinatol 1985; 9: 130–135.
36. Chervenak F A, McCullough L B. Does obstetrics ethics have any role in obstetricians' response to the abortion controversy? Am J Obstet Gynecol. In press.
37. Committee on Ethics, American College of Obstetricians and Gynecologists, 1987. Committee opinion. Washington DC.
38. Evans M I, Johnson M P, Holzgreve W. Fetal therapy. The next generation. Women Health 1990; 1: 31–33.
39. Macklin R. Maternal-fetal conflict: An ethical analysis. Women Health 1990; 1: 28–30.
40. Robertson J A. Gestational burdens and fetal status: Justifying Roe v. Wade. A J Law Med 1988; 189: 201–202.
41. Weir R F, Bale J F, Jr. Selective nontreatment of neurologically impaired neonates. Neurol Clin 1989; 7: 807–822.
42. Brody B. Abortion and the sanctity of human life: A philosophical view. Cambridge: MIT Press, 1975: 109.
43. Goldenring J. The brain life theory – Towards a consistent biological definition of humanity. J Med Ethics 1985; 11: 198–204.
44. Beller F K, Czaia K. Hirnleben und Hirntod, erklärt am Beispiel des Anenzephalen. Bochum, Germany: Med Materialien, Zentr Med Ethik, 1988 (17 April).
45. Sass H M. Zukünftige Möglichkeiten und ihre Bewertung. Arch Gynecol Obstet 1985; 238: 89–105.
46. Sass H M. Brain life and brain death: A proposal for normative agreement. J Med Philos 1989; 14: 45–61.
47. Downie J. Brain death and brain life: Rethinking the connection. Bioethics 1990; 4: 216–227.
48. Truog R D, Fletcher J C. Brain death and the anencephalic newborn. Bioethics 1990; 4: 199–215.
49. Jonas H. Against the stream. Comments on the definition and redefinition of death in philosophical ethics: From ancient creed to technological man. New York: Prentice Hall, 1974.
50. Beller F K, Johnson S R. Abortion and contraception: Is there actually an ethical dilemma? Second International Conference, Future of Medicine, Asian and Western Perspective 2000. Washington DC, 1990 (Sept. 9–14).
51. Barzellatto J. Reflections about ethics and human reproduction and the sense of the conference. In: Bankowski Z, Barzellatto J, Capron A M, eds. Ethics and human values in family planning. Geneva: CIMS, 1989: 63.

ROBERT M. VEATCH

The Beginning of Full Moral Standing

An extraordinary amount of philosophical effort and raw emotion has been expended on the question of when human life begins. It seems safe to say that something very important must be at stake. Yet from a strictly linguistic point of view it is not obvious why the question would be perceived as one commanding such high-pitched controversy. One dictionary I consulted defines life as "an organismic state characterized by capacity for metabolism, growth, reaction to stimuli, and reproduction." It defines human as "of, relating to, or characteristic of man." Aside from the potential controversy over the use of the term "man," it seems hard to imagine expending emotional energy over figuring out whether an organismic state has the capacity for metabolism characteristic of a human. Yet something of vital importance concerns those willing to become agitated over the question of when human life begins.

The Problem of Language

The Beginning of Life and Full Moral Standing

Even the most militant defender of late-term abortion should be willing to concede that human metabolism, growth, and reaction to stimuli are present in the early embryo. What is really worth fighting about is not whether that metabolizing entity exists, but rather what moral and legal status, if any, it has. The confusion arises because some people understand when they make a claim about the beginning of human life that they are making a claim only about the existence of an entity, leaving open the question of what moral or legal status the entity possesses. Holders of this view believe it is linguistically possible to say life has begun without taking a stand one way or the other about the moral or legal standing of that entity. For them, if the existence of life is linked to moral standing, it is linked synthetically. It is linked by some further argument purportedly showing that all life that exists has standing. Others, however, believe that when they claim a human life has begun they are *by definition* at the same time making a claim about the being's moral or legal

F.K. Beller and R.F. Weir (eds.), The Beginning of Human Life, 19–33.

status. Moral and legal status are sometimes linked analytically to the claim that life has begun. Users of this form of the term believe that when they say life has begun, they are simultaneously saying that moral or legal standing exists. They believe that to say life has begun *means* moral or legal standing has begun.

I would like to make a radical proposal in an effort to get us through the discussion of the beginning of life without needless combat. I would like to propose that we banish the phrase "the beginning of human life" and speak more directly of "the beginning of full standing." If we speak about human entities that have standing and those, if any, who do not, we may save ourselves some needless bloodshed.

In fact, the linguistic problem is even more difficult for two reasons. First, sometimes when we claim a human has standing, we mean standing in the eyes of the law – what I will call legal standing. In other cases we may mean standing in a moral community. One need not imply the other. A conservative on the issue of abortion might want to say that even though an embryo ought to be seen as having moral standing, it presently has no legal standing. As extreme liberal might, on the other hand, admit that a late fetus has legal standing even though, in the speaker's opinion, it has no moral standing.

In addition to the difference between legal and moral standing, there is a second difficulty. We need to distinguish between full standing and something less than full standing. Even those who acknowledge full standing quite narrowly might be willing to concede that early fetuses or newly dead human corpses have standing in some degree. They might be said to possess some rights, moral or legal, or if the notion of such entities being rights bearers is conceptually difficult, it might be said that living humans have certain duties regarding them. Thus I urge that we distinguish not only between moral and legal standing, but also between full and partial standing. Full legal standing should then be taken to mean that all of the legal protections given to human beings apply to the individual. It is the group to which the Constitution and its rights apply.

Full moral standing should be taken to refer to those human beings who are full members of the human moral community. They are bearers of all rights that attach to individuals simply by being members of the human community. They bear all "human rights." Exactly what those rights are will remain open to debate, but, for purposes of this conference, I believe we can assume they include the right not to be killed (at least not to be killed nonvoluntarily when one is innocent). They also include the right not to have one's organs and tissues taken without consent and probably certain more controversial entitlement rights, including the right to a certain decent minimum of health care, the right to have certain interests protected, and the right to have commitments made to one fulfilled.

The Possibility of Living Non-Persons

Closely related to the problem of linking the beginning of life with full standing is another linguistic confusion. The term *person* and its plural, *people*, is at least at ambiguous as the term *beginning of life*. As much irrational harangue takes place over the question of whether a particular human is a person as whether that human's life has begun. Some speakers assume that the claim that someone is a person carries with it as part of its meaning the claim that that person has full moral or legal standing.[1] For them persons are, by definition, those living humans with full standing. Others assume that the term *person* can be defined independent of the presence of this full standing, leaving to later argument whether all persons have such standing. In the latter case *person* can be linked to *standing* synthetically just as being alive can be. *Person* in this case is defined by some nonmoral characteristics. Persons are those able to think, feel, reason, manipulate language or other symbol systems, etc., leaving open the question of whether all who can do these things have full standing.[2] Such synthetic linking of the category of person with the category of those who have full standing permits one to speak of living persons who lack full standing as well as living nonpersons who might have such standing. If persons are defined by the ability to manipulate language, then one who believed that babies had full standing but no ability to manipulate language would hold that babies are nonpersons with full standing.

The language problem becomes still more complicated when one realizes that standing could be linked analytically or synthetically with either the concept of being alive or that of being a person, or both. For one who rejects either analytical link, there would be the possibility of human living persons who lacked standing as well as living non-persons who possessed standing.

It seems that the only way to retain our sanity and civility is to forswear the use of the terms *life* and *person* and instead speak directly about the question of whether humans have full moral or legal standing. That, I believe, is really what those who ask about the beginning of life or the beginning of personhood are interested in.

All of the questions posed in this conference have in common legitimate controversy over moral standing. Some critics of the new reproductive technologies argue against in vitro fertilization because they believe that the embryos have full moral standing and therefore have a right not to be exposed to manipulation or to the risks of the in vitro process. Abortion of those who have full standing is seen as homicide of the innocent, virtually universally unacceptable once full standing is posited. Prior to full standing, some right to abort is possible. (In the special case of extrauterine embryos, such as in the Davis case,[3] the right to abort, if there is one, would plausibly go equally to each parent.[4]) The ethics of maternal-fetal relations often hinges on whether the fetus has full standing. Sometimes even the question of whether the pregnant woman has full standing can be decisive, as in the case of Angela Carder, a woman who was near death at the time her fetus was delivered by cesarean.[5] If the fetus had standing and Angela Carder did not (for example, because she was already dead according to some definition of death), it would be easier to argue that a court-ordered cesarean would be justified.

The debates over neuromaturation and transplantation of fetal tissues as well as those over the status of anencephalic and other severely disabled newborns are in large part debates over whether embryos, fetuses, and postnatal humans have full standing. Although it is widely believed that it might be acceptable to withhold or withdraw disproportionately burdensome life-prolonging treatment of those who have full standing,[6] it is almost universally accepted that those who are full members of the human community cannot be killed (at least if they are innocent and do not consent). It is illegal to do so, and is generally thought immoral as well.[7] Even for a minority who accept voluntary suicide and homicide on request from competent full members of the human community, nonvoluntary killing of innocents with standing is almost universally condemned morally. Thus it will be critical to know which among the human beings discussed in the conference should be considered for moral and legal purposes to have full standing.

The Relevance of the Definition-of-Death Debate

While the emotional tension is extraordinarily high as we debate these issues in the context of fetuses and infants, our society is contemporaneously going through a very similar debate at the other end of life that might help shed some light on the matter. We have, for the past twenty years, been trying to clarify our definition of death.[8] While that debate is much more complicated than we realized and is far from resolved even after twenty years of argument, it is at least a calmer and sometimes more rational discourse. The question – who shall be deemed to have full moral and legal standing – is precisely the same as the one we are facing in the discussion of the standing of fetuses. The only difference is that in the case of the definition of death we are attempting to determine when this standing ceases while in the case of the issues for this meeting we are attempting to determine when the standing begins.

The Cardiorespiratory Definition of Death

The traditional concept of death was based on irreversible loss of cardiac and respiratory function. A human was said to have died when there was an irreversible loss of these so-called vital functions. Sometimes people, even skilled medical professionals, have spoken carelessly. They have talked of humans dying when their hearts or lungs stop. This is wrong, even based on the traditional definition of death, on two counts.

First, it is quite clear that individuals can lose their hearts or their lungs and still be members of the human community. Someone who has lost the ability to control lung function may still obviously be very much with us if his or her blood is being oxygenated mechanically using a heart-lung machine or a ventilator. We treat such individuals the way we treat the living. Likewise, someone whose heart has stopped beating can continue to carry out all essential bodily functions through the use of the heart-lung machine or a heart transplant. If cardiac and circulatory functions are maintained, an individual may be part of the community of the living even if heart and lungs do not function.

It is wrong for another reason for defenders of the traditional concept of death to consider those who have lost heart and lung function to be dead. Sometimes these functions are lost temporarily, but will return. As long as there is a possibility that they will return or be replaced by transplant or artificial organs, the individual may not be dead. What is critical according to this view is the flowing of fluids – the vital fluids of blood and breath.

Holders of this cardiorespiratory view are committed to the philosophical/theological claim that the minimal necessary condition for a human to be a part of the human community in full standing is the flowing of these fluids. Within the past twenty years this view has become increasingly problematic and, in fact, has been seen as an excessively animalistic, mechanical notion of humanness. More and more people doubt that either moral or legal full standing is contingent precisely on the flowing of any fluids. While the loss of these capacities surely seems consistent with loss of the status of being part of the human community in the full sense, their mere presence does not seem to be enough to count. Insofar as those who are considered "alive" cannot have organs removed and will otherwise receive the full protection of the law, it seems that the presence of mere cardio pulmonary function is not enough. Insofar as we are concerned about the question of who is a full member of the moral community, we are increasingly led to the conclusion that the presence of blood and breath flow are not a sufficient condition.

What are the implications for the beginning of full moral standing and the technologies of interest to this conference? The connections between them are important, but not necessarily straightforward. In particular, when one has irreversibly lost the cardiopulmonary functions – when one is called dead – then by definition they can never return in the future. On the other hand, if we want to know when full moral standing begins, we have to know whether those who have never had these critical functions, and cannot have them at the existing stage of embryological development, can be given status as members of the human community in full standing on the grounds that these functions will one day develop. In more traditional language, we need to know whether it is the presence of these functions or the potential for them that is critical morally and legally. This is a fundamental distinction; we shall reserve further discussion of it until later.

For now it seems clear that we can conclude that if one holds that it is the actual presence of cardiac and respiratory function that makes one a member of the human community in full standing for moral or legal purposes, then early embryos have not yet achieved full standing. They may command respect. They may have some partial standing. As with Aquinas, their destruction may be considered an offense. It would not be homicide, however.[9]

Early interventions involved in the new reproductive technologies could not be proscribed on the grounds that a full member of the human community was having its rights violated. If one holds that the critical feature is the capacity to perform cardiopulmonary functions, the destruction of a frozen embryo could not be forbidden on the grounds that a member of the human community was being killed. Surely, the interests of others who *do* have full standing could be violated. The disrespectful disposal of a frozen embryo might be offensive in a sense similar to the way the disrespectful disposal of a human cadaver is. For one committed to the actual capacity for the flowing of vital fluids, however, the destruction of embryos could not be direct violation of the claims of a full member of the human community.

In fact, all contraceptive and abortive interventions would have to be viewed as something less than interventions on a human in the full sense. Neuromaturation would be ultimately important in the sense that its study might be able to tell us when these critical cardiac and respiratory functions could be present.

The neurological question would appropriately focus not on when cardiac cells are able to contract spontaneously, but on when cardiac tissues and organs can carry out the functions of circulation. Likewise, we are interested not in when the first lung tissue is present, but when respiratory function can be performed.

The implications for fetal research and transplantation are important as well. Research on fetuses prior to the development of these functions would not be research on "living" beings in the full moral and legal sense of the term. There may still be reasons to regulate and even proscribe these activities. Research on living early fetuses might be proscribed because of concern about the effects on beings that will one day develop these critical functions. It might be proscribed if it were believed that tolerating research or transplantation involving early fetuses would be likely to have a spill-over effect encouraging analogous interventions on late fetuses, i.e., those who had developed these critical functions. It might even be proscribed because if involves some offense that one might commit on those who are not full members of the human community. After all, we proscribe certain harms to non-human animals. Our concern with nonhuman animals, however, is primarily with pain and suffering. If the fetus were so young that it lacked not only cardiac and circulatory function, but also the capacity to perceive pain, then this argument would not succeed.

For premature and disabled newborns the cardiorespiratory concept of what it means to be a member in full standing of the human community seems to have rather meager implications. No one is contemplating interventions of significance for newborns who lack cardiac and respiratory function (except the intervention to pronounce death). On the other hand, however, those who possess such function would be considered living members of the community with all of its moral and legal protections. This does not mean they could never be "allowed to die." Even conservative religious commentators often recognize the legitimacy of allowing critically and terminally ill patients to die – Roman Catholics when the burdens are disproportionate to the benefits,[10] and for some Orthodox Jews, when the patient is *goses* or moribund.[11] The point would be that newborns with cardio-pulmonary function should be treated using the same moral and legal criteria that are applied to other members in full standing of the moral and legal community.

What is striking is that the traditional concept of death grounded in irreversible loss of cardiac and respiratory functions is often considered the most conservative of plausible concepts of death, but nevertheless it has quite liberal implications for those who apply it to the beginning of life (at least for those who apply it in its "capacity" form). If one believes that abortion is proscribed at and not before the point of full moral standing, then abortions may be performed quite late in pregnancy – probably up to around the twenty-fourth week. New birth technologies, fetal experimentation and transplant, and other interventions might be tolerated up to a similar point, at least for those who consider something less than full moral standing inadequate to provide an absolute prohibition.

The Whole-Brain-Oriented Definition of Death

A second major position regarding the loss of full moral standing has emerged within the past twenty years and has largely replaced the cardiorespiratory formulation. Many, offended by the philosophical/theological claim that what is really important about being a human is that one can pump blood and circulate oxygen, have sought some more sophisticated concept of what it means to be living in a full moral and legal sense. By 1968 some of us had developed the idea that what is really critical is the development of integrated neurological functioning, normally related to the human brain.[12] It is now legally specified in all states in the United States and most other countries that, for legal purposes, an individual ceases to be a member in the full sense of the legal community when that individual irreversibly loses all of the functions of the entire brain. Since brainstem reflexes and lower-brain-regulated breathing are included, as well as the higher-brain functions such as consciousness, ability to think, feel, and reason, this view about what it means to die is now often referred to as the whole-brain-oriented concept of death, a term I introduced in an article originally written in 1973 and published some years later.[13]

The position that what is critical for membership in the human community is some brain function has interesting implications. First, it is now well known that individuals may have lost these functions even if the ability to circulate blood and respire remains. According to this view, an individual is dead, i.e., he or she does not command the full protection of the law that we give to living individuals, when brain function has irreversibly ceased, even if cardiopulmonary function remains. By law death must be pronounced. There is no discretion on the part of family or physician. It is logically impossible to commit a homicide on an individual whose brain function is totally and irreversibly lost. One may, of course, still do terrible things. One may mutilate a corpse. One could even violate the rights of others (such as family members or a waiting heart transplant recipient) by certain actions, but legally one cannot kill a respiring human with a dead brain, at least not in a jurisdiction with a brain-oriented definition of death.

The general effect of the shift toward a brain-oriented definition of death is to make some individuals dead who would not have been dead based on cardio-pulmonary criteria. The implications for the beginning of life are intriguing. Assuming that one takes the capacity for integrated neurological activity (rather than the potential for it) as critical for being a member in full standing in the human community, a more liberal concept for the end of life has relatively modest implications for the beginning of morally and legally protected life. The capacity for neurological bodily integration begins at about the same time as the capacity for cardiopulmonary function (in part because the body needs those neurological capacities to be able to control circulation and respiration). Thus approximately the same implications for the interests of this conference can normally be drawn from the whole-brain concept as from the cardiac concept.

There is one special set of exceptions. There may be certain seriously afflicted fetuses and newborns who have the capacity for cardiopulmonary function but who nevertheless lack all capacity for neurological integration because of severe neuropathology. According to the cardiopulmonary concept of full standing in the human community, these beings would have full standing. They could be allowed to die or be killed only on the basis of criteria that would be justified for other living humans.

According to the neurological integrating capacity (whole-brain) concept, these individuals would literally not be "alive" as members of the community in the full sense. They could not be killed. If this neurological integrating capacity had never been present, the being would never have been part of the community in any morally or legally interesting way. If it had once been present, then the fetus or newborn would be deceased (though continuing to have a beating heart and circulating oxygen).

Fetuses in this condition technically could not be aborted (assuming abortion is the removal of a living fetus from a pregnant woman). The fetal remains could be removed. They, in fact, could and should be removed even in the case of a woman who was militantly opposed to abortion on moral grounds. She should have no reason to object to removing a deceased fetus even if she opposes abortion.

Regarding neuromaturation, there may be technical differences between those committed to a concept of full membership in the human community based on cardiopulmonary function and those committed to neurological integrating capacity. For the latter, the neuromaturation that matters is the evolution of the neurological integrating capacity, not simply enough neurological capacity to make the heart and lungs work. While these two points may be quite similar, they need not be exactly the same.

A word of warning is in order here. Before a fetus is considered dead according to a whole-brain-oriented definition of death, there must really be complete and irreversible absence of all functions of the *entire* brain. It is becoming commonplace to try to deal with the moral and legal status of the anencephalic fetus or infant by claiming that such beings are "brain absent."[14] That is simply wrong; it may even be purposely misleading. If, in fact, the brain were entirely absent, such an anencephalic fetus or infant would, of course, be legally dead (or more correctly would never have lived). The anencephalic fetuses and infants that are of interest, however, actually have considerable brain function. It is only those who are capable of brain function that pose questions of interest for research, transplant, and termination of treatment. All anencephalics who have any brain function are legally alive. They may not serve as a source for organs and tissues for transplant until they die. They may not be subjects of experiments any more (or less) than nonconsenting infants. They could, with morally and legally appropriate surrogate consent, be allowed to die, but that is true of all members of the human moral community. Whether that destroys organs and tissues that could be useful to others is a question that must be subordinated to the determination of whether they are alive in the sense we are speaking about.

A Higher-Brain-Oriented Definition of Death

The anencephalic infant has posed a particularly puzzling dilemma for sorting out the question of precisely who is living in the sense of being a full member of the human community. We have just seen that anencephalics who retain any brain functions are legally alive in all jurisdictions. They cannot presently be used as organ sources or as objects of research; they can only be allowed to die. Yet, some of us have lingering doubts that anencephalic infants really ought to be treated as living, full members of the moral community. The argument is not that great good would come in research and transplantation if only we changed the way we classify anencephalics. If that were the case we could simply legalize or declare moral the use of certain defined classes of living human beings, such as, for example, anencephalics.

If being alive means, as I have argued, nothing more than being a member of the human legal and moral community in the full sense with all the rights and claims of other members, then it makes no sense to legislate that some living members of the community can nevertheless be used as organ sources, as objects of life-ending research, or be killed for other purposes. That misunderstands what it means to be a member of the human moral and legal community *in the full sense*. I take having such status to mean that certain basic rights accrue, including the right not to be used exclusively for the welfare of others and the right not to be killed (at least killed for the good of another).

If this is correct then it is a contradiction in terms to say that there are some individuals who are alive (i.e., who should be treated as having the rights of full membership in the community) who nevertheless can be treated as not having the basic rights of membership in the community.

I think the advocates of procuring organs from certain "living" humans such as anencephalics really mean something else that makes much more sense. I think they really believe that even though some humans have full standing according to current law, they really should not have it. Put simply, holders of this view should be advocating still another definition of what it means to be alive or dead.

As early as the early 1970s I began advocating the position that what is really critical to being considered dead or alive is not whether there is an irreversible loss of all brain functions, but whether there is an irreversible loss of certain critical functions, those that, with purposeful vagueness, I call "higher."

Identifying exactly what those functions are is complex and beyond the scope of our work here. I have argued elsewhere that in rough terms the key functions are those responsible for consciousness or social interaction.[15] I have claimed further that, even though it is the capacity for social interaction that is the minimal necessary condition for being a member of the human community, for practical purposes that is tantamount to capacity for consciousness.

Some implications should be emphasized. This postion is not that rationality or the ability to reason is what is critical. Cognitive, sapient state is not essential. Those presumably could be other concepts of life and death, but only a few intellectuals really consider those formulations possibilities. It is capacity to function in community, at least to interact with another human being through consciousness, that is essential, according to my view.

Neurologically, this higher-brain concept will have to be given more precision in order to be made operational. What we are talking about is not the same as what is sometimes called cerebral, cortical, or neocortical function.[16] Clearly, one can have some cerebral, cortical, or even neocortical function and still have irreversibly lost capacity for consciousness. On the other hand, in theory one may have lost all cerebral tissue and still retain some capacity for consciousness, either through reprogramming of other brain centers, through some residual capacity for consciousness in the thalamus or other brain tissues, or even through an artificial brain. A human with such consciousness would still be human, at least if he or she remained embodied in human flesh. What this new position is committed to is the view that one is a member of the human community in the full sense if, and only if, there is some capacity for consciousness or social interaction.

If it can be determined that anencephalic infants truly lack that capacity, then they would not be full members of the community in any legal or moral sense. They would be dead (if they previously had had such capacity), or they would never have lived. That is not their present legal status, but holders of this view believe that that is the status they should have.

The implications for the interventions that are the theme of this conference are significant. At least, if full standing accrues with the development of this capacity rather than the potential for it, then any embryo or fetus or postnatal human who lacked this capacity would not be subject to the same moral and legal strictures as those who do. It may still command respect and be protected by certain moral and legal requirements, but it would not be automatically given the status of a full member of the community. Gametes and embryos, preembryos, and very early fetuses, even late fetuses and postnatal infants who lack this capacity are, according to this view, morally and legally different from fetuses and postnatal humans who have a capacity for consciousness.

Almost all new reproductive technologies would be carried out on human tissues morally and legally distinct from full members of the human community. The critical line for abortion would, in theory, be clear; it would be the point at which consciousness began. Neuromaturation would focus on whether we could diagnose the presence of capacity for consciousness. Lest one believe that this is a technical impossibility, we should note that major groups of importance, including the President's Commission for the Study of Ethical Problems in Medicine and Biomedical and Behavioral Research[17] and the American Medical Association,[18] have claimed that, at least in adults, a persistent vegetative state – one such permanently unconscious condition – can be diagnosed with extremely great, if not perfect, reliability.

The implications for maternal-fetal conflict are important as well. Fetuses prior to this time would have claims primarily insofar as treatments of them would have an impact on their well-being after this critical point is reached. On the other hand, they *would* have such claims against their mothers, their fathers, and the state. In fact, in the special case of the permanently unconscious pregnant woman, her body would be available for use under the terms of the Uniform Anatomical Gift Act, since she would be deceased. With her consent expressed while living, or absent her objection, with the consent of her next of kin, the body could be used to serve the interests of her fetus.

POTENTIAL VS. CAPACITY

This brings us to the critical unresolved problem of whether it is the actual presence of these critical functions that determines full standing or some potential for development of it in the future. On this question the definition-of-death debate can be of no help, since all definitions of death incorporate notions of irreversible loss of function.

In the case of the beginning of full standing one could rationally hold that it is not the actual presence of capacity, but the potential for it to appear in the future that is critical. After all, even holders of the most liberal definitions of death acknowledge that an individual is not dead when there is a potentially reversible loss of critical function. It is a terrible confusion to call someone who has transiently lost heart or brain function "dead" or "clinically dead." It is foolish to say that CPR brings someone back to life. If death is irreversible loss of critical function, the fact that function returns establishes, by definition, that death never occurred. It is the potential for its return that is considered decisive.

Is there any reason why the potential for initial appearance of cardiac, whole-brain, or higher-brain function gives any less standing than the potential for return of these functions that have been lost temporarily? I see absolutely no scientific or deductively rational solution to this question any more than to the question of which function loss is critical in deciding when an individual has died. Moral and legal authorities simply have to decide whether the potential for first appearance of critical function is morally equivalent to the potential for reappearance of temporarily lost function, or whether the fact that the critical function has never appeared previously in the being means that something less than full standing is assigned to the being. Of course, some will believe that they must decide this issue based on their understanding of a preexisting moral order created by God or in the laws of nature. It is not at all irrational to hold that this is the basis of such a decision. Finite human beings have no option other than to draw on their available sources of knowledge – reason, revelation, and empirical observation – to draw a conclusion about the significance of the difference between potential in those who have temporarily lost critical function and those who have never previously possessed it. It there were a clear-cut, knock-down, drag-out winner in this debate, it would have long since been apparent. The tragic human condition is that a choice must be made.

For those who believe that the presence of *potential* in those who have never possessed capacity for critical function is decisive for establishing full moral standing, some additional issues must be settled. Liberal critics have attempted at times to reduce the conservatives' position to an absurdity by claiming that the potential for critical function – for circulation, neurological integrating capacity, or consciousness – actually exists in gametes. Gametes have within them such potential, and yet it seems absurd to give gametes the standing of full members of the human community so that, for example, killing an egg or sperm cell would be considered homicide.

The most plausible response is that it is the establishment of *unique* potential as a specific individual human that is critical. It is when the biological substrate for this unique individual is established that real potential for an embodied individual's circulatory, neurological, and mental function exists.

For centuries this was taken as the equivalent of "the moment of conception" or, closely related, "the moment of fertilization." Recent defenders of this more conservative view based on unique potential for function have become much more sophisticated, however. Beginning in the late 1960s medical scientists such as Jerome Lejeune and Andre Hellegers realized that even after the moment of initial combining of genetic material from sperm and egg, there is a possibility of rearrangement and recombination of genetic material through processes such as the forming of a chimera or through twinning.[19] If one holds that the creation of a unique individual with genetically established potential for critical function is what establishes full standing, then single-cell embryos and the products of the first cell divisions really have not yet fully established uniqueness. In their view such beings, now often termed pre-embryos, have great importance and command considerable respect, yet they are not yet individuals with a unique potential. Establishing exactly which point is critical in embryological development is partly a scientific question. It has recently been suggested that the critical event is the development of the primitive streak.[20] For those who hold that uniquely individual potential is decisive, this would appear to be the moment of full standing as a member of the human community (provided the very high probability of genetic continuity prior to then is not sufficient). (Obviously for those who do not accept the importance of potential, but insist on presence of actual capacity, this modest movement in the days between fertilization and development of the primitive streak is of much less interest.)

Participants in this conference, like the rest of us who are members of the human community, face vital decisions about who among those beings at the borders of the moral and legal community should be included as members in full standing. These are absolutely crucial questions, but questions that in principle cannot be answered by scientific investigation or by definitive deductive argument. We must choose – drawing on whatever religious and philosophical authority we can muster – exactly which features of human existence are necessary for full standing as a member of the human moral or legal community. No one, no matter how cautious, is so conservative as to insist that all living human tissue has such standing. No one, no matter how liberal, is so liberal that no such standing is granted. Some tragic choice must be made.

For that choice the definition-of-death debate has identified for us three groups of answers that are plausible. The first group focus on circulatory and respiratory function; the second, on neurological integrating function; the third, on capacity for consciousness or social interaction. I say groups of answers because it is now apparent that each of these positions, in fact, is made up of many slightly different variants.[21]

Those focusing on circulatory function could divide over exactly which circulatory functions are critical, on whether the human heart must be part of the circulatory system, for example. Those focusing on neurological integrating capacity need to decide which elements of the neurological system provide real integration: whether any of the autonomic nervous system must be present, whether spinal reflexes are significant, whether all brainstem reflexes really count, whether the existence of cerebellar function is a sign of the presence of significant function, and so forth. Likewise, those committed to higher-brain formulations must decide exactly which brain functions are "high." It is now clear that there are countless variations on these positions.

Given the infinite nuances among the positions, it seems very likely that no one position can ever really win in the public policy debate. For this reason, I and others have advocated a conscience clause in the definition of death that would pick one default definition as public policy, with the proviso that individuals who, based on religious or philosophical convictions, feel committed to some other view about which function is critical will have the right to opt for certain other definitions of death for their own cases, provided they were within the range of the reasonable. In cases of incompetents, surrogates would have a choice within reason.

Our crucial choice is not limited to the question of which function is critical for full standing. We must also decide whether it is the presence of capacity for that function or the potential for that capacity that matters and, if it is potential, exactly what constitutes potential.

The necessity for such a range of crucial, yet necessarily nonscientific choices should make all reasonable people humble in the face of the issues being addressed in this meeting. The fact that we as a society must reach some operating public policy consensus should make us approach the task at hand in a spirit of cooperation.

Notes

1. Among those who appear to claim or to imply that the term *person* carries with it moral standing are Michael Tooley. Abortion and infanticide. Philosophy and Public Affairs 1972; 2: 37–65; and Mary Anne Warren. On the moral and legal status of Abortion. Monist 1973; 57: 43–61.
2. Among those who appear to define *person* independent of moral standing are Lawrence C Becker. Human being: the boundaries of the concept. Philosophy and Public Affairs 1975; 4: 349, 334–359; Michael B Green and Daniel Wikler. Brain death and personal identity. Philosophy and Public Affairs 1980; 9(2): 105–133; and Joseph Fletcher. Medicine and the nature of man. In: Robert M Veatch, ed. The Teaching of Medical Ethics, Hastings-on-Hudson, N.Y.: Institute of Society, Ethics and the Life Sciences, 1973: 51, 47–58.
3. *Davis v. Davis*, No. E-14496, Cir. Ct. Blount County, TN, Sept. 21, 1989.
4. This view suggests that in principle the male and female parents are co-equally responsible and co-equally entitled to be decisionmakers. While in the case of normal uterine pregnancy a paternal decision to terminate a pregnancy could only be effectuated with a gross violation of the maternal body, in the case of an extrauterine embryo a symmetry exists in which each stands in identical relation to the embryo, equally entitled to "abort" or to insist that the life be maintained.
5. *In Re* AC, 533 A.2d 611 (D.C. App. 1987).
6. President's Commission for the Study of Ethical Problems in Medicine and Biomedical and Behavioral Research. Deciding to Forego Life-Sustaining Treatment: Ethical, Medical, and Legal Issues in Treatment Decisions. Washington, DC: US Government Printing Office, 1983.
7. Ibid.
8. For a history of the debate and summary of the issues see Robert M Veatch, Death, Dying, and the Biological Revolution rev. ed. New Haven, CT: Yale University Press, 1989; and President's Commission for the Study of Ethical Problems in Medicine and Biomedical and Behavioral Research. Defining Death: Medical, Legal and Ethical Issues in the Definition of Death. Washington, DC: US Government Printing Office, 1981.

9. Thomas Aquinas. Summa Theologica II–II, q. 64, a. 8; also see John T Noonan ed., The Morality of Abortion: Legal and Historical Perspectives. Cambridge, MA: Harvard University Press, 1970: p. 23.
10. Congregation for the Doctrine of the Faith. Declaration on Euthanasia. Rome: Sacred Congregation for the Doctrine of the Faith, May 5, 1980.
11. David J Bleich. The Obligation to Heal in the Judaic Tradition: A Comparative Analysis. In: Fred Rosner and J David Bleich, eds. Jewish Bioethics. New York: Sanhedrin Press, 1979: pp. 1–44.
12. Harvard Medical School. A definition of irreversible coma. Report of the Ad Hoc Committee of the Harvard Medical School to Examine the Definition of Brain Death. Journal of the American Medical Association 1968; 205: 337–340.
13. Robert M Veatch. The whole-brain-oriented concept of death; an outmoded philosophical formulation. Journal of Thanatology 1975; 3: 13–30.
14. Michael Harrison. Organ procurement for children: the anencephalic fetus as donor. *Lancet* 1986; 2: 1383–1386; Fritz K Beller and Julia Reeve. Brain life and brain death – the anencephalic as an explanatory example. A contribution to transplantation. Journal of Medicine and Philosophy 1989; 14(1): 5–23.
15. Robert M Veatch. Death, Dying, and the Biological Revolution.
16. Robert M Veatch. Whole-brain, neocortical, and higher brain related concepts. In: Richard M Zaner, ed. Death: Beyond Whole-Brain Criteria. Dordrecht, Holland: D. Reidel Publishing Company, 1988: pp. 171–186.
17. President's Commission, Deciding to Forego Life-Sustaining Treatment. pp. 176–177.
18. Council on Scientific Affairs and Council on Ethical and Judicial Affairs. Persistent vegetative state and the decision to withdraw or withhold life support. Journal of the American Medical Association 1990; 263: 426–430.
19. Lejeune J. Wann beginnt das Leben de Menschen? Padiatrie und Padologie 1981; 16: 11–18; A Hellegers. Fetal development. Theological Studies 1970; 31: 3–9.
20. Richard A McCormick. Who or what is the preembryo? Kennedy Institute of Ethics Journal 1991; 1: 1–15, esp. 4, 9, 11–12.
21. Robert Veatch. The definition of death: unresolved controversies. In: Howard H Kaufman, ed. Pediatric Brain Death and Organ/Tissue Retrieval, New York: Plenum Publishing Corporation, 1989: pp. 207–218.

BERNARD M. DICKENS

Legal Aspects of the Beginning of Human Life

The claim of this paper to be international is modest. It considers legal aspects of the beginning of human life in the context only of the English Common Law tradition, as opposed to that, for instance, of the Civil Law tradition of continental Europe, and approaches the Common Law through the legal experiences of the United States, Canada, and England. The legal systems of these countries often invoke the ethical and moral principles of Judeo-Christian culture, but they are essentially secular in their modern forms. In contrast, the legal systems of Islamic countries often not only reflect Islamic values but actively center their legal rules on such values. That is, the contrast between secular and religious law that is apparent in Western legal systems is not drawn, and Islamic sacred texts provide the content of applied law. Common Law systems tend to be pragmatic and empirical in their approach to the beginning of human life, neither self-conscious about nor embarrassed by their indifference to the spiritual status of unborn human life. Political legislatures have occasionally enacted that human life is to be recognized from conception,[1] but insofar as such legislation has an effect it is to change the general law. Some U.S. state courts have recently allowed claims on behalf of stillborn fetuses, but have thereby done some violence to the logic and justice of their laws.[2]

The law evolves as a consequence of developments in other spheres of knowledge and understanding. Historically, pregnancy was recognized from "quickening,"[3] but today pregnancy is recognized from completion of implantation of an embryo in a woman's uterus.[4] It does not follow, however, that the embryo acquires legal protection of its integrity and potential for development from that point. The traditional position has been, and widely remains, that live birth is the legal precondition to protection of existence, although in the U.S. the point of viability has gained some ascendancy following the U.S. Supreme Court decision in *Roe v. Wade*.[5] Widely supported is the observation of an English judge in 1979:

> The foetus cannot, in English law, in my view, have a right of its own at least until it is born and has a separate existence from its mother. That

F.K. Beller and R.F. Weir (eds.), The Beginning of Human Life, 35–48.

> permeates the whole of the civil law of this country . . . and is, indeed, the basis of the decisions in those countries where law is founded on the common law, that is to say, in [the United States of] America, Canada, Australia and, I have no doubt, in others.[6]

The English Court of Appeal has since endorsed the point, finding no jurisdiction to make a fetus a ward of court,[7] and, in a criminal case, that a fetus is not a person for the purpose of the crime of making a threat to kill the individual threatened "or a third person."[8] Similarly in Canada, the Supreme Court has approved the 1979 observation,[9] and, significantly, has interpreted the Quebec Civil Code, based on the Civil Law system of France, consistently.[10] The High Court of Australia has reached the same conclusion that a child must be born alive to acquire rights of its own to legal protection.[11]

Legislation that restricts abortion exists in these countries, but its function is to protect not the fetus itself but the state's interest in fetal life.[12] Accordingly, where the state is found to have no interest or where that interest is superseded by that of another, such as a pregnant woman, separate interests of a fetus cannot be asserted.[13] Of greater legal significance is the reference in the English judgment of 1979 to a fetus having "a separate existence from its mother."[14] Biologically, preembryos and embryos or zygotes are distinguishable from fetuses, but legal definitions are not necessarily congruent with biological distinctions, and in some jurisdictions "fetus" may be a generic expression or term of art that includes products of human conception that have the potential to be born. A preembryo in vitro is alive and has a separate existence from women who may gestate it, raising the question, to be addressed below, of the legal régime that is applicable to preembryos in vitro.

Persons and Human Beings

The Canadian Criminal Code embodies centuries of consistent Common Law understanding in its provision in section 223(1):

> A child becomes a human being . . . when it has completely proceeded, in a living state, from the body of its mother whether or not
> (a) it has breathed,
> (b) it has an independent circulation, or
> (c) the navel string is severed.

Compatibly with this definition, section 238(1), which addressed the offense of deliberately causing the death of a child in the process of its birth, speaks of "any child that has not become a human being." This confirms the so-called "born alive" rule of the Common Law, namely that, for the commencement of its legal rights and protection, a child must be born alive. Before it is born alive it is clearly a human child, but it is not "in being."

The legal distinction between a human child that is in being and one that is not in being has been confused by modern rhetoric outside legal analysis that concludes that to possess a human life is to be a human being, and that equates the status of being a human child in utero with being a human being in law. The fallacy arises through the failure to appreciate the legal significance of the qualification "being," meaning "in being," in the expression "human being." Since a child in utero is not a human being, *a fortiori* a preembryo in vitro is not a human being for purposes of the Common Law as traditionally applied.

The philosophical question of what constitutes personhood has been given legal relevance by the modern tendency in a number of the U.S. states to recognize wrongful death claims brought on behalf of viable fetuses through techniques of interpreting the language of legislation.[15] Classical Common Law considered that death was not a civil injury for which compensation could be awarded,[16] but legislation from the mid nineteenth century responded to the dysfunction of a legal position in which it was cheaper to kill persons than to injure them by permitting claims "whensoever the Death of a Person shall be caused by wrongful Act, Neglect, or Default."[17] U.S. jurisdictions adopted this language in legislation, and a judicial practice has evolved in a number to read the word "person" to include a viable fetus.[18] The practice predated *Roe v. Wade*, but this 1973 U.S. Supreme Court judgment, often presented as curtailing fetal rights, gave impetus to recognition of the damage claims of viable fetuses that suffered stillbirths through negligence or other wrongs.

The pervasive practice in Common Law jurisdictions outside the U.S. is to find the legislated words "human being" and "person" to be synonymous,[19] and accordingly to apply the "born alive" rule to claims. In the U.S., however, an interesting literature exists on the legal personhood of those who are not human beings, such as the unborn, which is contrasted with the historical denial of personhood to those who were human beings, notably slaves.[20] The fact that slaves were legally persons for purposes of liability to criminal punishment but not for purposes of pursuing legal claims of others' liability to them indicates how the legal recognition of personhood is applied instrumentally, to achieve predetermined objectives. In Canada, for instance, although such artificial entities as corporations were considered "persons" for many purposes, the Supreme Court held in 1928 that the language regarding a "person" who could be appointed to the Senate was to be interpreted not to include women, consistent with the restricted access to public office that women had at that time. Further appeal was available to the Judicial Committee of the Privy Council, which reversed the judgment.[21] The same flexibility or pragmatism could apply, of course, to the legislated words "human being," but these words are most likely to be understood in their historical sense developed over centuries of consistent judgments.

THE COMMON LAW STATUS OF THE UNBORN

The definition of a human being in section 223(1) of the Criminal Code of Canada, above, appears among provisions relevant to homicide, meaning murder, manslaughter, and infanticide. The universal understanding in the Common Law tradition is that there can be no homicide liability unless the alleged victim is proven to have been born alive. In a leading 1976 case in Massachusetts, for instance, a jury conviction was reversed for manslaughter alleged to have been committed in the course of a legal abortion. The prosecution claimed that upon detachment of the placenta, the fetus still in utero became a "person" within the manslaughter statute, even before birth through complete delivery clear of the mother's body. The judge directed the jury, however, and the appellate court agreed, that "manslaughter assumes that the victim was a live and independent person. . . . Destruction of a fetus in utero is not a manslaughter."[22]

It has been seen that abortion prohibitions protect not fetuses in themselves, but the interest that the state takes in them. Another measure of states' interest in the unborn is the proportion of health care, social service, and related resources that states dedicate to prenatal and neonatal care. This measure of practical concern may show a difference between public rhetoric and political commitment, but in law a state may be recognized to enjoy an unqualified interest in fetal life simply by asserting it. Abortion laws cease to operate when delivery commences, whether by natural or induced means or, indeed, by cesarean section, but homicide liability does not begin until complete extraction of the child from the mother's body. To cover the intervening time when the child is in the process of being born, many countries have an offense of deliberately causing a child to die in the act or process of birth. This crime is usually subject to an exception from liability when the child's death is caused "in good faith with the intention of saving the life of the mother."[23]

Acting before a child's birth in a way that causes it to die after it has been born alive is convictable as homicide, since the action causes the death of a human being. It is interesting to note, however, that in the U.S. before the 1946 decision in *Bonbrest v. Kotz*[24] it was doubtful whether a child born alive could sue successfully for injuries suffered while in utero. In little more than twenty years all U.S. jurisdictions had come to allow such claims,[25] but it cannot be said that this was a recognition of fetal rights, for two reasons. First, the "born alive" rule was widely still in effect, limiting claims to human beings legally defined so as to exclude fetuses. Second, a number of jurisdictions allowed like claims by children born alive for injuries inflicted on their mothers before they were conceived that caused them to suffer harm.[26] In one case, for instance, an infant recovered damages for injuries conditioned when its mother was transfused with negligently mislabeled blood eight years before the child was born.[27]

Uncritical legal commentators and, for instance, journalists who appear to have become absorbed with fetuses as, through medical technology, they have been made visible, tangible, and operable, sometimes find "fetal rights" in inheritance law. When a testator bequeaths gifts such as money to beneficiaries designated not by their individual names but by a class description, such as "my grandchildren," children in utero are usually held to be within the class. A portion of the bequest will be held for them, which they will receive on live birth. Legal language is employed to the effect that such children *en ventre sa mère* are deemed to have been born, leading to inadequate analysis that concludes that such unborn children have thereby acquired property rights as fetuses. The purpose of this legal technique is not to reward fetuses nor to give protection to their rights, however, but rather to give effect to the presumed intention of the testator that distribution of the estate be suspended in part, for no longer than nine months and usually for less, in order to accommodate all members of the class of beneficiaries.

In the past, such bequests often took the form of leaving gifts to, for instance, "the male heirs of my daughters." Historically there was no determination of fetal sex, of course, and a portion of the gift capital would be undistributed pending birth of a daughter's child that was in utero at the time of the testator's death. If the child proved to be male he would inherit, but if female the portion would be distributed among the previously determined class of beneficiaries. In any event, inheritance was dependent on live birth. Had true fetal rights of inheritance come into being, then on stillbirth the gift would pass to legal successors of the fetus, namely its parents. In fact, however, on stillbirth the portion held back pending live birth goes back to the testator's estate and forms part of the property to be distributed according to his or her wishes. The gift to the child has failed because the fetus never became a human being capable of inheritance. The fetus per se never acquired legal interests or rights.

A modern issue that challenges the Common Law understanding of the unborn arises from the possibility of fetal surgery. When it is performed on a fetus in utero, no new legal issues are raised, but when a fetus is removed for surgical or other care and is then replaced in the uterus for completion of gestation and birth, its legal status on return might be problematic. If "a child becomes a human being . . . when it has completely proceeded, in a living state, from the body of its mother whether or not it has breathed, it has an independent circulation or the navel string is severed,"[28] the fetus becomes a human being on removal from the uterus, and might seem to retain that status on return. Accordingly, it would be one human being residing within another, and its deliberate injury resulting in death, such as in abortion, might be convictable as murder, and the negligent causing of stillbirth might be convictable as manslaughter. Lawful, therapeutic abortion might become limited to instances of strict necessity, when the life of the fetus endangered the very life of the mother. This limitation might be more illusory than real, however, in the case of advanced pregnancy and the birth process, since a purely elective abortion or child destruction in delivery would be very unlikely to be medically undertaken except under such compelling circumstances.

The "born alive" test of legal status as a human being will probably be understood in future as meaning permanent as opposed to temporary removal from the mother's body. That is, the sense in which a human being has "completely" proceeded from its mother's body may refer to both physical and temporal completeness, so that a fetus removed for surgical or other care in order to be replaced in utero will not be considered to have proceeded completely from the body. If an option develops of using an artificial womb to carry viable or pre-viable fetuses outside mothers' wombs, they may have to be analogized to prematurely but permanently born human beings. The idea that their status is governed by the intention with which they are managed is not novel. The difference between legal and illegal abortion in the Common Law tradition has always turned on the question of intent, abortion intended to save the woman's life or permanent health constituting a lawful procedure.[29]

Modern Distortions of Principle

England, Canada, and other Common Law systems outside the U.S. have maintained their jurisprudence with consistency, but in the U.S. many jurisdictions have succumbed to instrumental arguments designed not only to widen the scope of physicians' civil liability but also to resist resort to abortion by recognizing the personhood and legal status of the unborn. This development has been apparent since the 1973 U.S. Supreme Court decision in *Roe v. Wade*.[30] The abortion issue has had a colonizing effect on U.S. law in that areas of law other than abortion have been taken over by advocates of positions on abortion who have made these areas of law serve the interests of their abortion-directed agendas. The fact that fetuses are now so visible and capable of personification has persuaded some courts not simply to distinguish "persons" from "human beings," but to depart from historical understanding and find that fetuses are human beings and are therefore persons. In particular, the court that determined the *Edelin* case so consistently with principle in 1976[31] observed in 1984 that

> an offspring of human parents cannot reasonably be considered to be other than a human being, and therefore a person, first within, and then in the normal course outside, the womb.[32]

This judgment was the first in which a U.S. court had included viable fetuses in a general definition of the word "person" in judicial interpretation of a penal statute. This result was accomplished by "giving terms their ordinary meaning,"[33] as opposed to the meaning that the drafters of legislation would have understood through longstanding legal usage. The statute in issue addressed vehicular homicide, but the question arises of whether the *Edelin* decision would accordingly be decided differently. It is a note of political interest that abortion opponents seek to fashion a conservative U.S. Supreme Court by being hostile to nominated justices who would "legislate from the bench," as the majority of the Court is claimed to have done in *Roe v. Wade*. However, the blatant legislating from the bench and ignoring of settled legal principles through which the Massachussets Supreme Judicial Court in 1984 reversed established jurisprudence and gave the law a novel meaning has not been condemned by abortion opponents.

The extent to which U.S. laws have become weapons in the abortion conflict is apparent in other areas. A number of state legislatures have enacted legislation designed to protect fetuses in utero and preembryos in vitro by declaring that individual human life begins at conception.[34] A number of these laws, such as the provision of the Illinois abortion law that banned experimentation on human fetuses, have on challenge been held unconstitutional.[35] Legislation remains, however, that seeks to prohibit such actions as so-called wrongful birth claims not because they are legally unsound but because they are perceived to create reasons why abortion might be favored.

Wrongful birth actions claim that a health care provider violated a legal duty owed to a parent to give information or to perform a medical procedure with due care, resulting in the birth of a handicapped child. The action emerged after biological means of genetic diagnosis and prognosis made it possible to counsel prospective parents on a child's likely genetic status, and abortion law developments had enabled such parents to terminate pregnancy in the face of an adverse genetic condition being determined during pregnancy. The action was reinforced when such techniques as amniocentesis, ultrasonic examination and fetoscopy enabled detection of nongenetic anomalies of fetuses in utero.[36]

Legislation in states including Minnesota, Missouri, and Utah has been enacted to prevent courts from accommodating the action, however, in the belief that doctors facing suits for the birth of a predictably handicapped child acquire an incentive to advise and perform abortions of affected pregnancies. This belief ignores the counterperception that parents who are aware that the birth of a handicapped child following their negligent testing and counseling would not entitle them to financial compensation may acquire an incentive of their own to abort pregnancy. It also suggests that doctors control patients' choices of medical treatments, and that doctors will or should conceal from patients their knowledge of negligently induced injuries to fetuses until they are born alive.

The greatest distortion both of legal principle and of common justice concerns approaches to actions for "wrongful life" and for wrongful death before birth that have been conditioned by opposition to abortion. Wrongful life is the misdescription given to claims through which handicapped children injured through negligence seek compensation to provide for their care after their parents no longer bear legal duties towards them for shelter, food, maintenance, and medical care. Negligence might consist in inadequate care, genetic counseling, or prenatal diagnosis afforded to their parents, as a result of which pregnancies were started or continued of children suffering predictable or diagnosable handicaps.

The name of the action, which understandably antagonizes the anti-abortion or pro-life movement, arose as a derisive and dismissive parody of the wrongful death action. The claim received little serious attention following its comprehensive rejection in the 1967 New Jersey case of *Gleitman v. Cosgrove*,[37] although academic commentary explored the extent to which it was a legally feasible action that would compensate negligently caused injury that otherwise would be uncompensated. It was shown that the wrong complained of in the action is not the child's life, but the child's predictable pain, suffering, and disability resulting from negligence.

The action was first allowed in *Curlender v. Bio-Science Laboratories*,[38] a 1980 decision in California, and subsequently refined in *Harbeson v. Parke Davis*[39] and other cases. Most significantly, New Jersey reversed its dismissive decision of 1967 and accepted the action in 1984.[40] Even before this, however, a number of states, pursuing a pro-life ideology that doctors' liability for not advising and performing abortions added to the number of abortions undertaken, legislated against courts allowing the action. A wrong would therefore be compelled to be without a remedy.

In contrast, in order to encourage protection of fetal life up to live birth, the pro-life philosophy endorses acceptance of claims on behalf of stillborn fetuses that perish due to negligence or other legal wrong. It has been seen above that, because the classical Common Law considered infliction of death a noncompensable injury, mid nineteenth-century legislation was enacted, and widely copied in the U.S., to give a statutory claim for compensation to the estates of deceased "persons" who, in the absence of negligence, would be alive. A number of states' courts have come to include stillborn fetuses within the meaning of "persons." Interpretations of such enacted laws in fact vary widely, reflecting uncertainty about whether they exist to deter wrongdoing resulting in death or primarily to provide for survivors who depended financially on the deceased person.[41] Insofar as actions brought on behalf of stillborn fetuses allow those who lost opportunities to know and parent fetuses following their live births to recover compensation, they are unobjectionable and even meritorious, although the law would do better to recognize the claims of victims of fetal losses acting directly on their own behalf rather than through the device of wrongful death actions brought on behalf of stillborn fetuses. Several jurisdictions will allow both types of claims, but seek to prevent double payments occurring when people recover for their own losses and also inherit through laws on intestacy the compensation paid to the estates of stillborn fetuses.[42]

The anomaly in some jurisdictions is that they deny wrongful life actions through which living people seek compensation for negligently inflicted injuries, but allow wrongful death claims on behalf of fetuses that are stillborn. That is, actions are dismissed by those who are rendered incapable of supporting themselves after their parents' legal maintenance duties end, but may succeed on behalf of estates of stillborn fetuses. Such a distortion is tolerable only when it serves an ideology whose values are not derived from a popular sense of justice.

CONTRACEPTION AND ABORTION[43]

The classical Common Law took no position on contraception, which in its medical forms is a product of relatively recent times. Early approaches to its development were prohibitive; for instance, in Canada until 1969 supplying information about contraceptive means and supplying such means themselves were characterized in the Criminal Code, along with abortion, as crimes against morality. In recent decades, however, family planning through chemical and mechanical contraceptive means has been found acceptable and, more positively, personally and socially responsible. Abortion tends to remain under some forms of legal control, although in most countries the controls have become increasingly relaxed.[44] It is frequently important both in law and in the practice of medicine and health care delivery, for instance, to know the difference between contraception and abortion.

Judges have not had occasion to address the difference, but in England in 1983 the attorney-general authoritatively confirmed what academic speculation had concluded, namely that acting to end pregnancy is abortion whereas acting to prevent pregnancy is contraception. The issue arose in the belief, which is unestablished, that intrauterine devices (IUDs) operate by preventing uterine implantation of a fertilized ovum, otherwise called a preembryo or pre-zygote. Activists opposed to abortion asked the attorney general to confirm that, in law, an IUD could be fitted only in accordance with provisions of the British Abortion Act 1967 on procurement of miscarriage. The attorney-general, in a parliamentary Written Answer, declined to make the declaration, and observed instead that

> the phrase procure a miscarriage cannot be construed to include the prevention of implantation. . . . The ordinary use of the word miscarriage [in the nineteenth century] referred to interference at a later stage of pre-natal development than implantation.[45]

While not judicially binding, this is a reliable and persuasive legal opinion.

In New Zealand, for avoidance of doubt on the issue, legislation was enacted. Following the 1977 report of the Royal Commission of Inquiry into Contraception, Sterilisation and Abortion in New Zealand, the Crimes Act that consolidates the law of offenses, including procurement of miscarriage, was amended to include the provision that

> the term "miscarriage" means
> (a) The destruction or death of an embryo or fetus after implantation, or
> (b) The premature expulsion or removal of an embryo or fetus after

> implantation, otherwise than for the purpose of inducing the birth of a fetus believed to be viable or removing a fetus that has died.[46]

This concern with implantation, meaning completion of the process of implantation, as the dividing line between abortion and contraception, reflects widespread understanding in countries in the Common Law tradition. It does not follow, however, that a preembryo is necessarily without legal significance. Particularly with the attachment of preembryo freezing or cryopreservation facilities to in vitro fertilization programmes, the legal regime that governs preembryos in vitro and in cryopreservation needs to be determined. A number of jurisdictions in the U.S. and, with high specificity, in Australia have legislated protective regimes for preembryos outside the uterus, including limits on research.

The Preembryo In Vitro

The classical Common Law dealt with the unborn from the point of quickening, but had no awareness of earlier stages of human reproductive biology. Legal responses to new awareness have therefore tended to come from legislation rather than judge-made law, although how judges have construed legislation has clearly been influenced by evolving perceptions. Some legislation can appear very contemporaneous or advanced. The Infertility (Medical Procedures) Act passed in 1984 in Victoria, Australia, for instance, includes provisions that center on the biological point of syngamy, meaning the time at which the genetic material of an ovum combines with the genetic material of the sperm that has entered it (whether naturally or by microinjection of a selected sperm into the ovum).[47] How contemporaneous and biologically informed the law should be is a contentious matter. In 1923 a judge in Wisconsin who upheld the legal decisiveness of quickening observed as follows:

> In a strictly scientific and physiological sense there is life in an embryo from the time of conception, and in such sense there is also life in the male and female elements that unite to form the embryo. But law for obvious reasons cannot in its classifications follow the latest or ultimate declarations of science. It must for purposes of practical efficiency proceed upon more everyday and popular conceptions, especially as to definitions of crimes that are *malum in se* [inherently wrong, in contrast to wrongs created to serve social administration]. These must be of such a nature that the ordinary normal adult knows it is morally wrong to commit them. That it should be less of an offence to destroy an embryo in a stage where human life in its common acceptance has not yet begun than to destroy a quick child is a conclusion that commends itself to most men.[48]

How well this proposition has withstood the test of time is a matter of personal judgment. In a modern world where embryos or preembryos are the subject of common news media discussion, their status is a matter of deep social division. Some believe that from conception the ensouled preembryo enjoys full human status and respect, others that, if not birth then viability is the mark of human status, and yet others that emergence of the fetal primitive streak, development of the central nervous system, or some other point of biological evolution is the mark of full membership in the human race. It may accordingly be less clear than it once was what "everyday and popular conceptions" are. Judges may have considerable scope to interpret the law by their own subjective perceptions invoking the name of an objective and detached jurisprudence.

The very language and descriptions that judges and others use are not neutral, but indicate personal dispositions. Embryologists and reproductive biologists increasingly speak of a preembryo or a pre-zygote to describe a fertilized ovum, or an ovum that has achieved syngamy, and describe it as an embryo when it has become implanted in the lining of a woman's uterus. Those who are sympathetic to or at least tolerant of the goals and techniques of such scientists are usually accepting of their language, but those who are unsympathetic and who attribute full human status to a product of human conception, often reflecting religious notions of ensoulment, refuse to recognize any qualitative distinctions among preembryos, embryos, fetuses, and human beings, but may differentiate born and unborn human beings by reference to their locations rather than their status. Indeed, in a 1989 Tennessee decision, a trial judge referred to a cryopreserved preembryo as "a human being existing as an embryo, in vitro."[49]

This decision, in the case of *Davis v. Davis*, was subsequently reversed by the Tennessee Court of Appeal and the Tennessee Supreme Court (under the name *Snowe* v. *Davis*), but it may be contrasted with the decision of the U.S. District Court for the Eastern District of Virginia in *York v. Jones*.[50] The latter decision's rational approach to control of preembryos in vitro offers the basis of sound legal policy, whereas the eccentric approach in the *Davis* trial court demonstrates confused legal reasoning, propelled by ideology rather than jurisprudence, and supports legal policies that adherents of the favored ideology deplore.

The *Davis* case concerned a couple whose marriage failed after they had attempted in vitro fertilization (IVF) by induced superovulation. Nine preembryos had been produced by IVF, and seven remained in cryopreservation when the couple separated and eventually divorced. Mrs. Davis, who had earlier had her fallopian tubes tied on health grounds, considered the preembryos to offer her only chance to have her own genetic child, and sought a court order that they be available to her for implantation. Mr. Davis resisted the order on the ground that he wanted some control over whether and when he became a father.

The trial judge was influenced by an expert witness whose testimony had earlier been rejected by a Canadian court in an antiabortion challenge,[51] and found that the preembryos were human beings, whose custody he awarded to Mrs. Davis. The judge observed that "it is to the manifest best interest of the children, *in vitro* that they be made available for implantation to assure their opportunity for live birth."[52] He ignored the fact that, had a preembryo become implanted in Mrs. Davis, she would have been legally entitled to an abortion without regard to its best interests. More significantly, had Mrs. Davis favored destruction of a preembryo when Mr. Davis had paid a woman to act as a surrogate mother to his child, the judge would have to approve the transaction since it would be in the preembryo's best interest. Indeed, had Mrs. Davis wanted implantation when she suffered from a disability that placed continued pregnancy in peril but Mr. Davis had hired an unimpaired surrogate mother, the judge would presumably have favored Mr. Davis over Mrs. Davis to assure the opportunity for live birth. In short, the judge inadvertently paved a judicial pathway to the uncritical approval of commercial surrogate motherhood.

In *York v. Jones*,[53] a couple whose cryopreserved preembryo was held by a clinic in Norfolk, Virginia, moved to Los Angeles and asked for the preembryo to be sent there for implantation into the wife. The clinic declined, primarily on the ground that IVF was subject to a protocol that required the clinic to maintain control of a preembryo. The couple's action for breach of contract and, among other claims, recovery of personal property unjustly detained, was successful. The court looked to the terms the parties had agreed for cryopreservation of the preembryo, which was named the pre-zygote in the contract, and gave effect to its terms, which placed control of its use in the couple. The court found that principles of both contract and property law supported the same conclusion.

The judgment is consistent with sound practices in IVF clinics of having couples make advance directives for disposition of their stored preembryos in anticipation of such circumstances as one or both partners' death, disability, separation, or divorce, or their disagreement.[54] The court's willingness to uphold and apply the terms of the prior agreement reinforces the policy of making choices in the event of anticipated occurrences. This minimizes uncertainty and the risk of conflict, placing control of the preembryo under the law not of crime but of contract and, to some extent, of property.[55]

The invocation of property law is provocative and offensive to those who extend the Kantian imperative that people not be treated as objects to preembryos. The private law model of contract, through which individuals may obtain services for themselves and their families and bring order to the chaos of individual initiatives through the exchange of commitments, offers a preferable legal basis of regulation of management of preembryos in vitro. It appears sound legal and social policy to promote agreements and to respect and give effect to their terms. *York v. Jones* may quickly come to represent the orthodox approach of the law to the question of who controls the destiny of preembryos in vitro.

NOTES

1. A number of antiabortion or pro-life states in the U.S. have such legislation, as have several Roman Catholic countries in Central and South America; see Cook RJ, Dickens BM. International developments in abortion laws: 1977–88. Am J Public Health 1988; 78: 1305 at 1308–09.
2. See Dickens BM. Abortion and distortion of justice in the law. Law, Medicine and Health Care 1989; 17: 395.
3. Williams G. The Sanctity of Life and The Criminal Law. London: Faber, 1957: 144, 148.
4. Cook RJ. Legal abortion: limits and contributions to human life. In: Ciba Foundation Symposium 115. Abortion: Medical Progress and Social Implications. London: Pitman, 1985: 211 at 212.
5. *Roe v. Wade*, 410 US 113 (1973).
6. Sir George Baker P. In: *Paton v. British Pregnancy Advisory Service Trustees*, [1979] Q.B. 276, at 279.
7. *In re F. (in utero)*, [1988] Fam. 122 (Eng. C.A.).
8. *R. v. Tait*, [1989] 3 W.L.R. 891 (Eng. C.A.).
9. *Tremblay v. Daigle* (1989), 62 D.L.R. (4th) 634 (Sup. Ct. Can.) at 661.
10. *Id.*
11. *Attorney-General v. T.* (1983), 46 A.L.R. 275.
12. See *R. v. Morgentaler* (1988), 44 D.L.R. (4th) 385 (Sup. Ct. Can.).
13. See the judgments in *Webster v. Reproductive Health Services*, 109 S. Ct. 3040 (1989).
14. Note 6 above.
15. See Dickens BM. Wrongful birth and life, wrongful death before birth, and wrongful law. In: McLean SAM, ed. Legal Issues in Human Reproduction. London: Gower Medico-Legal Series, 1989.
16. *Baker v. Bolton* (1808), 170 Eng. Rep. 1033 (Court of King's Bench).
17. The Fatal Accidents Act, 1846, 9 & 10 Vict., ch. 93.
18. See Special Project. Legal rights and issues surrounding conception, pregnancy, and birth. Vanderbilt Law Rev 1986; 39: 597 at 771 *et seq.*
19. See *Tremblay v. Daigle*, note 9 above.
20. See Baron CH. The concept of person in the law. In Shaw MW, Doudera AE eds., Defining Human Life: Medical, Legal and Ethical Implications. Ann Arbor, MI: AUPHA Press, 1983: 121.
21. *Edwards v. Attorney-General of Canada*, [1930] A.C. 124 (Privy Council).
22. *Commonwealth of Massachusetts v. Edelin*, 359 N.E.2d 4 (Mass. Sup. Jud. Ct. 1976) at 12.
23. See the English Infant Life (Preservation) Act, 1929, 19 & 20 Geo. V, ch 34, and, for instance, section 238(2) of the Criminal Code of Canada.
24. *Bonbrest v. Kotz*, 65 F. Supp. 138 (D.D.C. 1946).
25. See Baron CH. note 20 above at 129.
26. See *Jorgensen v. Meade-Johnson Laboratories*, 483 F.2d 237 (10th Cir. 1973.)
27. *Renslow v. Mennonite Hospital*, 367 N.E.2d 1250 (Ill. 1977).
28. See section 223(1) of the Canadian Criminal Code in text above, codifying the general Common Law.
29. See *R. v. Bourne*, [1939] 1 K.B. 687 (Eng.).
30. Note 5 above.
31. Note 22 above.
32. *Commonwealth of Massachusetts v. Cass*, 467 N.E.2d 1324 (Mass. Sup. Jud. Ct. 1984) at 1325.
33. *Id.*
34. See, for instance, the Missouri legislation at issue, although not in this regard, in the *Webster* case, note 13 above.
35. *Lifchez v. Hartigan*, 735 F. Supp. 1361 (D.C. Ill. 1990).

36. See Dickens BM. Abortion, amniocentesis and the law. Amer J Comparative Law 1986; 34: 249.
37. 227 A.2d 689 (N.J.S.C. 1967).
38. 106 Cal. App. 3d 811 (Cal. S.C. 1980).
39. 656 P.2d 483 (Wash. S.C. 1983).
40. *Procanik v. Cillo*, 478 A.2d 755 (N.J.S.C. 1984).
41. See Dickens BM. note 2 above at 400.
42. See, e.g., *Endresz v. Friedberg*, 248 N.E.2d 901 (N.Y.C.A. 1969).
43. For a fuller discussion, see Rebecca Cook, Contraception and abortion: distinctions and dynamics, in this volume.
44. See Cook RJ, Dickens BM. note 1 above.
45. The Times. London, 11 May 1983.
46. Crimes Act, 1961, No. 43, sect. 182A.
47. See Buckle S, Dawson K, Singer P. The syngamy debate: when *precisely* does a human life begin? Law, Medicine and Health Care 1989; 17: 174.
48. *Foster v. State*, 196 N.W. 233 (1923).
49. *Davis v. Davis* (1989), 15 F.L.R. 2097 (Tenn. Cir. Ct.) at 2103.
50. *York v. Jones*, 717 F. Supp. 431 (E.D. Va. 1989).
51. See *Borowski v. Attorney General of Canada*, [1984] 1 W.W.R. 15 (Sask. Q.B.), affirmed by the Saskatchewan Court of Appeal, at (1987), 39 D.L.R. (4th) 731.
52. Note 49 above at 2104.
53. See Robertson JA. In the beginning: the legal status of early embryos. Virginia L R 1990; 76: 437 at 461.
54. See Robertson JA. Prior agreements for disposition of frozen embryos. *Ohio State L J* 1990; 51: 407.
55. See Andrews LB. Control and compensation: laws governing extracorporeal generative materials. *J Med Philos* 1989; 14: 541.

RODRIGO O. KULJIS

Development of the Human Brain: The Emergence of the Neural Substrate for Pain Perception and Conscious Experience

This paper was designed to review some of the major aspects of the development of the human brain for non-neuroscientists, as a preamble for discussions on ethical, legal, philosophical, and religious dilemmas posed by new reproductive technology. The present review is limited to the key biomedical aspects of brain development as they may be pertinent to current moral, legal, ethical, and other humanistic concerns raised about the potential of modern reproductive technology. For didactic purposes, the text is divided into four sections: (1) an overview of the neural substrate for human conscious experience and pain perception, the main goal of brain development, (2) the early events during the development of the nervous system, (3) the development of the cerebral cortex, and (4) concluding remarks.

The Cerebral Cortex: Neural Substrate of Human Conscious Experience and Pain Perception

One of the major issues pertaining to the utilization of current reproductive technology rests on the understanding of the neural substrate for conscious experience and pain perception. These concerns can be posed as a series of questions on the neurological abilities of the fetus. For example, when can the embryo/fetus be considered to have a brain? When can the fetus experience pain? Does the fetus eventually become capable of self-awareness and conscious perception (and if so, when)? Can any of the temporal landmarks of the development of the central nervous system be used as unequivocal criteria for the onset of "personhood," "brain life," and to redefine when the fetus "becomes human"? In order to consider these issues appropriately, it seems necessary to address first the substrate of consciousness and pain perception in adults.

Despite the fact that we have known for at least 37 centuries that the brain is the substrate of human cognition, motor behavior, and emotion (Breasted, 1930), a precise understanding of the underlying mechanisms is still lacking. Current biomedical understanding of such substrate holds that conscious

F.K. Beller and R.F. Weir (eds.), The Beginning of Human Life, 49–56.

experience, pain perception, and voluntary movements depend critically on the integrity of the cerebral cortex, the folded sheet of gray matter estimated to contain 10^{10} neurons that covers the surface of the cerebral hemispheres. In fact, at least 200 years of progressively more scientific observation demonstrates that localized lesions of various parts of the cerebral cortex tend to result in selective deficits, such as paralysis, amnesia, and loss of sensory perceptual ability, such as blindness. While small, circumscribed cortical lesions invariably produce selective – and, in some cases undetectable – deficits in an awake and alert patient, increasingly extensive lesions of the cortex progressively obliterate consciousness and lead to irreversible coma (Plum and Posner, 1982). Nonstructural processes that transiently inactivate cortical activity, such as barbiturate intoxication, likewise preclude conscious experience and pain perception, but in a potentially reversible manner. The conclusion seems inescapable that an intact, normally functioning cerebral cortex is indispensable for human cognitive abilities. These abilities can survive, however, in the presence of some major insults, such as complete loss of voluntary motor function in one side of the body (hemiplegia) consequent to a stroke affecting the contralateral motor cortex, so long as most of the rest of the cortex remains intact. The latter provision is emphasized by conditions such as multi-infarct dementia (Hachinski et al., 1974), where usually small but numerous strokes distributed throughout both hemispheres produce generally mild motor and sensory symptoms yet progressively undermine multiple circuits which are collectively responsible for cognitive functions.

Virtually all other parts of the nervous system provide more or less important support for the preeminent role of the cerebral cortex in cognitive functions. In fact, the numerous sensory pathways that provide input to the cortex, and the motor pathways that provide an output from this region, must reach all the way from receptor organs and into muscles far from the cerebral hemispheres. Yet, the isolated loss or absence of just one, or even a few of these pathways – although leading to localized loss of sensation or paralysis – does not impair consciousness. It is important to emphasize here, however, the major role of the brain stem in activation of the cerebral hemispheres, which is essential to maintain alertness and wakefulness. Most lesions of the upper part of the brainstem result in stupor and coma, the severity of which is roughly proportional to the amount of tissue destroyed. Processes such as stroke, tumors, and trauma of this region frequently destroy ascending pathways to the cortex that are essential to maintain the level of physiological activity necessary for a wakeful state. Consequently, patients suffering from lesions of the upper brainstem often lapse into coma and eventually die. The lower half of the brainstem, while not essential for cortical wakefulness, contains vital nuclei responsible for the coordination of respiratory activity and cardiovascular regulation. Lesions of this region often result in respiratory arrest (apnea), severe drops in blood pressure (hypotension and shock), and cardiac arrest. Such lesions therefore often result in death of the patient, where the intercurrent disturbance of consciousness is due mostly to deprivation of blood and oxygen to the brain consequent to apnea, hypotension, and cardiac arrest, rather than to the original anatomical damage to the brain stem (Plum and Posner, 1982).

Pain is a sensation that depends on the integrity of pathways that convey information indicative of peripheral tissue damage to the cerebral cortex. Painful stimuli cannot be perceived if the cerebral cortex is not awake, as in coma or surgical anesthesia, and when the cortex has been subjected to extensive structural damage or is lacking (as in anencephalic infants). An important feature of the experience of pain is that it has two components: one is the awareness of a painful stimulus, the other is the emotional response (suffering) associated with it. It is known that awareness of pain can survive the destruction of many discrete regions of the cerebral cortex. However, the suffering associated with this sensation can be minimized or eliminated by means of rather small, strategically placed lesions. In fact, this is the basis for using controlled lesions of the thalamus (which provides all but olfactory input to the cortex), hippocampus, and frontal lobes to control otherwise intractable pain. Patients subjected to the now abandoned operation known as frontal lobotomy, for example, report being aware of painful stimuli, yet do not have the profound emotional response associated with what normal individuals would experience as excruciating pain. In a word, these patients "feel" pain but do not "suffer" from it (White & Sweet, 1969). This is an important factor in considering the potential for physical suffering in fetuses and infants that lack or have undergone significant destruction of parts of the brain necessary for the emotional response to pain. Presumably, such individuals are incapable or less capable of suffering pain than a child or an adult with an entirely normal brain.

The concepts subsumed above in a highly schematic fashion must be taken into consideration when interpreting the potential capabilities of the normal embryonic and fetal brain, as well as those that cannot possibly be attained by abnormal brains as a result of malformations in utero.

EARLY STAGES OF THE DEVELOPMENT OF THE NERVOUS SYSTEM

The development of the human brain starts with the formation of the embryonic disc during the 18th day of gestation (E18). At this time, part of the ectoderm (one of the three embryonic layers) that will give origin to the skin and nervous system – among other tissues – begins to form the neural plate, a thickened part of this layer. During the next two days, differential growth between the center and the edges of the plate results in the formation of the neural groove, the lips of which begin to fuse at the prospective cervical region during the 21st day of gestation (E21). This event marks the beginning of the formation of the neural tube, a cylindroid aggregate of neuroepithelial cells from which the entire central nervous system will be formed. Fusion of the lips of the neural groove progresses both anteriorly (rostrally) and posteriorly (caudally), so that the tips of the neural tube are the last to close. The rostral opening (anterior neuropore) closes about E25, and the posterior neuropore closes about E28. These events are important, in that failure of the neuropores to close results in various malformations collectively designated as dysraphism (*dys*-altered, abnormal; *raphe*-seam). Posterior dysraphism tends to result in defects of the spinal cord, such as spina bifida, while anterior dysraphism tends to result in brain defects such as anencephaly. The defects can vary from mild and asymptomatic to severe and incompatible with postnatal life, such as complete absence of fusion of the borders of the neural groove (craniorachischisis).

Anencephaly is a malformation that affects approximately 3 of every 10,000 births in the United States, and whose nature poses important medical, ethical, and legal problems. The condition consists in the congenital absence of the brain, skull, and overlying scalp, and is thought to result from failure of the anterior neuropore to close. As a result of the anterior dysraphism, a brain is formed that may be normal in size, or even oversized, but that is structurally abnormal and not covered by meninges, skull, or skin. This pseudobrain may be structurally quite elaborate, yet unprotected and supplied by abnormal blood vessels, so it becomes eroded and is eventually destroyed in utero (Hunter, 1934). Thus, only remnants of the brain, abnormal blood vessels, and scar tissue remain at the base of the brain as an "*area cerebrovaculosa*" (Lemire et al., 1978).

Anencephalic infants commonly have associated malformations of the brainstem, other regions of the nervous system, major defects of the cardiovascular system (4–15%), minor developmental abnormalities (2–31%) such as single umbilical artery and patent ductus arteriosus, hypoplastic lungs (5–34%), hypoplasia of the adrenal glands (up to 94%), and major urinary tract malformations (up to 16%) such as horseshoe kidney, polycystic or dysplastic kidneys, and unilateral or bilateral renal agenesis. Approximately 65% of anencephalic fetuses die in utero. Labor and delivery are commonly complicated for both mother and fetus, and most anencephalic infants die within the first few days after birth. In most cases cardiorespiratory arrest occurs before cessation of brainstem functions. Because these infants lack a functioning cerebral cortex, they are permanently unconscious. Brainstem function is present in varying degrees, yet they exhibit many behaviors formerly ascribed to cerebral hemispheric activity indicating their brainstem origin. These behaviors include responses to painful stimuli, feeding reflexes such as rooting, sucking, and swallowing, respiratory reflexes, interactions involving eye movements, and facial expressions seen in newborns with intact cerebral hemispheres (Medical Task Force on Anencephaly, 1990).

Since anencephalics have no functioning cerebral cortex, difficulties in documenting cerebral death relevant to other newborns are not encountered (Task Force for the Determination of Brain Death in Children, 1987). However, the frequent presence of abnormalities of eyes, ears, and cranial nerves may often interfere with the unequivocal diagnosis of brainstem death (Medical Force on Anencephaly, 1990). In these circumstances, the possibilities of performing research in these patients, withholding extraordinary life-support measures, and using anencephalics as organ donors has produced many medical, ethical, legal, moral, and religious dilemmas (Beller and Reeve, 1989; Sass, 1989a, b, 1991).

Development of the Cerebral Cortex

Given the preeminent role of the cerebral cortex as the biological substrate of human conscious experience, a detailed examination of the salient aspects of its development is particularly relevant to the objectives of this volume. In general, many aspects of the development (ontogenesis) of this region of the brain have been well characterized during mid and late gestation, particularly in nonhuman primates and other mammals. However, less information is available about early stages of the ontogenesis of this structure. According to Marín-Padilla (1978, 1983), one of the earliest signs of the impending development of the cerebral cortex is the appearance of the primitive internal capsule about E41 (Fig. 1). This structure consists of ascending nerve fibers from the brainstem, which in the adult includes thalamic fibers to the cortex, as well as descending fibers from the cortex into the brainstem and spinal cord. This primitive internal capsule carries fibers that enter the cerebral vesicle and are temporally related with the appearance of the embryonic Cajal-Retzius neurons in this region about E43. The source of these neurons is unclear.

Phenomenon	Days of Gestation
* primitive internal capsulo	41
* entrance of corticalpetal fibers into the cerebral vesicle and differentiation of the embryonic Cajal Retzius neurons	43
* ultrastructurally evident primitive synaptic contacts (Larroche, 1981)	49
* establishment of the primordial plexiform layer with complex fibrillar neuronal ("premammalian") organization	50
* appearance of the cortical plate	54
* ultrastructurally-proven synapses in the cortical plate (Molliver et al., 1973)	151

From: Marín-Padilla M. Structural organization of the human cerebral cortex prior to the appearance of the cortical plate. Anat Embryol 1983; 168: 21–40.

Fig. 1. Landmarks in the early stages of ontogenesis of the cerebral cortex.

However – according to Marín-Padilla – these are the first cortical neurons, destined to form both the most superficial and the deepest layers of the cortex. Larroche (1981) has reported that the first synaptic contacts in the prospective cortex can be observed electron-microscopically about E49. This may be consistent with Borkowski & Bernstine's (1955) report that electrocerebral activity may be recorded ex utero at E43–45, although it is difficult to be certain that this activity arises from the cortex and not from deeper regions of the brain. Only slightly thereafter, at about E50, a "primordial plexiform layer" has been observed by Marín-Padilla in the region of the future cerebral cortex, which in this author's formulation resembles the "premammalian" organization of the homologue of the cerebral cortex in reptiles. It is not until about E54 that the cortical plate appears in this region, which consists in a progressively thickening layer of primitive neurons (neuroblasts) that occupy the mid portion of the primordial plexiform layer, splitting it into a superficial and a deep half (Marín-Padilla, 1978).

The cortical plate arises from cells that originate in a germinal matrix lining the inner wall of the neural tube. The latter is an actively proliferating layer that spans the length of the neural tube, where cells first multiply and from which they escape, migrating to their final destination more or less far away from the inner wall of the neural tube. Neuroblasts cannot divide and multiply after leaving the germinal matrix, which disappears towards the end of gestation. This explains why neurons cannot be replaced once they have died (e.g., trauma, stroke) in the adult. Cells destined to form the cortical plate originate from the germinal matrix of the telencephalic vesicles, the *anlage* of the cerebral hemispheres, from E54 to about midgestation. Even shortly before escaping from the germinal matrix, the neuroblasts display growing processes that travel variable distances – from a few micrometers to almost 50 centimeters – to begin to establish synaptic contacts with neurons in the cortex, or in targets as distant as the lower spinal cord. This process, however, takes time, and it is not until E151 that the first synapses can be demonstrated electron-microscopically in the cortical plate, although synapses just above and below this structure can be seen as early as 8.5 weeks of gestation (Molliver et al., 1973). The precise functional role of these synapses is uncertain. They are not essential for the appearance of reflex responses about E49 (O'Rahilly and Gardner, 1977), and apparently are not essential either for the responses to pain, feeding, and respiratory reflexes, eye movements, and facial expressions seen in anencephalics. As mentioned previously, such behavior appears to be mediated by the brainstem, which has important implications for regarding the development of this structure as the landmark for "brain life" (Goldenring, 1985; Shea, 1985; Jones, 1989; Beller and Reeve, 1989; Sass, 1989a, b, 1091).

Recent findings in macaque monkeys by Rakic et al. (1986) indicate that cortical synapses are overproduced (2–3 times the density in adults) until 2–4 months postnatally and the excess eliminated over 1–3 years thereafter. These observations imply a significant amount of synaptic modeling during both pre- and postnatal development, such that initially the mere presence and number of synapses cannot have a direct correlation with behavioral and cognitive capabilities. Put in very simplistic terms, the infant brain does not perform better than the adult brain in spite of the fact that it has up to three times as many synapses per unit of tissue volume. On the contrary, progressive refinement in the behavioral repertoire and cognitive abilities is attended by a significant reduction in the number of cortical synapses, presumably due in part to selection of the most useful among such contacts. Given the protracted timespan of these synaptic rearrangements in nonhuman primates and humans, it is very difficult to ascertain exactly what functional capabilities – if any – are enabled by the primitive synaptic contacts in the primordial cerebral cortex. On purely speculative grounds, one may imagine that they may serve more for the elaboration of the primitive cortical structure and function, rather than for high-order information processing, as is believed to occur in adult brains.

One final important point pertains to exactly when the cerebral cortex becomes capable of mediating both the sensation of pain and the suffering associated with it. This question has, so far, no definitive answer. However, given the relative immaturity of cortical circuits until late in gestation, and the considerable difficulty in distinguishing the behavioral response to pain between normal newborns and anencephalics, it seems likely that fetuses lack the neural machinery to experience pain consciously until at least midgestation – in a very conservative estimation – and perhaps not even until much later. In fact, this question may remain unanswered forever, since newborns and even young infants apparently lack the ability to communicate verbally and to remember such experiences.

The preceding account consists of a brief summary of some of the major events in the development of the human brain, focused principally on aspects directly relevant to the emergence of the biomedical substrate of higher cerebral functions. The key elements in this formulation are the timing and mode of elaboration of the structure and function of the cerebral cortex, given the evidence from child and adult neurology that the integrity of this structure is essential for conscious experience and the complete experience of pain (sensation and associated suffering). Accordingly, it appears unlikely that the neural apparatus with which the fetus is endowed is capable of much more than unconscious reflex activity until at least midgestation and perhaps much later. Such activity – including the response to pain – is virtually indistinguishable between normal neonates and anencephalic infants that lack a cerebral cortex. In the latter, it is often only the grossly evident brain malformation that betrays the noncortical source of such behavior, which therefore appears to originate entirely from the brainstem and spinal cord.

REFERENCES

Beller FK, Reeve J. Brain life and brain death – The anencephalic as an explanatory example. A contribution to transplantation. J Med Philos 1989; 14: 5–23.
Borkowski WJ, Bernstine RL. Electroencephalography of the fetus. Neurology 1955; 5: 362–365.
Breasted JH. The Edwin Smith Surgical Papyrus. Chicago: University of Chicago Press, 1930.
Goldenring J. The brain life theory: Towards a consistent biological definition of humanness. J Med Ethics 1985; 11: 198–204.
Hachinksi VC, Lassen NA, Marshall J. Multi-infarct dementia. A cause of mental deterioration in the elderly. Lancet 1974; 2: 207–209.
Hunter RH. Extroversion of the cerebral hemispheres in human embryo. J Anat 1934; 69: 82–85.
Jones DG. Brain birth and personal identity. J Med Ethics 1989; 15: 173–178.
Larroche JC. The marginal layer in the neocortex of a 7-week-old human embryo. Anat Embryol 1981; 162: 301–312.
Lemire RJ, Beckwith JB, Warkany J. Anencephaly. New York: Raven, 1978.
Marín-Padilla M. Dual origin of the mammalian neocortex and the evolution of the cortical plate. Anat Embryol 1978; 152: 109–126.
Marín-Padilla M. Structural organization of the human cerebral cortex prior to the appearance of the cortical plate. Anat Embryol 1983; 168: 21–40.
Medical Task Force on anencephaly. The infant with anencephaly. N Engl J Med 1990; 322: 669–674.
Molliver ME, Kostovic I, Van der Loos H. The development of synapses in the cerebral cortex of the human fetus. Brain Res 1973; 50: 403–407.
O'Rahilly R, Gardner E. The developmental anatomy and histology of the human central nervous system. In: Vinken PJ, Bruyn GW, eds. Congenital Malformations of the Brain and Skull. Part 1. Handbook of Clinical Neurology. Amsterdam: North-Holland 1977; 30: 15–40.
Plum F, Posner JB. The Diagnosis of Stupor and Coma. 3d edition. Philadelphia: Davis, 1982.
Rakic P, Bourgeois JP, Eckenhoff MF, Zecevic N, Goldman-Rakic P. Concurrent overproduction of synapses in diverse regions of the primate cerebral cortex. Science 1986; 232: 232–235.
Sass HM. Brain life and brain death: A proposal for a normative agreement. J Philos Med 1989a, 14: 45–59.
Sass HM. Hirnleben und Hirntod. Medizin und Ethik. Stuttgart: Redam 1989b: pp. 160–183.
Sass HM. The moral significance of brain-life criteria. 000.
Task Force for the Determination of Brain Death in Children. Guidelines for the determination of brain death in children. Pediatr Neurol 1987; 3: 242–243.
White JC, Sweet WH. Pain and the Neurosurgeon: A Forty-Year Experience. Springfield, IL: Thomas, 1969.

HANS-MARTIN SASS

The Moral Significance of Brain-Life Criteria

While many moral and medical challenges at the end of life have found wide consensus on brain-based criteria for death, the abortion issue still causes great personal and societal moral uncertainties and conflicts. It was Andre Hellegers (1970) who stressed that

> it is not a function of science to prove, or disprove, where in this process [fetal development] *human* life begins, in the sense that those discussing the abortion issue so frequently use the word "life," i.e., human dignity, human personhood, or human inviolability. Such entities do not pertain to the science or art of medicine, but are rather of societal judgement.

on the other hand, consensus formation in nontotalitarian multicultural societies must respect the conscience of each and every citizen and his or her "inalienable right to follow one's own conscience and to profess and practice one's own faith . . . people must not attempt to impose their own 'truth' on others'" as Pope John Paul II underlined in his address of January 1, 1991, "If You Want Peace, Respect the Conscience of Every Person": When religious law becomes synonymous with civil law, it

> can stifle religious freedom, even going so far as to restrict or deny other inalienable human rights. . . . Intolerance can also result from the recurring temptation to fundamentalism, which easily leads to serious abuses, such as the radical suppression of all public manifestations of diversity. (John Paul II, 1990)

The four most important tools to be used in the respect for and the development of individual moral competence and cultural, legal, and moral consensus are (1) the history of moral argumentation, (2) cultural tradition, (3) moral evaluation of scientific evidence, and (4) the analytical and evaluative methods of assessing specific moral scenarios at the beginnings and ends of human life. A bioethical evaluation of the moral significance of neuromaturation, using these four methodological tools, will have to assess biomedical facts and biomedical technologies according to moral and cultural values. These values can be established by differential value diagnosis of

F.K. Beller and R.F. Weir (eds.), The Beginning of Human Life, 57–70.

concrete moral scenarios and by the hermeneutics of value history. I will proceed in three steps: (1) review the moral argumentation which led to widely accepted brain-death criteria, (2) evaluate the role of neuromaturation as a biomedical correlate to and indicator for the moral recognition and legal protection of the nasciturus, and (3) present a formula for consensus formation in public policy regarding issues of contraception, abortion, embryo research, and the protection of early human life.

It will be my thesis that the moral assessment of maturation and cessation of neuro-neuronal functioning, based on biblical, philosophical, and theological tradition, favors a Uniform Determination of Life Protection Act, legally protecting personal life (animate life) from the beginning of brain functioning (brain life) to its end (brain death).

A Uniform Determination of Life Protection Act could read as follows: *An individual developing or having integrated brain functions has the right to moral recognition and legal protection. A determination of integrated brain function must be made in accordance with accepted medical standards.*

Bioethical assessment of established biomedical facts suggests the protection of human life from the presence of neuro-neuronal integration in the cortical plate zone (around the 70th day after conception), when personal life becomes imminent, up to the absence of integrated brain functions, when somatic death becomes imminent.

H93While the ontological and ethical interpretation of biomedical facts of brain functioning can find wide cultural and moral consensus, teleological arguments from the "potentiality" of unborn life are logically inconclusive and morally invalid, as they favor one ontological potential (conception) over others (gametes, genome expression, nidation, individualization, synapsis formation, viability, birth).

For the stage prior to approximately the end of the 10th week of gestation (day 70 PC) the abortion decision must be left to the pregnant woman, following medical consultation and spousal discussion, where necessary. For the stage subsequent to the 10th week, the state, in promoting its interest in the protection of unborn human life, may, if it chooses, regulate and even proscribe abortion except where it is necessary, in appropriate medical judgment, for the preservation of the life or health of the mother. Public policy based on a Uniform Determination of Life Protection Act would allow for abortion up to the end of the 10th week of pregnancy and the withdrawal of life support from patients diagnosed to be brain-dead according to established criteria; competent adults should be allowed to opt for higher brain-death criteria for themselves, if they so choose. Research on inanimate human life would require bioethical guidelines and review boards. Individuals or groups holding stricter philosophical or religious views regarding the moral recognition of inanimate life would have every right to act accordingly.

Bioethical Reasoning Supporting Brain-Death Criteria

The shift from circulatory and respiratory indicators of death to brain-related indicators can serve as a case study in successfully applying differential ethics and value assessment to new bioethical challenges developed by biomedical technologies. Traditionally the death of a person was identical to the death of his or her organs. It was not necessary to differentiate between the cessation of functioning of particular organs and the death of the person as long as cessation of breathing and heartbeat caused a chain reaction, at the end of which all other organs had to stop working. But intensive-care technology supporting pulmonary and cardiovascular functions and the technical availability of heart transplantation and the artificial heart made it necessary to morally and culturally define the end of personal life in correlation with the functioning of particular organs.

In 1968 an ad hoc commission of the Harvard Medical School after bioethical evaluation of biomedical facts of the processes of dying came forward with a new and more precise biomedical criterion for bioethically defining the death of a person: brain death (JAMA 1968; 205: 337–340). This criterion has since been accepted, with technical refinements, in most countries.

The relatively smooth and widely accepted bioethical shift from cardiopulmonary death to whole-brain death was made possible by dominant values and principles in Western tradition, supported by the humanist Greco-Roman as well as the religious Judeo-Christian traditions. These values predetermined an anthropological understanding of the ontological "nature" of humans, to be related to the differentia specifica of reasoning, communicating, and self-communicating. The concept of man in Greek philosophy was that of *zoon logon echon*, i.e., the animal having as its specific difference reason and communication, cognition and consciousness; the Roman term *animal rationale* confirmed this concept, as do the dominant anthropological and ontological positions of modern philosophy since the Age of Reason. The Old Testament reports the creation of Adam after God's own image. God, in blowing his own breath (*ruach Jahwe*) into his creature after basic gestation, made the human corresponding, communicative to the creator, and different from the rest of creation. The general pattern of the image of God, the special relationship of the creator to his image, was reaffirmed and deepened in Christian belief in Jesus as the son of God, in his suffering and resurrection, and in the eternal kingdom of heaven as something spiritual, not biological. Additionally, the Christian doctrine that teaches the departure of the soul from the body at the moment of death strongly supports the brain-death concept.

Secular as well as religious Western ontological and anthropological concepts recognize "human dignity" and "personal life" as something different from the mere biological existence of human flesh, tissue (germline, fetal, somatic), vegetative human life, or the mere functions of bodily fluids; the

Christian tradition differentiates between inanimate and animate or ensouled fetuses. The U.S. President's Commission (1981, 42) summarizes: "A statute incorporating a brain-based standard is accepted by theologians of all backgrounds." It was not philosophical curiosity, but rather medical and moral need to differentiate morally and culturally between medical-moral scenarios of heart life, brain life, brainstem life, cerebral life, etc. The new definition did not create new moral principles or values; rather, it interpreted new technologies and new medical findings in the light of traditional principles and values, making the newly acquired scientific and technical wealth instrumental for strengthening the wealth of values.

The shift to a brain-oriented definition of death had the following five medical, moral, legal, and cultural advantages: (1) human life that meets the strict and well-defined biomedical criteria of whole-brain death does not deserve the same moral recognition and legal protection as other humans, while other forms of comatose or vegetative human life, including cessation of neocortical functions, are not covered under this formula; (2) moral, emotional cultural, social, and economic costs that would have been associated with the artificial extension of brain-dead life can be saved; (3) organs become available for patients who otherwise would die or face severe suffering, hardship, or inconvenience; (4) one single biomedical criterion serves as a correlate for a bioethical consensus on one specific scenario at the end of human life and the traditional difference between animate and inanimate life: "cessation of all functions of the entire brain"; (5) those whose system of belief does not support whole-brain-related criteria of death will not be required to change their belief and conduct and may choose to be diagnosed by traditional circulatory and respiratory criteria of death.

The Uniform Determination of Death Act states:

> An individual who has sustained either (1) irreversible cessation of circulatory and respiratory functions, or (2) irreversible cessation of all functions of the entire brain, including brain stem, is dead. A determination of death must be made in accordance with accepted medical standards. (US, President's Commission, 1981, 2)

The Moral Significance of Synapsis Formation as the Criterion for Brain Life

In strong contrast to the consensus regarding the end of life, we do not have a uniform understanding regarding the beginning of human life that has to be morally recognized and legally protected. On the contrary, we have a variety of rational and irrational, biological, religious, political, and legal positions, more or less developed, fighting each other, and creating great moral uncertainty for individuals and professionals involved, as well as moral risk to the fabric of societies torn apart by the friends and foes of pro-life and pro-choice advocates. If we did not have the Uniform Determination of Death Act, based on the bioethical interpretation of biomedical criteria of brain functioning, we definitely would have the same moral uncertainties regarding organ transplantation, prolongation of the process of dying, feeding vegetative human life, and terminating intensive care as we now have at the beginning of human life in the absence of a Uniform Determination of Life Protection Act. Moral obligations and agreements, based on similar criteria related to brain functioning and regarding the protection of early human life, the use of embryonal tissue or organs for farming or transplantation, and embryo experimentation, must and can be reached if we apply the methods of consensus formation which led to the widely accepted criteria of brain death.

If the special difference of humans in regard to other living beings is our rational capacity for conscience and self-consciousness, for communications and traditions, for arguing over right and wrong, then criteria related to the functioning of the brain will provide a moral and cultural basis for a societal moral consensus with regard to the beginning of morally significant human life. A symmetry between brain life and brain death has been discussed for twenty years now (Beller, 1989; Brody, 1982; Goldenring, 1985; Kannegiesser, 1988; Jones, 1988; Sass, 1985, 1989). Such brain life-based criteria would eliminate morally unacceptable different, even double standards regarding the protection of early human life. In the United States different states have different laws and legal rulings; in the Federal Republic of Germany an Embryo Protection Law was passed by the federal parliament to protect oocytes, fertilized eggs, zygotes, and blastocysts from experimentation, while reaffirming the right to abort under easily met criteria up to the end of the first trimester. Those discrepancies and differences in moral assessment and management are morally unacceptable, socially hazardous, legally unwarranted, and politically risky. A better way must be found to assure the protection of morally significant early human life and the moral and social fabric of a society based on commonly shared values and principles. Any criteria which would establish a consensus as broad as the whole-brain–oriented definition of death have to meet at least the following requirements: (1) compatibility with most of the major cultural traditions in existing pluralistic societies, (2) compatibility with the medical understanding and explanation of the process of human embryonal development and gestation, (3) simplicity of definition and diagnosis, and (4) a high preponderance of moral, medical, and cultural advantages over disadvantages. These criteria can be met only by a definition of brain life or brain birth which would function in "a consistent and evenhanded fashion," as the President's Commission (1981, 43) proposed for brain-death criteria.

In analogy with the definition of human death as brain death, all these criteria are best met by relating human life to brain life. The absence of brain-specific cells in early embryonal development could be understood as the absence of brain life. Following the Aristotelian-Thomist tradition, we may call prenatal human life prior to brain life inanimate, while developing brain can be interpreted as animating life, and stages of developed brain functions as animate, ensouled, or personal life. Information on neuromaturation will provide the biomedical facts which call for bioethical interpretation.

Animate human life, allowing for significant and adequate functioning of the cerebral-cortex presence of sensory telereceptors, central control of body functions and movements, logical communication with other persons, handling of tools, etc., occurs quite a while after birth (Kuljis, 1991); essential controls for bodily functions, the feeling of pain, and the distinct capacities to develop mature functions with the help of parents, guardians, and society are present earlier. We do not know yet when the process of animation ends or whether or not it ever ends. In searching for a statute to protect early human life we want to go a morally less risky road, to morally recognize the first ontological evidence of animating life; we leave the discussion of the transition from animating life to fully animate life to be debated by later generations.

Ontologically the earliest possible manifestation of biomedical facts, the beginning of synapsis formation between postmitotic stationary neurons in the subplate zone, can be interpreted as a biological correlate to the beginning of brain life. According to the Carnegie stages of neuromaturation (O'Rahilly and Mueller, 1987; Kostovic, 1990; Kuljis, 1991) we can identify in stage 7 (day 18 PC) the first appearance of the neural plate, in stage 15 (day 33 PC) the development of cerebral vesicles, and in stage 22 (day 54 PC) the appearance of the cortical plate formed by a single layer of postmitotic cortical neurons. No functional cortical brain tissue can be recognized at this time, even though spinal reflexes and brainstem activities have been documented at stage 22. The cortical neuroblasts, which lost the ability to divide and multiply and which cannot be replaced once they have died (e.g., trauma, stroke) will soon start to interconnect by forming neurites, dentrites, and synapses during the so-called process of synaptogenesis. These beginnings of neuro-neuronal interconnecting structures are the precondition of communication between individual neurons, neuron conglomerates, higher-brain hemispheres, and the parts of the brain, and between the brain and the other parts of the body. The first appearances of synapsis formation in the cortical plate zone and subplate zone occur in isolated areas around day 70 PC (Kostovic, 1990), but may be transient (Korein, 1986, 339). The "stabilization of interneuronal synapses" around and after day 151 PC will be the prerequisite for "interneuronal information processing required for learning, memory, awareness, and other complex mental processes" (Korein, 1986, 341, 339).

The first stages in the structural ontogenesis of the cerebral cortex, the formation of synapses, are the precondition for all further intercommunicating between neuroblasts and the development of the functioning higher brain. Synapsis formation can be interpreted as the beginning of animating life. Prior to the day 70 PC we have only biological, inanimate life. During the early stages of animating life, there definitely can be no functional higher-brain life, i.e., no reasoning or controlling of bodily functions, no feeling of pain, no consciousness or self-consciousness. The isolated networks must grow and grow together, to interconnect and to connect with other parts of the brain and the organs. This takes a long time and continues postnatally, but it happens in an evolutionary way, without precisely identifiable steps which would be of essential developmental or moral relevance.

A morally conservative assessment of neuromaturation suggests that inanimate embryonal life prior to day 70 PC, i.e., higher-brain-absent life, would be the symmetrical correlate to brain death at the end of human life. Consequently, only animating life (after the 70th day PC) and animate life at a later stage of neuromaturation ("operational brain life," Korein, 1986, 335) should be morally recognized and legally protected, as only from these stages onward can one identify neurons, which start interconnecting and finally will represent what the tradition calls *imago Dei*, *animal rationale*, the ensouled body.

Uniform brain-life criteria for morally recognizing unborn human life have been suggested recently by physicians (Goldenring, 1985; Beller, 1989; Jones, 1989), theologians (Overhage, Rahner, 1961; Haering, 1973), and philosophers (Brody, 1982; Sass, 1985; Kannegiesser, 1988; Sass, 1989a, b). Some identified the closure of the anterior neuropore (Rahner, 1961; Beller, 1989; Sass, 1985), others "brain-wave" activity measured by EEG (Goldenring, 1985; Jones, 1989) as the morally significant step in embryonal development. Jones argues that the first synapses "are very few and far between and they are unlikely to be functional," he suggests that stages after day 151 PC, from the 23d week of gestation up to 18 months after birth, develop a more "distinctive characteristic" of the networks in the human brain. EEG activity has been demonstrated as early as during the 14th week, with more generalised activity during the 22d week, but this activity is "discontinued with long periods of electrocerebral silence" up to the 32d week. He concludes: "If the EEG is to be taken as a guide to brain birth it is a highly conservative tool, placing the emergence of the semblance of an adult pattern at 32–36 weeks' gestation" (Jones, 1989, 176f).

Goldenring, a noted pediatrician and student of Andre Hellegers, concludes that functioning cortical brain, which according to our terminology would be the first manifestation of animating life, does not occur prior to the 22d to 28th week of gestation (Goldenring, 1985, 202), while Jones, anatomist and neuroscientist, interprets the period between the 24th and 28th week of gestation, "when most developmental sequences" of the brain have started, as the period of "brain birth," which "demarcates the transition from non-personhood to personhood", following the maxim "Whenever a functioning human brain is present, a human being is alive" (Jones, 1989, 178, 200).

Some problems in accepting Goldenring's and Jones's concept of morally recognizing the earliest stages of functioning brain, i.e., animated life, are related, as mentioned, to inconclusive interpretations of early fetal EEG activity and the fact that their moral assessment might have to be reassessed in close contact with steadily exploding new information regarding neuromaturation. Our proposal is more conservative, as it does not venture to medically or morally interpret early EEG activity or the moral significance of various states in cortical synapsis formation, thereby providing for a "safety net" in moral assessment. Actually, our proposal stops short of venturing into the moral evaluation of the stages of the evolutionary processes of the development of neuro-neuronal interconnecting and of forming the structures and ultrastructures of the higher brain. It only recognizes the ontological differences which become manifest in the first transition from isolated neurons to interconnected neurons in the cortical plate zone. These interconnected neurons will subsequently and gradually form functional higher-brain tissue during a long, complex, and not yet fully understood process. In searching for the widest possible societal consensus regarding the protection of animate human life, it is a morally very safe and conservative judgment to refer only to the first biological evidence of synapsis formation among postmitotic cerebral neurons as the prerequisite for cortical differentiation, which is the necessary physiological substratum and correlate to personal life.

Noted Roman Catholic theologians Karl Rahner and Bernhard Haering recognized that "hominization" (Haering, 1973; Overhage, Rahner, 1961) and personal life cannot at all be demonstrated theologically without the development of the biological conditions and presuppositions of personal life; both identify the cerebral cortex as the biological correlate to the Christian concept of personhood and *imago Dei*. Grobstein argues that because prior to the eighth week of gestation the embryo cannot be affectively recognized by others nor be consciously aware of him- or herself, it is a pre-person, not a person (Grobstein, 1981). Kushner also relates brain activity to personhood in differentiating between "life" and "subjective life": "Until it has developed a brain capable of consciousness the fetus's biography is not yet started. There is no life (bios) of which the fetus is subject, although there are lives of which the fetus is a part" (Kushner, 1984). She recognizes the eighth week of gestation as a stage where a previous incapacity for consciousness has developed into a capacity for consciousness. Similar arguments related to the beginning of the organizing capacities of the brain in regard to organs and the body as a crucial prerequisite for personhood are voiced by Shea (Shea, 1985); his arguments find strong support in the traditional Christian semantics of differentiating between the inanimate or unformed and the animate or formed fetus. Kannegiesser, who is closest to our own moral assessment of neuromaturation, concludes that "from about 10 weeks after conception until death, most human beings have sufficient moral value to warrant both care and protection . . . the beginning of brain activity heralds the beginning of moral value while the cessation of brain activity (brain death) signals the end of the individual as a morally relevant entity." He proposes to replace criteria related to personhood by those related to brain functioning because of culturally different concepts of personhood (Kannegiesser, 1988, 412). Brody

(1982, 245f.), in using an ontological "theory of essentialism," argues that fetal humanity can only be based on brain functioning because "a functioning brain (or at least, a brain that, if not functioning, is susceptible of function) is a property that every human being must have because it is essential for humans," as evidenced by a wide consensus on brain-death criteria, and that "one ought to conclude that the fetus becomes a human being at some time between the 6th and the 12th week after its conception."

Some have suggested (Haering, 1972; Sass, 1985; Beller, 1989) that the closing of the neural tube would be a significant stage of neuromaturation, as the closing of the neural tube, which does not occur in anencephalics, is preconditional for the development of brain cells other than brainstem tissue. But the closing of the neural tube marks just one of a variety of necessary conditions for transforming possibility into reality, while postmitotic stationary neurons in the cortical plate forming synapses are a reality. Even though cell death will be the fate of a great number of postmitotic brain cells later on, during the process of the closing of the neural tube no single cell exists which will be among the survivors of neuronal cell death, for there are no postmitotic cells yet.

At the beginning of life we should find greater consensus for a definition of cortical life than we have up to now been able to find for a definition of cortical death. Among the arguments favoring cortical brain-life statutes are the following: (1) other parts of the brain are still in development and maturation, even though the brainstem shows earlier functions, some of transient nature which in adults will be taken over by higher-brain structures; (2) there is no significant functioning of interrelation between developing and differentiating parts of the brain, so that the criteria proposed by Truog and Fletcher would not apply (Truog, Fletcher, 1990); (3) other organs are not yet functioning in a meaningful manner or connected to the brain, so the criteria discussed by Shea would not apply (Shea, 1985); (4) Aristotelian-Thomist ontology and anthropology, differentiating between inanimate and animate unborns, suggest cortex-related criteria rather than whole-brain-related criteria for recognizing personhood (Overhage, Rahner, 1961); (5) where the medical and ethical technicalities of interpreting biomedical criteria of comatose or persistent vegetative people do not exist, higher-brain-related criteria represent a "conceptual clarity" (Sorenson, 1988, 246) over whole-brain death definitions (Veatch, 1986; Sorenson, 1988).

A Uniform Determination of Life Protection Act, based on strong cultural tradition and consequent moral argumentation, considering integrated brain functioning, beginning with the presence of neuro-neuronal synapses in the subcortical plate and ending with the absence of brain functioning (whole-brain or higher-brain options) includes the following moral, cultural, legal and political benefits: (1) one single statute protects the moral value of human life from the beginning to the end; (2) the symmetry between brain-life and brain-death criteria represents conceptual clarity; (3) brain-life and brain-death criteria translate the ethos of strong ontological and moral traditions into the scenarios of modern biomedicine and its bioethical challenges; (4) moral criteria of differentiating between abortive, contraceptive, and contraimplantative techniques become irrelevant, and these techniques will have to be assessed on grounds other than those of "killing a person"; and (5) inanimate and postanimate forms of human life do not deserve the same moral recognition and legal protection as animating and animate life, reducing moral uncertainty and emotional stress in dealings with the beginning and end of human life.

Diagnosis of animating life can be done in accordance with accepted standards of determining the age of the fetus by ultrasound measurement of its size, by calculation of post-ovulation days, following HCG testing, or by other yet-to-be-established methods, depending on progress in directly diagnosing stages of neuromaturation. Given the accuracy of correlating the size of the embryo to its gestational and neuronal development, ultrasound diagnosis seems to be a good and sufficient indicator for determining the stage after which fetal life should be protected.

Thus the proposed uniform determination of Life Protection Act, could be expanded as follows: *An individual developing or having integrated brain functions deserves moral recognition and legal protection. A determination of integrated brain function must be made in accordance with accepted medical standards. Bioethical assessment of established biomedical facts suggests the protection of human life from the presence of neuro-neuronal connections in the cortical plate zone, when personal life becomes imminent, to the absence of integrated brain functions, when somatic death becomes imminent.*

As long as the technical diagnosis of irreversible cessation of higher-brain functions is not available or inconclusive, and insofar as different religious and philosophical positions are uncertain about the significance of higher-brain criteria versus whole-brain criteria, it would be advisable to have a uniform public statute mandating the "irreversible cessation of all functions of the entire brain, including brainstem" definition of the Uniform Determination of Death Act (U.S. President's Commission, 1981) as a default position; this would allow competent citizens to opt out of this position by specific advance directives or living wills demanding the application of other criteria for death (e.g., higher-brain criteria) for themselves. Such an option, however, cannot be applied to the strict and unconditional moral recognition and legal protection of early human life from around the seventieth day PC on, but would allow for individuals and religious groups to morally recognize and protect earlier stages of fetal development.

Public Policy Issues and Uniform Determination of Life Protection

The moral assessment of neuromaturation offers unique opportunities for moral and societal consensus formation on abortion and embryo research and for a symmetry with moral criteria based on the cessation of brain function at the end of life. A Uniform Determination of Life Protection Act can find the widest possible cultural, moral, and legal support. But the determination of the beginning and the end of morally recognized and legally protected human life has to be deliberately conservative rather than liberal. As has been discussed, moral assessment of neuromaturation, as well as dominant forces in philosophical and theological tradition, represented by authorities such as Aristotle, Saint Augustine, and Saint Thomas, favor moral and legal criteria for protecting animate life from the beginning of the first appearance of animation, based on brain functioning and covering the beginning (brain life) as well as the end (brain death) of human life.

Public policy consensus cannot be based on notions of "potentiality." Rather, as in the case of the Uniform Determination of Death Act, court decisions, legislation, regulation, and public morality and policy should be based on a moral and legal interpretation of biomedical facts. While the ontologically interpreted biomedical fact of synapsis formation in the cortical plate zone of what will become the cerebral cortex, occurring around or after day 70 PC, suggests that personal life cannot begin prior to neuro-neuronal interconnections, teleological arguments from the "potentiality" of unborn life are logically inconclusive and morally invalid as they favor one ontological potential (conception) over others (gametes, individual genome expression, nidation, individualisation, synapsis formation, quickening, viability, birth).

A Uniform Determination of Life Protection Act would protect unborn human life earlier and more strictly than the *Roe v. Wade* decision (*Roe v. Wade*, 41 LW, 4229), which does not protect the embryo prior to the 12th week and suggests, if the state so chooses, the legal protection of the fetus only after the 24th week of pregnancy. In contrast to *Roe v. Wade* our proposal recommends the following: For the stage prior to approximately the end of the 10th week of gestation (day 70 PC) the abortion decision must be left to the pregnant woman, following medical consultation and spousal discussion where necessary. For the stage subsequent to the 10th week, the state, in promoting its interest in the protection of unborn human life, may, if it chooses, regulate and even proscribe abortion except where it is necessary, in appropriate medical judgment, for the preservation of the life or health of the mother.

A national consensus formation body, similar to the ad hoc Harvard committee on brain death in 1968, could set up the argumentative framework for the diagnosis of biomedical criteria of brain life, allowing for the bioethical evaluation and legal protection of the beginning of personal human life. A uniform statute should address the protection of human life from its beginning to its end.

Individuals or groups holding stricter philosophical or religious views regarding the moral recognition of inanimate or vegetative life must have every right to retain their views and act accordingly. Philosophical or religious convictions applying more liberal concepts of animate life versus inanimate life should be tolerated if the acts based on these beliefs will affect themselves only, not others; they could do so by means of advanced directives or living wills requesting higher-brain death criteria for themselves in decisions of termination of medical intervention or organ transplantation.

A Uniform Determination of Life Protection Act would legalize abortion of inanimate life, as well as the use of contraceptives or devices which prevent nidation, and the termination of treatment after all brain functions, including those of the brainstem, have ceased. Naturally, it will not suppress the right of each individual to morally recognize earlier stages of fetal development. We owe respect to inanimate unborn life as we owe respect to human corpses and cadavers; the specifics of this respect will be expressed in different ways, given the multitude of diverse cultural and moral positions in a pluralistic society. No woman shall ever be forced to accept abortion or contraception, as the moral assessment of those interventions will depend on her particular system of values and beliefs. Legislative or regulatory bodies might require mandatory consultation for pregnant juveniles prior to abortion. On the other hand, no individual or group shall be allowed to dominate public policy, regulation, or legislation with their particular views on the beginning and the end of human life, life after life, or the moral status of the fertilized or unfertilized egg.

Research on inanimate human life will require bioethical guidelines and the involvement of bioethical experts or committees. Research on inanimate life or its use for diagnostic or therapeutic purposes will require the consent of those providing sperm, ova, or zygotes, the same way organ transplants may not be done without the consent of the donor.

References

Ad Hoc Committee of the Harvard Medical School. A definition of irreversible coma: report of the Harvard Medical School to examine the definition of brain death. JAMA 1968; 205: 337–340.

Beller FK, Reeve J. Brain life and brain death – the anencephalic as an explanatory example. J Med Philos 1989; 14: 5–23.

Bettenson H. Documents of the Christian Church. Oxford: Oxford U. Press, 1963.

Bole TJ. Human beings, substances, souls and persons. Unpub. ms.

Bondeson WB, et al., eds. Abortion and the Status of the Fetus. Dordrecht, Holland: D. Reidel Publishing Company, 1983.

Braude P, et al. Human gene expression first occurs between the four- and eight-cell stages of preimplantation development. Nature 1988 (Mar); 332: 459–461.

Brody B. The morality of abortion. In: Contemporary Issues in Bioethics. Beauchamp TL, Walters L, eds. Belmont, CA: Wadsworth 1982: 240–250.

Brody B. Religious perspectives on the beginning of human life. Unpub. ms.

Buckle SK, Dawson, Singer P. The Syngamy Debate: When Precisely Does a Human Life Begin? In: Embryo Experimentation. Singer P, et al., eds. Cambridge: Cambridge U. Press 1990: 213–225.

Colby WH, et al.. Cruzan: clear and convincing? Hastings Center Report 1990; 20: 5–11.

Congregation for the Doctrine of the Faith. Instruction on Respect for Human Life and Its Origins and the Dignity of Procreation. Vatican.

Dagi FT. Death-defining Acts. In: Historical and Cultural Observations on the End of Life, Pediatric Brain Death and Organ/Tissue Retrieval. Kaufman HH, ed. New York: Plenum Publ, 1–30.

Dagi FT. The beginning of life. A Talmudic view. Unpub. ms.

Dawnie J. Brain death and brain life: rethinking the connection. Bioethics 1990; 4: 216–231.

General Synod Board for Social Responsibility. Personal Origins. London: Church Information Office Publ., 1985.

Gervais KG. Advancing the definition of death. Med Humanities Review 1989; 3: 7–19.

Goldenring J. The brain life theory: towards a consistent biological definition of humanness. J Med Ethics 1985; 11: 198–204.

Grobstein C. From Chance to Purpose. An Appraisal of External Human Fertilization. Reading MA: Addison-Wesley Publ., 1981.

Haering B. Medical Ethics. Fides, Notre Dame IN.

Hare RM. Embryo experimentation: public policy in a pluralistic society. Proceedings of the IVF Conference. Center for Human Bioethics, Clayton, Australia Monash University 1987: 106–123.

Hellegers A. Fetal development. Theological Studies 1970; 31: 3–9.

Hellegers A. Allowing anencephalics to die. Obstet Gynecol News 1974; 9: 48.

Hinrichsen KV. Realisationsstufen in der vorgeburtlichen Entwicklung des Menschen. [Medizinethische Materialien Nr. 55]. Bochum: Zentrum für Medizinische Ethik, 1990.

John Paul II. If you Want Peace, Respect the Conscience of Every Person. Vatican City, 1990 (Dec).

Jones DG. Brain birth and personal identity. J Med Ethics 1989; 15: 173–178, 185.

Kannegiesser H. Conception in the Test Tube. South Melbourne: Macmillan, 1989.

Korein J. Brain states: death, vegetation, and life. In: Cottrel and Turndorf, eds. Anesthesia and Neurosurgery 1986: 293–351.

Kostovic I. Entwicklung des Zentralnervensystems, Humanembryologie. Hinrichsen KV ed. Heidelberg: Springer Publishing Company, 1990.

Kuhse H. Thinking about destructive embryo experimentation. Proceedings of the IVF Conference. Center for Human Bioethics, Monash University, Clayton, Australia, 1987: 96–105.

Kuljis RO. Development of the human brain: The emergence of the neural substrate for pain perception and conscious experience. In this volume.

Kushner T. Having a life versus being alive. J Med Ethics 1984; 10: 5–8.

Lockwood M. Warnock versus Powell: when does potentiality count? Bioethics 1988; 2: 187–213.

McCormick R. How Brave a New World? London: SCM Press, 1981.

Noonan JT. The Morality of Abortion: Legal and Historical Perspectives. Cambridge MA: Harvard U Press, 1970.

O'Rahilly R, Mueller F. Developmental Stages in Human Embryos. Meriden CT: Meriden Press, [Carnegie Inst. of Washington, Publ. No. 637], 1987.

Overhage P, Rahner K. Das Problem der Hominisation [questiones disputatae, no. 12(3)]. Freiburg: Herder, 1961.

Sass HM. Extrakorporale Befruchtung und Embryotransfer. Zukünftige Möglichkeiten und ihre Bewertung. Arch Gynecol 1985; 238: 81–105.

Sass HM. Brain life and brain death: a proposal for a normative agreement. J Philos Med 1989a; 14: 45–59.

Sass HM. Hirnleben und Hirntod. In: Medizin und Ethik. Stuttgart: Reclam 1989b: 160–183.

Shea MC. Embryonic life and human life. J Med Ethics 1985; 11: 205–209.

Singer P, H Kuhse, et al. Embryo Experimentation. Cambridge: Cambridge U Press, 1990.

Sorenson JH. The determination of death: the need for a higher-brain death definition. In: Monagle JF, Thomasma DC, ed. Medical Ethics. Rockville MD: Aspen Pub, 1988: 234–248.

Truog RD, Fletcher JC. Brain death and the anencephalic newborn. Bioethics 1990; 4: 199–215.
U.S. President's Commission for the Study of Ethical Problems in Medicine and Biomedical and Behavioral Research. Defining Death. Washington DC: Government Printing Office, 1981.
Veatch RM. Whole-brain and neocortical definitions of death. In: Edwards RB, Graber GC, eds. Bioethics. New York: Harcourt Brace, 1988: 414–424.
Zaner RM, ed. Death: Beyond Whole-Brain Criteria. Dordrecht, Holland: D. Reidel Publishing Company, 1988.

PART TWO

Assisted Reproductive Technology

RICARDO H. ASCH

Assisted Reproductive Technologies of the 1980s and 1990s: The State of the Art and a Look at the Future

The present paper is concerned with the problem of infertility in the United States and presents an overview of the new technologies available to help infertile couples who have successfully tried conventional treatments.

Demographics

Infertility is conventionally classified as ovulatory, tubo-peritoneal, uterine, or cervical. Immunologic factors are also considered, as is endometriosis. The male contributes to roughly one-third of all infertility cases. The category of unexplained infertility is decreasing because of modern technology. The numbers in the various categories as published in four series are listed in Table I. According to Mosher (National Center for Health Statistics) there are 4.5 million infertile couples in the United States (Table II). However, the

Table I
Etiology of infertility: Percentages

	Hull et al[1]	Collins et al[2]	Dor et al[3]	DCI[4]
Ovulatory disturbances	21	31	31	27
Tubo-peritoneal	14	16	16	15
Cervical	3	5	1	2
Uterine	–	–	4	2
Endometriosis	6	4	2	4
Immunologic	10	–	–	3
Male	26	31	28	28
Unexplained	28	14	18	19
Number of cases	708	1145	665	750

Sources:
[1] Br Med J 1985; 291: 1693.
[2] N Eng J Med 1983; 309: 1201.
[3] Fertil Steril 1977; 28: 718.
[4] February 1987, University of California, Irvine

F.K. Beller and R.F. Weir (eds.), The Beginning of Human Life, 73–88.

Table II
Distribution of infertile couples by etiology in the USA

Etiology	%	Estimated no.
Tubo-peritoneal	15	675,000
Ovulatory disturbances	27	1,215,000
Cervical	2	90,000
Uterine	2	90,000
Endometriosis	4	180,000
Immunologic	3	135,000
Male	28	1,260,000
Unexplained	19	855,000

Source: Mosher W and Pratt W. Fecundity and infertility in the United States: Incidence and trends. Fertil Steril 1991; 56: 192.

view that we can simply link infertility to a single problem is simplistic, since many couples have more than one problem. In recognizing the complexity of infertility, a listing such as in Table II is of value, both statistically and clinically. When treated by conventional approaches, many couples will be cured, i.e., become pregnant (by "conventional" is meant anything short of the new technologies, such as no treatment at all – many infertile patients get pregnant without treatment – or treatment to correct particular problems such as ovulation disturbances, cervical factors, etc.).

The percentage of couples pregnant after three years of conventional therapy is listed according to etiologic category in Table III. Patients with problems of ovulation, the most common problem of infertile couples, with become pregnant in 87% of cases. If, however, the problem is located in the fallopian

Table III
Distribution of infertile couples by etiology and results from treatment in the USA

Etiology	Estimated no. of couples	Cure rate %	Eligible for GIFT	Eligible for IVF
Tubo-peritoneal	765,000	19		546,760
Ovulatory disturbances	1,215,000	87	157,950	
Cervical	90,000	44		50,400
Uterine	90,000	50		
Endometriosis	180,000	30	126,000	
Immunologic	135,000	70		40,500
Male	1,260,000	20		1,080,000
Unexplained	855,000	61	333,450	
Donor insemination	25,000	20	5,000	
Oocyte donation	147,000	0	147,000	
Total number of potential couples			769,400–1,940,300	546,750–1,717,650

Based on data available concerning pregnancy rates after three years of conventional therapy.

tubes, only 9% will become pregnant. Another problem with a low success rate is that of male infertility (oligoasthenospermia). Only 20% of wives become pregnant, regardless of the treatment modalities. This means that a large population (80%) needs additional treatment. We believe that after three years of unsuccessful treatment, new reproductive technologies should be used.

NEW ART (ASSISTED REPRODUCTIVE TECHNOLOGIES)

By now there are thousands of scientific articles, chapters, and books published about the new reproductive technologies. All of them go back to two original techniques: the first, developed in England in 1978 by Drs. Steptoe and Edward, and referred to as IVF-ET, in vitro fertilization and embryo transfer, and the second, developed by our group in 1984 in San Antonio at the University of Texas, and called GIFT or gamete intrafallopian transfer. Figure 1 is a diagrammatic representation of both IVF-ET and GIFT. The IVF-ET process entails removing the oocytes, or unfertilized eggs, from the ovaries,

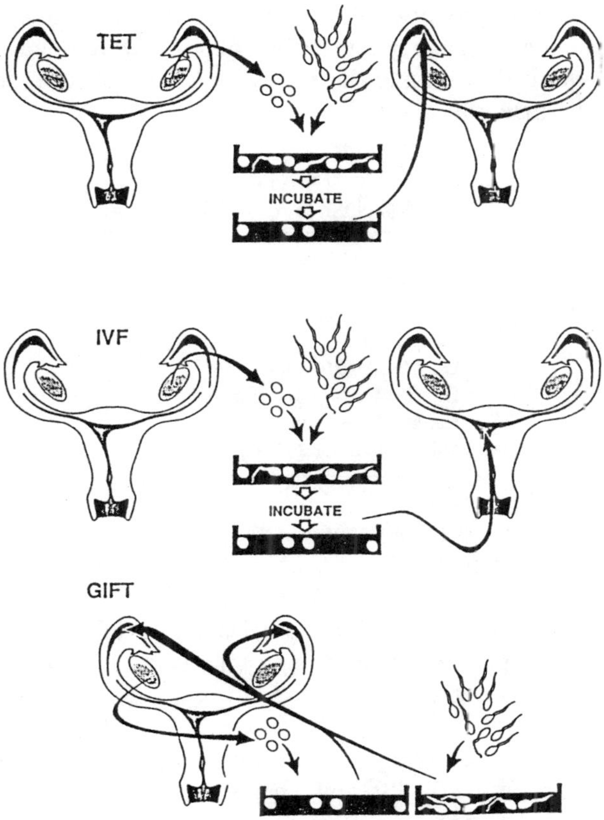

Figure 1.

placing them in a petri dish or a test tube, adding asperm is culture medium, allowing both gametes (sperm and egg) to incubate for about 48 hours, and then transferring the resultant embryos into the uterine cavity, hoping that in another five days some of those embryos will implant in the endometrial cavity.

In the GIFT technique, the eggs obtained from the ovaries are combined with the sperm inside the fallopian tube (where we believe fertilization takes place in the human). We expect that fertilization will occur, and that the embryos will move into the uterus, implant, and produce a pregnancy.

Table IV shows the chronology of a GIFT cycle; an IVF-ET cycle is very similar. It begins with induction of follicular development, that is, stimulation of multiple follicles in the ovaries. In the past, we used a protocol of stimulation that was a combination of clomiphene citrate and human menopausal gonadotropin. However, in the last five years we have used a new drug on the market, a luteinizing hormone-releasing hormone (LH-RH) agonistic analogue, leuprolide acetate. We can give leuprolide acetate either in the follicular phase of the treatment cycle (flare-up or up-regulation) or during the luteal phase (desensitization or down-regulation) of the preceding cycle. The treatment of ovarian stimulation with the aid of LH-RH analogues has helped greatly to produce more eggs, highter-quality eggs, fewer cancellations, and a better pregnancy rate. After follicular development is achieved, patients receive hCG to mimic the midcycle LH surge, in order to produce the final oocyte maturation.

Table IV
Chronology of a GIFT Cycle

1.	Induction of follicular development
2.	hCG administration
3.	Sperm preparation
4.	Oocyte pick-up
5.	Oocyte identification
6.	Gamete loading and transfer
7.	Luteal phase support
8.	Diagnosis of pregnancy

In most units, oocyte retrieval is carried out by laparoscopy or by ultrasound-guided aspiration. At UCI, we obtain the eggs exclusively via vaginal ultrasound. Their quality is judged microscopically. Dependent upon the protocol of stimulation, the size of the follicles, the estradiol levels in the blood, and the age of the patient, different egg quality will be observed, ranging from preovulatory (mature), grades 4–5, to immature or germinal vesicles, grades 1–2.

Sperm are obtained generally by masturbation prior to egg collection, and the specimen is processed by different types of laboratory techniques, according to the quality of the specimen. Basically, there are three techniques available: (1) sperm wash and swim-up, (2) percoll gradient, and (3) egg yolk technique. A team of biologists decides which of these techniques is appropriate, according to the characteristics of the semen sample. All three techniques have the same goal: to select from the entire ejaculate the most active fraction of sperm with the highest concentration of normal forms. Sperm are prepared prior to the oocytes being aspirated, then loaded into a catheter with the eggs, and transferred into the fallopian tubes.

In most units GIFT procedures are performed on an outpatient basis, via laparoscopy or mini-laparotomy, with similar results. In the last few years, good results have also been obtained in nonsurgical tubal gamete transfers by ultrasound-guided tubal cannulation transcervically. Figure 2 is a translaparoscopic view of the gamete transfer. It shows the fimbria being pulled from the dorsum (antimesosalpingeal area) with an atraumatic forceps; a catheter is inserted approximately 3 cm inside the fibria; then, very slowly, very gently, we inject an average of 2 eggs and about 100,000 mobile sperm per fallopian tube. This procedure is repeated in the other fallopian tube. In the IVF-ET technique, rather than transferring the gametes into the fallopian tubes, the sperm and egg meet in a test tube and are placed in an incubator. Approximately 60–70% of the time they will form an embryo, and the embryo/embryos (maximum of 4) are transferred, in a nonsurgical manner, through the cervix into the uterus.

IVF-ET and GIFT are the basis of all techniques available today in assisted reproductive technology. One additional available technique is a hybrid of IVF-ET and GIFT. Originally developed by our team in 1984, it is called tubal embryo transfer (TET), zygote intrafallopian transfer (ZIFT), or pronuclear stage transfer (PROST), according to the moment of embryogenesis in which embryos are transferred to the fallopian tubes. Basically, eggs are inseminated in the incubator (such as in IVF-ET), and then one or two days later, after fertilization can be confirmed, those embryos are transferred into the fallopian tubes, as in GIFT.

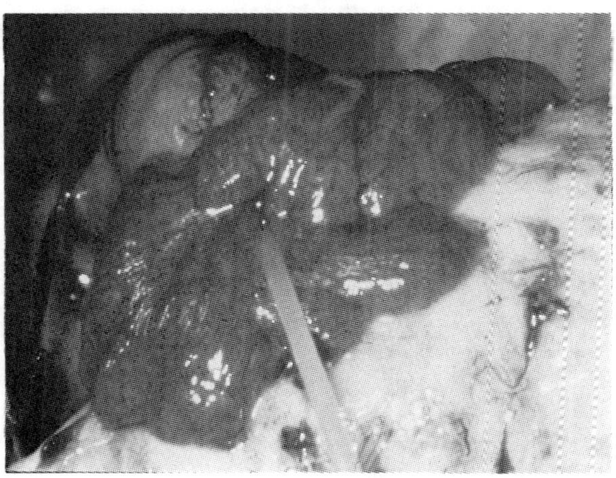

Figure 2.

Results

Multinational and AFS Data: IVF-ET and GIFT

The results of a multinational cooperative study carried out in 1987 in 12 different centers throughout the world are shown in Table V. Out of 2,092 cases there were 601 pregnancies, giving a 28.7% clinical pregnancy rate per attempt. According to the etiology of the infertility, the pregnancy rate varies with a given technique. In Table VI, the pregnancy outcome from GIFT conceptions is shown: 16.7% were miscarriages in the first trimester, 3.9% were ectopic pregnancies, and approximately 80% of pregnancies entered the second trimester.

Table V
Multinational cooperative GIFT study results: Clinical pregnancies

Etiology	No. of cases	No. of pregnancies	% Success
1. Unexplained infertility	796	247	31
2. Male	397	61	15
3. Endometriosis	413	132	32
4. Failed AID	160	66	41
5. Tubo-peritoneal	210	61	29
6. Cervical	68	19	28
7. Immunological	30	5	10
8. Premature ovarian failure	18	10	56
Total	2092	601	28.7

Source: Asch RH, Balmaceda JP, Cittadini E. Gamete intrafallopian transfer. International cooperative study of the first 800 cases. Ann NY Acad Sci 1988; 541: 722–7.

Table VI
Multinational cooperative GIFT study results: Pregnancy outcome

Etiology	Miscarriage (%)	Ectopics (%)	Live Births (%) or ≥ 12 weeks
1. Unexplained infertility	16.1	2.4	81.5
2. Male	12.7	3.9	83.4
3. Endometriosis	20.8	3.3	75.9
4. Failed AID	21.2	0	78.8
5. Tubo-peritoneal	16.3	11.0	72.7
6. Cervical	15.8	21.0	63.2
7. Immunological	20.0	0	80.0
8. Premature ovarian failure	10.0	0	90.0
Total	16.8	3.9	79.3

Source: Asch RH, Balmaceda JP, Cittadini E. Gamete intrafallopian transfer. International cooperative study of the first 800 cases. Ann NY Acad Sci 1988; 541: 722–7.

There are two factors that influence whether a patient will become pregnant or not through a GIFT cycle: the number of eggs, and the quality of those eggs. The multinational study revealed that if in a given cycle 14 or more eggs are retrieved, the patient should have, in that particular GIFT cycle, at least a 40% chance of becoming pregnant. Guzick et al. of the University of Pittsburgh, in a collaborative study with UCI, analyzed statistically all the factors that determine whether a pregnancy will take place or not during a GIFT cycle. They determined that the main variables associated with a successful GIFT were the quality of eggs transferred and the motility of sperm. In summary, both quantity and quality of eggs are important, as is therefore the induction of controlled ovarian stimulation.

The results published in the international literature comparing GIFT and IVF-ET outcome represent the world experience (Table VI). In the AFS registry of 1987, the pregnancy rate with IVF in all of the United States was 16% and with GIFT 25%, with take-home baby rates of 11% and 18%, respectively. In 1988, at the same centers performing GIFT and IVF, the pregnancy rates were 28% for GIFT and 16% for IVF, according to the United States IVF Registry reports (Medical Research International). Australia and Japan also have looked at GIFT and IVF data together. The Australian study reports a 25.6% pregnancy rate with GIFT, and 13.2% with IVF. In Japan, Mori's data revealed a pregnancy rate for IVF of 10%, and for GIFT 31%.

Improving Results

The Use of TET in Male Factor Infertility

After five years of experience with GIFT, we asked ourselves how we could improve the results of GIFT (Table VII). We found, first, that whenever we performed GIFT with very low sperm count and motility the results were very disappointing. All these cases are now switched to TET, which is producing excellent results.

We analyzed the first consecutive 135 cases of TET performed at UCI for severe male factor infertility, and we compared these results with the outcome

Table VII
How can we improve results?

1. Better patient selection	TET in male and immunological factor
2. Less invasive	US and hysteroscopic transfer
3. Safety	Avoid multiple pregnancies; limit no. of oocytes to 2–3
4. Effectiveness	LHRH analogues; cryopreservation of sibling embryos
5. More practical	NET programming (see text)

of GIFT in similar cases. The pregnancy rate per GIFT attempt was very low, only 16%. However, when TET was performed the pregnancy rate went up to 53% per transfer, a change that was statistically highly significant in favor of TET. In cases without the male factor, there is no apparent increase in the pregnancy rate from TET over GIFT, 36% versus 35% overall, respectively; therefore, in the non-male factor cases of infertility, we do not recommend TET over GIFT. Of the 47 pregnancies obtained in the initial study, 9 (19%) ended in spontaneous abortion, 1 was an ectopic pregnancy, and 12 (45%) were multiple pregnancies (all twins). The take-home baby rate, perhaps the most relevant datum, was 39% per attempt.

The development of the technique of TET, which places embryos in the fallopian tubes rather than in the uterine cavity (as in IVF-ET), gave us the opportunity to learn more about the ability of embryos to develop and implant after different transfer sites during early embryogenesis.

We examined data from patients at our institution in the assisted reproductive technology program, analyzing 232 cases of IVF-ET and 126 cases of TET. We obtained 51 pregnancies in the IVF series, and 67 from TET: that is, 22% per attempt for IVF versus 53% per attempt for TET ($p < 0.001$).

In this study, an embryo transferred to the fallopian tube had a chance of implanting in the uterus (implantation rate) of about 17.8%, compared with the 8.8% chance of an embryo transferred to the uterus. Again, there was a marked difference in favor of TET over IVF for the chance of an embryo implanting in the uterus ($p < 0.001$). Overall, of 232 cases of IVF, 51 pregnancies were produced with a 29% miscarriage rate and a take-home baby rate of 16%. That means that of every 100 couples undergoing IVF in our unit, 16 go home with a baby. With 126 cases of TET, 67 pregnancies were obtained with an 18% miscarriage rate, and a 44% take-home baby rate. There is an overwhelming difference in the take-home baby rate in favor of TET over IVF ($p < 0.001$).

The conclusion of our study is that in the human, transfer of the embryos into the fallopian tube results in a higher chance of implantation, pregnancy, and live birth. These findings are irrespective of the number and quality of embryos transferred. We believe that the reasons for improved success with TET include the following: (1) there are some factors in the fallopian tube that have a protective role in early embryo development and implantation; (2) the uterus may have some deleterious effects on the early embryo which prevent implantation or development; (3) the chances of "embryo loss" after transfer to the tubes may be much lower than when the embryos are introduced into the uterine cavity via the cervix.

Nonsurgical Transfer

In addition to the use of TET in male factor infertility, another possibility in improving the efficiency of a GIFT cycle is to be less invasive and safer, i.e., to attempt a nonsurgical transfer.

Considering safety, it is obvious that nonsurgical access to the fallopian tubes is highly desirable. There are three possibilities: with the aid of the hysteroscope, by ultrasound-guided catheterization of the fallopian tube, and by blind transcervical gamete or embryo tubal transfer. Janus and Anderson demonstrated that with the aid of vaginal ultrasound, catheterization of the fallopian tube through the vagina, cervix, uterine cavity, and the uterotubal junction is possible with good training of the operator. It is possible to transfer either sperm and eggs or embryos to the tubes, performing a nonsurgical GIFT or TET, respectively. In March 1990 most of the scientists performing these nonsurgical procedures met in Paris to review the data gathered in the last three years. The 12 reporting centers had an overall 22% pregnancy rate performing either GIFT or TET nonsurgically.

A great advantage of these new techniques is the important clinical and scientific information gathered therefrom. AT UCI Balmaceda led an original study to determine the volume capacity of the human fallopian tube. Most of the experiments were carried out combining either hysteroscopic and laparoscopic procedures, or by digital hysterosalpingography and hysteroscopies. These studies showed that the total volume of fluid injected into the uterotubal junction of the fallopian tube to obtain spillage at the fimbria is always around 120–150 microliters. At the very beginning of the history of the GIFT technique, we injected 100–200 microliters of fluid into the fallopian tube, so it is very likely that much of it was either passing to the uterus or refluxing into the peritoneal cavity.

Recently, Diedrich and co-workers in Bonn, Germany, reported that they can gain access to the fallopian tubes by blind transcervical catheterization using no control at all in over 75% of the attempted trials. Their pregnancy rates for nonsurgical blind GIFT or TET are very similar to those reported with conventional routes of transfer. Even though all data of nonsurgical tubal catheterization for gamete or embryo transfer appear very encouraging at this time, it would be prudent to gain more clinical experience before deciding whether these routes of transfer should be used routinely for all patients.

The Use of NET

In order to improve further the efficiency of a GIFT cycle, we have studied the effectiveness of a progestin, norethindrone acetate (NET), in controlling the onset of menses in a group of patients undergoing controlled ovarian hyperstimulation. Twenty patients were given NET to program the initiation of controlled ovarian hyperstimulation and to coordinate follicular aspiration with surgery to obtain spermatozoa from the husband. Patients received NET, 10 mg/day orally, starting between days 2 and 4 of the cycle. The duration of NET therapy varied from 9 to 37 days. The mean time of onset of vaginal bleeding after cessation of NET was 2.9 ± 0.7 days. Ovarian stimulation was carried out with a combination of a luteinizing hormone-releasing hormone analog, follicle-stimulating hormone, and human menopausal gonadotropin.

The day on which human chorionic gonadotropin (hCG) administration occurred ranged from day 8 to day 15 of the cycle (10.1 ±1.7). On the day of hCG injection, the mean E_2 level was 2188 ± 1126. The mean number of follicles aspirated was 18.4 ± 9.9 per cycle. The mean number of oocytes collected per cycle was 15.5 ± 8.5. There was no correlation between duration of NET suppression and the number of days of gonadotropin therapy needed to reach hCG administration. The large number of oocytes retrieved is probably related more to the fact that the patient couples had purely male factor infertility than to the specific drug protocol utilized. Our results indicated that ovarian response to gonadotropin stimulation was not affected by NET administration. The main advantages of the use of this drug for cycle control are that its administration is oral, simple, and inexpensive.

Cryopreservation of Extra Eggs

There are still other ways by which the efficiency of a particular GIFT cycle can be increased. Tables VIII and IX are from a prospective study by Alam, Weckstein and colleagues. They studied patients who had a single GIFT procedure, dividing them into two groups whether they became clinically pregnant or not. In this particular study, 50% became pregnant, and 50% did not in each GIFT attempt. In each of these attempts, most patients produced

Table VIII
Outcome of 121 patients initiating a GIFT cycle

	No.	% of A	% of C	% of E
A. Initiated a GIFT cycle	121			
B. Cancel/poor response	20	17		
C. Oocyte Aspiration	101	83		
D. Switch to IVF/FET	23	19	23	
E. GIFT transfers	78	64	77	
F. Pregnant from GIFT	34	28	34	44
G. Not pregnant from GIFT	44	36	44	56

Table IX
Cumulative pregnancy rate from one GIFT cycle with cryopreservation of supernumerary embryos

A. GIFT transfers	78
B. Pregnant from GIFT	34 (44%)
C. Pregnant from frozen ET	2 (2%)
D. Cumulative pregnancy rate	46%
E. Not pregnant from GIFT; no frozen ET yet	6
F. Pregnant from GIFT, with frozen embryos remaining	22

Source: Alam V, Weckstein L, Ord T, Stone S, Balmaceda JP, Asch RH. Cumulative pregnancy rate from one gamete intrafallopian transfer (GIFT) cycle with cryopreservation of embryos: A practical mathematical calculation. Human Reprod 1992. In press.

more eggs than the four transferred in the GIFT cycle. These extra eggs, "sibling eggs," were subjected to conventional IVF techniques, and if embryos were formed, they were cryopreserved in 1,2 propanediol. The pregnancy rate from frozen embryo transfers was about 30–35%. Thus the pregnancy rate from the GIFT program, if we add together the cycle of GIFT and all the potential pregnancies arising from future transferred cryopreserved embryos, could reach 56% per attempted GIFT cycle – obviously a very high success rate.

ART in Women over Age 40

A topic that has attracted the attention of the media recently is that of pregnancy in women over 40 produced with the aid of the new reproductive technologies. The data from our unit on this subject are interesting and provocative. We divided 152 patients over 40 years of age according to the ART they underwent and whether they used their own eggs (group 1) or unfertilized eggs donated to them by a younger subject (group 2). In group 1, in 35 cases of GIFT we obtained 10 pregnancies, of which 5 went to term and 5 were miscarried. In 35 cases of TET, 16 pregnancies were achieved and 8 were lost. In 41 patients who underwent IVF, only 2 pregnancies were obtained, and only one ended in a term delivery. Overall, despite a 25% pregnancy rate in women over 40 using new reproductive technologies, 50% of their pregnancies were lost in the first trimester.

These findings show clearly that in women over 40 years of age there is an overwhelming advantage in using the fallopian tubes rather than the uterus for a selective route of gamete or embryo transfer, if patients were stimulated to use their own eggs.

In group 2, 41 patients over 40 years of age underwent GIFT, TET, and IVF, but received eggs donated by younger volunteers. Six GIFT cases resulted in 4 pregnancies, 7 TET in 4 pregnancies, and 28 IVF in 8 pregnancies, for an overall 40% pregnancy rate with a much-reduced abortion rate of only 25%. In summary, women over 40 years of age became pregnant using their own eggs to a much lesser degree than if they used donated younger eggs. This study corroborates a recent report of a collaborative effort of our UCI unit with that of Steptoe and Edwards in Bourn Hall that demonstrated clearly for the first time that the uterus does not appear to age in the human. Under identical conditions of steroid preparation of the endometrium and age of embryos, the chances of implantation and pregnancy are identical in women of all ages.

The Use of Egg Donation

It is well known that the infant girl is born with millions of eggs in her ovaries. Throughout her years of reproductive life, these eggs disappear in a process termed attrition of oocytes (Table X). At the age of 50 to 53, when menopause

Table X
Attrition of oocytes in the human

Fertilization age	No. of oocytes
6 weeks	600,000
20 weeks	7,000,000
Newborn	2,000,000
3 years	800,000
6 years	600,000
12 years	400,000
22 years	300,000
50 years	Just a few

occurs, there are very few oocytes left in the ovary. The curve describing the number of eggs available in the ovary peaks before birth and ends at menopause. Unfortunately, this curve is sometimes shifted to the left, and a woman can reach menopause at an earlier age. This could occur at age 30, or at the time the girl is ready to start her menarche, or even before that baby girl is born. We know that in the U.S. premature ovarian failure (POF) is the cause of 28% of all cases of primary amenorrhea, and that 1% of all women will cease having their menses before the age of 40. We estimate that about 150,000 women in the U.S. have undergone premature menopause. Until a few years ago, these women had no possibility of being treated for permanent sterility.

In 1984, Lutjen of Monash University obtained an egg from a donor, fertilized it in vitro with sperm from the recipient's husband, then transferred the embryo to the recipient (a subject with premature menopause); fortunately, she became pregnant. Other units, including ours at UCI, using different techniques, have achieved pregnancies with egg donation, either with GIFT or TET. Possible recipients of egg donation, in addition to patients with POF, include subjects who have undergone surgery, radiation, or chemotherapy for cancer and whose ovaries have become nonfunctioning; poor responders to fertility drugs; subjects whose ovaries we cannot reach because they are inaccessible in scar tissue; subjects who do not want to transfer their genetic disease to their progeny; and patients who continue to attempt IVF, but whose eggs never fertilize (Table XI).

We analyzed the data of 186 patients who consulted our unit, 72 of whom underwent egg donation for a total of 84 transfer cycles. The average age of recipients was the mid 30s. Both donor and recipient sign separate legal consent forms for donation or receipt. (There are two types of egg donation: First, some patients who undergo GIFT or IVF produce many more eggs than could be transferred to them, and they are willing, anonymously and altruistically, to give those to other patients. The second type of donation is not anonymous, as, for example, when a patient has a sister who is willing to donate eggs to her.) Patients receiving egg donations not only need eggs but, because they

Table XI
Indications for oocyte donation

- Premature ovarian failure
- Gonadal dysgenesis
- Iatrogenic: Surgery, radiation, chemotherapy
- Poor responders to controlled ovarian hyperstimulation
- Carriers of undesirable genetic traits: x-inked or autosomal dominant
- Repeated failure of fertilization in vitro
- Unexplained repeated pregnancy wastage

Source: Alam V, Weckstein L, Ord T, Stone S, Balmaceda JP, Asch RH. Cumulative pregnancy rate from one gamete intrafallopian transfer (GIFT) cycle with cryopreservation of embryos: A practical mathematical calculation. Human Reprod 1992. In press.

have no endogenous estrogen or progesterone production, require treatment to create the environment of a normal menstrual cycle. We prescribe exogenous estradiol and progesterone in different doses, obtaining blood levels very similar to those of a normal spontaneous ovulatory menstrual cycle. Endometrial biopsies performed during evaluation mock cycles revealed a secretory endometrium in the majority of cases, and in about 60% of them we have noted a delayed luteinization (of 1 to 4 days) based on clinical endometrial dating. Of 39 cases of IVF with egg donation, 17 pregnancies occurred, for a 43.5% pregnancy rate; 28 cases of GIFT resulted in 14 pregnancies (50% pregnancy rate). For 17 cases of TET, there were 10 pregnancies, for a 59% pregnancy rate. The take-home baby rate for IVF was 36%, for GIFT 44%, and for TET 36%. These numbers are not statistically significantly different; apparently, in this particular model of a patient who is not hyperstimulated with gonadotropins, who has a normal or delayed endometrium and levels of progesterone and estrogen similar to those of a normal menstrual cycle, there appears to be no advantage to one technique of embryo transfer over the other. We believe that the high pregnancy rates in our egg donation program are due to the following: (1) lack of endometrial hyperstimulation; (2) lack of hyperestrogenism; (3) lack of underlying infertility disorders; (4) lack of premature luteinization; (5) better control of window of receptivity; (6) incubation of oocytes in vitro prior to GIFT.

Micromanipulation of Gametes

Microinjection of Sperm

The success of treatment for male infertility by GIFT, TET, and IVF is limited in cases in which a radically reduced number of immotile and highly abnormal sperm exist. In these instances, the placement of a capacitated spermatozoon in direct contact with the oolemma of the oocyte, or inside the oocyte, should increase the chance of fertilization for patients with severely reduced semen quality. This new approach, called microinjection of sperm in human oocytes, represents a future option for male factor infertility. However, to date the results obtained by microinjection are controversial, and a definite role in the treatment of male factor infertility cannot yet be substantiated. This technique could also provide important information concerning the physiology of the fertilization process, including sperm-oolemma contact, oocyte activation, sperm decondensation, and pronuclear formation.

Zona Pellucida Drilling

Zona drilling and partial zona dissection (PZD) entail the use of micromanipulation to create a gap in the zona pellucida – either mechanically or by localized application of a zona solvent from a microneedle. The theoretical advantage of this technique is that a semen sample with low count, low motility, and highly abnormal forms can fertilize an oocyte in vitro through the creation of a hole in the zona pellucida.

However, as with the microinjection approach, more experience is required before this technique can be utilized as a routine clinical offering. A high incidence of polyspermy is related to zona drilling, suggesting that in human oocytes the zona pellucida serves as a mechanism to block polyspermy. Recently Tadir assessed the potential use of laser microbeams for controlled, "non-contact" zona drilling. A well-shaped controlled crater in the zona pellucida was produced. The accuracy of this method enables drilling several neighboring apertures, without causing damage to the vitelline membrane and the ooplasm content. Ongoing experiments in our unit are exploring the increase in fertilization following laser drilling of oocytes in cases of severe male factor infertility.

Microsurgical Epididymal Sperm Aspiration (MESA)

Until recently, men with congenital absence of the vas deferens, failure of previous vasoepididymostomy, and congenital ejaculatory block could not produce their own genetic progeny because of the impossibility of achieving active sperm. Four years ago, we reported the achievement of two pregnancies and the first two births to couples where the husband presented with congenital absence of the vas deferens. In these cases the sperm, under 10X to 40X magnification with an operating microscope, were retrieved directly from the distal or proximal part of the blind-ending epididymis. The aspirate was immediately diluted and examined for sperm motility and quality of progression. If sperm were not found or if motility was absent, another aspiration was made 0.5 cm more proximally, and the process was continued until an area of motile sperm was reached. The recovered sperm were treated utilizing either the previously mentioned swim-up or minipercoll techniques. The resulting embryos were transferred to the fallopian tubes (TET) approximately 51 hours after the insemination.

The results accumulated thus far with MESA are very promising. After performing more than 100 MESA and TET procedures our pregnancy rate is approximately 28%, with a fertilization rate of over 30% per oocyte. The retrieval of sperm from the epididymal-vasa efferentia may potentially benefit other patients on whom surgery cannot be performed to restore the normal anatomy of the male genital tract (Table XII). A fascinating and exciting aspect of this technique is the fact that it has long been assumed that sperm must pass through a certain length of epididymis to mature, gain progressive motility, and become capable of fertilization. However, the pregnancies obtained with sperm aspirated from a proximal epididymal area, and two pregnancies reported with sperm from vasa efferentia, open once again the question raised by Orgebin-Crist in 1969: Are the factors governing the maturation process intrinsic to sperm, or do they reside in the epididymis? Further work in this area is needed to answer this longstanding query.

Table XII
Potential US cases benefiting from epididymal sperm aspiration

Congenital absence of the vas	41,000
Failed reversal at vasectomy	60,000–300,000
Other non-operable obstructions	41,000
Severe oligoasthenospermia	690,000
Total	832,000–1,072,000 men

References

Alam V, Weckstein L, Ord T, Stone S, Balmaceda JP, Asch RH. Cumulative pregnancy rate from one gamete intrafallopian transfer (GIFT) cycle with cryopreservation of embryos: a practical mathematical calculation. Human Reprod 1992. In press.

Asch RH, Balmaceda JP, Cittadini E, Cases PF, Gomel V, Hohl MK, Johnston I, Leeton J, Rodriguez Escudero FJ, Noss U, Wong PC. Gamete intrafallopian transfer: International Cooperative Study of the First 800 Cases. NY State J Med 1988; 541: 722–727.

Asch RH, Balmaceda JP, Ellsworth LR, Wong PC. Gamete intrafallopian transfer (GIFT): a new treatment for infertility. Int J Fertil 1985; 30: 41–45.

Asch RH, Balmaceda JP, Ellsworth LR, Wong PC. Preliminary experiences with GIFT (gamete intrafallopian transfer). Fertil Steril 1986; 45: 366.

Asch RH, Balmaceda JP, Ord T, Borrero C, Cefalu E, Gastaldi C, Rojas FJ. Oocyte donation and gamete intrafallopian transfer (GIFT) as a treatment for premature ovarian failure (POF) [Letter]. Lancet 1987; 3: 21.

Asch RH, Balmaceda JP, Ord T, Borrero C, Rodriguez-Rigau LJ, Rojas FJ. Gamete intrafallopian transfer (GIFT) and oocyte donation: a novel treatment for infertility in premature ovarian failure. Gynecol Endocrinol 1987; 1: 105–111.

Asch RH, Balmaceda JP, Wong PC, Ellsworth LR, Daich EA, Zuo WL, Remogida V, Santos R, Garcia M. Gamete intrafallopian transfer (GIFT): use of minilaparotomy and an individualized regimen of induction of follicular development. Acta Eur Fertil Steril 1986; 14: 187–193.

Asch RH, Ellsworth LR, Balmaceda JP, Wong PC. Birth following gamete intrafallopian transfer [Letter]. Lancet 1985; 2: 163.

Asch RH, Ellsworth LR, Balmaceda JP, Wong PC. Pregnancy following translaparoscopic gamete intrafallopian transfer (GIFT). Lancet 1984; 2: 1034.

Asch RH, Wong PC, Borrero C. LH-RH and its analogues. Gynecol Fertil 1987; 10: 1–45.

Australian In Vitro Fertilization Collaborative Group. High incidence of pre-term birth and early in pregnancy after in vitro fertilization. Br Med J 1985: 291–1160.

Balmaceda JP, Gastaldi C, Remohi J, Borrero C, Ord T, Asch RH. Tubal embryo transfer as a treatment for infertility due to male factor. Fertil Steril 1988; 50: 476–479.

Borrero C, Ord T, Balmaceda JP, Rojas F, Asch RH. The GIFT experience: an evaluation of the outcome of 115 cases. Human Reprod 1988; 3: 227–230.

Borrero C, Remohi J, Ord T, Balmaceda JP, Rojas F, Asch RH. A program of oocyte donation and GIFT. Human Reprod 1989; 4: 275–279.

Cefalu E, Balmaceda JP, Guastella G, Ord T, Rojas FJ, Cittadini E, Asch RH. Successful GIFT following failed AID: evidence for a defect in gamete transport. Fertil Steril 1988; 50: 2.

Diedrich K, Bauer O, Van der Ven H, Al-Hasani S, Krebs D. Transvaginal intratubal embryo transfer: a new treatment of male infertility. Human Reprod 1991; 6: 672.

Gerli S, Remohi J, Patrizio P, Borrero C, Balmaceda JP, Silver S, Asch RH. Programming of ovarian stimulation with norethindrone acetate in IVF/GIFT cycles. Human Reprod 1989; 4: 746–748.

Guidetti R, Balmaceda JP, Ord T, Asch RH. Non-surgical tubal embryo transfer [Case report]. Human Reprod 1990; 5: 221–224.

Guzick D, Balmaceda JP, Ord T, Asch RH. The importance of egg and sperm factors in predicting the likelihood of pregnancy from Gamete Intrafallopian Transfer. Fertil Steril 1989; 52: 795–800.

Lutjen P, Trounson A, Leeton J, Findlay J, Wood C. The establishment and maintenance of pregnancy using in vitro fertilization and embryo donation in a patient with primary ovarian failure. Nature 1984; 907: 174.

Medical Research International, Society for Assisted Reproductive Techniques. In vitro fertilization, embryo transfer in the United States, 1989 results from IVF/ET Registry. Fertil Steril 1991; 55: 14–23.

Mori T. An overview of recent advances in reproductive medicine. Nippon Sanka Fujinka Gakkai Sasshi 1989(Aug); 39(8): 1254–59.

Patrizio P, Silber S, Ord T, Balmaceda JP, Asch RH. Two births after microsurgical sperm aspiration in congenital absence of vas deferens. Lancet 1988 (Dec 10); 1364.

Rotsztejn DA, Remohi J, Weckstein LN, Ord T, Moyer DL, Balmaceda JP, Asch RH. Results of tubal embryo transfer in premature ovarian failure. Fertil Steri 1990; 54: 348–350.

Silber SJ, Asch RH, Balmaceda JP, Borrero C, Ord T. Pregnancy with sperm aspiration from the proximal head of the epididymis: A new treatment for congenital absence of the vas deferens. Fertil Steril 1988; 50: 525–528.

Silber S, Ord T, Balmaceda JP, Patrizio P, Asch RH. Congenital absence of the vas deferens: studies on the fertilizing capacity of human epididymal sperm. New Eng J of Med 1990; 323 (26): 1788.

Silber S, Ord T, Borrero C, Balmaceda JP, Asch RH. New treatment for infertility due to congenital absence of vas deferens [Letter]. Lancet 1987; 10: 2 (8563): 850–1.

Steptoe PC, Edwards RG. Birth after reimplantation of a human embryo. Lancet 1978; ii: 366.

Tadir Y, Wright WH, Vafa O, Ord T, Asch RH, Berns MN. Force generated by human sperm correlated to velocity and determined using a laser generated optical trap. Fertil Steril 1990; 53: 944–946.

Wong PC, Balmaceda JP, Blanco JD, Gibbs RS, Asch RH. Sperm washing and swim-up technique using antibiotics removes microbes from human semen. Fertil Steril 1986; 45: 97.

H. TRISTRAM ENGELHARDT, JR.

Human Reproductive Technology: Why All the Moral Fuss?

An Introduction to an Endless Debate

Discussions concerning the morality of the new reproductive technologies are interminable. The various parties to the debate speak past each other. There is strong disagreement but little dialogue. Moreover, the debates are never settled. There always remain moral holdouts and conflicting communities of moral opinion, and no clear basis upon which the disputes could ever be settled. Those who come to such debates arrive as moral strangers with fundamentally different understandings of the foundations of morality and the significance of human sexuality. The moral and public policy disputes concerning the new reproductive technologies illustrate the postmodern predicament: we do not possess a content-full universal moral narrative that can disclose the morally appropriate use of these new technologies. Instead, one finds a cacophony of concrete moral viewpoints and a diversity of content-full moral understandings unmediated by a canonical content-full moral view that can be justified in general secular terms.

An appearance of consensus is often achieved by artfully excluding from discussion individuals with stridently disparate moral visions. Or one can achieve a content-less moral consensus if one restricts one's focus to the resolution of disputes among moral strangers in terms that can be understood within that language of moral strangers, recognizing that nothing can be said within the bounds of that discourse about the meaning of life, the purpose of human relationships, or the significance of human sexuality (Engelhardt 1986, 1991). One is faced with the choice between focusing on strident disparities or making do with a moral language evacuated of content. One is faced with the choice of discovering meaning within a particular belief, tradition, or cultural context or negotiating a modus vivendi with moral strangers. The choice is not an exclusive choice, for even if one can discover content-full moral guidance through the gift of grace or the accident of history, one will still confront moral strangers.

The disputes regarding the new reproductive technologies disclose the failure of the modern rationalist project to discover either in nature or in reason

F.K. Beller and R.F. Weir (eds.), The Beginning of Human Life, 89–100.

content-full secular guidelines for human living in general or for human sexuality in particular (Engelhardt, 1991). Human nature is, after all, in each of its characteristics the outcome of the interaction among various natural forces, such as mutation rates, natural selection (which may include social forces), genetic drift, catastrophic occurrences, and constraints set by the laws of physics, chemistry, and biology. Human nature is, as such, a fact of the world that could have been otherwise, and which persons can imagine redesigning in order better to achieve the purposes they endorse. Human nature outside of a particular moral vision does not deliver moral constraints. Nor can one turn to reason itself to discover constraints on human action. One can envisage various ways in which humans may regard sexual intimacy, sexual reproduction, and the status of early human biological life. However, absent a way of choosing among these various visions, no conclusive sound secular arguments can be advanced to endorse a particular understanding without begging the question at stake. One cannot appeal to consequences without knowing how to rank or compare different sorts of consequences. One cannot appeal to preferences without knowing how to rank present versus future, well-considered versus impetuous preferences. One must already know how one should order basic human goods and/or social desiderata in order to be able to justify a particular thin theory of the good, moral sense, or moral vision. This failure to establish a concrete, canonical, general moral understanding characterizes the postmodern predicament. There is no generally established concrete, morally canonical vision of how humans should use their capacities, including their technologies. We lack a universal moral narrative, and the recognition of this condition marks the postmodern age (Lyotard).

In short, one cannot appeal to rational arguments to resolve content-full moral disputes among moral strangers without begging the question as to which ranking of goods, values, or preferences, or which moral sense, should be endorsed. Such moral resolution presupposes that one already shares a moral vision, however thin a vision, in common. At the most, one can indicate a grammar for the resolution of disputes insofar as moral strangers appeal to or create a fabric of mutual moral authority through common agreement. The authority of any such particular moral fabric springs from mutual consent, not from the authority of a canonical, content-full moral vision, however thin the content. Moreover, this authority will always be limited, for when moral strangers meet, they are unlikely to convey consummate authority, one to the other, over issues about which they have strong disagreement (Engelhardt, 1986, 1991).

All of this serves as an introduction to exploring the moral issues raised by the new reproductive technologies, not so much in order to say what ought to be done, but instead to disclose the moral limits of a secularly justifiable public policy. Though there are no conclusive secular rational grounds to justify a particular content-full moral vision about how one ought to use the new reproductive technologies, there is the possibility of adopting a policy of live and let live. That is, one can recognize that there will always be disagreements and therefore policies must be created that underscore the central role of rights to privacy as shorthand indicators of areas where common agreement is impossible and where moral authority for intervention is dubious or nonexistent. To embark on the project of secular moral discourse, many of the partners to the dispute will have to qualify the ways in which they enter into general secular disputes. To illustrate this point, I will in what follows contrast what can be termed an instrumentalist view of human sexuality (which I will somewhat playfully term "yuppie sex") with a particular content-full view of human sexuality, that advanced by the Roman Catholic church. I choose the Roman Catholic view not just because of its well-articulated position and its influence, but because of its mixture of claims from faith and reason. Each person, the yuppie and the Roman Catholic, will in his or her own way need to qualify his/her claims in order for a secularly justifiable accommodation to be made to the postmodern predicament.

On the one hand, the defenders of rationally justified traditional or religious morality such as the Roman Catholic view of sexuality will need to recognize that their natural-law arguments depend on a particular content-full vision in terms of which human nature is endowed with special moral or transcendent significance. The peculiarity of Catholic religious arguments in this and other areas is that the arguments claim to be more than religious, that is, to depend on premises that should be accessible to all men and women, even those untouched by belief, including Roman Catholic belief. For Roman Catholics to frame their moral claims, given philosophy's postmodern predicament, they will need to recognize that one must believe in order to understand, that an interpretation of nature that can give content-full moral guidance is an interpretation already framed within a moral vision.

On the other hand, those who regard human sexuality in fully secular terms, if they wish to be intellectually honest, may not smuggle fragments of religious and traditional cultural understandings of sexuality into their general secular claims. For example, they must recognize that in purely secular understandings of sexuality, where neither God nor content-full reason can play a role in resolving disputes, one will be left with peaceable agreements setting the only constraints that can be justified in general secular terms. One of the particular consequences will be a failure to be able to justify any conclusive secular rational arguments against surrogacy for hire. In such a context, human sexuality takes on an instrumentalist significance. Human sexuality achieves its value and significance in terms of allowing the achievement of whatever goods individuals peaceably decide to pursue together.

Despite the values introduced by many cosmopolitans into their secular vision, their moral vision contrasts with moral visions such as Roman Catholicism's regarding sexuality and the use of the human reproductive technologies. In the section that follows, I will lay out some of these differences. In the third section of this essay, I will outline some of the implications of these differences for the establishment of secular public policy. I will then conclude with a reminder why a peaceable, secular accommodation cannot exorcise the profound moral disagreements that will persist regarding the moral significance of the new reproductive technologies.

CONFLICTING VIEWS OF THE NEW HUMAN REPRODUCTIVE TECHNOLOGY

The Cosmopolitan View: Yuppie Sex

For the individual who views life unconstrained by transcendent or content-full traditional moral concerns, the new reproductive technologies offer a generally unalloyed benefit. They allow persons to overcome the biological constraints set by the imperfections of their nature. Technological interventions such as in vitro fertilization, perhaps augmented by partial zona dissection (PZD) in order to enhance fertilization of the ovum, followed by transfer of the embryo to the uterus, enable persons to overcome the surd, merely factual restraints set by biological maladventure on their desires to have children. The new reproductive technologies personalize nature. They personalize nature in the sense of informing nature with the goals of persons. They restructure things so that the goals of persons, such as the goal of having children, can be realized. The achievement of such goals will often require not just separating the act of intercourse from the event of fertilization, it will in addition require the use of gametes from outside of the couple seeking to have a child. Also, at times, besides the physicians and other technologists involved in augmenting reproduction, and in addition to the contributions from gamete donors, it will be necessary to involve women who will provide gratis, or for a fee, use of their uteruses in order to bring a child to birth. The new reproductive technologies thus introduce technical modalities and third parties in the otherwise intimate act of reproduction. For the cosmopolitans, this should provide no difficulty, as long as the technologies are not stolen and the third parties consent.

This technological and cooperative triumph of persons over nature is an epiphany of an ethos that celebrates those modalities that allow persons to achieve their own goals. It is this instrumentalist ethos that I somewhat playfully refer to as the ethos of the cosmopolitan or the yuppie. It is an instrumentalist ethics in that there are generally no intrinsic restraints other than that of not using others without their consent. At times claims will be introduced in favor of equality over freedom or in favor of autonomy as a value over free choice, though such claims will not be justifiable outside of a particular moral perspective. Such an augmented secular ethos contrasts with the sparse ethos of secular ethics as a means of negotiating moral disputes among moral strangers.

Within the latter ethical standpoint, one notes that moral authority can still be generated for moral strangers when they enter into collaborative endeavors. Moral strangers, insofar as they are interested in resolving moral controversies peaceably and with moral authority, can create a fabric of moral authority on the basis of mutual agreement, even when God is not heard and secular moral reason contentless (Engelhardt, 1986, 1991). Since there will be a limit to the authority one may assume that persons have explicitly communicated to joint endeavors, one will find, as the three salient practices of post-modernity, free and informed consent, the free market, and limited democracies.[1] Within the third, large areas of rights to privacy will open, where individuals will be free consensually to choose as they wish without the intrusion of the state. Rights to privacy are here not introduced as a concept in constitutional law, or because of a special value assigned to privacy, but rather in terms of the limited moral authority of the post-modern state. Rights to privacy, including the right to use the new reproductive technologies as one wishes with consenting others, mark the limited plausible moral authority of states. They represent areas where one may act peaceably with collaborators in the absence of others having the moral authority to interfere coercively. In such areas, one will appropriately note that people have secular rights to use the new reproductive technologies, even if most individuals hold such employment to be wrong. A general secular ethic provides a matrix for moral authority, even when individuals meet as moral strangers, but it does not have or convey the authority or substance to reach into all areas of the lives of persons.

Here an important ambiguity must be underscored. For the cosmopolitan, secular morality usually functions as more than a language for peaceable negotiation among moral strangers. For cosmopolitans, secular morality also provides a fabric of morality. It furnishes a morality for those who no longer have a canonical content-full morality, such as can be provided by religious viewpoints or traditional cultural understandings. For such individuals, secular morality is not simply an expedient for reaching out from one's moral community to engage in projects with individuals from other moral communities (as, for example, devout Muslims may engage in commerce with devout Christians in Beirut). Instead, secular morality supplies an increasing number of individuals with a way of articulating their own moral lives. In such circumstances, human nature, human sexuality, technology, the world at large, gain their meaning and significance from the immanent conjoint endeavors and choices of particular individuals. Secular morality thus enables individuals who endorse no transcendent interpretation of reality and who are unconstrained by established traditional moral understandings to collaborate together and enjoy this life. These individuals, free of particular religious and traditional constraints, I somewhat provocatively term "yuppies," in order to designate those cosmopolitan individuals who find themselves at peace, unlimited by what they would understand as parochial, content-full moral visions. They are the people whom Alasdair MacIntyre describes as speaking the international languages of modernity (MacIntyre, 1988, p. 384).

Cosmopolitans often, if not usually, incorporate into their secular vision shards and rests of religious, traditional, or, from their perspective, parochial moral content regarding sexuality. They find it difficult to live in the sparse moral perspective of a rigorously secular general ethic. It is therefore necessary to distinguish (1) secular ethics as the language of the bargaining and cooperation of moral strangers from (2) a particular secular ethics that is constituted by common agreement (e.g., a code of medical ethics for a secular reproductive clinic) and (3) a secular ethics as a thin, but still content-full moral understanding of sexuality that directs, however nominally, the consciences of cosmopolitans.

The first sense of secular ethics identifies the grammar of peaceable moral cooperation among moral strangers. It endorses no particular values, nor does it celebrate any particular good. It provides only a matrix for collaboration. Still, it often engenders a tension between the content-full moral life shared by individuals within particular moral communities and the sparse ethics of secular bioethics. Secular bioethics in the second sense identifies an ethics that arises out of an agreement as to when a community or clinic decides to provide third-party-assisted reproduction free for selected individuals. Secular bioethics in the third sense identifies an ethos for individuals who do not share a transcendently grounded or traditional ethic, who celebrate the immanent enjoyments of this life and endorse the instrumentalities needed for the achievement of their goals, but who bring to the interpretation of their experiences usually unrecognized fragments of once robust moral viewpoints. Individuals import shards, pieces, residues from concrete and once powerful moral visions (MacIntyre, 1981), such that their cosmopolitan, secular vision has a sense of greater substance than that which results from more common agreement or convention. The difficulty with importing such shards and pieces of moral visions is that they are introduced without the theoretical moral structure to justify their governance. The claims of a secular ethic in this third sense may collide with a generally justifiable secular ethic, just as may occur with a traditional morality. However, in this case there is not the same capacity to provide a moral narrative to justify the governance of the claims advanced.

General secular morality does not provide a basis for requiring one to endorse the values associated with the noncommercialization of surrogacy over the value of respecting the rights of women to decide freely whether and under what circumstances they will lease or rent their wombs. Outside of a particular moral vision, it will not be possible to determine which is a greater secular affront to the dignity of women: being used as surrogates for hire or being used in order to satisfy a particular moral vision through being forbidden to contract freely as a surrogate for hire. Because it is impossible to determine the correct moral ranking, in the absence of agreements to the contrary, women should in secular terms be free to choose their own ranking. They are therefore free in terms of general secular morality to act as surrogates for hire. More broadly put, men and women should be free, in terms of general secular morality, to use the new reproductive technologies as they wish. Attempts to limit such free use, if couched in secular terms, betray the importation of a particular thin theory (or perhaps thick theory) of proper reproductive deportment. The use of human reproductive technologies thus discloses often-unnoticed importations of values and the difficulty involved in giving justifications for these values or for particular moral constraints (other than requiring the consent of the participants) within a general secular context.

The Roman Catholic View

Roman Catholicism offers a content-full view of the value of human reproduction. It offers this view embedded within a set of transcendent claims and understandings. Roman Catholicism provides a moral interpretive fabric through which nature can be understood, human relationships valued, and human actions judged. The difficulty from a secular philosophical point of view with Roman Catholicism is that it claims to be able to justify its moral constraints not only by appeal to faith, but by reason. As already suggested, this appeal to reason cannot by itself succeed, because it requires either the endorsement of certain presuppositions regarding the significance of nature, or the content found within reason itself. But one does not have a basis for choosing one view over others without either begging the question or making an act of faith. Credendum est ut intelligere.[2]

Despite these difficulties, or perhaps because of them, Roman Catholicism provides a well-articulated set of judgments about the meaning of human reproduction, which contrasts with that of the cosmopolitan.

The Status of Preembryos

Because of the value assigned traditionally by Christianity to life from conception, and because of the current Roman Catholic view that even embryos must be treated as if they were persons, in vitro fertilization and embryo transfer involving direct embryo wastage are strongly condemned by the Congregation for the Doctrine of the Faith.

> Thus the fruit of human generation, from the first moment of its existence, that is to say from the moment the zygote has formed, demands the unconditional respect that is morally due to the human being in his bodily and spiritual totality. The human being is to be respected and treated as a person from the moment of conception; and therefore from that same moment his rights as a person must be recognized, among which in the first place is the inviolable right of every innocent human being to life. (Congregation for the Doctrine of the Faith, pp. 13–14)

Though in general secular terms there will not be the possibility of justifying such claims with regard to embryos, that is, one will not be able to show that embryos are persons, within this religious viewpoint they are given a status that precludes their direct destruction.

Unnatural Acts

Because the Catholic church is a moral community that provides a framework giving transcendent meaning to the actions and relations of individuals, sexuality has goals beyond the choices of the individuals directly involved. Unlike those who live in a secular post-Darwinian world, Roman Catholics can speak of particular actions as being unnatural, deviant, and perverse. They are unnatural, deviant, or perverse in departing from the goals set by God and understood to constitute the proper moral context for reproduction. The Congregation for the Doctrine of the Faith thus condemns in vitro fertilization and embryo transfer because they unnaturally separate fertilization from conception.

> Fertilization is licitly sought when it is the result of a conjugal act which is per se suitable for the generation of children to which marriage is ordered by its nature and by which the spouses become one flesh. But from the moral point of view procreation is deprived of its proper perfection when it is not desired as the fruit of the conjugal act, that is to say of the specific act of the spouses' union. (Congregation, p. 27)

Most significantly, the moral point of view to which reference is made is not one of secular reason outside of any tradition or set of commitments, a view from nowhere and outside of any particular context of belief, but one that requires very particular commitments. Human reproduction is thus set within a particular content-full, interpretive moral framework.

Sex Should Not Be Objectified

This moral framework endorses the value of sexual intimacy and rejects sexual acts which objectify reproduction. The Congregation thus condemns the use of the new reproductive technologies, holding that the child "cannot be desired or conceived as the product of an intervention of medical or biological techniques; that would be equivalent to reducing him to an object of scientific technology" (p. 28). This condemnation is in fact an endorsement of a particular vision or understanding of humans, of nature, and of the proper way in which human activities are to be understood.

The Unit of Sexual Intercourse and Reproduction

The Congregation develops the theme of preserving the unity of sexuality in terms of a particular understanding of value integrity. The Congregation possesses a content-full understanding of good sex. Because of that understanding, the Congregation holds that

> The Church's teaching on marriage and human procreation affirms the inseparable connection, willed by God and unable to be broken by man on his own initiative, between the two meanings of the conjugal act: the unitive meaning and the procreative meaning. Indeed, by its intimate structure, the conjugal act, while most closely uniting husband and wife, capacitates them for the generation of new lives, according to laws inscribed in the very being of man and of women. (Congregation, p. 26)

Sexuality and reproduction are construed, appreciated, and experienced within a particular concrete moral viewpoint that gives a robust account of morally good sex.

Adultery
Finally, in a purely secular context, adultery can only be understood in terms of the particular agreements of a particular couple. Thus, the use of gametes from outside the marriage would not, in general secular terms, constitute adultery if it met with the agreement of the couple. In contrast, the Roman Catholic perspective limits the free agreements of the parties by making God party to the contract. The marriage contract is imbedded in a set of prior, rich, and content-full constraints. The Congregation states:

> Respect for the unity of marriage and for conjugal fidelity demands that the child be conceived in marriage; the bond existing between husband and wife accords the spouses, in an objective and inalienable manner, the exclusive right to become father and mother solely through each other. Recourse to the gametes of a third person, in order to have sperm or ovum available, constitutes a violation of the reciprocal commitment of the spouses and a grave lack in regard to that essential property of marriage which is its unity. (Congregation, p. 24)

Because of obligations to God, which cannot be justified in general secular terms, choice is restricted for the believer.

Reciprocal Culture Shock: The Yuppie and the Devout Roman Catholic

The yuppie and the devout Roman Catholic regard sex in radically different fashions. For the yuppie, the cosmopolitan, freed from particular religious and traditional understandings of sexuality, sexuality has only instrumental significance. Sexuality has that meaning which individuals bring to it or invest in it by their mutual agreement. If one wishes to determine the meaning of sexual relations, it is usually sufficient simply to ask the individual involved. The cosmopolitan will therefore have no argument in principle against consensual premarital or extramarital sex. There may be prudential considerations regarding the medical risks of promiscuity. There may be sociological studies to show the destabilizing effects of open marriages. But there will be no constraints that in principle limit that to which men and women freely may agree with regard to sexual relationships.

Against this general understanding of sexuality, major secular moral problems do not surface with respect to in vitro fertilization, embryo transfer, and other means by which individuals, married or unmarried, would seek the open, free, and non-fraudulent cooperation of third parties in enhancing the opportunity to reproduce as wished. At times, cosmopolitans may carry with them poorly articulable residua of past religious or traditional commitments, which will make them uneasy regarding surrogacy in general or surrogacy for hire in particular. But they will not be able to offer general secular arguments to show in principle why such practices should be forbidden. Instead, they will indicate certain likelihoods of risk to the surrogates, to the children they will produce, etc. They will not usually bother to compare the risks of such less traditional activities (i.e., surrogacy) with the risks to children, etc., of other consensual activities such as divorce, adultery, and fornication. It is quite likely that the risks to couples, and to the children they will produce from a marriage that may end in divorce, are much greater than the risks likely to ensue from surrogacy for hire. In short, it will not be possible for cosmopolitans to develop a general secular argument that would provide a general secular basis for restricting the use of third-party technologically-assisted reproduction beyond those constraints set by the consent of the parties involved. However, because of the often-unnoticed influence of moral traditions and religious assumptions, cosmopolitans will frequently be misguided into believing that secular morality provides more than it in fact offers.

There will be considerable grounds for misunderstanding. The person who lives faithfully within the moral framework of Roman Catholicism will understand certain actions as perverse, others as proper, some as immoral, others as blessed and sacred. In contrast, the person who lives within a cosmopolitan framework will have difficulty developing any account of perversity or of immorality outside of the use of persons without their consent. Cosmopolitans may have secularly poorly articulated and articulable notions of exploitation, but these will collide with the notion of individuals as the source of authority for their own peaceable projects in collaboration with others.

The cosmopolitan may be shocked if not outraged when the Roman Catholic condemns as immoral certain consensual activities in human reproduction such as the use of gametes from outside the marriage. The Roman Catholic, on the other hand, will regard the cosmopolitan's life in general, and the cosmopolitan's view of sexuality in particular, as both morally misdirected and vacuous. The cosmopolitan will be affronted by constraints set upon free choice by a normative understanding of nature, as well as by a view of God's will. In fact, the cosmopolitan may regard the Roman Catholic as holding invidious prejudices against individuals with sexual life plans that do not conform with the teachings of the Catholic church. The Roman Catholic, on the other hand, will have principled grounds for holding the cosmopolitan to be adrift without appropriate moral direction regarding sexuality. Each will be shocked by the other. Up to a point, insofar as each appeals to generally defensible, rational arguments, there will be a possibility for dialogue. However, insofar as the Roman Catholic finds justification for the church's views in the revealed word of God, there will not be common grounds to settle the controversy.

Public Policy and the Central Place of Rights to Privacy

Because one cannot discover rational grounds for a canonical secular content-full vision of the moral life, or of human sexuality in particular, there will not be generally defensible bases for restricting the peaceable free choice of moral agents. Still, individuals live within particular cultural traditions and accept religious revelations. As a result, some will bring to their understanding of life in general, and human sexuality in particular, a moral interpretive framework that will not be open to general sexual criticism as long as it does not use others without their consent. Particular choices about the use of human sexuality will thus fall beyond general secular communal authority. There will not be secular grounds to judge them to be proper or improper, moral or immoral, well directed or perverse. From a secular perspective, one will simply see numerous ways in which individuals can compose the mosaic of their lives, including their reproductive sexuality. The secular perspective will therefore need to be tolerant and limited. It will justify large areas of private choice, where individuals will be at liberty either to sell themselves as surrogate mothers or morally to condemn certain reproductive arrangements as perverse and ethically forbidden. The central virtue in the secular ethics of human reproduction will be toleration, and the cardinal practice will be that of protecting robust rights to privacy, rights to areas of private peaceable choice with collaborating others.

The Irradicability of Moral Stridency: Some Postmodern Conclusions

In secular reflections on human reproductive sexuality, one major liberal goal will be achieved and another which is tied to Enlightenment notions of progress will be disappointed. First, there will be good grounds for toleration, for a policy of live-and-let-live. From a secular point of view, there will not be grounds for forbidding the use of gametes outside the compass of marriage, but there will also not be general secular grounds for forbidding the use of surrogates for hire. Because of the unavoidable centrality of persons as the source of moral authority when no canonical moral vision can be established, the appeal to the choice of individuals will both authorize such undertakings and undermine the legitimacy of coercive interventions to interdict them. However, because there is no canonical content-full vision of human sexuality justifiable in secular terms, those who embrace a particular vision from cultural dedication or religious conviction will not find a conclusive argument to undermine their convictions. Nor will there be grounds for their muting their moral condemnation of others. Instead, the vision of a postmodern world opens, in which many will have no great conviction about how they should use their sexuality and will live easily as cosmopolitans employing third-party, technologically assisted reproductive technologies. There will, though, remain communities of moral understanding and vision concerning human sexuality who will raise a constant call to critique and an invitation to conversion. There are no grounds to be convinced that the liberal Enlightenment goal of all having grounds to agree concerning a particular canonical understanding of sexuality will ever be realized. Controversy will continue and, as in most areas of morality, there will be nothing approaching consensus.

Notes

1. The reference to postmodernity does not imply that these considerations regarding secular ethics did not obtain in the past. It is rather that the postmodern age presents the philosophical unavoidability of these considerations (Engelhardt, 1991).
2. The reader should note that, though the author is critical of the rationalist excesses (and other errors) of the Roman patriarchate, he, as an Orthodox Catholic, albeit a sinner, does not reject the disciplines and teachings of the Fathers.

References

Congregation for the Doctrine of the Faith. Instruction on Respect for Human Life in Its Origin and on the Dignity of Proceation. Vatican City, 1987.

Engelhardt HT Jr. The Foundations of Bioethics. New York: Oxford University Press, 1986.

Engelhardt HT Jr. Secular Humanism: The Search for a Common Morality. Philadelphia: Trinity Press International, 1991.

Lyotard J-F. The Postmodern Condition: A Report on Knowledge. Bennington G, Massumi B., trans. Minneapolis: University of Minnesota Press, 1991.

MacIntyre A. After Virtue. South Bend, Indiana: University of Notre Dame Press, 1981.

MacIntyre A. Whose Justice? Which Rationality? South Bend, Indiana: University of Notre Dame Press, 1988.

KAREN H. ROTHENBERG

Gestational Surrogacy and the Health Care Provider*

Medical advances in new reproductive technologies continue to raise complex legal and ethical issues. In October 1990, a California Superior Court judge issued his opinion on the first contested case in this country involving gestational surrogacy.[1] Upholding the surrogacy contract as valid and declaring that the genetic parents had exclusive custody and parental rights, Judge Richard Parslow observed: "The IVF genie is out of the bottle and you're not going to be able to put it back."[2]

I contend that we must put part of the genie back into the bottle. Gestational surrogacy is not an acceptable option for the extension of in vitro fertilization (IVF). This is not a reaction to the facts of the California case, but rather a recognition that the medicalization of surrogacy as a reproductive technology attempts to legitimize a practice that professionals should not support.

Following a brief discussion of *Johnson v. Calvert*, the California case, I will summarize the status of U.S. and international laws and policies on surrogacy, with particular attention on gestational surrogacy. I will also discuss ethical positions on surrogacy issued by organizations of health care professionals. With this background established, I will outline my position on why the ethical and legal risks inherent in gestational surrogacy require professionals to reject it as a reproductive alternative.

Johnson v. Calvert

Crispina Calvert, who had had a hysterectomy, worked as a registered nurse in the same hospital as Anna Johnson, an ex-Marine and licensed vocational nurse. A mutual friend introduced them, believing that Anna wanted to be a surrogate. Anna was black and a single parent of a three-year-old girl. She had had two prior miscarriages and two stillbirths. Crispina was Filipino and her husband, Mark, was white. The Calverts claimed that they could not afford to go to a surrogacy agency, but paid $3,500 for the agency's standard contract and some legal advice. Johnson signed the contract.[3]

It is unclear whether Anna was ever screened as an "appropriate"

F.K. Beller and R.F. Weir (eds.), The Beginning of Human Life, 101–113.

surrogate. Crispina and Anna both began hormonal therapy to mesh their ovulation cycles. Crispina had a number of eggs removed and fertilized with Mark's sperm, and three were transferred into Anna. Against the odds, one embryo implanted. For weeks, Anna received hormonal injections to maximize her chances of maintaining the pregnancy. She was hospitalized more than once for complications during the pregnancy. She was also advised to seek psychiatric help for emotional problems.[4]

The deal seemed to be working. Anna would receive $10,000 for her gestational services and for relinquishing the baby, the Calverts would have a genetic child, and the IVF program would contribute to another expansion of IVF for women who would otherwise not be able to benefit from such technology. But Anna, for whatever reason, changed her mind, and the deal began to fall apart. Seeking to invalidate the contract, she claimed among other things that she had bonded with the fetus and sought the court's protection of her future parental rights. Unwilling to recognize the possibility of three parents and Anna's role as the gestational mother (and probably doubting her claim that she had, in fact, bonded), the judge declared the contract valid and granted full and exclusive custody to the Calverts.[5] Anna Johnson filed an appeal on October 24, 1990.[6]

U.S. and International Developments in Policies on Surrogacy

Since the Baby M case made headlines a few years ago, policies on surrogacy continue to evolve around the world.[7] In the United States, legislation has been introduced in Congress and in thirty-nine states, as well as the District of Columbia, to deal with various aspects of commercial surrogacy.[8] To date, only thirteen states have passed laws dealing with surrogate parenting contracts and their legality. Eleven states have either declared commercial surrogacy illegal and/or made it impossible to enforce a contract as contrary to public policy.[9] A few of these states specifically include gestational surrogacy within their definitional sections.[10] Arkansas allows for a birth certificate to be changed to recognize that the intended mother rather than the surrogate is the legal mother, but is vague about the parameters of the legality of surrogacy.[11] New Hampshire's recent statute permits, but with extensive regulation and pre-approval by the court, both forms of surrogacy.[12] No statute gives more rights to the surrogate with a genetic connection than to the gestational surrogate.[13]

Bioethical task forces in both New Jersey and New York have also recommended that surrogacy not be allowed, particularly in the commercial setting, and that the surrogate be given the right to keep the child.[14] In fact, the New Jersey Task Force recommends that it be criminal for professionals to participate in commercial surrogacy. The prohibition can subject the professional to a charge of unprofessional conduct and prosecution.[15] Such participation in surrogacy might include screening of candidates and performing artificial insemination and embryo transfer with a gestational surrogate.

The most recent survey of international laws and policies clearly establishes that surrogacy contracts, especially if commercial, are illegal, unenforceable, contrary to public policy and/or void.[16] Furthermore, most laws establish that the birth mother is deemed the legal mother.[17]

Of particular interest, Bulgaria declares that motherhood is determined by birth, whether or not conception is with another's genetic material.[18] Israeli regulations establish that a fertilized egg may be implanted only in the intended mother.[19] In Norway and Sweden, a fertilized egg may only be placed back into the woman from which the egg was removed.[20] In Spain, surrogacy with or without money is null and void, but if there is a contract for gestation, it declares that the mother who gave birth is still the mother.[21] The United Kingdom bans commercial surrogacy agencies from engaging women to act as surrogate mothers,[22] and the German parliament just passed a law banning both surrogate motherhood and embryo transfer.[23]

The Council of Europe has declared that "maternity should be determined by the fact of giving birth, rather than genetics (origin of the ova), firstly because of the relationship between the child and the woman giving birth to him and, secondly, because of the necessity of giving the child a clear legal situation at birth."[24] Furthermore, absent an exceptional case, surrogate motherhood should be banned and such contracts should be deemed null and void.[25] The council cautions that physicians should be prohibited from bringing together an infertile couple and a surrogate mother.[26]

Health-professional organizations both in the United States and abroad have also taken positions. The American Medical Association in December of 1988 incorporated its earlier report on surrogacy into the official opinions of its Council on Ethical and Judicial Affairs. Whether genetic or gestational, the opinion states that surrogacy "does not represent a satisfactory reproductive alternative for people who wish to become parents."[27] This past June, the Ethics Committee of the American Fertility Society also reissued, with minor changes, its position recommending that surrogacy and gestational surrogacy be continued only as a "clinical experiment".[28] The Committee on Ethics of the American College of Obstetrics and Gynecology (ACOG) just issued its revised opinion in "Ethical Issues in Surrogate Motherhood."[29] The committee found that the surrogate who both carries the fetus and delivers the infant should be the sole source of consent for all questions regarding prenatal care and delivery, and that she should have a specified time after birth to decide whether or not to place the child for adoption with the commissioning couple. The opinion specifically addresses, in part, gestational surrogacy and recognizes that while the genetic link to the couple is important, it deems it "less weighty than the link between the surrogate mother and the fetus or infant that is created through gestation and birth."[30] Thus, the opinion makes no ethical distinction between what it describes as "the usual pattern of surrogate parenting and surrogate gestational motherhood."[31]

The ACOG committee further states that the physician, when approached, should assure all disclosure of medical and ethical risk and that the provider may justifiably decline participating in a surrogacy arrangement. If the physician does agree to participate, strict ethical guidelines should be followed. Of particular interest is that the surrogate and the commissioning couple should be regarded as distinct parties and should be separately represented, both medically and legally.[32]

In August 1990, the Working Party on Human Infertility Services of the British Medical Association (BMA) adopted extensive ethical guidelines on surrogacy.[33] These guidelines supersede a 1987 ruling that doctors should not take part in surrogacy arrangements until the BMA had agreed upon ethical controls.[34] The BMA guidelines warn physicians that surrogacy arrangements are unenforceable in law and that neither of the parties can be prevented from breach.[35] The guidelines provide that surrogacy be a last resort, that doctors consider as surrogates only those women who have a partner and already have one child. Physicians should also warn the commissioning couple, the surrogate, and her partner of all risks (which the BMA outlines in great detail), including the possibility that the surrogate may refuse to relinquish the child and that the commissioning couple may refuse to accept a child born with any defects.[36] The Working Party makes no ethical or legal distinction between "partial" (genetic) and "full" (gestational) surrogacy. In fact, they note that "whatever the genetic origins of a child, and regardless of the wishes of the participants, the law regards the child as belonging to the mother who delivered it."[37]

Gestational Surrogacy: Ethical and Legal Problems

The American College of Obstetrics and Gynecology and the British Medical Association both have accepted the political reality that infertility specialists fear restrictions on their practice. In fact, some IVF programs are part of the created demand for legalized surrogacy. Surrogacy in this medical context reduces gestation to a technological tool. This is understandable, considering the increasing expectation of the couple believing that with enough technology anyone can have a baby.

At the same time this medicalization reduces the role played by the gestational mother in the creation of life. The surrogate is deemed to be making a healthy adjustment if she remains unconnected – the most unnatural of feelings. This is too great a risk for health care professionals to contribute to reducing women to extensions of a medical process.

Furthermore, as an international matter, gestational surrogacy has the potential to exploit poor women from Third World countries, perhaps raising the false hope of immigration to the United States. Rich white couples, in turn, desperate for a genetic connection, can use poor women to achieve the result. Health care professionals cannot condone using women in this way.

I would strongly urge that health professionals resist any support of the use of a gestational surrogate. Obviously we all want to satisfy the infertile couple with the option of IVF. But we have to set limits when another woman, also being treated as a unit by the IVF program, is involved. We are pitting mothers against each other, and the health care provider is potentially in the middle of the conflict. The right law, the right contract, and the right counseling will not be able to correct the problems with gestational surrogacy.

I do not make this argument in defense of Anna Johnson, or in reaction to that case. Although I am surprised that we have not seen more cases to date, they will come, and the health care provider will be in a no-win position.[38] Let me highlight the specific issues that gestational surrogacy poses for the health care professional throughout the process.

Screening

Proponents of surrogacy believe that with enough screening by qualified professionals, surrogacy can be a success. The recent New Hampshire statute,[39] in fact, provides for professional screening of both the couple and the surrogate to assure a court in a pre-approval process that the contract will work. Yet what are we screening for?

For example, how does a psychologist assess whether a gestational surrogate is a good risk?[40] If she is less willing to want to bond because there is no genetic connection, will she remain this way throughout the gestational process? And what if she continues to feel removed, because there is no genetic connection? Will this influence her prenatal behavior to make her a bad risk and a noncompliant patient? The data does not exist to develop the perfect profile of the surrogate and the commissioning couple who can cope with IVF and embryo transfer. What are the measures of motivation, self-esteem, family support, and experience in coping with childbearing loss? What relationship will the genetic and the gestational mother have to each other? What perception does the surrogate have of the father and the future of a unit relationship? Certainly we do not have experience with genetic parents dealing with loss to the gestational mother.

We do have some experience that supports the possibility of motivation to deny or omit feelings and relevant medical information. And there may be unconscious motivation not to hear or appreciate all the risks when the motivation is so strong for both the couple and the IVF program to achieve a pregnancy, and for the surrogate to be successful and to be paid.

In the first medical malpractice case filed that involved the treatment of a surrogate, *Mounce v. Hanson*,[41] the surrogate admitted to the physician who took her medical history that she had had two prior miscarriages and no live births. She was not screened out. Perhaps more important, she did not state that she had had a history of heart trouble. She was desperate to serve as a surrogate, perhaps as a way to deal with her prior losses, and to make some money. In her eighth month of pregnancy, she died of heart failure following a number of warning signals, and the baby died too. The sperm donor never came forward, but her family has sued Genesearch, the surrogacy program, the physician who screened her and provided her prenatal care, and the consulting cardiologist.[42]

The Calverts claimed that Anna Johnson also failed to provide important medical information, in not revealing her two miscarriages and two stillbirths.[43] Clearly, she was not an ideal candidate, either medically or psychologically, for surrogacy. When money is involved, and when we all want something bad enough, screening may be of limited use without all the facts. And even if we think we have all the facts, we have to decide which facts are the ones that matter.

Thus, in spite of the call for screening to assure that the arrangement has the Good Housekeeping Seal of Approval, the process is flawed. First of all, we have no consensus on what we are screening for. Medically, what are the standards for an acceptable surrogate? The existence of a uterus and a willing carrier are not enough. Rather, I would argue that at the present time an infertile couple is not a candidate for IVF if the woman is not able to be the birth mother. As noted earlier, Norway, Sweden and Israel require that IVF be allowed only if the woman is implanted with her own genetic material.[44]

Secondly, we do not know what the acceptable psychological profile is for a low risk couple and surrogate. And finally, professionals are not qualified to determine what information is meaningful. The ethical and legal, not to mention medical and psychological, risks are not clear, and by definition, they may never be.

Informed Consent

Assuming that both the couple and the surrogate pass the screening requirements, an elaborate informed consent process is to follow. ACOG, for example, recommends that the medical and the ethical risks be carefully spelled out to the couple and the surrogate.[45] The New Hampshire statute also requires an extensive evaluation, counseling, and an informed consent process.[46] But are health care providers qualified to do the job? And do they have enough information to make the process meaningful? How does a gestational surrogate consent knowingly to relinquishment of a future child? She may have experienced a birth, but is it easier or harder to relinquish if you have no genetic connection? Is the lack of a genetic connection relevant at all? Obviously, genetics matter to the couple, who may feel more strongly about losing their wholly genetic child.

In fact, how does a provider describe the ethical and legal risks? Fewer than a quarter of the states have laws that either hold surrogacy contracts unenforceable or heavily regulate them.[47] Under traditional family law, rather than contract law, the birth mother is the mother. Yet, in *Johnson v. Calvert* the lower court in California found that genetics is all that matters, and the gestational mother has no rights.[48]

Clearly, informed consent based on legal risks is risky at best. There are no guarantees. Nor are there any guarantees with respect to psychological risk for the couple, the surrogate, or the surrogate's family. Medically, there are unknown long-term risks associated with fertility drugs, IVF procedures, risk to the child, and risks to the gestational surrogate from multiple gestation. Obviously, the medical risks are more significant for the gestational surrogate than for the surrogate who is artificially inseminated and usually carries just a single fetus to term. Again, it is one thing to risk your own body. It is quite another to achieve "voluntary" consent to experiment with another woman's body for the couple's benefit.

Conflict of Interest and the Embryo Transfer

Assuming some form of informed consent is attempted, there still remain problems with the conflict of interest inherent in an IVF program promoting embryo transfer with a gestational surrogate. The couple and their surrogate are treated like a unit with the same interest – the achievement of a successful pregnancy. The client, however, is not the surrogate but the paying couple. The surrogate is needed to allow the provider to extend the potential of IVF use into a "uterine carrier." The surrogate is a means to an end. How can the physician maintain a confidential relationship with two women who are both potential mothers of the same baby or babies?

Furthermore, the medical risks are significant for both the genetic and gestational mother. First, their ovulatory cycles must coincide. Drugs are necessary to manipulate their cycles. Fertility drugs also may help to stimulate the production of eggs by the genetic mother-to-be so that a number of eggs can be retrieved. The husband's sperm is then combined with the eggs, and any resulting embryos are transferred into the gestational surrogate. The surrogate continues to receive hormonal injections for a number of weeks to maximize the chances of a successful implantation and pregnancy. The IVF program has a responsibility for the well-being of all members of this unit.

This is a risky business. Once the IVF process is finished, the IVF program may think its job is over. A pregnancy (or pregnancies) has been achieved, yet there is potential for future maternal morbidity and mortality for both mothers-to-be. It is one thing to assume these risks when the genetic mother is also to be the host uterus. It is different, however, when there is potential for conflict within the unit. In fact, all the parties cannot be treated as a unit. They are individual patients, with individual needs, and the provider must avoid any appearance of conflict of interest. Yet by definition, IVF and embryo transfer with a gestational surrogate is a case of potential conflict of interest. The ACOG committee opinion states that conflict of interest must be avoided by the use of separate medical providers for infertility and care to the surrogate.[49]

For the process to work, will we tolerate inherent conflict which clearly favors the interests of the consumers of the IVF technology over the surrogate? Does the IVF provider have, in fact, a physician-patient relationship with the surrogate, or does the provider take the surrogate as a mere extension of the procedure? How much responsibility will the IVF program take for screening a surrogate? If the surrogate is good enough for the couple, is the surrogate good enough for the IVR provider? It is the responsibility of the provider to warn the surrogate of all risks, but is this not in conflict with the couple's goals and interests?

The ACOG committee opinion provides that the surrogate is the source of all medical decisions with respect to the pregnancy.[50] For in fact, once the transfer is complete, all biological connections are made by the gestational mother-to-be. She is more than a uterine container.[51] She provides all the nutrients and bodily functions necessary to make this embryo grow into a fetus and then a baby. Clearly the interest of all is in her physical and emotional well-being. And any psychological counseling necessary during pregnancy must be directed to doing what is best for the pregnant woman.

Multiple Embryo Transfer

It is common IVF practice to transfer at least three fertilized embryos. Some IVF programs transfer up to six.[52] Obviously, this practice attempts to maximize the chances of achieving a pregnancy. However, twins, triplets, and maybe more are to be expected. A World Health Organization study on IVF found that with the potential for multiple births, maternal morbidity and mortality, as well as infant morbidity and mortality, significantly increase.[53] If the genetic mother chooses to take this risk with her body, it is one thing. But health care professionals should not impose such risks on the gestational surrogate whose body is being used for the couple's benefit.

Multiple gestation and its risks raise problems for gestational surrogacy that were not considered with genetic surrogacy, in which single gestation is the norm. The risks to all parties, including the liability of the IVF physician, increase. It is more likely that the gestational surrogate will become a high risk pregnancy, will require a cesarean section delivery, will have more complications and more monitoring, and will be unable to continue working throughout the pregnancy. And how do we then compensate fairly for this additional burden of gestational service and for relinquishing more than one baby?

Obviously the potential conflict of interest for the IVF provider is raised again. Just how many embryos should be transferred? On the one hand, selective termination of the "extra" fetuses might be the answer for the genetic couple.[54] But what about the surrogate's view? Perhaps she will not want to abort and will risk carrying three or four to term. Of course, this decision also raises the risk to her and the fetuses.

Ultimately, if the gestational surrogate is the decisionmaker for medical care, she and not the genetic couple must decide what is best for her health and the health of the fetuses, including selective termination of pregnancy. This is not to say that the couple and provider will not exert pressure on her.

Prenatal Diagnosis and Genetic Testing

A standard surrogate contract will require the surrogate to undergo genetic testing, including amniocentesis, to establish whether or not there are any genetic or chromosomal abnormalities. Yet is this not a strange requirement for the gestational surrogate? The gestational surrogate is not the genetic carrier of the problems being screened for. Obviously genetic counseling has no function for her. Such counseling is relevant to the genetic couple, but it is the surrogate who is subjecting herself to the testing. Once again she would have the right not to abort a defective fetus, but if the couple then rejects the fetus, who gets the child? Unless the surrogate chooses to keep the child with no genetic link to her, the child may become a ward of the state. What if she does choose to abort the fetus, because she does not want to carry a "defective" pregnancy, and the couple still wants the pregnancy to continue? It is the couple's genetic material, and they are willing to accept the result. Yet, if they desire the surrogate to have genetic testing, it would seem that the couple would have to accept her decision to abort. Regardless of the result, the use of genetic testing with gestational surrogates raises unique ethical and legal challenges for the provider.

Control of Behavioral Lifestyle and Work Environment

In addition to genetic testing, surrogate contracts often require that surrogates do not drink, smoke, or take illicit drugs. Obviously enforcement of such provisions is problematic. Such provisions require that the physician take on the role of spy rather than fiduciary toward the patient. In fact, the ACOG committee opinion clearly provides that the confidential relationship remains with the surrogate.[55]

However, with gestational surrogacy it would seem that the couple, and perhaps the physician, will feel more a hold on the gestational surrogate. Since she has no genetic connection to the pregnancy, they may fear she will be less concerned with taking care of herself and the fetus. There have been cases in which health care providers have gone to court to try to force certain treatments or cesarean section deliveries.[56] A couple, with the support of the provider, having invested so much time, emotional energy, and money in achieving a pregnancy, may feel they have no recourse other than to go to court to protect their genetic material from the negative behaviors of the surrogate. The couple might try to argue that their intention to rear the child, as well as the force of the contract, gives them legal standing to seek an injunction to get the surrogate to undergo a medical procedure or to stop smoking, drinking, or taking drugs during the pregnancy. It is not clear whether the court would be more or less concerned about the autonomy of the pregnant woman to control her own body when she has no intention to rear the child and to accept the consequences of her actions. One also wonders what the psychological impact of not carrying a genetic fetus has on the acts and behavior of the surrogate, as well as on the health of the uterine environment. If in fact it is easier to separate, is it easier to ignore other concerns for the fetus?

Furthermore, what will be the implications for employment of the surrogate? Is gestating her only job? Does she have the right to continue any other employment? If she works in a lead factory, must she be forced to be transferred or fired?[57] What if she is having twins and is told "to get off her feet?" If she stops working, will the couple pay her lost earnings? Will she be barred from disability payments if her pregnancy resulted from an embryo transfer for hire? What role will the provider play in helping her to obtain disability coverage? With the increase in medical risks come increasing economic risks.

Birth Defects and Causation

Unfortunately, no one can guarantee the birth of a healthy child. With gestational surrogacy, it may be more difficult to determine the cause of a problem at birth. Was it a genetic problem? Was it the surrogate's work environment? Was it the one drink? Was it caused by a sexually transmitted disease that she caught during relations with her husband? Gestational surrogacy takes genetics out of the picture, but it may be difficult to pin the problem on a particular cause. In the end, will the couple and/or the surrogate, if she retains custody, look to the physician for a financial solution through a liability claim? With so much that cannot be controlled in the birth process, and with such high expectations and expenses generated from IVF and embryo transfer, a liability threat from both the surrogate and commissioning couple should not be minimized.

CONCLUSION

State courts and legislatures, health-professional organizations, and policymakers throughout the world are struggling to develop laws and guidelines to address the complex questions raised by the expansion of new reproductive technologies. Clearly, infertility specialists are sincerely devoted to trying to help couples have their own babies. But health care professionals must resist the temptation to expand the use of IVF and embryo transfer with gestational surrogacy. The medical, ethical, and legal risks of using another woman to serve the interests of the infertile couple cannot be minimized. Gestational surrogacy is not a cure for infertility, but rather a course to be avoided.

NOTES

* Another version of this paper was published in *Law, Medicine and Health Care* 1990 (Winter); 18: 345–52.

1. *Johnson v. Calvert*, No. 63–31–90 (Orange Cty. Super. Ct. Calif. October 22, 1990). Gestational surrogacy is used in combination with in vitro fertilization. The fertilized egg of the genetic mother with the sperm of the genetic father or a sperm donor in vitro is transferred into the uterus of the surrogate, who is the birth mother. This differs from what I will term "genetic surrogacy" in which both the egg and gestation are provided by the surrogate, as was the case with Mary Beth Whitehead.

   Since the first birth in 1986, there have been about 80–100 births by gestational surrogates in this country. Noncommercial gestational surrogacy is also practiced at Bourn Hall Clinic, Britain's leading IVF clinic, near Cambridge, England. See the *Sunday Times* 19 Aug 1989.
2. *Id.*
3. Facts reported in the *Los Angeles Times* 1990 Oct 23; Sect A: 1 (col 5).
4. Additional facts about the case provided through personal interviews with the lawyers for Anna Johnson and the Calverts (October 1990).
5. *Johnson v. Calvert*, supra note 1.
6. See the *National Law Journal* 1990 Nov 5: p. 36 (The trial court was affirmed, and further review is pending in the California Supreme Court).
7. Since the New Jersey Supreme Court declared the surrogacy contract unenforceable in *In re Baby M*, 109 N.J. 396, 537 A.2d 1227 (1988), I have been cautioning health professionals to seriously consider the unanswered ethical and legal questions raised by surrogacy. See, e.g., Rothenberg. Surrogacy and the Health Care Professional: Baby M and Beyond. In: Gostin, ed. *Surrogate Motherhood: Politics and Privacy* (Ind Univ Press, 1990).
8. See, e.g., Adams. State legislative report: surrogate parenting contract legislation enacted: 1987, 1988 and 1989 legislative sessions. National Conference of State Legislatures 1990; 15(2) and see also 1990 update. 1990 (Jul).
9. *Id.* Arizona (1989 Ariz. Sess. Laws 14); Florida (Fla. Stat. Sec. 63.212(1) (1988) although allowing for pre-planned adoption arrangements with specific terms; Indiana (Ind. Code Sec. 31-8-2-1- to 31-8-2-3) (1988) sets out rights for the surrogate if an agreement is entered into; Kentucky (Ky. Rev. Stat. Sec. 199.590 (1988); Louisiana (La. Rev. Stat. Ann. Sec. 9: 2713 (1987); Michigan (Mich. Comp. Laws, Sec. 722.851–722.863 (1988); Nebraska (Ne. Rev. Stat. 674 (1988); Nevada (Nev. Rev. Stat. 127.303.5 (1987); North Dakota (1989 N.D. Sess. Laws 184); Utah (1989 Utah Laws 140); Washington (1989 Wash. Laws 404).
10. Louisiana and Kentucky just discuss surrogacy by insemination, with no discussion of gestational services and/or surrogacy by embryo transfer.
11. 1089 Ark. Acts 647.
12. New Hampshire, HB–1426–FN, Chapter 87 (1990).
13. The Uniform Status of Children of Assisted Conception Act, drafted by the National Conference of Commissioners on Uniform State Laws (1988), provides for one alternative that declares surrogacy contracts unenforceable (the alternative adopted by North Dakota) and it establishes that the birth mother is the legal mother. The other alternative, not adopted by any legislature, does provide that a surrogate who also provides the egg can change her mind within 180 days after the last insemination, but makes no similar provision for the gestational surrogate. There is no discussion on why the distinction was made, but this provision was a major political compromise.
14. See New York State Task Force on Life and the Law. Surrogate Parenting: Analysis and Recommendations for Public Policy. New York; New Jersey Task Force on New Reproductive Practices. Policy recommendations on surrogacy. New Jersey, 1990 (Jul).
15. New Jersey Task Force, *supra* note 14 at 2.
16. See generally Stepan (ed.), International Survey of Laws on Assisted Procreation, Zurich, 1990 (hereinafter Survey). The Ontario Law Reform Commission and a recent Australian

National Bioethics Consultative Committee report do recommend limited approval and strict regulation of supervised, noncommercial surrogacy contracts.

17. See Survey, *supra* note 16.
18. Bulgaria Family Code, Art. 31 (May 1985), reprinted in Survey, *supra* note 16 at 95.
19. Israeli Public Health (In Vitro Fertilization) Regulations, Ministry of Health (1987) at sec. 11, reprinted in Survey, *supra* note 16 at 121, 124.
20. Norwegian Law on Artificial Fertilization, No. 68, Chapter III, 1987, reprinted in *Survey* at 139, 141; Swedish Law on Fertilization Outside the Human Body, No. 711, at 2, 1988, reprinted in Survey, *supra* note 16 at 172.
21. Spanish Law on Assisted Reproduction Procedures, No. 35/1988, Chapter 10, 1988, reprinted in Survey, *supra* note 16 at 157, 161.
22. United Kingdom Surrogacy Arrangements Act, 1985, reprinted in Survey, *supra* note 16 at 184.
23. See Reproductive Rights Reporter 1990 (Oct 26) II, 19 at 8.
24. Council of Europe, Human Artificial Procreation Strasbourg, 1989, Principle 14 at 28–29.
25. *Id.* Principle 15 at 29–30.
26. *Id.*
27. Opinions of the A.M.A. Council on Ethical and Judicial Affairs (Dec. 1988).
28. Ethics Committee of the American Fertility Society, Ethical Considerations of the New Reproductive Technologies. 'Surrogate gestational mothers' (Chapter 21 at 64S–67S) and 'Surrogate mothers' (Chapter 22 at 68S–73S). Fertility and Sterility 1990, 53.
29. American College of Obstetrics and Gynecology, Committee on Ethics. Ethical issues in surrogate motherhood. 1990 (Nov): 88 (hereinafter, ACOG committee opinion).
30. *Id.* at 2.
31. *Id.*
32. *Id.* at 4–5.
33. British Medical Association. Surrogacy: ethical considerations – Report of the working party on human infertility services. 1990 (Aug) (hereinafter, BMA).
34. In fact, the Swiss Academy of Medicine continues to express general hostility to the use of IVF and embryo transfer in conjunction with surrogacy.
35. BMA, *supra* note 33 at 28. See Human Fertilization and Embryology Law, 1990.
36. BMA, *supra* note 16 at 28–30.
37. *Id.* at 41.
38. There are at least five other cases pending in lower and appellate courts around the country, according to Sharon DeAngelo, co-founder of the Washington, D.C.–based National Coalition Against Surrogacy. National Law Journal Oct. 1990.
39. HB 14260–FN, New Hampshire Laws. 1990; 87.
40. See generally Harrison. Psychological ramifications of Surrogate' motherhood. In Scotland, ed. Psychiatric Aspects of Reproductive Technology 1990; 97.
41. No. 89–045388 (Harris Cty. Tex. 1990).
42. *Id.* Follow-up discussions with the attorneys representing the estate of Ms. Mounce and Dr. Hanson, October 1990.
43. Numerous newspaper accounts of the testimony and discussions with the lawyers state that this information was not shared. In fact, the court opinion notes that "the Calverts were relying on Anna's representations, and arguably omissions, because there are some things she didn't tell them about her experience." National Law Journal 1990; 5.
44. See *supra* notes 19–20 and accompanying text.
45. ACOG committee opinion, *supra* note 29 at 4–5.
46. HB 1426–FN, New Hampshire Laws 1990; 87.
47. See *supra* note 9 and accompanying text.
48. See *supra* note 1. The appeal was filed to the 4th District Court of Appeals on October 25, 1990.
49. See ACOG committee opinion, *supra* note 29 at 5. The committee did not specifically address the inherent conflict of interest of the IVF program provider at the time of embryo transfer. Discussion with Elaine Locke, staff to ACOG Committee on Ethics, (Oct).

50. *Id.*
51. The more we view her as a container, the more we also separate her interests from those of the fetus, rather than seeing them as a union growing together.
52. See, e.g., Wagner. Is in-vitro fertilization appropriate technology?. World Health Organization, 1989. Reported in the Age 1989 (May 15): 1.
53. *Id.*
54. For a discussion on the difficult issues raised by selective termination, see Overall. Selective termination of pregnancy and women's reproductive autonomy. Hastings Center Report 1990 (May/June); 6.
55. ACOG committee opinion, *supra* note 29 at 4–5.
56. See Kolder et al. Court-ordered obstetrical interventions. N Engl J Med 1987 (May); 316(19): 1192. *In re A.C.*, 573 A.2d 1235 (D.C. App. 1990).
57. See generally, International Union UAW v. Johnson Controls, Inc., 111 S.Ct. 1196 (1991) in which the Supreme Court determined that an employer's fetal protection policy in the work place violated sex discrimination law.

PART THREE

Contraception and Abortion

LUIGI MASTROIANNI, JR.

The Beginning of Human Life: Contraceptive Implications

Contraception by its very definition implies prevention of the formation of a conceptus. On the surface, therefore, it would seem that contraception is clearly separated from the issue of when human life begins. Nevertheless, attitudes on contraception are often influenced by attitudes toward pregnancy termination and at what stage of pregnancy the effect of a given contraceptive is exerted. In the early stages of reproduction, the events that finally result in a successfully implanted embryo are not always clear. For example, a contraceptive agent might exert its action during the early phases of fertilization but before its completion. This approach might be looked upon by some as thwarting the process and hence would raise serious concerns. For others, the whole matter is a non-issue until after fertilization is complete. For still others, implantation and not fertilization is the point at which the line is drawn. It is not always possible to separate contraceptive methods according to their mechanism of action, although, increasingly, information is available to help in such delineations.

Even in the pluralistic society of the United States willingness to accept research on newer and possibly better contraceptive methods is influenced by attitudes towards abortion. At the political level, the impact of the lack of delineation between contraception and abortion has already been felt. For example, at present the United States provides no support for the World Health Organization's Special Programme in Contraceptive Development. The fear that monies might be used to support abortion research overrides any humanitarian concerns. There is no uniform enthusiasm for the development of family planning methods even when they clearly work prior to the completion of conception. Paradoxically, better methods of contraception could contribute to a decrease in the incidence of unintended pregnancy and hence of pregnancy termination.

Mechanisms of Conception

Development, conditioning, and release of spermatozoa are early progressive stages in reproduction. Each pregnancy is preceded by the normal

F.K. Beller and R.F. Weir (eds.), The Beginning of Human Life, 117–127.

development of spermatozoa in the testis, conditioning of spermatozoa in the male reproductive tract, transfer of spermatozoa either through intercourse or insemination to the environment of the female reproductive tract, and transport of spermatozoa from the vagina into the cervical mucus and past the cervix through the uterus to the fallopian tube, where fertilization occurs. The testes are a veritable factory. Spermatogenesis is initiated at the time of puberty and continues well into senescence.

Each ejaculate contains between 100 million and 200 million spermatozoa. A large percentage of these have the potential to move and, in fact, eventually to fertilize an egg.

Spermatozoa are living cells. When they are released they contain half of the normal complement of chromosomes. They are equipped with an effective mechanism for movement in the form of a tail, or flagellum. Their movement constitutes clear evidence that they are living cells. When spermatozoa are released from the testes into the transporting ducts of the male reproductive tract, they are not as yet capable of fertilization. Within the male reproductive tract they continue to mature and acquire an additional ability to function in fertilization. Yet, even after ejaculation, the spermatozoon is still not capable of penetrating an egg. It must be modified further through exposure to the female reproductive tract, where it acquires additional capacity to fertilize. Thus, there is progressive maturation from the time the spermatozoon is formed in the testis on through the time it comes under the influence of the female reproductive tract. Throughout this process, spermatozoa acquire greater and greater potential to fertilize, and hence a greater potential for continued life through the fertilization process. Are we to believe, then, that this conditioning endows the spermatozoon with increasing respect as a living human cell with the potential of creating new life? Admittedly the spermatozoon contains only half of the normal complement of chromosomes. At the same time, the initiation of a conceptus will not occur unless the spermatozoon undergoes maturation during which it is endowed with a progressively greater potential for fertilization. One could take the position that fertilization actually begins with conditioning of the spermatozoon in the male reproductive tract.

At the level of the ovary, the total number of oocytes, more than a million in late embryonal life, begins to recede at or before birth in a process of atresia. This loss of oocytes continues through the time of the menopause. At menarche, the normal human ovary is endowed with between 400,000 and 500,000 oocytes. In the normally menstruating woman, usually one oocyte is released each month from puberty through menopause. Thus, during the entire reproductive life of a woman, no more than 500 oocytes are ovulated. This is in stark contrast to the incredibly greater reproductive potential of the male.

Ovulation is preceded by the maturation and development of a follicle, the ovarian structure containing the oocyte. These events are influenced by cyclic changes in hormones through a delicately balanced and carefully programmed series of endocrine events which culminate in the release of an ovum. Following ovulation, the follicle from which the oocyte is released is converted into a special structure, the corpus luteum. The corpus luteum produces the hormone progesterone, so named because it favors gestation. This is the hormone which supports implantation and early pregnancy.

The oocyte which is destined to ovulate undergoes a process of maturation in the ovary prior to ovulation, during which it is prepared for fertilization. At the time of its release, it is surrounded by a thick layer of specialized cells. These sticky cells, referred to as cumulus cells, are responsible for the efficient transport of the egg from the ovulating follicle into the fallopian tube. The cumulus mass containing the oocyte is picked up by the delicate fingerlike fimbriated end of the fallopian tube and transferred efficiently into the tubal lumen. Fertilization takes place in the fallopian tube.

Fertilization involves not only the ovum itself, but the various investments which surround it. The sequence of events during penetration, although not completely understood, has been studied intensively in recent years in laboratory animals and, to some extent, in the human. Suffice it to say that the fertilizing spermatozoon must penetrate the cellular coats which surround the oocyte and must find its way to and attach itself to the zona pellucida, a protein layer which immediately surrounds the oocyte. The penetrating spermatozoon must have been conditioned further such that it can traverse the zona pellucida. It then attaches itself to the egg membrane and finally penetrates into the egg cytoplasm. It is then modified further to form a pronucleus. Thereafter, the male pronucleus and the female pronucleus, formed at about the same time, join, and at some point thereafter there is division to the two-cell stage. The fertilization process is not really complete until the ovum becomes a two-cell structure.

It is now known that the ovum and the spermatozoon destined to penetrate it communicate with each other through biochemical signals. The zona pellucida contains special proteins. As the spermatozoon reaches the level of the zona pellucida, some of these are released to condition the spermatozoon so that it is able to penetrate. After one spermatozoon has attached and penetrated, biochemical and bioelectrical processes prevent penetration by additional spermatozoa. In this way, polyspermy, incorporation of more than one spermatozoon, is avoided. An oocyte penetrated by more than one spermatozoon is abnormal, although early development can be initiated. Such oocytes uniformly abort, even when implantation occurs.

There is division within the environment of the fallopian tube, and at the 16- to 32-cell stage the conceptus is delivered into the uterine cavity. Therein it continues to develop. Its cells are divided into two separate functional elements: those which are destined to form the embryo, and those which will form the placenta. A fluid-filled cavity is formed. This structure is referred to as a blastocyst. On the sixth to seventh post-fertilization day some of the outermost layers of cells of the blastocyst attach to and begin to invade the endometrium. Thereafter, the conceptus continues to develop and eventually establishes contact with maternal blood. The embryo itself consists of undifferentiated cells early on, and it is not until the fourteenth post-fertilization day that the primitive streak, the anlage of the nervous system, is formed. The Ethics Committee of the American Fertility Society and the Warnock Committee of the U.K. have suggested the term "preembryo" for the conceptus through the formation of the primitive streak on day 14. [1, 2] The conceptus is not unique until well after the implantation process is complete. Twinning can occur many days following the initial attachment of the embryo to the endometrium.

The points at which the process is interfered with by a method of family planning are of more than passing interest. For those who look upon the whole process as a continuum, the mechanism of action of a contraceptive is less of an issue. Fertilization and implantation engender the most intense discussion.

Procreation as a Continuum

Those unfamiliar with the events associated with early reproduction might take a position based on definitions, i.e., a contraceptive should work before fertilization or perhaps before implantation, which, for some, represents completion of the process. One could also take the position that it is the *potential* for completion of the fertilization process that is important. The fallacy here is that a high percentage of oocytes which have been penetrated never proceed to further development. Many oocytes are thwarted so early in their development that pregnancy is not recognized in the form of a skipped menstrual period.

It is increasingly difficult for scientists familiar with the details of fertilization to establish a clear definition of the beginning of life during the course of fertilization. Even after implantation is completed, 30 percent of concepti fail to develop through a skipped menstrual period. This high rate of pregnancy loss is nature's way of protecting the species when there is an unfortunate combination of chromosomes.

The issues which separate contraception from abortion are beclouded further by definitions of abortion and contraception. Are we to consider abortion to have occurred when fertilization has been abnormal and the conceptus ceases to develop beyond one or two cell divisions? Has an abortion occurred when the implanted conceptus fails to progress to the point when a menstrual period is skipped? Under natural conditions, well over 50 percent of pregnancies are thwarted for one reason or another at various stages in this process. Is there less unease when we can know precisely about the impact, if any, of a given method of family planning on the early stages of development? Do we redefine our position with increasing levels of knowledge concerning the early phases of human reproduction? It is unlikely that a scientist with genuine expertise in this field would be able to label one event or another as the pivotal one on which to base the decision on exactly when human life begins. This issue has been considered by numerous bodies in the United States and abroad. In 1981, the American Fertility Society's Public Affairs Committee drafted the following statement for distribution to membership for approval:

> Human life is a continuous process, and therefore the exact moment at which a new person is formed cannot be defined in purely scientific terms. The definition of a person necessarily involves metaphysical (religious, philosophical) judgment.

Nonetheless, the mechanisms by which contraceptives work are of more than passing interest. Most people are more comfortable when they have information on mechanisms of action which would place them in a position to judge for themselves the acceptability of one form of contraception or another.

Contraceptive Choices

A variety of contraceptive methods are available in most modern societies. Their availability worldwide is affected by economic conditions and also by attitudes on contraception. In some countries in the developing world, family planning is given high priority. The most effective contraceptive program is that provided in China. There, the intrauterine device is a commonly used method. Abortion backup is generally available. In Japan, a highly developed country, barrier methods are the most commonly used. Abortion backup is widely available and socially acceptable. The array of methods used in the United States through 1990 along with a summary of their frequency of use and failure rates are listed in Table I. The estimated annual number of contraceptive failures is in excess of 1.5 million. In the United States, more

Table I
Method failures in USA

Method	% users	No. (millions)	% accidental pregnancies	No. accidental pregnancies (1st year)
Male steril	14	4.2	0.15	6,300
Female steril	19	5.7	0.40	22,800
OCP's	32	9.6	3	288,000
IUD	3	0.9	6	54,000
Condom	17	5.1	12	612,000
Diaphragm	5	1.5	5	75,000
Sponge	3	0.9	18	162,000
Natural	4	1.2	20	240,000
Vaginal contra	2	0.6	21	126,000
Total:				1,586,100

Based on est. 30,000,000 contraceptors in U.S.

than half of the 1.2 million annual pregnancy terminations are carried out for women who have suffered a contraceptive failure. This then speaks to the lack of efficiency of many of the methods being used. Even the most effective methods are associated with some failures, which, although low in number, are devastating, especially among those for whom abortion is not an acceptable alternative. Given the importance of human procreation, there is no doubt that contraceptive development has received but scant attention.

Oral contraception is the most commonly used method in Western Europe. At this point, Europeans have wider choices than do contraceptors in the United States. The modern intrauterine device is more common in Europe than it is in the United States, where it is marketed by only one small specialty company. Permanent sterilization is, in fact, now the most common U.S. method. Overall, 32 percent of contraceptors have been sterilized, with tubal sterilization being somewhat more popular than vasectomy.

Despite widespread contraceptive use in the United States, concerns persist about safety, effectiveness, cost, convenience, and acceptability. Those methods which are available are not uniformly suited to the religious, social, economic, or health circumstances of many Americans. Outside of the United States, particularly in less-developed countries where medical services are not consistently available and systems for the management of contraceptive-related side effects are sparse or absent, there is even greater concern over the ability of individuals to use existing methods. Attitude ranks high among the impediments to the development of additional contraceptives.

Methods and Mechanisms of Action

Contraception and abortion are inexorably linked. This makes it all the more important to explore mechanisms of action. Although those with grave reservations over mechanisms represent a minority, their opinions play a vital role in setting national policy in the United States. Misunderstandings often lead to a lack of willingness to support and fund contraceptive development initiatives.

Permanent sterilization can be looked upon as contraception in the purest sense. It clearly prevents the union of sperm and oocyte by creating a barrier in the transport system. Vasectomy involves occluding the vas, the structure which leads from the site of sperm production in the testis to the urethra, through which semen is delivered during ejaculation. When the vas is obstructed, spermatozoa are prevented from entering the ejaculate. Hence, the ejaculate is sperm-free and therefore sterile. Vasectomy has received increasing acceptance. It is associated with a very low method failure. Its disadvantage is that it is a permanent method. Reversal requires skilled microsurgical techniques which are successful in approximately 50 percent of cases. Fourteen percent of U.S. contracepting couples elect male sterilization.

The most commonly used method of female sterilization involves occlusion of the fallopian tubes. Blockage of the fallopian tubes prevents the sperm and egg from meeting. The fallopian tubes can be occluded with bands, clips, or electrocautery, or by cutting and tying. The procedure can be carried out using a laparoscope, a telescope which allows visualization of the fallopian tubes. By and large, laparoscopy is done under general anesthesia. Complications include bleeding, infection, injury to other organs, and anesthesia complications. Reversal of tubal sterilization requires a microsurgical procedure. At least 10 percent of sterilized women regret their decisions and many elect to have the sterilization reversed, or even proceed to such high-tech solutions as in vitro fertilization. Vasectomy and tubal sterilization leave no doubt as to the mechanism of action. They clearly prevent contact between spermatozoa and oocyte.

The development of oral contraception was one of the most dramatic events in the history of contraception. Over the three decades during which the Pill has been available, it has been modified significantly. Lower and lower doses have been shown to be effective. Even the Pill, the most effective method available short of sterilization, is associated with some failures. Oral contraception is associated with an accidental pregnancy rate of 3 percent in the first year of use. Most pregnancies occur because two or more pills have been omitted in a given menstrual cycle.

The Pill offers certain other health advantages. There is decreased amount of flow during menstruation. This is especially important when dietary intake of iron is limited and nutrition is not ideal. There is also a somewhat decreased risk of pelvic infections and decreased incidence of ovarian and uterine cancer. There are some disadvantages, especially among subsets of the population. Oral contraceptives inhibit lactation, and hence are not generally recommended for nursing mothers. Infrequent side effects include breast tenderness, nausea, depression, headache, and occasional spotting between periods. Earlier high-dose formulations were associated with a greater risk of cardiovascular disease and blood clots, heart attack, and stroke. The Pill is not recommended for women over age 35 who smoke or for those suffering from hypertension.

By and large, the Pill works through inhibition of ovulation. There is also an effect on the cervical mucus and on the endometrium. During the normal menstrual cycle, there is a change in the quantity and quality of cervical mucus. As ovulation approaches, the cervical secretions become abundant and clear. They are very receptive to spermatozoa and encourage the efficient progression of spermatozoa into the endometrial cavity. Following ovulation, under the influence of progesterone, the mucus becomes thick, viscous, and cellular and provides a much less amicable environment for spermatozoa. Upward progression of spermatozoa into the uterus is impeded. The Pill modifies the normal cyclic changes in cervical mucus, making it much less receptive to spermatozoa, interfering with upward migration. As the dosage in the Pill has been decreased, occasional breakthrough ovulation can occur. Even when ovulation does occur, sperm migration is adversely affected such that spermatozoa do not reach the site of fertilization.

A third possible mechanism of action of the Pill relates to its influence on the endometrium. In the normal menstrual cycle, the endometrium is first stimulated to proliferate by estrogen. Following ovulation, the progesterone produced by the corpus luteum causes secretary changes in the endometrium, preparing it for implantation. The Pill modifies the cyclic changes in the endometrium and hence theoretically, could prevent implantation. However, even if ovulation does occur occasionally, there is no evidence that there is sufficiently efficient sperm migration to allow fertilization.

A new method for the delivery of a progestational agent has recently been introduced. Norplant, progestin-containing capsules, are placed subcutaneously. Once in place, they provide a slow, continuous release of a progestational agent, levonorgestrel. The Norplant system provides contraceptive efficacy for up to five years.

Eighty to ninety percent of Norplant users are anovulatory during the first two years of use. The incidence of ovulation increases in time, and by the fifth year 55 percent of cycles display a hormonal pattern consistent with ovulatory suppression. In the remainder, the progesterone level in the latter half of the cycle is by and large lower than normal, and one cannot be sure that ovulation is in fact occurring.[3] As with oral contraception, Norplant consistently interferes with sperm migration as determined by postcoital tests.[4] Endometrial development is also suppressed, and this has served as the basis for the unsubstantiated suggestion that in some cases "menstrual abortions" may be occurring. This issue has been explored using sensitive hCG assays capable of detecting a pregnancy as early as nine days post ovulation.[5] In a controlled and statistically valid study, there was absence of evidence of pregnancy even when ovulation was not completely suppressed. Over and above ovulation inhibition and production of a mucus hostile to sperm penetration, it has been postulated that there is impaired maturation of the oocyte because of low levels of pituitary hormones, rendering it not fertilizable.

Of all the presently available methods, the intrauterine device has engendered the greatest controversy. One of the issues surrounding IUD use is the putative increase in pelvic infection. This issue surfaced with the use of an early IUD, the Dalkon Shield, which did have some unfortunate design defects. The Dalkon Shield has long been withdrawn from the market. The modern copper-containing IUD has been shown to be associated with markedly increased effectiveness and safety. There is no evidence that there is an increased incidence of pelvic infection except in those who are at greater risk for infection anyway, i.e., women with multiple sexual partners.

Located as it is within the uterine cavity, it has been suspected that the IUD works by preventing implantation. In early monkey studies, fertilization was not observed to occur.[6] Under some experimental circumstances, some fertilized cleaving monkey oocytes were recovered, albeit significantly fewer than in controls.[7]

Systematic search for embryos and oocytes has been carried out between the second and fifth day after ovulation in women using IUDs and in controls.[8] In only 1.5 percent of IUD users were ova found in the uterus, in contrast to 22 percent in the control group, providing evidence that the intrauterine device in humans acts before ova enter the uterus. In a more recent study,[9] the uterus and fallopian tubes of 115 controls and 56 women using various IUDs were explored at the time of surgical sterilization. This study provided results again concordant with the conclusion that the IUD exercises its effect through mechanisms as yet unknown but prior to fertilization.

Human chorionic gonadotropin studies have been carried out in IUD users. These have been done using positive controls (i.e., women seeking pregnancy) as well as negative controls (i.e., sterilized). After ovulation, hCG was found only in the group seeking pregnancy.[10,11]

These studies, taken together, are concordant with the conclusion that the IUD exercises its effect through mechanisms as yet unknown but prior to fertilization.

Contraceptive Methods under Development

A number of newer approaches to fertility control are in various stages of clinical investigation. A progestin-containing silastic ring has been devised. It is placed in the vagina to provide slow release of a progestational agent. The vaginal ring exerts an effect similar to that of Norplant, inhibiting ovulation and modifying the cervical mucus. It is in the late phases of clinical trial.

At the other end of the spectrum, a contraceptive vaccine is being developed. This is an anti-hCG vaccine which has as its point of attack the production of hCG by the early embryo. The net effect is demise of the embryo, if one is present, prior to the skipped menstrual period. Immunization results in the continuous presence of antibodies which would carry out their mission as needed. The immunized women would be completely unaware that conception had occurred. This method works after fertilization and during early implantation. Its mechanism of action is clear, and judgments as to its acceptability can be made on that basis.

Human in vitro fertilization has opened new avenues for exploration of methods which might act to prevent the initiation or completion of the fertilization process. By and large, these are immunological, with antibodies directed at specific proteins found in spermatozoa or in the zona pellucida of the ovum. Efforts have been made to identify the agents which would impair the ability of the spermatozoon to mature in the male. These approaches offer exciting avenues for the development of new contraceptives which actually would prevent fertilization.[12]

The controversy over contraception continues. Dr. John Rock, the Boston physician who has often been referred to as the "father of the Pill," was vitally concerned with the ethical issues surrounding contraception. In 1963, he collected his thoughts in a volume entitled *The Time Has Come: A Catholic Doctor's Proposal to End the Battle over Birth Control.*[13] He made a very good case for the importance of family planning, but not solely in terms of world population. As a caring physician, he also spoke with great eloquence on the health and well-being of women in the reproductive age group for whom pregnancy prevention is a pivotal issue. His was a balanced review – pessimistic in terms of what could happen if we did not focus attention on contraceptive development, but optimistic in terms of increasing world recognition of the importance of the issue. He stated:

> I am convinced that the birth control issue can be resolved to everyone's satisfaction and benefit. Indeed, it must be. I don't mean by this that Catholics, Protestants, Jews, and others will see eye to eye on this subject in the immediate future. I *do* mean that solutions can and must be worked out which obviate the distressing quarrelsome public paralysis we have witnessed during the last few years and which will permit us at least to begin action on the population problem. I mean also to imply that the time may not be far distant when a closer harmony will be evolved even among the doctrines of the various religious groups.

Sadly, Dr. Rock's prophecy was premature. In 1990, the National Academy of Sciences and its Institute of Medicine convened a committee to review the status of contraceptive development in the United States. The committee concluded that there are many serious impediments to contraceptive development. In the committee's report, attention is focused on attitudinal issues and values as they affect family planning.

> The contraceptive development process could not be adequately understood by focusing only on the potential gained in effectiveness or safety of a new method or on the profits a manufacturer projects for a new product. It is also important to understand the attitudes and values that influence the perception of individuals and groups regarding contraceptive practice and the need for new methods, as well as the desire for certain levels of risk, convenience and cost, and their willingness to support efforts to develop new contraceptives.[14]

Public policy is influenced in a dramatic way by abortion-related issues. These have spilled over to the field of contraceptive development. The paradox is that, were better methods of family planning available, the incidence of abortion might be substantially reduced. Certainly, the lives of couples who face the prospect of an unintended pregnancy would be much less complicated.

References

1. Ethical Considerations of New Reproductive Technology. Report of the Ethics Committee of the American Fertility Society. Fertil Steril 1986; 46 Supplement 1.

2. Warnock M. A Question of Life. Oxford: Blackwell Ltd., 1985.
3. Segal SJ, Alvarez-Sanchez F, Brache V, Faudes A, Vilja P, Tuohimaa P. Norplant Implants: The Mechanism of Contraceptive Action, 1991. In press.
4. Brache V, Alvarez-Sanchez F, Faundes A, Tejada AS, Cochon L. Ovarian endocrine function through five years of continuous treatment with Norplant subdermal contraceptive implants. Contraception 1990; 41: 169.
5. Brache V, Faundes A, Johansson E, Alvarez F. Anovulation, inadequate luteal phase and poor sperm penetration in cervical mucus during prolonged use of Norplant implants. Contraception 1985; 31: 261.
6. Mastroianni L Jr, Suzuki S, Manabe Y, Watson F. Further observations on the influence of the intrauterine device on ovum and sperm distribution in the monkey. Am J Obstet Gynecol. 1967; 99: 649.
7. Hurst PR, Wheeler AO, Eckstein P. A study of uterine embryos recovered from rhesus monkeys fitted with intrauterine devices. Fertil Steril 1980; 33: 69–76.
8. Croxatto HB. The duration of egg transport and its regulation in mammals. In: Coutinho EM, Fuchs F, eds. Physiology and Genetics of Reproduction (Part B). NY: Plenum Publishing, 1974.
9. Alvarez F, Brache V, Fernandez E, Guerrero B, Guiloff E, Hess R, Salvatierra AM, Zacharias S. New insights on the mode of action of intrauterine contraceptive devices in women. Fertil Steril 1988; 49: 768–773.
10. Segal SJ, Alvarez-Sanchez F, Adejuwon CA, Brache de Mejia V, Leon P, Faundes A. Absence of chorionic gonadotropin in sera of women who use intrauterine devises. Fertil Steril 1985; 44: 214–218.
11. Wilcox AJ, Winberg CR, O'Connor JF, Baird DD, Schlatterer JP, Canfield RE, Armstrong EG, Nisula BG. Incidence of early loss of pregnancy. N Engl J Med 1988; 319(4): 189–194.
12. Alexander NJ, Griffin D, Spieler JM, Waites GMH. Gamete Interaction: Prospects for Immunocontraception. New York: J Wiley & Sons, 1990.
13. Rock J. The Time Has Come: A Catholic Doctor's Proposals to End the Battle over Birth Control. New York: Knopf, 1963.
14. Mastroianni L Jr, Donaldson PJ, Kane TT, eds. Developing New Contraceptives: Obstacles and Opportunities. Washington, DC: Committee on Contraceptive Development, National Research Council, National Academy Press, 1990.

ALLAN ROSENFIELD AND HILLARY KUNINS

Abortion: A Public Health Perspective*

No single health-related issue today engenders more controversy, debate, and even violence than does the topic of abortion. Recent policy and legal changes, developments in medical technologies, and continuing maternal deaths from illegal abortion are some of the indicators of the centrality of abortion as an issue in women's reproductive lives. Since the 1973 landmark U.S. Supreme Court decision on abortion, *Roe v. Wade*, the issue of abortion has generated a vast literature, spanning many disciplines. This essay will summarize the history of abortion in the United States and will review relevant recent research generated from the field of public health and from several other related disciplines on such topics as the safety of abortion, the new "abortion pill", RU 486, and abortion in the developing world.

Criminalization of Abortion in the United States in the Nineteenth Century

In the midst of the current debates regarding abortion, a historical analysis lends insight into the contemporary discussion. Decriminalization of abortion in the United States began in the late 1950s and culminated with the *Roe v. Wade* decision in 1973. The forces that helped lead to legalization include health professionals' concerns about the dangers of illegal abortions, the women's movement, and changing social mores, as well as, in the minds of some, concerns about overpopulation.[29,50,52,59,69,72] These forces all coalesced in the 1960s to form a powerful social movement to decriminalize abortion. A major concern of health professionals today, however, is the possibility of the recriminalization of abortion. Thus, in reviewing the current legal and public health status of abortion, it is particularly useful to look first to an earlier period of U.S. history when the criminalization of abortion had its origins.

During the latter half of the nineteenth century the practice of abortion in the U.S. shifted from one governed by earlier British common law to a heavily regulated and criminalized medical procedure. This period matched our own

F.K. Beller and R.F. Weir (eds.), The Beginning of Human Life, 129–144.

in the amount of controversy and debate surrounding abortion. Many of the themes which characterize the current controversy emerged from that which occurred in this earlier period.

In the U.S. prior to the nineteenth century, no legislation had yet been passed regarding the legality of abortion. American courts relied on British common law doctrine to hand down decisions.[52] Under common law, abortion was a criminal act only after the pregnant woman felt fetal movement (quickening). Prior to quickening, however, abortion was not criminal, since at that time it was medically impossible to confirm a pregnancy with certainty before quickening had occurred.[52]

During the first half of the nineteenth century, many state legislatures began for the first time to pass laws that regulated the practice of abortion. For the most part, these laws preserved the common law doctrine of quickening, but set precedents for the practice of abortion to be subjected to statutory rather than common law regulation.[52]

From 1860 to 1880, state legislatures again intervened in the issue of abortion. As several historians point out, the legal status of abortion for most of the twentieth century was largely formulated by legislative action during this period of the nineteenth century.[50,52] The statutes then enacted overturned the quickening doctrine and abortion was made illegal at any point during pregnancy. Some state laws, however, made an exception for abortions to preserve the life of the mother.[50,52] In addition, many laws held the woman, as well as the abortionist, criminally liable.

The major advocates for criminalization of abortion were an emerging group of organized doctors primarily associated with the American Medical Association and antiobscenity crusaders led by Anthony Comstock. Surprisingly, feminists supported doctors in their antiabortion stance, while religious groups were virtually absent from the debates. A review of the major arguments and individual motivations are helpful in attempting to understand both the basis of these groups' positions and how the abortion debates were constructed.

Physicians associated with the A.M.A., which had been formed in 1847, were a dominant, if not the major, force in criminalizing abortion. Through their writings, lectures, and, perhaps most important, their successful lobbying of state legislators to pass antiabortion statutes, these doctors galvanized efforts to restrict the practice of abortion.[52,59,72] Historians attribute a variety of motivations to their antiabortion positions, ranging from doctors' explicit concern for maternal health (with many believing that abortion was a greater risk to health than childbirth) and for issues of morality (in effect an early expression of concern about fetal rights and an interpretation of the Hippocratic Oath) to more subtle and often unstated designs for professional power (in competition with the nonmedical practitioners who most often performed abortions and often in the process "stole" patients for other medical treatment) and for control over women's fertility.

Nineteenth-century feminists disagreed about the desirability of traditional sex roles for women, but they supported the doctors' campaign to criminalize abortion. These feminists advocated a concept called "voluntary motherhood," which meant that women should have the choice whether or not to become mothers. They believed that by limiting their fertility women would have more freedom to participate in spheres other than the domestic one. But here their argument parts ways with that of many contemporary feminists: the method of fertility control they generally advocated was abstinence. The availability of abortion, these feminists argued, allowed male sensualism to go unchecked and created a situation where women had to comply with their husbands' sexual demands.[52] The nineteenth-century feminists' assumption was that male and female sexuality was innately different; while men were inherently sexual beings, women were asexual. Engaging in sexual activity as often as men would like would compromise women's inherently asexual nature. The availability of abortion meant women would no longer have a convenient excuse, that of limiting the number of children, to avoid sexual activity.

Religious leaders comprised another group which had a considerably different stance from that of their twentieth-century counterparts. Prior to the 1860s, the clergy, including Catholics, were generally unwilling to speak out against the practice of abortion. In 1869, for the first time, a council of American bishops condemned abortion; later that year the pope reiterated the condemnation. According to one historian, the pronouncements received little public attention.[52] The church was hardly a leader in the nineteenth-century campaign to criminalize abortion in the United States. Antiobscenity crusaders were a second group crucial to the success of the campaign to criminalize abortion. The best-known figure associated with the crusade was Anthony Comstock, who began his antiobscenity career in 1872 as a member of the Committee for the Suppression of Vice (under the auspices of the Young Men's Christian Association of New York City). Comstock successfully lobbied at the federal level for the passage of "An Act for the Suppression of Trade in, and Circulation of, Obscene Literature and Articles of Immoral Use." Among its provisions, the Comstock Law, as it came to be known, prohibited the advertising of abortion by mail, as well as the distribution of drugs or instruments used for abortion purposes through the postal system. It also made it a federal crime to sell or advertise abortion services if the person providing such services was not a physician acting "in good faith."[43,52]

Although the Comstock Law was stringent, it held little power without diligent enforcement. Appointed as a "special agent" of the Post Office Department, Comstock himself became the primary enforcer. Endowed with a badge and the authority to issue warrants for arrests, he helped to indict 55 people for their activity as abortionists between 1872 and 1880.[52] His entrapment of perhaps the most infamous New York City abortionist, Madame Resell, is said to have led to her suicide in 1878.[43] After she died, Comstock was said to have "boasted that she was the fifteenth malefactor he had driven to suicide, in less than five years on the job."[43] Comstock's vigilance in enforcing the provisions of the antiobscenity law helped secure the success of the antiabortion campaign. By involving the federal government in the suppression of abortion advertising and services, the state lobbying conducted by those doctors opposed to abortion gained credibility. The antiobscenity campaign also decreased the public visibility of abortion services by criminalizing their advertisement.[52]

By 1900, the criminalization of abortion was complete. Virtually all states and territories had passed restrictive abortion statutes. Courts were more willing to mete out stricter fines and sentences to convicted abortionists.[52] While the criminalization process itself was successful, however, the doctors' goals of achieving greater maternal health was undermined by that very process. Since by 1890 doctors regularly used antiseptic procedures, "at the very time abortion might theoretically have become a safer procedure than it had been earlier in the century, it came instead to be perceived as more dangerous than ever."[52] The consequence of criminalization was to force the practice underground, where less-reputable practitioners could not or would not avail themselves of the safer methods. The legacy of the nineteenth century, increasing the physical health risks associated with abortion, would persist into the twentieth century, until legal and legislative actions in the 1960s and 1970s reversed it.

Abortion in the nineteenth century was a battleground for conflicting ideas about fetal life as well as women's fertility and sexuality, public health, and physicians' professional position in society. The historical literature reveals the complexity of the debates which raged during that time. While the actors and some of the issues were different from those involved in the abortion debate today, the intensity and degree of societal disruption which took place in the nineteenth century is quite similar to that of the late twentieth century. The nineteenth-century example shows us there are no simple resolutions to the conflict surrounding abortion, for the conflict stems from the tangled interplay of social, economic, and moral concerns.

Two Supreme Court cases in the latter half of this century marked the end of outright legal bars to abortion in the United States. In the 1965 case of *Griswold v. Connecticut*, the Supreme Court articulated a constitutional right of privacy that would ultimately lead to a successful challenge of the constitutionality of antiabortion laws.[27] This was followed in 1973 by the landmark *Roe v. Wade* decision and the subsequent controversies and further Supreme Court decisions.[6,23,28,36,38,41,58,64,70,77–79,81]

One decision, *Harris v. McRae*, had a particularly negative impact on poor women by affirming the congressionally mandated Hyde Amendment, which prohibited the use of Medicaid funds for abortions, except to save the life of the mother. By this decision, the health status and reproductive choices of poor women are compromised by restricting their normal source of funding for medical care. Researchers have found that between 18 percent and 35 percent of Medicaid-eligible women who would choose to terminate their pregnancies are unable to do so because of lack of funds.[70,78] Some of these women are forced to undergo childbearing simply because of their economic status. Poor women who manage to obtain abortions often delay the procedure while collecting sufficient funds.[36] Unfortunately, the data are clear that abortions after the first eight weeks are associated with somewhat higher health risks, risks that rise with each additional week of gestation.[10]

Similarly, the more recent *Webster v. Reproductive Health Services* decision, which limits access to public facilities and personnel for the purposes of abortion, will primarily affect low-income women.[2,3,15] While wealthier women can afford to pay the cost of an abortion at a private medical institution or to travel to distant abortion facilities, poorer women may not be able to do so. Further, it has been noted that *Webster*'s requirement that physicians test for fetal viability after twenty weeks LMP may constrain sound medical practice by requiring invasive, unnecessary testing, such as amniocentesis, in an effort to ascertain fetal lung maturity at a point in pregnancy at which such testing is not reliable.[15]

Another potential consequence of *Webster* may be to limit the training in the techniques of abortion in obstetrics-gynecology residency programs (at least for those who are training in public facilities). The resultant decrease in surgical skill in this area could lead to complications from abortion procedures as the number of experienced personnel decreases.[15]

Public Health and Medical Aspects of Abortion

Since its decriminalization in 1973, the subject of abortion has generated vast amounts of research on public health and medical issues. Researchers' interests have ranged from descriptive studies of demographic characteristics and morbidity and mortality rates to studies of how those rates and characteristics change over time.[4,10,33,73] The U.S. Centers for Disease Control in Atlanta and the private Alan Guttmacher Institute collect on an ongoing basis the most comprehensive demographic data about abortion seekers, incidence, complication rates, mortality rates, and availability of abortion services. Other researchers have examined the physical and emotional sequelae of abortion.[37,46,56] Still others have carried out social science studies on the reasons women choose to abort, and on contraceptive attitudes and practices regarding contraception.[35,76] The abundance of studies is such that Willard Cates, a prominent researcher in the field, has stated, "We have come to know more about [abortion] than any other surgical operation."[10]

Abortion-related Complications and Mortality

Abortions have been among the most commonly performed surgical procedures since the *Roe v. Wade* decision in 1973. When performed by properly trained personnel, they are also among the safest. Prior to federal legalization (or, for several states, prior to state liberalization of abortion laws preceding 1973) abortion was not the relatively risk-free procedure it has become today. It is impossible to know with certainty the number of induced abortions that took place prior to the liberalization of the abortion laws. Since the total number of abortions would be the denominator for constructing both morbidity and mortality rates, it is also difficult to make comparisons between these rates before and after legalization. However, many researchers have been concerned with precisely these issues, and their estimates and calculations are considered to be valuable approximations.

The difficulty of estimating the incidence of abortion prior to legalization is exemplified by the wide range presented in the published report of the first medical conference devoted to illegal and therapeutic abortion in 1958. The statistics committee of that conference reported that "a plausible estimate of the frequency of induced abortion in the United States could be as low as 200,000 and as high as 1,200,000 per year."[8]

Estimates for the death-to-case ratio in 1972 were 30 to 40 deaths per 100,000 abortions.[12,74] These ratios are similar to the maternal mortality ratios in the United States in the 1950s. Writing in 1975, Christopher Tietze calculated the risk of mortality from illegal abortion to be eight times greater than the risk from legal abortions.[74] Since his writing, the mortality ratio for legal abortions has further decreased, widening the safety gap between legal and illegal abortions.

Health-care providers who practiced prior to 1973 report many anecdotes about the women who presented with hemorrhage, fever, shock, or a foreign object in the uterus as a result of attempted induced abortion by either an incompetent abortionist or the individual herself.[8,24] In 1975, an Institute of Medicine report stated that "medical complications associated with illegal (nonmedical or self-induced) abortion appear to have declined markedly since abortion legalization, based on hospital admissions due to septic and incomplete abortion, two adverse consequences of the illegal procedure."[49] Clearly, then, the federal legalization of abortion has resulted in the availability of safer abortions, thus promoting the health of women of childbearing age.

A slow decline in abortion-related mortality began as early as 1940, when the abortion mortality ratio (the ratio of abortion-related deaths to live births) decreased at a rate of 11 percent per year until 1950.[13] Researchers have speculated that this decline was the result of the utilization of antibiotics. From 1951 to 1965, the ratio continued to decline, albeit at the greatly reduced rate of 1.7 percent per year. But from 1965 to 1976, the period of legalization, the mortality ratio dropped at a rate of 25 percent per year. This rapid rate of decline has been attributed to the availability of legal abortion as well as to the availability of effective contraceptives.[13]

The decline in the actual number of abortion-related deaths further demonstrates the effect of federal legalization on public health. From 1958 to 1962 there were approximately 290 deaths annually in the United States due to other-than-legal abortions ("other-than-legal" abortions include spontaneous, criminal, and undetermined abortions.[74] That number dropped to 142 deaths in 1969, at a time that abortion had become available in a number of states, and further, to 27 deaths, in 1973.

After the federal legalization of abortion in 1973, abortion-related mortality continued to decrease. It is estimated that abortion-related mortality in 1973 was 3.4 deaths per 100,000 legal abortions. In 1980, the figure was 0.5 deaths per 100,000 legal abortions – an 85 percent decrease.[75] The same study estimates the mortality due to childbirth to be 11 deaths per 100,000 births. Although the denominators are different, it appears that legal abortion is many times safer than childbirth.[75]

The continued decrease in abortion-related mortality may be attributed to several causes. The shift from riskier later abortions to safer earlier ones certainly helped to reduce mortality. For example, in 1974, 10 percent of abortions were performed on women with gestations of more than 15 weeks, while 43 percent were in gestations of less than 8 weeks. In 1985, however, only 5 percent of abortions occurred in women with gestations of more than 16 weeks, while slightly more than half of all abortions took place when the woman was less than 8 weeks LMP.[14] Since the earliest abortions are least risky, the shift to earlier abortions contributed to the decrease in mortality.[4] Increases in the use of local rather than general anesthesia also made the typical abortion procedure safer.[75] Finally, the physicians providing abortions had received better training and had gained experience. Their skill further enhanced the safety of abortion.[75]

The change in the techniques used to perform both first- and second-trimester abortions since 1973 has contributed significantly to the increased safety of abortion procedures. As of 1985, more than 97 percent of all abortions were primarily performed using instrumental evacuation, which includes vacuum aspiration (or suction curettage), dilation and evacuation, and sharp curettage.[14] In the first trimester, the majority of instrumental evacuations are now performed using suction curettage. A number of studies have demonstrated the decreased morbidity and mortality rates associated with its use compared to dilatation and sharp curettage.[42] In 1985, approximately 95 percent of all abortion procedures were performed using this method.[14]

The percentage of abortions performed by intrauterine instillation has decreased over time; in 1975, 6 percent of abortions were performed using this method, while in 1985 only 2 percent were.[14] Correspondingly, the number of second-trimester abortions performed using dilatation and evacuation, a form of instrumental evacuation documented to be safer than medical instillation when carried out by experienced practitioners, has increased.[11,26] In 1985, slightly more than 50 percent of abortions at more than 21 weeks LMP were performed using dilatation and evacuation and nearly two-thirds of abortions between 16 and 20 weeks LMP were performed with this method. Hysterectomies and hysterotomies as methods of abortion were documented as having virtually disappeared in 1982.[14] These two methods were the only ones requiring major abdominal surgery, conferring on the woman having the abortion all the attendant risks of major surgery; the disappearance of these methods contributes to the current level of safety of the abortion procedure.

Demographic and other Characteristics of Abortion Patients

Nearly two decades after *Roe*, we are able to construct a picture of abortion rates and ratios in an environment where the procedure is safe and legal. Official abortion rates increased from 1973 until 1981, at which time the annual rate stabilized at approximately 28–29 abortions per 1,000 women (aged 15–44) or about 1.6 million abortions annually.[34]

According to 1987 data, approximately one-quarter of the women obtaining abortions were teenagers, more than 80 percent of whom were unmarried. Over half of the women had not had a previous live birth, and nearly half, about 43 percent, had had at least one prior abortion.[35] Poorer women with family incomes of less than $11,000 were more likely to have abortions than women with higher income levels.[35] Younger women had higher abortion rates than older women, with 18–19-year-olds having the highest rate of all age groups. Hispanics had higher rates than non-Hispanics; nonwhites had higher rates than whites.[35]

The relationship between contraceptive use and abortion is another question which has been recently studied. According to data from 1987, the vast majority (91 percent) of abortion patients reported that they had used a birth control method at some point in their lives. Slightly more than half reported using a method in the month before they became pregnant.[35] Among 1987 abortion patients, students and working women were more likely to be in the group of recent users of birth control. The same study found that the women seeking abortion who were younger, had less income, fewer years of education, or who were black or Hispanic were more likely to report not having used contraceptives.[35]

Consequences of Abortion

The psychological and physical sequelae of abortion have been the subject of many studies. While research on the physical consequences of abortion is conclusive in demonstrating a very low rate of morbidity and essentially no long-term physical sequelae, the results of studies of the psychological sequelae are somewhat less firm. Many of these latter studies suffer from serious methodological flaws which limit their generalizability and reliability. Experts believe however that, given the great number of abortions performed each year and the absence of ensuing and obviously related mental health sequelae, significant psychological problems are unlikely to be associated with abortion.[40]

In one of the most comprehensive reviews of the physical consequences of abortion, Hogue and colleagues examined over 150 studies regarding the association between induced abortion and subsequent reproductive outcomes.[37] They concluded that the weight of the evidence shows no association between induced abortion and subsequent infertility, midtrimester spontaneous abortion, shortened gestation, or ectopic pregnancy. (Two later studies confirm this finding with regard to ectopic pregnancy.[7,39] However, Hogue and colleagues note that effects of repeated induced abortions remain unknown. The studies they reviewed contained contradictory findings; many of them may have shown effects only because of the failure to control for confounding variables. Some evidence, however, indicates that procedures which require wider dilatation of the cervix may be associated with negative outcomes such as increased risk of spontaneous abortion. The introduction of laminaria to dilate the cervix slowly helps to avoid this risk. Hogue and colleagues call for future studies to examine the "technical subtleties" of various abortion methods in order to understand the effect, if any, on subsequent reproductive function.[37]

Findings on the psychological effects of abortion have been politicized by those on both sides of the abortion debate. As Rogers and colleagues note, "Both advocates and opponents of abortion can prove their points by judiciously referencing only articles supporting their political agenda."[63] These researchers find that many studies of psychological sequelae suffer from methodological flaws, such as inadequate sample size, lack of an appropriate comparison group, and the use of data-collecting instruments which do not have known reliability or validity.

A more recent examination of the medical and psychological sequelae of abortion was conducted in 1987 by then U.S. Surgeon General C. Everett Koop at the direction of President Ronald Reagan. The implicit agenda behind Reagan's directive was for the surgeon general to accumulate evidence to support the overturning of *Roe v. Wade*.[40] Koop interviewed members of twenty-seven groups with interests in abortion (both antiabortion and pro-choice) and reviewed over 250 scientific articles to complete his project. Although his full report was never released, a congressional subcommittee gained access to it and then heard testimony from some of the groups and individuals with whom Koop had consulted. These hearings were made public in 1989. The information gleaned from them indicates that Koop, despite his admitted antiabortion stance, had essentially concluded that there are no negative medical or psychological consequences for women undergoing abortion. The subcommittee found that Koop had "expressed doubts about the existence of Postabortion Stress Syndrome," the condition often used by antiabortion groups to argue the deleterious after effects of abortion.[40] The subcommittee also reported that the American Psychological Association had submitted a review paper to Koop concluding that "despite the flaws in the research, there is so little evidence of psychiatric problems following abortion, and so much evidence of relief, that therefore abortion does not cause more psychiatric problems than unwanted pregnancy."[40] The subcommittee report made public the fact that Koop had failed to uncover serious medical or psychological consequences for women who have had abortions.

Medical Termination of Pregnancy: RU 486

For many years researchers have sought an agent that would function as an antiprogesterone, interfering with the critically important role played by progesterone, particularly in early pregnancy.[5] With the discovery by scientists at Roussel-UCLAF in France of the antiprogestin RU 486 (commercially marketed as mifepristone), for the first time the possibility of the medical termination of pregnancy became a reality. The abortion pill, as RU 486 is known in the mass media, holds great promise as an alternative to surgical first-trimester abortions. When RU 486 is used in combination with a prostaglandin within the first 49 days of pregnancy, successful and safe termination of the pregnancy occurs in 96 percent of cases.[62,71]

As of mid 1990, however, the drug was available only in France. While there are discussions about introducing the drug in England and the Scandinavian countries, Roussel-UCLAF and its parent company, Hoechst, have been unwilling to have the drug introduced into the United States, apparently because of fear of controversy and protest by antiabortion groups.**

RU 486 also generated much controversy in France, with public protests by antiabortion activists. Soon after the French government approved the marketing of RU 486 on September 23, 1988, Roussel announced that it was abandoning plans to distribute the drug in France. Their announcement made it clear that their decision was in response to public pressure. Two days later, however, the French health minister offered a powerful statement that RU 486 was "the moral property of women, not just the property of the drug company," and ordered Roussel to make the drug available in France.[44] In taking this action, the health minister made use of a French law that gave him the authority to withdraw a company's license to a drug if the company refuses to make it available, and then offer it to another company to distribute.

While the development of RU 486 poses difficult moral questions, there is clear medical evidence suggesting the drug is safe and efficacious when used in combination with a prostaglandin for early abortion.[5,9,62] (Prostaglandin encourages uterine contractions, thereby increasing the probability of expulsion of the contents of the uterus.) A recent clinical study of more than 2,000 women reported an overall efficacy rate of 96 percent, with efficacy defined as the complete expulsion of the products of conception without the need for additional procedures.[71] The study was conducted on women who were no more than eight weeks from their last menstrual period.

The most obvious advantage of RU 486 is that it avoids surgery and anesthesia and their attendant risks. In addition, greater privacy is afforded to the patient. One disadvantage of RU 486 is the number of visits to a medical facility – four – required in France; three of these are medically necessary. The first visit is to request the abortion, because, according to French law, the applicant must then wait one week to be sure she is certain of her decision. She returns to the clinic a second time to take RU 486. On the third visit, two days later, she is given the prostaglandin analogue. At that time, she remains in the clinic to be monitored for four hours. Finally, she returns 8 to 12 days after the administration of RU 486 for follow-up.[18,71] Fewer visits are generally required for the surgical procedure in the United States, and thus abortion using RU 486 may pose problems of access for women who must travel a distance to a medical facility.

Other applications of RU 486, both for contraceptive and noncontraceptive indications, are the subject of current research. One potential use is as a once-a-month contraceptive pill taken late in the menstrual cycle.[51,53] Other potential uses include treatment for breast cancer,[65] Cushing's syndrome,[48] and glaucoma.[16] RU 486 may also be useful in inducing labor after fetal death.[57]

While the future for RU 486 in the U.S. is unclear, its development is a remarkable advance from a scientific, as well as a societal point of view. Clearly, with a woman's right to an abortion still constitutionally protected in the U.S., women should have the option to choose a medical procedure, once this new agent has been reviewed by the FDA. Unfortunately, an FDA review can be initiated only at the request of the drug company and, at least for the present, Roussel has been unwilling to do so. Were the company to reverse its present stance, it has been suggested, antiabortion advocates in Congress and in the Bush administration may attempt to prevent the FDA from undertaking its normal review process for a new drug.

Abortion in an International Context

The worldwide trend in the last decade is toward the liberalization of abortion laws.[17,32] As of 1990, approximately three-quarters of the world's population lives in countries where abortion is available for health reasons, but only about 40 percent live in countries where it is available on demand.[30] The most restrictive abortion policies are in effect in Latin America, sub-Saharan Africa, and some of the fundamentalist Arab nations. Abortion policies in western, central and eastern Europe are generally nonrestrictive, with the exception of Ireland and Malta.[31]

Approximately 33 million legal abortions are performed every year. When illegal abortions are added, the total number rises to an estimated 40–60 million.[31] Fourteen million and eleven million abortions, respectively, are performed each year in China and the Soviet Union. The Soviet Union, with an approximate abortion rate of 181 abortions per 1,000 women, has the highest rate among all developed countries.[31]

Romania provides an often-cited example of the effect of changing abortion policy on population fertility rates and abortion-related mortality rates. During the last forty years, the abortion policy there has changed tremendously with accompanying social and health consequences. Abortion policies were first liberalized in 1957, and birth rates declined following this step.[82] In 1966, abortion laws were tightened in the first pronatalist policy changes. The birth rate rose from 14.3 per 1,000 population in 1966 to 26.7 in 1968, suggesting that women were no longer terminating pregnancies at the same rate.[19] By 1983, however, the birth rate had again dropped to its original rate, mainly because of contraceptive practice and illegal abortion.[61] Increased abortion-related mortality rates accompanied the restrictive abortion policies – the rates increased from 19 per 1,000,000 women aged 15–45 in 1966 to 69 per 1,000,000 in 1970.[82] The pronatalist policies of the Ceaucescu government were so onerous that liberalization of the abortion policy was one of the very first actions of the new government formed in December 1989 after Ceaucescu was overthrown. The drastic changes in abortion policy should predict changes in the maternal mortality rate, which is much higher than in the rest of Europe, probably as a result of the high rate of illegal abortion.

In many developing countries, complications of illegal abortion are one of the five leading causes of maternal mortality.[67] The absence of good data in the developing world, however, makes it difficult to assess quantitatively the relationship between abortion and health status. Much of the information about maternal deaths is based on hospital studies, which include only a self-selected group of patients who actually come to a hospital.[68] Studies of maternal deaths show a range in the proportion attributed to abortion. In sub-Saharan Africa in the 1960s, induced abortion was thought to be less common than in most other parts of the world.[54] In a large, urban-community study conducted in the early 1980s in Addis-Ababa, Ethiopia, however, it was found that 54 percent of maternal deaths in that city were due to complications of illegal abortion.[47] Similar high rates of abortion have been found in a number of other recent African studies, particularly in urban areas.[68] In Latin America, despite the lack of reliable data, it has been suggested that abortion-related complications are the leading cause of maternal mortality in many countries of the region.[68]

The cost of treating complications from illegal abortions is high, particularly in countries with scarce material resources. In Nigeria, for example, abortion-related complications are said to account for approximately 60 percent of acute gynecological beds.[1] Similarly, a study in Latin America found that septic abortion accounts for a disproportionate share of expenditures for transfusions, operating room costs, and total bed-nights.[22]

Overall, it has been suggested by WHO that between 20 percent and 40 percent of all maternal deaths in developing countries are due to complications of illegal and/or unsafely performed abortion procedures.[67] Thus, somewhere between 100,000 and 200,000 women are estimated to die each year from unsafe abortions, a public health tragedy of immense proportion, but one that has been essentially ignored by the public health and obstetrical communities, by policymakers, and by the media. It has been suggested that together with the other causes of maternal mortality, women's reproductive health is one of the great neglected diseases of the tropics.[68]

Abortion is a highly politicized issue in the United States and internationally. The availability of abortion is often a crucial determinant of the health status of women, affecting maternal morbidity and mortality rates. In many parts of the world, however, its availability is shaped by political, cultural, and religious factors. Depending on the resources and health-care system of a particular country, availability will vary with the socioeconomic status of the woman seeking an abortion.

Despite efforts on the part of the antiabortion movement to make abortion an illegal criminal offense, in the opinion of the authors the issue should not be a question of legal versus illegal status of abortion, but rather whether abortion will be safe or unsafe. Throughout known history, women have attempted to terminate unwanted pregnancies, no matter what the risk to their health and life, no matter the woman's religion, and no matter the local cultural factors. And, unfortunately, illegality or restrictions disproportionately affect the poor and disadvantaged. The data are clear; legal first-trimester abortion procedures, performed by properly trained personnel, are among the safest of surgical procedures and are safer than delivering a pregnancy. For these reasons, abortion constitutes one of the most significant public health issues of our time.

NOTES

* Adapted from Kunins, H and Rosenfield, A. Abortion: A legal and public health perspective. Annual Review Public Health 1991; 10: 361–82.

** As of early 1993, RU 486 is also available in England and Sweden. Further, with a prochoice Clinton Administration, Roussel has indicated its willingness for an American organization, the Population Council, to undertake clinical trials and plans for its introduction in the U.S. after an FOA review.

REFERENCES

1. Aggarwal VP, Mati JKG. Epidemiology of induced abortions in Nairobi, Kenya. J Obstet Gynecol East Cent Afr 1992; 31: 67–70.
2. Allen AE, Pearse WH. The implications of Webster for practicing physicians. J Am Med Assoc 1989; 262: 1510–11.
3. Annas GJ. The Supreme Court, privacy, and abortion. J Am Med Assoc 1989; 321: 1200–3.
4. Atrash HK, MacKay T, Binkin NJ, Hogue CJR. Legal abortion mortality in the United States: 1972 to 1982. Am J Obstet Gynecol 1987; 156: 605–12.
5. Baulieu EE. RU-486 as an antiprogesterone steroid: from receptor to contragestion and beyond. J Am Med Assoc 1989; 262: 1808–14.
6. *Bellotti v. Baird* 443 US 622 (US Supreme Court 1979).
7. Burkman RT, Mason KJ, Gold EB. Ectopic pregnancy and prior induced abortion. Contraception 37(1): 21–27.
8. Calderone MS, ed. Abortion in the United States. New York: Hoeber-Harper, 1958.

9. Cameron IT, Baird DT. Early pregnancy termination: a comparison between vacuum aspiration and medical abortion using prostaglandin (16, 16 dimethyl-trans 2-PGE1 methyl ester) or the antiprogestagen RU-486. Br J Obstet Gynecol 1988; 95: 271–76.
10. Cates W. Legal abortion: the public health record. Science 1982; 215: 1586–90.
11. Cates W, Grimes D A. Deaths from second-trimester abortion by dilation and evacuation: causes, prevention, facilities. Obstet Gynecol 1981; 58: 401–8.
12. Cates W, Rochat RW. Illegal abortions in the United States: 1972–1974. Fam Plann Perspect 1976; 8(2): 86–92.
13. Cates W, Rochat RW, Grimes DA, Tyler CW. Legalized abortion: effect on national trends of maternal and abortion-related mortality (1940–1976). Am J Obstet Gynecol 1978; 132: 211–14.
14. Cent Dis Control. Abortion surveillance, United States, 1984–1985. Morbid Mortal Wkly Rep. 1989; 38(SS-2): 11–15.
15. Chavkin W, Rosenfield A. A chill wind blows: Webster, obstetrics and the health of women. Am J Obstet Gynecol 163: 450–52.
16. Cheeks L, Green K. Distribution of a steroid antagonist in the eye following topical administration. Curr Eye Res 1986; 5: 705–9.
17. Cool R. Antiprogestin drugs: medical and legal issues. Fam Plann Perspect 1989; 21: 267–72.
18. Cook R, Dickens BM. International developments in abortion laws: 1977–8. Am J Public Health 1989; 78: 1305–11.
19. David HP. Eastern Europe: pronatalist policies and private behavior. Popul Bull 1982; 36(6): 1–48.
20. Donovan P. The 1988 abortion referenda: lessons for the future. Fam Plann Perspect 1989; 21(5): 218–23.
21. Ely JH. The wages of crying wolf: a comment on Roe V Wade. Yale Law J 1973; 82: 920–44.
22. Fortney JA. The use of hospital resources to treat incomplete abortions: examples from Latin America. Public Health Rep 1981; 96: 574–79.
23. Fujita B, Wagner NN. Referendum 20 – Abortion reform in Washington State. In: Osofsky JD, Osofsky HJ, eds. The Abortion Experience: Psychological and Medical Impact. New York: Harper & Row 1973: pp. 232–60.
24. Furth P. A piece of mind: Roe v Wade. J Am Med Assoc. 1989; 262: 1519.
25. Gordon L. Woman's Body, Woman's Right. New York: Penguin, 1977.
26. Grimes DA, Schulz KF. The comparative safety of second-trimester abortion methods. In; L Porter R, O'Conner M, eds. Abortion: Medical Progress and Social Implications. London: Pitman 1985 PP. 83–96.
27. *Griswold v. Connecticut*, 381 U.S. 479 (US Supreme Court, 1965).
28. *Harris v. McRae*, 100 Supreme Court 2671 (1980).
29. Hodge HL. Foeticide, or criminal abortion: a lecture introductory to the course on obstetrics, and diseases of women and children[1869]. Reprinted in Abortion in Nineteenth-Century America New York: Arno, 1974.
30. Henshaw SK. Induced abortion: a worldwide perspective. Fam Plann Perspect 1986; 18(6): 250–54.
31. Henshaw SK. Induced Abortion: A World Review. 6th ed. New York: Alan Guttmacher Inst, 1986.
32. Henshaw SK. Induced Abortion: a world review. Fam. Plann Perspect 1990; 22(2): 76–89.
33. Henshaw SK, Binkin NJ, Blaine E, Smith JC. A portrait for American women who obtain abortions. Fam Plann Prospect 1985; 17(2): 90–96.
34. Henshaw SK, Forrest JD, Van Vort J. Abortion services in the United States, 1984 and 1985. Fam Plann Perspect 1987; 19(2): 63–69.
35. Henshaw SK, Silverman J. The characteristics and prior contraceptive use of United States abortion patients. Fam Plann Perspect 1988; 20(4): 158–68.

36. Henshaw SK, Wallisch. The medicaid cut-off and abortion services for the poor. Fam Plann Perspect 1984; 16(4): 170–80.
37. Hogue CJR, Cates W, Tietze C. The effects of induced abortion on subsequent reproduction. Epidemiol Rev 1982; 4: 66–94.
38. Holt R. Current challenges to U. S. abortion: the Webster case. Unpublished paper.
39. Holt VL, Daling JR, Voigt LF, McKnight B, Stergachis A, et al. Induced abortion and the risk of subsequent ectopic pregnancy. Am J Public Health 1989; 79: 1234–38.
40. Hum Resour Intergov Relat Subcomm. *The federal role in determining the medical and psychological impact of abortion on women*[report]. Exerpted in Fam Plann Perspect. 1989; 22(1): 36–39.
41. Isaacs SL. Population Law and Policy: Source Book and Related Materials. New York: Human Science, 1981.
42. Joint Program for the Study of Abortion/Cent. Dis. Control CDC abortion survey, 1974. Fam Plann Perspect 1976; 8(2): 70–72.
43. Kendrick W. The Secret Museum: Pornography in Modern Culture. New York: Viking Penguin, 1987.
44. Kiltsch M. RU 486: The Science and the Politics. New York: Alan Guttmacher Inst, 1989.
45. Kolata G. After large study of abortion pill, French maker considers wider sale. NY Times, 1990 Mar 8.
46. Koop CE. A measured response: Koop on abortion. Fam Plann Perspect 1989; 21(1): 31–32.
47. Kwast BE, Rochat RW, Kidane-Mariam W. Maternal mortality in Addis Ababa, Ethiopia. Stud Fam Plann 1986; 17: 288–301.
48. Laue L, Chrousos GP, Loriaux DL, Barnes K, Munson P, et al. The antiglucocorticoid and antiprogestin steroid RU 486 suppresses the adrenocorticotropin response to ovine corticotropin-releasing hormone in man. J Clin Endocrinol Metab 66: 290–3.
49. Lincoln R. The Institute of Medicine reports on legalized abortion and the public health. Fam Plann Perspect 1975; 7(4): 185–88.
50. Luker K. Abortion and the Politics of Motherhood. Berkeley: Univ of Calif Press, 1984.
51. Luukkainen T, Heikinheimo U, Haukkannaa M, Lahteenmaki P. Inhibition of folliculogenesis and ovulation by the antiprogesterone RU 486. Fertil Steril 1988; 49: 951–62.
52. Mohr J. *Abortion in America: The Origins and Evolution of National Policy*. New York: Oxford Univ Press, 1978.
53. Nieman LK, Choate TM, Chrousos GP, Healy DL, Morin, et al. The progesterone antagonist RU 486: a potential new contraceptive agent. N Engl J Med 1987; 316(4): 187–91.
54. Ono OA, Savage VY. A ten-year review of maternal mortality rates in the University College Hospital, Ibadan, Nigeria. Am J Obstet Gynecol 1974; 118: 317–322.
55. Osofsky JD, Osofsky HJ, eds. The Abortion Experience: Psychological and Medical Impact. New York: Harper & Row, 1973.
56. Osofsky JD, Osofsky HJ, Rajan RR. Psychological effects of abortion with emphasis upon immediate reactions and followup. In: Osofsky JD, Osofsky HJ, eds. The Abortion Experience: Psychological and Medical Impact. New York: Harper & Row, 1973: pp 188–205.
57. Padayachi T, Norman RJ, Moodley J, Heyns A. Mifepristone and induction of labor in second half of pregnancy. Lancet 1988; i: 647.
58. *Planned Parenthood of Central Missouri v Danforth*, 428 US 52 (US Supreme Court 1976).
59. Petchesky RP. Abortion and Women's Choice. Boston: Northeastern Univ Press, 1984.
60. Powell-Griner E, Trent K. Sociodemographic determinants of abortion in the United States. Demography 1987; 24(4): 553–61.
61. Roberts M. trans. Romanian population policy. Popul Devel Rev 1984; 10(3): 570–73.
62. Reproductive Freedom Project. First circuit finds Title X gag rules unconstitutional. Reprod Rights Update 1990; ACLU 2(7): 3.

63. Rodger MW, Baird DT. Induction of therapeutic abortion in early pregnancy with Mifepristone in combination with prostaglandin pessary. Lancet 1987; 2: 1415–18.
64. Rogers JL, Stoms GB, Phifer JL. Psychological impact of abortion: methodological and outcomes summary of empirical research between 1966 and 1988. Health Care Women Int 1989; 10: 347–76.
65. *Roe v. Wade*, 410 US 113 (US Supreme Court 1973).
66. Romieu G, Maudelonde T, Ulmann A, Pujol H, Grenier J, et al. The antiprogestin RU 486 in advanced breast cancer: preliminary clinical trial. Bull Cancer 1987; 74: 455–61.
67. Rosenfield A. Maternal mortality in developing countries: an ongoing but neglected "epidemic." J Am Med Assoc 1989; 262: 376–79.
68. Rosenfield A, Maine D. Maternal mortality – A neglected tragedy: Where's the M in MCH? Lancet 1985; 2: 83–85.
69. Ross AS, Sitarnon B. Abortion in context: historical trends and future changes. Fam Plann Perspect 1988; 20(6): 273–81, 301.
70. Rubin GL, Gold J, Cates W. Response of low-income women and abortion facilities to restriction of public funds for abortion: a study of a large metropolitan area. Am J Public Health 1979; 69: 948–50.
71. Silvestre L, Dubois C, Renault M, Rezvani Y, Baulieu, E, Ulman A. Voluntary interruption of pregnancy with Mifepristone (RU 486) and prostaglandin analogue: a large-scale French experience. N Engl J Med 1990; 322: 645–48.
72. Smith-Rosenberg. The abortion movement and the AMA, 1850–1880. In: Disorderly Conduct: Visions of Gender in Victorian America. New York: Oxford Univ Press 1985, pp. 217–44.
73. Stewart GK, Hance F. Legal abortion: influences upon mortality, morbidity and population. Adv Plann Parent 1974; 9: 1–7.
74. Tietze C. The effect of legalization of abortion on population growth and public health. Fam Plann Perspect 1975; 7(3): 123–27.
75. Tietze C. The public health effects of legal abortion in the United States. Fam Plann Perspect 1984; 16(1): 26–28.
76. Torres A, Forrest JD. Why do women have abortions? Fam Plann Perspect 1988; 20(4): 169–76.
77. The Cent Popul Options. Adolescent Abortion and Parental Involvement Laws: Encouraging Communication or Conflict? Washington, DC, 1989.
78. Trussell J, Menken J, Lindheim BL, Vaughan. The impact of restricting medicaid financing for abortion. Fam Plann Perspect 1980; 12(3): 120–30.
79. *Webster v. Reprod. Health Serv.* 109 (US Supreme Court 3040 1989).
80. Wigglesworth JS, Desai R. Is fetal respiratory function a major determinant of perinatal survival? Lancet 1982; 264–67.
81. *Williams v. Zbaraz*, 100 (US Supreme Court 2694, 1980).
82. Wright NH. Restricting legal abortion: some maternal and child health effect in Romania. Am J Obstet Gynecol 1975; 121: 246–56.

HELGA KUHSE AND PETER SINGER

Abortion and Contraception: The Moral Significance of Fertilization

It is widely believed that there is a world of difference between contraception and abortion. For many people contraception raises no serious moral issue. Abortion, on the other hand, is frequently compared to and even equated with the most serious wrong: the intentional killing of an innocent human being.

What distinguishes the morality of contraception so radically from abortion, it is often thought, is that contraception prevents fertilization and the coming-into-existence of an as yet unidentifiable human individual; abortion, on the other hand, terminates the life of an identifiable human individual whose existence began at fertilization.

The purpose of this paper is to question that conventional dichotomy. In the first part, we shall present some of the additional challenges posed by new reproductive technologies for traditional arguments that purport to show that fertilization is the point when moral status is achieved. We conclude that these traditional arguments fail. In the second part, we shall ask why killing is wrong and look at some of the reasons traditionally advanced for the wrongness of abortion. We conclude that the very same reasons that make abortion seriously wrong would also make contraception seriously wrong. If our argument is sound, "traditionalists" may continue to hold that abortion is seriously wrong; but in that case, they should also think that contraception is seriously wrong. Alternatively, they may continue to think that contraception raises no comparatively serious moral issue; in that case, they should also think that abortion, in itself, raises no serious moral issue. What traditionalists will no longer be able to hold is that the morality of contraception and abortion are quite distinct. Finally, in the third part, we shall defend criteria that make entities "morally considerable"[1] and killing them directly wrong. Fetuses do not, we shall argue, have a "right to life," although they may well be morally considerable in some other respects.

In short, then, we are here concerned with the central question regarding the permissibility or otherwise of abortion: whether the embryo or fetus is the kind of entity whose life it is seriously wrong to end; and with the link between the answer to this question and the morality of contraception.

F.K. Beller and R.F. Weir (eds.), The Beginning of Human Life, 145–161.

This will involve us in some intricate and esoteric arguments about eggs, sperm, and embryos. Some might criticize us for this; what we should be talking about, these critics might say, is not mere human cells, but rather about the rights of women. Women as a group still do not have access to safe and effective contraceptive agents, and many of them die as the result of unsafe abortions. To devote so much time and intellectual energy to the debate of whether eggs, sperm, or zygotes have rights, and whether there is a moral difference between destroying those cells and not bringing them into existence in the first place, may seem almost an obscenity when conducted in a world in which women cannot control their reproductive processes, and in which there are already too many people, and thousands of children are dying each day because their parents can't feed them. Surely, what's important is not whether there is an intrinsic moral difference between abortion and contraception, but rather what role both these techniques can play in curbing the population explosion.

These objections are well taken, but misplaced. In adopting what has been labelled the "fetalist"[2] perspective, we are not denying the importance of women's claims, nor would we want to detract from the enormous problems posed by current population trends. We do, however, also take the view that issues such as these cannot be resolved in a morally satisfactory way until and unless we have given a prior answer to what we have called the *central* question: whether the embryo or fetus is the kind of entity whose life it is very seriously morally wrong to end. For if it were the case, as is so frequently asserted, that the fetus, and even the human zygote, has the same "right to life" as is possessed by any normal adult person, then it would seem to follow that most abortions are seriously wrong; it would also seem to follow that the use of some very popular "contraceptive" devices, such as the IUD, would be seriously immoral.[3] This means that unless the question of the moral status of the fetus has been settled, we cannot even begin to talk about contraception and abortion as means of curbing the population explosion, or as means of empowering women. For if the fetus were, morally, just like us, there would be little difference between a population policy that allowed or encouraged abortion and a population policy that allowed or encouraged the killing of more mature members of a family or group.

This, then, is the fundamental reason why we find ourselves arguing about the status of the embryo or fetus. The view that fertilization marks the time when a human being with a strong moral claim to life comes into existence is still widely held and the source of important policy decisions.[4] By clearing up some of the conceptual and moral confusions that surround discussions of the central question of abortion and contraception, we feel we can contribute most not only to the theoretical debate, but ultimately also to the resolution of some undeniably very pressing practical problems.

"From the Moment of Fertilization"

We shall begin, not by examining the standard cases of contraception and abortion themselves, but rather by looking at the analogue of the two in the laboratory situation.

In 1978, Louise Brown was born. She was the first child conceived by in vitro fertilization. Some nine months earlier, Robert Edwards and Patrick Steptoe had succeeded in removing an egg from Mrs. Brown, fertilizing it with the sperm of her husband, and replacing the egg in the uterus where it continued to develop and led to the birth of a child, Louise. Since then, scientists have been able to examine the process of human fertilization and development in a way that, up to then, had been quite impossible. This has been important not only scientifically, but also ethically, for it has shown us how to think more clearly about the nature of fertilization and the moral difference it may, or may not, make to what we do.

For opponents of abortion, the natural and apparently irresistible impulse has been to carry their opposition to abortion over to opposition to the destruction of the in vitro embryo, from "the moment of fertilization onwards." This, in their eyes, is the deliberate killing of an innocent human being and seriously wrong. On the other hand, and consistent with typical approaches to contraception, they do not object to the destruction of the egg and sperm before fertilization has taken place. This leads to some strange results, as we have pointed out on an earlier occasion by considering three imaginary stories:[5]

First Story

> Doctors working on an IVF program have obtained a fertile egg from a patient and some semen from the patient's husband. They are just about to drop the semen into the glass dish containing the egg, when the doctor in charge of the patient calls to say that it has been found that she has a hopeless medical condition which makes pregnancy impossible. The egg could be fertilized and transferred to the womb, but implantation would not occur. The couple are asked whether they would agree to the creation of an embryo, which could then be frozen and donated to another couple. But they do not want their genetic material to become someone else's child. There is therefore no point in proceeding to fertilize the egg. So the egg and semen are tipped, separately, down the sink.

According to the traditional view nothing wrong has been done. Now consider a second story:

Second Story

> Everything happens exactly as in the first story, except that the doctor in charge of the patient calls with the bad news some time *after* the egg and sperm have been placed in the glass dish and fertilization has already taken place. The couple ask that the fertilized egg by disposed of as soon as possible.

If the newly fertilized egg has the moral status of a human being, its disposal would raise moral questions quite different from the ones raised in the first scenario. But how plausible is the belief that it was not wrong to dispose of the egg and sperm separately, but wrong to dispose of them just after they have united?

For those who believe that there is a real moral distinction between the two actions, here is a third story, not to be taken too seriously, but intended to bring out the peculiarities of that belief:

> *Third Story*
>
> This story begins just as the first one does. The doctor's call comes before the egg and sperm have united and so they are tipped, separately, down the sink. But as luck would have it, the sink is blocked by a surgical dressing. As a result, the egg and semen are not flushed away but remain in the sink. Later, a nurse notices the blockage and is about to clear it away when a thought occurs to her: perhaps fertilization has occurred!
>
> What ought she, morally, to do?

If fertilization had occurred, or if there is even a significant chance of that having happened, it would seem that those who hold that a human zygote has the same status as any other human being must hold that it would be wrong to clear the blockage, thereby contributing to the certain death of the zygote. Instead, it would seem, the egg would have to be rescued from the sink, checked to see if fertilization had occurred, and if it had, efforts should presumably be made to keep it alive.

This seems, in our view, a very awkward consequence, awkward enough to lead one to question very seriously the view that the "moment of fertilization" is morally significant in itself.

It is, however, not only on the intuitive level that the implications of our stories are odd. The laboratory situation also raises doubts about the reasons traditionally advanced for attributing moral status to the zygote or early embryo. In the following, we shall consider three such arguments which seek to attribute moral status on account of some of the embryo's actual characteristics. Other arguments rely on the notion of the embryo's potential or of its future existence. We shall consider the latter type of argument in the section entitled 'WHAT MAKES SOME KILLINGS WRONG?'. Here we shall deal solely with arguments which suggest that fertilization is the moral Rubicon when the newly fertilized egg acquires moral status – not because of what it has the potential to become or because of what the future may hold for it – but because of what it currently is.

The Genetic Argument

According to the "genetic argument," fertilization marks the time when moral status is acquired because it is then that entities that "are genetically human beings" are created.[6]

Before fertilization, the genetic identity of the possible future child is still relatively indeterminate. Any one of the hundreds of thousands of sperm in a single ejaculate may fertilize the egg. After fertilization, on the other hand, genetic identity remains relatively fixed.[7] This means, according to proponents of this argument, that the union of the two gametes to form the single zygote at fertilization is the only stage at which it can be held that a new human entity begins to exist. If a zygote is being destroyed, one could sensibly ask whether the embryo was male or female, if the child that might have grown from it would have had blue eyes or brown ones, if it possessed the genetic basis for musical ability like that of Beethoven, a talent for chess like that of Fisher, or possibly the megalomaniacal tendencies of Hitler. In the case of the egg surrounded by sperm – either in vitro or in vivo – such a question is less appropriate, for the answer can only be: it depends on which sperm will fertilize the egg.

But can the fact that the genetic identity of an embryo has already been determined provide a good reason for giving it a moral status different from that accorded to the egg and sperm before they are united? Taken together, the egg and sperm also have a determinate genetic identity (there are no genetically indeterminate human beings) and no matter which sperm fertilizes the egg, the resultant embryo will always have a determinate genetic identity. Can it really make a moral difference that before fertilization we ordinarily do not know which particular sperm will fertilize the egg?

A new mode of laboratory fertilization accentuates the difficulties for those who want to hold that determinate genetic identity arises at fertilization, thus conferring moral status on the embryo but not on the egg and sperm prior to fertilization. Some forms of male infertility are due to the inability of sperm to penetrate the outer layer of the egg, the *zona pellucida*. In attempts to overcome this type of male infertility, scientists have developed a technique which allows them to take an egg and hold it in a special pipette, and then to pick up a single sperm in a very fine syringe and, under the microscope, inject that sperm under the *zona pellucida* of the egg. If things go well, fertilization will take place, followed by subsequent normal development.

This technique of microinjection shows, it seems to us, why the genetic argument is not an appropriate basis for moral status. Consider the moment at which the scientist has the egg in the holding pipette and the sperm in the needle, but has yet to inject the sperm into the egg. At this point, the genetic identity of the future possible child is, other things being equal, as determinate as the genetic identity of the zygote: we could ask whether it would be male or female, have brown eyes or blue ones, and so on.

To further emphasize this point, we want to return to the first two of our previous stories and change them somewhat to fit the situation of microinjection.

First Story

In the first story, a scientist has an egg in the holding pipette, and the sperm in the syringe, when she learns that no embryo is wanted. She abandons the procedure and does not carry out the injection.

Second Story

In the second story, the scientist has just carried out the injection, when the bad news about the woman's incurable condition reaches her.

Can there really be a moral difference between disposal of the egg and sperm separately, and of the egg with the sperm already inside it?

Here we must note a complicating factor, which we have so far ignored. Fertilization is a complex process, not an event. It requires some 24 hours for completion. It begins with a sperm penetrating the zona pellucida of the egg, and culminates in a process called syngamy, when the female and male chromosomes are combined. This sharpens the question of what exactly the difference between the first and second scenario amounts to. It appears that the only difference between them is that in the first case the sperm is outside the zona, and in the second case it is under it. Would a supporter of the genetic argument want to insist that a moral Rubicon divides the first scenario from the second, or would she want to hold that a new genetic entity comes into existence not when the sperm has entered the egg, but only at syngamy, some 22–24 hours later? The first answer is decidedly odd. Why should it make a moral difference whether two as-yet-separate entities are inside or outside a particular boundary, such as the zona pellucida? We can think of no plausible reason for such a belief.[8] The second answer points to an additional problem to which we shall now turn.

The Numerical Identity Argument

The genetic argument seldom stands on its own. It is usually advanced in tandem with what we want to call the "numerical identity argument," the view that a numerically distinct new genetic entity comes into existence at fertilization and that this entity is, in some clear and obvious sense, the same entity as the developing fetus and future child. It is, from the first moment of its existence until death, the very same thing. Were we to ask "When did we, Helga or Peter, come into existence?" the answer would be, on this view: "At fertilization when the gametes of your parents united to form a zygote." That is why the destruction of the embryo is regarded by those who take this view as much more serious than the prevention of conception.

If supporters of the genetic argument were to agree that there is no moral difference between the first and the second scenario just outlined, but maintain that a moral Rubicon is being crossed at syngamy, when the male and female genetic components are truly merged, then they would be relying not so much on the genetic argument (because the genetic identity of any future child was already fixed in the two scenarios), but rather on the view that fertilization is a "transformation"[9] of two entities into one, after which there is a continuum of development towards maturity.[10] In other words, the zygote does not just have the potential to produce an individual, rather it is, from the first moment of its existence, already a particular individual – Tom, Dick, or Harry. But is this a plausible view?

Let us assume, with supporters of the numerical identity view, that a particular individual, call him Tom, comes into existence at fertilization. In other words, the zygote *is* Tom. Eight days after fertilization, spontaneous twinning occurs. "Tom" divides into two separate identical cell groups. Nine months later, identical twins are born. Is either of them Tom? There are no good reasons for thinking of one of the twins as Tom and the other as Not-Tom; the twinning process is quite symmetrical and both twins have the same genetic blueprint as the original Tom. But they can't both be Tom; that conflicts with numerical continuity: there was one zygote and now there are two babies.

Did Tom cease to exist when the original embryo split? Perhaps two new individuals, Dick and Harry, came into existence then? But this won't help the supporter of the numerical identity view, for then it would of course no longer be true that the existence of the babies Dick and Harry began at fertilization: their existence as distinct and numerically continuous individuals did not begin until eight days *after* fertilization. Moreover, if Tom died on the eighth day, how is it that he left no earthly remains?

New scientific findings make the situation even more complex. We now know that early embryonic cells are totipotent; that is, up to the eight-cell stage, the embryo is a loose collection of distinct cells, held together by the zona pellucida. Animal studies on four-cell embryos suggest that each of these cells has the potential to produce at least one fetus or baby. So the kind of spontaneous twinning that occurs sometimes in nature can *always* be artificially created in the laboratory, and any "Tom" will always have the potential to give rise, not merely to a Dick and Harry, but to an Adam and Brian as well.[11]

All this shows, we think, that fertilization cannot reasonably be regarded as the beginning of a particular human life. Those who see the coming-into-existence of a genetically determinate and numerically continuous human entity as the time when moral status is achieved would be on much safer ground were they to argue that moral status is not achieved at fertilization but rather at around day 14 after fertilization. By that time, totipotency has been lost and the development of the primitive streak precludes an embryo from becoming two or more different individuals through twinning. Once the primitive streak has been formed, it would be easier to argue that it is Tom, Dick, or Harry that is developing – or all three of them – as distinct and numerically continuous individuals.

If we are correct in this, it would mean that there is, on the view we have been discussing, no intrinsic moral difference between deliberately destroying a set of gametes, a fertilizing egg, a zygote, or a totipotent embryo. It would also mean that contraceptive methods that prevent fertilization and abortifacients that prevent implantation (which normally happens around day 14) would be on a par. If the use of contraceptive agents is permissible, so must be the use of abortifacients. On the other hand, if one wanted to argue that the use of abortifacients is impermissible, then one would also have to accept that it is impermissible to use contraceptive devices.

The Probability Argument

Not everyone agrees that probability is relevant for the moral evaluation of actions. Those who do might want to argue that even if the arguments we have so far advanced are conclusive in certain artificial reproduction contexts, they do not lead to the conclusion that there is no morally relevant distinction between contraception and abortion.

One such argument has been put by John Noonan. He asserts that the distinction between abortion and contraception marks a sharp difference in the probability of embryos and sperm developing into persons. Abortions are wrong because there is a high probability that the entities they destroy will become persons; certain contraceptive methods are not wrong because of the small probability of any one sperm participating in fertilization and becoming a person.[12]

Let us accept that probability is sometimes morally relevant. Noonan suggests that a single sperm would have a chance of only 1 in 200 million of becoming a moral agent; a fetus, on the other hand, would have an 80 percent chance of developing into a baby. While these figures would need to be revised in line with more recent scientific findings, they will suffice for the purposes of our present discussion.[13]

Noonan makes his point this way: Assume that someone – the "agent" – knows that there is an 80 percent chance of an innocent person lying behind some bushes, and that the agent nonetheless shoots into the bushes, thereby killing the person. Contrast this with another agent shooting into the bushes but knowing that there is a chance of only 1 in 200 million that an innocent person is hiding in the bushes. We would, Noonan thinks, regard the first person as morally blameworthy but not the second.

Noonan's argument faces several problems. One has recently been raised by Mark Strasser. Strasser points out that Noonan's focus on a single sperm participating in fertilization is wrong-headed. When a male contraceptive, such as a spermicide, is being used, its action is not analogous to that of someone shooting into bushes when there is only a 1 in 200 million chance of hitting a person. Rather, if a spermicide were to prevent an otherwise certain conception, its action would be like that of a bomb, blowing up a forest with an 80 percent probability of killing the person that is hiding behind one of 200 million trees.[14]

One might, of course, also ask why we should concentrate on the probability of a sperm participating in fertilization, rather than on the probability of the egg participating in it. If we were to do this, we would obviously get a very different result. Even if not every act of intercourse leads to conception, during the period when a woman is most fertile the probability of fertilization taking place after intercourse without contraception would not be so greatly different from the probability of a newly fertilized egg developing into a child, and would still be morally significant.[15] Hence, if abortions are impermissible because, as Noonan says, there is a significant likelihood that fetuses will develop into moral agents, then contraception must also be wrong for the very same reason.

Of course, what hasn't been shown as yet – by Noonan or by anyone else – is that abortions are wrong; but neither has it been shown that they are morally permissible.

What Makes Some Killings Wrong?

Societies like ours do not regard all killings as wrong, or wrong to the same degree. Most people believe it is seriously morally wrong to kill innocent people against their will. On the other hand, hardly anybody would think that it is of great moral moment when we harvest a cabbage or lettuce for our table, thereby killing it. When it comes to animals, such as cows, pigs, rats, or monkeys, feelings may become more ambivalent; nonetheless, most of those who dine on the flesh of animals, or who use them in research, would also think that the killing of animals is morally much less serious than the killing of people. This raises the issue of the moral basis for the wrongness of killings. What makes it wrong to kill some entities, but not wrong (or not wrong to the same degree) to kill others?

These questions are fundamental to the abortion debate. If we accept that it is most seriously wrong to kill innocent people, against their will, does it also follow that it is most seriously wrong to kill human embryos and fetuses?

Two Senses of "Being Human"

For some antiabortionists the answer is clear. They will start with the widely accepted premise that it is wrong to kill innocent human beings, then point out that the embryo or fetus is an innocent human being, and conclude that it is therefore seriously morally wrong to kill the fetus.

This syllogism is logically valid. But for the moral conclusion to follow, it is also necessary to establish the validity of its premises. While we may accept that the embryo is an innocent human being (at least once individuality has been established at around day 14 postfertilization), our earlier comments should have made it clear that there is a need to establish the validity of the first premise: why is it wrong to kill innocent human beings, but not wrong to kill other innocent nonhuman beings?

One thing is certain: we cannot simply assume that human beings are morally different from other beings simply because they are *human* beings, that is, that the term "human being" is taken to be a biological category which denotes membership in a particular species. It would mean that the number of chromosomes, a particular sequence of DNA, or whatever else one takes to be the biological criterion of humanhood, would have to be regarded as the morally significant criterion that delineates human beings from other beings. Here an obvious question presents itself: why should a biological category be morally relevant in itself? After all, why should it be any more reasonable to base a moral judgment on the number of chromosomes in a particular cell than, say, on race, sex, or the color of one's skin?[16]

This means that the first premise of the antiabortion argument – that it is seriously wrong to kill innocent human beings – cannot rest on the simple biological basis of what it is to be a human being. What is needed is a substantive argument which will point to nonarbitrary morally relevant features that are possessed by human beings and which make killing them seriously wrong.

Such common-sense reasons are not difficult to find when we think about those features that distinguish human beings from most, if not all, nonhuman beings. Human beings, one might say, are valuable beings (or deserve respect) because they have superior mental powers – they are conscious, have a sense of their personal identities, rationality, a moral sense, autonomy; they are able to experience emotions and have the ability to form strong and lasting relationships; they have plans, goals, and projects, and the like. In short, people have a stake in their own future, a personal life not possessed by (most) other beings.

It seems very plausible that the particular objection (that is, the objection one would have to killing human beings, over and above any objections one might have to killing other living things) rests on these special human attributes. This becomes obvious when we focus on two very different examples from the spectrum of living things. Consider a person who is engaged in numerous activities, projects, experiences, and the like, who is part of a network of friends, and who is looking forward to what the future may bring. Compare the life of such a person with the life of a cabbage or lettuce which, we can safely assume, has no feelings, experiences, desires, no inner life at all. It is easy to see that the difference in the kinds of mental life possessed by persons and by lettuces will make a moral difference in the seriousness of killing them.

For the moment, we do not want to sharpen this point. We merely want to note that it is plausible to base the claim about the moral seriousness of killing human beings on the fact that human beings typically possess mental qualities that other living entities do not possess (or do not possess to the same degree). We shall call human beings who possess this cluster of attributes "persons."

This, then, would seem to lend some support to the first premise of the antiabortion argument. After all, who could seriously doubt that it would be gravely wrong to kill innocent human beings, who have lives of the kind just described?

But the time has come to draw some distinctions. We may well accept that it is seriously wrong to kill persons who have distinctively "human" qualities, such as rationality, self-consciousness, and the like, without thereby accepting the conclusion that it is also seriously wrong to kill innocent human beings who do not (yet) possess these qualities. Thus, while human zygotes and embryos are undoubtedly human beings, they are lacking all the qualities which are generally taken to be the basis for the special moral status of persons. Zygotes and early embryos have no brain, no central nervous system, and, like a cabbage, no mental life at all. This means that even though embryos are human beings, we can draw no valid conclusions about how we ought to treat them.

Unlike members of the *Brassica* family, embryos do, however, have the potential to develop into mature human beings and will, if things go well, one day possess the mental qualities thought relevant for moral status.[17] Can the claim that abortion is seriously morally wrong be based on the embryo's potential?

Thwarting a Future

There are two ways in which we cannot argue about potential: firstly, by simply asserting that potential just *is* morally relevant, by arguing, that is, that since it is wrong to kill mature human beings or persons, it is also wrong to kill potential persons. This is to confuse potentiality with actuality. Secondly, it will not do simply to assert that potential has *no* moral relevance just because it is only potential. For if it is seriously morally wrong to kill persons because person are loci of moral value, then it may also be seriously morally wrong to kill potential loci of value.

The vexed question of potential cannot be resolved, it seems to us, without further filling in the answer we have sketched in the preceding section about the wrongness of killing. We had arrived at the intuitively plausible conclusion that killing persons is seriously morally wrong because persons are self-conscious beings with life plans, goals, and so on. To kill a person against her will, one might say, will thwart all her goals and unfulfilled desires: it will deprive her of her future.

If killing is wrong because if deprives a person of her future, it seems clear that abortion also deprives a person of her future, a person who would one day exist if the pregnancy were not terminated. This recognition has led the former Oxford philosopher R. M. Hare to write that as far as the fetus is concerned, the central issue in the abortion debate is this one: "that . . . if not terminated, the pregnancy is highly likely to result in the birth and growth to maturity of a person just like the rest of us."[18]

To support this contention, Hare appeals to a type of formal argument, captured in the ancient Christian and pre-Christian Golden Rule, that has been the basis of almost all theories of moral reasoning: that we should do to others as we wish them to do to us. In other words, given that we are glad that nobody destroyed us when we were embryos, we should, other things being equal, not destroy an embryo or fetus that would have a life like ours.[19]

It might seem that the Golden Rule applied to the question of abortion would impose on us an extremely conservative position, for it would seem to make most abortions seriously morally wrong. But before we too readily embrace that conclusion, we should also note another of Hare's points: when we are glad to exist, we do not confine this gladness to the fact that we were not aborted when an embryo or fetus. Rather, we are also glad that we were brought into existence in the first place – that our parents had intercourse when they did, without contraception.[20] In other words, if it is wrong to have an abortion, it is also wrong and, other things being equal, wrong to the same degree, to prevent the existence of a future person, be this through the use of a contraceptive or through sexual abstinence.

On a view like Hare's, then, the wrongness of abortion lies not in what it does to the embryo or fetus, but rather in what it does to a potential or possible person – a person who will not exist either because we have chosen to abort her or because we have chosen not to conceive her in the first place.

Many of those opposed to abortion will want to reject this conclusion. On the one hand, it equates the seriously immoral, in their view, act of abortion with the less-serious issue of contraception, thereby trivializing it; and, on the other, it seems to rest on an absurdity. While there is an identifiable victim in the case of an abortion, there is no identifiable victim in the case of contraception.

Don Marquis has recently undertaken a valiant attempt to rescue the traditional position on abortion and contraception: that abortions are, except possibly in rare cases, seriously immoral, but that this does not entail that contraception is also seriously immoral.[21] We shall examine these claims in turn.

Marquis argues that killing a fetus is wrong for the same reason that it is wrong to kill a person:

> The loss of one's life is one of the greatest losses one can suffer. The loss of one's life deprives one of all the experiences, activities, projects, and enjoyments that would otherwise have constituted one's future. Therefore, killing someone is wrong primarily because the killing inflicts [one of] the greatest possible losses on the victim. To describe this as the loss of life can be misleading, however. The change in my biological state does not itself make killing me wrong. The effect of the loss of my biological life is the loss to me of all those activities, projects, experiences, and enjoyments which would otherwise have constituted my future personal life.[22]

Because most fetuses have futures like those we have – with sets of experiences, projects, activities and the like – Marquis draws the conclusion that abortion is prima facie morally wrong. His analysis does not, he asserts, rely on the notion of potential and on the invalid inference that if it is wrong to kill persons it must also be wrong to kill potential persons. Rather, abortion is prima facie seriously immoral because fetuses already are the kinds of beings who have futures like ours.

One may readily accept that fetuses will, other things being equal, *come to have* futures like ours. But do they already now, qua fetuses, have or "possess" a future-like-ours? There seems to be a very clear sense in which we can distinguish between persons and fetuses "having" a future. Persons are self-conscious beings who already have a personal or autobiographical past which is linked, through overlapping chains of memory, continuity of character, and intentions to their own autobiographical future. Zygotes, embryos, and early fetuses, on the other hand, have no memory, no knowledge of their own present existence, no intentions, plans, or goals for their future. They are not autobiographical beings and thus cannot be said to be beings with a future-like-ours.[23]

But if this is correct, then it is not possible to deprive an embryo or fetus of its future in the way in which it is possible to deprive a person of her future. This means that Marquis's argument for the wrongness of abortion fails. If it is wrong to kill those of us who are persons because it deprives us of our future, it does not follow that it is also wrong to kill entities which do not have a future-like-ours.

There is, of course, a different and more plausible sense in which embryos and fetuses can be said to have a future. If an abortion is not performed, and things go well, a fetus will develop into a person and *will come to have* a future in an autobiographical sense. On this understanding, abortion would be wrong because it "cuts off" this future. It would be wrong not because of what it does to the fetus qua fetus, but wrong because it deprives a potential person of a valuable future.

This understanding of the wrong-making feature of abortions is substantially close to Hare's analysis. This presents a serious problem for Marquis and the traditional position. For if abortion is prima facie seriously morally wrong because it deprives a potential person of a valuable future, could it not also be said that contraception is seriously morally wrong because it, too, deprives a potential person of a valuable future?

Marquis accepts that "contraception prevents the actualization of a possible future of value" and that, were one to accept the claim that such futures should be maximized, it would seem to follow that contraception is prima facie immoral. Nonetheless, he claims, the obligation to maximize does not exist. It would exist only if "something were denied a human future of value by contraception. . . . [However], nothing at all is denied such a future by contraception."[24]

There is a sense, Marquis admits, in which one might think that contraception deprives the combination of egg and sperm of a valuable future like ours. But here, he thinks, "the definite article misleads":

> At the time of contraception, there are hundreds of millions of sperm, one (released) ovum and millions of possible combinations of all of these. There is no actual combination at all. Is the subject of the loss to be a merely possible combination? Which one? This alternative does not yield an actual subject of harm either. Accordingly, the immorality of contraception is not entailed by the loss of a future-like-ours argument simply because there is no nonarbitrarily identifiable subject of the loss in the case of contraception.[25]

There are many problems with this argument. First, we wonder what Marquis would say about the egg and sperm when singled out for microinjection, using the technique we described earlier. Then there is only one ovum, and one sperm, so there is no problem about choosing among possible combinations of egg and sperm. These *is* a nonarbitrarily identifiable subject of the loss – the person who would have developed from that egg and sperm. So it seems that Marquis would have to regard a decision to discontinue such a procedure as equivalent to an abortion, at least in so far as his loss of a future-like-ours argument is concerned.

Next, why should it matter so much whether the subject of the loss is *identifiable* at the time the loss is inflicted? If the loss of a life like ours is a bad thing, the fact that there is no identifiable victim at the time seems irrelevant. Suppose I leave toxic waste in a steel drum near a river. About a century from now, the drum will rust through, the waste will run into the river, and those living downstream will become ill. Can I in any way mitigate the wrongness of my action by saying that the people wronged are not now identifiable? Of course not; they will be identifiable when the drum rusts. Similarly, if my partner and I decide to stop using contraceptives in order to conceive a child, that child is not now identifiable; but the child will be identifiable when she or he comes to be living a future-like-ours. Being presently identifiable does not seem to be a necessary condition either for being harmed, or for being benefited, by an action.

If the fetus were *already* a being who could be aware of its own existence, and could be enjoying the experiences, projects, and activities of which Marquis writes, that would make a relevant difference. Then we might indeed feel that the fetus was a morally significant subject, and that to end its existence would be to wrong it in a personal way, a way that frustrates its wants and plans. But we know that that is not the case. The fetus has no awareness of its existence, and has no future plans or projects. It is an impersonal being, and in depriving it of its future, we are not inflicting a personal wrong on it. So all that we can possibly be doing is causing impersonal harm; and this, as we have seen, we can do by preventing a presently unidentifiable future being from coming into existence, just as surely as we can do it by preventing a presently identifiable future being from coming into existence.[26]

Thus we cannot agree that abortion is worse than contraception because it alone thwarts a future. Both abortion and contraception prevent the existence of a future being. So, for that matter, does celibacy. That alone is not enough to show that any of those actions is wrong. Especially in an overpopulated world such as the one in which we are now living, it is simply not desirable for us to set ourselves a goal of actualizing as many possible future beings as we can.

Killing Persons and Other Beings

What, then, does make some killings wrong? Here we return to some points that we began to develop earlier in this paper. We have argued elsewhere that sentience – the capacity to feel pleasure or pain, to suffer or to enjoy life – is the minimum needed to make a being morally considerable. If a being is not – and never will be – sentient, we cannot harm it, as a subject. We can imagine what it is like to be a cat, and so we can imagine that to leave a cat without food is to make it feel hungry, and to suffer. Before the brain of a fetus is sufficiently developed for there to be a "what it is like to be a fetus," however, there is nothing we can do to the fetus that is going to make it suffer. We can harm the being that the fetus will develop into, but we cannot make life go worse for the fetus, from the fetus's own point of view. From evidence assembled by researchers at the Centre for Human Bioethics at Monash University, it appears that it is only quite late in its development – possibly in the third trimester of pregnancy – that the brain of the fetus is sufficiently developed for the fetus to be sentient.[27]

Even sentience, however, is not enough to provide a basis for saying that killing is necessarily wrong, or that the entity has a right to life. If normal mature human beings have a greater right to life than cats or pigs, that right must be grounded in their distinctive capacities. In particular, it would seem plausible to draw a distinction between beings who are capable of understanding that they exist over time, with a past and a future, and beings who are incapable of this understanding, and exist only in a kind of eternal present, on a moment-by-moment basis. We call the former kind of being a person, using the term in a sense used by philosophers for many centuries. To kill a person capable of having wishes and desires, plans and projects, for the future, is to wrong the person by cutting off these wishes and desires, plans and projects, leaving them unfulfilled and perhaps rendering meaningless much that has gone before. A being not even conscious that it has a future cannot suffer this kind of loss. That is why, if one is going to use the language of rights at all, it would be reasonable to say that a person, as we have defined the term, has a serious right to life not possessed by those who are not persons.[28]

What does this mean for the morality of abortions, as compared with the morality of contraception? It means that, at least for early abortions, where there is no likelihood of the fetus's being sentient, there is no intrinsic moral difference between contraception and abortion. This does not mean that there is no moral difference at all between the two of them. There may well be an extrinsic moral difference – that is, a difference in the external circumstances of abortion and contraception, rather than in their central feature. For example, there seems to be, in the case of abortion and contraception, an important difference in the way they are perceived by the women involved, and by attending health professionals; it seems clear that the psychological aspects of abortion, and even to some degree the physical aspects of the procedure, will generally mean that it should not be regarded as an alternative to contraception, but rather as a means of last resort. Nevertheless, putting such external factors aside, we repeat, in our view there is no intrinsic moral difference between preventing the development of a morally significant being by contraception, and preventing the development of such a being by aborting a pre-sentient embryo or fetus. Once the fetus is capable of feeling pain, it is a morally considerable being. This does not mean that late abortions are always wrong, because, as we have just indicated, to be morally considerable is one thing; having a right to life is a different thing altogether. It does mean, however, that to perform a late abortion which may cause distress to the fetus requires a stronger justifying reason than contraception.

RU 486 (in conjunction with prostaglandins) is, we understand, an effective abortive agent, up to day 49 of a pregnancy. At that stage, it seems clear that the brain of the fetus is insufficiently developed for the fetus to be sentient. Therefore the use of RU 486 to terminate a pregnancy is, in the central moral issue it raises, not different from the use of a contraceptive to prevent a pregnancy.

As we said at the beginning of this paper, our aim has been to compare the morality of contraception and abortion, rather than to justify or criticize them both. This we have now done. We have shown, we believe, that the attempt to draw a sharp moral distinction between contraception and abortion is unsuccessful, unless the abortion is a late one. Morally speaking, contraception and early abortion stand or fall together. With that conclusion, our paper is complete. Since we see no virtue in keeping our own views secret, however, we shall close by remarking that, in our opinion, contraception and early abortion stand, rather than fall, together. Perhaps in a different world, one with few human beings or other sentient creatures, we might consider that it is morally desirable to bring more people into existence so that they could enjoy the good things of life. We might then hold that, at least when other things are equal, both contraception and abortion are to be avoided. That, however, is very far from our situation today. The population crisis is at the root of many of the world's most serious environmental and political problems, and is one major reason why poverty is so difficult to eradicate. In these circumstances both contraception and early abortion are essential for our survival, and should be available to every woman. Restrictions on their use are an unjustifiable infringement on the reproductive freedom of women, a threat to the survival of the ecology of our planet, and an obstacle to our hopes of providing a better future for all human beings.

NOTES

1. The term "morally considerable" is borrowed from Kenneth E Goodpaster, On being morally considerable. J Philosophy 1978 (Jun): 308–325.
2. Janice G Raymond, Fetalists and Feminists: they are not the same. In: PP Spallone and DL Steinberg, eds. Made to Order. Pergamon Press, 1987: 58–66.
3. An IUD prevents not fertilization but implantation. This makes it an abortifacient.
4. Both in the area of antiabortion laws, and in laws relating to embryo experimentation on in-vitro embryos. On the latter see: A summary of legislation relating to IVF. In: P Singer, H Kuhse *et al.*, eds. Embryo Experimentation. Cambridge University Press, 1990: 227–236.
5. In slightly different form, these stories first appeared in Helga Kuhse and Peter Singer; The moral status of the embryo. In: W Walters & P Singer, eds. Test-Tube Babies. Oxford University Press, 1982: 57–64.
6. See, for example, Werner R, Abortion: the moral status of the unborn. Social Theory and Practice 1974; 3: 201–222. For a fuller discussion of the "genetic argument" see Karen Dawson, Fertilization and moral status: a scientific perspective. In: Embryo Experimentation. Cambridge University Press, 1990: 43–52.
7. Genetic changes can and do occur after fertilization. See Dawson, pp. 46–47.
8. See Stephen Buckle and Karen Dawson, Individuals and Syngamy. Bioethics News 1988 (Apr); 7: 15–30.
9. See, e.g., Hellegers AE. Fetal development. Theological Studies 1970; 31: 3–9; Curran GE. Abortion: Contemporary debate in philosophical and religious ethics. In: Reich WT Encyclopedia of Bioethis. Free Press, I: 17–26.
10. See, e.g., Santamaria J, *In vitro* fertilization and embryo transfer. In: Brumby, MN ed. Proceedings of the Conference – In Vitro Fertilization: Problems and Possibilities. Centre for Human Bioethics, 1982: 48–63.
11. See also Michael Coughlan, 'From the moment of conception . . .': The Vatican instruction on artificial procreation techniques. Bioethics 1988 (July); 2. For a more detailed discussion, see Norman Ford, When Did I Begin? Cambridge University Press, 1988.
12. John T Noonan, Jr. An almost absolute value in history. The Morality of Abortion: Legal and Historical Perspectives. Harvard University Press, 1970: 56–57.
13. Noonan, pp. 56–57. For more recent figures see Peter Singer and Karen Dawson, IVF technology and the argument from potential." In Embryo Experimentation, pp. 85–86.
14. Mark Strasser, Noonan on contraception and abortion. Bioethics 1987 (Apr); 1: 199–205.
15. See Singer and Dawson, p. 86.
16. See Peter Singer, Practical Ethics. Second edition, Cambridge University Press, 1993, chapter 3.
17. On the vexed notion of potential see Singer and Dawson, and Stephen Buckle, Arguing from potential. Both in Embryo Experimentation.
18. Hare RM, Abortion and the Golden Rule. Philosophy and Public Affairs 1975; 4: 207.
19. *Ibid*, p. 208.
20. *Ibid*, p. 211.
21. Don Marquis, Why abortion is immoral. Journal of Philosophy 1989 (Apr): 183–202.
22. *Ibid*, p. 189.
23. See also McInerney Peter K, Does a fetus already have a future-like-ours? Journal of Philosophy 1990: 264–268.
24. Marquis, p. 201.
25. *Ibid*, pp. 201–202.
26. See also Alastair Norcross, Killing, abortion, and contraception – A reply to Marquis. Journal of Philosophy 1990: 268–277.
27. Susan Taiwa, When is the capacity for sentience acquired during human fetal development? The Journal of Maternal-Fetal Medicine 1: 153–162, 1992.
28. See Helga Kuhse and Peter Singer, Should the Baby Live. Oxford University Press, 1985, chapter 6.

REBECCA J. COOK

Contraception and Abortion: Legal Distinctions and Dynamics

The practice of medical contraception and that of medically conducted abortion are essentially products of the twentieth century. Historical instances exist of physicians being concerned with the prevention or termination of life-endangering pregnancies, but these tended to be seen as part of desperate efforts to preserve existing lives, and were legally explicable and defensible under the legal doctrine of necessity to save human life. Recourse to contraception and abortion with medical assistance as an element of reproductive choice, designed to enhance the experience of life of women, their dependent children, and, for instance, their dependent parents, is a development of at most recent decades, and in many countries still not a legal possibility. In Canada, for instance, before 1969 the Criminal Code addressed both procuring miscarriage and spreading information about contraceptive methods under the classification of Crimes Against Morality.

The last two decades have coincided with rapid developments in knowledge of embryology, of reproductive physiology and endocrinology, and also of techniques of overcoming infertility and assisting reproduction by artificial reproductive means. Most legal systems have maintained a traditional lag-time in adjusting to these scientific developments, and are not necessarily to be condemned for that, since legal endeavors to predict and regulate anticipated developments have proven as likely to be misguided as to be protective of specified interests.[1] The law, formulated and interpreted by judges, often functions well in responding pragmatically to established experiences, although legislatures may prove slow and uncertain in learning from experience and acting in timely and perceptive ways. Indeed, the modern history of legislative responses to evolving perceptions of women's reproductive health needs is not encouraging.

An increasingly sensitizing factor in the advancement of modern legal systems is awareness of the role of women as possessors of rights and actors in communal advancement not confined to the home and family. The so-called "feminization" of law is evolutionary rather than revolutionary, and is therefore occurring unevenly among countries. Where courts are being opened to the experiences of women as, for instance, wage earners and competitors

F.K. Beller and R.F. Weir (eds.), The Beginning of Human Life, 163–178.

for opportunities in economic, educational, industrial, and business life, they are perceiving that bearing children can be a differential factor between men and women that constitutes unlawful discrimination when not appropriately accommodated in economic and related practices.

The law institutionally is coming to play an increasingly significant role in influencing attitudes and values in relations between the sexes, through national constitutional and human rights provisions and through international human rights instruments that are receiving growing support in international assessments. At least 118 national constitutions now have provisions calling for women's equality. At least 100 of these constitutional provisions have been enacted in the last two decades.[2] The international legal instrument most sensitive to the promotion of women's reproductive health is the Convention on the Elimination of All Forms of Discrimination Against Women (Women's Convention) adopted by the General Assembly of the United Nations in 1979. This convention is now ratified by over 104 countries.

If the past two decades are characterized as the decades during which a constitutional foundation for equality between women and men was established, the next two decades might well be those during which constitutional remedies might be used to correct discriminatory wrongs, particularly in the area of reproductive health. The role of national and international law is more important because of the twin effects of rising religious fundamentalism that oppresses women in some parts of the world and the decline in influence of the Roman Catholic church, whose moral authority is compromised by its systematic devaluation of women's status, lives, and experiences.[3]

Legal Distinctions: Contraception and Abortion

Discussions of the legality of abortion are frequently so animated, volatile, and divisive that it may be overlooked that little more than half a century ago the moral issue in many societies was the threat to the promotion of family life posed by contraceptive means. Contraceptive information was the knowledge of the whore, that of which respectable women knew nothing and men kept their wives innocent. This period of promotion of family values was also a time of devastation of families through high rates of maternal mortality and morbidity. Today, even when the wisdom of family planning is questioned, it is rarely doubted that individuals enjoy, or should enjoy, the legal power to choose recourse to safe and effective contraceptive methods. Laws, largely in the form of legislation rather than judicially made or interpreted provisions, accommodate the lawful practice of contraception.

In contrast, almost every country has restrictive legislation on abortion. In the last two decades, these laws have been progressively liberalized in at least 65 countries around the world by making exceptions to prohibitions of abortions.[4] Some expressly accommodate abortion on request throughout gestation, many permit wide areas of choice in the earlier months of pregnancy, and almost all permit abortion when medically indicated to preserve a woman's life or enduring health. Without further elaborating the grounds on which the laws of different jurisdictions accommodate medical termination of pregnancy, the contrast may be drawn that most laws regulate contraception by health and welfare criteria of safety and efficacy, whereas they approach abortion initially as being criminally unlawful, but permissible under exceptions of different degrees of liberality.

Accordingly, the contrast between contraception and abortion appears to be of significance, not only for purposes of legal regulation but primarily for purposes of medical provision of conscientious and lawful care of patients. Drawing the contrast is confounded, however, by both medical progress and the contrasting lexicons of lawyers and legislators, on the one hand, and doctors, scientists, and related health professionals on the other. The different meanings given to language are frequently concealed when legal and medical people employ the same words and fallaciously presume that they mean the same in other disciplines. Differences may be aggravated in sophisticated regulatory systems when legislation permits refined regulations to be made under its authority by administrative agencies whose personnel are guided by, and in part composed of, medical scientists accustomed to the language not of the law but of their own discipline.

Medical regulations may be written in words designed to bear the definitions of medicine, under the aegis of laws that use the same words for purposes of law. For instance, provincial regulation of abortions permitted by the federal Criminal Code of Canada, when the code had no gestational limits, frequently referred to abortion as termination of pregnancy before twenty weeks of gestation, later terminations being classified as induced stillbirths. Accordingly, there was confusing and disruptive dissonance between lawyers' and doctors' understanding of the rate and implications of abortions.[5]

The Uncertainty of the Legal Scope of Abortion

The historic law identified pregnancy by the crude measure of "quickening." This had the merit of being based on the woman's experience, although knowledge of quickening could be imputed to a woman by the observation of her pregnancy by others, or for purposes of criminal law could be determined by a Jury of Matrons.[6] Inadequacies of the statutory language "procuring a miscarriage" include the fact that it left unclear whether abortion was of a woman, a fetus, or a pregnancy. For instance, a woman who suffered interference of a multiple pregnancy might miscarry one fetus, which would be stillborn, but not another. Having been induced to miscarry, she would remain pregnant. One fetus had been aborted, but not another. The need for medical clarification would not arise in those many legal systems in which abortion was defined by reference only to the intent with which a person acted, and not by reference to the result. It remains uncertain, therefore, whether deliberate reduction of a multiple pregnancy, perhaps following hormonal treatment of infertility, is legally classified as abortion; if it is, however, it would not be punishable if it were classified as therapeutic abortion performed to save life or health.

Medical practice tends to describe as abortion the induced termination of a proven or reliably evidenced pregnancy, and as contraception the use of means, whether pre- or postcoitally, for preventing pregnancy. In contrast, many laws treat abortion as actions taken "with intent to procure the miscarriage of any woman whether she be or be not with child."[7] Doctors may prescribe and undertake as contraception what in law may questionably be abortion, and equally may fear liability for abortion when dealing, for instance, with threatened spontaneous (or unlawfully initiated) miscarriage when in law they would be innocent of the intention of the crime of abortion.

Some laws, particularly those in the English-speaking world that were influenced historically by the Indian Penal Code of 1860, make it a precondition of liability for abortion that the woman claimed to have been aborted was actually pregnant. Because the burden of criminal proof falls on the prosecuting authority and has to be satisfied beyond reasonable doubt, enforcement of the law is very difficult when procedures are undertaken early in pregnancy. For instance, when a procedure is undertaken shortly after a missed menstrual period, doubt about whether pregnancy exists would be reasonable. Further, even when a pregnancy test is done and proves positive, doubt about whether it was a false positive, and about whether it indicated only a chemical pregnancy, might also be reasonable. Accordingly, the particular requirements of the law might warrant study for their accommodation of medical procedures undertaken either to prevent or terminate any pregnancy that could arise. That is, such procedures would be punishable under the English-derived law but not under the Indian Penal Code.

The developments that most affect the legal distinction between contraception and abortion are those of means that operate after fertilization of an ovum for the purpose of preventing completion of the process of implantation of the resulting preembryo in the woman's uterine lining. These means are not strictly contraceptive, in that they do not prevent conception, and they are not abortifacient in the medical sense of inducing miscarriage, because they prevent carriage from commencing. They raise fundamental concerns in religious circles that inquire when the soul enters the conceptus, because wastage of a product of human conception that no soul has entered is less grave than deliberate wastage of an ensouled embryo.

The religious distinction between contraception and abortion, and the sad eternal consequences for the soul of an unbaptized being that is lost through abortion, underlie the criminal abortion laws of many countries. The development of medical means that obscure this distinction by preventing implantation and gestation of products of conception that may or may not have achieved ensoulment may explain religious objections to all such means, but requires that laws be comprehended or designed that turn on the resolution of pressing temporal questions concerning women's health care. Religious approaches reflect spiritual concerns that may be worthy in themselves, but they must remain secondary to secular realities in societies where women face disadvantage and discrimination aggravated by their inability to control unwanted pregnancy.

Contragestion

Recently developed techniques of preventing pregnancy that may operate after fertilization are sometimes described as being contragestive in that they oppose not necessarily conception, but gestation of any ovum that may be fertilized. Contragestion introduces a new concept into discussion of human reproduction that some may consider unwelcome or false. In contrast, the value of this term to others is that it is an accurate description of the mode of action of certain fertility control measures devoid of the emotions that are associated with abortion.

It may be anticipated that as women become assertive of their health concerns, they will describe medical procedures less in terms of embryology or the spiritual preoccupations of religions and more in terms of how they view their reproductive health interests. For example, instead of using the term "abortion" the term "methods for treatment of contraceptive failure" might be more productive regarding women's reproductive health. Such usage accepts the scientifically proven fact that contraceptives fail and that methods are available to treat failure. They might or might not have an abortifacient effect.

Legal Dynamics

Historical

The motivation of early laws that condemned both contraception and abortion is demonstrated in the pre-1969 language of the Criminal Code of Canada, which considered both to be Crimes Against Morality. Morality was conceived in law almost exclusively in terms of sexual license, and means that would permit individuals to engage in illicit sex, meaning sex outside lawful marriage, and to escape the consequences of pregnancy, childbirth, and child maintenance, were regarded as endangering the moral order. This attitude is reflected in the censorious language a celebrated English judge used in 1954 regarding vasectomy. He observed:

> Take a case where a sterilisation operation is done so as to enable a man to have the pleasure of sexual intercourse without shouldering the responsibilities attaching to it. The operation then is plainly injurious to the public interest. It is degrading to the man himself. It is injurious to his wife and to any woman whom he may marry, to say nothing of the way it opens to licentiousness.[8]

The moral danger to society and to the integrity of family life was perceived to arise more through the unrestrained sexual activity of women than of men, because the men who dominated values and decisions in public life were aware that their own infidelities and those of their sons were mere titillation, but that the unfaithfulness of their wives and the sexual indulgence of their daughters jeopardized the family's good name; this behavior was to be repressed for the sake of preservation of everything that made society decent and stable and that founded the basis of family life.

Accordingly, it was considered essential to prohibit legally or to regulate strictly any means of contraception and abortion that would allow women to conceal infidelity and sexual license. The first relaxation of the prohibition against the supply of knowledge and means of contraception came about through recognition of the burden on family life of excessive childbearing. The early pioneers of family planning won their first legal victories by persuading courts that contraceptive counseling and assistance were lawful for married partners. When contraceptive practice was first legislated in affirmative terms as a health service, it was limited to married people.[9]

Similarly, an early English report recommending the legalization of therapeutic abortion was primarily motivated by evidence of harmful effects on families having resorted to unlawful abortion. The Birkett Committee observed in 1939 that

> in cases of poverty or unemployment, the task of maintaining another child may be felt to be intolerable. When the family is wholly or largely dependent upon the earnings of the pregnant woman, there may be an added incentive to criminal abortion. Among parents of moderate or comfortable means, fear that a lowering of the family's standards may result from the advent of another child may be responsible for the desire for abortion . . . Purely selfish motives predominate in only a small proportion of cases.[10]

Motivations of family protection remain applicable to family planning. The Birkett Committee addressed recourse to abortion in the absence of alternative recourse to family planning, which was obstructed by the law, among other forces. Today, wise policy would encourage facilitated access to contraceptive means in order to reduce the incidence of unwanted pregnancy and abortion. A longstanding religiously conditioned cultural assumption that the birth of a baby is always a blessing continues to be invoked by conservative and doctrinaire commentators, but the Michigan Court of Appeal was appropriately pragmatic in a case in 1971 concerning negligent delivery of a contraceptive service, when it observed that

> contraceptives are used to prevent the birth of healthy children. To say that for reasons of public policy contraceptive failure can result in no damage as a matter of law ignores the fact that tens of millions of persons use contraceptives daily to avoid the very result which the defendant would

have us say is always a benefit, never a detriment. Those tens of millions of persons, by their conduct, express the sense of the community.[11]

Modern Dynamics: Contraception

Availability of Contraception

Epidemiological data from individual regions and countries may offer evidence that contraceptive services are inadequately available and that rates of induced abortion are unnecessarily high. The history of repressive abortion legislation has not been adequately observed in a context of denial of access to alternative means of reproductive self-determination. Repressive abortion laws have developed a culture in which true rates of induced abortion are concealed and disguised. The determination of true rates remains in many countries the subject of interpretations and interpolations from other data, so that an understanding of the results of epidemiological inquiry often depends on an interpretation of an interpretation. Nevertheless, epidemiological data can be used to provide assessments of reproductive practice that reflect on health service delivery and that can be a credible foundation for improved programs that can be delivered within a framework of law.

Comparisons among cities, regions, and nations may provide a sense of whether a specific rate of abortion is excessive, taking account of such factors as the age-structure of the population and usual ages of marriage. Where abortion rates recorded in health facilities are increasing or appear uncomfortably high, the conclusion may be entertained that contraceptive health services are inadequate. Similarly, where the known incidence of septic abortion is high, an association with unskilled interference with pregnancy may be inferred, with the same conclusion regarding access to contraception. Historically, criminal abortion statistics consisted less in prosecutions for abortion than in statistics of prosecutions for abortion-related manslaughter. It remains tragically true today in many regions of the world that maternal mortality rates indicate failures of contraceptive health care planning and delivery.

Epidemiology may provide more subtle evidence of the need for contraceptive services and their delivery within a sympathetic setting. High rates of adolescent pregnancy and abortion may suggest that women about to enter their reproductive years are inadequately aware of or familiar with contraceptive services and counseling. Similarly, high rates of second-trimester abortion may indicate not only barriers to abortion services, but also late identification of pregnancy associated with poor contraceptive and sex education.

Henshaw says that in 1987 legal abortion rates "ranged from a high of at least 112 per 1,000 women of reproductive age in the Soviet Union to a low of 5 per 1,000 in the Netherlands."[12] He states that the U.S. rate is 28 per 1,000 women, and in recent years abortion rates have been increasing in

Czechoslovakia, England and Wales, and Sweden, and declining in France, Iceland, Italy, and the Netherlands. The Dutch situation, with a liberal abortion law, public accommodation of sex education, and accessible contraceptive information and services resulting in low and declining abortion rates, presents an impressive model that bears examination and duplication. The Dutch law enables postcoital treatment in the event of contraceptive failure and characterizes interceptive methods used before the preembryo has implanted in the uterus as contraception and not abortion. This characterization encourages women to come for treatment as soon as possible in the event of contraceptive failure, unprotected intercourse, or a missed period. The Dutch model, as a matter of law and policy, thus facilitates and encourages contraceptive, interceptive, contragestive, and early abortion services, and so reduces the need for more costly and far less desirable treatment later in pregnancy.

Contraceptive failure

Acceptance of the legality of contraceptive practice should accommodate the scientific reality of an irreducible minimum failure rate of conscientious contraception. It has been estimated that rates of contraceptive failure range from 6 percent of women using oral contraception experiencing failure during the first twelve months of use, to up to 16 percent for the condom, diaphragm, and rhythm methods, and 26 percent for spermicides.[13] A common response to the failure of contraceptive practice is resort to abortion, but historically this has been barred by law even when contraception was lawful, leaving women the losers in a reproductive lottery. Even today no jurisdiction expressly permits abortion on the legal indication of failure of conscientious contraception.[14]

The Legal Limits of Contraception

Increasing attention is being given within the concept of contraception to postcoital and other methods that prevent completion of the process of uterine implantation of a preembryo. The legality is recognized of the use of what are sometimes euphemistically described as "morning-after" methods, reflecting a cultural belief that human reproduction is a nocturnal activity undertaken by couples who "sleep together." Such means as pills and intrauterine devices may be undertaken as lawful contraception within a period of 72 hours from unprotected intercourse, but a respected legal commentator in England has claimed that postcoital contraception is lawful as contraception during "that time period which the consensus of informed medical scientific opinion states is the maximum time after intercourse before implantation takes place. This may be 7 days or 8 or 9 or 10."[15]

Accommodation of a maximum time for contraceptive intervention before abortion liability arises is encouraged by legislation that makes it clear that such liability arises only on completion of implantation. In New Zealand, for instance, the Royal Commission of Inquiry into Contraception, Sterilisation and Abortion reported in 1977 that "a doubt exist as to whether certain devices and techniques are contraceptive or abortifacient."[16] By a consequently enacted amendment to the criminal law, it is provided that in the provision on procuring miscarriage the term "miscarriage" means

(a) The destruction or death of an embryo or fetus after implantation; or
(b) The premature expulsion or removal of an embryo or a fetus after implantation, otherwise than for the purpose of inducing the birth of a fetus believed to be viable or removing a fetus that has died.[17]

Legislation of this type, which also is found in Austria, the Netherlands, and Germany, expresses for the avoidance of doubt what is increasingly found to be the law elsewhere, even where no legislation exists, namely, that lawful contraception consists in the deliberate use of either precoital, coital, or post-coital methods to prevent completion of the process of implantation.

A 35-Day Presumption

In practice, a doctor treating a woman may be uncertain whether implantation is complete, since there is at present no biological way to ascertain this point with absolute certainty. An aid to contraceptive employment of preimplantation methods would be a presumption of contraceptive intention when they are used within the longest possible interval between a woman's last menstruation and completion of implantation. Evidence indicates that while implantation is frequently completed at 28 days after the last menstrual period (LMP) in women with a standard 28-day cycle, it may not be completed until up to 35 days.[18] Late ovulation, medical intervention, or, for instance, emotional factors may present clinical circumstances postponing menstruation.

Such a presumption of contraceptive intent up to 35 days after the LMP is consistent both with traditional law and modern public policy. Since the criminal law limits freedom of individual action, courts respecting individual liberty have a tradition of interpreting the criminal law conservatively, in order to minimize state intrusion on freedom.[19] Any uncertainty in the scope of criminal law is resolved in favor of the individual and against a prosecuting authority. Further, prosecuting authorities themselves lose credibility by pursuing cases at the margins of the law. In practice, they prefer pursuit of clear wrongs and are uncomfortable when prosecuting reputable professionals in speculative cases.

Encouraging and facilitating women to seek timely contraception is compatible with sound public health policy. Recourse to contraception is preferable to abortion, particularly by illicit means and unqualified practitioners. Epidemiological data confirm that public health is well served by encouragement of child spacing, and that women's health is advanced by avoidance of unwanted pregnancy in adolescence and at advanced maternal age.[20] Expansion of contraceptive opportunities through last-chance contraception is likely to decrease national statistics of maternal mortality and morbidity[21] and also, because of advantageous child spacing, infant mortality.[22]

Modern Dynamics: Abortion

Postimplantation intervention is in law abortifacient, but the modern tendency of legislation is to accommodate abortion as being lawful on therapeutic and several other indications, such as severe handicap in an embryo of fetus that would otherwise result in the birth of a severely disabled child. In addition to recognizing traditional health indications for abortion, a number of countries have recognized other indications, such as family welfare, adolescence itself, the state of being unmarried or separated, AIDS or HIV, women's distress regarding pregnancy, and lack of housing. Some of these indications reinforce traditional indications of abortion on therapeutic or mental health grounds, and others establish completely new grounds for abortion, such as adolescence.[23]

Modern Dynamics: Constitutional and Human Rights Law

Directed by international human rights conventions, related provisions in countries' constitutional laws and general legislation, and the decisions of international and leading domestic courts, a recognition is arising that control of individual fertility is a necessary condition of women's reproductive health care, and indeed of women's collective and individual welfare in areas of activity beyond health care. The human rights claims implicated in the removal of restrictive laws on contraception and abortion may be classified in a number of different ways.

An influential literature exists in the area of those ethical values and principles that underlie the leading international human rights instruments, such as the Universal Declaration of Human Rights, the several legally enforceable international and regional human rights conventions (including the International Covenants on Civil and Political Rights and on Economic, Social and Cultural Rights) and, particularly, the Women's Convention. The latter gives prominent recognition and expression to women's legal rights to take advantage of methods of family planning. The rights discussed below are drawn from a combination of at times differently expressed legal endorsements of human rights.

The Right to Integrity and Security of the Person

The legal right that the law protects through restrictive abortion laws is not that of a fetus per se but of the state when it chooses to protect its own interest in fetal life. The state has no less an interest in the welfare of women, including pregnant women. When the state limits women's freedom of action on behalf of fetuses, women may invoke their own rights of bodily integrity and security of the person to seek therapeutic abortion, and perhaps abortion on grounds other than therapy, in order to curtail the state's promotion of its interests over theirs. A number of courts have ruled that, under many conditions, the state's interest in fetal life is subordinate to the rights to integrity and security of pregnant women and that women's legal rights to abortion prevail.

This point was made explicit in 1988 by the Supreme Court of Canada when the restrictive abortion provision of the Criminal Code of Canada was found unconstitutional and inoperative because it violated the provision of the Canadian Charter of Rights and Freedoms guaranteeing to everyone the right to life, liberty and security of the person.[24] Chief Justice Dickson observed that

> forcing a woman, by threat of criminal sanction, to carry a foetus to term unless she meets certain criteria unrelated to her own priorities and aspirations, is a profound interference with a woman's body and thus a violation of security of the person.[25]

The Court recognized the legitimacy of the state's interest in fetal life, suggesting that it might be given effect if applicable at an appropriate point in gestation, perhaps in the second trimester, but subordinated the state's interest to women's rights of access to necessary health services, which it found that the Criminal Code provisions obstructed. Subject to its observance of such superior interests, however, the state was acknowledged to have an interest to protect fetal life within constitutional limits.

Limitations on a state's powers would be illustrated if a person widely revered in the community were to be sick and in need of a kidney transplant. Computerized medical records might be available to show that a particular woman was perfectly matched by tissue typing to donate a kidney for transplantation, and legislation might be enacted by democratic approval that she was to be operated upon to remove a kidney, her personal objections notwithstanding. It is clear that such legislation, even though reflecting the overwhelming will of her community, would be a fundamental violation of the human right to bodily integrity and security. Equally, it may be claimed that the state's protected interest in a fetus does not entitle it to conscript a woman's body for gestation. This would be evident if an embryo were preserved in vitro, and is no less true of an embryo in utero. It may accordingly be argued in law that legislation that compels a woman unwillingly to continue gestation is a violation of her human rights. Contrary arguments would invoke the state's power rather than its just claim to bar abortion, and interests of fetuses themselves that are believed to supersede the rights of women. The most obvious of the fetal rights that may be invoked is the right to life.

The Right to Life

There are several international and national cases that invoke the right to life of the unborn in order to argue that liberal abortion laws are contrary to right-to-life provisions of national constitutions or international or regional human rights treaties. Such arguments in general have not been successful. For instance, in its decision to uphold the Austrian Penal Code's 1974 provision permitting abortion on request during the first trimester, and on specified grounds thereafter, the Constitutional Court of Austria based its reasoning on Article 2 of the European Convention of Human Rights, which provides that "everyone's right to life shall be protected by law." The Court held that this article does not recognize a right to life before live birth.[26]

A similar interpretation of Article 2 was applied in a review of an English judicial decision on the legality of abortion practice under the British Abortion Act of 1967. The European Commission on Human Rights affirmed this decision and concluded that "both the general usage of the term 'everyone' in the Convention and in the context in which it was employed in Article 2 tend to support the view that it does not include the unborn."[27]

The Inter-American Commission on Human Rights gave a similar ruling of the right-to-life article of the American Declaration of the Rights and Duties of Man. Case 2141[28] involved a petition against the United States and the Commonwealth of Massachusetts by several complainants who alleged that the "right to life" of the victim ("Baby Boy," an aborted male fetus), had been violated, contrary to Article 1 of the American Declaration of the Rights and Duties of Man. The petitioners alleged that the U.S. Supreme Court's decision in *Roe v. Wade*, in limiting the legal protection of the unborn, set the stage for the deprivation of the right to life of "Baby Boy."

The Commission, relying on the *travaux preparatories* of the American Declaration, rejected an interpretation of Article 1 that would have protected unborn life more stringently than U.S. law under *Roe v. Wade*. It decided that Article 1 of the American Declaration did not incorporate the notion that the right to life exists from the moment of conception, since the drafters chose not to adopt language which clearly stated that principle.

The Constitutional Court of Italy in 1975 invoke the constitutional right-to-life provision to protect the interests of the woman in an abortion case. The Court declared the abortion provision of the Italian criminal code unconstitutional because it restricted lawful abortion to life-threatening pregnancies.[29] The Court observed that women's health prevails over fetal life, because "there is no equivalence between the right not only to life but also to health of one who – like a pregnant woman – is already a person, and the safeguard of an embryo which has yet to become a person.[30]

The Rights to Liberty, Privacy, and Family Life

Justice Wilson in the Canadian *Morgentaler* case struck down the restrictive abortion law because it violated women's rights not just to security of the person, but to liberty itself, showing that the abortion legislation was objectionable on wider grounds than obstruction of access to health services. The justice acknowledged the state's interests in fetal life, but took a developmental view of when that right could be enforced. She observed that

> the undeveloped foetus starts out as a newly fertilized ovum; the fully developed foetus emerges ultimately as an infant. A developmental progression takes place in between these two extremes . . . in balancing the state's interest in the protection of the foetus . . . against the right of the pregnant

> woman . . . greater weight should be given to the state's interest in the later stages of pregnancy than in the earlier. The foetus should accordingly . . . be viewed in differential and developmental terms.[31]

Justice Wilson based her concurring judgment in large part on a woman's right to liberty, which she construed to grant an individual considerable autonomy, and observed that

> liberty in a free and democratic society does not require the state to approve the personal decisions made by its citizens; it does, however, require the state to respect them.[32]

The liberty interest was considered to include a right to sanctity of the family and of privacy.

The liberty interest was found to be inextricably tied to the concept of human dignity, which includes the right of individuals to choose their own philosophies of life and to make fundamental personal decisions without interference from the state. The power to exclude the state from individual decisions is also described as the right of privacy, which was the constitutional value to which the U.S. Supreme Court gave effect in the landmark decision in *Roe v. Wade.*[33] In this case the Court concluded that the right to privacy found in the Fourteenth Amendment guarantee of liberty "is broad enough to encompass a woman's decision whether or not to terminate her pregnancy."[34] The right was not found to be absolute, because at some point the state enjoyed a legitimate interest in the protection of health, proper medical standards, and prenatal life.

In *Paton v. United Kingdom,*[35] Mr. Paton appealed the decision of the English court in which he was precluded from preventing his wife from having an abortion pursuant to the British Abortion Act of 1967.[36] Mr. Paton alleged that his inability to regulate his wife's decision or to be consulted on the issue was a violation of his right to respect for family life protected by Article 8(1) of the European Convention on Human Rights. The European Commission on Human Rights dismissed Mr. Paton's appeal, explaining that the English decision, "in so far as it interfered in itself with the applicant's right to respect for his family life, was justified under paragraph (2) of article 8 as being necessary for the protection of the rights of another person."[37] In addressing Mr. Paton's alleged right to be consulted, the commission did "not find that the husband's and potential father's right to respect for his private and family life can be interpreted so widely as to embrace such procedural rights as claimed by the applicant, i.e., a right to be consulted, or a right to make applications, about an abortion which his wife intends to have performed on her."[38]

The Right to Sexual Nondiscrimination

The principle of nondiscrimination on grounds of sex furnishes a seamless web that connects different aspects of offensive discrimination against women, including the aspect of reproductive health. Pregnancy-based discrimination created by law is discrimination based on sex. It deliberately or inadvertently targets one sex only for disadvantage, and such laws are therefore offensive to sexual antidiscrimination principles. Article 1 of the Women's Convention goes beyond any discriminatory intention of laws to consider whether, intentionally or unintentionally, they have discriminatory effects:

> The term "discrimination against women" shall mean any distinction, exclusion or restriction made on the basis of sex which has the effect or purpose of impairing or nullifying the recognition, enjoyment or exercise by women, irrespective of their marital status, on a basis of equality of men and women, of human rights and fundamental freedoms in the political, economic, social, cultural, civil or any other field.

Criminalizing a medical procedure needed only by women to preserve their life and health "excludes and restricts" them on the "basis of sex" and, according to this definition, would constitute sex discrimination. In no other area does the law impose criminal penalties on individuals in order to compel them to afford the benefits of their bodies to others. The reasons for the existence of prohibitive abortion laws are many, and include the need to control women's sexuality. The effect is to impair or nullify the recognition, enjoyment, or exercise by women of many of their fundamental rights, such as their rights to life, integrity and security of the person, liberty, privacy, and family life. In addition to violations of these fundamental rights are the denials of their rights to reproductive health and to the benefits of scientific progress, outlined in the International Covenant on Economic, Social and Cultural Rights.

There are many ways to protect prenatal life that are consistent with women's rights to nondiscrimination, such as through prenatal care, better nutrition programs, and sufficient funding for research in human reproduction that provides insights into the high rate of natural wastage of prenatal life. Spontaneous abortions can range as high as 62 percent of fertilized ova, depending on the stage of gestation.[39] To think that the only way to protect unborn life is through criminal prosecutions and the use of women's bodies against their will is to oppress women in the most fundamental of ways. The emerging standard of sexual nondiscrimination requires that prenatal life be protected only in ways that are consistent with women's enjoyment and exercise of their rights equally with men.

The historical oppression of woman through their reproductive functions is too pervasive to entrust their reproductive health and self-determination to the votes of legislatures. History has also shown, however, that constitutional and international human rights principles and their enforcement by national and international courts are essential for the protection of individual rights against administrative and political oppression, including that by democratically composed legislatures. Without such safeguards, fragile though they may appear before totalitarian and authoritarian governments, women's rights, their reproductive health, and the welfare of their families have been swept away by majoritarian rule.

NOTES

1. Brahms D. The hasty British ban on commercial surrogacy. Hastings Center Report 1987 (Feb); 16.
2. Cook R. et al. Progress towards equality. People (IPPF) 12(2) (1985).
3. Steinfels P. Split, catholic bishops shun proposals on women's issues. New York Times 1990 Sep 14.
4. Cook R. et al. Abortion law and policies: challenges and opportunities, Int J Gynecal Obstet 1989; Supp 3: 61.
5. Dickens BM. Abortion I: definitions and implications Can Med Assoc J 1981; 124: 113–4.
6. Dickens BM. Abortion and the Law. London: MacGibbon and Kee, 1966: 26.
7. See the English Offences Against the Person Act, 1861, Section 58, which remains the prohibitive basis of the criminal abortion laws of many jurisdictions in the (British) Commonwealth and beyond.
8. *Bravery v. Bravery* [1954] 3 All E. R. 59 [English Court of Appeal] at 67–68.
9. The first accommodation of legal contraception in Ireland was limited to married people.
10. Report of the (British) Inter-Departmental Committee on Abortion 1939 (Chairman, Norman Birkett), Main Conclusion 6.
11. Troppi v. Scarf (1971), 187 NW 2d 511 (Mich CA) at 517.
12. Henshaw SK. Induced abortion: a world view. Family Planning Perspective 1990; 22: 76.
13. Jones EG, Forrest JD. Contraceptive failure in the United States: revised estimates for the 1982 National Survey of Family Growth. Family Planning Perspectives 1989; 21: 103.
14. The Indian Medical Termination Pregnancy Act of 1971 explains that contraceptive failure might be a reason for abortion but does not cite it as an indication as such.
15. Kennedy I. The legal and ethical implications of postcoital birth control. In: Grahame H, ed. Postcoital Contraception: Methods, Services and Prospects 1983, 62 at 66.
16. Contraception, Sterilisation and Abortion in New Zealand: Report of the Royal Commission of Inquiry. Wellington: Government Printer, 1977: 22.
17. Crimes Act, 1961, No. 43, Sect. 182 A.
18. Yen SSC. The human cycle. In: Yen SSC, Jaffe RB. Reproductive Endocrinology, Physiology, Pathophysiology, and Clinical Management. Philadelphia: Saunders, 1986: 220, 202.
19. Packer HL. The Limits of Criminal Sanction. Stanford, CA: Stanford University Press, 1969.
20. Maine D. Family Planning: Its Impact on Health of Women and Children. New York: Center for Population and Family Health, Columbia University, 1981.
21. Prevention of maternal mortality, Report of a World Health Organization Interregional Meeting: 1985 Nov 11–15; Geneva: WHO, 1985.
22. Maine D, McNamara R. Birth Spacing and Child Survival. New York: Center for Population and Family Health, Columbia University, 1985.
23. Cook RJ, Dickens BM. International developments in abortion laws: 1977–88. Am J Public Health 1988; 78: 1305.
24. Section 7.
25. *R v. Morgentaler* (1988), 44 DLR (4th) 385 (Sup. Ct. Can.) at 402.
26. Judgment of October 11, 1974. Constitutional Court, Erklärungen des Verfassungsgerichtshofs 221 (Aus.).
27. *Paton v. United Kingdom* 3 E.H.R.R. 408, 413(1980) (Eur. Comm'n Hum. Rts.)
28. Inter-Am. C. H. R. 25, OEA/ser. L./V.1154, doc. 9 rev. 125 (1981).

29. Judgment of February 18, 1975, Corte Costituzionale e Civile, no. 27, 98 Foro It. I, Giurisprudenciea Costituzionale e Civil 515 (Italy), translated in part in M. Cappelletti and W. Cohen, *Comparative Constitutional Law: Cases and Materials* (1979): 612–4.
30. *Id.* at 613.
31. Morgentaler, at 499, Wilson, J.
32. *Id.* at 487.
33. 410 U.S. 113 (1973).
34. *Id.* at 153.
35. *Paton v. United Kingdom,* 3 E.H.R.R. 408, 413 (1980) (Eur. Comm'n Hum. Rts.).
36. *Paton v. British Pregnancy Advisory Service* [1979] Q. B. 276.
37. *Id.* at para 26.
38. *Id.* at para 27.
39. Wilcox A J. et al. Incidence of early pregnancy loss. N Engl J Med 1988; 319: 189; Edmonds D K, et al. Early embryonic morality in women. Fertil Steril 1982; 38: 447.

PART FOUR

Fetal Research and Fetal Tissue

KENNETH J. RYAN

The Use of Human Fetal Tissue for Research and Therapy

For years, research on the human fetus or its tissues has been conducted to advance knowledge in the area of fetal growth and development, in the diagnosis of fetal disease or abnormality, and in treatment of the fetus in utero, and to promote better understanding of the management, physiology, and pathology of human pregnancy. In these instances, the fetus or the pregnancy has been the subject and as a class the beneficiary of the research, although usually only in future generations. Examples of such research would include diagnosis, prevention, and treatment of fetal lung immaturity caused by premature birth, development of amniocentesis for prenatal diagnosis of birth defects and chromosomal and metabolic disorders, development of treatment for premature labor or preeclampsia, and the prevention and treatment of Rh blood group incompatibility.

Alternatively research with human fetal tissue and organs has been used to advance knowledge for general human biology involving cancer, immunology, cell culture, and transplantation. The fetus in these cases is the object of the research and the wider human community is the beneficiary. Examples of this research include development of the polio vaccine by growth of the virus in human fetal kidney tissue and transplantation of fetal cells or tissues to recipients with deficiency diseases such as diabetes.[1,2]

Fetal Research and Abortion

Research on a fetus that might benefit that individual fetus directly or research on cadaveric tissue derived from a fetus dead of natural causes provokes little controversy as long as the research is conducted within generally accepted ethical guidelines. Research on a fetus or with fetal issue obtained after an induced abortion has, however, resulted in social discord and national and international political debates, because of strong feelings about abortion itself and about how the fetus derived from an abortion is treated. After World War II there was a marked increase in all aspects of biomedical research, especially in developed nations. At the same time, there was a loosening of

F.K. Beller and R.F. Weir (eds.), The Beginning of Human Life, 181–187.

restrictions on the availability of induced abortion for non-life-threatening medical and social indications in the Scandinavian countries, England, and several U.S. states. As a result, research on aborted fetuses increased and raised ethical concerns because of the association with abortion.

One of the earliest, if not the first, responses to such social concerns about the conduct of fetal and fetal tissue research in association with abortion was the creation of the Peel Advisory Group in England (1970–1972), which was asked to consider the ethical, medical, social, and legal implications of such research. Their recommended code of practice allowed for the conduct of research on tissues from dead fetuses as long as full records were kept, no monetary exchange took place, and provisions of their Human Tissue Act were observed. They also accepted research on the whole pre-viable fetus of less than 300 grams but prohibited research on the viable fetus unless it was necessary to promote its life.[3]

After *Roe v. Wade* made abortion generally available in the United States in 1973, the political fallout has resulted in repeated national and local attempts to prevent the use of the aborted fetus or its tissues for any form of medical research. The National Research Act (P.L. 93–348) imposed a moratorium in 1974 on federal support for research conducted on a fetus before or after an induced abortion except to assure the survival of the fetus. The law also created a national commission to study the nature and extent of research involving the living fetus, to recommend whether and under what circumstances the government might support such research, and to determine whether the congressionally imposed moratorium should be lifted. The commission was given four months to respond. The concerns expressed publicly were largely over a limited number of research projects involving perfusion of the living pre-viable fetus ex utero, or on the fetus or pregnancy in anticipation of an abortion. The commission decided that for living human fetal research to be ethically acceptable it should meet certain requirements:

1. Appropriate studies on animal models and nonpregnant humans should be completed.
2. The knowledge to be gained should be important and not otherwise reasonably obtainable.
3. Risks and benefits should be evaluated.
4. Informed consent should be obtained appropriately.
5. Subjects should be selected fairly so that risks and benefits will not be inequitably distributed because of race, social class, or economic status.

The commission outlined the circumstances under which such research might be performed, favoring instances in which knowledge gained would be important and risk of harm minimized. The commission further recommended that research on the dead fetus and fetal tissue be permitted consistent with local law, the Uniform Anatomical Gift Act, and commonly held convictions about respect for the dead. By 1973, essentially all states had adopted the Uniform Anatomical Gift Act. In 1975, the federal government issued regulations on the conduct of human fetal research based on the commission's recommendations.[4]

THE USE OF FETAL TISSUE FOR TRANSPLANTATION

The only type of fetal tissue transplantation currently accepted as therapy is the transfer of the fetal thymus to patients with DiGeorge's syndrome. This syndrome comprises severe immunodeficiency due to absence of the thymus, hypoparathyroidism, and cardiac anomalies. Although the hypoparathyroidism can be treated with supplemental calcium and vitamin D, and the cardiac defects can be surgically corrected, absence of the thymus generally leads to infections which can be fatal in the first year of life. Animal studies demonstrated that the neonatally removed thymus could be replaced by thymus transplants, and fetal tissue was much preferable to adults tissue for this purpose. In the human, successful transplants of fetal thymus to two human infants with DiGeorge's syndrome was first reported in 1968. At least 27 infants have been treated, with 9 surviving for prolonged periods. The tissue was obtained from fetuses at 12 to 20 weeks' gestation and transplanted into muscle, the peritoneum, or a millipore chamber. Results occurred rapidly – within hours to a few weeks. Since the transplanted thymus tissue can cause a graft-versus-host reaction in the recipient if the donor is over 14 weeks' gestation, tissue is sought from fetuses at earlier periods.[5]

Another use for fetal transplantation is in attempts to treat diabetes. There are at least one million juvenile (Type I) insulin-requiring diabetics in the United States. Diabetes may lead to shortened life span, blindness, loss of limbs due to poor circulation, or heart and kidney defects. Although insulin is the current standard treatment, transplantation of insulin-secreting cells into the diabetic might effect a cure or amelioration of the disease process. In animals it is possible to transplant fetal pancreatic tissue without immunosuppression and reverse experimentally induced diabetes. Human fetal pancreatic tissue can also produce such an effect when transplanted into animals with diabetes. Human diabetics have received fetal pancreatic tissue transplanted under the kidney capsule at the time of a kidney graft. Such tissue appears to grow and differentiate and secrete insulin, but it is too early to tell whether such transplanted tissue can control diabetes in the human.[6]

Perhaps the most dramatic use of fetal tissue for transplantation is associated with attempts to treat Parkinson's disease. This disease afflicts almost 400,000 patients in the United States and is associated with muscle rigidity, loss of posture, difficulty and slowness of motion, and uncontrolled tremors. The disease is progressive and severely crippling. Parkinson's disease is believed to be associated with loss of dopamine-secreting cells in the central nervous system caused by genetic susceptibility and environmental toxins. Current therapy is with the drug L-dopa, but the response is limited. An objective of fetal transplantation would be to provide cells that could produce the missing dopamine. Dr. Redmond from Yale reported in public testimony that Dr. Gilman Thompson attempted to graft mature brain tissue into the brains of dogs as long ago as 1890. Elizabeth Dunn first reported that neonatal brain tissue could successfully be grafted into the adult rat brain, and in 1940 Le Gros Clark reported grafting fetal brain tissue in animals.[7]

In Sweden, Lars Olson demonstrated that human fetal cells transplanted into animal models of Parkinson's disease could be functionally integrated into the brain, produce dopamine, and reverse symptoms. Redmond at Yale developed a subhuman primate model that developed Parkinson-like symptoms which could be ameliorated by transplantation of fetal brain tissue from the substantia nigra. Fetal tissue transplantation into human Parkinson's disease patients had occurred in Sweden, Mexico, China, England, and Cuba by 1988. Results were reported in mostly anecdotal fashion and, although they were promising, it was clear that more careful documentation was needed. Two studies reported in 1990 were even more promising. In a report from Sweden, fetal brain tissue from four fetuses of 8–9 gestational weeks was injected into a 49-year-old man with a 13-year history of Parkinsonism. After one year, there was evidence of improvement and a suggestion by brain scanning that the cells were producing dopamine.[9] A case reported from Denver involved a 52-year-old male with 20 years of Parkinson's disease who received cells from a 7-week fetus. He was not immunosuppressed and showed improvement after the procedure.[10]

It might reasonably be asked why fetal tissues seem to be more effective in transplantation than tissues derived at a later stage of develoment. As described by Auerbach in testimony at public hearings, fetal tissues have plasticity. They can adapt to a new host environment, change their shape, migrate, and assume proper orientation and location, as well as integrate functionally into new surroundings. Fetal cells can divide more frequently and for more generations, and retain their capacity to divide better than cells from other individuals. Fetal tissues provoke an angiogenic response which supports their growth in a new environment. Fetal cells are immunologically more compatible than adult cells. They lack many of the antigens and cells of the immune system which cause tissue incompatibility and rejection. For all of these reasons fetal tissue provides a special advantage for transplantation.[11]

Human Fetal Tissue Transplantation Research Panel

In 1987, investigators at the National Institute of Neurological and Communicative Disorders and Stroke proposed transplantation of fetal tissue to an adult patient with Parkinson's disease as a research project in the Clinical Center. In the course of review, the director of the National Institutes of Health, although not required to do so, asked the assistant secretary for health for approval of the procedure because of the ethical and scientific issues which might be raised. Assistant Secretary for Health Robert E. Windom responded by imposing a moratorium on federal funding for research on fetal transplantation and requesting the formation of one or more advisory committees to consider the matter. Although there was no prohibition of federal funding for other forms of fetal research, there was much confusion within the scientific community about exactly what was covered under this new moratorium.[12]

In the summer and fall of 1988, a panel of 21 members was convened at the request of the director of the National Institutes of Health to deliberate on the questions posed by Assistant Secretary Windom, to hold public hearings, and to make recommendations. Public testimony provided evidence that research on fetal tissue transplantation held promise for relief of human problems, especially diabetes and Parkinson's disease, although much work needed to be done before the feasibility of transplantation as a form of therapy could be considered. It was suggested that substitutes for fetal tissue such as self-replicating cells in culture were possible, but not in the immediate future. It was generally accepted that sufficient work with animals had been done with diabetes and Parkinson-like models to justify study with humans. Presentations at the public hearings favored lifting the moratorium and funding of research by most who represented the scientific and medical communities, some ethicists, and the public support groups that represented patients with diabetes, Parkinson's disease, and other conditions that might be benefitted. Funding of research was generally opposed by right-to-life advocates and those opposed to abortion. The panelists themselves could be separated into three categories: those who found abortion and the use of fetal tissue morally acceptable; those who found abortion problematical or immoral but the use of fetal tissue acceptable and separable from the abortion; and, finally, those who found both abortion and the use of fetal tissue immoral and inseparably evil. Essentially all panelists agreed that the research offered opportunity for medical progress and relief of suffering, but differed on whether it could be justified because of the issue of abortion. The clear majority of the panelists favored lifting of the moratorium with the imposition of rules to separate the source of the tissue from its ultimate use. These guidelines included the following:

1. The decision to terminate the pregnancy and the procedures of abortion should be kept independent of the retrieval and use of the tissue.
2. All payments for fetal tissue should be prohibited except for the reasonable cost for handling.
3. Full disclosure on the source of the tissue should be made available to recipients and handlers of the tissue.
4. Fetal tissue should be accorded the same respect as other cadaveric human tissues.

In general, these guidelines are in accord with an international consensus as set out by nine other review panels from the United Kingdom, Australia, Netherlands, France, Sweden, the Council of Europe, and Canada.

The minority report which favored the moratorium did so on the grounds that one could not separate the immorality of abortion from the use of the fetal tissue, invoking a Nazi Holocaust analogy. Members of the minority also felt that the women consenting to abortion relinquished kinship rights and therefore the ability to consent for the subsequent use of the fetal tissue. Finally, it was argued that the benefit from the use of such tissue would induce women to have abortions who otherwise might not do so. These contentions were rejected and rebutted by the panel and by the advisory committee to the director of the National Institutes of Health, which also considered the panel report and all the arguments. In any case, the Department of Health and Human Services has continued the ban, claiming with the minority that support of such research might lead to more abortions.[13]

Postscript

In the fall of 1989, Dr Louis W. Sullivan, Secretary of Health and Human Services, indicated the ban would stand indefinitely. Thirty-four medical and scientific organizations wrote to him, protesting his action. Congressional committees held hearings, and a bill to lift the ban on federal financing of fetal tissue transplantation research failed passage. In the meantime, the American College of Obstetricians and Gynecologists and the American Fertility Society have tried to create a public ethics advisory board to fill the moral vacuum created by government inaction in this area.[14]

References

1. Summary, Fetal Research and Fetal Tissue Research, Association of American Medical Colleges, 1988 (June).
2. Mahoney MJ. The nature and extent of research involving living human fetuses [appendix]. Research on the Fetus, National Commission for the Protection of Human Subjects of Biomedical and Behavioral Research: 1975: 1–1 – 1–48. DHEW Publication No. (OS) 76–128.
3. Peel J. The Use of Fetuses and Fetal Material for Research. London: Trinity Press, 1972.
4. Research on the fetus, report and recommendations. National Commission for the Protection of Human Subjects of Biomedical and Behavioral Research; 1975. DHEW Publication No. (OS) 76–127.
5. Buckley RH. Fetal thymus transplantation for the correction of congenital absence of the thymus (DiGeorge's Syndrome). Report of the Human Fetal Tissue Transplantation Research Panel 1988 Dec; 3: D50–D57.
6. Lafferty KJ. Diabetic Islet Cell Transplant Research, Basic Science. Report of the Human Fetal Tissue Transplantation Research Panel, 1988 Dec; 2: D142–D144.
7. Redmond DE. Testimony. Report of the Human Fetal Tissue Tranplantation Research Panel, 1988 Dec; 2: D231–D244.
8. Olson L. Parkinson's disease fetal tissue transplant research, basic and clinical studies. Report of the Human Fetal Tissue Transplantation Research Panel, 1988 Dec; 2: D219–D299.
9. Lindval O et al. Grafts of fetal dopamine neurons survive and improve motor function in Parkinson's disease. Science 1990; 247: 574–577.

10. Barrett JN, et al. Transplantation of human fetal dopamine cells for Parkinson's disease: results at one year. Archiv Neurology 1990; 47: 505–512.
11. Auerbach R. Qualities of fetal cells and tissue. Report of the Human Fetal Tissue Transplantation Research Panel, 1988; 2: D27–D31. 2, D27–D31.
12. Report of the Advisory Committee to the Director. National Institutes of Health, Human Fetal Tissue Transplantation Research, 1988 Dec 14.
13. Report of the Human Fetal Tissue Transplantation Research Panel, vol. 1, 1988; 1.
14. Hilts PJ. Groups set up panel on use of fetal tissue. New York Times 1991 Jan 8; col 3.

JOHN C. FLETCHER

Restriction and Suppression of Fetal and Pre-Embryo Research, 1974–1990

The thesis of this paper is that a state of unjustifiable suppression exists in one area of science in the federal sector. The area involves three related but conceptually distinct research activities: (1) investigational research (to gain knowledge not directly beneficial to the subject of research) involving the human fetus in the first trimester from implantation through twelve weeks of gestation; (2) investigational research involving the human preimplantation embryo during the first 14 days after fertilization outside the human body and before any attempt to transfer the embryo for possible implantation in the uterus; and (3) therapeutic experiments to transplant tissues and cells from dead fetuses to patients with neurological and other disorders.

Assuming that these three activities ought to be done, research ethics requires voluntary informed consent of (1) the woman carrying the fetus in the first trimester, as well as at least the lack of objection of the biological father, if available; (2) the woman and man whose egg and sperm were sources of the preembryo(s) to be involved in the research; and (3) at any stage of gestation, the woman who chose an abortion or suffered a spontaneous abortion, and the nonobjection of the biological father, if available. However, the tenet of voluntary informed consent can be challenged if the research activities are basically unethical. What is their moral status? Should they be done at all?

Collective ethical judgments in an open, public forum were made about fetal and preembryo research in the 1970s.[1] Two national ethics commissions recommended that fetal[3] and preimplantation embryo[4] research could ethically be done if carefully restricted to prevent abuses. Further, federal guidelines in effect since 1975 direct that research activities and therapeutic uses of fetal material, cells, tissue, or organs excised from a dead fetus "shall be conducted only in accordance with . . . state or local laws regarding such activities.[5]

This paper will show that despite such backing in the 1970s, federally sponsored research in these three vital areas in the U.S. has been suppressed in a pattern that began in 1980 and continues. Excellent research in these areas, which is being done in other nations, *can* be done in the United States. The

F.K. Beller and R.F. Weir (eds.), The Beginning of Human Life, 189–206.

research promises to lead to safer and more effective diagnosis and treatment of genetic diseases, infertility, cancer, neurological disorders, and AIDS.

This paper traces the historical causes and harmful effects of this situation on clinical research, academic freedom, and the public welfare. It also proposes reforms in federal fetal research guidelines. My goal in the proposals is to combine respect for diverse moral traditions within a set of internally consistent policies and practices for research involving the human pre-embryo, pregnant women, and fetuses, including the nonviable or viable fetus ex utero.

From Restriction to Suppression

The Belmont Report, an important source of ethical guidance for research with human subjects composed in 1976, begins as follows:

> Scientific research has produced substantial benefits. It has also posed some troubling ethical questions. Public attention was drawn to these questions by reported abuses of human subjects in biomedical experiments, especially during the Second World War.[6]

Among the troubling ethical questions that continued after the war was an apparent pattern of excessive risks with and abuses of human subjects in the United States and elsewhere that was identified by Beecher and other experienced researchers.[7] As a result, since the late 1960s a policy of restriction of research activities with human subjects has been in effect that is accepted by the vast majority of scientists in the United States.

A policy of restriction of scientific activities involving human subjects has two goals. One is to protect human subjects and investigators. A second is to raise and answer questions, as well as resolve disputes, about whether particular research activities ought to be done at all. The United Sates was the first nation to shape a set of ethical and public policy guidelines for federally sponsored research involving human subjects, required by federal law, to provide for a local and national process to accomplish both of these goals.

At the local level, an institutional review board (IRB) has the duty to evaluate risks and benefits that may result from the specific proposals of research to involve human subjects.[8] The IRB has authority to decide whether a proposed research project should be done at all or be altered to reduce risks and increase benefits. An IRB is also the sole source of approval for arrangements for informed consent and the language to be used therein. Any major change in the research project after its initial approval can be made only by a scientist's own IRB.

The IRB was specifically charged in public policy not to consider the "long-range effects" of knowledge to be gained from research or its effects on public policy or morality.[9] Such effects include questions about the moral and public policy implications of investigative research with the fetus, the embryo, or therapeutic research with fetal tissue. Consideration of these questions was to be done by "one or more" ethical advisory boards [EAB] established by the secretary of the Department of Health and Human Services (HHS).[10] This twin process of local and national oversight of research activities grew out of a foundational policy of restriction.

The Belmont Report's opening words rested on two premises. One was explicit, i.e., the benefits of research to society. The second premise was unstated. It concerned the dominant approach to the "troubling ethical questions" that was taken by the commission that endorsed the Belmont Report, described later by Jonsen and Toulmin as "casuistical."[11] This approach, also described by Toulmin at the time,[12] examines ethical controversies and cases by analogical reasoning to other cases, discourse marked by standards of reasonableness, and careful attention to the circumstances of the case or problem. Casuistry strongly eschews ethical absolutism. The commission's hope for an HHS ethics advisory board was that it could become an experienced, continuing national resource to study, debate, and resolve controversial proposals for research that raised social-ethical questions.

The history of the commission and the example it set for the nation in its reasoning would oppose the suppression of research based on the imposition of claims impossible to weigh reasonably, a disregard for evidence, and the obstruction of due process to resolve conflicting scientific and moral views about specific research proposals. This paper will show that each of these has occurred.

I choose the word "suppression" with care. Webster's[13] defines "suppress" as: "1a: to put down or out of existence by or as if by authority, force, or pressure; b: to force into impotence or obscurity." Both definitions apply. "Forced into obscurity" describes the present situation in federally supported fetal research. Only a tiny amount of federally funded investigational fetal research has occurred since it was permitted by federal fetal research guidelines.[14] Although technology for fetal diagnosis and treatment has improved vastly since fetal research became a controversial issue in the early 1970s, very little research and development of the technology has been federally funded. A review of extramural grants of the National Institute of Child Health and Human Development (NICHD) for projects on high-risk pregnancy and fetal pathophysiology for 1983–84 showed that of 183 projects, only three involved the human fetus, none is the context of abortion.[15]

Federal fetal regulations need three reforms, discussed at greater length below: (1) provision of a specific framework for the definition of "minimal risk" in fetal research, (2) provision for greater than minimal research risks in the first trimester of pregnancy, and (3) provision for selective exposure of fetuses to be aborted to higher research risks before exposing fetuses intended for delivery to such risks.

"Forced into impotence" aptly describes the status of the use of federal funds for research with the human preembryo since 1975 since most funding today would be used to study the causes and treatment of *infertility*. The National Institutes of Health (NIH), the nation's premier biomedical research agency, is impotent to provide peer review and funding in research activities affecting not only infertility, but human genetics, cancer, and AIDS.

"To put down . . . by authority" best describes the mode of action of a moratorium first imposed in May 1988 by the Assistant Secretary for Health on any research funded by the Public Health Service using fetal tissue obtained after elective abortion for transplantation into human beings. The moratorium became a ban by order of the secretary, HHS, in November 1989, overriding the December 1988 recommendations of an expert advisory panel convened by the NIH.

The National Commission and Fetal Research

In 1974, the National Research Act (Public Law 93–348) created IRBs and the National Commission for the Protection of Human Subjects of Biomedical and Behavioral Research, which was chaired by Kenneth J. Ryan, M.D. The first of the commission's several mandates was to recommend guidelines for fetal research that became federal regulations.[16] After the 1973 *Roe v. Wade* decision, Congress was concerned about potential abuse in fetal research. News stories from abroad about research with live fetuses ex utero raised questions about whether the NIH had funded the projects. Eunice Kennedy Shriver led a demonstration to NIH. NIH leaders denied such funding but placed a moratorium on all but directly beneficial fetal research.[17] The moratorium was in effect when the commission began its work.

The commission considered an appropriate ethical framework both to encourage fetal research, because of its benefits (e.g., in the development of a vaccine against rubella, and in amniocentesis, treatment of Rh isoimmunization disease, and respiratory distress syndrome), and to restrict it, especially to protect the fetus to be aborted from opportunistic exploitation. Several invited ethicists and theologians gave arguments to the commission. Richard McCormick[18] and LeRoy Walters [19] probably had the most lasting influence on the commission's ethical perspective, although philosopher Stephen Toulmin[12] of the University of Chicago finally framed the commission's conclusions.

Walters advised the commission to use the principle of *equality of protection in research* as the framework for fetal research, whether fetuses were destined for abortion or delivery. Do no more and no less to a fetus to be aborted than what ought to be done to a fetus to be delivered – a "Golden Rule" approach to protect all fetuses in research. Walters noted that any policy based on the equality principle would be "formal and therefore flexible."

McCormick, a Roman Catholic moral theologian, advised against conventional moral reasoning that balances social benefits against risks to the fetus, as this approach could not avoid "utilitarian" subjugation of the individual to the collective. He began his arguments from the practice of parental proxy consent for research with children.[20] Was it ethical to give proxy consent for strictly investigational research with children, since it would not benefit them? McCormick answered in the affirmative. Why? Because children themselves should want to participate in it to help others, simply "because we are members of the human community."[21] He then extended this reasoning to fetal research, including the few examples of "tragic" abortions that he found morally acceptable. McCormick concluded that the ethical arguments for investigational research in children supported such research in the fetus. His major proviso on investigational fetal research was that it should be done only when there is "no discernible risk or undue discomfort." An additional factor in McCormick's argument was a belief that "the fetus is a fellow human being, and ought to be treated . . . exactly as one treats a child."

Sisela Bok took a position[22] similar to that adopted by a British commission in 1972.[23] She gave four reasons why society must protect life: (1) to protect the victim from harm, fear, anguish, suffering, and loss of continued experience, (2) to protect the agent from the brutalization and criminalization entailed by the act, (3) to protect the victim's family from grief and loss, and (4) to protect society from the greater harm that would follow from permissive killing. She argued that up to a point well before viability such reasons have no moral relevance to fetuses, because claims for the "humanity" of the early fetus fail to make sense. Based on this reasoning, Bok argued to allow a higher level of research risk before 18 weeks[1] gestational age.

A position advanced by Joseph Fletcher[24] favored no restrictions on risks of investigational research prior to or after elective or spontaneous abortion, assuming that the design of the research was scientifically meritorious and clinically indicated. The key criterion to him was whether fetal survival was purposed and waned. If not, "any use" of the fetus was justified.

Toulmin[12] preferred McCormick's and Walters' reasoning to Bok's. He recommended what he believed to be a moderate, restricted approach to investigational fetal research. Toulmin favored McCormick's approach because it had opened a way conceptually for those giving primary rights to the fetus to accept investigational studies. However, with McCormick's argument came his risk standard, developed for children and extended to the fetus: "no discernible risk, no notable pain, no notable inconvenience, and . . . promise of considerable benefit."

Rather than draw a "hard and fast line" between classes of fetuses and the risks to which they could be exposed in investigational studies, Toulmin endorsed McCormick's risk standard, applied equally to all fetuses at all stages of development. In doing so, Toulmin anticipated, as did the commission, that in "actual practice" IRBs would probably base their decisions about investigational fetal research less on a "single, hard-and-fast index of permissibility" than on an emerging body of "case law" and "precedents." He expected that a national body (the EAB) would "keep a watchful eye" on the development of that case law.

So a large compromise framed the commission's recommendations. On the one hand, it restricted fetal research through the equality principle and a "minimal risk" standard for investigative research. It would become public policy that each fetus was a protected research subject. On the other hand, the commission encouraged fetal research with commitment to an open due process to resolve specific research proposals referred from local IRBs to a national body. In compromise, the commission did not discuss the moral status of the fetus and focused on a process to resolve specific conflicts that lay ahead.

For example, commissioners discussed the question of first-time investigational research with fetuses, e.g., to learn about the complications of amniocentesis. Could unknown but presumably higher risks be imposed, selectively, first on fetuses to be aborted and subsequently to fetuses to be delivered? Most members said that if research carried some risk but was acceptable to offer to fetuses to be carried to term, initial studies should be done selectively with fetuses to be aborted. Other members disputed this approach, preferring to distribute the risks equally over both groups of fetuses. The commission's report noted this moral dilemma but left it unresolved, pending further national review. The report stated:

> Anticipating that differences of interpretation will arise over the application of the basic principles of equality and the determination of "minimal risk," the Commission recommends review at the national level . . . the appropriate forum for determination and public merit of such research. In addition, such review would facilitate public discussion of the sensitive issues surrounding the use of vulnerable non-consenting subjects in research.[25]

The commissioners were understandably glad to achieve a compromise at all in this ethically troubled area. Their recommendation for a new national body to review specific proposals by request of the secretary, HHS, was approved. The EAB was authorized to recommend that the secretary reserve or use a waiver of the minimal risk requirements in specific cases. The commission's other major recommendations–with one notable dissent by lawyer David Louisell – advised that federal support be provided in six categories of therapeutic and investigational research involving pregnant women and fetuses, including research with the dead fetus as guided by state and local law. All funding was to be conditional on approval by a local IRB, the informed consent of the pregnant women, and the lack of objection of the father. As the next section will show, the support for fetal research that existed on the commission was obscured in subsequent regulations on fetal research.

"Minimal Risk" Definitions: Suppression by Obscurity

The commission recommended, and federal regulations for fetal research require, that all investigational research meet the test of "minimal risk." However, no specific definition of minimal risk for the actual context of fetal research has ever been written. The commission's report stated that "the term 'minimal' is a value judgment. . . . Determination of acceptable minimal risk is a function of the review process."[26] However, true to its casuistical approach, the commission later included a specific frame of reference for minimal risk in research with *children*:

> "Minimal risk" means that the risks of harm anticipated in the proposed research are not greater, considering probability and magnitude, than those ordinarily encountered in daily life or during the performance of routine medical or psychological examinations of *healthy children*.[27] (italics added)

Federal attorneys and others who redacted the commission's recommendations decided to use most of the commission's language in defining minimal risk. However, they dropped any specific frame of reference for all populations, save one. In current federal regulations, the definition of minimal risk is the same in research with fetuses, children, and adults:

> "Minimal risk" means that the risks of harm anticipated in the proposed research are not greater, considering probability and magnitude, than those ordinarily encountered in daily life or during the performance of routine physical or psychological examinations or tests.[28]

That federal redactors were aware of the ethical potency of frames of reference is clear, because in the regulations to be followed for research with prisoners, one finds a framed definition of minimal risk as the commission might have worded it:

> "Minimal risk" is the probability and magnitude of physical or psychological harm that is normally encountered in the daily lives, or in the routine medical, dental, or psychological examination of *healthy persons*.[29] (italics added)

Why does not each vulnerable group – fetuses, pregnant women, and children – deserve its own definition of minimal risk, such as the one enjoyed by the prisoner population? The reader is asked to assume the role of a federal regulation writer using the commission's definition of minimal risk. Should the definition of minimal risk for fetal research have its own frame of reference, e.g., "in the daily lives of pregnant women and fetuses (receiving routine prenatal care"? What does "routine medical or psychological test" mean in the context of fetal-maternal medicine? Federal redactors not only omitted any frame of reference, but they substituted "physical" for "medical" test. Were they worried that if they framed the definition of minimal risk for children, e.g., a frame of reference for "healthy children," a similar framework might have to be worked out for fetuses and pregnant women? More to the point, were they concerned that at the time of this redaction amniocentesis was being found by a NICHD-supported study to be a safe and accurate "routine medical test"?[30] If fetal researchers assumed that amniocentesis was within a "minimal risk" standard, more fetal research would occur.

When the regulations on fetal research were later revised in 1983, the term "minimal risk" appeared in the section on investigational research.[31] However, no definition of minimal risk appears in a section on definitions that prefaces the subpart on fetal research.[32] The general and unframed definition cited above applies. What conclusion can be drawn? Choosing words is a moral choice, and the reader may recall a meaning of suppression as "to force into . . . obscurity."

To complicate matters further, federal regulations permit a higher level of investigational research risks with living children than with the fetus. A category permitting "research involving greater than minimal risks and no prospect of direct benefit to individual subjects" was recommended by the National Commission in 1977[33] and subsequently adopted as a federal regulation.[34] If there can be a higher level of investigational research risks with living children, why can there not be one with fetuses, especially in the first trimester?

The regulations present fetal researchers with an obscure, unframed definition of minimal risk and inconsistently permit a higher degree of investigational research risks with the living child than with the fetus in the first trimester. Whose "daily life" is supposed to be taken into account when considering the probability and magnitude of harm in fetal research? The current definition of minimal risk falsely conveys that (1) the risks of daily fetal-maternal life are comparable to those in the daily life of other "healthy persons," and that (2) "medical tests" for fetuses (e.g., ultrasonography, amniocentesis, chorionic villus sampling, etc.) that do meet a standard of minimal risk are not applicable because they are in a different category from "physical tests." The reader is asked to assume the role of a researcher who must use these regulations to make proposals for research in fetal medicine. Do these obscurities and inconsistencies encourage or discourage investigational fetal research?

The Fate of the First Ethics Advisory Board

HHS Secretary Califano was the only secretary who used the "waiver" of minimal risk for investigational fetal research. He was also the first to consider HHS approval of research in the preimplantation embryo. An EAB was chartered in 1977 but did not convene until 1978, chaired by James C. Gaither, J.D. A de facto moratorium on investigational fetal research and on pre-embryo research continued from 1974.

In May 1978 the EAB agreed to review a proposal from Vanderbilt University received by NIH in 1977 and approved by a study section. In May 1979 the EAB recommended approval[4] for federal funding of research on the safety and efficacy of IVF and embryo transfer when used to treat infertility. This approval was also for study of untransferred pre-embryos, provided researchers had IRB approval and the informed consent of women who would receive any transferred but studied embryos. The EAB set a 14-day cut-off for studying preembryos in vitro and required that sperm and eggs be obtained only from lawfully married couples. McCormick, then an EAB member, crafted this compromise. He courageously broke with a Vatican position against *any and all* technological assisted pregnancies, even in lawfully married couples. Mr. Califano then published the EAB's report for public discussion. He resigned at President Carter's request in late September 1979. No secretary, HHS, has approved the EAB's recommendations, and no federal support of IVF research has ever been permitted.

The EAB reviewed only one proposal for investigational fetal research. In 1978, researchers at the Drew Postgraduate Medical School in Los Angeles proposed to assess the safety of fetoscopy for prenatal diagnosis of hemoglobinopathies in pregnancies of women who had elected abortions for reasons unrelated to the research. Earlier data on fetoscopy suggested a risk of fetal loss, due to the procedure, of about 5 percent. The EAB did not apply the equality principle in this case. The value of the biomedical information, unobtainable any other way, led to an EAB recommendation that the secretary waive the minimal risk standard for this study.[35] The EAB also stipulated that the timing of the planned abortions not be altered by the research. Mr. Califano granted a waiver for this project in September 1979, shortly before his resignation.

Secretary Barbara Harris allowed the EAB to lapse on September 30, 1980, when its charter and funding expired. One view[36] is that she did so to avoid overlap with a successor to the National Commission, the President's Commission for the Study of Ethical Problems in Medicine and Biomedical and Behavioral Research. Congress had created it but as of 1980 had not yet appropriated funds for operations. She disbanded the EAB and transferred its budget to the new commission, fully aware that this step removed the only lawful body that could recommend use of the waiver in fetal research.

Harris saw her role primarily as to direct HHS efforts to benefit poor and disadvantaged people. She opposed any Medicare support for heart transplantation, observing that no transplants were being done for poor people. She regarded IVF research in the same vein, writing in response to a decision-memo on the EAB recommendations and IVF research:

> I need greater justification for such research. Whether the research will take place with or without government support is not really relevant. Why should government support such as area as this! (I have read the material. It is not persuasive.)[37]

NIH directors in the 1980s appealed to various secretaries to recharter and approve the original EAB's recommendations on IVF. There was no action until, under pressure from Congress, Dr. Robert Windom, Assistant Secretary for Health, announced on July 14, 1988, that a new charter for an EAB was to be drafted and discussed in public, and a new EAB appointed.[36] A draft of a charter was published in the Federal Record and comments invited, but no approval was given before the transition to a Bush administration, which has not moved on the issue.

In early 1991, the American College of Obstetricians and Gynecologists and the American Fertility Society moved to establish a national advisory board to monitor embryo research and fetal tissue transplant research.[38] This step was seen as necessary to provide some oversight to an area that has been abdicated by federal authorities.

Fetal Tissue Transplant Research (FTTR)

In 1986, neurosurgeons at the Clinical Center, NIH, designed a research project to give patients with Parkinson disease the choice of an adrenal autotransplant or a fetal neural cell transplant. After the proposal had been approved within the NIH, Dr. James Wyngaarden, NIH director, decided in October 1987 to seek higher departmental review of FTTR. In March 1988, Dr. Windom withheld approval and (there being no EAB) asked that the NIH convene an outside advisory panel to consider a list of ten questions, among which was a concern that FTTR would induce women who were ambivalent about abortion to have one. In December 1988, a 21-member advisory panel approved a report by a vote of 18–3 recommending federal funding of this research.[39] The majority argued that the use of fetal tissue was separable from the morality of abortion. Three panel members objected and dissented. This report, submitted to the director, NIH, was rejected in November 1989 by Secretary Louis B. Sullivan, who continued the earlier moratorium "indefinitely," citing as his major reason that the administration and Congress opposed any funding of activities by HHS which "encourage or promote abortion."[40] The press[41] and a letter from Rep. Weiss to Dr. Sullivan[42] cited a memorandum from HHS counsel saying that the extension of the moratorium was on a "shaky legal base" in that it does not conform with federal law requiring that such decisions be published in the Federal Register and made the subject of rule making.

Causes of the Situation

Today, virtually all federal support for research in their three areas has ceased. There is a growing wall of separation between federal and private support for any clinical research associated with elective abortion or studies of human embryos in vitro.[43] For the federal sector of science, this period recalls the Lysenko affair in the U.S.S.R. A dedicated Marxist biologist who became the dictator of Soviet biology under Stalin, Lysenko denied the physical existence of genes and elevated the influence of environmental factors on heredity. His views from 1940 to 1964 wreaked havoc with the scientific basis of Soviet agriculture and contributed to a weakened medical genetics in that nation today.

Contemporary moral opposition to research with embryos and fetuses is a type of reverse Lysenkoism. It elevates over all other considerations the fact that cells in a human preembryo and the implanted embryo have 46 human chromosomes.[44] This doctrinalized biology minimizes all later fetal development and cancels out all other moral claims except those based on the genetics of the embryo and the projection of the potential for personhood. One consequence is the abandonment of research activities related to diseases and conditions that affect millions of human sufferers. Why? There are four main causes for this situation.

Causes: Moral Status of the Embryo and Fetus

The first cause is a relatively new ethical position that appeared in the nineteenth century, especially in Roman Catholic moral reflection, holding that a human preembryo and early fetus are equal in every respect to living persons and deserve the same degree of social protection. Gordon Dunstan recalled[45] the older moral tradition from which this new idea arose, writing that it "attempted to grade the protection accorded to the nascent human being according to the stages of its development."[45] Dunstan noted that neither Christian nor Jewish morality, nor English law, gives human life absolute protection at any stage, since to do so would unfairly rule out other valid moral claims. Human life is not an end in itself but a means to other values and commitments.

To use the term "child" or impute personhood to preembryos, as does a draft executive order of the Reagan administration cited below, is a profound logical error. Michael Lockwood[46] argues that the idea of "person" is not a biological concept at all. He writes:

> A person is a being that is conscious, in the sense of having the capacity for conscious thought and experiences, but not only that: it must have the capacity for reflective consciousness and self-consciousness.[46]

Further, the claim that the preembryo and early fetus are human beings, Lockwood continues, cannot be true, because "newly fertilized human ova and week-old embryos *do not yet have brains*." The criterion of "sufficient brain life" is the most rationally compelling test of the supremely important question, "When is there a human being?" Sufficiency of brain life is clearly a researchable question that can be approached on a rational basis. To be a human being characteristically means to have a significant part or all of a brain. Before the twelfth week of pregnancy, in biologist Clifford Grobstein's view,[47] there is no evidence of enough neural substrate to posit any kind of inner experience or pain during the entire first trimester. More discussion is needed to flesh out this position, but if "brain life" is necessary for an adequate definition of a human being,[48] then claims made for equal protection of the preembryo and early implanted embryo in research have no logical standing.

In late 1988, on the eve of the NIH's panel vote on FTTR, Gary L. Bauer, then President Reagan's Assistant for Policy Development, drafted an executive order, "The Equal Protection of Children."[49]

> By the authority vested in me as President by the Constitution and laws of the United States of America, and in order to ensure that unborn and newborn children receive the same protection that is afforded other children from potentially harmful biomedical and behavioral research activities and transplantation procedures, it is hereby ordered as follows:
>
> *Section 1.* It shall be the policy of the Federal Government, to the extent permitted by law, to respect the humanity and dignity of living unborn and newborn children from the time of fertilization by protecting them from biomedical and behavioral research activities that involve greater than minimal risk of suffering, injury, or death, unless such activities are intended to directly benefit the individual research subject and the risk is justified by the anticipated benefit to the individual subject. This policy shall not be construed as restricting activities whose purpose is the development of important biomedical knowledge which cannot be obtained by other means, when such activities involve no greater than minimal risk to the subject. In determining risk, a child intended for abortion or who has been aborted may not be subjected to risk which would not be imposed on a child intended for survival. This Order also shall not be construed as overriding Federal, state or local policies which provide additional protections for unborn or newborn children.

This order was never issued. However, it is an example of that reasoning about the equality of the embryo and fetus with living human beings which has prevented research activities in the federal sector.

Causes: A Politics of Abortion

The second cause is found in a politics of abortion that began to dominate scientific and ethical considerations of research in the same period that the EAB was formed and dismantled. Ethical issues associated with fetal and embryo research were politicized and associated with partisan politics, rather than considered as issues that faced the American people to be resolved by processes other than legislative or decisions by executive order. In the earlier period in which the National Commission was formed, political leaders in both parties saw their role as "wise sponsors" of a public debate about serious issues that faced society. The commission and the EAB that followed were appointed to do a societal task. Elected or appointed officials did not politicize the issues, try to join the debate, or determine the outcome. However, once the EAB was abandoned, a moral (and political) vacuum was created which had to be filled. In a period of high abortion politics that ensued, however, elected and appointed officials have become actors in determining policy affecting ethical issues in research. This change is especially apparent in the HHS response to the FTTR debate.

A politics of abortion has its origins in opposition to the *Roe v. Wade* decision. In response, Congress separated the federal share of the costs of elective abortions for Medicaid-eligible women from other forms of state, local, and private funding. The Hyde Amendment[50] limits federal funding only to cases where two physicians attest that continuation of the pregnancy will result in severe and long-lasting damage to the woman's physical health, and in cases of reported rape and incest. From a beginning in the area of federally funded medical services, all activities in research that are associated with abortion or the loss of embryos have become unsupported and suspect in the federal sector.

The Health Research Extension Act of 1985[51] was notable for two important actions in this area: it prohibited the secretary, HHS, from using the waiver in fetal research, and it created the Congressional Biomedical Ethics Board (CBEB) with members from the House and Senate, along with a public advisory board to conduct studies and debate on fetal research, among other issues. In 1989, the CBEB collapsed under the weight of controversies about abortion before being able to begin its public work.[52] There has been no viable national forum in which to debate a score of issues related to fetal and embryo research since the President's Commission ceased to function in 1983. One more serious sign of the politics of abortion is that more than two years of the Bush administration have passed without appointment of a director of the NIH. This hiatus is largely due to the abortion politics that have dominated the decade.

Causes: Abandonment of a Due National Process

The situation's third cause is that, because of the political causes discussed above, the national dimension of the conflict resolution model required by federal regulations to debate and resolve such problems, and EAB, was abandoned in 1980. The history of the EAB and the moral vacuum created by its abandonment has been told above. To remedy this situation, Rep. Waxman introduced the Research Freedom Act of 1990 in the 101st Congress.[53] This measure would nullify the FTTR moratorium and prohibit officials in the executive branch from imposing such a policy on the NIH. The bill will establish an authority within current law for support of FTTR by or through the NIH, after proposals have been reviewed by local IRBs and scientific and technical review has occurred at the NIH. FRRT can be conducted in accordance with the several recommendations of the NIH panel, unless an EAB convened by the HHS secretary advises the withholding of funds on ethical grounds.

Causes: Problems in Federal Fetal Research Guidelines

A fourth cause is that U.S. research policy lacks a balanced set of ethically and procedurally consistent public policies to encourage and restrict federal support of investigational research in the human preembryo, pregnant women, and the fetus at all stages whether in utero or ex utero. The best point of departure for the whole project is to correct problems in the existing federal guidelines for fetal research. In my view, the commission compromised too much with a radical view of the moral status of the fetus, especially in the first trimester, which led to guidelines rooted in an untenable proposition, i.e., that the early implanted embryo is a human being deserving of equal protection with other liveborn human beings. For this reason, the first reform would be a provision for a standard of "greater than minimal" research risks in investigational research in the first trimester with all fetuses. The arguments for a higher level of acceptable research risks in the first trimester are that (1) it accords with the dominant moral tradition on fetal status, if Bok's and Dunstan's position accurately reflect this tradition, (2) it agrees with McCormick's original argument that no more and no less risk ought to be taken with a fetus than with a living child, and (3) it encourages more investigational fetal research involving only minimal risk in the context of prenatal diagnosis and fetal therapy.

The second reform would be a requirement that the only fetal research projects to be referred to an EAB for study of secretarial waiver be those that propose selectively to expose fetuses to be aborted to a level of "greater than minimal risk." The arguments for the second reform are that (1) the proposal continues the intent of the National Commission to assure protection in research of fetuses before and during abortion procedures, and (2) only the most controversial protocols will require national review.

The third reform is a clearly framed definition of minimal risk for fetal research. Arguments for clarifying the minimal risk definition were given above. Ryan and this author proposed this definition of minimal risk in the context of fetal research:

> "Minimal risk" in Subpart B means that the risks of harm anticipated in the research are not greater, considering probability and magnitude, than those encountered in the daily life of pregnant women and fetuses (receiving routine prenatal care) in the stage of gestation in which the activity is planned, or during the performance of routine obstetrical or other medical examinations or tests appropriate to that stage of gestation.[53]

Results: Five Areas of Loss

Continuation of suppression of fetal and embryo research in the federal sector results in great losses in five areas. First, the scientific knowledge base for the practice of reproductive medicine and medical genetics is stunted in comparison to the demand placed upon these specialties for clinical services. Examples abound: In the U.S. chorionic villus sampling could not be compared with amniocentesis in an optimal way, e.g., in an early, timely, randomized clinical trial in which the sponsors of the trial pay for the procedures, thus reducing the subjective biases of the patient and physician. However, in Canada and in several European nations, truly randomized trials were able to be mounted. IVF, a method of last resort to treat infertility, expensive and with very poor results, cannot be scientifically evaluated or improved using federal funds. Research on pre-embryo diagnosis, which would benefit infertile couples now, and if IVF were as effective as natural fertilization would benefit couples at higher genetic risk, is not supported by federal funds in the U.S.

An example of meritorious pre-embryo research not receiving federal support is a study submitted to the NIH from Washington University by O. H. Lowry and colleagues.[36] This study would directly address the poor results of human IVF, recognizing that today in vitro culture media are based on metabolic characteristics of animal ova and preimplantation embryos, especially those of the mouse. Lowry's laboratory can measure between 20 and 30 enzymes and as many metabolites in untransferred embryos after IVF and compare these measurements with findings already available from the mouse. The Lowry proposal cannot be approved without an EAB. An Office of Technology report[54] on infertility stated that NIH would receive at least 100 grant applications on IVF if the EAB were extant.

Secondly, health benefits to infertile couples, families at higher genetic risks, and to future fetuses needing diagnosis and possible treatment are being lost by this situation. Fetal research must precede effective fetal therapy.

Thirdly, the NIH cannot give routine scientific peer review or support such research. The NIH-private sector partnership, of such inestimable value in other areas of science, has been disrupted in reproductive medicine, medical genetics, and fetal treatment. The NIH is supported by taxes from all citizens, including those deprived of its participation, which is grossly unfair to them.

Fourth, the U.S. is not carrying its fair share of fetal and embryo research in comparison to the rest of the world, especially Australia, the United Kingdom, and some European nations. Standards of international justice, in terms of the selection of subjects and the allocation of the benefits and burdens of research, are being violated. The U.S. is a debtor nation in more than an economic sense.

Of most concern is the fifth area of loss, violation of the one of the core tenets of research ethics, scientific freedom. Suppression of the freedom of clinical research, wherever it occurs, is unethical for two reasons. First, it violates the imperative to learn to prevent harm, to alleviate human suffering, and to increase health benefits. Secondly, it hampers the obligation to learn about the true significance of risks in procedures such as prenatal diagnosis and treatment of infertility. Suppression of the search for truth in clinical research hampers the obligation to tell the truth to patients.

This paper has explained how investigational fetal research and pre-embryo research in the federal sector has been suppressed by the calculated dismantling of due national processes designed to resolve conflicts in research ethics and instituted in the 1970s. Recently, FTTR has also been subjected to unjustifiable and possibly illegal suppression. Legitimate, clinically relevant research on the causes of human infertility, diagnosis of chromosomal and genetic disorders, and treatment for these disorders is being suppressed. The causes and effects of this situation have been traced. The basic thrust of the argument is that a moral line between restriction and suppression of research has been breached by those who espouse a moral idea of embryonic-fetal equality. This situation is a moral blight on American society and its scientific community that cries out to be corrected. Scientific freedom and properly restricted research must be restored in these areas.

The author is grateful for comments on an early draft by James F. Childress, Ph.D., and Mary Faith Marshall, Ph.D.,Alexis Pinto and Felicia G. Cohn also assisted in research and revisions of this paper.

NOTE

1. I use the term preembryo following McClaren [1] and the Ethics Committee of the American Fertility Society [2].

REFERENCES

1. McLaren A. Prelude to embryogenesis. In: Ciba Foundation. Embryo research: yes or no? London: Tavistock Publications, 1986: 5–17.
2. Ethics Committee of the American Fertility Society. Ethical considerations of the new reproductive technologies. Fertil Steril 1986; 46 Suppl: 26–8.
3. National Commission for the Protection of Human Subjects of Biomedical and Behavioral Research. Report and recommendations: Research on the fetus. Washington, DC: US Government Printing Office, DHEW Publication No (OS) 76–127, 1975: 61–88.
4. Ethics Advisory Board of the U.S. Department of Health, Education, and Welfare. Report and conclusions: DHEW support of research involving in vitro fertilisation and embryo transfer, May 4, 1979; also, Fed Reg 1979; 44: 35.
5. Title 45 Code of Federal Regulations Part 46. 210 (revised March 8, 1983). National Institutes of Health: Office of Protection from Research Risks.
6. National Commission for the Protection of Human Subjects of Biomedical and Behavioral Research. The Belmont Report. April 18, 1979. U.S. Government Printing Office: 1986–181–296: 41238.

7. Beecher HK. Ethics and clinical research. N Engl J Med 1966; 274: 1354–1360. Pappworth MH. Human guinea pigs. London: Routledge & Kegan Paul, 1967.
8. 45 Code of Federal Regulations 46. 103 (2).
9. 45 Code of Federal Regulations 46. 111 (2).
10. 45 Code of Federal Regulations 46. 204 (a).
11. Jonsen AR, Toulmin S. The abuse of casuistry. Berkeley, CA: University of California Press, 1988.
12. Toulmin S. Fetal experimentation: Moral issues and institutional controls. Appendix. Research on the fetus. Washington, DC: US Government Printing Office, DHEW Publication No (OS) 76–128, 1976: 10: 1–26.
13. Webster's Third New International Dictionary, 1981.
14. 45, Code of Federal Regulations 46, Protection of Human Subjects, Subpart B, Additional Protections Pertaining to Research Development, and Related Activities Involving Fetuses, Pregnant Women, and Human In Vitro Fertilization (revised March 8, 1983).
15. Fletcher JC, Schulman JD. Fetal research: The state of the question. Hastings Cent Rep 1985; 15: 6–12.
16. Federal Register 1975; 40: 33528, August 8.
17. Cohn V. NIH vows not to fund fetus work. Washington Post, April 13, 1973: A1.
18. McCormick RA. Experimentation on the fetus: Policy proposals. Appendix. Research on the fetus. Washington, DC: US Government Printing Office, DHEW Publication No (OS) 76–128, 1976: 5: 1–11.
19. Walters L. Ethical and public policy issues in fetal research. Appendix. Research on the fetus. Washington, DC: US Government Printing Office, DHEW Publication No (OS) 76–128, 1976: 8: 1–18.
20. McCormick RA. Proxy consent in the experimentation situation. Perspec Biol Med 1974; 18: 2–20.
21. McCormick RA. How brave a new world? Washington, DC: Georgetown University Press, 1981: 76.
22. Bok S. Fetal research and the value of life. Appendix. Research on the fetus. Washington, DC: US Government Printing Office, DHEW Publication No (OS) 76–128, 1976: 2: 1–18.
23. Department of Health and Social Security. Report of the Advisory Group. The use of fetuses and fetal material for research. London: Her Majesty's Stationery Office, 1972.
24. Fletcher JF. Fetal research: An ethical appraisal. Appendix. Research on the fetus. Washington, DC: US. Government Printing Office, DHEW Publication No (OS) 76–128, 1978: 3: 1–14.
25. National Commission for the Protection of Human Subjects of Biomedical and Behavioral Research. Report and recommendations. Research on the fetus. Washington, DC: US Government Printing Office, DHEW Publication No (OS) 76–127, 1975: 67.
26. National Commission. Research on the fetus. 1975: 66.
27. National Commission for the Protection of Human Subjects of Biomedical and Behavioral Research. Research involving children. Report and recommendations. 1977: xx, DHEW Publication No (OS) 77–0004; Fed Reg 1975; 40: 33529.
28. 45 Code of Federal Regulations 46. 102 (g).
29. 45 Code of Federal Regulations 46. 303 (d).
30. The NICHD National Registry for Amniocentesis Study Group. Midtrimester amniocentesis for prenatal diagnosis: Safety and accuracy. JAMA 1976; 236: 1471–1476.
31. 45 Code of Federal Regulations 46. 206 (2).
32. 45 Code of Federal Regulations 46. 203.
33. National Commission. Research involving children. 1977: 7–8.
34. 45 Code of Federal Regulations 46. 406.
35. Steinfels M. At the EAB. Same members, new ethical problems. Hastings Cent Rep 1979; 5:2.
36. Norman C. IVF moratorium to end? Science 1988; 241: 405.

37. Department of Health, Education, and Welfare. Memorandum to the Secretary. Action: In vitro fertilization and embryo transfer. October 29, 1979.
38. Squires S. Groups plan advisory board for fetal tissue research. Washington Post 1991 Jan 8; Sect A.
39. Report of the Human Fetal Tissue Transplantion Research Panel. Vol. 1. Bethesda, MD. National Institutes of Health, Dec. 1988; Specter M. Draft report backs fetal tissue use. The Washington Post 1988 Oct 22; Sect A: 10.
40. Sullivan LB to Raub WF. [Letter] Nov. 2, 1989.
41. Hilts PJ. US aides seek shaky legal basis for ban on fetal tissue research. New York Times, January 30, 1990: A1.
42. Weiss T to Sullivan LB. [Letter], January 26, 1990.
43. Fletcher JC. Fetal tissue transplantation research and federal policy. A growing wall of separation. Fetal Diagnosis and Therapy 1990; 5: 211–225.
44. Blechschmidt E. Human being from the very first. In: Hilgers TW, Horan DJ, Mall D, eds. New perspectives on human abortion. Frederick: MD: University Publications of America, 1981: 1981: 6–28.
45. Dunstan GR. The moral status of the human embryo. A tradition recalled. J Med Ethics 1984; 1: 38–44.
46. Lockwood M. When does a life begin? In: Lockwood M, ed. Moral dilemmas in modern medicine. Oxford: Oxford University Press, 1985: 9–31.
47. Grobstein C. From chance to purpose. Reading, MA: Addison-Wesley, 1981: 75–103; also see Grobstein, Science and the unborn. New York: Basic Books, 1988: 54–55.
48. Sass HM. Brain life and brain death. A proposal for normative agreement. J Med Philos 1989; 14: 45–59.
49. Bauer GL. Executive Order. The Equal Protection of Children (draft). September 2, 1988.
50. The language of the original Hyde Amendment as introduced is found in the House Congressional Record, p. 20410 (June 24, 1976). The Hyde Amendment became law in 1976 but did not take effect until after a Supreme Court ruling. Depts. of Labor and Health Education and Welfare Appropriations Act of 1977. Pub. Law 94–439, Sec. 209, 90 Stat. 1418, p. 1434 (signed into law Sept. 1976).
51. Health Research Extension Act of 1985, Public Law 99–158, November 20, 1985.
52. The story of the rise and fall of this congressional attempt to establish a national ethics body is told by Robert Cook-Deegan, Kennedy Institute Newsletter, Fall 1990.
53. Fletcher JC, Ryan KJ. Federal regulations for fetal research: A case for reform. Law, Med & Health Care 1987; 15: 136.
54. US Congress, Office of Technology Assessment. Infertility. Medical and social choices. OTA-BA-358. Washington, DC: US Government Printing Office, 1988: 297.

JOHN A. ROBERTSON

Two Problems in Embryo Research

Controversies over prenatal human life also extend to the use of fetuses and embryos in biomedical research. These concerns first arose around 1973, when abortion in the United States was first recognized as a constitutional right, and reports surfaced that fetuses destined for abortion were the objects of experimentation, and that live aborted fetuses were being used inappropriately in research.

A national ethical commission examined these questions in 1975, and developed a set of guidelines for fetal research that were incorporated into regulations for federally funded research.[1] Its distinctions between research on fetuses going to term, fetuses destined for abortion, and on live and dead fetuses are ethically sound, and widely accepted. Their much-applauded work, however, has not made federal funds available for fetal research.[2]

The most recent controversy in fetal research – transplantation of tissue from aborted fetuses – appeared to be an easy case in 1975. The national commission's recommendation that dead fetal tissue be treated like other cadaveric tissue is also part of current federal regulations.[3] It may be used in research if obtained in accordance with the consent requirements of state or local law. When the possibility of using fetal tissue to treat Parkinson's disease arose in the late 1980s, antiabortionist groups challenged this provision as encouraging women to have abortions. Although a National Institutes of Health task force found that use of cadaveric fetal tissue in experimental transplants was ethically acceptable, the secretary of Health and Human Services agreed with the antiabortion groups and banned federal funding for such research.[4] Until the Clinton administration overturned this ban in January, 1993, this position left researchers free to proceed with fetal tissue research if non-federal research support were available.

Lost in the debates about fetal research has been considered attention to research at postconception prefetal stages of development – with fertilized eggs, zygotes, blastocysts, and other preimplantation stages of human life. While addressed initially in 1978 by the Ethics Advisory Board in the United States, and subsequently by ethics advisory boards in other countries, embryo research has received little recent attention.[5] Developments in in vitro fertil-

F.K. Beller and R.F. Weir (eds.), The Beginning of Human Life, 207–223.

ization (IVF), in cryopreservation of embryos, and in preimplantation genetic diagnosis should bring renewed interest to issues of embryo research, thus making a survey of the field of interest.

After briefly discussing the interest in and need for embryo research, I will comment on two questions in embryo research: (1) is embryo research ethical? and (2) is such research legal?[6] I will then illustrate problems related to these two questions with a discussion of preimplantation genetic diagnosis of embryos.

The Interest in and Need for Embryo Research

Preimplantation embryos are potentially valuable research vehicles for many issues in prenatal development, organogenesis, cancer research, birth defects, and a variety of issues related to contraception and assisted reproduction.

Of most immediate interest, however, is the need for research with human embryos in order to improve the efficacy of assisted reproductive techniques. As diagnostic tests improve, embryos will also be used in research directed to screening of embryos and eventually to gene therapy on the embryo. For example, some forms of assisted reproduction involve creating embryos and placing them in the uterus of a woman with the intent that they will implant and come to term. At least in the earliest stages of use of these techniques, such actions might constitute research on the embryo, the women, or the resulting child.

In other cases, research might occur on spare embryos produced in the IVF process, with studies of those embryos occurring before they are discarded or allowed to divide without placement in the uterus. Finally, there are instances where egg and sperm will be brought together solely for experimental purposes, to see if fertilizations might occur, as with microinjection of sperm or attempts at fertilization of eggs that have been frozen and thawed. In these cases the embryos are created for research purposes with no intention or possibility of later transfer.

The most recent example of embryo research is occurring in the area of preimplantation genetic diagnosis.[7] Couples at risk for serious genetic disease in offspring have been offered the possibility of undergoing IVF, with the resulting embryos then biopsied and genetically diagnosed, and only nonaffected embryos placed in the uterus. The first efforts at embryo biopsy are clearly experimental on the embryo, because they may affect its well-being and its ability to implant and come to term. This area holds promise for couples at risk, since it could enable them to avoid the burdens of later prenatal diagnosis and abortion. A ban on embryo research would prevent these techniques from becoming available.

With these needs and possibilities, we can see that use of embryos in research is an area of growing interest and importance. Even if federal government funding of such research is not forthcoming, more embryo research can be expected at private hands. Questions of its ethical and legal acceptability are likely to arise once again, and therefore deserve new attention. These are the two problems in embryo research which I wish to address.

Problem One: Is Embryo Research Ethically Acceptable?

The central question in embryo research is whether it is ethically acceptable at all, and if so, under what circumstances and with what safeguards. While some commentators continue to ask this question as if it were a novel issue of bioethics, the question is neither new nor novel. With the advent of IVF in the late 1970s and early 1980s, prestigious and authoritative government ethical advisory bodies in the United States, Great Britain, Canada, Australia, and other Western nations examined this question. The resulting consensus shows the major fault lines of this debate.

The Consensus on Embryo Research

At the most general level, these bodies uniformly agreed that embryo research for valid scientific purposes, conducted as part of an IRB-reviewed research protocol, was ethically acceptable.[8] Since embryos were not persons or subjects with interests, and were at too rudimentary a stage to be harmed, such research could ethically occur. Thus there was no need to treat embryo research more restrictively than research on infants or adults, or other human-subject research.

There was also widespread agreement that embryo research to improve the safety and efficacy of IVF was a legitimate and acceptable purpose.[9] Some reports, however, suggested that this was the only acceptable purpose for embryo research, while others made no such restriction. But the purpose of the research should not affect its ethical acceptability if it otherwise meets ethical guidelines.

Third, there was clear consensus that such research was acceptable on embryos that were not going to be placed in a uterus, e.g., were going to be discarded or allowed to deteriorate without transfer.[10] If embryo discard were planned, the research could not then affect the well-being of resulting children, a major concern with in utero fetal research when a pregnancy was going to term. Indeed, some reports went so far as to recommend against any research on embryos that would be placed in a uterus, because of the feared impact of experimental procedures on future offspring. But it should now be clear that if the research is designed to avert harm to future offspring – is done for their benefit – the fact that it is done at the embryo level should not matter. Research on embryos or fetuses for the benefit of the resulting child is clearly ethical (when the other conditions of ethical research are met).

Fourth, there was almost universal agreement that no embryos should be kept alive in the laboratory without the possibility of transfer for more than 14 days.[11] Since 14 days would have marked the end of implantation and the development of the primitive streak and first signs of a nervous system, it was thought that this limit would prevent actual harm to more mature embryos and early fetuses. At present, this limit is easy to live with, since no researcher appears able to maintain an embryo in vitro for that period of time. When that ability develops and the need to experiment for longer periods appears, then this line should be reassessed. If there is a legitimate need for such research, the question of whether embryos at peri-implantation stages can be harmed, and thus whether such research should be permitted, can be addressed.

Fifth, many ethical advisory bodies also agreed that embryos could be created solely for research purposes with no intention to implant them afterwards. This issue led to strong dissents on the Warnock Committee, and to prohibition in Australia and in some other European countries.[12] It has been the most contentious issue in the whole embryo research debate. But in most places, there was seen to be no significant moral difference between doing research on embryos that were going to be discarded, and creating them for research and discard.

Given the remarkable consensus that emerged from these prestigious ethical advisory bodies, there should be no question in 1993 that research with embryos to improve assisted reproduction, as well as for other legitimate biomedical purposes, is ethically acceptable as part of a research protocol that has been reviewed by an IRB, and has the informed consent of the gamete providers, etc. It should also be acceptable in some cases to implant embryos that have been the object of research in order than they may come to terms, and even to create them for research (though there is more controversy on this point). While maintenance beyond 14 days is not currently acceptable, that barrier should be reevaluated as progress occurs and the need for such research arises.

However, because these issues have been controversial, and are likely to heat up again, I would like to address further the two central issues: the ethical acceptability of embryo research, and the ethical acceptability of creating embryos for research with no intention to transfer.

The Ethical Acceptability of Embryo Research

The most basic question is why embryo research is ethical at all. The question is raised, not because there is any doubt about possible benefits, but because of the costs or harms to embryos which, by definition, cannot consent to the research. The normative acceptability of embryo research thus depends upon whether such research harms the embryos in an ethically unacceptable way.

This issue is usually presented as a problem of research with an unconsenting subject, which is ordinarily considered ethically problematic, if not prohibited. Since embryos are human subjects, and cannot give consent to research on them, some persons argue that their use in research would violate the basic norm of no research with unconsenting human subjects.

But this claim is wrong on several counts, as the ethical advisory commissions intuited, even if they did not say so directly. The embryo is human in species, but that fact alone does not make it a human subject to which consent and other rules apply. While a minority of persons believe that fertilized eggs and embryos are persons or human subjects with all the rights of human subjects, the overwhelming ethical and legal view is that embryos are not yet persons or moral subjects in their own right.[13] Because of their very rudimentary biologic development, they consist of a few undifferentiated cells. There is no nervous system or developed organs. The first differentiation is to a trophoblastic or placental layer, and only then do organs and a nervous system develop. Indeed, individuality is not assured until after implantation.

Given this state of development, embryos are too rudimentary to have interests in their own right, much less rights. At this stage, they cannot be harmed, for they lack the very requirements for harm – the capacity to have interests. Because of their potential to develop into fetuses and newborns, embryos have more symbolic importance than other human tissue. But they have no rights or interests in themselves.

At this stage, then, the question of consent simply is not relevant. Nor is the concept of harm. Embryos are not human subjects in the sense that that term has meaning in the ethics of human experimentation, because they lack interests or the capacity to be harmed. Therefore, research with them is not unethical, because it cannot harm them. While symbolic concerns may arise, issues of rights or justice toward embryos do not. Indeed, given their very rudimentary development, the symbolic harms or costs to notions of respect for human life appear to be very small, compared to the scientific and medical benefits of using them in many kinds of research. It they are used in a legitimate research project in order to increase usable medical knowledge, the symbolic harm is neither so clear nor so certain that it outweighs the benefits to others to be derived from the research.

Finally, it should be noted that even if one believes that embryos are persons or human subjects, it would not follow that no research should occur because they cannot give consent. Research may ethically be done on nonconsenting subjects as long as it poses minimal risk to them or is for their benefit.[14] On this principle, minimal-risk research on embryos should also be permitted. Since embryos are too rudimentary in development to be harmed, embryo research is necessarily of minimal risk and should be permitted. The mere fact that they are being used as a means does not in itself make research unethical, because may acceptable human activities, including human experimentation, involve treating the subject as a means. The important question is whether use as a means is sufficiently respectful of the subject's other interests so that they are not treated as a "mere" means. If the embryos will be placed in the uterus, with the intent of bringing them to term, then the research does not harm them. If likely to benefit resulting offspring, it should also be permitted. If the research is on embryos that will be discarded, the concept of respect or harm in terms of the embryo's own rights or interests simply does not apply.

Given this analysis, it is not surprising that embryo research is deemed ethically acceptable for reproductive or other purposes. It would also be acceptable whether or not transfer to the uterus is intended, within the 14-day limit. Most embryo research should therefore be ethically acceptable.

Creating Embryos Solely for Research Purposes

Even if research on some embryos is deemed ethically acceptable, some persons would draw the line at creating embryos solely for research purposes. They find embryo research ethically acceptable if performed on embryos created in the IVF process that will not be transferred to a uterus. However, they object to research on embryos created solely for research purposes, with no intention of placement in the uterus.

They vigor with which this distinction is drawn is seen in the dissenting opinions in the Warnock Committee.[15] While the Committee agreed on a wide range of novel noncoital reproductive techniques, including egg and embryo donation and embryo freezing, it sharply disagreed on this issue. Victoria also saw a significant moral boundary here, and outlawed such research, as have certain European countries.[16] It is thus useful to examine this claim to see if there is an ethically significant difference between research on unwanted embryos created in the IVF process and research on embryos created solely for research purposes.

The issue thus posed is whether creating embryos solely for research and discard is unethical, even if it is granted that research on embryos resulting from IVF that will not be transferred is ethically acceptable. I do not see a morally significant difference in the two cases. Any difference is purely symbolic. Since symbols do not make the same moral claim on us that subjects with interests do, we are not morally required to pursue symbolic goals.[17] If we deem them outweighted by other concerns, such as the benefits to persons of the resulting research, then such research may ethically occur.

It should be clear that there is no moral difference – in terms of impact on embryos – in the two cases. If research on embryos created for reproductive purposes is ethically acceptable because they are too rudimentary to have interests and hence be harmed, then it should not matter – in terms of impact on embryos – whether the embryos are created for that purpose or were created for other purposes. In either case the research will be occurring on a rudimentary entity that lacks the capacity for harm. If the embryo cannot be harmed when already existing, then it cannot be harmed if it is created solely for research purposes. As a matter of morality or justice toward embryos, no harm occurs in either case. Therefore, it is not morally significant whether embryos are created for research or for other purposes and then used in research.

The difference in the two cases is symbolic only. While symbolic values or interests are also important, they are not obligatory and can be given up to serve other goals without injustice to anyone. Choosing not to obtain a symbolic goal does not violate anyone's rights, and may be chosen or not as a matter of policy.[18]

Persons who accept research on embryos created for other purposes but object to creating embryos solely for research are, in my view, making a symbolic statement about embryos. Their concern is not with the rights of embryos as such, but rather with the meaning or attitude toward human life which such actions, in their minds, symbolize. They believe that creating embryos solely for research is wrong because it denotes or symbolizes an attitude that all forms or stages of human life are not worthy of protection.[19] To them, it shows an attitude of willingness to sacrifice human life for other, utilitarian goals.

Now it may be that persons holding that view are being inconsistent if they accept research on embryos created for other purposes. One may also disagree with their claim about what the practice of creating embryos solely for research conveys. But even if we grant some such symbolic message from this form of embryo research (indeed, from other forms of embryo research as well), the question is now one of policy, not of ethics. Is the knowledge likely to result from the research in question of sufficient importance that it justifies the symbolic costs perceived in undertaking the research? Is the symbolic message so important, given that other embryo research is accepted, that important scientific or medical benefits should be forgone in order to make that symbolic point?

In my view it is inconsistent to say that the symbolic cost of research on spare embryos created for reproductive purposes is acceptable, but not if the research occurs on embryos created solely for that purpose. Since research will be occurring on embryos at exactly the same stage of development, and there may be no other way to carry out the research in question, the more persuasive position is that such research should be permitted. Given that many kinds of research cannot occur unless embryos are created solely for research purposes, a reasonable case can be made that the benefits of that research outweigh any symbolic cost to life from creating embryos solely for research purposes.[20]

It may be useful to compare deliberate creation of embryos for research with deliberate creation of fetuses to be aborted in order to obtain tissue for transplant. The fear that women will do precisely that has lurked in the background of the debate in the United States over the use of tissue from aborted fetuses for transplantation. A careful analysis of the competing ethical considerations, however, shows that a reasonable case permitting abortion to obtain tissue for transplant can be made.[21] For example, in a case where no other source of tissue for transplant is available, as where a genetic match is necessary, a woman might ethically conceive and abort in order to obtain the necessary tissue to save the life or health of herself, her husband, her children, or her parents. If abortion is otherwise permissible, e.g., for family planning reasons, and tissue from aborted fetuses may be used for transplant, then conceiving and aborting for transplant should also be permissible.

Abortion to save the life of a close family member would seem to be as worthy a purpose as aborting because the pregnancy is unwanted. However, there may be a significant symbolic difference in attitudes toward human life and fetuses. The importance of that symbol must then be weighed against the need to save a person's life. One might thus reasonably find that conception and abortion to obtain tissue for transplant is ethically acceptable in certain cases.

But while the analysis is similar in both cases, accepting that embryos may be created solely for transplant purposes does not necessarily entail that one also accept conception and abortion to procure tissue for transplant. The most important difference in the two cases is that one concerns embryos and the other fetuses. Given the rudimentary nature of embryos, the notion that they lack interests and that discard and manipulation of them has little symbolic cost is more easily accepted. One may so argue about fetuses as well, but they are a different entity, at a more advanced stage of development. The symbolic costs as well as the possibility at some point in the pregnancy of harming the fetus in its own right are higher at this later stage of development. But if fetuses are viewed as not having interests, then the reason or motivation for the abortion should not matter (except symbolically). On the other hand, if fetuses can be harmed to avert the burdens of unwanted pregnancy, why could they not be harmed to achieve the even more important goal of saving one's own life or that of a close relative?

Problem Two: Is Embryo Research Legal?

Having seen that the first problem of embryo research – whether it is ethical at all – must be answered in the positive, and that even creating embryos solely for research purposes is ethically acceptable, I now turn to the second problem of embryo research – its legality.

I would like to focus on the legal situation in the United States, and ask two questions: (1) is embryo research now legal? (2) may the state constitutionally ban such research? Before addressing those questions, however, let me note that embryo research with spare embryos is generally legal around the world, and in most countries research on embryos created solely for research purposes is also legal. Only West Germany appeared to ban embryo research for all purposes, but that position has not yet been officially adopted into law. A few jurisdictions do limit research with embryos created solely for that purpose, but allow it with embryos created for other purposes.[22]

The Legality of Embryo Research in the United States

The question of the legality of embryo research in the United States must distinguish between funding restrictions and direct prohibitions of such research. At the present time the federal government does not fund embryo or fetal research, but there is no federal law against the conduct of such research with nonfederal funds. Indeed, the lack of federal funding is not even direct, but results from the absence of the Ethics Advisory Board, which under federal regulations is needed to approve applications for federal funds for embryo and fetal research.[23]

Although not federally supported, embryo research is lawful in the United States except in those states that have enacted legislation that restricts that research. In the middle 1970s twenty-five states enacted laws to restrict fetal research. Although these laws were inspired by concerns about research on fetuses, fifteen of the states used such terms as "embryo," "conceptus," "product of conception," "unborn child," or other language that might appear to apply to research activities with embryos.[24]

A closer look at these statutes, however, leads to the conclusion that they are most likely to apply to preimplantation embryo research in only four states. First, they were written with the purpose of restricting fetal, not embryo, research. Second, terms that could be read to include preimplantation embryos are either specifically defined as or used in a context where the use of implanted embryos, fetuses, or aborted fetuses is contemplated, not preimplantation embryos.

In four states (Minnesota, Massachusetts, North Dakota, and Rhode Island), one could argue that the operative definitions of the fetal research laws would include prohibitions on embryo research. However, even here the ban is not as broad as it might seem. Massachusetts (North Dakota and Rhode Island copy its statute) does not prohibit "diagnostic or remedial procedures the purpose of which is . . . to preserve the life or health of the [embryo] involved."[25] Thus embryo research designed to enable that embryo to be transferred to a uterus and brought to term would not be prohibited if, absent the research, the embryo would not be transferred. Arguably, then, embryo research (such as research in embryo biopsy and genetic diagnosis) that will enable those embryos to be transferred would be permitted in Massachusetts, even if research on embryos that will be discarded is prohibited.

Even that limit might not apply in Minnesota, which exempts from its ban on "any type of . . . research or experimentation" on "a living human conceptus" that research "which verifiable scientific evidence has shown to be harmless to the conceptus."[26] Since early embryos do not have a nervous system and are clearly not sentient, one could reasonably argue that research could not harm them, and thus might be permitted. Of course, persons who view the embryo as having interests and rights would argue the opposite. Given Minnesota's current ban on embryo discard, the dispute on this point may be academic.[27]

Two other states – New Mexico and Pennsylvania – have laws that restrict fetal research with such broad language that some kinds of embryo research, including preimplantation genetic diagnosis, might not be permitted. For example, Pennsylvania, which defines "unborn child" to include fertilized eggs, bans "any type of nontherapeutic experimentation upon any unborn child."[28]

New Mexico, which has a comparably broad definition of fetus, specifically excludes any IVF research that does not "insure that each living fertilized ovum, zygote or embryo is implanted in a human female recipient."[29]

Both Pennsylvania and New Mexico, therefore, would appear to prohibit nontherapeutic embryo research. Thus preimplantation diagnostic research on embryos that will not result in the transfer of the embryos may be illegal in those states, though research that does lead to transfer may be acceptable.

A reasonable conclusion is that embryo research, including preimplantation genetic-diagnosis research with embryos, whether followed by transfer or discard, is legally permissible in all but four to six states at the present time. In those states, however, such research might be permissible if designed to enable transfer to the uterus to occur. While research on embryos to be discarded is more clearly prohibited in those states, there may be some leeway for research on spare embryos created in the IVF process that will not be transferred.[22] Such research might be viewed as "harmless" to the embryo and be permitted in Minnesota. It may even be acceptable in Pennsylvania and New Mexico if the embryos were not created specifically for research purposes.[30]

It should be noted that these restrictions apply only to research or experimentation with embryos. They would not apply to procedures with embryos that are done primarily to enable a healthy child to be born, and not to acquire information as part of a research protocol. In any event, researchers in any of the fifteen states that might conceivably ban embryo research should seek further legal advice before embarking on research that uses human embryos.

Constitutional Limits on State Restriction of Embryo Research

While only a few states have enacted laws that appear to restrict embryo research, more laws may be enacted as new forms of embryo research occur and public controversy over abortion continues. An important question, therefore, is whether there are constitutional limits on state restriction of embryo research. The requirement that statutes be precise and that they not interfere with reproductive freedom are the main constitutional barriers to such state laws.

Vagueness

Laws must be sufficiently precise that they give a reasonable person fair notice of what is permitted. Precise laws also prevent arbitrary enforcement. Two state laws on fetal and embryo research have been struck down on grounds of vagueness, suggesting that others may be vulnerable.[31]

The most recent decision was handed down in April 1990 by a federal district court in Illinois confronted with a challenge to an Illinois law that banned "experiment(s) upon a fetus produced by the fertilization of a human ovum by a human sperm unless such experimentation is therapeutic to the fetus thereby produced."[32] Although the court could have found that the term "fetus" was vague, in that it was unclear that it included fertilized eggs and embryos, it found vagueness in the terms "experimentation" and "therapeutic." A reasonable physician would have no way of knowing whether prenatal diagnostic procedures or extensions of basic IVF or experimental procedures for the benefit of a pregnant women were banned or permitted.[33] Accordingly, the law was void for vagueness.

The decisions in *Margaret S. v. Edwards* and *Lifchez v. Hartigan* suggest that there are major constitutional problems with existing embryo research laws. None of them appear to give a clear idea of which procedures are permitted and which are not, and indeed, whether they apply only to implanted embryos or fetuses or to extracorporeal embryos as well. The reasoning of these cases suggests that it would be difficult to enact a law that defined "experimentation," "research," "therapeutic," and "nontherapeutic" precisely enough to meet constitutional requirements of precision.[34] However, if a state is willing to spell out distinctions in circumstances and procedures, it is possible that laws banning some kinds of embryo (or fetal) research could be drafted to a reasonable degree of certainty.

Procreative Liberty

Embryo research laws, even if precisely drawn, may be open to constitutional attack on the ground that they interfere with reproductive decision making. Laws that prohibit embryo biopsy or embryo discard impinge on the procreative liberty of couples at risk for genetic disease. They bar access to information essential to the couple's decision to reproduce. If the information is available, they may require that embryo transfer occur and thus prevent a couple from avoiding reproduction.

Although not mentioned specifically in the Constitution, some degree of procreative liberty seems to be constitutionally protected. A person's right, prior to conception, not to procreate is well established, and continues until viability of pregnancy has occurred.[35] A right to reproduce no doubt would be recognized for married couples seeking to reproduce coitally, and arguably would exist for noncoital reproduction with their own gametes.[36] A cogent argument for extending the right of noncoital reproduction to gamete and embryo donors and even to surrogates can also be articulated.[37]

State restrictions on the use of preimplantation diagnostic techniques directly interferes with procreative liberty by limiting a couple's access to information essential to make procreative decisions. They limit information that is material to a couple's decision whether to proceed with or to avoid reproduction.[38] Embryo research laws that prevent preimplantation genetic research or other research that is central to a couple's decision about having a family are thus constitutionally suspect, even if they are precisely drawn. Maintaining symbolic respect for early embryos or preventing eugenic decisions are not sufficiently compelling interests to justify such restrictions. Indeed, the court in *Lifchez* also found the Illinois ban on fetal research to be invalid because it intruded upon constitutionally protected choices about procreation.[39]

Is Regulation Needed?

One may ask whether legislation is needed to regulate research with embryos. From my analysis it should be clear that I think that a wide range of embryo research is permissible, and should not be banned. Indeed, a legal ban runs the risk of being found unconstitutional.

What forms of regulation are needed? One is to assure that consent of the gamete providers is obtained. A second is to assure that embryo research has prior approval of institutional review boards, just as other human-subjects research does. A third issue concerns whether money should be paid to donors. Since creation of embryos is itself expensive, I think that some payment to help recoup the costs of embryo production would not be amiss. However, bans on payments for embryos donated to research would be acceptable as long as an adequate supply of embryos is forthcoming.

Application: The Case of Preimplantation Genetic Diagnosis

Let us now apply this analysis of ethical and legal issues in embryo research to one area in which research with embryos is now likely to occur – research in preimplantation genetic diagnosis of embryos. With many advances in human genetics and micromanipulation of embryos occurring, many centers are now exploring the possibility of combining the two. Genetic diagnosis of embryos will allow those embryos with serious genetic defects to be screened out, and either not transferred or eventually to be the subject of embryonic gene therapy.

At present, however, the main focus of the research is to provide preimplantation screening for couples at risk for offspring with serious genetic disease as an alternative to later prenatal diagnosis and abortion. A team in Great Britain has reported two births of children who had been examined at the embryonic level and found to be negative for the genetic disease for which they were at risk.[40] An international symposium on this topic was held in September 1990 in Chicago, suggesting that rapid progress and endeavors in this area are likely.[41]

Preimplantation genetic diagnosis of embryos occurs by drilling the zona pellucida of four- to eight-cell embryos, aspirating one or two blastomeres, subjecting them to genetic diagnosis through polymerase chain reaction, and, depending on whether the results are positive or negative, either placing or not placing the embryo in the uterus. It functions as a very early form of prenatal diagnosis, substituting embryo examination and discard for chorion villus sampling/amniocentesis and abortion.

Ethical Issues in Preimplantation Embryo Research

Preimplantation genetic diagnosis of embryos raises several ethical issues beyond issues of embryo research. Concerns have been raised about its eugenic nature, its burdens on women (who might not be undergoing IVF), and its opening the door to more questionable procedures, such as gene therapy or engineering of offspring characteristics.[42] In addition, some persons will object to preimplantation diagnosis because it will cause embryos to be discarded rather than placed in the uterus.

In my view, the claim that preimplantation genetic diagnosis should not, on ethical grounds, be available to couples at risk for offspring with severe genetic disease cannot be sustained. If established as safe and effective, it will offer carrier couples an attractive alternative to their current options of adoption, donor gametes, no children, or possible abortion. Some women will prefer to undergo ovarian stimulation, egg retrieval, and in vitro conception rather than taking the risk of carrying an affected fetus that will then be aborted.

Preimplantation diagnosis is no more eugenic than genetic screening at the carrier or prenatal level. While it can lead to the discard of affected embryos, including those that have a 50 percent risk of being affected, it seems preferable to have prenatal selection occur at this stage rather than at a later stage when abortion is necessary. Discard of embryos is clearly preferable to later abortion, and should be an available option for those couples who are willing to undergo IVF rather than coital conception. Nor do slippery slope concerns justify a brake on preimplantation genetic diagnosis. Many of the alleged fears may not turn out to be so horrible when closely examined, e.g., germline therapy, or may not be so likely to occur that they justify excluding couples from a technique that in itself is acceptable.[43]

But developing and perfecting preimplantation diagnosis will require research with embryos. Research is essential to perfect micromanipulation techniques, to determine whether the genetic diagnosis of blastomeres is accurate, and to identify the best conditions for assuring that biopsied embryos will implant and come to term. Would embryo research to perfect preimplantation diagnosis be ethically acceptable? Is it currently lawful in the United States? May it constitutionally be banned?

If embryo research is ethically acceptable, then there should be no objection to embryo research in the service of preimplantation diagnosis. The goal of developing embryo screening techniques to deselect embryos with serious genetic defect is clearly a legitimate research goal. It carries forward the general obstetrical project of providing to women at the earliest possible time information about the characteristics of potential offspring so that therapeutic or avoidance measures may be taken. If this option is ethically acceptable once shown to be safe and effective, research to develop that option should also be acceptable.

Several kinds of embryo research directed to this goal should then be ethically acceptable. For example, research on spare IVF embryos to determine how best to drill the zona and aspirate blastomeres would pose no additional ethical problems to research on spare embryos generally. Indeed, as I have argued above, creating embryos solely for this research purpose, if spare embryos were not available, should also be acceptable.

Nor would the impact of such research on embryos that might be placed in the uterus make such research unethical. Embryos that test negative after biopsy would be placed in the uterus; those that test positive would be discarded (that is, not transferred). Transfer of embryos that test negative is designed to enable the couple to have a healthy child. Although biopsy might lead to some normal embryos being damaged and not implanting, the research is nevertheless for the purpose of enabling those embryos to be implanted and to come to term. It clearly benefits resulting offspring, and the couple seeking a healthy child. If preimplantation diagnosis were not available, these embryos might never have been created or been implanted. Thus such research may be reasonably viewed as enabling the embryos created to be implanted, even though some may be damaged in the process.

What about the impact on embryos that are not transferred because they test positive? If the embryos that test positive have the genetic disease in question, one cannot easily argue that it is unethical to discard them. If abortion of fetuses with this condition is acceptable (as it would be for all except persons generally against abortion) certainly it should be acceptable to discard or not transfer embryos, which are at a much earlier stage of development. Even if one rejected abortion of fetuses with this condition, one might still accept embryo discard because the embryo is so different developmentally from the fetus.[44] Given that most people and commentators find embryo discard ethically acceptable, discard of affected embryos *a fortiori* follows.

But half of the embryos that test positive will in fact be normal, as in the case of determining the sex of embryos at risk for X-linked genetic disease. In that case only female embryos will be placed in the uterus.[45] Male embryos will not be transferred, because of the 50 percent risk that they have the condition sought to be averted. But discard of embryos with a 50 percent chance of being normal is not per se unethical. Given that nontransfer of spare IVF embryos is accepted by most people and commentators, even though the embryos appear normal, nontransfer of embryos that have a 50 percent risk of being affected should also be acceptable. The fact that embryo biopsy research will lead to the nontransfer of some embryos that may be normal is not therefore a compelling reason against conducting such research.

In a strict sense the research does not benefit those embryos. But neither does it harm them. The ethical acceptability of embryo research does not depend on showing that research benefits the embryo – it is at too rudimentary a stage to be benefited or to be harmed. Transfer of embryos that have been the object of research is not essential to make embryo research acceptable. If it were, one could still argue that the research is beneficial to the embryos as a whole, even though some will be transferred and some will not be, because it enables some embryos to be transferred that, but for the preimplantation genetic screening, would not have been created and transferred at all.

Legal Issues in Preimplantation Embryo Research

Having seen that embryo research designed to make preimplantation diagnosis safe and effective is ethically acceptable, I want to comment briefly on the legality of such research in the United States.

As noted previously, some states have laws restricting research with fetuses and embryos that might apply to some kinds of preimplantation embryo research. This will depend upon the definition of fetus in the jurisdiction, and whether the research is seen as benefiting or harming embryos. In a very few states, such research might presently be illegal, even though the same procedures done with therapeutic rather than research intent would not be illegal.[46]

But even if state laws do ban embryo research, the question of their constitutionality remains. Such laws would be vulnerable to attack on grounds of vagueness and as interferences with procreative liberty. The latter ground would invalidate even precisely drawn prohibitions on preimplantation genetic diagnosis research. Since a general ban on prenatal diagnostic techniques would violate procreative liberty, a ban on preimplantation diagnosis would violate procreative liberty as well.[47] Since research is necessary to develop those techniques, a ban on research that interfered with women obtaining access to prenatal diagnosis would also violate constitutional rights. A woman's fundamental right to reproduce or not protects the right to the information essential to make that decision. The state's concern with protecting embryos and demonstrating respect for human life would not justify interference with fundamental constitutional rights.

Two major problems in embryo research are (1) whether it is ethical, and (2) whether it is legal. This article has shown that it is ethical in most circumstances, and is also generally legal in the United States. State laws which ban such research are vulnerable to constitutional attack on grounds of vagueness and interference with reproductive liberty.

Given this conclusion, there should be no major barriers to physicians, institutions, and patients participating in such research, as the example of embryo research aimed at developing preimplantation genetic diagnosis of embryos shows. Careful attention to the competing considerations leads one to conclude that embryo research is indeed an ethically acceptable and constitutionally available technique for acquiring medical knowledge.

NOTES

1. For an account of these developments, see Fletcher and Ryan, Federal Regulations for Fetal Research: A Case for Reform, 1987; 15:126, 127 Law, Medicine and Health Care. See also 45 C.F.R. 46 (Subpart B-Additional Protections Pertaining to Research, Development, and Related Activities Involving Fetuses, Pregnant Women, and Human In Vitro Fertilization). This subpart requires the approval of the Ethics Advisory Board for projects involving IVF or embryos, but no Ethics Advisory Board exists at the present time, so no such projects can be funded.
2. *Id.*
3. 45 C.F.R. # 46.210 (1987).
4. National Institutes of Health, Report of the Human Fetal Tissue Transplantation Research Panel, Dec. 1988.
5. Note 1 *supra* at 129–30.
6. The term "embryo" is used here to refer to all stages from fertilization to implantation, rather than technically more accurate terms such as zygote, blastocyst, or preembryo.
7. See, e.g., Handyside et al., Pregnancies from Biopsied Human Preimplantation Embryos Sexed by Y-Specific DNA Amplification, Nature 1990; 344; 768.
8. For an account of the ethical issues in embryo research generally and applicable citations, see Robertson, Embryo Research, 24 West. Ontario L. Rev. 15, 26–27 (1986).
9. *Id.* at 30–33.
10. *Id.* at 28–30.
11. *Id.* at 33–35.
12. *Id.* at 35–36.
13. American Fertility Society, Ethical Considerations of the New Reproductive Technologies, 46 Fertility & Sterility 1S, 32S (Supp. 1 1986); Robertson, In the Beginning: The Legal Status of Early Embryos, 76 Va. L. Rev. 437, 44–48 (1990).
14. See, e.g., 45 C.F.R. 46; Robertson, note 13 *supra* at 504.
15. Robertson, note 8 *supra* at 35–36.
16. *Id.*
17. *Id.*
18. Aside from promises of one person to another to uphold certain symbolic values, etc. The point being made in the text is a more general one.
19. See Robertson, note 13 *supra* at 448–50 for discussion of symbolism.
20. At least where no other source of embryos is available to conduct the research.
21. Robertson, Fetal Tissue Transplants, 66 Wash. U.L. Rev. 443, 455–63 (1988).
22. See note 16 *supra*.
23. See note 1 *supra* at 129.
24. Office of Technology Assessment, Infertility: Medical and Social Choices 324 (1988).
25. Mass. Stat. Ann. c. 112 # 12J (West 1983). See also R. I. Gen. Laws # 11–54–1E (1981); N. D. Cent. Code # 14–02.2 (West 1989).
26. Minn. Stat. Ann. # 145.421–422 (West 1990).
27. If embryos may not be discarded, however, research on embryos that will be discarded is unlikely.
28. 18 Pa. Cons. Stat. Ann. ## 3203, 3216 (Purdon 1983).
29. New Mexico State. Ann. # 1978, 24–9A–1 (1989).
30. If the embryos were otherwise going to be discarded (which is not prohibited in either state), then one could argue that using them for research first would not harm them.
31. Margaret S. v. Edwards, 794 F.2d 994 (5th Cir. 1986) (Margaret S. III); Lifchez v. Hartigan, 735 F. Supp. 1361 (N.D. Ill. 1990).
32. Ill. Rev. Stat., Ch. 38 Para. 81–26, #6(7) (Smith-Hurd 1989).
33. Lifchez v. Hartigan, 735 F. Supp. 1361, 1365–67 (N.D. Ill. (1990).
34. A state could solve the precision problems by specifying the exact procedures that could

not be done on embryos or fetuses, rather than use these broad terms. Such a tactic would then raise directly questions of procreative liberty.

35. Robertson, Procreative Liberty and the Control of Conception, Pregnancy and Childbirth, 69 Va. L. Rev. 405–6 (1983).
36. *Id.* at 406–7.
37.
38. Here the information is necessary for them to decide whether to go ahead with IVF, and if they do, to have the embryos placed in the uterus or not transferred at all. Whether or not they end up with offspring may depend upon access to the genetic information in question.
39. Lifchez v. Hartigan, 735 F. Supp. 1361, 1376–77 (N.D. Ill. 1990).
40. See note 7 *supra*.
41. The proceedings of this conference have been published as Preimplantation Genetics, ed. Y. Verlinsky (New York: Plenum Press, 1991).
42. Robertson, Ethical and Legal Issues in Preimplantation Genetic Diagnosis of Embryos, in Verlinsky, ed, note 41 *supra*. See also M. Michael, S. Buckle, Screening for Genetic Disorders: Therapeutic Abortion and IVF, J Med Ethics 1990; 16: 43–47.
43. *Id.* at 8–12.
44. For example, some couples might object to abortion of a fetus with cystic fibrosis but be willing to deselect such an embryo for implantation.
45. See note 7 *supra*.
46. However, state laws against embryo discard (four states arguably) might prevent destruction of embryos found to be genetically defective on the basis of preimplantation diagnosis. See Robertson, note 42 *supra* at 17–22.
47. Diagnosis and disposition as a result of the diagnosis are two different things. The right to diagnose would not necessarily give a right to dispose, though it often would. See note 46 *supra*.

MARY B. MAHOWALD

Fetal Tissue Transplantation and Women

During the last few decades, fetuses have often been considered apart from the women in whose bodies they develop. Earlier in history this was not so: the term "fetus" was rarely used, in part because fetuses were neither observed nor observable. Pregnancy was viewed as an essential relationship between a woman and her potential baby. The recent tendency illustrates the fallacy of abstraction, i.e., consideration of an object as if it exists without a context.[1] The fact that such thinking is fallacious supports a feminine model of moral reasoning, with its essential emphasis on context as crucial to moral judgment.[2] It also supports feminist critiques of the neglect of women's central role in discussions of reproductive issues.[3]

Developments that have influenced the shift from concerns about pregnant women to debates about fetuses and embryos include the legality of abortion, techniques for "assisted reproduction," and possibilities for "fetal therapy." Recent discussions of fetal tissue transplantation provide another example of the tendency to consider fetuses apart from women.[4] In what follows, therefore, I want to examine the issue of fetal tissue transplantation with a particular emphasis on women. To do so, I will first examine some of the terms in which the issue has been framed and addressed, suggesting (among other things) that lack of pertinent distinctions and consistent usage reinforce the tendency to consider fetuses apart from women. I will then scrutinize some of the practical ramifications for women of fetal tissue transplantation, comparing and contrasting this with surrogate motherhood and prostitution. Finally, I will briefly apply different feminist theories to the issue, defending one of these as more cogent than the rest.

Some Distinctions Not Made

While the abortion debate has generally centered on the moral status of the fetus, with one side denying and the other affirming a fetal "right to life," the debate about fetal tissue transplantation has triggered reconsideration of the same positions. Although the fiery rhetoric of abortion discussions has

F.K. Beller and R.F. Weir (eds.), The Beginning of Human Life, 225–232.

hardly needed impetus to continue, the issue of fetal tissue transplantation has added fuel to the fire. Pro-life rhetoric compares abortion to a silent holocaust;[5] early on in my own involvement with the issue of fetal tissue transplantation, I was accused of fomenting another holocaust. The accusation assumes what I argue against, i.e., the moral inseparability of abortion decisions from decisions to use fetal tissue for transplantation.[6] It also assumes that abortions, at any stage of pregnancy, are morally equivalent to the slaughter of adults and children by the Nazis. The latter assumption bypasses the fact that human lives were separately and collectively terminated in the Holocaust, whereas terminations of fetuses occur only through women's bodies. It also ignores the different legal and moral status of adults and children as compared with fetuses. Adults and children are universally regarded as persons, while fetuses are not.

The term mother is prevalently and misleadingly used for pregnant women whose fetuses could serve as sources of tissue for transplantation. The term father is similarly used for men who have impregnated women who have not given birth. Obviously, the two terms are not entirely parallel because men cannot be pregnant or give birth, and their only tie to a fetus is genetic. In ordinary language, however, neither women nor men are considered parents until a child is born. As Webster puts it, a mother is "a woman who has borne a child," and a father is "a man who has engendered a child."[7] Since a child is not a fetus or an embryo, a woman who undergoes abortion, whether spontaneously or electively, is not a mother, and neither is the provider of the sperm that fertilized her ovum a father. Perhaps we should use the term "pregnant man" (rather than father or even semen donor) to refer to the status of the one whose sperm has produced a fetus or embryo in the uterus of a woman. Since the decision in the Anna Johnson case,[8] however, Webster's definition and the common perception of what it means to be a mother is in question. By that ruling, motherhood is defined by the genetic relationship to one's offspring, and by that rationale, fatherhood could be defined in a manner parallel to motherhood. Genetic relationship represents the crucial component of either definition of a parent.

How are these labels relevant to fetal tissue transplantation? Mainly with regard to determination of whose consent (if any) is necessary for use of fetal tissue. If the term mother is used for a pregnant woman, it suggests that she and the fetus are separate individuals despite the tie between them. It further suggests special rights and responsibilities on the part of the pregnant woman, that of a mother towards her child. If the term mother is used for a nonpregnant woman who has provided the ovum producing a pregnancy, this also suggests, along with the notion that she and the fetus are separate individuals, special rights and responsibilities on her part. One parental right relevant to mothers (along with fathers) is that they may consent to their living children's participation in low- or non-risk scientific research or therapy intended to benefit others (e.g., bone marrow donation). They may also consent to use of tissue or organs from their deceased children for research or therapeutic purposes. The Uniform Anatomical Gift Act specifies that this parental right applies to fetuses as well as children.[9] Mothers may not, however, agree to exposing their living children to serious risks; to do so would mark them as negligent or abusive. Hence, consent of a pregnant woman regarded as mother to removal of neural tissue from her fetus might also be considered negligence or abuse.

Suppose, however, that we take the term mother to mean what it has traditionally meant, and then ask about consent to fetal tissue transplantation. Now we're left with the simple fact of a pregnant woman, who may or may not be genetically related to the fetus whose nurturance has depended on her. Although this woman is not a mother, the developing fetus is part of her body. In fact, if she is not considered a mother, the argument that the fetus is not separate but part of her is stronger, and her consent to fetal tissue transplantation is not consent for (in behalf of) the fetus but consent for herself. Arguments about property rights with regard to one's own bodily tissue or organs are also valid in this context. We will return to this point later.

Since the association between abortion and fetal tissue transplantation has been targeted as the main difference between this and other types of transplant,[10] different concepts of abortion need to be considered.[11] Clinically and legally, abortion is defined as termination of pregnancy before the fetus or embryo is viable. Popularly it has long been understood as termination of the fetus or embryo. The latter definition allows us to view disposal of in vitro embryos as abortions, and if it became possible in the future to develop embryos in vitro into fetuses that could provide tissue useful for transplantation, abortion might present a moral and legal problem in connection with it. In fact, however, most people do not construe disposal of in vitro embryos as comparable to abortion. While that construal seems inconsistent with the popular definition, it may be mainly influenced by a view to which the majority of people subscribe: that termination at later stages of development is more morally problematic than termination of very early embryos or preembryos.[12] Disposal of fetuses would then be considered more difficult to justify than disposal of embryos, regardless of their in vitro status.

Empirically, because it is now possible for zygotes to develop in vitro to a multicellular stage, and for second-trimester fetuses to survive ex utero, the moral parameters of decisions regarding their disposition involve others besides women. The term fetus may thus need to be redefined, or modified in order to distinguish between in vitro and in vivo status. Traditionally, (human) "fetus" means "the offspring in the womb from the end of the third month of pregnancy until birth."[13] Clinically, the fetus is defined as a "post-embryonic organism contained within the body of a pregnant person."[14] When a fetus is expelled from the uterus, it is either an abortus or a newborn. If these distinctions were utilized in language about fetal tissue transplantation, it would be more appropriate to speak of tissue transplantation from abortuses than from fetuses. Such a distinction entails recognition of the difference between a pregnant woman agreeing to use of tissue from her fetus, and a woman who has aborted her pregnancy agreeing to use of the aborted tissue. The former involves use of tissue from her own body; the latter refers to use of discarded tissue. The property right argument may apply ex utero, but possible claimants include gamete providers as well as the (gestational) parent. So long as the fetus remains within the body of a woman, however, her claims regarding its disposition are more compelling than others' claims. They become more compelling still if possibilities of prolonging a pregnancy, or of a riskier or more uncomfortable method of abortion, are proposed in order to optimize the chance of successful fetal tissue transplantation.[15]

Surrogacy and Prostitution

In 1987 I suggested three paradigms with which the issue of fetal tissue transplantation may be compared: transplantation from cadaveric donors, transplantation from living donors, and surrogate motherhood.[15] Although the first two are generally accepted practices in specific (limited) circumstances, the third remains controversial, and few discussants on the issue of fetal tissue transplantation pay any attention to it. Yet it is that model, rather than the others, that points to the particular vulnerability that fetal tissue transplantation imposes on women. In this section, therefore, I want to elaborate more fully on the correlation between the two, and their correlation with an even less enticing paradigm, prostitution.

Some years ago I received a letter from a teacher who had Parkinson's disease. The man, whom I will call Mr. M, was in his early fifties, and was still able to teach his classes and enjoy other aspects of his life. His family consisted of a wife and two adult daughters. Mr. M knew that his disease would progress and become debilitating. He had read about possible treatment of Parkinson's through transplantation of neural fetal tissue.

Mr. M made two principal points in his letter. One was that he would not want either of his daughters to become pregnant and abort her pregnancy in order to provide him with fetal tissue for experimental treatment. The other was that the availability of so many electively aborted fetuses in this country creates an important resource that should not be left unutilized for research and therapeutic purposes related to his and other diseases.

Mr. M's daughters had considered the possibility of providing their father with experimental treatment of a disease that had no known cure. He did not want them to use their bodies in this way for his sake. What fetal tissue transplantation has in common with surrogacy and prostitution is this *use* of women's bodies, through their reproductive capacity, for the sake of others.

Because Mr. M's daughters would not have sold but given fetal tissue for transplantation, their potential gesture does not seem as crass as commercial surrogacy or prostitution. In fact, their action might well be construed as generous and loving. Commercial surrogacy and prostitution are generally viewed as morally problematic because of their connection with money; in a sense, both involve the rental of body parts. To gestate a fetus and *sell* its tissue is a more radical or "final" expression of bodily commerce because one thereby disowns what one had previously chosen to be part of oneself. Selling, unlike renting, means transfer of ownership and not mere use of another's property.

Surrogate motherhood (whether gestational, genetic, or both), is more likely to receive moral approbation if it is practiced for so-called altruistic reasons such as the desire to provide an infertile couple with a child. Similarly, if a woman has sexual intercourse with someone without receiving money in return, she is not considered a prostitute because she has not sold sex or rented her body to a man. In fact, her act may be seen as a loving or positive gesture, and morally commended. Yet some authors have compared marriage to prostitution for women who thus agree to sex with their husbands in exchange for their financial support.[16] And noncommercial surrogacy is not necessarily undertaken for altruistic reasons. A woman who volunteers to carry a pregnancy for her sister who has cystic fibrosis may do so for altruistic reasons, but she may also do so to overcome a sense of guilt, because she likes to be pregnant, or because of pressure from other members of her family. Even when money is exchanged, it is unlikely that a surrogate is adequately paid for "services" rendered. As the Whitehead case suggests, in such situations elements of altruism are probably mixed with motives of self-interest.[17]

Mr. M's daughters are more likely to be commended for undertaking pregnancy for the sake of their father than they would be for developing a business for selling tissue from their own fetuses to others. Suppose, however, they pooled their savings and their fetuses to form a nonprofit corporation to provide the tissue without charge to those whose health or lives might benefit most from it? Wouldn't that be more altruistic than their offer to help their father, whose will might be influenced by their gesture, or lack thereof? If impartiality is a characteristic of ethical decision making, might it be more moral to provide fetal tissue to an unknown person who is needier than one's parent, or to someone whose health or life is less likely to constitute a benefit to the provider of tissue as well as to its recipient?

Because motives for human behavior are generally mixed, it is simplistic to assume that exchange of money is an adequate criterion for determining whether surrogacy or provision of fetal tissue is morally appropriate. Even if self-interest were the only criterion for either behavior, this does not imply that the behavior is wrong. In a society whose economic foundation is capitalism, which in turn is based on individualism, acting in one's own interests is expected and respected. While most organs may not legally be sold, some human tissue is routinely provided in exchange for money, e.g., blood, semen, and ova. Although prostitution is generally condemned in this same individualistic society, other uses of one's body and sexuality are encouraged and rewarded – e.g., in athletic achievements and beauty contests.

The use of women's bodies through surrogacy and prostitution treats women as means rather than ends (fetal containers or vessels of pleasure);[18] in addition, both of these practices dramatically illustrate the socioeconomic disparity between the users and used. In surrogacy, the disparity occurs between affluent couples and a lower socioeconomic class of women; in prostitution, although there are rare exceptions, the disparity is between men (johns) who can pay for sexual pleasure and women who depend on that pay for their survival. The main worry of advocates for women about the prospect of fetal tissue transplantation is that a new opportunity for economic and psychological exploitation is herein provided. Moreover, because women are either naturally prone or conditioned to be caregivers, and comprise by far the majority of caregivers,[19] some at least may feel additional pressure to care for those in need through use of their own bodies. Without any encouragement on Mr. M's part, his daughters might have felt that pressure.

Feminist Theories

The issues of surrogacy and prostitution illustrate the diversity of contemporary feminist theories. What different versions of feminism have in common is a critique of sex inequality.[20] However, the equality affirmed may be one that allows for disparities among individuals so long as equal liberty is preserved. Or it may start with recognition that men and women are not created equal, and call for rectification of the inequalities between them as a social goal. Some versions of feminism interpret equality as sameness, while others view it as equal respect for differences. While there are diverse theories of feminism, I will discuss only two orientations with which different theories can be aligned: individualistic and communalistic.[21] Individualistic versions of feminism occur in both liberal and libertarian contexts; postmodern feminism also appears individualistic. Communalistic versions may be socialist or Marxist. Radical and existentialist feminism may be related to either orientation, depending on the issue addressed.[22]

Lori Andrews has argued in behalf of a consumer model for assisted reproduction, claiming that this is consistent with a woman's right to control her reproductive life. Feminists who reject the practice of surrogate motherhood, according to Andrews, deny the fundamental principle of women's liberation, the right to dispose of one's own body as one wishes.[23] The same argument is applicable to prostitution and to provision of fetal tissue for transplantation. The individualistic concept on which the argument is based is "My body, my property."[24] This version of feminism emphasizes equal liberty and minimization of governmental interference in the lives of individuals. In an individualistic society such as ours, no change is advocated except to insure that women in general have the same access as men to opportunities for economic advancement.

A communialistic version of feminism targets the practice of private property as an obstacle to social equality, including sexual equality. It thus involves a critique of the capitalist structure of U.S. society, which inevitably leads to economic disparities between classes. The role of government, on this account, is to minimize inequalities that arise from the different needs of individuals and groups, by taking from each according to ability and distributing to each according to need. Liberty is one among other social goods to be distributed equally. Thus individual liberty is subordinated to equality as a social goal. The goal of socio-economic equality requires something that appears to have happened in no socialist regime as yet, namely, dissolution of the private/public split that results in women working in both spheres while men work only in one.

Andrews is right in that individualistic versions of feminism support women's right to surrogacy arrangements, both as surrogates and as prospective "consumers" of their services. They also support, as already suggested, the right to prostitution and the right to sell fetal tissue. However, the majority of feminists do not subscribe to an individualistic orientation because sex equality is seen as integrally connected to the larger social equality on which communalistic versions insist. The argument here is that sex equality can only be achieved within the context of human equality, and that unless racism, classism, and other forms of inequality are eliminated, sexism will continue to prevail as well.

The problem, then, is that individualistic versions of feminism are not sufficiently egalitarian for most of us feminists. Neither do they appear sufficiently concerned with interpersonal and social relationships, which a feminine model of reasoning regards as essential to moral decision making. From a communalistic feminist perspective, fetuses are to be valued, in part because of their relationship to the women who gestate them, and in part because of their potential for social relationships, but not to the same extent as those who are clearly already persons who have established relationships with many others. To communalistic feminists, the difference between decisions regarding a fetus (i.e., within a woman's body) and decisions regarding an abortus or in vitro embryo is morally significant. A critique of private property is not to be identified with a critique of the notion of control over one's own body. The inevitable connection between economic and sexual inequality is also morally significant, as is well illustrated in the case of prostitution. Communalistic feminists note something similar happening with regard to surrogacy, and potentially happening with regard to fetal tissue transplantation.

As a feminist who subscribes to a communalistic orientation, I believe it is possible to have intercourse, become pregnant, gestate a fetus, and deliver a baby, or to abort a fetus and consent to use of its tissue for others without reinforcing sexual double standards or social inequality. I think, however, that all of these situations increase the probability that women's needs, desires, and interests will continue to be generally subordinated to those of men. Fetal tissue transplantation, as an area of research as well as therapeutic possibility, is yet another example of medical technology for which women bear a disproportionate burden and risk.

NOTES

1. Cf. Mary O'Brien. Reproducing the world. Boulder Co.: Westview Press, 1989: 39–40.
2. Carol Gilligan. Moral orientation and moral development. In: Eva F. Kittay and Diana T. Meyers, eds. Women and Moral Theory. Totowa, NJ: Rowman and Littlefield Publishers 1985: 19–33.
3. E.g., Laura Purdy, ed. Ethics and reproduction. Hypatia 1989 Fall: 4(3).
4. A recent egregious example of this is the following: "When we are led to the conclusion that fetal research is ethical . . ., we ignore the basic issue that has never been adequately considered by the court, namely the question of when *the highly valued producer of fetal tissue* comes into existence" (my italics). When I first read this sentence, I assumed that the author was characterizing the pregnant woman as "the highly valued producer." Wrong. He goes on to identify the highly valued producer with the fetus, totally ignoring the woman's essential reproducing/producing role. Monte Harris Liebman. The fetal tissue debate on complicity. Hastings Center Report 1990 Mar/Apr; 20(2): 50.
5. E.g., James T. Burtchaell. Rachel Weeping. New York: Harper and Row Publishers, 1982: 141–238.
6. Mary B. Mahowald, et al. The ethical options in transplanting fetal tissue. Hastings Center Report 1987; 17: 9–15.
7. *Webster's New World Dictionary*. 2d college edition, 928, 509.
8. Seth Mydans. Surrogate loses custody bid in case defining motherhood. New York Times 1990 Oct 23; Sect A: 1; Sect A: 8.
9. Patricia King, Judith Areen. Legal regulation of fetal tissue transplantation. Clin Res 1988; 36: 205–208; Lori B. Andrews, Feminism revisited: fallacies and policies in the surrogacy debate. Logos 1988; 9: 81–96. Dorothy E. Vawter et al. The Use of Human Fetal Tissue: Scientific, Ethical and Policy Concerns. Minneapolis: University of Minnesota, 1990 Jan: 169–187; US Congress, Office of Technology Assessments. Neural Grafting: Repairing the Brain and Spinal Cord OTA-BA-462 Washington DC: US Government Printing Office, 1990 Sept: 113–145.
10. Mary B. Mahowald et al. Transplantation of neural tissue from fetuses. Science 1987; 235: 1308–1309; Consultants to the Advisory Committee to the Director, National Institutes of Health, Report of the Human Fetal Tissue Transplantation Research Panel 1988 Dec.
11. Mary B. Mahowald. Concepts of abortion and their implications for the abortion debate. Southern Journal of Philosophy 1982; 20: 195–207.
12. EJ Dionne, Jr. Poll on abortion finds the nation is sharply divided. New York Times 1989 Apr 26; Sect A: 1.
13. *Webster's*: 517.
14. Mary B Mahowald. Neural fetal tissue transplantation: should we do what we can do? Neurol Clin 1989; 7: 746.
15. Mahowald MB. The ethical options, 9–15.
16. E.g. Esther Vilar. The Manipulated Man. New York: Farrar, Strauss & Giroux, 1972; cf. Catherine MacKinnon. Feminism Unmodified. Cambridge: Harvard University Press, 1987.
17. Cf. Philip J Parker. Motivation of surrogate mothers: initial findings. Am J Psychiatry 1983, Jan; 140(1) 117–118; Richard Lacayo. Whose child is this? Time 1987, Jan 1957: "She had wanted to become a surrogate mother to help a childless couple."
18. George Annas. Pregnant women as fetal containers. Hastings Center Report 1986 Dec; 16: 13.
19. Mary B Mahowald. Sex-role stereotypes in medicine. Hypatia 1987; 2: 21–38.
20. Alison Jaggar. On sexual equality. Ethics 1974 Jul; 84: 275.
21. Mary B Mahowald. Feminism: individualistic or communalistic? Proceedings of the American Catholic Philosophical Association 1976; 50.
22. Rosemarie Tong. Feminist Thought. Boulder, Co. Westview Press, 1989.
23. Lori B Andrews. New Conceptions: A Consumer's Guide to the Newest Infertility Treatments. New York: St. Martin's Press, 1984; cf. Andrews. Feminism revisited.
24. Lori B Andrews. My body, my property. Hastings Center Report 1986 Oct; 28–38.

SUSAN R. JOHNSON

Fetal Tissue Transplantation: An Institutional Review Board Perspective

In this essay, I consider fetal tissue transplantation research from the point of view of an American institutional review board (IRB). The literature in this area, although meager, provides the foundation for my views. This perspective is supplemented by my experience as both an IRB chair and a gynecologist who performs abortions. I focus on three issues that may come before the IRB at an institution where fetal tissue transplantation research is proposed. Two are related to the tissue donor, and the third to the recipient.

Each local IRB operates within the constraints of relevant federal and state regulations. Currently (except for the prohibition of funding for fetal transplant research), federal rules are nonrestrictive. In contrast, some states either do not allow this research or they have in place legal obstacles (Greeley, 1989). The IRB may choose to be *more* stringent than the federal and state regulations, and in the absence of uniform federal regulations, it is likely that there will be a variety of institutional approaches to the conduct of fetal tissue research.

In this discussion, I make several assumptions. First, the fundamental question that must be addressed by the IRB is whether to permit fetal tissue transplantation research at all. Here, I assume approval. This is not a foregone conclusion, however, as demonstrated by the experience at Notre Dame (Burtchaell, 1988).

Second, I assume that tissue will be obtained primarily from elective pregnancy termination procedures. While I agree that tissue from spontaneous abortions or ectopic tubal pregnancies is more ethically acceptable (Fung and Lo, 1990), this option is not feasible (Annas and Elias, 1989).

Third, I assume that certain restrictions, intended to reduce the possibility that abortions will be encouraged by a policy allowing use of the tissue from elective abortions, will be required by the IRB. As stated by the Committee on Ethics of the Stanford Medical Center, the principle underlying these restrictions is that neither the donor nor the operator should benefit from the performance of the abortion (Greeley et al., 1989). The report of the Human Fetal Tissue Transplantation Research Panel to the National Institutes of Health (1988) spells out the practices derived from this principle. Briefly, the woman who consents to tissue donation should not be paid or reimbursed for abortion

F.K. Beller and R.F. Weir (eds.), The Beginning of Human Life, 233–240.

expenses, the procedures should be performed by a physician not otherwise involved in the research, and the donor should not be allowed to designate a recipient.

THE DONOR: CONSENT

The IRB spends much of its effort scrutinizing the process proposed by the investigator for obtaining informed consent. In the case of fetal tissue transplantation research, the consent of the tissue donor must be considered in addition to that of the recipient. There has been extensive discussion in the literature as to whether consent is required from the woman having the abortion. Most commentators conclude that consent should be obtained; indeed, consent is required by the Uniform Anatomical Gift Act (UAGA), which provides (by default) guidelines for this situation.

The arguments supporting consent are grounded in three premises: the dead fetus is the same as a dead *person*, so relevant next-of-kin consent requirements apply; societal mores will be violated if fetal tissue use is exempt from a consent requirement; and consideration for the woman requires her consent. Although the first two arguments, focusing on the fetus and society, are more commonly used, I believe they are less compelling than the third, derived from the interests of the woman donor.

Why does it matter which premise is used? The first premise is vulnerable to attack in several ways. First, if the Uniform Anatomical Gift Act were revised to allow use of organs for transplantation without the consent of kin, this change could apply to fetal tissue. Albert Jonsen (1988) points out that the requirement for next-of-kin consent for cadaver organ donations is *not* morally required, but is simply a matter of public policy. Second, the woman undergoing an abortion has a different relationship to the fetal tissue than that of next of kin, so that the UAGA requirements may be inappropriate. Third, fetal tissue obtained at an elective procedure fulfills the criteria for "discarded surgical tissue" for which consent is not required by current federal research regulations.

The societal premise is derivative, dependent on a particular perception of societal sensibilities. It would disappear if and when society were no longer offended by the idea of not obtaining consent.

These first two positions, then, seem to me to be unstable. In contrast, a requirement for consent based on the principle of "respect for persons," in this case the woman having the abortion, does not depend on a particular view of the fetus or the donation process. This position obviates even Burtchaell's claim (1989) that the woman may not give consent because she has no moral claim to give permission *for the fetus*, because the investigator would be required to get permission solely out of respect *for the woman*.

Roberton (1988) concluded that consent should be required, in part because the woman should retain the right to dispose of fetal tissue as she wishes, and in part because she will benefit from knowing that the tissue is being used for a good purpose. Although these two points are "woman-focused," they are off-target. In most abortion clinics, the woman is not involved in the decision about tissue disposition; indeed, the tissue is usually handled as any other surgically discarded tissue.

The second justification assumes a feeling on the part of the woman that may not exist. Indeed, the process of obtaining consent may impose an emotional *burden* on many women. Imagine: a woman arrives at the abortion clinic after spending weeks agonizing over her decision. Her anxiety over the upcoming procedure makes it difficult to concentrate during the routine counseling. When presented with the standard surgical consent, she tells the physician that she wants to "just sign it and get it over with." Then a two-page document is presented, perhaps (as described in the Yale IRB-approved procedure) by an investigator she has never met, which describes "her" fetus, and what uses might be made of it (Levine, 1988). She is asked to sign her name again.

In practice, many women prefer to hear as little as possible about the abortion procedure that they are about to undergo. The addition of extensive information, at a vulnerable time, about a matter that has no direct personal benefit, is more likely to be emotionally disruptive than beneficial. At the least, it is unlikely that thoughtful "informed" consent will be a result.

The requirement for consent should be motivated by the principle of respect for persons rather than some notion of "moral salvage." Respect dictates that the woman's own sense of the moral appropriateness of fetal tissue transplantation be taken into account. Because fetal tissue is not "merely" surgically discarded tissue and human transplantation is not "merely" research, individual women may have religious, moral, or other reasons for not wanting the tissue used in this way. Respect also requires treating vulnerable groups with greater care. One way to minimize exploitation of the vulnerable woman about to undergo an abortion is to give her a choice about this use of the tissue.

Finally, women should be asked for permission in a way that does not impose an undue burden. Nelson (1990) suggests that information about possible research be placed in the standard consent document. This could consist of a brief statement including the information that (1) the tissue obtained during the procedure may be used for research; (2) this could include transplantation into another person; (3) anonymity is guaranteed; (4) she may decline to allow the tissue to be used for research by (for example) checking the box after the statement; and (5) more information can be provided if she desires.

This procedure would be satisfactory, of course, only if no alterations in the abortion procedure were planned (Mahowald, 1988). If alterations are planned, complete disclosure of the changes and associated risks, along with separate consent, would be preferable.

The Donor: Assessment of Risks

Investigators may request changes in the abortion procedure in order to obtain fetal tissue suitable for the planned research. How should the IRB assess additional risks to the woman undergoing the procedure, and are there specific changes that are unacceptable?

Redmond et al. (1988) observed that most reports of transplantation research do not describe how the tissue was obtained. The range of possible alterations has been described in the ethical literature (Mahowald, 1987). Types of change include (1) making alterations in the standard technique, (2) delaying the procedure, and (3) changing to a different type of procedure. The ramifications of these changes to the woman undergoing the abortion have not been considered (Annas and Elias, 1989).

There are two published reports which contain sufficient detail to examine the question of changes in standard technique. In research proposed at Yale, the investigators required no change in the usual first-trimester suction curettage procedure (Redmond et al., 1988). In contrast, a Swedish investigation required substantial alterations (Gustavii, 1989). General, rather than local, anesthesia was used, a larger suction cannula was required, and the procedure was done under ultrasound direction because of a need to remove the fetus isolated from the placenta and other tissue. These alterations result in a procedure that is riskier, lengthier, and more expensive.

The relative risk of general compared to local anesthesia has been reported. In the largest study from the United States, suction curettage performed with general anesthesia was more likely to be associated with blood transfusion (relative risk 5), uterine perforation (relative risk 2.2), and hysterectomy (relative risk 5.7) (Grimes et al., 1979). Damage to the cervix from mechanical dilatation is directly related to the amount of dilatation required, so that the need to use a larger-than-usual cannula increased this risk. A longer procedure may not be a problem for the patient if she is under general anesthesia, but it would increase discomfort if performed under local anesthesia. A difference of a few minutes is insignificant, but more than 10 or 15 minutes (since a suction curettage typically takes less than 5 minutes) is something about which the woman should be informed.

Presumably the woman donating tissue would not be responsible for any increased procedural costs. Someone needs to pay, however, and the difference between local and general anesthesia (which includes the cost of an anesthesiologist and an operating room) may be as much as two thousand dollars. Additional costs would be incurred if ultrasound (and technician) were required. The IRB will need to ascertain the source of funding for any alterations in procedure, and verify that patients are not directly assessed as individual donors, or indirectly through an overall increase in fees. Third-party payers (e.g., insurance companies) should not be billed for any increased costs, unless, of course, it is the insurer of the tissue recipient.

The use of ultrasound to view the fetus raises the additional issue of increased emotional discomfort. It seems obvious that the screen should be shielded from the woman if this is necessary, but even hearing the operators talking about the fetus as they try to locate it, or simply being aware that the fetus can be seen and is being "targeted," may be a problem.

Although there are no empirical examples of either requiring delay in the procedure or changing to a different technique, the potential need for each has been raised in the ethical literature. What do we know about risks associated with these alterations? Cates (1984) describes the three main determinants of risk in abortion procedures as (1) operator skill, (2) gestational age, and (3) type of procedure. There is considerable information about each of these factors, and IRBs must be aware of this data in order to make appropriate decisions.

Delay in performing a procedure to a later gestational age could be requested in order to obtain tissue more acceptable for transplantation. In general, risks of suction curettage increase linearly between 8 and 20 weeks, by about 15 to 30 percent per gestational age week (Cates, 1982). Grimes et al. (1984) examined a specific serious complication, hysterectomy, and found that the rate increased from 1.5/10,000 at 8 or fewer weeks to 10/10,000 at 16 to 20 weeks. The largest increment in risk occurred between 12 and 13 weeks (from 2.5/10,000 to 6.8/10,000).

A related issue is the "supply" of fetal tissue available at the needed gestational age. For example, it appears that for neurological indications, fetal tissue from 10 to 12 weeks (LMP) is optimal. It may not be necessary to consider delay if a sufficient number of abortions are being done at this gestational age to provide the needed tissue. Gero and Giordano (1990) point out that there are about 1.6 million abortions performed per year in the United States, and that 78 percent are in the first trimester. Based on this data, sufficient late first-trimester tissue should be available if methods of distributing it to investigators are found. If tissue from second-trimester fetuses were required, there would be more potential for a supply problem.

What should an IRB allow? I believe that delay is not acceptable if the natural distribution of elective abortions results in sufficient tissue at the required gestational age. If the supply is low, a delay of up to two weeks within the first trimester could be defended since risk is not appreciably altered. In contrast, delay into the second trimester is accompanied by an increase in risk that cannot be justified for research. If an IRB denies a request to allow procedural delays, it will face the practical question of how to monitor compliance. Because of full schedules, abortion clinics frequently schedule procedures several weeks after the request.

An investigator may need tissue that is not damaged as it would be after suction curettage or dilatation and evacuation. Two alternate procedures are available: intra-amniotic instillation, and hysterotomy. Hysterotomy is essentially a mini-caesarean section, and is medically unacceptable as an elective abortion procedure (Cates, 1982). It must be performed under a major anesthetic, has the highest complication rate among abortion procedures, requires a postoperative hospitalization of several days, and is expensive.

Intra-amniotic instillation, on the other hand, is widely used for second-trimester abortion. A substance (hypertonic saline, urea, or prostaglandin) is injected into the amniotic fluid surrounding the fetus, resulting in uterine contractions. After several hours (sometimes up to 24) the intact stillborn fetus is delivered. However, the alternative procedure, dilatation and evacuation (D&E), has less than half the rate of major complications (Grimes et al. 1977), is more rapid (a typical procedure takes about 15 minutes), and is less expensive. For these reasons, D&E is the procedure of choice in many centers for second-trimester pregnancy termination. If the knowledge (or clinical benefit) to be gained were great enough, use of an instillation procedure could be defensible. However, full informed consent would be required from the donor.

In summary, the IRB must be cautious about requests by investigators to alter the abortion procedure in any way. There is sufficient information available in the literature regarding the risks of most possible changes to allow for rational decisions. Changes that increase either risk or discomfort should generally be disapproved.

THE RECIPIENT: REGULATION OF TRANSPLANTATION RESEARCH

The protection of the recipient of fetal tissue is also the concern of the IRB. This protection is best achieved by appropriate scientific oversight of the research. Although IRBs focus most of their attention on the consent content and process, they must first be assured that the proposed research meets acceptable scientific standards. Most funded projects are subjected to stringent scientific peer review, and the IRB usually proceeds on the assumption that this is adequate. however, when work does not require outside funding, there is often no peer review.

Most committees do not have the expertise to perform a thorough scientific review. Early fetal tissue transplantation research is apt to be non-externally funded work (especially given the current ban on federal funding). Coupled with the fact that IRBs rarely disapprove protocols, it is likely that protocols of questionable merit will be approved and carried out. Also, some clinician-investigators might try to avoid IRB review by claiming that transplantation is "novel therapy," and therefore exempt from IRB oversight.

In the preface to the report of the Human Fetal Tissue Transplantation Research Panel (National Institutes of Health, 1988), Arlin A. Adams suggests that restoring the availability of federal funding for fetal tissue research will provide the needed supervision. While this would be an improvement, it would apply only to federally financed research, and would not be the comprehensive solution.

Annas and Elias (1989) have proposed that fetal tissue transplantation research be regulated by federal guidelines. Although I am not in favor of excessive federal influence in the research sphere, I think there is merit in this suggestion. The use of transplanted fetal tissue for treatment is not dissimilar to the use of drugs. A requirement that research involving transplantation of tissue into humans be certified by a federal agency would correspond to the current process for investigational drugs and devices. This mechanism would provide assurance to the IRB that the science was adequate, and would improve protection to subjects.

Fetal tissue transplantation research will no doubt be conducted in the United States even if federal funding is not available. For this reason, institutional review boards must familiarize themselves with the issues. Currently, the recommendations of the Human Fetal Tissue Transplantation Research Panel (1988) provide the best guidance. While consent from the woman donor should be obtained, IRBs must insure that the process is not onerous. Protocols that request a change in abortion procedure must be carefully scrutinized, and any increased risk to the woman donor should be discouraged. In the absence of federal regulations, the IRB must be prepared to obtain expert review of protocols in order to fulfill the moral obligation to the tissue recipient.

References

Annas GJ, Elias S. The politics of transplantation of human fetal tissue. N Engl J Med 1989; 320: 1079–1082.

Burtchaell JT. University policy on experimental use of aborted fetal tissue. IRB: a review of human subjects research 1988; 10(4): 7–11.

Burtchaell JT. The use of aborted fetal tissue in research: A rebuttal. IRB: a review of human subjects research 1989; 11(2): 9–12.

Cates W. Induced abortion. In: Perinatal Epidemiology MB Bracken, ed. New York: Oxford University Press, 1984, 301–324.

Freedman B. The ethics of using human fetal tissue. IRB: a review of human subjects research 1998; 10(6): 1–4.

Fung CHK, Lo JW. Alternatives to using fetal tissue from induced abortions [letter]. JAMA 1990; 264: 34.

Gero E, Giordano J. Ethical considerations in fetal tissue transplantation. J Neurosci Nurs 1990; 22: 9–12.

Greeley HT, Hamm T, Johnson R, Price CR, Weingarten R, Raffin T. The ethical use of human fetal tissue in medicine. N Engl J Med 1989; 320: 1093–1096.

Grimes DA, Schulz KF, Cates W, Tyler CW. Local versus general anesthesia: which is safer for performing suction curettage abortions? Am J Obstet Gynecol 1979; 135: 1030–1035.

Grimes DA, Flock ML, Schulz KF, Cates W Jr. Hysterectomy as treatment for complications of legal abortion. Obstet Gynecol 1989; 63: 457–462.

Grimes DA, Schulz KF, Cates W, Tyler CW. Mid-trimester abortion by dilatation and evacuation: a safe and practical alternative. N Engl J Med 1977; 296: 1141–1145.

Gustavii B. Fetal brain transplantation for Parkinson's disease: technique for obtaining donor tissue [letter]. Lancet 1989 Mar 11: 565.

Jonsen AR. Transplantation of fetal tissue: an ethicist's viewpoint. Clin Res 1988; 36: 215–219.

Levine RJ. An IRB-approved protocol on the use of human fetal tissue. IRB: a review of human subjects research, 1989; 11(2): 7–8.

Mahowald MB. Placing wedges along a slippery slope: use of fetal neural tissue for transplantation. Clin Res 1988; 36: 220–222.

Mahowald MB, Silver J, Ratcheson RA. The ethical options in transplanting fetal tissue. Hastings Center Report, 1987 Feb.

National Institutes of Health, 1988. Consultants to the Advisory Committee to the Director. Report of the Human Fetal Tissue Transplantation Research Panel. 2 vols. Washington, DC: U.S. Government Printing Office.

Nelson RM. A policy concerning the therapeutic use of human fetal tissue in transplantation. West J Med 1990; 152: 447–448.

Redmond DE, Naftolin F, Collier TJ, Lernath C, Robbins RJ, Sladek CD, Roth RH, Sladek JR. Cryopreservation, culture and transplantation or human fetal mesencephalic tissue into monkeys. Science 1988; 242: 768–771.

Robertson JA. Fetal tissue transplant research is ethical. IRB: a review of human subjects research 1988; 10(6): 5–8.

PART FIVE

Medical, Ethical and Legal Aspects of Maternal/Fetal Relationships

CARL P. WEINER

Primary Care Fetal Medicine

Though only recently proposed as a subspeciality[1], primary care fetal medicine began in the late 1950s with the development of techniques for the evaluation and subsequently the treatment of fetal hemolytic anemia.[2–4] With several exceptions, further developments in fetal medicine were limited to the diagnosis of abnormalities and the characterization of their natural histories until the early 1980s. These obligatory first steps continue today, since it is impossible to treat without an accurate diagnosis and unwise to treat without knowledge of the likely outcome. Though the subspeciality is still in its early development, the fetus is no longer hidden and unapproachable. The emergence of the fetus as a patient generates the potential for conflict between the autonomous woman and her dependent fetus.

While this paper focuses on one advantage of fetal diagnosis, the potential for therapy, there are a number of other salient advantages which should be acknowledged: (1) Alleviation of anxiety. Ninety-eight percent of tests confirm normality, providing reassurance and perhaps dissuading a woman from terminating an at-risk pregnancy. (2) Improvement in both maternal and neonatal care. Obstetric and neonatal care may be modified specifically to support the ill fetus/neonate. (3) Improved likelihood of family adjustment to a fetal problem. Without question, learning that their future child is not perfect constitutes a traumatic event for the parents. Prenatal diagnosis provides time to activate coping mechanisms and to initiate appropriate medical and psychological counseling of the couple while there is still time for reflection.

Fetal Diagnosis

The first step in fetal therapy is diagnosis. Most patients who conceive a fetus with an anomaly or whose fetus experiences a complication during pregnancy, such as a viral infection or uteroplacental insufficiency, were not known to be at risk at the outset of their pregnancy. Screening is thus of the utmost importance. To deny a patient access to effective screening when

F.K. Beller and R.F. Weir (eds.), The Beginning of Human Life, 243–255.

available, whatever the modality, is to directly deny the patient and, indirectly, her fetus access to medical care.

Noninvasive Diagnosis

Hormonal Screening

Current hormone screening during pregnancy consists of measuring maternal *a*-fetopotein (MSAFP), estriol, and hCG between 16 and 20 weeks' gestation. This "triple screen" is valuable for the identification of (1) a variety of fetal anatomic defects including open spina bifida and abdominal wall defects, (2) fetal chromosome abnormalities; (3) fetal infection, and (4) pregnancies with normal fetuses but an abnormal placenta placing the fetus at risk for preterm delivery, growth retardation, and stillbirth.[5–10]

MSAFP is usually elevated when the fetus has an open spine or abdominal wall defect. The measurement of MSAFP permits the identification of almost all fetuses with abdominal wall defects and approximately 80% of fetuses with a neural tube defect. The expected outcome of a fetus with an abdominal wall defect unaccompanied by another malformation is very good after postnatal repair. In contrast, the long-term prognosis for children with a neural tube defect depends upon both the location and the extent of the lesion. Counseling must take these elements into consideration.

Women whose fetuses have one of several chromosome abnormalities have a low MSAFP. Application of the "triple screen" to the detection of fetal chromosome abnormalities permits the identification of 60% of all trisomy 21 fetuses compared to only 24% if maternal age alone is used as the criteria for amniocentesis. Though the information on the detection of chromosome abnormalities other than trisomy 21 is preliminary, it appears that a similar number of other aneuploidies will also be detected. The percentage of screened women who undergo amniocentesis remains constant since the triple screen allows modification of the predicted risk for the older gravida. A woman who might have chosen to undergo amniocentesis because of her age may now decline if the predicted risk after triple screening is similar to that of a much younger woman. Because the positive yield from amniocentesis is higher with the triple screen than that achievable using other screening criteria, the cost per case identified and the number of normal fetuses lost per case identified are also significantly reduced.

Ultrasound

Primary care fetal medicine could not exist without high-resolution diagnostic ultrasound to illuminate this previously dark and forbidden area. Initially, sonographic resolution was poor and the examinations focused primarily on the documentation of gestational age. With technologic improvements, it became possible accurately to identify a wide variety of malformations. High-resolution ultrasound now permits not just the determination of fetal viability, number, position, and gestational age, but also the near 100% accurate diagnosis of a wide variety of lethal or usually lethal malformations. These include anencephaly, iniencephaly, hypoplastic left or right heart syndromes, and renal agenesis.

There are a relatively small number of fetal structural malformations currently thought potentially amenable to antenatal therapy. The first lesion for which antenatal therapy was actually attempted was hydrocephalus.[11,12] Subsequently, many investigators collaboratively concluded that decompression of the hydrocephalic head antenatally did not improve outcome.[13]

Why would therapy so successful postnatally be unsuccessful antenatally? In hindsight, the failure of antenatal shunting to palliate hydrocephalus likely reflects poor patient selection. Available, safe imaging equipment did not permit an accurate anatomic diagnosis of obstructive hydrocephalus on a day-to-day basis. Metaphorically, ultrasound allows visualization of only the external problem, not the etiology. For example, if your left index finger was struck by a hammer and your right index finger run over by a truck, both would look black and blue and swollen on the outside. On the inside, it is likely that the finger run over by the truck would have sustained significantly more damage. With ultrasound, we see the black, blue, and swollen finger, but cannot tell how it got that way. While dilated ventricles can be imaged, we frequently cannot tell how they got that way. The lesson learned from the antenatal treatment of fetal hydrocephalus is not that therapy was inappropriate, but that attempts at therapy should follow the ability to accurately make a diagnosis of lesion whose natural history is clear.

Since most fetal abnormalities are unexpected, should routine diagnostic ultrasound be offered to all pregnant women? Recent randomized, prospective trials conducted in Europe suggest that routine screening of low-risk patients with ultrasound is associated with significant decreases in perinatal morbidity and mortality.[14,15] The reduction associated with singleton gestations results from the identification of major fetal malformations at a stage when pregnancy termination is still an option. The improved outcomes of multiple gestations may reflect early discovery. It is likely that as the cost of basic equipment declines and the expertise needed to use the equipment spreads throughout obstetrical training programs, routine ultrasound will be incorporated into the average obstetric practice in the United States as it already has been in several other countries.

Magnetic Resonant Imaging (MRI)

MRI is a method of imaging based on the innate magnetic fields of structural nuclei. In our experience, MRI is the ideal modality for the precise identification of fetal intracranial abnormalities.[16] With the ability to make a definitive, anatomic diagnosis of obstructive hydrocephalus, future studies will be able to focus on the efficacy of shunting appropriate hydrocephalic candidates.

Invasive Diagnostic Techniques

The need for invasive fetal testing is usually suggested by the results of non-invasive studies. In 1990, one cannot conceive of performing any type of invasive fetal/pregnancy procedure without the benefit of ultrasound guidance.

Amniocentesis

Amniocentesis is the insertion of a needle through both abdominal and uterine walls into the amniotic fluid. It may be performed safely from 11 weeks of gestation until term. Initially used to predict the severity of fetal hemolytic disease by measuring a bilirubin breakdown product (the ▲ OD 450) in the fluid, subsequent major applications include obtaining amniocytes for culture and karyotype, and fluid upon which a variety of biochemical tests are performed to predict the ability of the neonate to breath successfully. Other miscellaneous uses of amniocentesis include obtaining specimens to search for evidence of a fetal biochemical abnormality, to culture for viruses, to inject dyes to either enhance x-ray visualization of the fetus or to confirm rupture of the membranes, and to instill artificial amniotic fluid to improve sonographic visualization. Though by far the most common invasive procedure performed in fetal medicine, it now often takes a diagnostic back seat to chorion villus biopsy and cordocentesis.

Chorion Villus Biopsy (CVS)

CVS is performed either transabdominally or transcervically by either aspirating or pinching off a small quantity of placental tissue. Though the quantity is small, it is rich in DNA and mitotically active cells. CVS may be performed at almost any stage in pregnancy though the safest time appears to be around 11 weeks' gestation.[17] The most common indication for CVS presently is to obtain a specimen for determination of the fetal karyotype. However, if the tissue is cultured for a karyotype, CVS offers no advantage amniocentesis performed at 11 weeks' gestation. CVS is the method of choice to obtain material for the diagnosis of metabolic disorders and for genetic diseases whose diagnosis is amenable to DNA technologies (recently reviewed[18]).

Cordocentesis

Cordocentesis is the insertion under sonographic guidance of a needle into a fetal umbilical vessel. First reported by Daffos in 1983,[19] it is the single most important advance in the evolution of primary care fetal medicine since the application in the late 1950s of diagnostic ultrasound to obstetrics. Imagine trying to care for a postnatal patient from behind a barrier, unable to do such basic medical procedures as measuring blood pressure or obtaining a blood sample for the measurement of biochemical parameters. Cordocentesis provides a safe and efficient means of doing both.[20–22] Cordocentesis may be performed as early as 11–12 weeks' gestation and continued up until delivery.

Other blood sampling techniques which preceded cordocentesis carried a much higher risk of pregnancy loss and were less efficient. Thus, their indications were restrictive.

Indications for cordocentesis, too, are limited by the risks of the procedure. Fortunately, the risk of loss with cordocentesis in trained hands is reasonably low (in the appropriately grown fetus < 1/400). The most common significant complication of cordocentesis is a slowing of the fetal heart (bradycardia). It is more common when the umbilical artery rather than the umbilical vein is punctured or if the fetus is oxygen deficient (hypoxemic). On occasion, fetal bradycardia may necessitate emergency delivery or result in fetal death.[23]

At the University of Iowa, the most common indications per patient for cordocentesis are to obtain blood for a rapid karyotype, to search for fetal infection, and to evaluate fetal hemolytic disease or intrauterine growth retardation. The positive yield per first procedure (i.e., the result provides an explanation or/and changes patient care) for these indications ranges from 19–40%.[24] Clearly, the benefit of the procedure for these indications outweighs its risk.

A great deal of effort has been focused on the collection of normative fetal parameters. This information is extremely difficult to gather since normal fetuses are not purposefully subjected to cordocentesis. Normal values are acquired from studies of fetuses at risk for a variety of disorders which turn out to be absent. Nomograms must consider the impact of gestational age even for tests as basic as the electrolytes. Similar studies performed on blood samples obtained either from fetuses with mild disease, or by fetoscopy, or at the time of cesarean section without labor may be misleading since many of the parameters (including hematocrit) may be altered.

From the diagnostic standpoint, cordocentesis has had its greatest impact to date on two areas in fetal medicine. The first is the evaluation of fetal hemolytic disease. Direct examination of fetal blood permits the stratification of fetuses into risk groups for requiring antenatal transfusion.[25] About 50% of patients who undergo fetal blood sampling rather than amniocentesis for the evaluation of hemolytic disease require only one procedure; another 10% require only two procedures. This contrasts with the mandatory serial amniocenteses required when relying on the ▲ OD 450 measurements. Those fetuses in the highest risk group have a greater than 80% likelihood of requiring transfusion before birth. Since as many as 40% of fetuses whose ▲ OD 450 measurements are in the danger zone (zone III of the Liley curve) actually have a hemaotocrit high enough that an antenatal transfusion is not needed,[26] fetal blood sampling is mandatory prior to transfusion when the physician has relied on the amniotic fluid tests for diagnosis.

The second area where cordocentesis has dramatically improved diagnostic efforts is severe, early-onset growth deficiency (defined as growth deficiency sonographically identifiable prior to 32 weeks or symmetric growth deficiency at any time). The information obtained can have a dramatic and beneficial effect upon the care of the pregnancy.[27] Approximately 20% of severely growth-deficient fetuses have a chromosome abnormality and another 8% a major congenital infection. Excluding miscellaneous causes, about two-thirds of these fetuses are dangerously small because of utero-placental dysfunction. Thirty-five percent of these fetuses will be acidemic by non-laboring norms and 42% hypoxemic (Weiner, C.P., unpublished study based on 91 fetuses). The potential to supplement these fetuses is exciting and the subject of an intense research effort. About half of those fetuses with a chromosome abnormality have an abnormality incompatible with life. Thus, if fetal distress occurs during labor, cesarean section can be avoided. The antenatal diagnosis of fetal infection is important for several reasons. First, the fetal response to infection is often transient. If diagnostic efforts are delayed, it may be impossible to make a diagnosis postnatally. Second, medical therapy prior to birth may prevent or reduce the complications of the infection.

Fetal Therapy

Fetal therapy may be either medical or surgical. Though fetal surgery has clearly captured the eye of both the scientific and lay press, the indications for medical therapy will ultimately, like that for the postnatal patient, far exceed the indications for surgery. The development of fetal therapies is clearly at an early stage. There will inevitably be steps forward and backward.

Medical Therapy

Indirect Therapy

By indirect therapy it is meant that the therapeutic agent is administered to the pregnant patient and is transferred to the fetus by the placenta. Therapy consists of a drug (such as a corticosteroid to suppress the adrenal glands of a fetus with adrenogenital syndrome),[28] or oxygen (for the fetus who is hypoxemic secondary to severe uteroplacental dysfunction).[29]

One notable false start in the area of indirect medical fetal therapy was the use of digoxin to treat the fetus with a type of abnormal heart rate called supraventricular tachycardia. When the heart is beating fast (at almost twice the normal rate), there is too little time for it to refill with blood between contractions. As a result, fetal heart failure may occur. Maternal digitalization was widely reported in both research and lay publications as successful.[30–32] Not until a more detailed investigation of the fetal pharmacokinetics was done did evidence emerge indicating that the reports of successful conversion of the arrhythmia by maternal digitialization were likely serendipitous. This story shows how rapidly the field is evolving and provides a cautionary note.

The ill fetus produces a digoxin-like substance not readily distinguished from the medication derived from the foxglove plant. This led investigators to conclude that the digoxin administered to the mother had crossed the placenta.[33,34] Clearly it does cross when the fetus is healthy and there is little if any endogenous fetal digoxin being produced. However, study of blood samples obtained by cordocentesis from sick fetuses before, during, and after maternal digitalization clearly demonstrated that little, if any, exogenous digoxin crosses the placenta of these ill fetuses.[35] They do produce large amounts of endogenous digoxin.[36] However, if the digoxin is administered directly to the fetus (in whom its elimination half-life is less than 15 hours,[35,37] a rapid biologic effect can be demonstrated. Reinterpreting the reports of presumed *successful* transplacental digoxin therapy, we now know the natural history of fetal supraventricular tachycardia. Many affected fetuses will spontaneously convert to a sinus rhythm even after heart failure has developed. Current research is focused on drugs other than digoxin which may prove successful fetal antiarrhythmics.

One success story for indirect medical therapy is the use of immune globulin to treat alloimmune thrombocytopenia. Alloimmune thrombocytopenia may be thought of as the Rh disease of the platelet. The mother makes an antibody against her fetus's platelets, leading to their destruction. Fetuses with alloimmune thrombocytopenia are at significant risk to hemorrhage before birth.[38] High doses of immune globulin (1 gm/kg) administered to the pregnant patient at weekly intervals have been shown to increase the fetal platelet count in about 80% of treated fetuses.[39] It is occasionally necessary to supplement maternal immunoglobulin therapy with a corticosteroid. Medical failures are treated with weekly platelet transfusions.

One area of indirect medical therapy that has as yet barely been touched is the treatment of fetal infection. The most comprehensive work to date was reported by Daffos on the diagnosis and treatment of congenital toxoplasmosis.[40,41] Antenatal diagnosis of toxoplasmosis and likely all other agents capable of causing congenital infection requires a multifaceted approach. But a diagnosis can be reliably made and, in the case of toxoplasmosis, the fetus can be treated.

At least 8% of fetuses with early-onset growth deficiency have a congenital infection. It is likely that the true percentage is higher, but their identification will require new, sophisticated means of detection such as a search for a specific viral genome. With the development of effective antiviral agents for the treatment of patients with HIV, it may be possible to treat the asymptomatic, infected fetus in an attempt to decrease later sequelae.

Indirect fetal therapy has long been part of the treatment of maternal hyperthyroidism secondary to Graves' disease. Fetal hyperthyroidism results when the fetal thyroid is stimulated by a maternally produced immunoglobulin which crosses the placenta. In the past, the goal of maternal therapy was to maintain the pregnant patient on as low a dose of antithyroid medication as possible in order to prevent oversuppression of the fetal thyroid. It was reasoned that fetal hyperthyroidism could be identified by either decreased growth and/or increased heart rate. Recent study suggests that this approach is not completely reliable.[42,43] Direct evaluation of the fetal thyroid status permits refinement of maternal therapy to assure the delivery of a euthyroid fetus. It is likely that a variety of other illnesses will present themselves which will be amenable to indirect fetal therapy.

Direct Therapy

By direct therapy, it is meant that the medication is administered to the fetus. Pharmacologic interventions have been limited. In the future, fetuses with severe uteroplacental insufficiency may receive parenteral hyperalimentation. Digoxin and digitoxin have each been given directly to the fetus for the treatment of supraventricular tachycardia and congenital myocarditis.[35,37] The fetal pharmacokinetics of these drugs clearly differ from those of the neonate, child, and adult; likely, there will also be differences in the fetal responses. The findings of these trials serve as a reminder that the fetus is not just a low-birthweight neonate.

The most frequent indication for direct fetal medical therapy is treatment of anemia resulting from either hemolytic disease or, less commonly, congenital infection or fetal-maternal hemorrhage. In reference to hemolytic disease, simple intravascular transfusion therapy permits suppression of fetal blood cell synthesis, the complete replacement of antigen-positive blood with antigen-negative blood, and delivery at full term.[44] As a result, perinatal morbidity and mortality from fetal hemolytic disease have both been significantly reduced.[44,45] There have been several reports of fetuses with either aplastic anemia secondary to human parvovirus infection[46,47], or anemia secondary to fetal-maternal hemorrhage[48,49] who have been treated with intravascular transfusion.

Another potential application of fetal transfusion is the treatment of acute, early-onset twin-twin transfusion. This syndrome is particularly devastating when it occurs prior to 24 weeks. The outcome is almost uniformly lethal for both twins unless one of the co-twins dies. Several attempts have been made at the University of Iowa to transfuse one twin and phlebotomize the other. To date, each attempt has proven unsuccessful because the magnitude of the shunt was so large. Successful preservation of the pregnancy in *documented* cases of twin-twin transfusion prior to 24 weeks as of this writing in 1990 has resulted from only two types of therapy. The first is selective feticide – killing the donor twin.[50,51] The second is introduction into the uterus of a fiber-optic telescope through which a laser beam is directed to cauterize the communicating placental vessels.[52] It should be pointed out that the definitive diagnosis of twin-twin transfusion cannot be made without fetal blood sampling. The differential diagnosis of size discordance in twins includes twin-twin transfusion, discordant uteroplacental insufficiency, congenital infection, discordant aneuploidy, and discordant fetal structural malformations.

Surgical Therapy

Percutaneous Therapy

A variety of fetal abnormalities are potentially amenable to the placement of a catheter ("shunt") between an obstructed cavity and, usually, the amniotic cavity. The first shunt was placed, as noted earlier, for the chronic antenatal decompression of presumed obstructive hydrocephalus.[11] The second abnormality to be shunted was bladder obstruction by posterior urethral valves.[53] Though each indication has had its proponents, neither is presently of documented efficacy. The former suffers from both an inability to accurately identify the appropriate candidate and the lack of an effective percutaneously placed shunt. The latter suffers from a host of problems, including the possibility that the associated renal dysplasia and pulmonary hypoplasia has in some fetuses an etiology other than back pressure or compression.[54]

Perhaps the only documented indication for fetal shunting is the treatment of nonimmune hydrops secondary to a hydrothorax which has caused heart failure by mechanically obstructing the return of blood to the heart. The hydrothoraces may be secondary to a variety of abnormalities, including chylothorad, extralobar sequestration, cystic adenomatoid malformation, or mediastinal cyst. Drainage of the chest (or mediastinum) restores near-normal anatomy, permitting normal cardiac return, and allows the fetal lungs to develop normally.[55,56]

Open Surgery

On several occasions, a maternal laparotomy and hysterotomy have been performed, a portion of the fetus exteriorized, and either an ostomy done to relieve a urinary obstruction,[57] an attempt made to repair a diaphragmatic hernia,[58] or a mass removed from the chest.[59] The first procedure suffers the same pragmatic difficulties whether approached by percutaneous or open methods. Since the maternal morbidity of the percutaneous method is markedly lower than the open approach, and in almost all circumstances can be performed by trained operators, it is difficult if not impossible to justify open surgery as the initial approach to relieving fetal urinary obstruction.

The use of open surgery for the antenatal correction of diaphragmatic hernia is more controversial. Clearly, this operation has captured the imagination of both the scientific and lay press, having even been the subject of a made-for-television movie. To date, seven operations have been formally reported, of which two fetuses survived.[58] Though maternal fertility is said to be "unaffected," clearly maternal morbidity has occurred. A guiding rule of medicine is that therapy is undertaken only after the potential risks have been balanced with the potential benefits. In the arena of fetal therapy, this balancing act must also include balancing the good intentions of the physician and the strong maternal desire to do anything to help her fetus with a scientific understanding of the anomaly's natural history. As physicians, we must be willing to revise this risk-benefit ratio constantly, as new information is developed. In the case of fetal diaphragmatic hernia, the natural history studies upon which open surgery was justified appear to be flawed.

The argument for open surgery to correct fetal diaphragmatic hernia was based on the belief that the survival rate if untreated was between 20% and 33%.[60,61] This conclusion was based on physician and hospital surveys which clearly suffered from a variety of methodologic flaws. It was further suggested that the fetus at greatest risk for hypoplastic lungs could be identified antenatally and treated.

The state of Iowa has established a birth defects registry maintained by a nursing staff who examine the full medical records of all anomalous neonates weighing more than 500 grams at birth. Between 1985 and 1989, 65 fetuses with a diaphragmatic hernia were delivered after 20 weeks' gestation. The overall survival rate was 42%. Eighty-nine percent were delivered in community hospitals where 42% of the hernia repairs took place. However, 45% of the fetuses who died had one or more additional major anomalies that were detectable either by ultrasound or by karyotype. These fetuses would have been precluded from antenatal open surgery. Thus, the corrected survival rate was 56%.[62] Any counseling of women regarding the desirability/advantages of open fetal surgery compared to postnatal correction of diaphragmatic hernia should now be based on population studies rather than spotty physician surveys. In that circumstance, much of the attraction of open fetal surgery for the treatment of diaphragmatic hernia is lost.

I do not condemn open fetal surgery, only its first applications. Recently, two attempts were made to remove large cystic adenomatoid malformations in the mid second trimester.[59] This indication is much more attractive since the size of the malformation and thus the risk of fetal cardiac and pulmonary sequelae are more readily determined. It should be noted that macrocystic lesions have a far better prognosis than microcystic lesions have without intervention.[63]

Clearly, primary care fetal medicine is a specialty in its dawning. Much work remains to be done to ascertain normal values and to understand the natural history of the diseases we attempt to treat. Indications will change as the knowledge base grows. It should also be made very clear that the procedures alluded to above are but that – procedures. On the assumption that they are performed efficiently and safely, they can be performed by many. It is more important that there be a cohesive and experienced team to deal with the findings and specimens. A fetal diagnosis and treatment team should include not only the fetologist, geneticist, neonatologist, and nursing specialists, but also pediatric surgeons, neurosurgeons, infectious disease experts, and basic scientists. As the accuracy of diagnosis and the abilities of fetal diagnosis and treatment teams progress, it is essential that every attempt be made to balance maternal desire and physician good wishes with science, and to recognize that the weighting of that scale will change as knowledge accumulates.

References

1. Weiner CP. Introduction to fetal disease. Semin Perinatol 1989; 13: 251.
2. Liley AW. Liquor amnii analysis in management of pregnancy complicated by rhesus sensitization. Am J Obstet Gynecol 1961; 82: 1359.
3. Liley AW. Intrauterine transfusion of foetus in haemolytic disease. Br Med J 1963; 2: 1107.
4. Liley AW. Errors in assessment of hemolytic disease from amniotic fluid. Am J Obstet Gynecol 1963; 86: 485.
5. Cuckle HS, Wald NJ. Maternal serum alpha-fetoprotein measurement: a screening test for Down syndrome. Lancet 1984 Apr: 926.
6. Haddow JE, Knight GJ, Kloza EM, Palomaki GE. Alpha-fetoprotein, vaginal bleeding and pregnancy risk. Br J Obstet Gynaecol 1986; 93: 589.
7. DiMaio MS, Baumgarten A, Greenstein RM, Saal HM, Mahoney MJ. Screening for fetal Down's syndrome in pregnancy by measuring maternal serum alpha-fetoprotein levels. N Engl J Med 1987; 317: 342.
8. Robinson L, Grau P, Grandall BF. Pregnancy outcomes after increasing maternal serum alpha-fetoprotein levels. Obstet Gynecol 1989; 74: 17.
9. Williamson RA. Improved screening for fetal chromosome abnormalities. Iowa Med 1990 Mar: 125.
10. Wald NJ, Cuckle HS, Densem JW et al. Maternal serum screening for Down's syndrome in early pregnancy. Br Med J 1988; 297: 883.
11. Clewell WH, Johnson ML, Meier PR et al. A surgical approach to the treatment of fetal hydrocephalus. N Engl J Med 1982; 306: 1320.
12. Depp R, Sabbagha RE, Brown JT, Tamura RK, Reedy NJ. Fetal surgery for hydrocephalus: Successful in utero ventriculoamniotic shunt for Dandy-Walker syndrome. Obstet Gynecol 1983; 61: 710.
13. Manning FA, Harrison MR, Rodeck C. Catheter shunts for fetal hydronephrosis and hydrocephalus. Report of the International Fetal Surgery Registry. N Engl J Med 1986; 315: 336.
14. Waldenstrom U, Axelsson O, Nilsson S, et al. Effects of routine one-stage ultrasound screening in pregnancy: A control, randomized trial. Lancet 1988; ii: 585.
15. Saari-Kemppainen A, Kayalainen O, Ylostalo P, Heinonen OP. Ultrasound screening and perinatal mortality: Controlled trial of systematic one-stage screening in pregnancy. The Helsinki Ultrasound Trial. Lancet 1990; ii: 387.
16. Wenstrom KD, Williamson RA, Weiner CP, Sipes SL, Yuh WTC. Magnetic resonance imaging of fetuses with intracranial defects. Obstet Gynecol. In press.
17. Rhoads GG, Jackson LG, Schlesselman SE et al. The safety and efficacy of chorionic vilus sampling for early prenatal diagnosis of cytogenetic abnormalities. N Engl J Med 1989; 320: 609.
18. Daffos F. Access to the other patient. Semin Perinatol 1989; 13: 252.
19. Daffos F, Capella-Pavlovsky M, Forestier F. A new procedure for fetal blood sampling in utero: Preliminary results of 53 cases. Am J Obstet Gynecol 1983; 146: 985.
20. Daffos F, Capella-Pavlovsky M, Forestier F. Fetal blood sampling during pregnancy with use of a needle guided by ultrasound: A study of 606 consecutive cases. Am J Obstet Gynecol 1985; 153: 655.
21. Weiner CP. Cordocentesis for diagnostic indications: Two years' experience. Obstet Gynecol 1987; 70: 664.
22. Weiner CP, Heilskov J, Pelzer G, Grant S, Wenstrom K, Williamson RA. Normal values for human umbilical venous and amniotic fluid pressures and their alteration by fetal disease. Am J Obstet Gynecol 1989; 161: 714.
23. Weiner CP. Pancuronium protects against fetal bradycardia following umbilical cord puncture. Proceedings, Society of Perinatal Obstetricians, Abstract # 321, 1991.

24. Weiner CP, Williamson RA, Wenstrom KD, Grant SS. Risk factors for complications of cordocentesis and intravascular transfusion (IVT). Proceedings, Society for Gynecologic Investigation, Abstract #346, 1990.
25. Weiner CP, Wenstrom KD, Williamson RA. The results of direct evaluation and treatment of fetal hemolytic disease. Proceedings, Society of Perinatal Obstetricians, Abstract #33, 1990.
26. Frigoletto FD, Greene MF, Benacerraf BR, Barss VA, Saltzman DH. Ultrasonographic fetal surveillance in the management of the isoimmunized pregnancy. N Engl J Med 1986; 315: 430.
27. Weiner CP. Pathogenesis, evaluation, and potential treatments for severe, early onset growth retardation. Semin Perinatol 1989; 13: 320.
28. Chrousos GP, Evans MI, Loriaux DL, McCluskey J, Fletcher JC, Schulman JD. Prenatal therapy in congenital adrenal hyperplasia. Attempted prevention of abnormal external genitalia by pharmacologic suppression of the fetal adrenal gland in utero. Ann NY Acad Sci 1985; 458: 156.
29. Nocilaides KH, Bradley RJ, Soothill PW, et al. Maternal oxygen therapy for intrauterine growth retardation. Lancet 1987; i: 942.
30. Kerenyi TD, Meller J, Steinfeld L et al. Transplacental cardioversion of intrauterine supraventricular tachycardia with digitalis. Lancet 1980 Aug: 393.
31. Harrigan JT, Kangos JJ, Sikka A et al. Successful treatment of fetal congestive heart failure secondary to tachycardia. N Engl J Med 1981; 304: 1527.
32. Kleinman CS, Copel JA, Weinstein EM, Santulli TV, Hobbins JC. In utero diagnosis and treatment of fetal supraventricular tachycardia. Semin Perinatol 1985; 9: 113.
33. Rogers MC, Willerson JT, Goldblatt A, Smith TW. Serum digoxin concentrations in the human fetus, neonate, and infant. N Engl J Med 1972; 287: 1010.
34. Chan V, Tse TF, Wong V. Transfer of digoxin across the placenta and into breast milk. Br J Obstet Gynaecol 1978; 85: 605.
35. Weiner CP, Thompson MIB. Direct treatment of fetal supraventricular tachycardia after failed transplacental therapy. Am J Obstet Gynecol 1988; 158: 570.
36. Weiner CP, Landas S, Persoon TJ. Digoxin-like immunoreactive substance in fetuses with and without cardiac pathology. Am J Obstet Gynecol 1987; 157: 368.
37. Naides SJ, Weiner CP. Antenatal diagnosis and palliative treatment of non-immune hydrops fetalis secondary to fetal parvovirus B19 infection. Prenat Diagn 1989; 9: 105.
38. Mueller-Eckhardt C, Grubert A, Weisheit M et al. 348 cases of suspected neonatal alloimmune thrombocytopenia. Lancet 1989; ii: 363.
39. Bussel JB, Berkowitz RL, McFarland JG, Lynch L, Chitkara U. Antenatal treatment of neonatal alloimmune thrombocytopenia. N Engl J Med 1988; 319: 1374.
40. Desmonts G, Forestier F, Tulliez PH, Daffos F, Capella-Pavlovsky M, Chartier M. Prenatal diagnosis of congenital toxoplasmosis. Lancet 1985 Mar: 500.
41. Daffos F, Forestier F, Capella-Pavlovsky M et al. Prenatal management of 746 pregnancies at risk for congenital toxoplasmosis. N Engl J Med 1988; 318: 271.
42. Westrom KD, Weiner CP, Williamson RA, Grant SS. Prenatal diagnosis of fetal hyperthyroidism using funipuncture. Obstet Gynecol 1990; 76: 513.
43. Porreco RP, Bloch CA. Fetal blood sampling in the management of intrauterine thyrotoxicosis. Obstet Gynecol 1990; 76: 509.
44. Weiner CP, Wenstrom KD, Williamson RA. Intravascular transfusion for the treatment of nonhemolytic fetal anemia. Proceedings, International Society of Fetal Medicine and Surgery, 1990.
45. Harman CR, Bowman JM, Manning FA, Menticoglou SM. Intrauterine transfusion – intraperitoneal versus intravascular approach: A case-control comparison. Am J Obstet Gynecol 1990; 162: 1053.
46. Peters MT, Nicolaides KH. Cordocentesis for the diagnosis and treatment of human fetal parvovirus infection. Obstet Gynecol 1990; 75: 501.
47. Sahakian V, Weiner CP, Naides SJ, Williamson RA, Scharosch LL. Treatment of nonim-

mune hydrops fetalis secondary to human parvovirus B19 infection with intrauterine transfusion. Am J Obstet Gynecol. In press.
48. Fischer RL, Kuhlman K, Grover J, Montgomery O, Wapner RJ. Chronic, massive fetomaternal hemorrhage treated with repeated fetal intravascular transfusions. Am J Obstet Gynecol 1990; 162: 203.
49. Rouse D, Weiner C. Ongoing fetomaternal hemorrhage treated by serial fetal intravascular transfusions. Obstet Gynecol 1990; 76: 974.
50. Wittmann BK, Farquharson DF, Thomas WDS, Baldwin VJ, Wadsworth LD. The role of feticide in the management of severe twin transfusion syndrome. Am J Obstet Gynecol 1986; 155: 1023.
51. Weiner CP. Diagnosis and treatment of twin to twin transfusion in the mid-second trimester of pregnancy. Fetal Ther 1987; 2: 71.
52. DeLia JE. The neodymium-YAG laser and fetal/placental surgery. In: Keye WR, ed. Laser Surgery and Gynecology and Obstetrics. 2d ed. Chicago: Yearbook Medical Publishers 1990; 3.
53. Harrison MR, Golbus MS, Filly RA et al. Management of the fetus with congenital hydronephrosis. J Pediatr Surg 1982; 17: 728.
54. Weiner C, Wiliamson R, Bonsib S, Erenberg A, Pringle K, Smith W, Abu-Yousef M. In utero bladder diversion – Problems with patient selection. Fetal Ther 1986; 1: 196.
55. Weiner C, Varner M, Pringle K, Hein H, Williamson R, Smith W. Antenatal diagnosis and palliative treatment of nonimmune hydrops fetalis secondary to pulmonary extralobar sequestration. Obstet Gynecol 1986; 68: 275.
56. Rodeck CH, Fisk NM, Fraser DI, Nicolini U. Long-term in utero drainage of fetal hydrothorax. N Engl J Med 1988; 319: 1135.
57. Harrison MR, Golbus MS, Filly RA et al. Fetal surgery for congenital hydronephrosis. N Engl J Med 1982; 306: 591.
58. Harrison MR, Adzick NS, Longaker MT et al. Successful repair in utero of a fetal diaphragmatic hernia after removal of herniated viscera from the left thorax. N Engl J Med 1990; 322: 1582.
59. Harrison MR, Adzick NS, Jennings RW et al. Antenatal intervention for congenital cystic adenomatoid malformation. Lancet 1990; 336: 965.
60. Harrison MR, Bjordal RI, Langmark F, Knutrud O. Congenital diaphragmatic hernia: The hidden mortality. J Pediatr Surg 1978; 13: 227.
61. Adzick NS, Harrison MR, Glick PL, Nakayama DK, Manning FA, deLorimier AA. Diaphragmatic hernia in the fetus: prenatal diagnosis and outcome in 94 cases. J Pediatr Surg 1985; 20: 357.
62. Wenstrom KD, Weiner CP, Hansen J. A five-year statewide experience with congenital diaphragmatic hernia. Proceedings, Society of Perinatal Obstetricians, 1991.
63. Adzick NS, Harrison MR, Glick PL et al. Fetal cystic adenomatoid malformation: Prenatal diagnosis and natural history. J Pediatr Surg 1985; 20: 483.

FRANK A. CHERVENAK AND LAURENCE B. MCCULLOUGH

Court-Ordered Cesarean Delivery

An increasingly prominent topic in the literature of obstetric ethics is court-ordered cesarean delivery. Despite its rarity in clinical practice, the topic is nonetheless significant because it raises fundamental questions about the rights and obligations of pregnant women in the intrapartum period, the obligations of physicians to pregnant women and their fetuses, and the role of the law in regulating the behavior of pregnant woman and their physicians. The purpose of this paper is to advance a series of criticisms against those who hold that court-ordered cesarean delivery is not justified, tragic consequences for the imperiled fetus notwithstanding. We shall argue that well-documented, complete placenta previa is a counterexample to the arguments of opponents of court-ordered cesarean delivery.[1]

This paper has four parts. First, we provide a brief summary of the arguments of three of the most prominent opponents of court-ordered cesarean delivery: Annas,[2] Nelson and Milliken,[3] and Rhoden.[4]

Second, we address two fundamental conceptual considerations. The first of these concerns whether refusal of cesarean delivery in all cases constitutes a negative right, a right to noninterference, to be left alone to make private reproductive decisions. We shall argue that a negative right exists only when the pregnant woman refuses any longer to be a patient and leaves the care of her physician. By contrast, when the pregnant woman remains a patient, refusal of cesarean delivery in the intrapartum period amounts in all cases to the assertion of a negative right of refusal of one form of obstetric intervention, cesarean delivery, in conjunction with a positive right to another form of obstetric management, vaginal delivery, the only other alternative. This conceptual issue has been overlooked in the entire literature on court-ordered cesarean delivery. The second conceptual issue concerns epistemological uncertainty in clinical prognostic judgment. We shall argue that the nature of this uncertainty has been systematically misunderstood by opponents of court-ordered cesarean delivery. On the basis of these two conceptual considerations, we conclude that in the case of well-documented, complete placenta previa the physician has an ethical obligation not to accept refusal of cesarean delivery. This necessarily raises the question of whether

F.K. Beller and R.F. Weir (eds.), The Beginning of Human Life, 257–272.

this ethical obligation could justifiably take the form of seeking a court order.

In the third section of this paper we therefore address the arguments of opponents of court-ordered cesarean delivery. We focus most of our attention on Rhoden's arguments, because of their thoroughness.[5] In doing so, we assume that, if our criticisms of Rhoden's arguments succeed, they surely succeed against the arguments of others, because of the thoroughness and representativeness of Rhoden's arguments. We develop our criticism on the basis of the counterexample of well-documented, complete placenta previa.[5]

The first three sections of this paper force a reconsideration of the issue of court-ordered cesarean deliveries by shifting subsequent argument to new grounds. In effect, we mean to show that arguments pro and con, to date, have been conducted on the wrong grounds, mainly as a consequence of regarding all refusals of cesarean delivery as exercises of a protected negative moral and legal right to noninterference, to be left alone to make one's own reproductive decisions. Conceptually clarified grounds require that the right to refuse a cesarean delivery but not to refuse remaining a patient, exercised in the intrapartum period, should be understood as a negative right in conjunction with a positive right. The latter, like all such rights, is intrinsically capable of being limited in its exercises for both ethical and legal reasons.

The fourth section of this paper occupies less space than the preceding three sections, in an inverse relationship to its clinical importance. Here we argue that the focus of attention on the crude clinical instrument of court-ordered cesarean delivery fundamentally distorts obstetric ethics. When law and ethics are conflated, as they have been in most of the literature on this topic, ethics becomes exclusively retrospective, thereby sacrificing altogether its prospective character. Dramatic medical ethical dilemmas are intellectually stimulating to address but their most significant ethical feature for clinicians, patients, and society is that they ought to be prevented. By disentangling obstetric ethics from obstetric jurisprudence we mean to focus ethical attention to where it ought to be in the clinical setting: clinical strategies for preventive obstetric ethics.[6]

The Arguments of Opponents of Court-Ordered Cesarean Delivery

Among the most visible opponents of court-ordered cesarean delivery is Annas.[7] He holds the view that women's reproductive rights – ethical and legal alike – are absolute. Annas's argument in support of this view is essentially twofold. First, he points out that women have an "inalienable right" to abortion "that they retain ... up to the moment of childbirth if their life or health is in danger by continuing the pregnancy."[8] Second, all claims by physicians to know which obstetric management is in the interest of the fetus are epistemologically unfounded, because of their systematic prognostic uncertainty. Annas brings these two lines of reasoning together in the following way:

> In the face of such uncertainty – uncertainty compounded by decades of changing and conflicting expert opinion on the management of pregnancy and childbirth – the moral and legal primacy of the competent, informed pregnant woman in decision making is overwhelming.[9]

The argument of Nelson and Milliken follows Annas's argument about the ethical and legal implications of uncertainty in clinical judgment. Nelson and Milliken represent an advance over Annas's arguments, because they recognize the larger ethical context in which medical uncertainty must be analyzed, namely, the pregnant woman's "ethical obligation to accept reasonable, non-experimental treatment for the sake of her fetus and to behave otherwise in a manner intended to benefit and not harm her fetus."[10] This obligation, they claim, is rooted in the pregnant woman's influence on the health and development of the fetus.[11] Nelson and Milliken are correct to point out that, if clinical judgment is unavoidably uncertain in the sense of never being reliable, then neither the clinician nor the state can legitimately claim authority to define criteria for which obstetric interventions are reasonable and prudent. Their argument is to the effect that unavoidable clinical uncertainty makes it impossible to justify legal enforcement of any ethical obligations on the part of pregnant women to their fetuses. Moreover, they add, it would be dangerous to do so, because doing so would result in more harm than good, by discouraging pregnant women from seeking obstetric care. Their view is summarized in the following:

> Incompleteness of medical knowledge and the unavoidable uncertainty of medical diagnostic and therapeutic techniques make it impossible to define a clear, precise, and accurate medical model on which society could base a fair and uniformly applied legal policy that would sanction the use of force against pregnant women.[12]

Rhoden's arguments against court-ordered cesarean delivery are very thorough, indeed, masterful.[13] This is because, first, she directly addresses, and offers arguments designed to refute, those arguments that can be made in favor of court-ordered cesarean delivery, such as Robertson's,[14] and, second, with an important exception (exclusion of pregnant women from the provisions of living wills in a number of states), she addresses and rejects legal arguments in favor of court-ordered delivery that might be constructed on the basis of analogies to child neglect law, the law regarding obligations to rescue strangers, and abortion law, as well as providing a positive argument to support opposition to court-ordered cesarean delivery.

The core of Rhoden's positive argument comprises two closely related claims: (1) pregnant women have no legally enforceable ethical obligations to the fetus, and (2) court-ordered cesarean delivery treats the pregnant woman as a means and also as a "means merely," in that such court orders violate her autonomy without justification. A buttressing argument claims that prognostic obstetric judgment is systematically disabled by uncertainty.

Like Annas,[15] Nelson and Milliken,[16] and the ACOG Committee on Ethics,[17] Rhoden focuses almost exclusively on court-ordered cesarean delivery for fetal distress. She discusses other cases, notably *Jefferson v. Griffin Spalding County Historical Authority*[18] and *In Re Baby Jeffries*,[19] in which complete placenta previa was allegedly involved. By not subjecting the latter category of cesarean delivery to the same searching analysis she provides for the former, Rhoden fails to identify the marked heterogeneity between the two categories.

Two Fundamental Conceptual Issues

In this section we address and clarify two conceptual issues that have been systematically misunderstood in the literature on the subject and that are, moreover, fundamental for the development of our argument: refusal of cesarean delivery as a negative right and epistemological uncertainty in clinical prognostic judgment.

Refusal of Cesarean Delivery: Always a Negative Right?

A negative right is usually understood in ethics as a right of noninterference in decision making and behavior. A negative right therefore generates duties on the part of others to leave the individual in question alone.[20] In law, the rights to privacy and to self-determination, both pertinent to reproductive decision making, are negative rights in this sense. By contrast, positive rights involve a claim on the resources of others to have some need, desire, or want met. Such rights obligate others to act in specified ways in response. As a rule, positive rights are in all cases understood to be liable to limits by their very nature.[21] This feature of positive rights contrasts sharply with negative rights, where the burden of proof is on others to establish limits on negative rights, e.g., on the basis of preventing serious harm to innocent others. The entire debate about court-ordered cesarean deliveries has, to date, treated refusal of cesarean delivery as an instance of negative rights.

It is interesting that even proponents of court orders have accepted the basic framework of the courts and of opponents to court-ordered cesarean delivery. Robertson, for example, sees the issue of whether the woman's right to bodily integrity, a negative right based on her autonomy, can be overridden by "a compelling state interest, not attainable in any other way."[22] Robertson elaborates the issue in the following terms:

> The issue becomes whether the mother's interest in bodily integrity is great enough to override the unborn child's interest in life and well-being when parental autonomy alone is not. The answer depends in part on the extent and risks of forcible intrusion and the value granted to bodily integrity, a right the limits of which have not been identified.[23]

Elkins et al., in a broad-reaching defense of court-ordered cesarean delivery, characterize the issue in terms of a balance between a woman's autonomy-based negative right to refuse obstetric intervention and the ethical demands of "beneficence, non-malfeasance, justice, obstetric contract keeping, and acting in the patient's best interest."[24] In "rare situations" the latter combine "to challenge and override individual maternal autonomy."[25] To be fair we must admit that our own prior work framed the ethical issues in terms of whether beneficence-based obligations of the physician and of the pregnant woman to the fetus can justifiably override autonomy-based respect for refusal of cesarean delivery.[26]

We here identify the heterogeneous nature of such refusals.[27] Sometimes refusal is the exercise exclusively of a negative right; sometimes, importantly, refusal is exercised in conjunction with a positive right to request one particular obstetric management plan rather than another.

Refusal of cesarean delivery is exclusively a negative right when that refusal does not impose any obligation on the physician to employ an alternative obstetric management strategy. That is, refusal of cesarean delivery is a negative right when the pregnant woman refuses any longer to be a patient. Such a legal right was recognized by the *Jefferson* court when it declined to give the state custody of Mrs. Jefferson's fetus unless she returned to the hospital for further obstetric care.[28] This negative right in obstetrics has direct analogues in other specialty areas, e.g., when a patient refuses an electrocardiogram for workup of chest pain and leaves the doctor's office, or when ambulatory patients – as they frequently do – do not take prescribed medications (at all or for the full course).

When refusal of cesarean delivery is a negative right, what would a court be asked to do by issuing an order for a cesarean delivery? The answer seems to be that the physician or hospital or even the police would be sanctioned by the power of the state to go into the community, seize someone, and present that individual to a physician as a patient – all the while restraining an uncooperative individual if necessary.

Usually, individuals become patients if they consent to do so or, if they are incompetent, when others elect to present them to a physician. Court orders to seize competent individuals and make them patients against their will would do considerable violence to this central ethical tradition of becoming a patient in medicine. Moreover, such court orders would grossly overmedicalize the lives of individuals subject to those orders, undermining the very social conditions of the voluntary formation of patient-physician relationships. Violating a negative right involves all of the worries of opponents that court orders undercut the purpose they presumably are serving: seeing to it that fetuses are protected. That purpose will not be well served by forcing individuals to become patients against their will. Thus, the authors believe that the *Jeffries* court[29] erred in ordering Mrs. Jeffries to be seized by the police and presented to the hospital for further obstetric care.

When the pregnant woman does not leave the hospital and does not dissolve the patient-physician relationship, or when she returns to the hospital to continue that relationship, she is not simply exercising a negative right to refuse any longer to be a patient. That is, the patient is not refusing all intervention, but one of only two alternative obstetric management strategies. In effect, this amounts to a positive claim on the services of the physician and hospital to assist in vaginal delivery. "Refusal" of cesarean delivery is an accurate description of the woman's expressed decision, but only at the most superficial level of its verbal formulation. At a deeper level, i.e., at the level of its practical effect, "refusal" here is really the attempted exercise of a positive right in conjunction with a negative right. As noted above, however, positive rights cannot be intrinsically absolute, because they are intrinsically capable of being limited. Thus, it is appropriate – because conceptually necessary – to inquire into those limits.

Interestingly, there are direct analogues to other specialty areas. A hospitalized patient with gangrene of a toe, caused by insufficient blood circulation secondary to poorly controlled diabetes mellitus, who refuses amputation but wants the gangrene treated, is both refusing surgery and demanding the only other available alternative, namely, medical management. A Jehovah's Witness who refuses blood products in a situation in which volume expanders (which need not be constituted of blood products) may be therapeutic is demanding the former on the grounds of religious objection to the latter. Notice that in these two examples there may be no well-founded objection by a clinician to do as he or she has been requested by the patient. Thus, there may be no sufficiently compelling reason to seek to limit the patient's request.

This does not mean, however, that every patient's request for one management strategy as opposed to another is not intrinsically liable to limits in its ethical or legal force.[30] This is because the possibility that there can be compelling reasons to limit the exercise of positive rights is built into the concept of positive rights. No separate burden of proof must be satisfied in order to introduce the possibility of limits, only to introduce particular limits. This is quite different from the attempt to set limits on negative rights, e.g., when those rights are grounded in autonomy as a side constraint.[31] Thus, to argue in terms of refusal of cesarean delivery simply as a negative right – as if the physician were expected by the patient to do nothing and end the patient-physician relationship and as if the burden of proof were on the physician to show that questions of limits on "refusal" of cesarean delivery are relevant clinical considerations – involves a serious conceptual confusion. Once the true nature of "refusal" of cesarean delivery within the patient-physician relationship is properly understood, the counterexample that we will develop becomes salient.

Epistemological Standards for Clinical Prognostic Judgment

Annas's second main line of justification depends heavily on his conclusion that clinical prognostic judgment is so uncertain that it has no ethical or legal authority.[32] The uncertainty of clinical prognostic judgment also plays a central role in the argument against court-ordered cesarean delivery by Nelson and Milliken.[33] Annas, along with Nelson and Milliken and the ACOG Committee, who rely on Annas's analysis, make a fundamental mistake.

They hold clinical prognostic judgment to a standard of truth that it can never satisfy, namely, that clinical prognostic judgment never turns out to be false. On such a standard of truth, before the outcome actually occurs, all clinical prognostic judgments must be judged possibly false and therefore disabled by uncertainty. In effect, Annas, along with Nelson and Milliken and the ACOG committee, propose an impossible epistemological standard, one that bears little relation to reasonable tests of epistemological reliability of clinical prognostic judgments. This test emphasizes the reliability with which such judgments are formed because, prospectively, knowledge of the actual outcome is unavailable.

Reliability of clinical judgment involves two considerations: (1) the process of reaching a particular clinical judgment, and (2) the data upon which clinical judgment is based. In the first respect, a clinical judgment is reliable when that judgment would most likely be made again by a second competent, rigorous judger who was given the same data as the original judger. In the second respect, a clinical judgment is reliable when the data upon which it is based do not vary and are not expected to vary. These realistic tests of the reliability of prognostic judgments are pertinent to our foregoing comments about refusal of obstetric intervention as positive rights in the following way.

In our view, assessing the reliability of prognostic clinical judgment involves several considerations. First, the clinician must identify rigorously the probability of self-limitation or spontaneous resolution of the patient's condition. In addition, the clinician needs to specify as precisely as possible the expected outcomes of alternative management strategies.

Second, the clinician needs to realize that prognostic clinical judgment is not about individual cases but about the natural history of a particular disease under different management strategies. Thus, if an outcome of very rare incidence happens to occur, this does not mean that the prior prognostic judgment that the most common event would be the most likely outcome was wrong. In particular, given that spontaneous resolution of well-documented, complete placenta previa diagnosed in the intrapartum period is at best an extremely rare event, the clinician who makes a recommendation for cesarean delivery as the better obstetric management on this basis is making a reliable clinical judgment in both senses of reliability explained above. He or she was not "wrong" if the extremely unlikely event, spontaneous resolution, happens to occur.

Third, to say, nonetheless, that clinicians can be and often are "wrong" in their clinical prognostic judgments only makes sense if one is employing the clinical instrument medical students fondly dub the "retrospectoscope." It has a wonderful feature: it is always crystal clear. It also has an unfortunate feature: its findings always come too late. Our point in using this metaphor is not to entertain. Rather, we use it to underscore the epistemological status of prognostic clinical judgment. That status is not adequately captured in the two-valued logic of truth and falsehood about individual cases.

This analysis of the reliability of prognostic clinical judgment is crucial for our counterexample to the opponents of court-ordered cesarean delivery: well-documented, complete placenta previa. By well-documented, complete placenta previa we mean the following: (1) transabdominal or transvaginal ultrasound examination is performed by individuals competent in the technique and interpretation of its results; (2) the placenta is clearly visualized on ultrasound examination to cover the cervical os completely; and (3) to maximize reliability, ultrasound examination should be performed shortly before delivery.[34] (The reliability of the examination varies inversely with the length of time remaining before expected date of delivery, because of increased variability of data regarding outcome the earlier the examination is performed.) Satisfaction of these three criteria makes a false-positive diagnosis of complete placenta previa highly unlikely.

Fulfillment of these criteria also makes the following prognostic clinical judgments highly reliable. First, spontaneous resolution of the condition or an erroneous diagnosis is highly unlikely. Second, the outcome of vaginal delivery for the fetus is that there is a very substantial risk, approaching certainty, of fetal death. That is, fetal survival will with very high probability not occur.[35] Third, the outcome of cesarean delivery for the pregnant woman vis-à-vis vaginal delivery is a dramatic reduction of the risk of mortality.

Can the clinician say unconditionally that the fetus will not survive vaginal delivery? No. However, the issue for prognostic clinical judgment is its reliability, not its truth. The ethical issue regarding reliability here is this: Can any clinician competently claim to have documented evidence of a significant rate of fetal survival from vaginal delivery? No. Indeed, such a claim would properly be regarded as an irrational basis for obstetric management. Moreover, to study the question via a randomized clinical trial would be judged unethical by any IRB asked to review such a proposal, because of grave risk to fetuses in the vaginal delivery arm of such a clinical trial. The upshot of this ethical analysis is that the clinician is correct to conclude that the only obstetric management strategy consistent with the interests of the fetus is cesarean delivery.

With regard to the pregnant woman's interests, the reliability of prognostic clinical judgment here means that any clinical judgment that well-documented, complete placenta previa is most likely self-limiting and most likely to resolve spontaneously is unfounded and probably irrational. The only rational assumption to make is that vaginal delivery places the pregnant woman at grave risk for exsanguination. The gravity of such a risk is underscored by a long-standing obstetric dictum: Never perform a vaginal examination on a third-trimester patient who is experiencing vaginal bleeding, because of the rapidity with which uncontrollable blood loss might result from disruption of a placenta previa.[36]

Should bleeding occur, massive blood replacement may save some women.[37] However, this intervention may not be sufficient to prevent maternal death. In addition, there are significant risks of morbidity and mortality associated with massive blood transfusion, risks that exceed those of cesarean delivery. Finally, no one would seriously propose that studying this issue via a clinical trial is ethically justified, because the maternal risks are so well defined.

The upshot of this analysis of reliability is that vaginal delivery carries significant risks of material mortality that can infrequently be managed successfully. By comparison, cesarean delivery, despite its morbidity and mortality risks for the woman and despite its invasiveness, unequivocally produces net benefit for the pregnant woman. Any clinical judgment to the contrary borders on the irrational. Therefore, the clinician who recommends cesarean delivery to protect both the fetus and the pregnant woman is making a recommendation with the highest reliability that can be applied to clinical judgment: no competent, rigorous clinician would undertake the management of patients on the basis of a clinical judgment of expected spontaneous resolution.

The ethical implications of this level of reliability of clinical judgment and of refusal of cesarean delivery are the following: (1) no physician is justified in accepting such a refusal, because doing so would be based on unreliable clinical judgment; and (2) the physician is justified in resisting a patient's exercise of a positive right when fulfilling that positive right contradicts the most highly reliable clinical judgment. Patients do not have a positive moral right to obligate physicians to practice medicine in ways that are patently inconsistent with the most reliable clinical judgment.[38]

The Counterexample to Arguments of Opponents of Court-Ordered Cesarean Delivery: Well-documented, Complete Placenta Previa

These implications necessarily raise the issue of whether resisting a request during the intrapartum period for vaginal delivery to manage well-documented, complete placenta previa could justifiably take the form of seeking a court order to override the woman's verbal refusal of cesarean delivery. Addressing this issue requires an argument to show that the arguments of opponents to court-ordered cesarean delivery do not apply to the counterexample of well-documented, complete placenta previa.

For the reasons mentioned already, we focus on Rhoden's arguments. The first that we consider is Rhoden's claim that court-ordered cesarean delivery necessarily treats the pregnant woman solely as an instrument or means by which the fetus is benefited but by which the woman is not benefited, but only placed at risk. In Rhoden's terms, court orders treat the pregnant woman as a mere means to the benefit of her fetus, with no attention to possible benefit for the woman.

This is not the case, because cesarean delivery produces significant benefit in reducing maternal mortality risks, and significant benefit for the fetus, i.e., essentially complete elimination of risks of fetal mortality. Cesarean delivery for well-documented, complete placenta previa produces two *causally independent* effects: benefit for the pregnant woman is not "mere means" to the benefit of her fetus. Instead, she is an end and is, therefore, in no way whatever reduced to being simply a "fetal container," the dramatic but, in this context, totally misleading construct of Annas.[39] The pregnant woman is, and remains throughout the procedure, a patient in her own right, a status that is never compromised.

The preceding is not meant to imply that cesarean delivery is risk-free. To the contrary, because it is major abdominal surgery, it implicates risks, albeit small and usually manageable, of morbidity and rare incidents of mortality. The key feature in the present context of cesarean delivery for well-documented, complete placenta previa is that its *net effect* for the pregnant woman is to produce benefit. Because the risks involved in cesarean delivery are a means to benefit the pregnant woman, while at the same time benefiting the fetus, the pregnant woman is not a "mere means" for benefiting the fetus. By aggregating all cases of cesarean delivery – in particular, fetal distress and complete placenta previa – Rhoden is prevented from identifying this unique feature of cesarean delivery for well-documented, complete placenta previa. Annas, along with Nelson and Milliken and the ACOG committee, make precisely the same mistake.

Rhoden's next objection is that forced cesarean delivery treats pregnant women as a "means merely." That is, her autonomy is violated without sufficient justification. This objection can be defeated by the following two considerations.

We have argued elsewhere that the pregnant woman, in a pregnancy being taken to term, is ethically obligated to accept reasonable risks on behalf of the fetus in the management of her pregnancy.[40] Robertson argues for a similar legal obligation.[41] Nelson and Milliken,[42] as well as Rhoden,[43] accept an ethical obligation. If this view is reasonable in obstetric ethics, then it is all the more reasonable to hold that the pregnant woman is ethically obligated to accept obstetric interventions that *benefit the fetus while also benefiting her*. If she is obligated to accept reasonable risks, she is surely obligated to accept well-documented benefits for herself.

Another justification exists for constraining autonomy in these cases, the harm principle.[44] It is a well-understood tenet of ethical theory that an individual's exercise of positive, as well as negative, rights can justifiably be limited to prevent virtually certain, preventable, serious, and far-reaching harm to innocent others. This justification becomes even stronger when imposing such limits also benefits the individual who is subject to those limits.

On the basis of the above analysis, it is clear that the analogies employed by Rhoden to forced donation of tissue, such as bone marrow or one of a matched pair of solid organs, fail.[45] The analogies are used in the following argument: Just as courts have refused to order family members (more precisely, distant family members, namely, cousins) to donate tissue or organs, so too, courts should not order cesarean deliveries.

At first glance, these analogies possess a powerful intuitive appeal. On closer examination that appeal fails in the case of well-documented, complete placenta previa. In cases of tissue and organ transplantation, the donor is subject to significant harms, among which are risks of morbidity and mortality of the medical procedures, of hospitalization, and – in cases of organ donation – subsequent life without the donated organ. There may be psychological benefits to being a donor.[46] In the case of bone marrow transplantation, the benefits to the pediatric recipient seem not to be significant, given the high failure rate of this therapy.[47] In the case of pediatric kidney transplantation, it is regarded as the preferred management of end-stage renal failure, although it has persistent, significant rates of failure.[48] Moreover, even though independence is increased, pediatric renal transplantation can involve diminished quality of life in other respects.[49]

Cesarean delivery for well-documented, complete placenta previa produces clear-cut net benefit for the pregnant woman (the analogue of the tissue or organ donor) and clear-cut benefit for the fetus (the analogue of the pediatric recipient of tissue or an organ). Thus, the alleged analogies fail. Indeed, there is no such analogy in pediatrics to cesarean delivery for well-documented, complete placenta previa. In this respect, cesarean delivery for well-documented, complete placenta previa is ethically *sui generis*.

Rhoden considers at some length differences in beliefs about outcome between pregnant women and their physicians and understandable fears about major surgery on the part of patients. In the present context a belief on the part of the pregnant woman that vaginal delivery would be more beneficial for her or for her fetus than cesarean delivery is a matter of demonstrably false belief, not a difference of opinion. Fear of the cesarean delivery is, therefore, in all likelihood, an irrational fear. False beliefs and irrational fears are properly understood in bioethics not to be an expression of autonomy, but a factor that can significantly disable autonomy.[50] Thus, neither demonstrably false belief nor irrational fear should be treated as expressions of autonomy. Rather, they should be addressed as obstacles to the exercise of autonomy. Rhoden's argument on this score would, therefore, appear to fail.

Rhoden also considers and supports religious objections to forced cesarean delivery. Here we believe that there is an analogy to overriding parental refusal on religious grounds of well-documented lifesaving interventions for children who are patients, an analogy that defeats Rhoden's view. Rhoden points out that one reason that the courts are correct to protect pediatric patients in these circumstances is that no physical burden is imposed on the parents by a court order to treat their child. To be sure, cesarean delivery is invasive, major abdominal surgery. In the case of well-documented, complete placenta previa invasiveness should not be the sole criterion for assessing physical burdens, because invasiveness in this case is not associated with net harm. To the contrary, it is associated with net benefit, because it dramatically reduces the risk of maternal mortality. To be sure, parents may take moral or psychological offense in being overridden, but the courts apparently do not regard this as a sufficiently compelling invasion of their autonomy. The same would hold true in the present instance. The net effect, therefore, of cesarean delivery for this complication is to benefit the pregnant woman, not burden her. This would seem to complete the analogy to court orders to override religiously based objections of parents for well-documented saving interventions for pediatric patients.

We believe that we have shown well-documented, complete placenta previa to be a decisive counterexample to the school of thought that opposes court-ordered cesarean delivery. The development of our counterexample implies that legitimate grounds for court-ordered cesarean delivery may exist in the case of sustained refusal in the intrapartum period by the pregnant woman of cesarean delivery to manage well-documented, complete placenta previa. Court orders in such cases, when all else fails, do not treat the pregnant women as a "mere means" or a "means merely." She is and remains a patient, an end in herself. Clinical prognostic judgment meets the most rigorous test for reliability: no reasonable clinician would act as if spontaneous resolution occurs in any significant percentage of cases. Cesarean delivery for well-documented, complete placenta previa is *sui generis*, and, therefore, existing common law regarding pediatric transplantation is disanalogous. Finally, well-documented, complete placenta previa is a rare clinical entity.[51] Adamant refusal of cesarean delivery leaving court orders as the sole, last resort is rarer still. Thus, court orders as such a rare last resort cannot reasonably be expected to damage the patient-physician relationship in obstetric practice generally, nor to discourage pregnant women from seeking obstetric care. In summary, we believe that the preceding line of argument entails new grounds for analyzing the ethics and jurisprudence of court-ordered cesarean deliveries for at least one clinical entity, i.e., well-documented, complete placenta previa. These grounds are immune to Rhoden's argument to the contrary – because they defeat it – as well as to the arguments of Annas, Nelson and Milliken, and the ACOG Committee on Ethics.

Those grounds are three: (1) the pregnant woman's exercise of an autonomy-based positive right to vaginal delivery is justifiably limited because of the physician's obligations to avoid unnecessary harm to an innocent other (the harm principle); (2) there is an epistemologically well-founded ethical obligation on the part of the pregnant woman as the price for conferring dramatic benefit on the fetus; and (3) the pregnant woman is not treated only as a means to benefit her fetus – her status as a patient is not compromised in any ethically unacceptable fashion.[52]

Preventive Ethics in Obstetric Practice

The purpose of the preceding section is to force a shift in the grounds upon which further discussion of court-ordered cesarean delivery should be undertaken. If we are correct, both the courts issuing orders and those who oppose and who support court-ordered cesarean delivery have fundamentally misunderstood those grounds.

The courts and those who oppose and who support court-ordered cesarean delivery have, we believe, made an even more fundamental error, and so have served physicians, their pregnant patients, and intrapartum fetuses poorly. The error is to conflate ethics and law – Annas is the worst offender in this respect – with the result that *reaction* to ethical dilemmas, rather than their *prevention*, has received virtually all of the attention. To paraphrase Abraham Lincoln, obstetric ethics should disenthrall itself of the law and focus prospectively on ethical conflicts between pregnant women and their physicians. A judge can refuse to issue a court order to force a pregnant woman to have a cesarean delivery. By itself, however, such refusal – even if it should become the legal norm – will not encourage or foster respect for autonomy of the pregnant woman. In this respect the law is virtually impotent to promote respect for the autonomy of the pregnant woman as a basic principle in obstetric practice.

Ethics, however, can take a prospective posture in the form of preventive ethics. On the basis of preventive ethics the three fundamental skills of clinical obstetric ethics can be developed in clinical practice: the identification, prevention, and management of ethical conflict in obstetric practice. Because they will promote respect for the autonomy of pregnant woman, the clinical skills and strategies of preventive ethics should receive most of our energy and attention for the future, their lack of drama and intellectual excitement notwithstanding. Those strategies are based in an informed consent process in which the probabilities, nature, and management of high risk pregnancy are discussed in advance and in which the pregnant woman is invited to articulate her values for her pregnancy over time. A general strategy for managing her pregnancy can be developed on these bases. These values and the already disclosed information about cesarean delivery as a legitimate management strategy for some high risk pregnancies together constitute the foundation for the additional strategies of negotiation and respectful persuasion.[53] In this way a patient-physician relationship can be developed on the basis of respect for the pregnant woman's autonomy, on the basis of beneficence-based obligations to the fetus on her part and on her physician's part, and on the basis of the physician's beneficence-based obligations to the pregnant woman. In the authors' view, these together constitute the most appropriate framework for obstetric ethics.[54]

The authors want to thank the following individuals for their very helpful comments on earlier drafts: Thomas Bole, Baruch A. Brody, H. Tristram Engelhardt, Jr., B. Andrew Lustig, Joy H. Penticuff, and Stephen Wear.

Notes

1. This counterexample has been identified by others, e.g., Carson Strong. Ethical conflict between mother and fetus in obstetrics. Clinics in Perinatol 1987; 14(2): 313–328. However, Strong does not carefully define "placenta previa," whereas the more precise term is "well-documented, complete placenta previa." Nor does he provide a thoroughgoing argument for his claim that "when the mother's behavior is likely to cause serious harm to the fetus, she steps beyond her right to autonomy" (316). We also take exception to applying the concept of personhood to the fetus.
2. George J Annas. Protecting the liberty of pregnant patients. New Engl J Med 1988; 316(19): 1213–1214; Sherman Elias and George J Annas. Reproductive Genetics and the Law. Chicago: Year Book Medical Publishers, 1987: 253–262; Sherman Elias and George J Annas. Perspectives on fetal surgery. Am J Obstet Gynecol 1983; 145(7): 807–812; George J Annas. Pregnant women as fetal containers. Hastings Center Report 1986; 16: 13–14; George J Annas. Forced Cesareans: the most unkindest cut of all. Hastings Center Report 1982; 12: 16–17, 45.
3. Lawrence J Nelson and Nancy Milliken. Compelled treatment of pregnant woman: life, liberty, and law in conflict. J Am Med Assoc 1988; 259(7): 1060–1066.
4. Nancy K Rhoden. The judge in the delivery room: the emergence of court-ordered Cesareans. California Law Review 1986; 74: 1951, 1950–2030. A shorter version of this article appeared as Nancy K Rhoden. Cesareans and Samaritans Law, Medicine and Health Care 1987; 15(3): 118–125.
5. "Well-documented, complete placenta previa" is defined in the next section.
6. Frank A Chervenak and Laurence B McCullough. Clinical strategies for preventing ethical conflict between pregnant women and their physicians. Am J Obstet Gynecol 1990; 162(2): 303–307.
7. See note 2 above.
8. Elias and Annas. Reproductive Genetics and the Law, 260.
9. Annas. Protecting the liberty of pregnant patient. 1213.
10. Nelson and Milliken. Compelled medical treatment of pregnant women. 1065–1066.
11. Ibid., 1066.
12. Ibid., 1065.
13. See note 4 above.
14. John A Robertson. The right to procreate and in utero fetal therapy. J Legal Med 1982; 3(3): 333–366. See also John A Robertson. Legal Issues in Prenatal Therapy. Clin Obstet Gynecol 1986; 29(3): 603–611.
15. See note 2 above.
16. See note 3 above.
17. Committee on Ethics, American College of Obstetrics and Gynecology. Patient choice: maternal-fetal conflict. American College of Obstetrics and Gynecology Committee Opinion Number 55, 1987 Oct.
18. *Jefferson v. Griffin Spalding County Hospital Authority*, 274 Ga. 86, 274 S.E. 2d 457 (1981).
19. *In Re* Baby Jefferson, No. 14004 (Jackson County, Mich. P. Ct. May 24, 1982).
20. While he does not use the terms "positive rights" and "negative rights" in precisely this sense, Feinberg makes a distinction between moral rights that "a person can make in either or both of two directions." These two directions match what we call negative and positive rights. See Joel Feinberg. Rights: systematic analysis. In Warren T. Reich, ed. Encyclopedia

of Bioethics. New York: Macmillian, 1978: 1508–1509. See also Joel Feinberg. Harm to Self. New York: Oxford University Press, 1986: 53.
21. See Ruth Macklin. Rights: rights in bioethics. In Warren T. Reich, ed. Encyclopedia of Bioethics. New York: Macmillan, 1978: 1513.
22. Robertson. The right to procreate and in utero fetal therapy, 354.
23. Ibid., 353.
24. Thomas E Elkins et al. Court-ordered Cesarean section: an analysis of ethical concerns in compelling cases. Am J Obstet Gynecol 1989; 161(1): 153.
25. Ibid.
26. Frank A Chervenak and Laurence B McCullough. Perinatal ethics: a practical analysis of obligations to mother and fetus. Obstet Gynecol 1985; 66: 442–446.
27. Frank A Chervenak and Laurence B McCullough. Justified limits on refusing intervention. Hastings Cent Rep 1991; 21: 12–18.
28. See note 18 above.
29. See note 19 above.
30. Allen Brett and Laurence B. McCullough. When patients request specific interventions: defining the limits of the physician's obligations. N Engl J Med 1986; 315: 1347–1351.
31. H. Tristram Engelhardt, Jr. The Foundations of Bioethics. New York: Oxford University Press, 1986.
32. See, especially, Annas. Protecting the Liberty of Pregnant Patients.
33. See note 3 above.
34. Ott WJ. Placenta previa. In F. A. Chervenak, G. Isaacson, S. Campbell, eds. Textbook of Ultrasound in Obstetrics and Gynecology. Boston: Little, Brown. (1993, p. 1493); D. Farine, H. E. Fox, and I. E. Timor-Tritsch. Placenta previa: transvaginal approach. In Textbook of Ultrasound in Obstetrics and Gynecology p. 1503.
35. C. Crenshaw, D. E. D. Jones, and R. T. Parker. Placenta previa: a survey of twenty years' experiences with improved perinatal survival by expectant therapy and Cesarean delivery. Obstet Gynecol Surv 1973; 28: 461–470.
36. J. A. Pritchard, P. C. MacDonald, and N. F. Gant, eds. Williams Obstetrics, 17th ed. Norwalk: Appleton-Century-Crofts, 1985, 1493.
37. D. B. Cotton, J. A. Read, R. H. Paul et al. The conservative aggressive management of placenta previa. Am J Obstet Gynecol 1980; 137: 687–695.
38. See note 30 above.
39. Annas. Pregnant women as fetal containers.
40. See note 26 above.
41. See note 14 above.
42. Nelson and Milliken. Compelled medical treatment of pregnant woman, 1065–1066.
43. Rhoden. The judge in the delivery room, 1081 ff.
44. For a concise formulation of this principle, see Tom L. Beauchamp, Paternalism. In Reich, ed. Encyclopedia of Bioethics, p. 1195. See also Joel Feinberg. Harm to Others. New York: Oxford University Press, 1984, passim.
45. These analogies play a significant role in the arguments of those opposed to court-ordered cesarean delivery. Robertson (see note 14 above) believes that a legal justification can be developed for court-ordered tissue or organ donation. That argument is irrelevant in the present context, because of the irrelevance of the analogies.
46. Robert M House and Troy L Thompson. Psychiatric aspects of organ transplantation. J Am Med Assoc 1988; 260(4): 535–539.
47. C. Philip Steuber. Bone-marrow transplantation. In Frank A. Oski, ed.-in-chief, Catherine D. DeAngelis, Ralph D. Feigin, and Joseph B. Warshaw, eds. Principles and Practice of Pediatrics. Philadelphia: J. B. Lippincott, 1990: 1578–1579.
48. Edward C Kohaut. End-stage renal disease. In Oski et al. Principles and Practice of Pediatrics, pp. 1619–1624.
49. Larry M Gold, Beverly S Kirkpatrick, F Jay Fricker, and Basil J Zitelli. Psychosocial

issues in pediatric organ transplantation. Pediatrics 1986; 75(5): 738–744; House and Thompson. Psychiatric aspects of organ transplantation.

50. Ruth R Faden and Tom L Beauchamp. A History and Theory of Informed Consent. New York: Oxford University Press, 1986, especially chapter 7.
51. W. J. Ott. Placenta previa. In F. A. Chervenak, et al.
52. Some might worry at this point that these three grounds could be quite broad-reaching, thus initiating a "slippery slope," the chief result of which would be systematic erosion of the autonomy of pregnant women. This worry can be readily allayed. There is no slippery slope as a logical matter of the extent of satisfaction of these grounds, because these three grounds apply only to well-documented, complete placenta previa. Because of the rarity of well-documented, complete placenta previa, these three grounds will only rarely be satisfied. Thus, should they be adopted in common law, the effect could not rationally be expected to be broad-reaching.
53. See note 6 above.
54. See note 26 above.

BONNIE STEINBOCK

Pregnant Drug Addicts

Hardly a day goes by, it seems, in which one does not read an article about the impact of the crack epidemic on babies. In a recent column in the *New York Times*, Anna Quindlen describes the neonatal intensive care unit of Bronx-Lebanon hospital as "filled with baby misery: babies born months too soon; babies born weighing little more than a hardcover book; babies that look like wizened old men in the last states of a terminal illness, wrinkled skin clinging to chicken bones; babies who do not cry because their mouths and noses are full of tubes."[1] According to one commentator, "If cocaine use during pregnancy were a disease, its impact on children would be considered a national health care crisis."[2]

Two factors in particular contribute to the crisis: the rise in cocaine addiction and the devastating effects cocaine can have on a developing fetus. Crack has more than tripled the number of cocaine addicts in New York City since 1986. The number of cases in which parents under the influence of drugs abused or neglected their children has also tripled. Seventy-three percent of the deaths in abuse and neglect cases in 1987 resulted from parents abusing drugs, up from 11 percent in 1985.[3]

Use of crack is particularly prevalent among youth between the ages of 16 and 25, prime childbearing years, and is especially popular among women, perhaps because it is smoked rather than injected. The New York City Health Department estimates that births to substance-abusing mothers have increased 3000 percent during the past ten years.[4] In a typical week, Harlem Hospital reports that 50 percent to 70 percent of newborn infants in their neonatal intensive care unit test positive for cocaine.[5] Neonatal intensive care units experienced a 37 percent average annual increase in admissions between 1983 and 1987, leading the city's health department to project that by 1995 5 percent of all babies and 10 percent of nonwhite babies could require admission to neonatal intensive care units.[6]

Nor is the problem confined to New York City. A 1988 survey of 36 hospitals across the country indicated that 11 percent of women are using drugs during pregnancy, resulting in 375,000 drug-exposed infants annually. Other surveys indicate that 15 percent of women use some sort of illicit drug while

F.K. Beller and R.F. Weir (eds.), The Beginning of Human Life, 273–285.

pregnant. Use is not confined to urban areas or particular racial or socio-economic groups, although most women prosecuted for using illegal drugs while pregnant have been poor members of racial minorities.[7]

New evidence is emerging about the danger that cocaine can pose to fetal health. As recently as 1982, medical texts on high risk obstetrics maintained that cocaine had no deleterious effects upon fetuses.[8] Since that time, a number of studies have been done throughout the country, including over a dozen studies by Northwestern University's Perinatal Center for Chemical Dependence, under the direction of Dr. Ira Chasnoff. These studies indicate that the effects of fetal exposure to cocaine included retarded growth in the womb and subtle neurological abnormalities, leading to extraordinary irritability during infancy and learning disorders later. In more extreme cases, cocaine can cause loss of the small intestine and brain-damaging strokes. Cocaine-exposed babies face a tenfold increase in the risk of crib death. Some of the worst effects occur during the first three months of pregnancy, when the woman may not even know she is pregnant. Some researchers think that even a single cocaine "hit" during pregnancy can cause lasting fetal damage.

> Cocaine, which is soluble in fat, readily crosses the placenta, where the baby's body converts a significant portion of it to norcocaine, a water-soluble substance that does not leave the womb and that is even more potent than cocaine. Norcocaine is excreted into the amniotic fluid, which the fetus swallows, re-exposing itself to the drug. As a result, the researchers believe, almost no cocaine-exposed baby fully escapes its damaging effects.[9]

Not all researchers have found such clear evidence of harmful effects on the fetus from cocaine use.[10] It is often difficult to tell whether the symptoms in the child are specifically due to cocaine use or to other features of poverty, such as poor nutrition, poor maternal health, and little or no prenatal care. Some experts have expressed the concern that the media focus on "crack babies" enables society to blame the terrible women who impose such awful consequences on their children, while ignoring all the other factors that cause babies to be born damaged. This is certainly an important concern. Nevertheless, the evidence or far indicates that crack use during pregnancy poses special dangers to unborn babies, over and above the risks stemming from poverty.

We desperately need a framework for thinking about maternal and fetal rights. Typically, and unfortunately, the framework is derived from the abortion debate. Those who oppose abortion favor fetal rights, on the ground that fetuses – indeed, even preimplantation embryos – are "pre-born children" with all the rights of born children. Pro-choice advocates, on the other hand, deny that fetuses have rights. They regard the ascription of rights to fetuses as the first step in a campaign to make abortion illegal. This has led some feminists and civil libertarians to maintain that whatever a woman does during her pregnancy is her own business. Some have gone so far as to claim that even noncoercive measures such as warnings against alcohol consumption during pregnancy posted in bars violate women's rights.

I consider both of these approaches to be mistaken. The mistake of right-to-lifers is to ignore important and morally relevant differences between embryos and children. What one does to a child *matters* to that child. If children are mistreated or neglected, they suffer. This is not true of embryos or early-gestation fetuses. It isn't until late in the second trimester that the fetus becomes conscious and sentient.[11] Prior to this time, the fetus cannot experience anything, and so cannot suffer. Nor can it enjoy life. Although the fetus is *alive*, in a biological sense, he or she does not yet *have* a life, in a biographical sense.[12] If a fetus is killed prior to becoming conscious and sentient, he or she is deprived of nothing wanted, because the fetus wants nothing. For this reason, I maintain that embryos and early fetuses have no interest in continued existence, and so are not harmed by being killed.[13] By contrast, babies and late-gestation fetuses, who do have lives that are a good to them, can be harmed by death. The mistake of pro-lifers is to treat fetuses, and even embryos, as if they were babies.

Pro-choicers do not make this mistake. However, some of them ignore the fact that if a woman decides not to abort, but to carry to term, it is not the welfare of the fetus that is at stake, but rather the welfare of the future child. The unfortunate tendency of some pro-choice activists is to think that if a woman has the right to terminate a pregnancy, she also has the right to act in any way she pleases during pregnancy, regardless of the impact this is likely to have on the child she bears.

Most women who are expecting a child will voluntarily adapt at least some of their behavior to protect their babies. They drink alcoholic beverages only moderately or not at all. They try to eat regular nutritious meals and take daily vitamins. A few even manage to stop smoking.[14] They do all this because they want a healthy baby more than anything else. But what if the woman is an alcoholic or a crack addict? What if she is ignorant, or indifferent to the health of her baby? Does society have the right – indeed, the responsibility – to coerce the mother to protect the not-yet-born child?

Society clearly has a legitimate interest in the welfare of its children, both those existing today and those who will exist in the future. The mere fact that people do not now exist is no reason to discount the interests they will have, when they come into existence. We are morally required to consider actual, not merely potential, interests. If we do nothing about the deficit, if we allow the ozone layer to be depleted, if we do not solve our waste disposal problem, then actual, living people will suffer. We have a responsibility to these people not to destroy the world they'll live in, even though they do not yet exist.

The primary responsibility for protecting the interests of children belongs to their parents. Yet although parents have a great deal of discretion in deciding how to care for and raise their children, they do not have absolute freedom. They are morally and legally obligated not to inflict injury on their children, to feed and clothe them, to provide them with necessary medical care. Parents who fail in these obligations may have their children taken from them; they may even be criminally charged. If the coercive power of the state is justifiably used to protect children, why can't it be used against a woman whose behavior injures her child before it is born?

Notice that it is the future *child* – not the fetus – who would be the intended beneficiary of such protective legislation. Because of this, law professor John Robertson, who has argued in favor of some coercive measures to protect not-yet-born children, once said to me that I should not title a talk I was about to give "Maternal-Fetal Conflict." The conflict, he said, is not between mother and fetus, but between mother and surviving child.

I entirely agree with Professor Robertson about the nature of the conflict, but I did not change the title of my talk, because the behavior likely to harm the child occurs while the woman is pregnant, and the child still a fetus. We cannot remove the fetus from the woman, as a child can be put in protective custody. We can protect the future child only through the body of the pregnant woman or by controlling the woman's behavior during pregnancy. This raises concerns about privacy and bodily autonomy that simply do not exist in ordinary child welfare cases.

Thus, the issue of maternal-fetal conflict is both like and unlike the abortion issue. It is like abortion in raising the question of how much control the state should have over the bodies and lives of its citizens. It differs from abortion in remaining silent on the status of the unborn. It is not the fetus per se who is the object of moral concern, but rather the future child. Whatever one's position on the morality of abortion, one can and should recognize moral obligations to the children one intends to bring into the world.

Moral Obligations to the Not-Yet-Born

How shall we characterize moral obligations to not-yet-born children? It is useful to think about these obligations in the context of general parental obligations to children.[15] This prevents us from imposing especially stringent obligations on pregnant women, or thinking that pregnant women are morally required to subordinate all their interests to their fetuses. No one requires this of parents generally. Parents are supposed to take reasonable steps to protect their children's health and well-being. They are not morally required to avoid any and all risks to their children's health. If they were, they couldn't allow their children to ride in cars or learn to rollerskate. They couldn't even inoculate them against disease. So the obligation is rather to avoid *unreasonable* risks of *substantial* harm.

But which risks are unreasonable? How much harm is substantial? Consider, for example, drinking during pregnancy. Alcohol is a potent teratogen which can cause irreversible damage to the body and brain of the developing fetus. Alcohol crosses the placenta and the fetus's blood-alcohol level will equal that of the mother's. If the mother's blood alcohol reaches a certain level – the toxic threshold – the fetus is at risk. Heavy drinking during pregnancy – especially binge drinking – is particularly risky. It can cause fetal alcohol syndrome (FAS), which is often marked by severe facial deformities and mental retardation. Some researchers believe that even the children of moderate drinkers may have lifelong learning disabilities and behavioral problems. One study showed that moderate drinking – defined as one to three drinks daily – during early pregnancy can result in a loss to the child of as much as five IQ points.[16] In another study, children born to women who had one or two drinks a day were found to have slower reaction times and more difficulty paying attention in their early school years.[17]

There is no established safe level of alcohol consumption. The fetus may be more vulnerable on certain days of pregnancy, so that having two drinks on day 33 could be above the toxic threshold, but below it on day 39. While there is no evidence that a rare single drink during pregnancy does damage, there is no guarantee that it does not. The safest course is therefore total abstention. But is the safest course the morally obligatory one? We do not require this standard of parents regarding their already-born children. If we did, we could not justify leaving children with babysitters to go out to dinner. What if something should happen? It seems to me that having a single drink occasionally in pregnancy falls into the area of individual discretion, because the risk of causing harm is very low (perhaps nonexistent) and the documented harm (shorter attention span or a few IQ points) hardly devastating. The claim made by some writers[18] that "the only prudent course" for the pregnant woman is total abstinence seems extreme.

By contrast, binge drinking, which has a 35 percent chance of subjecting one's baby to full-blown FAS,[19] clearly qualifies as unreasonably risky for the health of one's baby. So does smoking crack. The difficulty with saying that women have a moral obligation not to drink heavily or to smoke crack during pregnancy is that these behaviors are often the product of addiction. They are less than fully voluntary – some would say not voluntary at all. If a woman *cannot* modify her behavior, then she cannot have a moral obligation to do so.

However, I think we should distinguish between being able to stop doing something *at will*, and not being able to stop at all. Although it is difficult to get over addictions, many smokers, alcoholics, and drug users do manage to change their behaviors. In a study done by the Boston University Fetal Alcohol Education Program, two-thirds of heavy drinkers who received counseling were able to cut down considerably or stop altogether.[20] We can recognize that it may be very difficult for some women to fulfill their moral obligations to the babies they intend to bear, and acknowledge that they will need help to do so, without denying that they have such obligations. Unfortunately, such help is often not forthcoming. Many in-patient alcohol rehabilitation programs exclude pregnant women. The situation is probably worse for pregnant addicts. Two-thirds of the hospitals surveyed by the House

Select Committee on Children, Youth and Families reported that they had *no* drug treatment programs to which their pregnant patients could be referred; *none* had special programs providing comprehensive drug treatment and prenatal care. Dr. Wendy Chavkin, of the Columbia University School of Public Health, surveyed 78 drug treatment programs in New York City (95 percent of the city's programs). She found that 54 percent categorically excluded pregnant women, 67 percent exclude pregnant women on Medicaid, and 87 percent had no services for crack-addicted pregnant women.[21] And even in areas where there are treatment programs for pregnant addicts, there are not nearly enough spaces for everyone who wants help. Odyssey House, virtually the only residential mother/child drug treatment program in New York City, has a waiting list of several months' duration. In 1988 the waiting time for a bed in Los Angeles County's rehabilitation program for pregnant women was seven months.[22] The absence of treatment programs makes it virtually impossible for substance abusers to fulfill their moral obligations to the children they intend to bear, even with the best will in the world.

My view posits moral obligations to the children one intends to bear. It has been objected that often women do not "intend to bear" children. Dr. Lorraine Hale, for example, maintains that the women she sees at Hale House regard pregnancy as something that happens to them, often as a result of bartering their bodies for drugs; it is not something they intend. Nor do they necessarily choose to give birth: they may not be able to afford an abortion or it may not be available in a particular geographical area. For some women, abortion is not a morally or culturally acceptable option. Do restrictions on the choice whether to bear a child affect the woman's moral obligations to the child she bears? It seems to me that these restrictions do not affect how the woman ought to act, but they may affect how much she is to be blamed if she acts wrongly. Consider a woman who deliberately gets pregnant, intending to have a baby. If she goes on drinking and smoking and using recreational drugs, making no effort to stop, she acts very wrongly indeed. She is selfishly indifferent to the health of her not-yet-born child, and she deserves harsh criticism. By contrast, consider a woman who has no responsibility for becoming pregnant (she was raped), and who is unable to obtain an abortion. She is the victim of two grave injustices – first, in being raped, second, in being denied an abortion. Still, that would not justify behavior likely to inflict severe damage on the child she will perforce bear. Ideally, she should behave as if the pregnancy were chosen, since she is prevented from terminating the pregnancy. That is, she should stop smoking, drink moderately or not at all, etc. However, her failure to do so is certainly less blameworthy than the failure of a woman who has chosen to conceive and bear a child. Obviously, most cases will fall somewhere in between the extremes of deliberate conception and forced childbirth. In general, the fewer options a woman has regarding pregnancy and childbirth, the less she deserves blame for failing to fulfill her obligations to her future child. At the same time, women are not relieved of moral responsibility simply because they do not see pregnancy as a choice.

LEGAL OBLIGATIONS TO THE NOT-YET-BORN

The next question is whether the moral obligations women have to their not-yet-born children should be made legal. There is a range of options. Women could be subject to civil liability for harm they cause their children by their behavior during pregnancy. It seems unlikely that many civil suits would be filed against women who used prohibited substances in pregnancy; the pocket of most drug addicts is not deep. In most cases in which a child has sued a parent for prenatal harm, the attempt has been to recover from an insurance company, through either an automobile or homeowner's policy.[23] Whatever the merit of these suits, it is doubtful such policies would cover damage caused by illegal drugs, even assuming the existence of well-insured drug addicts.

What about criminal prosecutions of women whose babies have been harmed, or exposed to the risk of harm, because of illegal drug use during pregnancy? More than 180 criminal proceedings against women for drug use during pregnancy have been instigated in 19 states and the District of Columbia since 1987.[24] In most the charges were ultimately dismissed or dropped, sometimes before indictment.[25] Criminal charges can take a variety of forms. Perhaps the most creative is charging the woman with the same charge prosecutors routinely use against drug dealers: delivering drugs. Whereas drug use itself is typically a misdemeanor punishable by probation, especially in a first-offense case, delivering drugs is a felony in most jurisdictions. In Michigan it carries a mandatory minimum jail term of one year and a maximum of 20 years.[26] In Florida it carries a maximum sentence of 30 years.[27] In July 1989, Jennifer Johnson of Florida became the first woman to be convicted of delivering cocaine to her newborn child through the umbilical cord. She was sentenced to one year in a rehabilitation program and 14 years' probation. The sentence was later overturned on appeal.

By charging Johnson with delivering a drug to her newborn, not her fetus, the prosecution avoided the issue of the legal status of the unborn. However, many experts regard as dubious the theory that cocaine is passed through the umbilical cord just before it is clamped. One of the skeptics is Dr. Ira Chasnoff, the founder and president of the National Association of Perinatal Addiction Research and Education. He says, "Good ethics and good law have to be based on good science, and we just don't have that kind of data."[28]

Even if the scientific basis were more solid, the legal basis for these prosecutions is shaky. Applying existing drug laws to the prenatal cases ignores very real differences between the two situations. For one thing, the intent ordinarily necessary for a criminal charge is missed. A woman who uses drugs during pregnancy does not intend to give her child drugs. It is absurd to treat her like a pusher in a schoolyard. At most, she is guilty of reckless endangerment, if she is aware of but simply ignores, the risk to her baby from her drug use. The charge of reckless conduct probably applies in few cases, since, as we have already seen, this implies a degree of *voluntary* risk-taking absent in most drug users. Moreover, some pregnant addicts may be ignorant of the extent of the risk their behavior poses to their babies. One woman, who smoked crack the night before she gave birth to a baby who weighed five pounds, was jaundiced, and couldn't keep his formula down, reportedly thought it would help her relax and go into labor. "The baby was so far along that a couple of hits couldn't possibly hurt."[29] Such a woman does not intentionally or even recklessly harm her baby. Rather, she is negligent in allowing her not-yet-born child to be exposed to harm from the drugs she takes.

Parents who are extremely negligent in their care of their children may be charged with child neglect or abuse. There have been several cases where mothers of babies who were born addicted were charged with child abuse. This is a less serious offense than the drug-delivery charge; in Florida, it generally carries a sentence of no more than 60 days.[30] So far, 12 states have expanded their definitions of child abuse to include fetal drug exposure. Aside from criminal charges, women who use drugs during pregnancy may face other legal penalties. A woman who smokes one joint of marijuana at the end of her pregnancy risks losing custody of her newborn in Nassau County, New York, even if there is no evidence of damage to the baby.[31] She could go to jail in Louisiana, if a currently pending bill that would make drug use during pregnancy a felony passes.[32] Such laws would leave untouched a woman who smokes three packs a day and gives birth to a very premature and very sick baby, or a woman who drinks a quart of bourbon daily and has a child with fetal alcohol syndrome. If we are going to prosecute women at all, why limit prosecutions to those who use illegal drugs when use of legal drugs, such as tobacco and alcohol, may cause just as much harm, if not more, to the developing fetus?

One reason for distinguishing between legal and illegal drugs is concern for the constitutionally protected right of privacy. The right of privacy covers both the right to make one's own decisions about procreation and the right to control one's own body. Laws prohibiting pregnant women from using alcohol or tobacco infringe on a woman's power to make decisions about how she will live her life during her pregnancy, and thus infringe on her privacy right.[33] A statute that infringes on a constitutionally protected privacy right must undergo strict scrutiny; it will be upheld only if it is narrowly tailored to achieve a compelling state interest.

Could laws prohibiting pregnant women from drinking or smoking survive strict scrutiny? On the one hand, alcohol and tobacco are legal substances which individuals have a right to use. On the other hand, judges might view the right to drink alcohol or smoke cigarettes as trivial, compared with the state's interest in seeing that children are born free of incapacitating disabilities. However, as a recent note in the *Harvard Law Review* plausibly argues,

> . . . more is at stake – the state in these situations is seeking to regulate the procreative aspects of particular decisions and thus the procreative process. In considering the constitutionality of fetal rights legislation, there-

> fore, courts should assign greater weight to maternal decisional rights than they might at first perceive as appropriate, in order to protect the woman's right of procreative autonomy.[34]

Under strict scrutiny, the burden would be on the state to show that the statute was likely to protect fetal health, and was the least restrictive means of doing so.

On the face of it, statutes that prohibit pregnant women from engaging in otherwise legal activities discriminate against women, since they impose a burden on women, who are the only people to get pregnant, that is not imposed on others. However, not all different treatment is discriminatory. Discrimination exists only when individuals are treated differently and there is no relevant difference between them. It would be discriminatory to forbid smoking by women while allowing men to smoke, because gender is not rationally related to allowing or prohibiting smoking. Pregnancy is a relevant difference, if the woman is carrying to term, because then she is going to have a child who could be harmed by her behavior.

The difficulty with such statutes is that they could only apply to women who were indeed going to term, but how can this be known in advance? Under *Roe v. Wade*, a woman has the right to choose abortion throughout the second trimester of pregnancy. There would be no basis for preventing a woman in her first or second trimester from drinking, since she still has the legal option of aborting. Ironically, the greatest harm to the fetus is probably caused by drinking early in pregnancy, so it is unclear what purpose would be served by laws prohibiting drinking in pregnancy.

The claim that such statutes are discriminatory would be weakened if parents of *both* sexes were subject to legal penalties for imposing health risks on their children by drinking or smoking. So far no one has proposed criminalizing such behavior. However, in September, a report appeared in the *New England Journal of Medicine* which maintained that children who are exposed to large amounts of tobacco smoke at home are more than twice as likely to develop lung cancer later in life than those who grow up in smoke-free households. Shortly afterward, in New York, a state judge ruled that a parent's smoking habit is a legitimate consideration in determining which parent should gain custody in divorce and other proceedings. Last year an appeals court upheld a LaPlace, Louisiana, lower court decision reducing a father's visitation rights because his smoking aggravated his child's bronchial problem. In August 1990, a California Superior Court judge conditioned the grant of custody to a mother on the promise that she would not smoke in front of her five-year-old son.[35]

Commenting on these cases, law professor and columnist Alan Dershowitz says that they raise the question of whether the law will next forbid parents who are not in a child-custody dispute from smoking in the presence of their children. "Another question is what effect this no-smoking decision could have on pregnant women who breathe smoke into their babies, or on anyone who smokes in the presence of pregnant women." Derschowitz notes that custody disputes are commonly the opening wedge into state monitoring of families, because in such disputes judges must decide which parent will be better for the child. Despite the fact that all children would be better off with parents who don't smoke, under present law the state has little power to intervene to protect children from parents who are not seeking a divorce or custody.[36] Why, Dershowitz asks, does the state tolerate behavior dangerous to children when it is committed by parents who are not seeking custody? Don't these endangered children deserve the protection of the state from parents who are abusing their health? "Of course they do," Dershowitz responds. "But the price of state intervention into intact families would be very great."

Thus, we allow parents to do things we wish they wouldn't do for the sake of the greater good of family privacy and integrity. A comparable argument can be made against criminalizing otherwise legal behaviors, such as drinking alcohol and smoking, during pregnancy. The costs to individual freedom and privacy would be very great. Moreover, because of the difficulty of monitoring women's consumption of legal drugs, and therefore of implementing the statute, it seems unlikely that the goal of protecting fetal health would be significantly advanced.

But what about illegal drugs that harm developing fetuses? Laws making it a crime for pregnant women to use illegal drugs, and holding them criminally responsible for the effects of such drug use on their offspring, are not discriminatory (since no one is allowed to use these drugs). Moreover, if a woman has no right to use cocaine, pregnant or not, she cannot complain that her right of privacy is invaded by a statute that imposes additional penalties on pregnant women who use cocaine. Such laws are therefore probably constitutional. Nevertheless, they can be criticized on grounds of policy.

First, what good would such laws do? It seems unlikely that laws making the use of drugs during pregnancy a crime would prevent women from taking drugs. If a woman is willing to risk criminal prosecution for drug use, why will she be deterred by additional penalties for harming her unborn child?

It may be objected that the same could be said of prosecuting women for postnatal child abuse. Obviously, people who abuse their children are not deterred by criminal sanctions. It is unlikely that laws prohibiting child abuse can have much deterrent effect, because most abuse is not deliberate or planned, but stems from inability to control frustration or anger. So, it might be said, why punish any child abusers? And if we do think that some abusers deserve to be punished, regardless of deterrent effect, why can't the same be said of some women who inflict prenatal abuse? This may not be the only way or the best way to protect babies, but some prosecutions might nevertheless be justified. They are justified when a woman is aware that her voluntary and noncompulsive behavior poses serious risks to the health of her not-yet-born child, yet she disregards these risks, causing her baby to be born seriously damaged. Perhaps a yuppie recreational cocaine user would come into this category. Her behavior is immoral; why shouldn't she be prosecuted? I concede that prosecution in such a case would be justified. My fear is that it is unlikely that prosecution would be confined to such cases – if they exist at all. There is a real danger that fetal abuse statutes, even constitutionally acceptable ones, would be used primarily to prosecute uneducated and low-income addicts who are less than fully responsible for their harmful behavior.

Another rationale for prosecution is that it is a way to pressure women to get into treatment. Tony Tague, a prosecutor in Muskegon County, Michigan, who has prosecuted a number of women whose newborns tested positive for crack cocaine, says, "When physicians make suggestions, it doesn't appear that's enough for them to seek treatment. The possibility of prosecution is a strong incentive."[37] However, seeking treatment may not help a woman avoid prosecution. One woman who was indicted after she tried to get help with her drug problem says, "I feel betrayed. Everyone I talked to about my drug problem has been subpoenaed.[38]

While there may be some women who will not seek treatment without fear of prosecution, many pregnant addicts have found that there are no treatment programs for them. Dr. Chavkin says, "The important thing to remember about the Jennifer Johnson case is that this is a woman who tried to get treatment and was turned away."[39] It makes no sense to spend resources prosecuting women in order to force them into treatment, when there are too few adequate programs for women who will voluntarily undergo treatment. Kary Moss of the ACLU asks, "Why is it that we have to make women criminals before we can get them drug treatment?"[40]

It might be argued that laws criminalizing drug use in pregnancy have an important symbolic function, even if they don't directly protect babies. They express society's outrage and convey the message that drug use during pregnancy is totally unacceptable. This is a legitimate function of law, but the social costs must be considered. The threat of prosecution may cause women to lie to their doctors about their drug use, preventing doctors from having information necessary to safeguard the baby's health. Drug users may even avoid hospitals and doctors altogether, for fear of being turned in to the authorities. In that case, the very purpose of such laws – to protect infants – would be subverted.

Despite the rhetoric, it does not seem that we as a society are serious about getting addicted women into treatment or protecting babies. Congress has mandated that states spend 10 percent of their federal Alcohol, Drug Abuse and Mental Health Services block grant funds on the development and expansion of prevention and treatment programs for alcoholic and drug-dependent women, with special emphasis to be given to services for pregnant women. Yet most states have failed to comply with this mandate.[41] We cannot solve the problem of damaged babies with a "win the war on drugs" mentality. Instead, the problem must be treated with a comprehensive approach that includes funding drug treatment programs for pregnant women, and by ensuring that all pregnant women have adequate prenatal care. I believe that a close personal relationship with a caring and nonjudgmental obstetrician –

the kind of care which middle-class women take for granted – would do more toward ending substance abuse, legal and nonlegal, in pregnancy than any number of prosecutions or fetal abuse laws.

NOTES

1. Anna Quindlen. Hearing the cries of crack. The New York Times 1990; Oct. 7; Fig.
2. Revkin, A. Crack in the cradle. Discover 1989 Sep: 63–69.
3. Michel Marriott. After 3 years, crack plague in New York only gets worse. The New York Times 1989 Feb 20; Sect A: 1. However, the crack epidemic appears to have peaked in 1988. The infant mortality rate in New York City has gone down in recent years.
4. French H. Rise in babies hurt by drugs is predicted: 4% in New York city could need care by '95. The New York Times 1989 Oct 18; Sec B: 1–2.
5. Revkin.
6. French.
7. A study done by the National Center for Perinatal Addiction Research and Education assessed the prevalence of drug use in pregnancy by collecting urine samples from all pregnant women who visited public health clinics or private obstetricians' offices in Pinellas County, Florida, for one month last year. In Florida, all drug use during pregnancy must be reported to health departments. The researchers found that about 15 percent of both the white and the black women used drugs, but black women were 10 times as likely as whites to be reported to the authorities, and poor women were more likely to be reported than middle-class women. Racial bias seen on pregnant addicts. The New York Times 1990 Jul 20; Sect A: 13.
8. Revkin.
9. Jane E Brody. Cocaine: litany of fetal risks grows. The New York Times 1988 Sep 6 (col 8).
10. See, for example, Tatiana M. Doberczak, Stefan Shanzer, Ruby T. Senie, and Stephen R. Kandall. Neonatal neurologic and electroencephalographic effects of intrauterine cocaine exposure. J Pediatr 1988; 113(2): 354–58.
11. It seems likely that third-trimester fetuses can feel pain. After examining the anatomical, neurochemical, and behavioral evidence, K. J. S. Anand and P. R. Hickey, researchers at Children's Hospital in Boston, conclude, "Numerous lines of evidence suggest that even in the human fetus, pain pathways as well as cortical and subcortical centers necessary for pain perception are well developed *late in gestation*, and the neurochemical systems now known to be associated with pain transmission and modulation are intact and functional." Pain and its effects in the human neonate and fetus. N Engl J Med 1987 Nov; 317(21): 1326 Emphasis added.

    It is very unlikely that a fetus can feel pain prior to the end of the second trimester, because the nervous system is insufficiently developed. Most sensory pathways to the neocortex, where pain and other experiences are registered, have synapses in the thalamus. The synaptic connections between the thalamus and neocortex are not completed until between 20 and 24 weeks of gestation.
12. The distinction between biological and biographical life comes from James Rachels. The End of Life: Euthanasia and Morality. New York: Oxford University Press, 1986, 25.
13. The view of moral status sketched out here is elaborated in my Life Before Birth: The Moral and Legal Status of Embryos and Fetuses. Oxford University Press, 1992.
14. Only a tiny fraction stop smoking when pregnant. 1989 Jan 6.
15. This point is made by Thomas H. Murray. In: Moral obligations to the not-yet-born: the fetus as patient. Clinics in Perinatology 1987 Jun; 14(2): 329–343.
16. A P Streissguth, H M Barr, P D Sampson, B L Darby, and D C Martin. I. Q. at age 4 in relation to maternal alcohol use and smoking during pregnancy. Developmental Psychology 1989; 25(1): 7–8.

17. Daniel Goleman. Lasting costs for child are found from a few early drinks. The New York Times 1989 Feb 16; Sect B: 16.
18. Elisabeth Rosenthal. Pregnant woman drinks. The New York Times Magazine 1990 Feb 4: 66.
19. Ibid.
20. Ibid.
21. Wendy Chavkin. Drug addiction and pregnancy: policy crossroads. Am J Public Health 1990 Apr; 80(4): 485.
22. Rorie Sherman. Keeping baby safe from mom. National Law Review 1988 Oct 3: 25.
23. For example, *Grodin v. Grodin*, Mich. App., 301 N.W.2d 869 (1981).
24. Jan Hoffman. Pregnant, addicted – and guilty? The New York Times Magazine 1990 Aug 19: 35.
25. Tamar Lewin. Drug use in pregnancy: new issue for the courts. The New York Times 1990 Feb 5; Sect A: 14.
26. Hoffman, 34.
27. Mother who gives birth to drug addict faces felony charge. The New York Times 1988 Dec 17: 9.
28. Hoffman, 35.
29. Ibid., 53.
30. Mother who gives birth to drug addict faces felony charge, 9.
31. Sherman, 24.
32. Women's Rights Project, American Civil Liberties Union, Memorandum: Update of state legislation regarding drug use during pregnancy, May 22, 1990.
33. Note, Maternal rights and fetal wrongs: the case against the criminalization of 'fetal abuse'. Harvard Law Review 1988; 101(994): 1000.
34. Ibid., 1007.
35. Amy Dockser Marcus. Parent's smoking becomes issue in child custody cases. The Wall Street Journal 1990 Oct 18; Sect B: 1.
36. "In the absence of immediate risk to life or health – such as physical or sexual abuse – the state will rarely try to take children out of an intact family home." Alan Dershowitz. Custody with smoking ban. Albany Times Union 1990 Oct 22: Sect A: 6. It is extremely unlikely that a court would remove a child from a home in which both parents smoked in the presence of a child, despite the heightened risk of lung disease. However, in Denton, Maryland, a judge placed a three-year-old girl with severe asthma in a foster home because her parents ignored medical advice to protect the child from their tobacco smoke. (See also Marcus.)
37. Hoffman, 55.
38. Ibid.
39. Lewin.
40. Hoffman, 57.
41. Women's Rights Project Memorandum, 11.

MARY ANNE WARREN

Women's Rights versus the Protection of Fetuses

The claim that human fetuses have rights once served primarily to underpin opposition to abortion. However, some of the newer fetal rights claims are neutral with respect to the morality of abortion. These involve the rights of fetuses which will *not* be aborted, but whose future well-being is thought to be endangered by the behavior of the pregnant woman. Fetal rights advocates argue that when the actions or nonactions of pregnant women endanger the health of the unborn child, coercive interventions of various kinds may be justified. John Robertson makes a useful distinction between two forms of coercion at issue here, i.e., prebirth seizures and postbirth sanctions.[1] Prebirth seizures include court-ordered cesareans or other medical interventions performed against the will of the pregnant woman, as well as the involuntary confinement of pregnant women to prevent their using alcohol or illegal drugs, or otherwise adversely affecting fetal development. Postbirth sanctions include criminal penalties for women whose infants are born with illnesses or injuries due to the woman's behavior during her pregnancy. I shall argue that these forms of coercion are unjustified.

Involuntary cesareans are already a reality. Since 1981 there have been dozens of cases in which physicians or hospital administrators have sought and obtained court orders to perform caesarean sections upon competent and unconsenting women, on the grounds that a vaginal delivery would be more dangerous for the fetus and/or for the woman herself. Some commentators have argued that as intrauterine surgery and other techniques for correcting fetal abnormalities become standard medical therapies, these too may rightly be performed upon unconsenting women for the benefit of the fetus.[2] There have also been cases in which judges have imposed unusually severe sentences upon pregnant drug users, in order to protect the fetus from (further) harm due to prenatal drug exposure.

It has long been known that children of alcoholic women may suffer from prenatal alcohol syndrome, and more recently it has been found that even moderate drinking by pregnant women can be harmful to fetal development. But the current calls for legal sanctions against "fetal abuse" are largely inspired by the recent and tragic increase in the number of infants born with

F.K. Beller and R.F. Weir (eds.), The Beginning of Human Life, 287–299.

mental or physical abnormalities due to prenatal exposure to cocaine or other illegal drugs. In 1986, Pamela Stewart was charged in San Diego with criminal child neglect when her son was born with brain damage and later died, allegedly because of Stewart's failure to follow her doctor's advice (e.g., to avoid sex and drugs). In that case, charges were dropped because the defense persuaded the court that the law under which Stewart had been charged was not intended to apply to cases of this kind. The implementation of criminal sanctions in such cases would probably require new legislation, defining certain actions as crimes – or as more severe crimes – when performed by pregnant women who do not subsequently abort.[3]

Fetal rights advocates maintain that these new forms of legal coercion are necessary to protect (future) persons from prenatal harms. In contrast, feminists and civil libertarians regard these forms of coercion as egregious violations of women's most basic moral and legal rights – including the constitutional right to privacy guaranteed by *Roe v. Wade* and other Supreme Court decisions. Ironically, the *Roe* decision (which established women's constitutional right to choose abortion in the first two trimesters of pregnancy) has often been used to argue for the legality of these forms of coercion. I will argue that this is a misinterpretation of that decision, and that these forms of coercion are both contrary to fundamental legal principles and morally unconscionable. First, however, it is necessary to comment upon an underlying conceptual issue.

Maternal and Fetal Interests

Some feminist theorists have questioned whether it is even conceptually coherent to assert that fetuses have interests or rights that are separate and distinct from those of the pregnant woman. For instance, Barbara Katz Rothman maintains that the perception of the fetus as a person separate from the mother is a consequence of patriarchal ideology – in particular the Aristotelian notion that women do not really produce children or contribute to their formation, but only nurture the seeds which men plant within them.[4] In Rothman's view, once we recognize that "the baby is not planted within the mother, but flesh of her flesh, part of her,"[5] we are forced to abandon the model of conflicting rights and interests. A pregnant woman is one person, not two. Third parties, therefore, may legitimately protect and care for the fetus only by protecting and caring for her.

I strongly agree that the fetus is not yet a person, and does not yet have a right to life comparable to that which an infant has once he or she is born.[6] If this is true, then abortion is not directly comparable to homicide. However, it does not follow from this that the interests of the pregnant woman can never come into conflict with those of the fetus qua future person. If the pregnancy is not to be aborted, then (nonlethal) damage to the fetus may cause harm to the future child. If serious harm to a future person is a predictable consequence of an action, then the fact that the person who will suffer that harm *does not yet exist* does not automatically excuse the action. Suppose, for instance, that a company's directors decide to bury toxic wastes in steel containers, knowing that these will disintegrate within a century or two, and knowing that the probable result will be the contamination of local water supplies and the poisoning of anyone who drinks the water. The directors' actions would surely be subject to moral criticism, even though the possible victims of their actions have not yet been born, or even conceived.

Thus, even if abortion is morally innocuous, inflicting damage upon fetuses which will not be aborted is not. If a pregnant women does not intend to abort, then she and involved third parties are morally obligated to consider not only her interests but also those of the future child. In most cases, there will be no conflict between these two sets of interests. Most women who expect to give birth are more than willing to make sacrifices for the sake of optimal fetal development. At the risk of belaboring the obvious, women *want* healthy babies. The mistake made by the thalidomide and DES mothers was not that of putting their own interests first, but of placing too much trust in their medical advisers, who proved all too fallible. Yet conflicts of interest between pregnant women and their future children sometimes occur. A pregnant woman will not harm her own health by taking an occasional drink, but her future child may suffer mental retardation as a result. A medical treatment that is potentially life-saving for the woman (e.g., chemotherapy for cancer) may be highly detrimental to the fetus. A woman who knowingly exposes her future child to avoidable danger is no more immune to moral criticism than is a physician who carelessly prescribes drugs that may have mutagenic or teratogenic effects.

Moral Duties vs. Legal Coercion

But to say this is not to imply that legal coercion is the best way to protect future children from harm due to maternal behavior during pregnancy. There are many actions which are morally suspect yet which are not and should not be illegal. Examples would include ordinary acts of unkindness, such as speaking harshly to someone who loves you, or refusing to help a friend in need. To act in these ways is to violate important moral obligations. But many moral obligations are better left to the conscience of the individual and to moral suasion than to the coercive force of the law. Thomas Murray notes that

> for good reasons, including moral ones, we are reluctant to allow the state to force its view of correct conduct on individuals unless the harm to be avoided is grave, especially when doing so requires coercion, bodily invasion, or incarceration.[7]

Of course the harms which some wish to prevent through coercive "pregnancy policing" policies *are* sometimes very grave. But that does not settle the issue. The appropriateness of legal coercion must be evaluated in the light of its probable effectiveness, as well as its social costs. Before examining the moral arguments for and against prebirth seizures and post-birth sanctions, I want briefly to consider a common legal argument in favor of these coercive measures.

THE ARGUMENT FROM *ROE V. WADE*

These are many legal arguments for prebirth seizures and postbirth sanctions; however, one legal argument stands out as particularly important. Courts and legal commentators have often appealed to *Roe v. Wade* to support the state's constitutional right to protect fetuses by coercive measures against pregnant women.[8] That decision permits states to protect "potential human life" by prohibiting third-trimester abortions, except when necessary to protect the life or health of the woman. This is sometimes held to imply that the state may also protect (at least) third-trimester fetuses by requiring the woman to submit to medical interventions that are thought to be in the best interest of the fetus. Often it is argued that, in deciding not to terminate the pregnancy in the first two trimesters, the women has voluntarily waived her right to refuse any such medical interventions. But the very fact that some women decline to undergo surgery which their physicians regard as potentially beneficial to the fetus shows that they have *not* voluntarily waived that right. The model which this argument presupposes is not that of the voluntary waiving of rights, but rather that of involuntary forfeiture.[9] The presupposition, in other words, is that any woman who elects to continue rather than abort a pregnancy thereby forfeits fundamental legal rights enjoyed by all (other) competent adults who have been convicted of no crime.

There is nothing in the *Roe v. Wade* decision to support such an interpretation. Fetal viability (which is assumed to occur around the start of the third trimester) is treated as a sufficient justification for the prohibition of third-trimester abortion *only when continued pregnancy poses no threat to the woman's life or health.* (This prohibition is one which states are permitted, but not required, to enact.) This in no way suggests that states may subject pregnant women to harmful and life-threatening surgery, in order to protect the potential human life within them. Indeed, it strongly suggests the opposite: that even in the third trimester of pregnancy, the protection of the woman's life and health supersedes the state's interest in protecting potential human life.[10]

Last year's Supreme Court decision in the case of *Webster v. Reproductive Health Services* has somewhat expended the states' power to restrict access to abortion, e.g., by permitting states to prohibit the use of state-supported facilities for abortion or abortion counseling, and by casting doubt upon the future of the trimester system established in *Roe*. However, nothing in this decision supports the claim that a state's interest in protecting potential human life authorizes it to commit violent physical assaults against pregnant women. Nor does there appear to be any reason to believe that the legal case for postbirth sanctions has been strengthened by *Webster*.

Moral Arguments for Prebirth Seizures and Postbirth Sanctions

The most common moral arguments for prebirth seizures appear to be of a naive utilitarian kind. Many people find it natural to reason in the following way: Suppose that a woman refuses to have a cesarean section, even though her physician believes that a vaginal birth is likely to damage or even kill the infant. (In some cases, caesarean birth might be medically safer for the mother as well; but for the moment let us focus on the more typical case, where it is the infant who is most at risk.) Of course, the physician might be wrong. But on the assumption that the physician is right, it seems likely that forcing the surgery upon the woman will do less harm to her than vaginal delivery will do to her infant. True, she will suffer significant physical harm and perhaps great mental anguish from the surgical invasion of her body, but the odds are good that she will survive with little permanent impairment.

Parallel arguments have made for other involuntary medical interventions against pregnant women. Robertson, for instance, hold that a variety of involuntary treatments – including intrauterine surgery, blood transfusion, or the administration of drugs – would be justified whenever "the benefits to the offspring clearly outweigh the burdens of the intrusion."[11] On such a view, it may seem reasonable that the weighing of those benefits and burdens not be left entirely to the woman (who is one of the interested parties), and that in disputed cases the decision should be made by a court of law (which is presumably capable of greater impartiality).

Similarly, it is argued that the involuntary incarceration of pregnant women who are addicted to legal or illegal drugs is justified because it will probably harm them less than their behavior, if they are left at liberty, will harm their future child. The woman, it is said, will lose only a few months of freedom, whereas her continued use of alcohol or cocaine may result in lifelong impairment for her child.

The utilitarian argument for postbirth sanctions may also seem quite strong. It may be argued that holding women criminally liable for actions that cause harm to their future children will help to deter such harmful behavior. After all, their parties – e.g., physicians and employers – whose negligent actions result in such harm are at least civilly liable, and this liability has probably served to deter some negligent behavior. In addition to this utilitarian argument for postbirth sanctions, there is the retributivist argument: that women who negligently harm their future children ought to be punished because they are guilty, and it is just that the guilty should suffer.

In what follows, I will develop three major objections to these arguments for coercion, each of which is, I think, independently decisive. First, prebirth seizures and postbirth sanctions are morally objectionable even in narrowly utilitarian terms – that is, even if little emphasis is placed upon individual rights.[12] Second, these forms of coercion entail such severe violations of women's rights to privacy, liberty, autonomy, and physical integrity that they would be unjustifiable even were it possible confidently to predict some net benefits to future persons or to society as a whole. And third, the racial and economic injustices that prevail in this country guarantee that these forms of coercion will most often be employed against poor women and women of color. As a result of this discriminatory impact, these coercive practices will be both more unjust and more socially harmful than might be the case in a more nearly just society.

Doubts about the Utility of Involuntary Medical Interventions

Consider, first, the alleged utility of force cesareans. The case for coercion rests upon the presumption that physicians are able reliably to identify those cases in which cesarean birth is necessary to protect the fetus and/or the mother. But the evidence suggests otherwise. In a 1981 Georgia case, a court issued an order for an involuntary cesarean after the woman's physicians testified that there was a 99 percent probability that the infant would die without the surgery;[13] yet before the order could be carried out, the woman gave birth without surgery to a normal infant. And this is not the only such case.[14]

Further evidence that American physicians are not highly reliable predictors of when nonsurgical birth will prove unsafe is found in the exceptionally high rate of cesarean deliveries in this country – as high as 31 percent in some hospitals.[15] These is widespread agreement that this rate is much higher than it ought to be. Whether we blame the physicians' fear of malpractice suits, the desire for greater profit and convenience for hospitals and physicians, the reliance upon fetal monitoring equipment (which can lead to the overdiagnosing of fetal distress), or a combination of these and other factors, it seems clear that there are too many cesareans being performed, not too few. The result is not just a waste of medical resources and money, but increased iatrogenic harm and risk for both women and infants. The maternal mortality rate for cesarean delivery is said to be somewhere between three and thirty times higher than for vaginal delivery,[16] with five to ten times the risk of infection or other complications.[17] Recovery is apt to be slower and caring for the infant more difficult after a cesarean. Infants are also placed at some risk by cesarean delivery, e.g., the risk of respiratory distress associated with prematurity, and perhaps with the absence of the compressing effect of the lungs by vaginal delivery.[18]

Since intrauterine surgery is still in the early stages of development, it is somewhat difficult to predict whether its imposition upon unconsenting women might eventually produce some net benefits for offspring. But the track record for cesareans – voluntary and otherwise – is sufficiently mixed that it would be rash to make such a prediction.

THE VIOLATION OF BASIC RIGHTS

For these reasons, I doubt that a strong case can be made, even on narrowly utilitarian grounds, for involuntary medical interventions against pregnant women. But let us suppose for the sake of the argument that physicians were able to identify precisely those cases in which the woman's refusal of medical treatment seriously endangers her fetus and/or herself. Perhaps in that situation the use of coercion would produce some net benefit. However, the narrowly utilitarian argument for coercion ought to shock us, because it ignores the fundamental moral and legal rights of competent adults to autonomy and security against physical assault. It presumes that merely by being pregnant the women has forfeited these fundamental rights.

Last year, doctors performed the first liver transplant in the United States using a live donor rather than a cadaver organ. The recipient was an infant girl, whose mother donated a part of her own liver in order to give her child a chance of survival. Her act was undoubtedly a generous and praiseworthy one. But suppose that she had declined to make such a donation. Should the child's physicians have sought a court order empowering them to seize the woman by force and cut out part of her liver? It is all but inconceivable that any American court would issue such an order. Legally, the infliction of surgery upon a competent and unconsenting adult constitutes a criminal assault. Morally, not even the laudable goal of saving a human life can justify the commission of a violent, damaging, and life-threatening physical assault upon a competent adult who has done nothing to deserve such abuse.

Sanctioning such an assault is so contrary to American legal tradition that there are very few clearly analogous cases in American legal history.[19] One such case of that of *McFall v Shimp*. In that case, a man who was dying of cancer petitioned the court to order his cousin to donate bone marrow, since there was no other compatible donor and no other therapy that promised a chance of his recovery. The judge refused to issue such an order, stating that

> to *compel* the Defendant to submit to an intrusion of his body would change every concept and principle upon which this society is founded. To do so would defeat the sanctity of the individual and would impose a rule which would know no limits.[20]

The point illustrated by this case is that one person's medical needs cannot readily override another person's rights to autonomy and physical integrity. Perhaps one person *ought* to be willing to donate bone marrow when that donation might save another person's life. But to use the force of the law to compel such a "donation" would be to treat the "donor" as a thing rather than a person. No clearer violation can be imagined of the principle that persons are to be treated as ends in themselves and never merely as means.

It is arguable that there are *some* cases in which it is right to impose involuntary medical treatment upon one person for the sake of others. For instance, requiring children or adults to be vaccinated against deadly and contagious illness might be justified under certain – rather rare – circumstances. If the vaccine is effective and the risk of harmful side effects slight; if any individuals who are harmed by the vaccine are well cared for and adequately compensated; and if the risk of widespread contagion without mandatory vaccination is very great, then perhaps the relatively modest invasion of the autonomy and physical integrity of unconsenting individuals can be justified. But a relatively safe and simple injection is one thing, and major surgery is another. The severity of the assault involved makes both involuntary organ donations and involuntary cesareans fundamentally different from mandatory vaccinations. People's bodies are not public resources that may be invaded and parts removed for the sake of some social good, or the good of some other person.

The Case against Postbirth Sanctions

Women who knowingly use unsafe drugs while pregnant, or otherwise risk harm to the future child, may sometimes be morally culpable. But it is not always wise to use the force of the law to punish the morally guilty. From a utilitarian perspective, punishment makes sense only if it is likely to produce some net social benefits. From a retributivist perspective, in contrast, it is inherently good that the guilty should suffer; hence punishment need not be justified in terms of other social benefits. But when punitive laws are almost certain to do much more harm than good; when they will predictably worsen the very problems they are intended to solve; and when innocent as well as guilty persons will be seriously hurt, then I think it is time to put aside the intuition that the guilty should be made to suffer and look for nonpunitive approaches. The following problems are inherent in any proposal to use the criminal law to penalize women for prenatal negligence.

First, any law or policy that required or permitted health care workers to provide evidence of fetal neglect by their clients would probably deter many women from seeking any prenatal or obstetrical care at all, and prevent many others from providing accurate information to their health care advisers. Pregnant women with drug problems might be wise to avoid medical care entirely, since even a simple physical examination might prove incriminating. Women with personal or religious convictions that preclude certain medical procedures would also have powerful reasons for avoiding medical care during pregnancy, lest they later be prosecuted for refusing suggested therapies. The probable results include more medically disastrous pregnancies, more premature deliveries due to the lack of prenatal care, more concealed pregnancies and unattended births, more infant abandonment, and perhaps a resurgence of infanticide, as women find themselves forced to destroy the evidence of their presumed wrongdoing.

Second, the use of health care workers to implement "pregnancy policing" policies is incompatible with an open, cooperative, and egalitarian relationship between women and health care providers. Women who are either pregnant or fertile would need to be extremely cautious about what they tell their health care advisers regarding their sex lives, diet, use of legal or illegal drugs, and anything else that could eventually lead to criminal charges against them, should they be unfortunate enough to give birth to a less-than-perfect infant. To the extent that doctors' advice takes on the force of law, and doctors function as police informants, the relationship between women and medical professionals can only be authoritarian, adversarial, and marked by mutual distrust. This relationship has long been a somewhat strained and authoritarian one. But coercive pregnancy policing policies would make it much worse, undoing much of the progress made in recent decades toward informed consent and respect for patient autonomy.

Advocates of fetal abuse laws argue that these would be no more destructive of the doctor/patient relationship than are contemporary child abuse laws. They point out that the legal requirement that doctors report suspected cases of child abuse does not seem to have prevented parents from taking their children to doctors.[21] But so-called fetal abuse is very different from child abuse. Because the fetus is physically located within the woman, almost anything that she does or does not do could conceivably affect it for better or worse. To hold her legally liable for behavior that others suspect may have harmed her fetus is to expose her entire private life to hostile scrutiny by doctors, lawyers, and police. Private acts of violence toward children *should* be exposed to hostile scrutiny. But women's personal decisions about how to care for themselves during pregnancy are not analogous to private acts of violence toward a child already born – even though they can occasionally have equally unfortunate results. For the actions that are said to constitute fetal abuse are, in the first instance, things that the woman does to or for herself, and the consequences of those actions for the future child are often very difficult either to prove or to predict. That fact does not eliminate her moral obligation to avoid actions that are likely to harm her future child, but it does undermine the assumption that "fetal abuse" is directly analogous to child abuse and amenable to similar legal approaches.

The third problem is that pregnancy policing policies could not be effectively enforced without infringing upon a wide range of basic civil liberties. Enforcement would be very difficult without resort to such measures as police surveillance of pregnant women, unannounced searches of their homes, mandatory tests for forbidden drugs, seizure of medical records, "sting" operations in which pregnant women are offered drugs or drink, the solicitation of damaging testimony from children and other family members – and so on through the list of devices dear to totalitarian governments. Remember that one of the charges against Pamela Stewart was that she had sex with her husband against her doctor's advice. How many of our basic civil liberties would survive intact if the law were seriously committed to detecting and punishing such actions?

Some of these ill effects could probably be minimized by carefully drafted fetal abuse laws. Health care workers could be prohibited from testifying against women accused of fetal abuse, and law enforcement agencies could be limited to minimally intrusive methods of gathering evidence. But the restrictions necessary to make fetal abuse laws compatible with decent medical care and basic civil liberties would also make them virtually impossible to enforce. Enforcement would be sporadic and often arbitrary, making any beneficial deterrent effect very slight.

INVOLUNTARY INCARCERATION

The involuntary incarceration of pregnant women, e.g., to prevent their continuing to use drugs, is subject to similar pragmatic and rights-based objections. In some cases, the future child might be saved from a harm greater than that inflicted upon the woman – who might even benefit in the long run from being prevented from continuing her habitual drug use. But there would inevitably be many other pregnant alcohol or drug users who would be deterred from seeking any medical care during pregnancy and birth, or from telling the truth to their medical advisers. Moreover, it is contrary to fundamental legal principles to imprison competent adults not for crimes of which they have been convicted but to prevent their behaving irresponsibly in the future. Voluntary treatment and education programs would reach far more women, and would be much more beneficial to them and their families, than such punitive and coercive approaches. Those are apt only to increase the total harm to future persons caused by inadequate prenatal care, while undermining the civil liberties of all women.

The Social Context

All of these arguments gain additional force when we consider the social context in which these coercive policies would operate. Rates of perinatal mortality and morbidity are high in this country in comparison with other industrialized nations. The most common cause of infant mortality or morbidity is premature birth, which is strongly correlated with poverty and inadequate prenatal care. The lack of adequate medical insurance, or adequately funded Medicaid or other social programs, makes it all but impossible for many women to obtain prenatal care. For poor women, minority women, and pregnant teenagers it is apt to be especially difficult. And yet it is, predictably, these and other particularly vulnerable groups of women who will most often be subjected to involuntary obstetric interventions.[22] As Laura Purdy points out,

> Under these circumstances, invading women's bodies to impose last-minute, heroic care is stupid, mean and unfair. . . . Until we as a society act to make good, inexpensive, convenient and respectful care a priority, punishing women for lack of prenatal care reeks of hypocrisy.[23]

Proposals to punish "fetal abuse" by pregnant women raise comparable issues of social justice. The harm to infants caused by maternal drug use is a symptom of ineffective social policies. The legal prohibition of recreational drugs that (rightly or wrongly) are considered particularly harmful has thus far done relatively little to deter their sale and use. Prohibition seems only to worsen drug-related social problems, creating warfare in the streets and political corruption in both supplying and consuming nations. While drug use is not confined to those who bear the burdens of racism and economic deprivation, it is they who are most likely to be imprisoned as drug offenders, or killed in the drug wars. So too, it is poor and minority women who would most often be prosecuted under fetal abuse laws. Such laws are not likely to deter drug use very much more effectively than do existing antidrug laws, and would tend to exacerbate rather than remedy the problems of families and individuals affected by drug abuse.

It is easy to understand why that those who observe firsthand the tragedy of "crack babies" and infants damaged by alcohol should want to punish those who seem most directly responsible, i.e., the mothers. But in practice this would be little more than an exercise in scapegoating. Such scapegoating distracts attention from the need for fundamental changes in social policies. The necessary changes include improved access to medical care, including contraception and abortion as well as prenatal and obstetric services; improved economic and educational opportunities for economically disadvantaged groups; adequate funding for voluntary drug therapy programs, with priority given to pregnant users; better education about sex and contraception, and legal and illegal drugs; and perhaps a cautious process of legalization and regulation to bring some sanity to the trade in now-illegal recreational drugs. All of this will require a massive realignment of social priorities; but nothing less will effectively reduce the number of avoidable prenatal injuries to future persons.

I have argued that both prebirth seizures and postbirth sanctions are medically counterproductive, destructive to the physician/client relationship, and unjust in their differential impact upon poor and minority women. Conflicts can occur between the interests of pregnant women and those of their future children. But jettisoning women's fundamental rights to autonomy, privacy, and physical integrity is not the answer to the dilemmas posed by those conflicts. The imposition of invasive and life-threatening medical interventions upon competent and unconsenting adults is unconscionable, regardless of whether it is done for paternalistic reasons or for the benefit of some other individual.

The case against postbirth sanctions is based less upon fundamental rights that on the fact that punitive approaches will do a great deal more harm than good. However, basic civil liberties are at stake here too, inasmuch as the effective enforcement of criminal sanctions for fetal neglect or abuse would require substantial violations of privacy rights, as well as the erosion of medical confidentiality.

The vast majority of women who intend to give birth fully recognize their obligation to care for the fetal life within them, and are willing to undertake substantial personal sacrifices in the fulfillment of that obligation. As Janet Gallagher points out, treatment refusals by pregnant women are quite rare; if anything, women have been "too compliant in their dealings with the medical profession, and too willing to accept cesarean sections and other invasive procedures,"[24] without sound evidence that they or their offspring will benefit. The best way to protect future persons from prenatal injuries is to provide all women with access to high-quality medical services, and to empower them to make informed decisions about their own prenatal and obstetric care. Empowering others – physicians, courts of legislators – to make those decisions is inconsistent with fundamental legal and moral rights, and ultimately more dangerous to the well-being of future persons.[25]

Acknowledgement

My thanks to Michael Scriven and Dianne Romaine, who made helpful comments on earlier versions of this paper.

Another version of this paper was published in Midwest Medical Ethics 7 (Winter 1991), 1–7.

Notes

1. John A. Robertson. Reconciling offspring and maternal interests during pregnancy. In *Reproductive Laws for the 1990s*, edited by Sherrill Cohen and Nadine Taub. Clifton, New Jersey: Humana Press, 1989: 259–76.
2. See John A. Robertson, The right to procreate and in utero fetal therapy. J Legal Med 1982; 3: 438–439.
3. Other fetal rights issues, which are beyond the scope of this apper, include civil liability for women whose children are harmed by the mother's behavior while pregnant; whether living will statutes should contain a pregnancy exception; and whether employers may exclude women from jobs where the working conditions might prove injurious to fetuses. For an excellent discussion of some of the issues involving civil liability and employment discrimination, see James W. Knight and Joan C. Callahan. Preventing birth; contemporary methods and related moral controversies. Salt Lake City: University of Utah Press, 1989. On the pregnancy exception for living wills, see Janet Gallagher. Fetus as patient. In Reproductive Laws for the 1990*s*, 193–35.
4. Barbara Katz Rothman. *The Tentative Pregnancy; Prenatal Diagnosis and the Future of Motherhood*. New York: Viking Penguin, 1986: 31–32.

5. Cited by Laura M. Purdy. Are pregnant women fetal containers? Paper delivered at American Philosophical Association convention, Atlanta, December 28, 1989.
6. See, e.g., M. Warren. On the moral and legal status of abortion, Monist 1973 Jan: 43–61; and The moral significance of birth. Hypatia 1989 Fall: 46–65.
7. See Thomas H. Murray. Moral obligations to the not-yet-born: the fetus as patient. In Ethical Issues in the New Reproductive Technologies. Edited by Richard T. Hull. Belmont, California: Wadsworth, 1989: 218.
8. See, for instance, *Jefferson v. Griffin Spaulding County Hospital Authority*, 247 Ga 86, 274 S.E. 2d 457 (1981), in which the court gave a local government agency temporary custody of an unborn infant, empowering the agency to order medical interventions on its behalf – including the performance of a cesarean section against the will of the mother.
9. See Knight and Callahan: 268–69.
10. See Gallagher: 195.
11. Robertson, 1989: 265.
12. Of course, not all utilitarian thinkers reject the concept of a moral right. In a broader utilitarian perspective, it can be argued that utility is best served by respecting individual moral rights even in cases where some immediate social goal might seem to be better served by dispensing with rights.
13. See n. 8.
14. Gallagher cites a similar case in Michigan; 186.
15. See, for instance, Knox and Karagianis. Caesarean births: high rates, impassioned debate. Boston Globe Magazine 1984 Oct 21, 10–1; cited by Gallagher, 233.
16. Gilfix. Electronic fetal monitoring: physician liability and informed consent. A J Law Med 1984; 10: 31, 42; cited by Gallagher, 233.
17. Knox and Karagianis, 58.
18. H. Marieskind. An Evaluation of Caesarean Section in the United States 64; cited by Gallagher: 233.
19. There have been cases in which Jehovah's Witnesses have been forced to accept blood transfusions, for paternalistic reasons and/or for the sake of a minor child. (See, for instance, *United States v. George*, 33LW 2518 (1965).) The severity of the infringement of personal autonomy and religious freedom in these cases creates grave doubt about the correctness of these decisions. Be that as it may, the case is not analogous to that of involuntary surgery, since the direct physical invasion and damage is far less severe.
20. *McFall v. Shimp*, Pittsburgh Legislative Journal 14 (July 26, 1978), 127.
21. Robertson, 1989: 265
22. Kolder et al. Report that of the 21 cases in which court orders had been sought for involuntary medical interventions, 81 percent of the women were black, Hispanic or Asian. (Veronika E. B. Kolder, Janet Gallagher, and Michael T. Persons. Court-ordered obstetrical interventions. New Eng Med 316 1987 May 7: 1192.
23. Purdy: 13.
24. Gallagher 187.

LAWRENCE J. NELSON

The Mother and Fetus Union: What God Has Put Together, Let No Law Put Asunder?

Some courts have ordered pregnant women to undergo medical treatment against their will and have restricted their liberty for the sake of their fetuses.[1] There is, however, no reliable way to determine the exact number of times courts have issued such orders because these judicial actions usually are not publicly reported. More important, for the same reason there is no reliable way to determine the number of times judges have *refused* to issue such orders: these decisions are almost never reported either. Consequently, it is impossible to ascertain what portion of courts faced with a request from a physician or hospital to compel a pregnant woman to do something for the benefit of her fetus have granted or refused such requests. It is thus manifestly wrong to claim that "the majority of courts faced with this issue have found that the state's compelling interest in protection of the unborn should prevail.[2]

The overwhelming number of these orders came only from trial courts and were never reviewed by an appellate court that published its opinion on the case. Trial court decisions, of course, do *not* establish binding judicial precedent as do appellate court decisions and can be a highly unreliable source for determining the state of the law in a given area.[3]

Moreover, these courts were not enforcing public policy articulated by a democratically elected body in a statute. In fact, not a single statute exits in any state that explicitly authorizes courts (or any other agency of the government) to intervene in the medical or life-style choices of a pregnant woman. With the exception of pregnant women using illegal drugs,[4] no state has a statute authorizing governmental interference with the liberty of a pregnant woman on the basis of her failure to act in a manner consistent with the well-being of her fetus. Instead of relying upon a statute to justify their orders, these courts created a state interest "in the life of [the] unborn, living human being,"[5] asserted that "the unborn child is entitled to the law's protection" with no citation to any statute or other judicial precedent to support this conclusion,[6] or interpreted a state's child abuse and neglect law to include fetuses despite the lack of any precedent for considering a fetus a "child" under such law.[7] In addition, these courts frequently have sanctioned bodily

F.K. Beller and R.F. Weir (eds.), The Beginning of Human Life, 301–317.

invasion of the pregnant woman in the absence of an adversarial hearing and representation of the pregnant woman by a lawyer.

The creation and use by courts of such poorly defined and understood concepts to require one person to undergo bodily invasion or restriction of liberty for the sake of another, whether fetus or live-born person, constitutes an extremely serious and unprecedented State enterprise. So serious, in fact, that it ought to be completely dismantled now – until the legislatures of the various states duly enact a statute that expressly empowers courts to issue orders forcing pregnant women to undergo medical treatment or change their behavior for the sake of their fetuses.

This essay explores the ethical, legal, and policy reasons why the courts (as well as physicians and hospitals) ought to avoid the use of State compulsion to force pregnant women to "do the right thing" by the fetuses they carry. First, it contends that the pregnant woman and her fetus are a union, an ethically and legally significant (and unique) union. In light of this notion, any intelligible positing of fetal "rights" or any enforceable State interest in the protection of fetal well-being must account for and respect this union. Next, it argues in greater detail and largely by analogy that no judge should ever render the mother and fetus union asunder (that is, divide it or tear it apart) by means of a court order forcing a pregnant woman to undergo medical treatment or to change her non-drug abusing behavior for the sake of her fetus – *unless* the judge is properly applying a constitutionally valid statute duly enacted by a state legislature. Furthermore, in the absence of such a statute, physicians and hospitals should not seek, and judges should not consider granting, court orders compelling pregnant women to undergo unwanted medical treatment or behavior changes for the sake of their fetuses because of the intolerable dangers inherent in such activities. In short, the legislatures of the various states, and not the courts, should be authorizing State intervention in the medical and life-style choices of pregnant women when these choices may adversely affect the fetus's life or health: only the legislature, and not the courts, should authorize the invasion by force of the mother and fetus union by the State.

Union and Unity

The pregnant woman and her fetus are a union and a unity, what will sometimes be referred to herein as "the mother and fetus union." The use of the term "mother" is not meant to be emotionally evocative, or to prejudge the moral status of the fetus. In fact, "mother" may not be the correct term in a strict logical sense,[8] but it is an accurate term phenomenologically. To take a cue from Oliver Wendell Holmes, the life of humans, like the life of the law, is not logic, but experience. Women who are pregnant and intend to bring the pregnancy to term often consider themselves to be mothers because they experience themselves as familially attached to their fetuses. These pregnant women often act maternally and are bonded to their fetuses in a close and loving manner. Fetuses can and do have mothers as a result of the experiences of the women who gestate them.

A "union" is a combination, a junction, a fusion, something formed by a combination of united parts. A pregnant woman and her fetus constitute a union in the sense that they are two genetically different human entities who are joined together for a period of time. They are a union, yet simultaneously distinguishable as two different entities who are intimately joined.

A "unity" denotes oneness, singleness, the state of being one – a totality. A unity plainly cannot be divided or separated without doing harm to or destroying that which is one. A pregnant woman and her fetus are also a unity. The fetus is literally inside the woman and completely dependent upon her for life itself for a minimum of about half a year. To be sure, these notions of "union" and "unity" overlap, but the former emphasizes that there are two put together into one, while the latter reminds us that they are truly one.

There are a number of different dimensions to this particular union, all of which point to the conclusion that it can be a grave mistake conceptually, ethically, and legally to put the mother and fetus union asunder.

First, the union is *epistemological*. We cannot even know anything of the fetus, except to infer its existence from observing a woman's abdomen, without something literally going through or into the pregnant woman, or at lest touching her in some way. We cannot gain knowledge of a fetus, much less know when a physician, society, or the mother herself might need to actively intervene to protect its well-being, without involving the body and the self of the mother.

Second, the union is *biological* or *physical*. The pregnant woman and her fetus are bound up together by nature or, for a theist, by God. It is just the way things are. The fetus develops inside the body of the mother, hooked up to her physically and dependent upon her for the substances he or she absolutely needs in order to live and develop into a child capable of living on his or her own outside the womb. Until the fetus reaches about 24 weeks of gestation, he or she will die if the physical bond with the mother is severed or badly damaged.

Living fetuses, then, do *not* exist in the abstract or on their own: they exist only inside the womb, inside the body, inside the very person of a woman. If the fetus is taken outside the womb, then he or she is no longer a fetus, but something else – maybe a live-born child, maybe a corpse – yet surely very different from what he or she was inside the womb. A fetus by definition is unborn, is still inside the mother. Birth (or an abortion) is the end of the mother and fetus union.

Third, the union is *personal*. As every human person is an embodied consciousness, every person *is* a body. I do not have a body: I am my body.[9] The fetus is inside the body, inside the very self, of the pregnant woman. Put differently, the fetus is vitally hooked into the self of the mother. The link between them is more than biologically mechanical; it is personal as well. However, the personal connection can be broken. A dead woman can still produce a live child, as long as medical science can keep her biological body and the fetus alive after the person has died.[10] Even here, the biological connection must remain. It cannot be prematurely severed, or the fetus dies.

Fourth, the union is *ethical*. The biological and personal connection between fetus and mother supports the conclusion that there is an ethical dimension to their relationship as well. Because the mother can radically affect her fetus's life and well-being and because the fetus can develop eventually into what we all would recognize as a live human person with rights and interests, pregnant women have a general ethical obligation to act reasonably to preserve the well-being of the fetus when they continue a pregnancy and do not have an abortion.[11]

Finally, and most important for present purposes, the union is *legal*. Assuming for the sake of argument that fetuses have some legally cognizable interests or "rights," it is a serious mistake for the law to understand these rights or enforce them as if they exist in reality apart from the mother's interests and rights.

Although it makes little sense to talk of a fetus's "rights" apart from the mother, it makes a great deal of sense to talk about a *live-born* child's rights apart from his or her mother. State-mandated medical treatment or alternative placement of a live-born child does *not* place the mother's life or health at risk, does not interfere with her personal privacy, liberty, or *self*-determination, and does not invade the mother's bodily integrity. In contrast, State-mandated medical treatment of a pregnant woman or modification of her behavior for the sake of her fetus can and usually does create such risk, interference, and invasion.

The unity of mother and fetus can be most plainly seen in the enforcement of fetal "rights." If the State is to enforce legal rights of a fetus (and enforcement is what makes legal rights meaningful), then it must necessarily do so by significantly affecting the mother's legal rights and interests as well. The paradigmatic case of a compulsory cesarean delivery makes this exceedingly clear. If a fetus has a legally protected interest in being delivered by cesarean section to preserve his/her life or health when the mother refuses consent to this surgical intervention, then the State can vindicate this interest only by interfering with the mother's well-established, legally enforceable interests in (1) the protection of her life and health; (2) the preservation of her constitutionally protected interests in privacy, liberty, and self-determination; and (3) the maintenance of her bodily integrity. All bodily invasions of a pregnant woman or restrictions on her liberty interfere with these interests to one degree or another.

The State's Interest in the Fetus

Instead of granting a fetus legally cognizable rights that can be called upon as a basis for compelling a pregnant woman to undergo medical treatment or change her behavior, the State can claim to have a compelling interest in protecting the fetus which justifies its ability to intervene in a pregnant woman's life and force her to do or not do certain things. To use *Roe v. Wade*'s odd and ill-chosen term, the State has an interest in protecting "the potentiality of life" which becomes compelling at the point of fetal viability.[12] After this point in gestation, *Roe* acknowledges, the states have an interest strong enough to outweigh whatever interests the woman might have and may, if it chooses to do so, ban abortions outright – except if an abortion is necessary to preserve the mother's life and health.[13]

The positing of a compelling State interest in protecting the life of the fetus as such – whether this interest begins at the point of viability according to *Roe v. Wade* or exists throughout pregnancy according to Chief Justice Rehnquist's plurality opinion in *Webster*[14] – ignores the significance of the mother and fetus union. It is yet another example of a misleading, wrong, and ultimately dangerous legal fiction. As demonstrated above, the interests of a mother and her fetus cannot be cleanly separated. They are a unity in the sense that the State cannot vindicate its interest in the fetus without simultaneously affecting the well-settled legal rights of the mother.

Too much talk about fetal rights makes the mother seem as if she is not there with the fetus in an intimate and indivisible union.[15] Similarly, there is too much talk about the State's interest in protecting fetal life as if the State simultaneously has no interests in the mother.[16] Surely the State must have an interest in (1) protecting the life and health of individual persons like pregnant women (whose legal status as holders of legal and constitutional rights is not in question); (2) preserving an individual's privacy, liberty, and self-determination; (3) maintaining the bodily integrity of its citizens. Whatever interest the State has in a fetus, the State simultaneously has an interest in protecting these rights of the individual woman from unjustified interference.

In sum, the mother and fetus union has to be reinserted into any legal consideration of the State's interest in protecting fetal (or, for that matter, embryonic) life. The sorting out of these potentially directly competing interest of the State in mother and fetus should largely be left to the legislature and not the courts. But that is not what is happening at present. Courts are invading the mother and fetus union on an unpredictable, case-by-case basis using highly questionable rationales and treading heavily upon what the American political system traditionally has considered sacred ground: the bodies and private lives of its citizens.

State Intrusion into Privacy and Bodily Integrity

Judicial Intervention in Obstetrical Cases

There are serious dangers inherent in the present system of ad hoc judicial intervention into the lives and bodies of pregnant women in the absence of specific laws permitting such intervention. First, in the absence of legislation requiring that all cases meeting certain specified criteria be brought to court for consideration of intervention, the most fundamental precept of justice and equal protection of the laws is being violated – similar cases are *not* being treated similarly. At present, physicians, hospitals, and their lawyers have unfettered discretion regarding if and when they seek the use of State compulsion in the life of a pregnant woman in order to benefit her fetus. It is offensive, indeed outrageous, that similarly situated women should be treated very differently by their providers of health care and by the State.

Second, physicians and hospitals can and apparently do discriminate on the basis of race, language, or socioeconomic status is deciding whether to seek State judicial compulsion. The leading national survey of court-ordered obstetrical interventions found that 81 percent of the women involved were black, Asian, or Hispanic; 44 percent were unmarried; 24 percent did not speak English as their primary language; and 100 percent were treated in a teaching hospital clinic or were receiving public assistance.[17] This is more than the unevenhanded administration of justice: it is invidious discrimination. It is telling that there has been no reported court case of a physician or hospital trying to force a pregnant lawyer or the wife of a rich and prominent businessman to have a cesarean section, or to stay in the hospital against her will, or to stop snorting cocaine.

Third, judges frequently are making their decisions about the fate of pregnant women under so-called emergency conditions with little time for reflection or legal research.[18] This invariably leads to bad results, particularly when there is no informed attorney arguing the patient's side of the question.

Fourth, as conflict over proper medical treatment has arisen suddenly in pregnancy cases and court orders are often sought under strict time constraints, judges typically hear a one-sided case in favor of intervention, and the woman is almost never represented by informed legal counsel. In short, the constitutional guarantee of procedural due process is ignored. Accused criminals, murderers for example, receive much greater consideration when judges hold lengthy adversarial hearings on a prosecutor's motion to compel surgical retrieval of a bullet.

The Case for Legislation

However frequently it occurs and whatever its inherent dangers, the State's use of coercive power to force a pregnant woman to undergo a cesarean section, to be hospitalized and bedridden against her will, to abstain from sex or alcohol under penalty of jail or fine, to quit her job in order to be free of exposure to potential fetotoxins – all for the benefit of her fetus – is an extraordinary, drastic, and uncommonly serious type of State intervention into the life of one of its citizens. Forcing medical treatment or any other type of bodily intrusion upon an unconsenting individual (whether pregnant or not) or restricting the liberty of one individual for the sake of another under any circumstances is an exercise of governmental power that cries out for clear and unambiguous justification. Almost one hundred years ago, long before anyone thought of forcing anyone to undergo surgery for any purpose, the U.S. Supreme Court recognized that the law ought to stay out of people's liberty and bodies in the absence of explicit authority. "No right is held more sacred, or is more carefully guarded, by the common law, than the right of every individual to the possession and control of their own person, free from *all* restraint or interference by others, *unless by clear and unquestionable authority of law*. As well said by Judge Cooley, 'The right to one's person may be said to be a right of complete immunity: to be let alone.'[19]

The unusual and radical character of this form of government intrusion into the life and person of individuals is the primary reason why it should be permitted only when a state legislature has explicitly authorized it by means of a statute that has passed constitutional scrutiny by the courts. There are other reasons for strictly requiring statutory authority for bodily invasions and restrictions of liberty for the sake of another (discussed below) that mostly have to do with justice and fairness. In any event, the failure to recognize the extraordinary, drastic, and serious nature of State-mandated medical treatment of pregnant women or State-enforced restrictions of their liberty for the sake of a fetus is not only dishonest, but plainly discriminates against women because of their unique reproductive capabilities. It is a sexism, a blind and ugly prejudice, that has no place in a country committed to freedom and equality for all. In other words, no judge should ever invade the mother and fetus union by means of a court order forcing a pregnant woman to undergo medical treatment or change her non-drug abusing behavior for the sake of her fetus – *unless* the judge is properly applying a constitutionally valid and duly enacted statute.

There are a number of important advantages to requiring legislative authorization of State intervention in the lives of pregnant women rather than permitting ad hoc judicial intervention.

First, a statue satisfying justice as fairness and the constitutional guarantee of equal protection would require health care providers (or some other persons) to seek court authority in *all* cases that meet certain specific criteria and would direct courts to grant them in certain specified instances. Consequently, all pregnant women would be treated evenhandedly. None of them need fear facing a judge because they just happen to be black, poor, or legally unsophisticated while another woman allegedly threatening her fetus's well-being in the same way would entirely escape State scrutiny of her choices.

Second, establishment of legislation would create clear legal authority for this type of drastic and dangerous State intervention instead of the murky and exceedingly elastic standards judges have created. The appellate cases of judicially compelled obstetrical intervention – *Anderson, Jefferson*, and *Maydun* – surely do not constitute "clear and unquestionable authority of law." *Anderson* relies upon the judge-created assertion that "the unborn child is entitled to the law's protection" unsupported by reference to judicial or statutory precedent, as well as the invalid analogy to court-ordered treatment of live-born children over parental objection.[20] *Jefferson* rests upon a strained interpretation of child abuse and neglect law as well as a hotly disputed view of the significance of *Roe v. Wade* to the question.[21] *Maydun* was implicitly, but unavoidably, overruled by the *In re A.C.* decision.[22]

Third, requiring legislative authority will permit all the lobbying and special interest groups to join in the debate and try to persuade our elected representatives one way or the other on this obviously controversial subject. The pro-lifers as well as the ACLU and Planned Parenthood could publicly make their cases for and against forcible State intervention into the lives of pregnant women. While state legislatures may not be the ideal place to work out such disputes, they are better places than courtrooms, particularly when the judge is being forced to make a decision under purportedly emergency circumstances.

Fourth, holding public debates on such legislation will help to smoke out the true differences (if any) between pregnant women who refuse medically indicated treatment and those who take illegal drugs, who legally consume vast quantities of alcohol, or who smoke many cigarettes – all to the potentially serious detriment to their fetuses.[23] If the goal of judicial intervention is to prevent harm to the fetus and vindicate the State's interest in the fetus, then there is no reason in principle why women who smoke or drink heavily to the detriment of their fetuses should not be brought before judges as well.

Fifth, legislation will permit the courts to adjudicate its constitutionality as reviewers of the form and substance of the forced State intervention rather than as its creators and agents. It is very likely there will be a much more careful, critical, and traditional examination of the constitutionality of State compulsion of pregnant women if the courts are reviewing the actions of the legislature rather than the actions of other judges.

Lastly, assuming such laws would pass constitutional scrutiny under the due process and equal protection clauses, they very likely would contain explicit procedural and substantive criteria that trial courts would have to use in deciding such cases and for appellate courts to use when reviewing cases on appeal. The existence of such criteria is much more desirable than the amorphous state of the present law of judicially compelled, but not statutorily authorized, obstetrical intervention.

Precedents for State Obstetrical Intrusions?

The extraordinary, drastic, and serious nature of State obstetrical intervention manifests itself in three fundamental ways. The first is the lack of significant similarity between accepted State intrusions into the body of an individual and judicial orders directed at pregnant women. The second is the absence of judicial orders in other areas of life that require nonpregnant persons to submit to State intrusion into their lives and bodies for the sake of another individual, even when that individual's life hangs in the balance. In other words, there is an almost complete absence of judicial orders mandating intrusion into the lives and bodies of nonpregnant persons that would be directly analogous to, and provide parallel justification for, the compulsory treatment or detention of pregnant women. The third is by way of analogy to the creation and enforcement of the criminal law in a democratic society.

Accepted State Action

The Military Draft

Involuntarily drafting persons into the armed services where they are at risk of death or serious bodily injury is a well-entrenched power of the State. However, it is an explicit constitutional power granted only to the democratically elected Congress and not to judges.[24] Conscription is utilized for the "pursuit of public purposes,"[25] not the good of any individual person. It would, for example, seem to be manifestly unconstitutional for Congress, much less a judge, to use the draft to take by force an inductee's kidney and order that it be transplanted into an army general dying of renal disease.

The power to draft citizens into the armed services for the national defense is reserved to the federal legislature and can be implemented only by statute. In contrast, no legislature has ever explicitly utilized whatever power it has under the federal Constitution and its state constitution to use force against pregnant women. The courts that have acted to coerce pregnant women have *never* done so pursuant to a statute properly enacted by the legislature that expressly authorized the use of coercion against pregnant women in designated circumstances. Also, citizens are drafted into the military for the common good, unlike a pregnant women who is being forced by the State to undergo treatment for the sake of a particular individual entity, her fetus.

Forcible Taking of Blood Samples for Criminal Evidentiary Purposes[26]

The courts regularly have permitted blood samples to be taken involuntarily from suspects, provided there was a valid arrest or at least probable cause for law enforcement's belief that the sample would produce needed evidence of conduct explicitly made illegal (such as drunk driving) by a criminal statute.[27] In approving of this result, the U.S. Supreme Court has emphasized that the physical intrusion involved is "slight"[28] or "minor,"[29] that a blood test "has become routine in our everyday life,"[30] and that the test "involves virtually no risk, trauma, or pain.[31] Furthermore, it required that such blood tests be conducted in a medically reasonable manner by trained personnel in order to be constitutionally acceptable.[32] The Supreme Court has also cautioned that its holding "that the constitution does not forbid the states *minor intrusions* into an individual's body under stringently limited conditions in no way indicates that it permits more substantial intrusions, or intrusions under other conditions."[33]

The involuntary taking of blood samples is a very small intrusion that is performed only for social reasons upon those who stand accused of a statutory crime. It poses no appreciable risk to the life or health of the suspect. In contrast, a forced cesarean section is by no means a "minor" intrusion into the privacy and bodily integrity of a pregnant woman, and it poses risks to the woman for beyond those of a blood test.[34] Like all of the accepted State intrusions, it is imposed for the public good, not the good of any individual.

Compulsory Surgery for Criminal Evidentiary Purposes

On a number of occasions, the courts have ruled that it is constitutionally permissible under certain circumstances for law enforcement officials to compel criminal suspects, despite their strong interests in personal privacy and bodily integrity, to undergo surgery involuntarily for the removal of evidence (usually a bullet) imbedded in their bodies. Generally speaking, the courts have approved of these involuntary "surgical searches" only when (1) the surgery would be "minor" and pose no substantial risk to the life, health, or well-being of the subject (viz., removal under local anesthesia of a bullet only superficially lodged beneath the skin);[35] (2) the State can establish a truly compelling need for the evidence;[36] and (3) the suspect has been afforded full procedural due process, that is, the suspect was represented by legal counsel, the surgery was preceded by a full adversarial hearing on the medical and legal issue involved, and appellate review was available.[37] The courts have refused to permit such surgery on criminal suspects if it endangered their life or health.[38]

Compulsory surgical searches are distinguishable from forced treatment or detention of pregnant women in two important ways. First, surgical searches are authorized only for minor procedures usually done under local anesthetic that pose no significant risk to the life or health of the suspect. If such risk is present, the procedure is prohibited. Second, the criminal suspect is afforded full procedural due process rights *before* the surgery is performed, including representation by legal counsel and an adversarial hearing. Pregnant women are almost never afforded such due process rights before they are forced to accept risks that can be far greater (as in the case of a cesarean section) than what the courts will permit in criminal cases.

Compulsory Vaccinations for Public Health Reasons
States have the constitutional power to require by statute that all citizens or only school-age children submit to vaccination for public health purposes,[39] although the sanction for noncompliance is apparently limited to a fine or jail sentence for adults, or exclusion from school for children.[40] When the Supreme Court decided *Jacobson* in 1905 and communicable diseases like smallpox were still prevalent, no state undertook forcible vaccination.[41] Vaccination is a minor physical invasion that is done for the public good, not for the benefit of an individual.

The most important difference between "compulsory" vaccination and forced treatment of pregnant women (besides the difference between receiving an injection and, for example, undergoing a cesarean delivery) is that the former is not really "compulsory" in the same sense as the latter. State laws regarding vaccination provide for some sort of sanction only after the fact for the person who refuses; pregnant women are literally forced to comply with the court order.[42] Furthermore, compulsory vaccinations are expressly authorized by a statute passed by a legislature, and these statutes commonly exempt those with religious or personal objections.[43] Pregnant women receive no such solicitude, despite the fact that their refusals are frequently religiously based.[44]

Analogies to Obstetrical Intrusions

It is significant that the presently accepted State intrusions into the privacy and bodily integrity of citizens described above do not provide strong support for compulsory treatment or detention of pregnant women. But it is striking, indeed shocking, that judges have not issued orders in cases truly analogous to that of the pregnant woman, that is, ordered nonpregnant persons to submit to State intrusion into their lives and bodies for the sake of another individual, even when that individual's very life or health is at stake. Consider the following five examples:

Forcing a Person to Give a Kidney, Bone Marrow, or Blood to a Close Relative in Dire Need Thereof
There have been two reported court cases in which someone has resorted to the courts (unsuccessfully) to force a nonpregnant relative to undergo a medical procedure for the benefit of another. In *McFall v. Shimp*, a 39-year-old man terminally ill with aplastic anemia sought a state court order compelling his first cousin to undergo tissue testing and to "donate" bone marrow for transplantation if compatible.[45] A bone marrow transplant was the plaintiff's only real hope for survival, while the testing and bone marrow extraction was very unlikely to harm the "donor's" physical health. Nonetheless, the court refused to grant the order and stated that legally forcing the cousin to submit to such bodily intrusion "would change every concept and principle upon which our society is founded." It ruled that establishing a legally enforceable duty

to undergo bodily invasion for the benefit of another "would defeat the sanctity of the individual, and would impose a rule which would know no limits, and one could not imagine where the line would be drawn."

In *Bosze v. Curran*, a father sought a court order compelling his former girlfriend and the mother of his 3-year-old twins to have them tested as potential bone marrow "donors" for his 13-year-old son who was dying of leukemia. The Illinois Supreme Court affirmed a lower court decision that the father could not force the children to undergo the testing.[46] As in the *McFall* case, the donation might have been lifesaving for the boy. Interestingly, in a different case, a lower court judge refused to order a woman to undergo a cesarean section after acknowledging that he lacked the legal authority to force her to donate an organ to a child of hers, even if that child were dying.[47]

Compelling Blood Extraction in Order to Meet Blood Bank Shortages
Blood for transfusion increasingly is in short supply,[48] and yet apparently no one has ever obtained a court order to force anyone, close relative or not, to give blood to a specific patient or to whoever was in need, even though the extraction poses no risk of harm and could greatly benefit others or save their lives.

Penalizing the Failure to Rescue Someone in Dire Need
It is still the law in the overwhelming majority of states that individuals have no legal duty to come to the aid of another who is at risk of harm or death from circumstances not of the potential rescuer's making, even if all that was called for was a phone call to 911 to summon help.[49]

Restricting the Liberty of One Person to Benefit Another
For example, courts have refused to compel an unwilling child to visit with a divorced parent even though the parent was providing support to the child.[50]

Compelling Organ "Donation" from a Corpse
Despite the facts that only about 13 percent of potential cadaver organ donors actually become donors and that many persons die waiting for an organ transplant, no physician or hospital apparently has ever obtained a court order authorizing them to take vital organs from a corpse over the objection of relatives or the previously stated wishes of the dead patient.[51]

Intrusions like these into the bodies and lives of unwilling persons (or even of corpses) are unheard-of in our society, even though they are materially analogous to forced treatment or detention of pregnant women. This striking absence of analogous State compulsions should give us pause. If they are not happening to other persons in materially analogous cases, why are they happening to pregnant women?

The Analogy to the Criminal Law

In the American governmental system, the democratically elected legislatures are the creators of crime and punishment. If one is to lose one's money to a criminal fine, one's freedom to prison, or one's life to capital punishment, he or she must be convicted by proof beyond a reasonable doubt of having committed a crime against society as set forth in a particular criminal statute authored by the legislature. This system does not recognize the creation of crimes by ad hoc judicial action. The reasons underlying this system of criminal punishment are analogous to the reasons why pregnant women should not be subjected to forced medical treatment or detention by the State in the absence of a constitutionally valid statute duly enacted by a state legislature that authorizes the use of force against them.

The general rule of American law is that the identification of crimes and the specification of criminal punishment is the exclusive province of the legislature.[52] Courts are not empowered to hear a State official complain of someone's alleged antisocial behavior and determine on a case-by-case basis whether this behavior constitutes a criminal offense punishable by loss of liberty, property, or life. The application of the criminal process to an individual has momentous consequences (loss of liberty, self-determination, even loss of life) and thus is too serious a matter to be done in an ad hoc manner.

The consequences of imposition of criminal sanctions on an individual are similar to the imposition of medical treatment (like cesarean delivery) on an unconsenting woman: invasion of protected interests in privacy and self-determination, loss of liberty, and perhaps loss of life, as can happen with capital punishment. Because it is such a serious matter for the State to adjudicate someone a criminal, criminal statutes are held to high standards of constitutional propriety. For example, a criminal statute can be found constitutionally void for vagueness when the conduct prohibited is expressed in terms so vague that "persons of common intelligence must necessarily guess at its meaning and differ as to its application."[53] Moreover, vague criminal statutes foster arbitrariness and discrimination in application, a result antithetical to justice. "If arbitrary and discriminatory enforcement is to be prevented, laws must provide explicit standards for those who apply them. A vague law impermissibly delegates basic policy matters to policemen, judges, and juries for resolution on an *ad hoc* and subjective basis, with the attendant dangers of arbitrary and discriminatory application.[54] In addition, accused criminals are afforded elaborate procedural due process rights, such as representation by effective legal counsel,[55] the right to cross-examination of witnesses,[56] and the right to a jury trial before criminal sanctions like loss of liberty are imposed.[57]

These elements fundamental to the constitutionality of any criminal law are clearly missing with respect to judicially sanctioned interventions in the lives of pregnant women. First, the commonly used standards for such intervention are hopelessly vague, and therefore women have no idea what is legally expected of them. For example, it is very difficult to see how a pregnant woman in Georgia could reasonably know what conduct might subject her to forcible State intervention when such intervention is triggered by an appeal to a "viable unborn child's . . . right under the U.S. Constitution to the protection of the State" and to the fetus as "a deprived child without proper parental care necessary for his or her physical health.[58] Such amorphous "standards" are as treacherous as vague criminal laws. "The view of vagueness in criminal statutes is the treachery they conceal either in determining what persons are included or what acts are prohibited. Words which are vague and fluid . . . may be as much as a trap for the innocent as the ancient laws of Caligula."[59]

Second, compulsory treatment can be imposed in an arbitrary and discriminatory manner when, for example, the undefined appeal to "the compelling interest[of the State] to intervene and protect the life and safety of a fetus"[60] is used by a judge. For example, the Supreme Court has invalidated as unconstitutionally vague a criminal law that prohibited "three or more persons [assembling] on any of the sidewalks . . . and there conducting themselves in a manner annoying to persons passing by."[61] The Court observed that this law "contains an obvious invitation to discriminatory enforcement against those whose association together is 'annoying' because their ideas, their lifestyle or their physical appearance is resented by the majority of their fellow citizens."[62] Similarly, vague standards can lead to discriminatory imposition of force on pregnant women because the physicians seeking the court order or the judge considering the matter may personally disagree with or find repugnant the particular reasons the woman is giving for her actions, while they may idiosyncratically find other reasons acceptable. For example, objections to cesarean delivery based upon minority religious values may be suspect for physicians and judges belonging to mainstream religions that do not acknowledge such values.[63]

Criminal statutes can also be constitutionally infirm as overbroad in that a proper governmental purpose may not be achieved by means which sweep unnecessarily broadly and thereby invade the area of protected freedoms, such as freedom of speech.[64] This is precisely what court orders can do with respect to pregnant women: the loose criteria for judicial intervention can easily invade traditionally protected freedoms such as the right of a competent adult to refuse unwanted medical treatment.[65]

If our society does not tolerate vague and overly broad State criminal laws that can take away persons' liberty or life, it should be similarly intolerant of vague and overly broad judicial standards that are used to take away the liberty – or perhaps the life – of a pregnant woman. This is particularly true when these objectionable standards are being applied to pregnant women who are not receiving the basic procedural due process protections afforded to the worst criminal. "The importance of informed, detached, and deliberate[judicial] determinations of the issue whether or not to invade another's body in search of evidence of guilt is indisputable and great."[66] The importance of careful and fair judicial determinations whether or not to invade the body of a woman to possibly help her fetus is no less indisputable and great.

Because of the seriousness of forced State intervention into the bodies and other legally protected interests of its citizens, courts should not be authorizing any such intervention using vague standards of their own creation in emergent circumstances and in the absence of procedural due process safeguards. Court orders compelling pregnant women to undergo medical treatment or to change their behavior for the sake of their fetuses are not the type of State action that should be created and enforced by the courts in the absence of explicit legislative authority. State action compelling one person to restrict involuntarily her freedom or to sacrifice her body for the interests of another is too drastic, too intrusive, and too dangerous to be created by judges on an ad hoc basis to meet the exigencies of individual cases.

The near-total absence of instances of judicially sanctioned State intrusion into the life and body of a nonpregnant individual for the sole benefit of another individual, whether they be familially related or strangers, should give everyone great pause when the propriety of State-compelled treatment or detention of pregnant women for the sake of their fetuses is considered. If the State does not require such bodily invasion or restriction of liberty in other, materially analogous cases, it should not impose such a requirement upon pregnant women merely because they are a convenient, and perhaps sometimes unsympathetic, target of coercion. But if there are sound policy reasons in favor of such drastic intervention into the privacy and bodily integrity of some pregnant women, then let the democratically elected bodies in our nation make that decision, and let the courts decide whether this decision is constitutionally valid and properly protective of the individual rights and liberties this country stands for.

REFERENCES

1. *Raleigh Fitkin-Paul Morgan Memorial Hospital v. Anderson*, 201 A.2d 537 (N.J. 1964), *cert. denied*, 377 U.S. 984; *Jefferson v. Griffin Spalding County Hospital Authority*, 274 S.E.2d 457 (Ga. 1981); *In re Maydun*, No. 189–86, (D. C. Super. Ct., July 26, 1986), as Appendix to concurring and dissenting opinion of Belson, J., 573 A.2d 1259 (D.C. App. 1990); *In re Application of Winthrop University Hospital*, 128 Misc.2d 804, 490 N.Y.S.2d 996 (N.Y. Sup. Ct. 1985); *In re Application of Jamaica Hospital*, 128 Misc.2d 1006, 491 N.Y.S.2d 898 (N.Y. Sup. Ct. 1985); *Crouse-Irving Memorial Hospital v. Paddock*, 127 Misc.2d 101, 485 N.Y.S.2d 443 (N.Y. Sup. Ct. 1985); *In re Unborn Baby Wilson*, No. 81–108 AV (Calhoun County P. Ct. Feb. 3, 1981), *aff'd*, No. 81–108 AV (Calhoun County P. Ct. Mar. 9, 1981), *leave to appeal denied*, No. 57436 (Mich. Ct. App. July 28, 1981); *In re Baby Jeffries*, No. 14004 (Jackson County P. Ct. May 24, 1982); Kolder, Gallagher, and Parsons, *Court-Ordered Obstetrical Interventions*, 316 New Eng. J. Med. 1192 (1987); *North Central Bronx v. Headley*, No. 1992–85 (Sup. Ct., Special Term, Bronx City, N.Y. Jan. 6, 1986).

2. *In re A.C.*, 573 A.2d 1235, 1257 note 8 (D.C. App., 1990) (Belson, J., concurring in part and dissenting in part). See also, Noble-Allgire, Court-Ordered Cesarean Sections, 10 J Leg Med 1989; 211, 236.
3. E.g., *Barber v. Superior Court*, 147 Cal. App. 3d 1006, 195 Cal. Rptr. 484 (1983); *Bartling v. Superior Court*, 163 Cal. App.3d 186, 209 Cal. Rptr. 220 (1984); *Bouvia v. Superior Court*, 179 Cal. App.3d 1127, 225 Cal. Rptr. 297 (1986); *Conservatorship of Drabick*, 200 Cal. App.3d 185, 245 Cal. Rptr. 840 (1988), cert. denied, 109 S. Ct. 299, reh. denied, 109 S. Ct. 828.
4. E.g., Minn. Stat. § 626.5561.
5. Jefferson, *supra* note 1, at 460.
6. Anderson, *supra* note 1, at 538; see Annas. Forced cesareans: the most unkindest cut of all. Hastings Cent Rep 1982; 12: 16.
7. Jefferson. *supra* note 1, at 459, 462.
8. Kaufman. The Fetus's Mother. Hastings Cent Rep 1990; 20: 3.
9. P. Ricoeur. Freedom and Nature: The Voluntary and the Involuntary 1966: 10–12.
10. Field, Gates, Creasy, Jonsen & Laros. Maternal brain death during pregnancy: medical and ethical issues. J Am Med Assoc 1988; 260: 816.
11. Nelson and Milliken. Compelled medical treatment of pregnant women: life, liberty, and law in conflict. J Am Med Assoc 1988; 259: 1060, 1065–66.
12. *Roe. v. Wade*, 410 U.S. 113, 162 (1973).
13. *Id.* at 163–64.
14. *Webster v. Reproductive Health Services*, 492 U.S. 490, 109 S. Ct. 3040, 3057 (1989).
15. E.g., Bowes and Selgestad; Fetal vs. Maternal Rights: Medical and Legal Perspectives, Obstetrics and Gynecology 1981; 58: 209; Shaw. Conditional prospective rights of the fetus, J Legal Med 1984; 5: 13.
16. E.g., *In re Application of Jamaica Hospital, supra* note 1.
17. Kolder, Gallagher & Parsons. Court-Ordered Obstetrical Interventions, 316 New Eng J Med 1987: 1192, 1195.
18. Annas, *supra* note 6, at 17.
19. *Union Pacific Railway. Co. v. Botsford*, 141 U.S. 250, 251 (1891) (emphasis added).
20. Nelson and Milliken, *supra* note 11, at 1062.
21. Nelson, Buggy, and Weil. Forced medical treatment of pregnant women: compelling each to live as seems good to the rest. Hastings L Rev 1986; 37: 703, 745.
22. Annas. Foreclosing the use of force: a.c. revisited. Hastings Cent Rep 1990; 20: 27, 28–29.
23. Bays. Substance Abuse and Child Abuse: Impact of Addiction on the Child, Ped. Clinics of No. Amer. 1990; 37: 881, 882; see Shaw, *supra* note 15.
24. U.S. Constitution Article I, § 8.
25. *Gillette v. U.S.*, 401 U.S. 437, 459 (1971).
26. See generally Michelle Gee. Propriety of search involving removal of natural substance of foreign object from body by actual or threatened force. ALR Fed 1990; 66.
27. See Gulbis. Admissibility in criminal case of blood-alcohol test where blood was taken despite defendant's objection or refusal to submit to test. ALR4th 1990; 14: 690, 694–695.
28. *Breithaupt v. Abram*, 352 U.S. 432, 439 (1956).
29. *Schmerber v. California*, 384 U.S. 757, 772 (1966).
30. Breithaupt, *supra* note 28, at 436.
31. Schmerber, *supra* note 29, at 771.
32. *Id.* at 771–772.
33. *Id.* at 772 (emphasis added).
34. J. Pritchard, P. MacDonald, N. Gant. Williams Obstetrics (17th ed) 1985: xi.
35. E.g., *Hughes v. State*, 466 A.2d 533 (Ct. Sp. App. Md. 1983); *United States v. Crowder*, 543 F.2d 312 (D.C. Cir. 1976), *cert. denied*, 429 U.S. 1062.
36. *Winston v. Lee*, 470 U.S. 753, 84 L. Ed.2d 662 (1985); *Hughes, supra* note 35, at 536.
37. Crowder, *supra* note 35.
38. E.g., *Bowden v. State*, 256 Ark. 820, 510 S.W.2d 879 (1974); *State v. Allen*, 277 S.C.

595, 291 S.E.2d 459 (1982); *People v. Richard*, 548 N.Y.S.2d 369 (N.Y. Albany Co. Ct. 1989).

39. *Jacobson v. Massachusetts*, 197 U.S. 11 (1905); *Zucht v. King*, 260 U.S. 174 (1922).
40. 39 Am. Jur. 2d Health § 27 (Supp. 1990); e.g., Smith-Hurd Illinois Annotated Statutes Ch. 111 1/2, Para. 24 (Supp. 1990) (misdemeanor); 79 C.J.S. Schools and School Districts § 453 (Supp. 1990).
41. Jacobson, *supra* note 39, at 15 (argument for appellant).
42. E.g., *In re Jeffries, supra* note 1.
43. Cal. Health & Safety Code § 3800 et seq.; Smith-Hurd Illinois Annotated Statutes Ch. 111 1/2, Para. 22.12(1) (Supp. 1990); *Mason v. General Brown Cent. School Dist.*, 851 F.2d 47 (2d Cir. 1989).
44. E.g., Jefferson, Anderson, *In re Baby Jeffries, North Central Bronx v. Headley, supra* note 1.
45. 10 Pa. D. & C.2d 90 (1978).
46. Court blocks forced bone marrow tests. San Francisco Chronicle 1990 Sep 29; Sect A: 8. Boy in leukemia case dies – he lost supreme court ruling. San Francisco Chronicle 1990 Nov 20; Sect B: 6.
47. Unpublished opinion, No. 84-7-50006-D (Super. Ct. Benton Cty. WA, April 29, 1984).
48. Roberts and Wolkoff. Improving the quality and quantity of whole blood supply: limits to voluntary arrangements. Health Polit Pol Law 1988; 13: 167.
49. Nelson, *supra* note 21, at 753, citing W Keeton, D Dobbs, R Keeton, D Owen. Prosser and Keeton on the Law of Torts (5th ed.) 1984: 375.
50. *Henshaw v. Henshaw*, 258 N.W.2d 289 (Ct. App. Mich. 1978); *Schmidt v. Schmidt*, 459 A.2d 421 (Super. Ct. Penn. 1983).
51. Nelson and Milliken, *supra* note 11, at 1065.
52. E.g., *People v. Jacobs*, 157 Cal. App.3d 797, 204 Cal. Rptr. 234 (1984); *People v. Brangofsky*, 181 Misc. 782, 50 N.Y.S.2d 32 (Mag. Ct. N.Y.C. 1943); *People v. Montgomery*, 669 P.2d 1387 (Colo. 1983).
53. *Connally v. General Construction Co.*, 269 U.S. 385, 391 (1926) (citations omitted); *Lanzetta v. New Jersey*, 306 U.S. 451 (1939).
54. *Grayned v. Rockford*, 408 U.S. 104, 108–109 (1972) (footnotes omitted).
55. *Gideon v. Wainwright*, 372 U.S. 335 (1963).
56. *Pointer v. Texas*, 380 U.S. 400 (1965).
57. *Duncan v. Louisiana*, 391 U.S. 145 (1968).
58. Jefferson, *supra* note 1, at 458, 459.
59. *United States v. Cardiff*, 344 U.S. 174, 176 (1952) (citation omitted).
60. Maydun, *supra* note 1, at 1264.
61. *Coates v. Cincinnati*, 402 U.S. 611 (1971).
62. *Id.* at 616.
63. See *In re Clark*, 21 Ohio Op.2d 86, 89, 185 N.E.2d 128, 132 (C.P. Lucas County 1962).
64. *Stromberg v. California*, 283 U.S. 359 (1931).
65. *Cruzan v. Director, Missouri Department of Health*, 497 U.S. 261, 111 L.Ed.2d 224, 242 (1990).
66. Schmerber, *supra* note 29, at 770.

MARK I. EVANS, MARK P. JOHNSON, NELSON B. ISADA
AND WOLFGANG HOLZGREVE

Coercion for Fetal Therapy?

The "fetus as a patient" has over the past two decades become an accepted concept in obstetrics.[1] A specific field of fetal medicine has developed as a recognized subspecialty.[2] There are, however, complex interactions that emerge from the alteration of roles and responsibilities that have evolved over the past decade. Maternal-fetal conflicts for standard and experimental indications are likely to abound in the coming decade.[3]

Pediatricians have long understood that their primary obligation is to the child, and in fact they have a moral as well as legal obligation to protect the child from the parents if need be.[3] Most American states have laws regarding the reporting of child abuse which require physicians to notify local authorities upon suspicion. The laws protect physicians from legal repercussions if they do so.

The obstetrician, however, has a much more delicate job, i.e., balancing the needs of two patients. Sometimes those needs will *not* be in concert. When a conflict arises, tradition has supported the mother against the fetus – presumably because until recently the fetus was not a visualized entity.[4] Since fetuses were "amorphous," there was no specific person to represent. Some may argue that American tradition supported the fetus, on the basis of traditional antiabortion laws in most states that lasted until the early 1970s.[7,8] However, despite political grafitti to the contrary, the basis for most of these laws was directed to maternal safety, not fetal rights.

With the development of fetal imaging techniques, however, in the minds of many the moral status of the fetus has risen to some degree.[9] Work in the early 1980s documented the parental bonding that is considerably accelerated by the first visualization of fetal form on ultrasound.[10] At that time ultrasound was just becoming a routine procedure, and many couples were amazed at the concept of seeing the fetus. Some studies have shown increased maternal compliance with medical treatment as a result of viewing the fetus.[11] We worried then that ultrasound could be misused as a tool in the abortion debate.[10] Not surprisingly, to some the rights of the fetus – at least politically – are equal to those of the child and greater than those of the mother.

F.K. Beller and R.F. Weir (eds.), The Beginning of Human Life, 319–324.

However, in practice even some obstetricians have been advocates in court on the fetal behalf.[5,6]

The 1980s saw several instances of obstetricians in the United States seeking judicial sanction to force women to undergo cesarean sections against their will for the supposed benefit of the viable fetus.[5] Unfortunately, analysis reveals that in many cases patients subjected to court orders either did not speak English well or were of minority groups and/or lower socioeconomic status.

The first known court-ordered cesarean section occurred in 1980 in Colorado.[12] An obese female with a fetus in distress refused cesarean section, citing fear of surgery in part because of her size. After several hours of unsuccessful attempts to convince the patient, a court order was readily obtained. The baby did well, but the mother had a wound infection which required several weeks to heal.

In 1981, a Georgia woman refused on religious grounds to have a cesarean section performed because of a placenta previa diagnosed on ultrasound.[13] Physicians told the court of a 100 percent fetal mortality risk and an 80 percent maternal mortality risk. A judge ordered the cesarean section and gave temporary custody of the fetus to the Family and Children's Services Bureau. While the order was being appealed to the Georgia Supreme Court, the woman delivered safely and vaginally; the diagnosis had been wrong.

Perhaps the most dramatic confrontation concerned a Washington, D.C., woman imminently dying of metastatic cancer. She was at approximately 26 weeks' gestation. She was told that cesarean section would likely reduce what little time she had left. She and her husband decided against cesarean section. However, her physicians were afraid of being abandoned by their hospital's legal protection in light of a concurrent, but unrelated instance. In the other instance, George Washington University had, to the perceptions of the physicians, abandoned the legal defense of one of its faculty. Thus, the physicians sought the approval of university counsel before agreeing not to intervene and, if necessary, allow the fetus to die with the mother. University counsel panicked and called a judge who hastily heard the case and called for the cesarean section to be done over everyone's objections.[14] Both mother and baby died.

A new element of conflict has also come to national attention over the past few years. Some zealous district attorneys have attempted to seek judicial intervention to coerce substance-abusing mothers to refrain from their abuses by incarcerating them. The mechanism for such incarceration has been to bring criminal charges of child abuse against pregnant women for exposing their fetuses to hazardous and illegal agents. It is likely, because of the tremendous potential for publicity, that legislators will introduce specific prenatal child abuse bills, and district attorneys will seek to prosecute women under the guise of trying to help prevent child abuse.

In 1986, a California woman was charged with causing her son's death (at 27 weeks of age) by failing to get proper medical care during her pregnancy.[15] Specifically, the prosecutor alleged that she had waited several hours after the onset of contractions and vaginal bleeding before seeking care, had intercourse with her husband during that time, and used amphetamines and marijuana. If convicted, a $2,000 fine and a one-year jail term were possible under the California child support statute under which charges were brought. That law, originally mandated in 1872, made "willful omission" without lawful exercise of proper child support a crime. Until 1986, it had been used only to argue financial issues. Before the charges were ultimately dismissed, the woman spent several days in jail and had the details of her sexual life published in the local newspapers.

At first glance, sanctions against women taking illegal substances such as cocaine may have considerable appeal. However, alcohol consumption, although potentially very damaging to the fetus, is nevertheless legal and within the guidelines of autonomous behavior for an adult. The "slippery slope" principle describes the phenomenon where by once one has jumped onto the "slope," the more that one struggles, the faster one slides "downhill." In discussing legal manipulation of personal autonomy, a slippery slope is created. The precedent is set for moving to impose sanctions not only upon egregiously unacceptable behaviors but, as momentum builds, more moderate ones. Finally, one can obstruct behaviors that are culturally or religiously appropriate under certain circumstances yet violate the mainstream of public opinion. The end result could be a state of extensive infringement upon individual autonomy. We prefer to trust in counseling and educating women so that they can make their own informed decisions regarding personal issues such as pregnancy.

Tremendous technologic advances in the late 1980s and early 1990s have perfected the prenatal diagnosis of numerous congenital anomalies.[16,17] In most cases, such diagnoses are performed early enough in pregnancy to allow couples the legal option of terminating the pregnancy. Many couples elect to do so when faced with major fetal anomalies or genetic disease.[18] In general, the likelihood of choosing abortion is related to the severity of the defect and the subsequent burden which would be placed on the parents. Now a new option has emerged: in utero treatment and correction of certain birth defects.[19] Publicized attempts have included (1) open fetal surgery, (2) the percutaneous placement of shunts to relieve obstructive uropathies and hydrocephalus, and (3) pharmacologic interventions to alter cardiac arrhythmias and hypothyroidism, and to prevent external genital masculinization in the adrenogenital syndrome. All of these procedures remain at least innovative if not experimental. The original fetal surgery, i.e., transfusion for hemolytic anemias,[20] has been practiced for over twenty years and is no longer considered experimental.

It is ordinarily a well-established ethical principle that no physician needs to offer, nor any patient accept, an experimental procedure.[21] However, as identification of fetuses with anomalies as well as the interpretation of the fetus as a separate entity have developed, mostly through ultrasonographic visualization, a separate identity of the *fetus as a patient* has emerged. Ultrasonographic visualization of the fetus has greatly accentuated the bonding process.[10] Since the early 1980s, it has become common for parents – both mother and father – to see the fetal image before its movements are first felt. The resultant identification with the fetus is often remarkable, especially for first-time parents or those who have previously had a poor pregnancy outcome. Some data have shown that maternal compliance with medical direction is increased following the positive encouragement of seeing the fetal image. This compliance is, we feel, very different from that secured under the threat of prosecution. Many ethical analyses have concluded that attempted coercion and prosecution of pregnant women are ultimately bound to fail.[5] These analyses are unlikely, however, to sway aggressive district attorneys from prosecution of such cases.

Parental decisions to withhold proven treatment modalities from their children have been overridden by the courts. Thus, it is not unrealistic, given the body of experience with cesarean section and "child abuse," to expect similar attempts to be made on behalf of a fetus for whom a proven or experimental therapy might be of benefit. It has been our collective experience that, when confronted with a treatable fetal defect, some parents elect to terminate the pregnancy and therefore the "problem." Many others, however, opt to attempt novel fetal therapeutic interventions, if available. We have been impressed by the degree to which women are generally willing to subject themselves to discomfort and sometimes risk for invasive procedures, even if the chances of success may be minimal. Given such general parental enthusiasm, we have occasionally been surprised and frustrated by the refusal of a few very well educated and sophisticated patients to attempt even innocuous therapies. As physicians in centers heavily involved in developing novel interventive fetal therapeutic modalities, we might easily become victims of our own zeal and consequently be tempted to impose our will on such patients. We have recognized this danger and have attempted to maintain our objectivity under these circumstances. Such frustrating circumstances have certainly tested our own ethical principles. We are further concerned that some party not directly related to a theoretical situation of parental refusal of experimental therapy might seek judicial relief on behalf of the fetus – over the objections of both parents and physicians. Such a situation has occurred in abortion circumstances (e.g., the Klein case in New York).[22] Third-party intrusions, while likely to be eventually denied on the basis of lack of standing,[22] could cause serious damage to the doctor-patient relationship and to women's rights in general.[23]

Recently we have worried that as the political football of the abortion rights debate continues to be kicked about, some extremists may see treatment of the correctable fetal defect in a viable or even a previable fetus as the next venue for establishing the "rights" of the fetus over the interests of the mother.[19] The argument goes that the failure to correct a correctable fetal defect could be considered prenatal child abuse. Yet what if the bodily integrity of the mother is violated? We must heighten our awareness to guard against the temptation of scientific advances when they conflict with the fundamental principle of maternal autonomy.

Autonomy must remain a key factor in any arguments about intervention on behalf of the fetus. The "slippery slope" only gets further greased, and issues become progressively more complicated, when one focuses exclusively on the potential benefits to a fetus. Without regard for the basic rights of the mother in making decisions about invasive interventions, impassioned physicians who focus unilaterally on the fetus as the individual, solitary patient could unintentionally do great harm to the hard-won gains of women in the last two decades. Recognizing that difficult situations exist when fetal interventions are proposed which potentially place the pregnancy at risk, we support the establishment of internal review forums where such issues can be discussed. Our institution has established a Fetal Therapy Board comprised of multidisciplinary specialists and ethicists who discuss each case and its unique set of surrounding issues. Although the physicians on the board can enthusiastically support possible interventive procedures, we are committed to the principle that the mother should retain the right of refusal for any potential procedure or in any conflict of interest between mother and fetus. There is no other circumstance, in medicine or elsewhere, in which one person has been forced to be violated for the benefit of another. No father has ever been forced to donate an organ – no even blood – for a child, even his own. No soldier has ever been told to give a kidney to a general. While parents can authorize the donation of material from one child to another, no court has ever forced a parent to do so. In fact, parents have deliberately conceived children in the hope of their becoming organ donors to save existing children. No court has ever told a women to have sex to become pregnant.

Why is it wrong to cut open a woman against her will? The classic slippery slope is in operation. Start from the potentially most acceptable extreme – the cesarean section for the normal, full-term baby. Next comes the premature baby (who dies anyway), next comes the drug user – to be followed by the woman who had sex with her husband before delivery. Fetal therapy is next – no matter how desperate or how little the chances of its success.

Unlike pediatricians, who can clearly distinguish who their patient is, obstetricians both by tradition and anatomy cannot. They must consider two competing forces, the rights of the mother and the rights of the fetus. While respect for both is important, there is a serious flaw in the logic of the pro-lifers who argue that all life is equal. Given the need to violate the body of the mother to gain access to the fetus, the rights of the mother and the fetus cannot be considered equally. One must eventually prove greater than the other. Consistent with the guidelines for the professional conduct of obstetricians, the rights of the mother must predominate.

NOTES

1. Kuriak A, ed. The fetus as patient. Excerpta Medica, Amsterdam, 1985.
2. Creasy R, Resnik R. Maternal-Fetal Medicine. 2d ed. WB Saunders, Philadelphia, 1990.
3. Robertson J. Legal issues in fetal therapy. In: Evans MI, Fletcher JC, Dixler AO, Schulman, eds. Fetal Diagnosis and Therapy: Science, Ethics and the Law. Philadelphia; JB Lippincott, 1989: 431.
4. Fletcher JC. Ethics of fetal therapy. In: Evans, Fletcher, et al, p 443.
5. Kolder VEB, Gallagher J, Parsons MT. Court-ordered obstetrical interventions. N Engl J Med 1987; 316: 1192–1197.
6. Engelhardt HT. Current controversies in obstetrics: wrongful life and forced fetal surgical procedures. Am J Obstet Gynecol 1985; 151: 313–318.
7. Fleming L. The moral status of the fetus: a reappraisal. Bioethics 1987; 1: 15–34.
8. Fletcher JC. The fetus as patient: Ethical issues. JAMA 1981; 246: 772–773.
9. Callahan D. How technology is reframing the abortion debate. Hastings Cent Rep 1986; 16: 33–42.
10. Fletcher JC, Evans MI. Maternal bonding in early fetal ultrasound examinations. N Engl J Med 1983; 308: 392–393.
11. Reading AE, Cox DN. The effects of ultrasound examination on maternal anxiety levels. J Behav Med 1982; 12: 237–247.
12. Levin T. When courts take charge of the unborn. New York Times 1981 Jan 19; Sect A: 14.
13. *Raleigh-Fitkin-Paul Morgan Memorial Hospital v Anderson*, 42 N.J. 421, 201 A. 2d 537 (1964).
14. *In re* A.C., 533 A2d611 (DC1987).
15. *People v Pamela Roe Stewart*, M508197 (San Diego Municipal Court, 1987).
16. Evans, Fletcher, et al.
17. Romero R, Pilu G, Jeanty P, Ghidini A, Hobbins JC, eds. Prenatal Diagnosis of Congenital Anomalies. Norwalk, CT: Appleton and Lange, 1988.
18. Drugan A, Koppitch FC, Williams JC, Johnson MP, Moghissi KS, Evans MI. Prenatal diagnosis following recurrent early pregnancy loss. Obstet Gynecol 1990; 75: 381–384.
19. Evans MI, Drugan A, Manning FA, Harrison MR. Fetal surgery in the 1990's. Am J Dis Child 1989; 143(12): 1431–1436.
20. Liley AW. Intrauterine transfusion of foetus in haemolytic disease. Br Med J 1963; 2: 1107–1109.
21. Fletcher JC. Ethical Issues. In: Evans, Fletcher, et al, p 4.
22. *Klein v NY.*
23. Hanft RS, Evans WJ. Government involvement in the doctor-patient relationship. In: Evans, Fletcher, et al, pp 509–519.

PART SIX

Rights and Obligations Related to the Beginning of Individual Human Lives

NEIL CAMPBELL

When Care Cannot Cure: Medical Problems in Seriously Ill Babies

Thankfully, most babies are born intact and healthy after a normal pregnancy, and thereafter they thrive. But a few, around 4–6%, are born seriously ill or become ill after birth.[1]

Illnesses in babies have two important characteristics: they are often life-threatening, and they can cause serious handicaps or chronic ill health (morbidity) in babies who survive. Advances in knowledge, organization of newborn health services, and technology are achieving cures or amelioration of many illnesses that in the past resulted in death or permanent severe handicap. With mechanical ventilators and other complex life-supporting treatment most extremely premature babies now survive. In the past most died. Complex surgery can now ensure survival of most babies with severe malformations, even those considered "monstrous."

We can take over the function of most organs, for days or weeks, when they temporarily fail. Mechanical ventilators and extra-corporeal membrane oxygenators can assume the functions of failing hearts and lungs. Hemofiltration and dialysis can take over the functions of failing livers and kidneys, and transfusions of red blood cells, white blood cells, and blood platelets, the functions of failing bone marrow. Intravenous nutrition can take over the functions of the diseased bowel. The only major organs we cannot yet transplant are brain and bowel, given donors.

However there are still many babies for whom modern techniques are less than successful. In some, new treatments achieve little more than delaying death. In others death is averted but survival results in permanent severe handicaps or lifelong ill health. When treatment falls far short of complete success, ethical questions arise. Are such treatments in babies' and families' best interests? How can costs be justified?

This paper describes a number of newborn illnesses to show how they create ethical problems. First, however, two caveats: It is conventional to describe newborn intensive care activities in medical-technical language, implying scientific objectivity, but this language does not accurately reflect reality. Many things we do in newborn intensive care involve value judgments and some of these have ethical content. Second, medical-technical language speaks of

F.K. Beller and R.F. Weir (eds.), The Beginning of Human Life, 327–344.

pathology and physiology, mechanical ventilators and blood gases, drug doses and brain functions. Such language can obscure the deeper context – that of hopes and fears, joys and grief, pleasures and pains, and life and death. Scientific objectivity has its place in newborn intensive care, but much is lost if it overshadows the human values and goals it is meant to serve.

Illnesses in newborn babies can be classified into three main diagnostic groups: extreme prematurity (babies born 8–17 weeks early); birth defects, including malformations, chromosomal disorders, intrauterine infections, and inborn errors of metabolism; and acquired diseases (babies normal at the end of pregnancy, but becoming ill during or after delivery. The most important acquired diseases are birth asphyxia and bacterial infections).

This paper concentrates on aspects of extreme prematurity and representative birth defects. These illustrate well the ways in which newborn illnesses create ethical problems. There are many areas of ethical concern in newborn care – informed consent, "standard" versus "experimental" treatments, pain, withdrawal of treatment, costs and resource allocation, and duties to impaired survivors. This paper confines itself to placing in context the ethical questions of withdrawal of treatment and resource allocation.

Extreme Prematurity

Normal babies are born after 38 to 42 weeks of pregnancy (gestation) and average around 3400 grams in birthweight. A few babies (about 1.2%) are born far too early, and have a characteristic set of problems resulting from immaturity of organ and tissue functions. Very low birthweight (VLBW) babies are those of birthweight less than 1500g, (usually less than 32 weeks' gestation). Within this group are the tiniest babies, the extremely low birthweight (ELBW) group, less than 1000g and usually less than 28 weeks' gestation. Live-born ELBW babies represent 0.3–0.4% of all live births. There are 11,000–14,000 in the U.S. each year.[2]

ELBW babies are usually critically ill in the hours and days after birth. Although they have a strange beauty to those experienced in their care, their skin is thin and leaks body fluids; the flesh is jellyish and bruises easily. Liver, kidneys, heart, and glands perform poorly: the babies have great difficulty even maintaining normal body warmth. They experience a variety of complex problems in the early weeks of life. Three will be described: respiratory distress syndrome (RDS), intracerebral hemorrhage, and necrotizing enterocolitis (NEC).

Respiratory Distress Syndrome (RDS)

Most ELBW babies develop lung disease, respiratory distress syndrome (RDS), within minutes, and their lungs are simply too immature and delicate to function normally. The baby's breathing in distressed and labored. Most affected babies must be placed on mechanical ventilators, and given extra oxygen and other life-sustaining treatments. The disease usually gets progressively worse in the first three days. Many babies die during this time. Their lungs are so affected the ventilator cannot support them, and other complications pile up. In some babies it is obvious hours in advance that they will die. In such situations, how long should care continue? Until the baby is moribund? Until the heart stops? Continuing maximal, intrusive, expensive therapies in babies who are dying is, to some, obscene. And yet, how can caregivers be sure death will occur? How much certainty is required?

In surviving babies RDS starts improving on the fourth day, but the lungs will have been injured to some extent by the physical effect of the pressure produced by the ventilator (barotrauma) and the toxic chemical effect of oxygen (oxygen toxicity). These iatrogenic injuries to the lung are called bronchopulmonary dysplasia (BPD). BPD slows the rate of recovery from RDS. In a few babies BPD gets progressively worse over many days, and a vicious cycle is set up: the baby must remain on the ventilator and oxygen because of his/her damaged lungs, but the ventilator and oxygen, while keeping the baby alive, exacerbate the lung damage.

BPD keeps some babies on the ventilator for weeks or months. Occasional babies become respiratory cripples: they never get off the ventilator.

When it becomes clear – at a month, or six months, or a year of age – that a baby will never get off the ventilator, parents and caregivers are faced with caring for a baby with poor quality of life and a dismal long-term outlook. A point may be reached where maximal therapy cannot keep the baby comfortable. Should therapy be withdrawn? If months of ventilator dependency have gone by, should caregivers withdraw *before* the point of failing maximal therapy has been reached? Does the presence of other complications which further reduce quality of life – for example, moderate brain damage – have relevance?

Ethical problems arising from the use of mechanical ventilators are well illustrated by the example of RDS in the ELBW baby, but similar problems arise in many other serious diseases of newborn babies. A mechanical ventilator is used to assist a baby's breathing when it is inadequate. Breathing may be inadequate because the lungs are severely diseased, or because the brain is diseased or injured in such a way that it no longer drives the lungs to breathe.

The ventilator pumps oxygen into the lungs many times per minute, hour after hour, day after day. It can keep a baby alive for weeks or months, even if most of the brain is dead or the lungs hopelessly damaged and incapable of healing. Ventilators achieve excellent results in babies with diseases which *temporarily* prevent their breathing adequately: the ventilator maintains life until treatment and nature allow the baby to cope alone. Dilemmas arise if babies are kept alive by ventilators when they have no hope of eventually recovering sufficiently to cope alone. Being on a ventilator involves many painful or frightening experiences throughout each day, only partially ameliorated by sedation or analgesia. Babies on ventilators are socially and emotionally isolated: it is difficult to pick them up for feeds and cuddles, and the necessary sedation depresses their awareness.

Intracerebral Hemorrhage

During the first week of life 40–50% of ELBW babies suffer bleeding of varying severity into the brain (intraventricular hemorrhage, IVH). Blood flow to the brain fluctuates widely during the unstable states ELBW babies experience in the first days after birth. During unstable episodes brain blood flow may temporarily cease, injuring areas of the brain (cerebral ischemia). Injured areas may die. When brain blood flow improves again, bleeding may occur into injured or dead areas of brain.

Small hemorrhages (small areas of ischemia) have little immediate or long-term effect on the baby. Large hemorrhages can cause sudden deterioration and, occasionally, death. When babies survive large hemorrhages, permanent serious intellectual and physical handicaps are common. Between 75% and 100% of babies with extensive intracerebral hemorrhages or ischemia have severe permanent handicaps.

The presence of areas of ischemia or hemorrhage in the brain can be seen by ultrasound or CAT scanners: ultrasound scans are usually performed daily or more often in sick ELBW babies. However, extensive ischemic areas may not be obvious to scanners in the first few days of life. Their effects may be detected only several weeks later, as the injured areas of brain dissolve or shrivel away. This process is called periventricular leukomalacia (PVL). Thus ischemic brain injuries occurring in the first few days, which will result in severe handicaps, may only be detected at several weeks of age.

Sometimes clotted blood from hemorrhagic areas of brain block the circulation of the brain's cerebrospinal fluid. The blocked fluid builds up within the spaces in the brain called the ventricles, producing hydrocephalus. The ventricles distend, further injuring the surrounding brain. Some ELBW babies with hydrocephalus need a surgical operation to insert a plastic tube into the distended ventricles, to drain the fluid blockage (ventriculo-peritoneal shunt; V-P shunt).

When an ELBW baby suddenly deteriorates in the first few days with a massive intracerebral hemorrhage, should life-supporting measures be discontinued? If so, what degree of risk of severe handicap should suffice for decision making? Only certainty? Fifty percent? When, at several weeks of age, a baby thought to have had only moderate cerebral ischemia in the first week is found to be developing extensive periventricular leukomalacia, with large areas of brain dissolving away, should life-sustaining treatment continue? At this stage the baby may be off the ventilator and other intensive life-supporting treatment. The only life-sustaining treatment the baby may be getting is scheduled feeding via a stomach tube, as he or she cannot suck or swallow. Should this scheduled feeding continue? Is it not life-supporting in the same way as is a mechanical ventilator?

The term "scheduled feeding," introduced above, requires explanation. Healthy normal babies are "demand" fed – that is, fed from breast or bottle whenever they show signs of hunger or thirst, rather than to a formal timetable or schedule. Ill babies may have no sense of hunger, nor be able to suck and swallow. For example, ELBW babies cannot suck or swallow effectively, as the brain mechanisms controlling these functions are immature and uncoordinated. Babies unconscious from brain diseases or medications do not demand feed. Also, major brain abnormalities often disturb the swallowing and sucking mechanisms. Babies with malformations of the mouth or throat also may not be able to suck and swallow. Babies with very distressed breathing from lung diseases or heart failure may be too short of breath to demand feed, or to swallow feed safely without breathing it into their lungs (aspiration).

To ensure effective nutrition in such babies, carefully planned feeding schedules, delivered by artificial means such as stomach tubes, must be prescribed. Waking and demanding, thirst and appetite, and sucking and swallowing, are replaced by scheduled feeding. For ill babies, such regimes are lifesaving. They ensure survival until the baby's recovery allows normal demand feeding. If it is acceptable to withdraw life-sustaining treatments such as mechanical ventilation from babies in whom hope for survival or meaningful life is gone, is it not also acceptable to withdraw scheduled feeding?

Necrotizing Enterocolitis (NEC)

After the first week of life 2–5% of ELBW babies develop a severe inflammation of the bowel, necrotizing enterocolitis (NEC). The inflammation may be so severe that it destroys varying lengths of the bowel – from a few centimetres to the entire bowel. Some babies are overwhelmed by the inflammation and quickly die. In survivors, when parts of the bowel have been destroyed, surgical operations are required to remove them. Loss of short lengths of bowel at operation have little practical consequence, but if greater lengths of bowel are lost, the baby may be left with insufficient bowel for normal digestion.

In mild cases of NEC the inflamed bowel is rested for 2–3 weeks by stopping milk feeds. The babies' nutritional requirements are provided with intravenous nutrition. When milk feeds are recommenced, they usually succeed. In worse cases, when substantial bowel has been lost, reintroduction of feeds results in diarrhea. It may take weeks or months for the shortened bowel to recover sufficiently for normal milk feeding to succeed. During the recovery period the baby's health and growth rely on intravenous nutrition.

Occasionally babies lose so much bowel at operation that they can never recover sufficient bowel function to see them through life. Such babies will always be dependent on intravenous nutrition. In some it is obvious at the surgical operation that there is insufficient bowel for life. In others it becomes apparent only after months of intravenous nutrition and repeated failures of milk feeding.

When it is found at surgery that too much bowel has died, what should caregivers do? The baby can survive only if she is given lifelong intravenous nutrition. She will never be able to be fed normally. She is usually critically ill, on a mechanical ventilator and other life-sustaining treatments. Should they be discontinued? When it becomes apparent only after months of intravenous nutrition that the bowel will never work successfully, what should caregivers do? Once again, the baby is faced with a life of total intravenous nutrition. By this time the baby is off the ventilator, but will have developed complications of intravenous nutrition.

Intravenous nutrition is a complex, expensive procedure in which all nutrition is administered through a catheter in a vein. IV Nutrition can keep a baby healthy and growing for weeks, months, or years without oral feeds, yet life-threatening infections of the intravenous catheter are common. IV nutrition also causes liver damage, worst in the most immature babies, which can cause progressive failure of the liver over several months. Thus a baby being kept alive by intravenous nutrition because his bowel does not work can die of liver failure at 6–12 months of age, a complication of the intravenous nutrition. Liver failure is a distressing condition: the baby swells up all over (edema), the abdomen becomes tense with fluid (ascites), the blood fails to clot, and frequent, distressing hemorrhages result.

When a baby develops liver failure after months of intravenous nutrition, what should caregives do? There is little hope of recovery of either the liver or the bowel. Life with progressive liver failure is very unpleasant. Should intravenous nutrition be withdrawn? IV nutrition achieves wonderful results when babies have bowel diseases which prevent normal milk feeding for weeks or months, but which eventually get better. It creates dilemmas when it keeps babies alive with bowel diseases which will never ameliorate sufficiently for the baby to feed naturally.

Given these complex problems, what is the overall outcome for VLBW and ELBW babies? Tables 1 and 2 show typical outcome figures for all babies from a single region (Victoria, Australia). Similar figures are reported from regions in North America and Europe.

Live-born ELBW babies constitute only 0.3% of all births, but 34% of all baby deaths. Care is nowadays offered at 23 weeks' gestation (around 600 g, 17 weeks early). Few survive. By 24–25 weeks' gestation (700–799 g) around 30% survive: around 25% of survivors have severe handicaps; the chances of surviving without handicap are about 10%. By 26–27 weeks' gestation (900–999 g) 75% survive: around 10% have severe handicaps; the chances of surviving without handicap are around 40%. As organization of care and methods of treatment improve, outcomes improve. Current extremely premature babies are likely to do better than babies born five or ten years ago.

Table I
VLBW and ELBW Outcomes

Birth weight, grams	Gestational age, weeks	Survival rate	Severe handicap	Normal survivor
1250–1500	29–31	> 95%	< 10%	60%
1000–1250	27–29	85%		
900–999	26–27	75%	10–15%	35–40%
800–899	25–26	45%		
700–799	24–25	30%	15–25%	5–15%
600–699	23–24	< 10%		

Table II
VLBW and ELBW Babies

Victoria 1987	61,000	live births
	292	neonatal deaths

Birth weight	Total births	Live births		Percentage of all births	Neonatal death		Percentage of all deaths
< 1500G (VLBW)	627	467	=	0.76%	139	=	47%
< 1000G (ELBW)	294	177	=	0.3%	100	=	34%

What of costs and resources? In our state (Victoria, Australia) VLBW babies constitute 0.6% of all live-born babies, and yet they make up 53% of all admissions to neonatal intensive care units, and 83% of patient ventilator days. Thus a tiny population is responsible for a substantial workload. Estimates of costs vary from country to country and with the methods of costing used. Typical costs for ELBW babies in intensive care units are around $A1,000 per day, and average hospitalization costs around $A50,000–$A80,000 per baby. The earlier the gestation, the higher the cost. To achieve a survivor at 24 weeks in our region costs around $A300,000.

Such cost estimates include only initial hospitalization after birth. They do not include costs for subsequent hospitalization, nor lifetime costs of care for handicaps. ELBW costs compare badly with costs of other patient populations. They are more expensive than VLBW babies and mature babies needing treatment for malformations: they are far more expensive than children needing intensive care for life-threatening conditions beyond the first year of life. The care of ELBW babies diverts scarce resources from other babies, children, and adults with better potential outcomes. Should costs be taken into account in treatment decisions?

Care is nowadays often offered at 23 weeks' gestation, when the chances of survival are less than 10%, the chances of serious handicap in survivors around 30%, and the cost for each survivor between $300,000 and $400,000. Caregivers know that termination of pregnancy for serious fetal defects is performed as late as 28 weeks' gestation, legal or not. Given all these considerations, many people ask whether there is a gestation and birth size below which care should not be offered. Do caregivers really have a mandate from their society to use such large resources when returns are so poor?

Severe Handicaps

In this discussion of VLBW and ELBW babies frequent reference has been made to severe handicaps (and there are many other serious illnesses in babies which also result in handicaps). Severe handicaps involve various combinations of mental deficiency, body paralysis, blindness, and deafness. Mental deficiency means varying degrees of reduced intelligence; lack of awareness of self, others, and "the meaning of life"; and lack of ability to interact socially and emotionally. Body paralysis means varying degrees of lack of control of muscles, body, and limbs, with resulting immobility and dependence on others for feeding, toileting, and other aspects of life's basics.

Survival of a baby with severe handicaps has a serious effect on his or her family. Marital breakdown is frequent, and when it occurs the mother is often left to cope as a single parent. There is a high incidence of psychiatric disturbances in affected families. Other children in the family can suffer emotional hardship and deprivation as a result. For some families, though, the care of a severely handicapped child can be an experience of moral growth and enrichment. Many parents, especially mothers, develop an extraordinary bond of love for a handicapped child, even when the child's existence leads to so much hardship. Indeed, to the outsider, the loving sacrifice by parents of self and family interests to the handicapped child is a central part of the tragedy.

It is widely held that when withdrawal of treatment is being considered, the best interests of the baby should prevail. Does a baby have interests which can be viewed in isolation, as separate from those of the family?

Birth Defects: Conditions That can be Fixed

The list of birth defects is very long.[3] Major categories include malformations of one or more major organs or body structures, the rest of the baby being normal; chromosome abnormalities, in which every tissue of the baby is abnormal; inborn errors of metabolism, in which there are malfunctions in one or more of the body's chemical processes; and intrauterine infections, which usually affect most of the fetus's developing tissues, causing abnormal tissue function and in some cases malformations.

To illustrate ethical dilemmas, birth defects are best classified according to prognosis – what effects they have on survival and function – rather than diagnosis.

Prognostically, birth defects can be divided into those conditions which can be fixed, and those which cannot. In the former conditions, there is a very high chance of survival if all available treatment is offered. With survival there is a normal or "acceptable" life span, with no handicaps, or an "acceptable" level of handicap and no chronic ill health, or an "acceptable" level of chronicity. Obviously, much hinges on the definition of "acceptable."

More, and more serious, newborn illnesses are moving into this category. Although outcomes in this group are good, treatment is often long and arduous for the baby. Intrusive, distressing treatments are often needed, and hospitalization may continue for months. Costs can be very high, especially in babies needing prolonged mechanical ventilation, surgical operations, or intravenous nutrition. On the other hand, the average stay in hospital for mature babies with esophageal atresia (failure of the gullet to form normally), who require major chest surgery on the first day of life, is nine days. Most babies requiring bypass cardiac surgery are home within three weeks.

Birth Defects: Conditions That Cannot be Fixed

Those conditions which cannot be fixed can be categorized as follows: (1) conditions in which death is inevitable, despite all available care. Active treatment only lengthens the period before death occurs; (2) conditions in which active treatment will ensure survival, but with severe handicaps, chronic ill health, or shortened life span; and (3) conditions in which survival *might* be achieved with prolonged, intrusive, distressing treatments, but with serious handicaps, chronic ill health or shortened life span. (Classification according to prognosis is helpful in ethical discussions about *all* baby illnesses – the ELBW baby, babies with birth asphyxia or infections – not just birth defects.)

Conditions in Which Death Is Inevitable

This group includes such conditions as Potter's syndrome and its variants (renal agenesis or dysplasia with pulmonary hypoplasia), anencephaly, chromosomal abnormalities such as trisomy 18, and some complex heart malformations.

Potter's syndrome and Its Variants

In this condition, for unknown reasons, the fetus's kidneys fail to form (renal agenesis). Fetal lung growth depends on the development of normal fetal kidneys. When the fetal kidneys fail to form, the fetal lungs fail to grow adequately. At birth Potter's syndrome babies look abnormal. They have very distressed breathing and cannot cope unless given oxygen and placed on a ventilator. These treatments are often started if the baby's condition is not recognized. Some die quickly despite ventilation and oxygen; in others survival is prolonged, but never beyond a day or so.

It is generally assumed that the lungs will never work satisfactorily, so that temporarily taking over their function with ventilators, oxygen, or extra-corporeal membrane oxygenation (ECMO) is inappropriate. Babies cannot survive long-term without kidneys. It is generally assumed that it is inappropriate to temporarily take over kidney functions with renal dialysis or hemofiltration, although renal transplantation might be technically possible if donors are available. Given all of these assumptions, death is inevitable.

Are these assumptions morally sound? If a Potter's syndrome baby is placed on a ventilator before the condition is recognized, is there an ethical problem in stopping? What should be done with the baby if ventilation is withdrawn? Such babies may be conscious and aware, and death from hypoxia is frightening until unconsciousness is reached.

Potter's syndrome occurs in about 1 in 10,000 births. There are therefore approximately 370 Potter's syndrome babies born in the U.S. each year.

Anencephaly

In anencephaly there is failure of development of most of the brain (the cerebral hemispheres and much of the midbrain) together with the covering skull and scalp. Two-thirds are born dead. Most born alive die within minutes or hours; a few live for days or months. It is generally assumed that the babies have no conscious awareness and that death is inevitable. They may, however, suck, cry, grimace, and even smile.

Because death is assumed to be inevitable, most caregivers withhold treatment likely to prolong life. However, recently anencephalic infants have been placed on mechanical ventilation and other life-supporting treatments, with a view to using them as sources of organs for transplantation. These babies have done better than expected. So, are assumptions about the inevitability of death soundly based? No one can say with certainty, since in the past no one has really tried to achieve survival.

Anencephaly occurs in about 3 in 10,000 births: there are about 1,100 born each year in the U.S., 350 of these alive at birth.

Trisomy 18

There are several chromosomal disorders, including trisomy 18, which result in profound mental insufficiency and a shortened life span. In trisomy 18 every cell in the developing fetus, from conception, has additional genetic material (an extra chromosome). This results in abnormality of all the developing tissues. The babies have an abnormal appearance. Their consciousness is depressed and it is assumed they are never aware of themselves, others, or their environment. Some have life-threatening malformations, especially of the heart or esophagus (esophageal atresia). The brain is so abnormal that its reflex nerve mechanisms controlling sucking, swallowing, and coughing do not function adequately. In some babies this results in frequent choking episodes, or blockages of the breathing passages with saliva or other secretions. Attempts at feeding often result in choking. Feeds may be breathed into the lungs (aspiration), causing pneumonia.

Half die in the first month; fewer than 10% survive the first year. It is assumed that death is inevitable from choking episodes, feeding difficulties, or pneumonia. Treatment for life-threatening malformations is therefore usually withheld. No one really knows how long life might continue if all available treatment were offered – ventilator support for poor breathing or pneumonia; surgery for life-threatening malformations, antibiotics for infections; and careful attention to nutrition. The view that death is inevitable may thus be a self-fulfilling prophesy.

What treatment should be offered to babies with trisomy 18 or other similar chromosomal abnormalities? Scheduled feeds by stomach tube, or intravenous fluids, will prolong life in some of them. In others, with choking episodes or a malformed heart, feeds and fluids may hasten death. Should caregivers clear out the throat with suction catheters when choking episodes occur? These episodes are distressing to watch, but it is assumed the baby is unaware and does not suffer. Regular sucking out of the airways can be lifesaving, but is this beneficial to the baby? Trisomy 18 occurs in about 3 in 10,000 births. There are about 1000 per year in the U.S.

When Death Is "Inevitable"

It will be seen from these descriptions of conditions in which death is considered inevitable that "inevitable" is a relative term. It is not known how long such babies might live if all available treatment were given. Technically, the only major organs not currently transplantable are brain and bowel: if donors were available, and ECMO tried, an occasional Potter's syndrome baby might be salvageable. If mechanical ventilation and other active treatment were offered, anencephalics might live weeks or months. If surgery and other forms of active intervention were offered, babies with trisomy 18 might live for years. Even when active treatment is not offered, some babies with "inevitably" lethal conditions survive for weeks or months.

Nevertheless most caregivers believe that life-sustaining treatments should be withheld from these categories. Given that survival prospects are not accurately known, since no one really tries for survival, are decisions in these babies based on the "inevitability" of death, or are they rather based on "quality of life" judgments? Caregivers who view quality-of-life judgments as unacceptable criteria for deciding to withdraw treatment usually accept that life-sustaining treatments are not morally mandatory in babies for whom death is "inevitable." Perhaps these are quality of life judgments after all.

Survival with Severe Handicaps

This category includes conditions in which active treatment will ensure survival but with severe handicaps, shortened life-span, and chronic ill health.

Diagnoses included in this group are severe spina bifida and a range of chromosomal abnormalities less severe in their effects than trisomy 18.

Severe Spina Bifida

Spina bifida (high meningomyelocoele with congenital hydrocephalus) results from failure of the brain and spinal cord to develop normally in the fetus (neural tube defect). The spinal cord carries all the nerves from the brain to all the other body structures. It is contained within the spinal column. In spina bifida one section of the spinal cord, together with the surrounding spinal column, fails to form properly. The backbone lies open with the malformed spinal cord exposed. This lesion is called a meningomyelocoele. All functions below the level of the lesion are severely abnormal, since they are normally controlled by the spinal cord nerves. Below the lesion there is no sensation: the muscles are paralyzed; organs such as urinary bladder, genitals, and lower bowel function abnormally. If the lesion is low on the back, the handicaps which result are mild. High lesions, midway up the back, result in a child who will never walk, may not be able to sit upright normally; and will have no feeling below the waist, marked disturbances (incontinence) of urine and bowel functions, and abnormal sexual function.

Most babies with meningomyelocoele also have brain malformations, i.e., hydrocephalus. In mild cases (the majority) this may require surgical operations (ventriculo-peritoneal shunts), but has no serious effects on the baby's future. In severe cases hydrocephalus can result in significant mental deficiency not correctable by surgery.

The child with a high meningomyelocoele and severe hydrocephalus has a difficult life. Surgery on the back lesion, to prevent infection, and on the head to prevent worse mental deficiency, and scheduled feeding in the early weeks of life, will ensure survival. Without these most die after weeks or months, depending on how they are cared for. Survivors spend much of their childhood in the hospital with complications. They are confined to bed or wheelchair. Their lives may be shortened by such complications as infections in the hydrocephalus shunt or kidney failure from the urinary bladder dysfunction.

The incidence of spina bifida varies from place to place, between 1 in 1,000 and 5 in 1,000 births. About one-quarter have high back lesions and serious hydrocephalus. Given the potentially poor quality of life, many caregivers practice selective treatment, withholding surgery or other lifesaving procedures from severely affected babies. However, not all such babies die: occasional babies survive, with worse handicaps than if they had been offered surgery at the beginning.

Can withholding treatment that would ensure survival be justified on the grounds of poor future quality of life? If an occasional baby might survive despite surgery's being withheld, can scheduled feeding, antibiotics, and other forms of life-prolonging care be withheld?

More than 95% of spina bifida fetuses can be detected in the womb.

Termination of pregnancy can be performed if parents wish. Although this is seen by many as the answer to the ethical problems arising in babies with severe spina bifida, it is really only a shift in the ethical framework, from the ethics of withholding treatment from babies to the ethics of abortion.

Babies Whose Outcome Is Uncertain

These babies might survive after long, complex, intrusive treatment, but they might not. Survival may result in a lifetime of chronic ill health or severe handicaps. Diagnoses in this group include multiple malformation syndromes not due to chromosomal disorders, and hypoplastic left heart syndrome.

Multiple Malformation Syndromes

There are many conditions in which babies have several major malformations. Consider a baby who has esophageal atresia (failure of the gullet to form); a major heart malformation; major abnormalities of the kidneys; and major malformations of the spine, arms, hands, and legs (VATER syndrome).

The esophagus can usually be easily repaired, but there may be annoying complications throughout childhood. Most heart defects can now be cured or improved by surgery, although some need more than one operation. The kidney abnormalities may be correctable, but there may be a risk of progressive kidney failure in childhood, with poor health and eventual need for transplantation. The spinal deformity may be correctable, but may result in a permanent marked twisting of the back. The arm, hand, and leg deformities may be improved but not corrected: walking without aids such as calipers or crutches may be difficult or impossible; the arm and hand abnormalities may make this and other functions harder. Brain function and intelligence will be normal unless diseases of the brain such as meningitis are acquired during treatment of the other conditions.

At best, such a baby will need lengthy hospitalization, with a number of surgical operations and other arduous treatments. If everything goes well, only the back, arm, hand, and leg deformities will persist as lifetime problems. At worst, complications of treatment of any of the malformations could result in death; partial success in these treatments could result in chronic ill health: kidney failure could lead to the need for transplantation; and complications of treatment causing brain damage could cause mental deficiency. Given the certainty of physical handicaps from arms, hands, legs and back, the uncertainty of survival despite months of arduous treatment, and the possibility of progressive kidney failure, could a case be made not to embark on any lifesaving treatment at the outset?

If life-threatening complications develop after weeks or months of care, how far should arduous treatment such as mechanical ventilation and surgical operations be pushed? Is a point reached where it is appropriate to say, "Enough is enough"?

Hypoplastic Left Heart Syndrome (HLHS)

This is a relatively common malformation of the heart in which the left half of the heart, the parts responsible for pumping blood around the body, fail to form properly. Babies with HLHS are usually beautiful babies. In the past they all died, most in the first week of life. Now a number of centers around the world offer surgery. Instead of dying, babies are placed on mechanical ventilators, given other complex, arduous treatment, and then have surgery to make the heart sufficiently functional to sustain life for the first year or two. If this first stage is successful, a second operation must be performed to improve long-term survival. An alternative to this two-stage treatment, advocated by some, is cardiac transplantation soon after birth.

Death rates after the first operation in various centers around the world vary from 50% to 95%, babies die hours, weeks, or months after surgery. Not many babies live to the second operation. It is too early to know how many babies will live, or for how long, after the second operation. No one knows the long-term outcome of cardiac transplantation in the first year of life, and finding donors is difficult.[4]

Before surgery was offered for HLHS, death was inevitable, but happened quickly and peacefully. With surgery, most babies still die (perhaps all will die in childhood – who knows?), but after hours, weeks, or months of intrusive, arduous treatments. Should babies and families be offered such treatment in the (so far) small hope of eventual survival? Or should it be accepted that, in some conditions, it may be better not to try? HLHS babies consume huge resources in health care systems where resources are finite. Is it fair on all that resources are used in this way? And yet, if surgeons do not try, how will advances ever be made?

Withholding Treatment

So far this paper has described a number of serious newborn illnesses to illustrate how ethical dilemmas arise, especially in relation to decisions for or against lifesaving treatment.

What happens in practice? Ways in which these problems are resolved vary around the world. In 1973 neonatologists at the Yale–New Haven Hospital (U.S.) reported that 14% of deaths in babies followed withdrawal of treatment.[5] In 1986 Hammersmith (U.K.) reported a figure of 30%.[6] Our own practices are outlined below. Discussions with neonatologists in several countries lead us to believe our practices are not unusual.

We believe that withdrawal of treatment should be considered when there is little hope of survival despite all care, or when quality of life may be unacceptably poor. When such is the case, the doctor in charge must inform parents about all relevant aspects of diagnosis and prognosis and give a clear view of what he or she thinks is best.

In the context of near-certainty of death or very poor quality of life, after all necessary advice and guidance has been given, the decision whether to continue or to stop active treatment belongs to the parents. If parents decide that treatment should be continued, contrary to caregivers' views, all measures should be continued in good faith, but the doctor in charge should tactfully continue to advocate his/her views.

The baby's interests are of central importance, but we do not believe they should (or can) be separated from the interests of the family. It is appropriate for the parents and their advisers to take into account the effects of the baby's continuing defects on the rest of the family, should the baby survive.

When everyone agrees it is best to withdraw treatment, no measures likely to prolong life inappropriately should be continued. This includes oxygen, antibiotics, intravenous fluids, and scheduled feeding. When all life-sustaining treatments are withdrawn, attention to the baby's comfort is paramount. Ensuring the baby's comfort will often require analgesics and sedatives which may as a side effect shorten the baby's life.

Withdrawal of Treatment at Royal Children's Hospital, Melbourne, Australia

We have studied all deaths in our unit in a recent two-year period. There were 1,362 babies admitted with complex problems during the period studied. Of these 132 (9.7%) died. Thirty-one (23.5%) of the deaths occurred despite all efforts to ensure the babies' survivals. The remaining 101 deaths (76.5%) occurred following withdrawal of life-supporting treatment.

Babies from whom treatment was withdrawn were classified in the three prognostic categories previously mentioned.

Babies in Whom Death Was Inevitable

There were 42 babies in this group (41.6%). They were almost certain to die despite all available treatment; withdrawal of treatment shortened the time to the babies' deaths. In this group were extremely low birthweight babies with RDS, and lungs hopelessly disrupted by high-pressure mechanical ventilation or massive brain hemorrhages; babies born without kidneys and with lungs too small to support life (Potter's syndrome); babies with chromosomal disorders such as trisomies 18 and 13. The ELBW babies would have died within hours, as would those with Potter's syndrome. Some of the babies with chromosomal abnormalities might have lived weeks or months. The medical and ethical assumptions guiding their care were that death was inevitable and so life-prolonging treatment was burdensome and not serving their interests.

Babies Who Would Almost Certainly have Survived with Life-Sustaining Treatment but with Severe Handicaps and Cronic Ill Health.

There were 17 babies in this group (16.8%). Diagnoses included babies with severe birth asphyxia, spina bifida with hydrocephalus, and Down's syndrome with life-threatening malformations. The medical and ethical decisions for these babies were based on judgments of the future quality of life of the babies and their families.

Babies in Whom Prognosis for Survival was Uncertain
With active, prolonged, and potentially distressing treatment they might have survived, but more likely would have died. If they had survived it would have been with serious handicaps and chronic ill health. Diagnoses in this group included severe birth asphyxia, ELBW babies with serious intracerebral hemorrhages, and various serious chromosomal abnormalities.

It can be seen that withdrawal decisions were based on prognosis – whether or not babies could survive, and what the quality of survival would be – rather than diagnosis. Many forms of treatment were withdrawn. Those essential to survival were as follows: Of the 101 babies who had active treatment withdrawn, 40 (39.6%) had withdrawal of mechanical ventilation. Forty-eight babies (47.%) had scheduled feeding withheld. These were babies unable to feed from breast or bottle, so that immediate survival depended on scheduled gavage (stomach tube) feeding, gastrostomy feeding, or other special techniques. Oral feeding was not withheld from babies who "demanded" feeding and in whom oral feeding would not itself be life-threatening. Feeding was not withheld; it was simply not imposed.

Eight babies not on mechanical ventilators had oxygen therapy withdrawn. Five babies had intravenous nutrition withdrawn.

It will be clear from what has been said so far that not all babies who are going to die, or to survive with severe handicaps, are extremely tiny or immature, or "monstrous" or malformed. Some are of normal size and pleasing to look at. Not all are brain-damaged or in coma: some are conscious, aware, and responsive. Even when most of the brain is malformed or injured, babies can exhibit "normal" baby behaviors such as gazing, feeding, crying, and smiling, since these are brainstem functions.

Not all are on mechanical ventilators or other complex high-technology support. Some are breathing unaided, in ordinary baby cots, receiving no life-support treatment except oxygen or scheduled feeding and fluids, or suctioning of secretions from the throat to prevent choking. Not all are desperately ill and in the first days or weeks of life: some are stable and several months of age.

Palliative Care: Fluids and Feeds

When life-supporting treatment is withdrawn from babies, palliative care to relieve pain or distress is essential. For many babies palliative care is straightforward: analgesics and sedatives are given even though they often incidentally shorten life. Many caregivers have ethical difficulties withholding feeds and fluids. To them feeding babies is a fundamental part of human nurturing, and seeing babies fade away dehydrated and starving seems morally repugnant.

In our experience, continuing feeds and fluids makes many dying babies worse. The dying process is prolonged. Babies who are breathless and distressed from lung disease, heart failure, or kidney failure remain distressed if fluids are continued, but symptoms improve as fluids are withdrawn and dehydration develops. Babies with abnormalities of brain or airway, which cause choking episodes and labored breathing, improve as dehydration develops and saliva and other secretions diminish. Babies with malformations of the mouth or throat, or brain abnormalities preventing them from sucking, swallowing, or coughing effectively, are made worse by feeding attempts. They may vomit and choke, or if feed is aspirated into the lungs it may cause death. Withholding feeds and fluids is sound palliative care for many dying babies.

When treatments directly supporting life, such as mechanical ventilation, oxygen, or drugs maintaining blood pressure or heart function, are withdrawn, death may follow in minutes or hours. Babies who are aware or in pain pose special problems. The symptoms resulting from withdrawal are distressing until consciousness is lost. Doses of analgesics such as morphine, sufficient to make relief of distress certain, may kill them – that is, cause immediate cessation of breathing and consciousness, whereas without analgesia they might breathe for hours. Arguments that such analgesia is not active euthanasia appear, to some bedside attendants, casuistic.

Slippery-slope arguments against euthanasia in such cases appear to many to be especially unjust. Such arguments appear to say to the baby, "As far as your interests are concerned it would be morally best if we induced a quick and painless death. But if we do, it will launch the rest of us down a slippery slope. So put up with your distress, and save us all from slippery slopes."

I have emphasized earlier that most babies with serious illnesses have good outcomes. It is these who make neonatology such a rewarding endeavor. As methods of treatment improve, further good outcomes should result, but that is not guaranteed. Unless sophisticated high-technology medicine is balanced by imagination (allowing us insight into other people's worlds), compassion, and forbearance (accepting that there are valid views other than our own), outcomes may well be worse.

Notes

1. For a brief account of medical problems in the newborn see Marshal H Klaus & Avroy A Fanaroff. Care of the high-risk neonate, 3d. edition. Philadelphia: W.B. Saunders, 1986. For a comprehensive account see Avroy A Fanaroff and Richard J Martin, eds. Neonatal-perinatal medicine. 4th edition St. Louis: C V Mosby, 1987.
2. For comprehensive accounts of VLBW and ELBW babies see David Harvey, ed. The baby under 1,000 g. London: Wright, 1989; and Dharmapuri Vidyasager, ed. The tiny baby. Clin Perinatol 1986; 13: 2.

3. For outlines of the majority of birth defects see Kenneth Jones. Smith's recognizable patterns of human malformations. 4th edition. Philadelphia: W B Saunders, 1988.
4. James H Moller, William A Neal, eds. Fetal, Neonatal, and Infant Cardiac Disease. Norwalk: Appleton and Lange, 1990; 35: 723–743.
5. R S Duff, A G M Campbell. Moral and ethical dilemmas in the special care nursery. N Engl J Med 1973; 289: 890–94.
6. Andrew Whitelaw. Death as an option in neonatal intensive care. Lancet 1986; ii: 328–331.

ROBERT D. TRUOG

Transplantation and the Anencephalic Newborn

Anencephaly, a severe developmental anomaly occurring early in gestation, results in the "partial or complete absence of the cranial vault as well as absence of overlying tissues and varying degrees of malformation and destruction of the exposed brain rudiments."[1] The possibility of using anencephalic patients as sources of transplantable organs has been the focal point of many debates in contemporary medical ethics. The controversy has attracted a wide audience and has appeared prominently in newspapers as well as in medical and ethical journals.

The driving force behind this debate has clearly been the need for transplantable infant organs. Techniques for pediatric organ transplantation have developed rapidly in recent years. Many infants and children previously destined for early death can now hope for a transplanted organ and a potentially normal life span. Unfortunately, the need for organs greatly exceeds the current supply. Each year in the United States, 400 to 500 infants and children with end-stage renal disease could be taken off dialysis regimens by renal transplantation. A similar number of infants born with fatal forms of congenital heart disease are potentially curable by heart transplantation. An estimated 500 to 1000 children with biliary atresia, cholestatic syndromes, and some inherited metabolic defects could survive with liver transplantation.[2]

Current strategies for organ procurement provide only a fraction of the need. Most organs are procured, at parental request, from newborns, infants, and small children who have been declared brain-dead. Neonatal asphyxia, sudden infant death syndrome, trauma, and drowning are the most frequent causes of death in these patients. Although fortunately only a small number of children succumb to these afflictions each year, the lack of transplantable organs is a hardship for those in need. Of all the children under two years of age who are awaiting organ transplantation, approximately 30 percent to 50 percent will die before suitable organs can be found.[3]

In an attempt to meet this need, for more than twenty-five years efforts have been made to transplant organs from anencephalic newborns. Goodwin and colleagues in 1963 were the first to attempt transplantation of kidneys obtained

F.K. Beller and R.F. Weir (eds.), The Beginning of Human Life, 345–352.

from an anencephalic.[4] Authors of many subsequent reports have detailed the technical aspects of the procedure and commented on its outcome. In many cases the kidneys were removed from anencephalics under anesthesia and prior to the cessation of either spontaneous respiration or heartbeat (personal communication from anonymous sources). Kantrowitz and colleagues reported the first attempt to transplant a heart from an anencephalic source in 1968.[5] In this case, when the anencephalic's cardiac rhythm became irregular at two days of life, the infant was taken to the operating room and cooled by immersion in ice water. When cardiac activity ceased forty minutes later, the heart was excised and transplanted into a neonatal recipient. Severe respiratory and metabolic acidosis developed rapidly, however, and the recipient died six hours after operation.

In the United States, publication of the Uniform Determination of Death Act in 1981 terminated the use of anencephalics for transplantation prior to the cessation of spontaneous respiration and the clear documentation of brain death.[6] Other countries, not bound by this restriction, have continued to transplant kidneys from anencephalic sources.[7] In 1987, for example, Holzgreve and colleagues from West Germany described three successful kidney transplants utilizing anencephalic sources.[8] This was the first report that included an extensive ethical justification for the approach employed. They generalized from the West German commentaries on abortion law to support their actions:

> The concept that the anencephalic fetus, because of the absence of brain development, has never been alive despite the presence of a heart beat is now accepted in the courts of the Federal Republic of Germany and allows termination of pregnancy involving an anencephalic fetus at any time of gestation.

By claiming that anencephalic infants have never been alive, this team avoided the question of whether these newborns met criteria for brain death. In addition, by removing the organs as soon as possible after birth they maximized the likelihood that the organs would function well after transplantation.

Perhaps encouraged by this report from their European colleagues in transplant surgery, surgeons at Loma Linda University Medical Center (LLUMC) performed the first successful heart transplant from an anencephalic source in October 1987.[9] Baby Gabrielle was prenatally diagnosed with anencephaly. Her parents elected to carry the fetus to term so the organs could be used for transplantation. Although born breathing, the infant soon developed respiratory failure and required intubation at approximately 12 hours of age. Despite full life support, her neurological condition deteriorated and she was declared brain-dead at two days of life. She was then flown to LLUMC where, at four days of age, her heart was transplanted into Baby Paul, a newborn with hypoplastic left heart syndrome. The transplant was successful, and Baby Paul was doing well as of follow-up at 20 months of age.[3] Baby Gabrielle's parents stated that the donation process shortened their grieving period: "We thought we'd be coming home from the hospital empty, but what she's done has taken away the pain."[9]

Following this success, LLUMC developed a protocol in December 1987 to support anencephalics with mechanical ventilation for seven days or until brain death, whichever came first.[3,10] If the infants did not meet brain death criteria within seven days, support was discontinued and they were allowed to die. If they did meet criteria, they were listed for organ transplantation. Six patients were enrolled, but only one became brain-dead within the specified time limit, and no organ recipients were available. The protocol was therefore modified to increase the likelihood that patients would become brain-dead. In the modified protocol (1) the newborns were not placed on respirator support at birth but only after respiratory failure occurred; (2) if brain death had not been determined after intensive support for 24 hours, mechanical ventilation was withdrawn and death was allowed to occur; and (3) if brain-death criteria were met within 24 hours, intensive care was continued and a confirmation of brain death by an outside neurologist was sought, which allowed for an additional 12 to 24 hours. Six more infants were enrolled under the new protocol, but again only one became an eligible organ source, and again no recipients were found. Because of these disappointing results, the protocol was suspended in August 1988. At present there are no active programs in the United States for the use of anencephalic infants as organ sources.

If it were possible to use anencephalic newborns as a source of transplanted organs, could they realistically contribute to the need for infant organs? Evidence indicates that the majority of their transplantable organs are morphologically and functionally intact. With regard to hearts, eleven of the twelve anencephalics enrolled into the program at LLUMC had hearts that were suitable for transplantation at time of admission (based upon both shortening fraction and CPK-MB criteria). Of the two anencephalics who became potential organ sources, one retained criteria acceptable for transplantation at the time of brain death.[3] This is consistent with a study of cardiac autopsies on seventy-nine anencephalic newborns, which found that only four of the hearts would have been anatomically unacceptable for transplantation.[11]

With regard to liver transplantation, there have been no attempts to transplant a liver from an anencephalic source in the modern era of transplantation. Nevertheless, there is no evidence to suggest that they would not be acceptable, particularly if the organs were available immediately after birth. Eleven of the twelve Loma Linda patients had hepatic function acceptable for transplantation at the time of admission to the protocol, but only one of the two who became potential organ sources retained adequate hepatic function at the time of the diagnosis of brain death.[3]

Renal transplantation from anencephalic newborns is more problematic. A recent review documented thirty-nine patients who received one or both kidneys from an anencephalic source; follow-up on thirty-one of these patients found that only one-third of the grafts had sustained long-term (>1 year) function.[12] This does not compare favorably with the current expectation of 75–80 percent one-year graft survival. Possible reasons for the poor results obtained with these kidneys from anencephalic sources include the fact that many of these transplants were performed before the advent of modern immunosuppressive therapy. In addition, many of the kidneys were not removed from the sources prior to cardiac arrest, a factor known to significantly diminish the likelihood of long-term graft function. It is likely, however, that the problem was not just the fact that the kidneys were from anencephalic sources. Recent studies suggest that kidneys obtained from all newborn and infant donors do not have acceptable long-term survival. At the Children's Hospital in Boston, for example, no kidneys are accepted from any donor less than three years of age. Therefore, it is unlikely that policies which would permit the use of organs from anencephalic newborns would have an appreciable effect on the current need for transplantable kidneys.

In assessing the impact of policies which would permit the transplantation of organs obtained from anencephalics, the number of organs that would potentially be available must be considered. Assuming an incidence for anencephaly of 0.3 per 1000 births and 3.75 million births per year, approximately 1,125 anencephalics are born in the United States each year. Only about 375 of these would be potential organ sources, since approximately two-thirds of anencephalics are stillborn.[13] This number will certainly decrease in the future as testing of maternal serum alpha-fetoprotein levels and early fetal ultrasound become more commonly employed, since most of these fetuses will be aborted early in gestation. It is unlikely that the number will become insignificant, however, since many couples are opposed to abortion for any reason. In addition, there are some altruistic couples who desire to carry their anencephalic pregnancy to term rather than have an abortion, in an attempt to salvage some good from an otherwise tragic situation through donation of their infant's organs. During the eight months that a protocol was available at Loma Linda University, for example, at least 24 couples with an anencephalic pregnancy sought the opportunity to donate their infant's organs,[3] and more have inquired at other medical centers.[14] The fact that most of the organs are anatomically and functionally normal combined with the likelihood that numerous couples will desire the option of donation suggest that organs obtained from anencephalic newborns could make a partial but significant contribution to the need for infant hearts and livers.

The investigators at LLUMC concluded that

> it is not feasible, within the restrictions imposed by current requirements of total brain death, to procure from anencephalic infants a substantial number of hearts and livers for transplantation. . . . Possible options include . . . a change in the current law to allow the procurement of organs from

anencephalic infants as a separate category of donors to whom the current standards for total brain death would not apply.[3]

Several different proposals have been suggested for making anencephaly "a separate category." The most straightforward approach is simply to define anencephalics as dead. They could then be treated as any other brain-dead organ donor and be maintained on life support until organ removal could be performed. This was essentially the ethical and legal approach adopted by the West German physicians for the renal transplants described previously.[8] A law to this effect was introduced in the California legislature by State Senator Milton Marks in 1986; the bill would have amended the UDDA to include a provision stating that an individual born with the condition of anencephaly is dead.[15] The noted Protestant theologian Paul Ramsey seemed to share this view when he stated that "such an infant (i.e., anencephalic) has not been born alive . . . and no more enters the human community to claim our care and protection than a patient remains in the human community when his brain death . . . is only disguised behind a heart-lung machine."[16] Alexander Capron, an ethicist who helped defeat the Marks amendment, opposes all of these approaches. "Anencephalic infants may be dying," he wrote, "but they are still alive and breathing. Calling them 'dead' will not change physiological reality."[17]

Another approach which seeks to avoid implications of defining them as dead is to regard anencephaly as a special case in which removal of organs is permissible without regard for brain death criteria. For example, pediatric surgeon Michael Harrison advocates the creation of a new category, "brain-absent," which would be limited exclusively to anencephalics.[18] He believes this designation should have the same medical and legal implications as brain death, but without actually defining anencephalics as dead. An advisory committee of Michigan's Transplant Policy Center recently advocated a similar position.[19] They concluded "that infants born with the top half of their brains missing are so very different from other living infants – and their future so radically limited – that it is permissible, with the fully informed and freely given consent of the parents, to remove their organs for transplantation." Although expedient, both of these proposals suffer from a lack of justification for their conclusions. Harrison's "brain-absent" category, for example, is technically inaccurate, because most anencephalics do in fact have a functional brainstem.

Bioethicist John Fletcher and I recently put forward a proposal that attempts to address many of the above concerns.[20] Similar to the recommendations of both Harrison and the Michigan group, it singles out anencephaly as a special case for organ transplantation, but differs from them by attempting to justify this approach through an interpretation of the Uniform Determination of Death Act. We proposed that "individuals are dead if they have a distinct and precisely definable condition characterized by the absence of integrative brain function such that somatic death is uniformly imminent." We further argued that brain death and anencephaly were the only two conditions that fulfilled this criterion.

Finally, a growing number of bioethicists hold that the anencephaly controversy is subordinate to the more fundamental problem of the "whole-brain" definition of death.[21] These writers maintain that our current conception of brain death, as articulated in the UDDA, is seriously flawed, both theoretically and empirically. They propose that the concept of death is best constructed (medically, morally, and legally) around the permanent and irreversible absence of consciousness.[22] This "higher-brain" concept of death has been articulated in various ways, with emphasis on different aspects of the same phenomena. One formulation stresses the capacity for memory and reasoning as well as consciousness,[23] another rests on the notion of personal identity ("a given person ceases to exist with the destruction of whatever processes there are which normally underlie that person's psychological continuity and connectedness"),[24] while another defines death as "the irreversible loss of the embodied capacity for social interaction."[25] The most significant implication of accepting this higher-brain criterion would be that individuals in a persistent vegetative state (PVS) would be considered brain-dead.

Most advocates of a higher-brain criterion acknowledge that we currently do not have the means to diagnose the persistent vegetative state with sufficient reliability for it to function as a standard for death. Adoption of a consciousness-based standard for brain death must wait, at the very least, for more definitive methods of diagnosing this condition. This is only a technical problem, however, and already new techniques (such as PET scanning) promise to make this diagnosis much more reliable in the near future.[26]

If acceptance of a consciousness-based standard is only contingent upon attaining highly reliable methods of diagnosis, then this reasoning provides another justification for regarding anencephalics as a separate category for organ transplantation. Like PVS, anencephaly is characterized by the permanent absence of consciousness. Unlike PVS, however, highly reliable methods of diagnosis are already available. Although Shewmon has reviewed some of the many pitfalls in the diagnosis of anencephaly, even he concedes that "in the vast majority of cases the diagnosis can be made easily and without risk of error."[13] Considering anencephalic newborns as brain-dead under this higher-brain standard would clearly be only a first step toward adoption of a more general consciousness-based standard for brain death.

All of these proposals for making anencephaly a "special case" share the problem of potentially giving the public the impression that doctors are "fiddling" with the definition of death. They may therefore do more harm than good for transplantation programs in the United States. A marked decline in organ donations occurred in England following a highly publicized television program that called into doubt the accuracy of brain death diagnoses.[27] These proposals must therefore be thoroughly scrutinized by the medical community and by the public at large. They must be analyzed not just in terms of the limited problem of organ shortage but with regard to their broad impact on society as well. As the President's Commission noted, "Policy conclusions . . . must accurately reflect the social meaning of death and not constitute a mere legal fiction."[28] If one of these proposals stands the test of this inquiry, however, anencephalic newborns may yet become a significant source of organs for many young patients who will otherwise certainly die.

REFERENCES

1. Lemire RJ, Beckwith JB, Warkany J. Anencephaly. New York: Raven Press, 1978: 1–9.
2. Fletcher JC, Robertson JA, Harrison MR. Primates and anencephalics as sources for pediatric organ transplants. Medical, legal, and ethical issues. Fetal Diagn Ther 1986; 1: 150–164.
3. Peabody JL, Emery JR, Ashwal S. Experience with anencephalic infants as prospective organ donors. N Engl J Med 1989; 321: 344–350.
4. Goodwin WE, Kaufman JJ, Mims MM, Turner RD, Glassock R, Goldman R, Maxwell MM. Human renal transplantation. 1, Clinical experiences with six cases of renal homotransplantation. J Urol 1963; 89: 13–24.
5. Kantrowitz A, Haller JD, Joos H, Cerruti MM, Carstensen HE. Transplantation of the heart in an infant and an adult. Am J Cardiol 1968; 22: 782–790.
6. Guidelines for the determination of death. Report of the medical consultants on the diagnosis of death to the President's Commission for the Study of Ethical Problems in Medicine and Biomedical and Behavioral Research. JAMA 1981; 246: 2184–2186.
7. Gutierrez Calzada JL, Martinez JL, Baena V, Laguna G, Arrieta J, Rodriguez J, Moncada A. En bloc kidney and bladder transplantation from an anencephalic donor into an adult recipient. J Urol 1987; 138: 125–126.
8. Holzgreve W, Beller FK, Buchholz B, Hansmann M, Kohler K. Kidney transplantation from anencephalic donors. N Engl J Med 1987; 316: 1069–1070.
9. Frewen T, Stiller CR, Hinton G, Lowry J. Clinical summary: Baby Gabrielle. Transplant Proc 1988; 20 (Suppl 5): 81–82.
10. Walters JW, Ashwal S. Organ prolongation in anencephalic infants: Ethical and medical issues. Hastings Cent Rep 1988; 18: 19–27.
11. Cabasson J, Blanc WA, Joos HA. The anencephalic infant as a possible donor for cardiac transplantation. Clin Pediatr (Phila) 1969; 8: 86–89.
12. Fine RN. Renal transplantation of the infant and young child and the use of pediatric cadaver kidneys for transplantation in pediatric and adult recipients. Am J Kidney Dis 1988; 12: 1–10.
13. Shewmon DA. Anencephaly: selected medical aspects. Hastings Cent Rep 1988; 18: 11–19.
14. Stiller CR. International Consensus Development Conference on Anencephalic Donors. January 5, 1987, London, Ontario, Canada. Proceedings. Transplant Proc 1988; 20 (Suppl 5): 1–83.
15. California Senate Bill No. 2018. Introduced by Senators Marks, Nielson, Rosenthal, and Watson on Feb 19, 1986; amended in Senate Apr 3, May 20, and Jun 12, 1986.
16. Ramsey P. Ethics at the edges of life: medical and legal intersections. New Haven, CT: Yale University Press, 1980: 213.
17. Capron AM. Anencephalic donors: separate the dead from the dying. Hastings Cent Rep 1987; 17: 5–9.
18. Harrison MR. The anencephalic newborn as organ donor. Hastings Cent Rep 1986 Apr 16: 21–23.

19. Ethics and Social Impact Committee Transport Policy Center. Ann Arbor MI. Anencephalic infants as sources of transplantable organs. Hastings Cent Rep 1988; 18: 28–30.
20. Truog RD, Fletcher JC,. Anencephalic newborns. Can organs be transplanted before brain death. N Engl J Med 1989; 321: 388–391.
21. Cefalo RC, Engelhardt HT Jr. The use of fetal and anencephalic tissue for transplantation. J Med Philos 1989; 14: 25–43.
22. Cranford RE, Smith DR. Consciousness: the most critical moral (constitutional) standard for human personhood. Am J Law Med 1987; 13: 233–248.
23. Engelhardt HT Jr. Defining death: a philosophical problem for medicine and law. Am Rev Respir Dis 1975; 112: 587–590.
24. Green MB, Wikler D. Brain death and personal identity. Philosophy and Public Affairs 1980; 9: 105–133.
25. Veatch RM. Death, dying, and the biological revolution. New Haven, CT: Yale University Press, 1989.
26. Cranford RE. The persistent vegetative state: The medical reality (getting the facts straight). Hastings Cent Rep 1988; 18(1): 27–32.
27. Potts SG. Headaches in Britain over brain death criteria. Hastings Cent Rep 1987; 17(2): 2–3.
28. President's Commission for the Study of Ethical Problems in Medicine and Biomedical and Behavioral Research. Defining death: a report on the medical, legal, and ethical issues in the determination of death. Washington, DC: Government Printing Office, 1981.

ROBERT F. WEIR

Life-and-Death Decisions in the Midst of Uncertainty*

A neonatal intensive care unit (NICU) is characterized by premature and disabled patients with life-threatening conditions, highly trained medical and nursing specialists, state-of-the-art medical technology, an endless stream of medical consultants, parents grappling with frightening possibilities, and numerous decisions that have to be made in the midst of impenetrable uncertainty. Whether made while looking down at an imperiled baby, in consultation with the baby's parents, or in a conference room near the NICU, many of these decisions are crucial because a baby will continue to live or will die as a consequence of them.

The context of uncertainty has several aspects. The primary uncertainty in many NICU cases is medical in nature, with the greatest medical uncertainty usually having to do with prognosis rather than diagnosis. Even with the availability of increasingly sophisticated diagnostic tools, neonatologists and other pediatric specialists sometimes find it impossible, literally impossible, to predict with any measure of confidence the long-term prospects of a child with severe neurologic, cardiac, genetic, or pulmonary disabilities. Such medical uncertainty most commonly arises with babies having known neurologic impairments, but with pediatric neurologists and developmental specialists having no way of accurately predicting the extent or severity of the developmental disability that the child will actually have if he or she lives.

The other aspects of the context of uncertainty in the truly difficult NICU cases have to do with ethics, the law, and the parents of the baby. Moral uncertainty arises for either of two reasons: the neonatologists, parents, and other participants in a case are not adequately informed about the work that has been done in neonatal ethics in recent years, or the uncertainty about the medical prognosis in a given case necessarily causes the ethical analysis of the case to be less decisive than it would normally be.

Uncertainty about the law takes many forms. Sometimes the decision makers in a case are insufficiently informed about how federal or state statutes apply to the case under consideration. Sometimes they are unsure of the meaning and applicability of the federal child abuse regulations. Sometimes they are unsure about the role that can or should be played by state child protective agencies

F.K. Beller and R.F. Weir (eds.), The Beginning of Human Life, 353–370.

in cases involving decisions by parents not to sustain the lives of severely disabled newborns. In some cases the legal uncertainty is focused on a particular question, such as the legal liability of physicians who refuse to abide by parents' requests regarding the administration or abatement of treatment, or the legality of transplanting organs from an anencephalic baby, or the legality of abating life-sustaining nutrition and hydration.

Uncertainty about the parents of an imperiled baby adds another level of complexity to some cases. At times neonatologists, NICU nurses, or consultants on particular cases raise questions about the parents' ability to grasp the relevant medical data, the parents' psychological conditions, the parents' desires related to the baby's life or death, the parents' abilities to cope with the ongoing management problems presented by their disabled child, and the parents' ability to pay for the hospital and medical expenses involved in the child's care. At other times much more specific case-centered questions are raised, regarding the mother's use of alcohol, cocaine, and other drugs during pregnancy, the absence of an identifiable father, the mother's earlier refusal of prenatal diagnosis, parental decisions made contrary to the advice of genetic counselors, problematic interactions between parents, or the likelihood that the parents may initiate legal action if their requests regarding treatment or the abatement of treatment are not carried out.

The commonality of uncertainty in its several forms will be illustrated in this paper by focusing on five questions. These questions address substantive aspects of decision making about neonates and other young infants that remain problematic for persons making life-and-death decisions at either the clinical or public-policy level.

(1) Do neonates count as persons?

The first question of uncertainty has two dimensions. One dimension is theoretical and has to do with the ontological status of neonates and young children, whether normal or neurologically impaired. Simply put, this aspect of the question asks, "What kind of entity is it whose life or death is at stake in the decisions made by clinicians and/or parents?" The other dimension is practical and pertains to the realities of decision making in NICUs, PICUs, and specialized chronic care units for young children. This second aspect of the more general questions asks, "What difference does an abstract question about personhood make in the real world of tough clinical decisions?"

The uncertainty surrounding the theoretical question of personhood could hardly be greater, especially among persons lacking training in philosophy. Although the debate about the ontological status of human beings in certain situations (both before and after birth) has been going on for centuries among philosophers and theologians, a question about the ontological status of neonates nevertheless elicits puzzled responses when raised in a modern medical center, university, or other social setting. The question often seems strange to health care professionals and others outside philosophy, partially because of its abstract nature and partially because many people simply assume that "person" and "human" are synonyms.

Sometimes the abstractness of the question about personhood can be alleviated by suggesting to individuals or groups that they try to articulate what they understand the term "person" to mean, especially in terms of the properties that persons possess. Then one can raise questions about the possession of those properties by patients in persistent vegetative state, or by severely demented individuals, or by dolphins, or by some apes, or by extraterrestrial beings, or by human babies. The central point in such a discussion is clear, namely whether any of the human or nonhuman candidates for personhood is correctly to be regarded as a person in the same ways that you and I are persons.

On other occasions the abstractness of the question about the personhood of neonates can be alleviated by pointing out that the language of personhood regularly surfaces in pro-life arguments about the morality and legality of abortion. For example, one of the many proposed amendments to the U.S. Constitution following the 1973 *Roe v. Wade* decision would have granted fetuses the legal status of persons:

> With respect to the right of life, the word "person" as used in this article and in the fifth and fourteenth articles of amendment to the Constitution of the United States, applies to all human beings, including their unborn offspring at every stage of their development, irrespective of age, health, function, or condition of dependency. (Perkins, 1974: 229)

Thus the question of personhood is with us, along with its abstractness, and its legitimate application covers the spectrum of human biological existence from fetuses to permanently unconscious adult patients to severely demented geriatric patients. The question of the personhood of neonates, at least among philosophers, has generally been framed so that it focuses on whether neonates possess the properties or intrinsic qualities generally ascribed to persons such as you and me (Tooley, 1972: 37; Tooley, 1979: 62; Tooley, 1983: 332; Warren, 1973: 43; Singer, 1979: 97). A few philosophers have suggested that the personhood of neonates, if they are to be counted as persons, can also include their social roles or extrinsic qualities (Engelhardt, 1986: 117; Jecker, 1990: 35).

To the extent that there is consensus among philosophers on the concept of personhood, that consensus focuses on the intrinsic rather than the extrinsic qualities of persons. Most philosophers agree on at least the core properties or traits of personhood, if not on all of their applications. Joel Feinberg (1986: 263), in his discussion of "commonsense personhood," puts forth the consensus view of personhood as being the possession of three necessary and jointly sufficient properties: consciousness, self-awareness, and at least minimum rationality. Such properties, for him and many others, represent "person-making characteristics."

The possession of personhood therefore has to do with neurological development and, at least among human beings, the absence of profound neurological dysfunction or impairment. The answer to the question of whether neonates are to be counted as persons depends on three interrelated factors: (1) how much neurological development is required for personhood, (2) how much neurological impairment is necessary to rule out personhood, and (3) whether any significance is to be placed on the principle of potentiality as it applies to personhood.

In my judgment, there are three basic positions regarding the personhood of neonates (and other human beings whose personhood may be questioned), and the positions are distinguishable largely because of their handling of the factors of neurological development, neurological impairment, and potential personhood (Weir, 1985: 1115; Weir, 1986: 48). The first position holds that *all neonates*, whether normal or neurologically impaired, *are nonpersons*. As initially described by Thomas Murray (1985: 1104), the philosophers who hold this view make four related claims: (1) personhood is a moral category attaching to beings (of any species) with certain characteristics, principally cognitive capacities; (2) neonates lack the cognitive qualities that make a human into a person; (3) being a *potential* person does not count; and (4) only *actual* persons are entitled to the moral benefits of personhood, including the right not to be killed.

The second position stands at the other end of a philosophical and political spectrum, and represents a very common view of neonates held by many physicians, nurses, and other people as well. This position, which holds that *all neonates are actual persons*, can also be presented in terms of four related claims: (1) personhood is a moral and legal category attaching to human beings at a chronological point determined by social consensus, with conception, viability, and birth as three alternatives for such a point; (2) neonates count as *actual* persons, as do all other human beings who are past the chosen chronological point; (3) being a *potential* person does not signify very much; and (4) neonates and all other *actual* persons are entitled to the moral and legal benefits of personhood, including the right not to be killed.

The third position stands between the other positions, differing from the first position's insufficient claims and the second position's excessive claims regarding the personhood of human newborns. This position, which holds that *most neonates are potential persons*, can be compared with the alternative views on the basis of its four claims: (1) personhood is a moral category attaching to beings (of any species) with certain characteristics, principally cognitive capacities; (2) neonates lack the intrinsic qualities that make a human into a person, as do fetuses; (3) having the potential to become a person through the normal course of development does count, and neonates without severe neurological impairment (and fetuses having exhibited brain activity) have this potential; and (4) all *potential* persons have a prima facie claim to the moral benefits of personhood, including the right not to be killed, because they will subsequently acquire an *actual* person's moral and legal right to life.

The last of these positions, in my view, is the correct way of describing the ontological status of neonates. This position is preferable to the neonates-are-not-persons view of some philosophers because it grants more than a species value to human newborns – and avoids the major weakness of having to allow, in principle, for the indiscriminate termination of an indeterminate number of neonatal lives, whether these lives are cognitively impaired, physically disabled, or normal. The third position is also preferable to the neonates-are-actual-persons view (especially as put forth by several pro-life groups) because it takes the philosophical and psychological concept of personhood seriously – and avoids the major weakness of having to say, in principle, that a baby has no more claim to the moral benefits of personhood than an early human embryo does.

Now we turn to the second aspect of the question about personhood: what difference does greater clarity about the ontological status of neonates make in the real world? Given the abstract, nonempirical nature of the concept of potential personhood, how can such a concept – even if philosophically sound – be used to make the tough clinical decisions about initiating, continuing, or abating life-sustaining treatment in an NICU?

The honest answer is, of course, that the philosophical view developed above cannot currently play a major role in clinical decision making, for a number of reasons. It is too abstract and subjective. It is not based on, nor is it likely to be based on, empirical studies. It is the sort of view about which reasonable people disagree. It opens up the possibility of using quality-of-life criteria for decision making in pediatric critical care units, which the "Baby Doe" regulations and subsequent Child Abuse regulations have expressly prohibited. Perhaps most important, it is not consistent with federal and state laws that tend to define citizens in this society as legally being persons from the time of their births.

Nevertheless, as graphically illustrated by the ongoing controversy in this society over abortion, questions about the ontological status of human beings in certain situations do not simply go away. In time, they occasionally influence changes in laws and public policy, as has already happened regarding abortion laws and may happen again.

I frankly doubt that public policy regarding severely disabled neonates will ever be based on the philosophical view that most neonates are to be regarded as potential persons. However, I remain convinced that the concepts of personhood and potential personhood have some merit in the prolonged, often agonizing deliberations that take place about neonates having severe to profound neurological impairments. At the very least, the concept of potential personhood provides an intellectual framework in which prognostic judgments about the future level of a baby's neurological development or the future degree of a baby's neurological impairment make some sense. After all, at least part of the uncertainty that everyone struggles to get a handle on has to do with who a particular baby has the chance to become or, put more bluntly, whether the baby in question has the potential even to become a who in the normal course of his or her development.

(2) What is the best ethical option for making decisions to initiate, continue, or abate life-sustaining treatment?

This question addresses the uncertainty generated by the pluralism of value perspectives over how life-and-death decisions should be made in pediatric critical care units, and by whom. This pluralism is often present as neonatologists discuss treatment options with parents, pediatric specialists and residents discuss problematic cases during rounds, professionals from multiple health care fields exchange views during case conferences, and pediatric ethics committees struggle to give appropriate advice regarding cases referred to them.

In cases of neonates or young children with life-threatening medical conditions, the adults involved have five ethical options available to them for deciding about life-sustaining treatment (Weir, 1984: 143). The options range from very conservative to very liberal, and they differ from one another regarding the substantive and, to a lesser extent, the procedural aspects of making life-and-death decisions for nonautonomous young patients.

The most conservative of these ethical options is the ethical perspective that was enacted into public policy by the Reagan administration through the "Baby Doe" regulations and subsequent Child Abuse regulations. Incensed that one "Baby Doe" (the 1982 Bloomington, Indiana, case) had died who could have lived with surgical intervention, and concerned that other disabled infants were unnecessarily being allowed to die in other hospitals, the leaders of the Reagan administration went to great lengths to advocate the ethical perspective held by then–Surgeon General Everett Koop and many of the administration's pro-life supporters.

This ethical position holds that there is one and only one acceptable moral reason for not sustaining an infant's life, namely the medical futility in a very limited number of cases of trying to do so. According to this ethical perspective, decisions not to sustain a severely disabled infant's life are acceptable only when such an infant is irretrievably dying (or, for some persons holding this position, an infant whose condition is some form of permanent unconsciousness). Therefore the only cases in which such decisions by physicians or parents are justifiable are those unusual cases in which there is actually no moral decision to make: God, nature, fate, the roll of the genetic "dice," or some force beyond our control prevents medical efforts at sustaining life from working.

The most liberal option is a position that carries significant weight in some philosophical circles, but not, as we have already discussed, among physicians and others who are more oriented toward a practical, empirically based view of reality. This position, in sharp contrast to the first position, is based on the ontological status of the young lives at risk in critical care units rather than on the severity of their medical conditions. Instead of calling for life-sustaining treatment to be administered to all neonates or young children who are not dying (or permanently unconscious), the philosophers holding this position (e.g. Michael Tooley, Mary Anne Warren, and Peter Singer) argue that physicians and parents are obligated to provide life-sustaining treatment only for neonates and young children who count as persons. The catch is, as we have seen, that according to this perspective no neonates meet the criteria for personhood and no moral weight is placed on the potential they may have to become persons later in the course of their development. An unresolved problem for these philosophers –and one of the reasons that this position will never become public policy – is that of defining the "magic moment" beyond the neonatal period when young children do meet the criteria for personhood and are thus protected from having their lives arbitrarily terminated.

The third position is the first of three positions that reside closer to the middle of the philosophical spectrum than either of the views just discussed. The physicians, philosophers, and other individuals who hold this view do not believe that all nondying neonates should be given life-sustaining treatment, nor do they believe that lives of neonates can be morally terminated on the basis of a definitional point about personhood. Rather, they are convinced that the most important aspect of decisions not to sustain some infants' lives is the procedural question of who should make these difficult decisions. The correct answer to that question, according to the advocates of this position, is that the appropriate decision maker is the parent or parents of the neonate or young child whose life is threatened by his or her medical condition, even though the current federal regulations do not permit this kind of parental discretion. Since the parents of a disabled infant are the ones who stand to gain or lose the most, depending on what happens to the infant, it is they – instead of the physicians, an ethics committee, or anybody else – who should have the right to make the life-or-death decision in all cases of disagreement over whether a disabled infant should continue to live with, or die in the absence of, life-sustaining treatment.

Advocates of a fourth ethical position are convinced that quality-of-life judgments are unavoidable in cases of severe neurological or physiological malformation, in spite of what federal regulations say to the contrary. All of the responsible parties in cases of serious neonatal abnormalities are morally obligated – and should be legally permitted – to raise important questions about the most likely future ahead of these children if their lives are to be prolonged with medical treatment. Of fundamental importance in such cases is not only the question of whether a given child can be salvaged with the abnormalities he or she has but also what kind of life he or she is most likely to have with those abnormalities. The most important abnormalities to consider are neurological in nature. If a neurological disorder is sufficiently serious that pediatric neurologists and neonatologists project a life with severe disabilities for the child, virtually all persons holding a quality-of-life position would find the abatement of life-sustaining treatment in such a case to be morally justifiable.

The fifth position is held by individuals who are convinced that life-sustaining treatment should be provided to normal and disabled neonates whenever such treatment is in their best interests, and that life-sustaining treatment should be abated in the care of severely premature or severely disabled neonates (and other young children) whenever such treatment is judged not to be in their best interests. Persons holding this position tend to be in agreement with quality-of-life advocates whose projections of a given child's future focus *entirely* on that child's likely abilities and disabilities, not on the child's impact on anybody else or ability to attain somebody else's minimal standard of acceptability for personal human life. By contrast, persons having a best-interests position disagree with quality-of-life advocates who tend to compare mentally and physically abnormal children with normal children, emphasize the problems that disabled children cause for their families and society, and try to protect families and society from having to deal with disabled children who cannot meet some arbitrary standard of acceptability. Like all advocates of the quality-of-life position, proponents of the best-interests position hold a view that is more liberal than the current federal regulations.

The best-interests position, in my judgment, is the preferable ethical perspective to take in regard to difficult decisions about initiating, continuing, or abating life-sustaining treatment with any patients having life-threatening medical conditions. Neonatal and other young pediatric patients are no exception. They, like other nonautonomous patients, should receive life-sustaining treatment whenever the decision makers are convinced that the treatments available provide a balance of benefit to burden for the child. Such decisions should focus on the child's medical condition, concern suffering and irremediable handicap rather than projected social worth, and involve comparative judgments about the continuation of the child's injurious existence as opposed to the child's nonexistence.

(3) What does "best interests" mean when patients are neonates?

Even though widely supported in theory, the best-interests position is not without problems. Some of the advocates of the position (President's Commission, 1983: 217; McCormick, 1986: 18; Jonsen, Siegler, and Winslade, 1986: 188; Bartholome, 1988: 39) admit that the concept of the patient's best interests is inherently vague, especially when the patient is a neonate. Nevertheless, they argue that the concept is helpful in decision making about life-sustaining treatment for neonates because it focuses the decision-making process on precisely the human lives that ought to be the primary focus of concern.

Some of the critics of the best-interests position, at least as it applies to neonates, think that the conceptual foundation on which it stands is fundamentally flawed. Martin Benjamin (1983: 5) argues that neonates simply do not yet possess the cognitive awareness, much less the specific wants and purposes, that are necessary for ascribing to them an interest in continued life. Howard Brody (1988: 37) is convinced that any attempt to apply the concept of best interests to infants is bound to fail, because the concept is either incoherent or inadequate as a guide for tough clinical decisions. He argues that even if infants can intelligibly be said to have interests, such interests would be unknowable by adult decision makers.

The third question of uncertainty thus has to do with the intellectual integrity and plausibility of the concept of the patient's best interests when that concept is used in the context of NICUs. Is "the best interests of the infant" only a symbolic slogan without substance? Is its only function that of oversimplifying the complex decisions that have to be made in NICUs?

I think not, and I will make three points briefly to try to demonstrate the importance and usefulness of the concept. To begin, it is necessary to say something about interests. One's "interests" consist of relationships, activities, and things in which one has a stake, and on which one places value. To have interests (as opposed to sensations or instincts) normally requires as necessary conditions that one be conscious, aware of oneself, and able cognitively to have wants and purposes. In other words, to have interests normally requires that one be a person.

Yet, as Joel Feinberg (1984: 96) points out in a discussion of fetal interests, it is plausible to ascribe *future* interests to a "prepersonal fetus." Even though a fetus "presumably has no actual interests," it can correctly be said to have future interests on the assumption that it will at some future point in its normal development (at birth or subsequent to birth) become a person and thus the possessor of actual interests. In a similar manner the law recognizes that fetuses can have "contingent rights," such as the right to property, that will become actual rights the moment the fetus becomes a baby. Any contingent right of a fetus is instantly voided if the fetus dies before birth.

The same kind of reasoning about interests can be used in analyzing the interests that are ascribable to neonates, even by philosophers who claim that all neonates are nonpersons. For even if neonates as nonpersons cannot correctly be said to be the possessors of actual interests, they can be said to have future interests (assuming that they will at some future point become persons) that can be interfered with or damaged by decision or actions by adults long before these developing human lives become persons. For example, a neonate with myelomeningocele could reasonably be said to have a future interest in physical mobility, but come to realize later in life that a decision by physicians or parents during the neonatal period not to have the lesion surgically corrected had preempted that future interest from being actualized.

An alternative conceptual framework for discussing the interests of neonates was presented earlier, namely the philosophical view that neonates without severe neurological impairments are to be regarded as potential persons. In this framework, an analysis of the interests of neonates does not involve the ascription of future interests to them because they are thought likely to become persons at some "magic moment" in the future, but ascribes future interests to them because they have the potential to become the possessors of interests through the normal course of their development.

The point is a fundamental one. Just as potentiality is an important aspect of the concept of personhood, so potentiality is an important feature of a philosophical understanding of interests (but not of legal rights). Interests change from time to time after one becomes a person, with some interests intensifying over time, others waning, and others appearing as though newly born. For that reason, a discussion of the future interests of any given neonate becomes problematic if one can only project the actual interests that child will have when he or she meets the criteria for personhood at some future time. By contrast, the principle of potentiality, as it applies both to the possession of personhood and the possession of interests, permits one reasonably to ascribe to any given neonate the most general and basic kinds of interests that most individuals tend to have as they develop from young children to older children and on through the various phases of personal life.

Second, even if it is not incoherent to discuss the general interests (in the sense of future interests) that neonates have, one must still make some sense out of the concept of "best interests." Simply put, persons tend to have a multiplicity of interests that help to define who they are and what they hold to be worthy of their expenditures of time, money, effort, and prolonged thought. Given this multiplicity of interests, some of the interests are necessarily regarded as being more important than others.

A common way of focusing on the interests that are most vital to a person, especially when that person is a patient in a hospital, is through the language of "best interests." Of course patients, at least those who are conscious and autonomous, do not lose their "regular" interests (e.g., in their families, personal goals, and work) when they are admitted to a hospital. However, their interests related to their own health tend to take on an immediacy and overall importance that transcend the range of other interests they have. In particular, if they have an injury or illness that is life-threatening in nature, their normal interests in the prolongation of their lives and the avoidance of suffering are greatly intensified, to the point of becoming the focal point of all their interests at that time. The concept of the patient's "best interests" captures this change in the ranking of personal interests, especially when the clinical circumstances concern decisions about administering or abating life-sustaining treatment.

When applied to neonates, the concept of "best interests" can obviously not refer to the specific wants and purposes any given neonate may have in continued life, much less to the specific wants and purposes that the neonate may have later in life. However, the concept of "best interests" can be used to capture the most fundamental future interest that persons have when they are patients, namely an interest in not being harmed on balance during the course of medical treatment. For most patients in most clinical situations, this vital interest in not being harmed on balance means that they prefer continued life to death – unless intractable pain and other suffering have made continued life more harmful than the prospect of death. To ascribe this general and basic interest to neonates is to claim that all neonates lacking severe neurological impairment can reasonably be said to have this future interest in not being harmed, an interest that will become actualized as they become persons during the normal course of their development.

Third, the toughest aspect of using the concept of best interests in decision making in NICUs is determining the factors that should be considered in any given case. How can physicians and parents assess the beneficial and detrimental aspects of medical treatment in a case? How can they decide if life-sustaining treatment is in a neonate's best interests, or is contrary to those interests?

My suggestion is to regard the patient's-best-interests standard as having eight variables (Weir and Bale, 1989: 818). In neonatal (and other young pediatric) cases, the variables are as follows:

1. the severity of the patient's medical condition
2. the availability of curative or corrective treatment
3. the achievability of important medical goals
4. the presence of serious neurological impairments
5. the extent of the infant's suffering
6. the multiplicity of other serious medical problems
7. the life expectancy of the infant
8. the proportionality of treatment-related benefits and burdens to the infant.

The last of these variables is, in many respects, a summation of the preceding variables. For decision makers in such cases, a consideration of the benefits of the treatment (both short-term and long-term) to the patient is the bottom line for determining whether life-sustaining treatment or the abatement of life-sustaining treatment is in a particular neonate's best interests. In making this assessment, decision makers arrive at a subjective judgment that includes objective factors but is not finally reducible to quantifiable information. For to decide in rare clinical situations that treatment is, on balance, harmful to the infant rather than beneficial, is to make a moral judgment.

(4) Should the lives of severely disabled neonates and other young children always be sustained with nutrition and hydration?

This question of uncertainty reflects the ongoing debate in this society over the morality and legality of abating technological feeding and hydration. The societal debate over technological feeding has been characterized by exchanges in the media, the professional literature, the courts, and the legislatures between the advocates of a mainstream position and the proponents of a large minority position on this issue.

The advocates of the mainstream position claim that technologically supplied nutrition and hydration may be abated on moral and legal grounds, in the same way that decisions are made about other life-sustaining technologies, whenever such treatment is contrary to the preferences of an autonomous patient or the best interests of a nonautonomous patient. The proponents of the minority view argue that the provision of nutrition and hydration, even if supplied by any of several kinds of feeding tubes, cannot correctly be regarded as a form of life-sustaining medical treatment or ever be discontinued in the care of nonautonomous patients (Weir, 1989).

In addition, this question of uncertainty reflects a fundamental ambiguity in the Child Abuse regulations (Department of Health and Human Services, 1985: 14878). Three exceptions to the requirement of providing medically indicated treatment are spelled out in the regulations: (1) infants who are "chronically and irreversibly comatose," (2) dying infants for whom the provision of medical treatment would be "futile in terms of the survival of the infant," and (3) infants for whom the treatment would be "virtually futile . . . and . . . inhumane." Each of these exceptions is described in ambiguous terminology, and each has been the subject of considerable discussion and debate since they were published in 1985.

An equally ambiguous part of the regulations immediately precedes the description of the three exceptions. The same sentence concerning medically indicated treatment indicates that effective treatment includes "appropriate nutrition, hydration, and medication." This statement, in contrast to the description of the three exceptional situations, has received relatively little attention in the literature on the regulations or in the more general literature on the issue of technological feeding.

For example, neither a questionnaire directed at Massachusetts pediatricians (Todres et al., 1988: 644) nor a national survey of neonatologists (Kopelman et al., 1988: 677) asked the physicians what they understood this portion of the regulations to mean. Likewise, the policy statements on technological feeding by medical and health-care organizations focus on adult cases and do not even raise, with the exception of the statement of the American Nurses' Association (1988), the issue of technologically supplied nutrition and hydration for infants.

One exception to this trend is a short chapter written by Joel Frader (1986: 180). Frader, a pediatrician at the University of Pittsburgh, argues that the same kind of reasoning about the provision of technological feeding "should apply equally well to infants and older persons, even though feeding babies has special social significance." He suggests that in at least a few instances (e.g., hydranencephaly or renal agenesis), the provision of fluids and nutrition to neonates will only prolong their dying or extend their suffering. In these rare cases, he suggests, "good medical practice, that is, palliation, could require allowing dehydration and malnutrition."

Another exception is an article written by John Paris and Anne Fletcher (1987: 367). Paris, an ethicist, and Fletcher, a pediatrician, emphasize that the language of "appropriate nutrition, hydration, and medication" allows for the kind of discretionary decision making that is required by complex NICU cases. They describe three clinical cases in which physicians and parents decided against the continuation of technological feedings: a premature baby with necrotizing enterocolitis, a neonate with severe birth asphyxia, and a three-month-old girl dying with multiple medical complications incompatible with long-term survival. In each of these cases, Paris and Fletcher think that the abatement of technologically supplied nutrition and hydration was medically and ethically appropriate.

These two publications notwithstanding, many neonatologists and nurses in NICUs have a great deal of uncertainty about the morality and legality of abating life-sustaining nutrition and hydration. They remain uncertain even when informed of the mainstream ethical and legal position that says (1) that the technological provision of nutrition and hydration is not morally or legally different from other life-sustaining care and (2) that decisions about abating life-sustaining treatment with neonates and other young children should follow the best-interests standard in a manner similar to decisions about life-sustaining treatment made on the behalf of nonautonomous adult patients. Their uncertainty is partially due to the ambiguities they perceive in the law, and partially due to the emotional and psychological realities of discontinuing nutrition and hydration in the care of babies with life-threatening conditions.

I anticipate that this uncertainty will be lessened as neonatologists and nurses in NICUs do more to address the question of when technological nutrition and hydration is and is not appropriate. At the present time, however, their uncertainty about this question is very real.

(5) Should life-sustaining treatment for neonates and other young children ever be abated for economic reasons?

Neonatologists and other pediatric specialists place considerable importance on providing good patient care. In terms of the patient's-best-interests position, this emphasis on the medical needs and interests of individual patients is the morally preferable perspective for pediatricians and other physicians. According to this view, the needs and interests of each patient related to continued life correctly outweigh any competing interests of parents, siblings, or society. Simply put, no neonate or other young, nonautonomous patient should die merely because the requisite medical and hospital care is expensive, even when the physicians and parents in a given case know that the family's income and insurance cannot cover the costs involved in the patient's care.

In the last few years, however, a number of factors have combined to create uncertainty about this basic moral premise for the provision of medical care, especially as it applies to cases of extremely premature or severely disabled neonates. Physicians, hospital administrators, and other concerned persons often question the importance that should be placed on the economic aspects of sustaining the lives of some neonates and other young children, especially when these lives predictably will be characterized by severe mental and physical disabilities. Case discussions in NICUs, PICUs, and specialized chronic-care units for young children increasingly have comments and questions by staff physicians, residents, nurses, social workers, and ethicists regarding the costs of the ongoing treatment and who will have to pay for those costs.

One of the factors contributing to this uncertainty about the economics of neonatal care has to do with the public policy regarding medically indicated treatment for disabled young children developed by the Reagan administration and continued by the Bush administration. Whether the legal framework for the policy was the 1973 Rehabilitation Act (for the now invalidated "Baby Doe" regulations) or the 1984 Child Abuse Amendments (for the current Child Abuse regulations), the public policy developed by the federal government has placed unprecedented pressure on neonatologists and parents to make treatment decisions without regard to cost.

The unfortunate and often tragic catch has been that the government, in mandating the administration of life-sustaining treatment for all neonates who are not dying or permanently unconscious, has never provided adequate financial coverage for that treatment for hospitals or for parents who are uninsured, underinsured, or have limited eligibility for state aid programs for disabled children. Moreover, given the drastic cuts by the Reagan administration in Medicaid funds and in funds for material and child health services, the various state aid programs for disabled children have much more restricted budgets now than they did in the early 1980s.

Another factor contributing to uncertainty about the role of economics in neonatal cases pertains to the escalating costs of the care needed by extremely premature or severely disabled newborns. This uncertainty is brought about not only by an awareness of the escalating costs of providing care for these babies, but also by the realization that efforts to provide comparative cost figures for neonatal care have proven less than satisfactory, that the application of diagnosis-related group (DRG) categories has not worked well in NICUs, and that the cost-effectiveness of neonatal care for low birthweight neonates is still questionable (Berki, Schneier, 1987: 874; Lichtig, et al., 1989: 49; Young, Stevenson, 1990: 549).

The escalating cost of providing neonatal intensive care is widely recognized by neonatologists and hospital administrators, even though the medical diversity of NICU cases and variation of financial charges from hospital to hospital (and country to country) make accurate comparative cost comparisons virtually impossible. At the very least, the figure of $8,000 that a 1981 study by the Office of Technology Assessment gave as the average expenditure per NICU patient now seems quite low (Budetti, 1981: 4).

Studies published in recent years all document the increasing cost of providing care for disabled neonates and young children in chronic-care units. For example, one study from Canada (using 1978 Canadian dollars) found that the costs of intensive care for infants weighing less than 1,000 g averaged $102,500 per survivor (Boyle, et al., 1983: 1330). A study from Australia (using 1984 Australian dollars) determined that the total direct cost for level 3, high-dependency care in one hospital was $690 per day (Marshall, et al., 1989: 568). Studies in the United States, varying greatly in methodology, have found the total cost for selected survivors of neonatal intensive care in a Boston hospital to range from $14,600 to $40,700 (Kaufman, Shepard, 1982:

172), for long-term survivors in a Washington, D.C., pediatric hospital to be $182,500 for a year (Battle, 1987: 422), and for extremely low birthweight survivors of NICUs in six medical centers to range from $72,110 to $524,110, with a mean cost of care per infant of $158,000 for 137 days (Hack, Fanaroff, 1986: 660; Hack, Fanaroff, 1989: 1642).

A third factor has been the increased recognition that the financial pressures created by expensive neonatal and pediatric treatment can greatly damage and sometimes destroy families (Strong, 1983: 168; Lyon, 1985: 237). For example, a 1988 Minnesota follow-up study of disabled infants and their families had a number of disturbing findings: the proportion of families who have young children but lack health insurance is increasing; 16 percent of the families in the study pay the entire cost of their health insurance; middle-income families have not qualified for state financial assistance; several of the families have filed for bankruptcy; and at least one family still owes the hospital and physicians over $300,000 for the care of their young child. The report concludes: "Families should not have to lose their homes, mortgage their future, or neglect other children's needs to pay for the care of a chronically ill or disabled child" (Van Allen, et al., 1988: 3).

A related but different factor has to do with the long-term costs of providing medical, nursing, and surgical care for severely disabled children who remain in hospitals for months and years. Sometimes called "boarder babies," these children have complicated, chronic medical conditions, are usually dependent on mechanical ventilation and other technological assistance for survival, and frequently come from low-income, single-parent families that simply cannot afford (in terms of money and time) to have the child at home.

If no other institutional home can be arranged (usually because of the cost and technology involved), and if foster parents are not a realistic option, such children may reside for several years in a specialized chronic-care unit in the hospital in which they were born. When that happens, the children become living symbols of a second-generation type of problem brought about by the successes of neonatal intensive care: they are survivors of the NICU, but remain captives of medical technology in an institution that nobody would choose to call home. They also become the focal point for an ongoing debate among health professionals about the justifiability of the high costs required to keep them alive.

Given the uncertainty generated by these variables, what should be done? For two of the ethical positions described earlier, the answer is reasonably simple: revise or ignore the federal regulations; abate life-sustaining treatment more quickly on the basis of (1) parental discretion or (2) projected quality of life for the neonates involved (including the impact of a neonate's later life on others); and thus cut down on the costs in NICUs, to families, and to institutions.

To go that way, for that reason, would be a mistake. The economic aspects of neonatal intensive care would become a dominant factor in decision making by parents and physicians, and many premature and disabled neonates would have their lives cut short to save money. To establish a policy that would encourage parents to make life-and-death decisions in individual cases as a money-saving strategy for themselves (or for physicians to do the same to save money for their hospitals) is not the best way to address the very real problem of escalating costs for neonatal intensive care, especially if that policy is to be guided by the ethical principles of beneficence, nonmaleficence, and justice.

There is, in my judgment, a better alternative. That alternative is a combination of (1) continued use of the patient's-best-interests standard in clinical settings, including increased emphasis on the eight variables that comprise the standard, (2) the establishment of a national policy, based on sound clinical evidence, that would restrict the use of neonatal intensive care in terms of infants' birthweights, and (3) the establishment of a national health insurance program that would pay for the catastrophic health-care expenses generated by caring for extremely premature and severely disabled newborns.

The results of this combined approach would be threefold. A more consistent application of the best-interests standard would result in an increased number of decisions, as difficult as they are, by parents and physicians to discontinue life-sustaining treatment in individual cases. Such decisions would not be made to save money, but would be based on an honest conclusion that the treatment available, although capable of sustaining a neonate's life, is contrary to the infant's best interests.

In addition, the establishment of a national policy that would limit life-sustaining treatment to neonates over a certain birthweight (e.g., 600 g) would not only cut down on the enormously high costs of caring for extremely low birthweight infants, but could also be defended, depending on the rationale and details of the policy, as meeting the requirements of justice. Such a policy would surely not solve all of the problems of uncertainty in NICUs, but could provide a measure of greater certainty, if based on a consensus among neonatologists, in establishing a minimum weight limit for neonates who would be given life-sustaining treatment.

Finally, by establishing a national insurance program, the federal government would help pay for the enormous costs that are involved in neonatal intensive care and specialized chronic-care units for young children. For the federal government to mandate that virtually all neonates, unless dying or permanently unconscious, be kept alive and then to make no serious effort to help parents and institutions pay for that expensive care is unjust. In the absence of such a program, parents and physicians will continue to be faced with the task of making life-and-death decisions for newborns in the midst of great uncertainty – including whether the family will be destroyed financially by costs of the medical care.

Note

* An expanded version of this paper was published in Arthur L Caplan, Robert H Blank, and Janna C Merrick, eds. Compelled Compassion: Government Intervention in the Treatment of Critically Ill Newborns. Totowa, N J.: Humana Press, 1992: 1–33.

References

American Nurses' Association. Guidelines on Withdrawing or Withholding Food and Fluid, 1988.

Bartholome WG. Contested terrain: in the best interest of . . . Hastings Cent Rep 1988; 18: 39–40.

Battle CU. Obligations to the survivors of technology. In: Clinics in Perinatology. Tomas J Silber, ed. Philadelphia: WB Saunders, 1987; 14: 419–25.

Benjamin M. The newborn's interest in continued life: a sentimental fiction. Bioethics Rep 1983; 5–7.

Berki SE, NB Schneier. Frequency and cost of diagnosis-related group outliers among newborns. Pediatr 1987; 79: 874–81.

Boyle MH, et al. Economic evaluation of neonatal intensive care of very-low-birth-weight infants. N Engl J Med 1983; 308: 1330–37.

Brody H. Contested terrain: in the best interests of . . . Hastings Cent Rep 1988; 18: 37–39.

Budetti P, et al. Case Study #10: The Costs and Effectiveness of Neonatal Intensive Care. Washington DC: Office of Technology Assessment, 1981.

Department of Health and Human Services. Child abuse and neglect prevention and treatment program. Federal Register 1985; 50: 14878–901.

Engelhardt H, Tristram Jr. The Foundations of Bioethics. New York: Oxford University Press, 1986.

Feinberg J. Abortion. In: Matters of Life and Death. Tom Regan, ed. New York: Random House 1986, 256–92.

Frader J. Forgoing life-sustaining food and water: newborns. In: By No Extraordinary Means. Joanne Lynn, ed. Bloomington: Indiana University Press 1986; 180–85.

Goldman GM, K Stratton, M Douglas Brown. What actually happened: an informed review of the linares incident. Law Med Health Care 1989; 17: 298–307.

Gostin L. Editor's introduction: family privacy and persistent vegetative state. Law Med Health Care 1989; 17: 295–97.

Hack M, AA Fanaroff. Changes in the delivery room care of the extremely small infant: effects on morbidity and outcome. N Engl J Med 1986; 314: 660–64.

Hack M, AA Fanaroff. Outcomes of extremely low-birth-weight infants between 1982 and 1988. N Engl J Med 1989; 321: 1642–47.

Jecker NS. Commentary: the moral status of patients who are not strict persons. J Clin Ethics 1990; 1: 35–38.

Jonsen A, M Siegler, WJ Winslade. Clinical Ethics. New York: Macmillan Publishing Company, 1986.

Kaufman SL, D Shepard. Costs of neonatal intensive care by day of stay. Inquiry 1982; 19: 167–78.

Kopelman LM, T Irons, A Kopelman. Neonatologists judge the 'baby doe' regulations. N Engl Journal of Med 1988; 318: 677–83.

Lichtig LK et al. Revising diagnosis-related groups for neonates. Pediatr 1989; 84: 49–61.

Lyon J. Playing God in the Nursery. New York: WW Norton and Company, 1985.

McCormick RA. The best interests of the baby. Second Opinion 1986; 2: 18–25.

Marshall PB et al. The cost of intensive and special care of the newborn. Med J Aust 1989; 150: 568–73.

Murray TH. Why solutions continue to elude us. Soc Sci Med 1985; 20: 1102–7.

Paris JJ, AB Fletcher. Withholding of nutrition and fluids in the hopelessly ill patient. In: Clinics in Perinatology. TJ Silber, ed. Philadelphia: WB Saunders 1987: 367–77.
Paris JJ, RK Crone, F Reardon. Physicians' refusal of requested treatment: the case of baby l. N Engl J Med 1990; 322: 1012–15.
Perkins RL. Abortion: Pro and Con. Cambridge, Mass.: Schenkman Publishing Company, 1974.
President's Commission for the Study of Ethical Problems in Medicine and Biomedical and Behavioral Research. Deciding to Forego Life-Sustaining Treatment. Washington, DC: US Government Printing Office, 1983.
Singer P. Practical Ethics. Cambridge: Cambridge University Press, 1979.
Strong C. Defective infants and their impact on families: ethical and legal considerations. Law, Med Health Care 1983; 11: 168–81.
Todres D, et al. Life-saving therapy for newborns: a questionnaire survey in the state of Massachusetts. Pediatr 1988; 81: 643–49.
Tooley M. Abortion and infanticide. Philosophy and Public Affairs 1972; 2: 37–65.
Tooley M. Decisions to terminate life and the concept of person. In: Ethical Issues Relating to Life and Death. John Ladd, ed. New York: Oxford University Press, 1979: 62–93.
Tooley M. Abortion and Infanticide. New York: Oxford University Press, 1983.
Warren MA. On the moral and legal status of abortion. Monist 1973; 57: 43–61.
Weir RF. Abating Treatment with Critically Ill Patients. New York: Oxford University Press, 1989.
Weir RF. Selective Nontreatment of Handicapped Newborns. New York: Oxford University Press, 1984.
Weir RF. Selective nontreatment – one year later: reflections and response. Soc Sci Med 1985; 20: 1109–17.
Weir RF. When is it justifiable not to treat? Second Opinion 1986; 2: 42–61.
Weir RF, JF Bale Jr. Selective nontreatment of neurologically impaired neonates. In: Neurologic Clinics. JL Bernat, ed. Philadelphia: WB Saunders 1989; 7: 807–22.
Young EWD, DK Stevenson. Limiting treatment for extremely premature, low-birth-weight infants (500 to 750 g). Ame J Dis Chil 1990; 144: 549–52.

LORETTA M. KOPELMAN

When is Medical Treatment Futile?

A recent article about an infant identified only as Baby L (Paris, 1990a) caused sharp differences about whether treatment had been futile: Baby L's condition had been so grave and her prognosis for survival so poor that her doctors and nurses tried to convince her mother that maximal life-support treatment was futile. Her mother, however, insisted that it was not futile, and that Baby L must receive heroic treatment. The doctors and nurses refused. Another facility and physician eventually took over her care and Baby L survived. Years later, this child is blind, deaf, and quadriplegic with an arrested developmental stage of a three-month-old. To some this outcome vindicates the original physicians' judgment that treatment was futile and not in Baby L's best interest; to others it justifies the belief that it was not futile because, unexpectedly, the infant survived (Paris, 1990a; Paris, 1990b; Grodin, 1990; Lantos, 1990; Murphy, 1990b).

When is the continuation of medical treatments futile or virtually futile? The answers to these questions require judgments that play key roles in many health-care treatment choices, allocation decisions, and policies. I will argue that all medical judgments about futility, to count as *medical*, use stable scientific data to justify their probability claims. But to be about *futility*, medical judgments must adopt some goal in order to say how or in what way the treatment is futile. While their scientific or medical component is well recognized, too little attention has been given to their value components. A value is something of importance for some goal, whether a moral, social, political, or self-interested purpose. Values are often obvious and clearly noncontroversial. But in the complex judgments surrounding life-and-death decisions in medicine, it can be especially important to identify and justify the value components.

I will show that value, or moral, judgments are incorporated into medical assessments about futility in several different ways: (1) in the *goals selected* to judge the way in which something is futile, (2) in the way the *data is collected*, such as what population to consider, (3) in the way the *data is used*, such as in how the line is drawn between required and optimal treat-

F.K. Beller and R.F. Weir (eds.), The Beginning of Human Life, 371–381.

ments, and (4) in clarifying how futility and virtual futility are *related to nonverified, experimental, or innovative treatments*.

Discussion of the issues will also show that moral or value judgments play a role in fundamental research and treatment methodology. This should undercut the belief that medicine is about facts alone, and that values enter into considerations independently of its findings. The dangers of not being clear about these points will be illustrated by the current, ill-considered U.S. federal "Baby Doe" regulations (DHHS, 1985). These regulations preselect an overriding goal of biological survival in considering whether treatments for sick infants are futile or virtually futile.

Different Goals

In this section I want to show that judgments about futility must be made in relation to some goal(s), and that these judgments are value judgments; they may be moral, social, or even political values, aims, designs, or purposes. Medical judgments about futility are distinguishable because they tend to appeal to professionally defined goals, such as trying to relieve pain, and because they rely upon professional standards on how stable scientific data must support the claims being made.

The obvious way to account for the controversy about Baby L is that different people used different goals to assess futility. If the goal is biological survival, then treatments for Baby L were not futile. They *were* futile, however, if the goal of prolonged support was a survivor with a better outcome than Baby L had.

The goal of prolonging biological life is unquestionably a central and important goal in medicine, but there are many other goals and values that are part of the internal morality of the medical and nursing traditions. These include seeking to provide the best available care, relieve suffering, prevent unnecessary pain, reduce morbidity and mortality, distribute resources fairly, and respect the wishes of patients and their families. Unfortunately these goals sometimes conflict, and we have to decide which will be the most important and for what reason. In the case of Baby L, some doctors and nurses believed that biological survival was the overriding goal, and some did not.

Using the same stable data, then, an action can be futile for one purpose but not for another. What is futile for aggressive care might be important for comfort care. Comfort care allows different treatment than aggressive life-prolonging care. If the goal is comfort care, a child might receive more pain medication or more time being held by family and friends, or time outside the intensive care unit, perhaps to sit with his or her family in the sunshine. Moreover, procedures that are futile for prolonging biological life in any meaningful way might not be futile for another purpose. Suppose the family had wanted Baby L to receive maximal treatment for a short time so that the extended family could gather for the baby's death. The treatments that are futile to prolong biological life may have great symbolic and emotional value to patients, families, or caregivers. Concern for the family and its needs might justify continuing futile treatments, at least for a short time. In some cases, however, the desire to continue futile treatments represents denial of imminent death, or an unreasonable desire to prove that family or caregivers have "done everything" or "not given up." This can create problems when the procedure is painful, expensive, or scarce, as well as futile.

Thus, what is futile for one purpose need not be futile for another. We might reasonably have different goals for treating people whose biological conditions are similar but whose circumstances are otherwise different. One reason why consent is important is that people come to understand the design of the treatment, and whether they agree with its aims.

The current U.S. "Baby Doe" regulations (DHHS, 1985) preselect the treatment goal for very sick infants and thus determine what treatments are futile (Kopelman, 1988). According to these rules, maximal life-support therapy may be withheld or withdrawn from extremely sick newborn infants *only* if the treatment would be "virtually futile in terms of survival" and therefore inhumane. In addition, maximal treatment is not required if the infant is irreversibly comatose. However, it is extremely difficult (some say impossible) to make the diagnosis of irreversible coma in the newborn period (Coulter, 1987). Thus, the comatose condition is *unusable*. The regulations also state that maximal treatment is not required if it would only "prolong dying . . . or be otherwise futile in terms of the survival of the infant." This is little different from saying that the treatment would be "virtually futile in terms of survival of the infant." If anything it is *more restrictive*, in that it must also be shown that the infant is dying and that the treatment is actually futile. In practice, therefore, using the Baby Doe regulations to stop or withhold maximal treatments requires showing that the treatment in question is virtually futile in terms of survival of the infant. Hence, I will focus simply upon virtual futility in terms of survival in discussing when the Baby Doe guidelines permit withholding or stopping medical treatments.

The goal preselected by the U.S. federal Baby Doe regulations, then, is that in order to stop or withdraw heroic care, treatments must be *virtually futile in terms of survival*. In light of these rules, Baby L's treatment was not futile; therefore, it was required. The Baby Doe regulations take the duty to prolong biological life to be more important than comfort care, relief of suffering, parental wishes, cost, resource allocation, and the needs of others. The rules, for example, recognize no duties to those outside hospital walls who cannot get care because facilities are being used for infants who may not survive but who consume large amounts of resources. Moreover, the cut-off for considering what is futile leaves little room for differences of opinion on ranking values such as prolonging biological life, relief of pain, or resource allocation. Short of the cut-off of virtual futility, the rules hold that maximal treatments must be provided. The Baby Doe regulations do not, however, acknowledge that they have preselected moral or social goals nor do they justify them. They imply that the relevant judgments are medical. In short, *the Baby Doe regulations preselect goals by a forced ranking of values, and they radically restrict standard medical practice because they preselect one goal, biological survival, as the most important.*

A survey my colleagues and I conducted of U.S. neonatologists found that the preselection of biological life as the only goal for judging futility is believed to lead to overtreatment, poor use of resources, and insufficient attention to suffering (Kopelman, 1988). Some criticized our results, however, arguing that neonatologists were likely to dislike regulations that restricted their autonomy; that neonatologists were inappropriately pessimistic about the prognosis of severely sick and handicapped infants, since they do not work with older children; that they probably did not understand the Baby Doe rules; and that the rules, properly understood, are innocuous since they permit any reasonable medical judgment (Freeman, 1988).

Let me respond to these charges. First, it seems unlikely that the responding neonatologists did not understand the rules since the key portions were written on the survey; respondents could study the regulations as they responded to our survey. Second, it cannot be said that the study showed merely the protests of neonatologists who fail to understand about older children because pediatricians who were not neonatologists responded similarly (Kopelman, 1991); pediatricians are familiar with outcomes for older children and cannot be accused of being unrealistically pessimistic about their prognoses. (In addition, the regulations do *not* restrict *their* practice of medicine.) Third, it is mistaken to believe that the Baby Doe rules permit any reasonable medical judgment. The Baby Doe rules permit only a reasonable medical judgment that the rules have been fulfilled. (This flexibility may have been the intention of *some* of those who drafted the final rules, but this is not what the rules say.) Comfort care or triage is not permitted unless it is compatible with maximal treatment, or unless maximal treatment is not obligatory because it is virtually futile.

The following additional data, collected at the time of our original survey, show that both neonatologists and pediatricians are critical of the Baby Doe regulations, and for similar reasons (Kopelman, 1991). The responses of the neonatologists are from 494 (49%) of the members of the Perinatal-Pediatric Section of the American Academy of Pediatrics, all of whom had received a survey. The responses of the pediatricians are from a randomly selected sampling of 3,000 non-neonatologist pediatricians supplied to us by the American Academy of Pediatrics; 730 (25%) responded (Kopelman, 1991). ("BDR-II" refers to the current "Baby Doe" rules [DHHS, 1985].)

1. The BDR-II will result in improved care for all infants:

	% Agree	% Uncertain	% Disagree
Neonatologists	5	14	81
Other pediatricians	6	16	78

2. The BDR-II was needed to protect the rights of handicapped infants:

	% Agree	% Uncertain	% Disagree
Neonatologists	14	10	76
Other pediatricians	20	12	67

3. The BDR-II will not affect parental rights to consent for or refuse treatment based upon what is in the infant's best interest:

	% Agree	% Uncertain	% Disagree
Neonatologists	19	15	66
Other pediatricians	19	17	65

4. The BDR-II allows adequate consideration of suffering:

	% Agree	% Uncertain	% Disagree
Neonatologists	29	11	60
Other pediatricians	30	14	56

5. Most critically ill infants are overtreated when the chances for their survival are very poor:

	% Agree	% Uncertain	% Disagree
Neonatologists	56	13	31
Other pediatricians	62	18	19

The respondents evaluated three cases of critically ill and profoundly cognitively impaired infants with a poor prognosis for survival. The neonatologists agreed overwhelmingly (75–86%) about what was in the child's best interest. But in those same three cases up to a third perceived a conflict between their duty to act in the infant's best interest and the legal requirement to act in accordance with the BDR-II. In each case, too, there was a significant difference ($p \leqq 0.001$) in their responses to what was the best way to take care of these infants and what the BDR-II required. The pediatricians' responses were similar, with the exception of one of the three cases (case 3). Even more pediatricians (66%) than neonatologists believed infants are overtreated in NICUs.

Thus, according to both the neonatologists and pediatricians who responded to our survey, the Baby Doe regulations restrict parental and medical discretion in trying to select the best treatment plans for very sick infants. The Baby Doe regulations do not acknowledge or justify their preselected, controversial moral goal. Neonatologists and pediatricians do not regard it to be in the best interest of infants to establish the single goal of prolonging life as a basis from which to judge futility.

It is not the mere fact that they agree, of course, that is important, but that their reasons are defensible, and that they are knowledgeable people committed to the children's well-being. Furthermore, their reasons match those of the Supreme Court in its rejection of an earlier set of Baby Doe regulations (Bowen, 1986; Kopelman, 1988). The agreement between medical experts in infant care and care for older children and legal experts is a powerful argument that the Baby Doe guidelines are faulty (Kopelman, 1991).

Judgments about medical futility, I have argued, cannot be value-free scientific claims about probabilities. To justify them, therefore, we need to defend the goals used to judge futility. These goals, we have noted, are usually one or more of the traditional goals that comprise the internal morality of the medical and nursing professions, such as prolonging biological life, relieving suffering, or distributing goods and services fairly. These goals, however, can conflict, and we may not agree about which to rank as most important. When this happens, the moral, social, or even political aspects of the judgments about medical futility need to be identified and defended.

Collecting Data

There is a second way in which value judgments must enter assessments about medical futility. In order to collect data we have to identify certain things as important or valuable for some purpose. This means there is no possibility of value-free science. Some hold that medical judgments about futility are *basic* scientific or value-free judgments about outcomes for groups. What this view ignores, however, is that many kinds of value or normative judgments are necessarily required in determining the population that is used in making any probability claims (Kopelman, 1989, 1990). Values are used in selecting tests and in picking criteria for inclusion in test groups.

For example, suppose one wants to know the mortality and morbidity of premature infants. One can change the results dramatically by changing the definition of "premature infant." The results look better if one includes larger babies, worse if one restricts the group to smaller infants. Grouping together all premature infants (however defined) would not show that extremely low birthweight infants have high mortality and morbidity rates when compared to larger infants. Someone interested in treating all infants aggressively might resist singling out the lowest-birthweight infants. In contrast, someone interested in showing that these very small premature infants do badly, cost more, and have poorer outcomes might wish to gather data on the smallest infants. This is not to say, of course, that people always have ulterior motives. How we select our groups is not an arbitrary matter, however, but is done in terms of what we consider important or value considerations.

USING DATA

Third, even when we agree about how we arrived at the stable data, we can disagree about the importance (value) of using the results for some purpose. Thus, we can still come to different judgments about when treatments are futile or virtually futile. Let me illustrate this.

According to some reports, the United States provides far more aggressive treatment for its extremely low birthweight infants than do England and Sweden (Rhoden, 1986). These three countries draw upon the same stable evidence and research data. They also define extremely low birthweight infants in the same way, as under 700–750 grams. The more aggressively infants in this group are treated, the greater the cost and the greater the likelihood of infants surviving with extremely serious morbidity. In Sweden infants weighing less than 700 g are not routinely offered maximal life support. In contrast to U.S. and Swedish practice, in England individualized treatment plans are adopted depending upon the particular infant's condition. It costs England more to take care of this group of infants than it does Sweden, and there is more resulting morbidity in England. In turn, in England the cost of caring for these infants is less than in the U.S.; fewer survive, and there is less serious morbidity from the treatments. To summarize:

For infants under 700 g

	Treatment	Cost	Mortality	Morbidity
Sweden	rarely given	low	high	low
England	individualized	medium	medium	medium
U.S.	given	high	low	high

Thus, three different countries using roughly the same scientific base and population have arrived at three different policies. Each is a balancing act between acceptable outcomes, resources, and costs. There are differences as well in the social support for infants who survive with serious handicaps, and of course many in the group do have such problems. Pediatricians and neonatologists in our survey of the Baby Doe regulations were critical of the U.S. for requiring maximal treatment but failing to provide funds for long-term care (Kopelman, 1988; Kopelman, 1991).

Claims about medical futility thus are more than probabilities. They are judgments about how to use the data, and these judgments require the use of values (aims, goals, plans, or designs). Suppose, for example, that only 6% of infants in some group will survive after five months of NICU treatment: Is that treatment virtually futile? Is it virtually futile if 1% survive this course of treatment, and many survivors have severe neurological damage? Is survival of .001% virtually futile? What if it would take a full year of maximal treatment that is burdensome and painful to have 1% of the infants survive.

Is that virtually futile? If non-virtually-futile treatment is required, the other 99% will pay a heavy price in anguish and suffering. The cut-off used might reflect our views about how fair it is to the other non-surviving infants to require the burdensome treatment. Adults would balk at such a requirement, and infants deserve equal protection. If it is wrong to do to others what we would not have done to ourselves, then it is wrong to prolong biological life and not consider the burden of the treatments.

Some may respond that there is a useable, well-established, value-free, scientific cut-off to distinguish between futile and nonfutile treatments. Physicians like to use the 5% out-off, and many regard it as a scientific, not moral, standard. If they are correct, this cut-off may be understood as follows: If the chances are less than 5% that the infant will survive with maximal treatment, then that treatment is virtually futile, according to this view.

However justified the 5% standard may be, it is not value free because this standard is really a moral judgment. In research this standard is typically an estimate about how long it is thought morally appropriate to continue a controlled trial. This standard is not value-free, but is a moral trade-off. If one continues the study too long, some are likely to receive what is increasingly known to be suboptimal care. If one does not continue the study long enough to get reliable results, then either good therapies may be discarded or bad therapies adopted (Wikler, 1981; Kopelman, 1986). There is, then, a moral trade-off about the cut-off for judging the futility of treatments.

Related Concepts

Fourth, moral or value judgments must be used to clarify how treatments that are called futile or virtually futile can be distinguished from the related concepts of "nonverified," "experimental," and "innovative" treatments.

There is a continuum between ideal therapy and futile "therapy":

Ideal Therapy

Standard

Innovative

Experimental

Unverified

Futile "Therapy"

Between them are standard, innovative, and experimental therapy at the one end, and futile "therapy" at the other. A wide range of unverified therapies stretches between. *Where do we put "virtually futile" therapies?* If one must provide all but virtually futile treatments, as the Baby Doe rules state, does this mean one must run through all the standard, innovative, experimental, last-ditch, and unverified therapies as a matter of legal obligation before one can withhold or withdraw treatments? This startling, counterintuitive question is yet another proof of the ill-considered nature of the Baby Doe requirement. It would be extremely troubling to suppose that physicians must engage in experimental, unverified, or last-ditch treatments where there is no evidence of efficacy or safety, and where no laboratory justification exists. Furthermore, such a requirement would violate policies that require approval and consent for experimental treatments and rules for the use of unverified treatments.

To conclude, I have tried to show how values are part of judgments about medical futility. First, values in the form of goals must be used to indicate how or in what way something is futile. In medicine and nursing these goals are often moral aims about prolonging life, relieving suffering, and distributing goods and services fairly. Sometimes these goals are controversial. The U.S. Baby Doe regulations were severely and, I believe, deservedly criticized by U.S. neonatologists and pediatricians for restricting the goals that could be selected in considering whether treatment is futile or virtually futile. Second, values are used in selecting tests and study populations in order to produce the data used as a basis for the medical judgment that something is futile. Third, the interpretation or use of the data is also value-laden. Moral, social, and even political aims are often apparent in the ways treatment thresholds are chosen. Finally, nonmedical, nonscientific assessments must be used in saying when a procedure should be regarded as a futile treatment as opposed to a standard, experimental, innovative, or unverified treatment. Often the key value component in a medical judgment about futility is one of several moral goals associated with the internal morality of medicine and nursing. The normative character of these judgments, I believe, has been largely ignored in the many discussions about futility. But they need to be identified and justified. The Baby Doe regulations, for example, incorporate moral and perhaps political goals, but fail to either acknowledge or justify them. The results are an unfortunate policy, and I believe that the views of pediatricians and neonatologists support my conclusion.

Judgments about medical futility cause controversies and dilemmas if we do not deal with their dual nature of science and values. As we have seen, not everyone agrees about how to make or use these judgments. Given their scientific basis, it seems imprudent to say that the judgments of physicians and nurses that further treatment of an infant is futile can always be overridden by parental demands. On the other hand, given our disagreements about their moral basis, it would seem to undercut the role of parental consent if professionals can entirely manage the options. In some life-and-death situations, there are genuine disagreements about which treatments are futile. Parents generally want to be told, for example, that professionals in the particular unit in which their infant is a patient have made a certain judgment about futility, or that they plan to discontinue treatments the parents have come to expect. Imagine their shock if they were to discover that someone had, without their knowledge, written do-not-resuscitate (DNR) orders for their child. On the other hand, if unreasonable parents are allowed to overrule professional assessments about the futility of treatments on their infant, the infant may suffer as high technology medicine is continued. Furthermore, it seems both unreasonable and unjust to give in to parental requests for futile "treatments" when the treatments are costly, painful, or scarce.

One way to help solve these dilemmas is to acknowledge fully the dual nature of judgments about medical futility. There should be a way to overrule patients or parents who demand procedures that either will not work or cannot work, or where third-party payers have previously set limits about the use of costly and scarce resources. Making a public policy about the use of resources gives us a chance to review and consider it, and minimizes the chance of being held hostage to unreasonable demands. Moreover, physicians and nurses have no duty to perform procedures that cannot work. These procedures by definition are not therapy since, by definition, in therapy one believes one acts in the patient's best interest. On the other hand, we need to recognize that even in the most uniform societies, we have different moral goals and differences of opinion about values. Some people are prepared to suffer more than others at the end of their lives in order to obtain longer biological survival. What seems immoral is to deny the importance of suffering as a consideration in making decisions about the well-being of infants, when most of us believe it to be of crucial importance in making decisions about ourselves. Infants deserve the same range of value considerations we want, and the right to have surrogates make reasonable medical decisions for them based upon what is in their best interest.

REFERENCES

Coulter DL. Neurological uncertainty in newborn intensive care. N Engl J Med 1987; 316: 840–4.

Department of Health and Human Services (DHHS). The child abuse and treatment amendments of 1984 (Public Law 98–457).

Fed Regist 1985; 50: 14878–901 (Referred to as BDR-II).

Freeman JM. The "Baby Doe" Regulations [letter]. N Engl J Med 1988; 319: 726.

Grodin MA. The case of Baby L [letter]. N Engl J Med 1990; 323(16): 1148.

Kopelman LM, Irons TG, Kopelman AE. Neonatologists judge the "Baby Doe" regulations. N Engl J Med 1988; 318: 677–683.

Kopelman LM. Moral problems in psychiatry. In: Medical Ethics. Robert Veatch, ed. Boston, MA: Jones and Bartlett Publishing Co, 1989: 253–290.

Kopelman LM. On the evaluative nature of competency and capacity judgments. Int J Law Psychiatry 1990 Fall; 13: 4: 309–329.

Kopelman LM, Kopelman AE, and Irons TG. Neonatologists, pediatricians and the Supreme Court judge the "Baby Doe" regulations harshly. (Forthcoming).

Lantos JD. The case of Baby L [letter]. N Engl J Med 1990; 323(16): 1148.

Murphy DJ, Matchar DB. Life-sustaining therapy: a model for appropriate use. JAMA 1990a; 264(16): 2103–2108.

Murphy DJ. The case of Baby L [letter]. N Engl J Med 1990b; 323(16): 1148.
Paris JJ, Crone RK, Reardon F. Physician's refusal of requested treatment: the case of Baby L. N Engl J Med 1990a; 322(14): 1012–1015.
Paris JJ, Crone RK, Reardon F. The case of Baby L [letter]. N Engl J Med 1990b; 323(16): 1148–1149.
Rhoden NK. Treating Baby Doe: the ethics of uncertainty. Hastings Cent Rep 1986 August; 16: 34–42.
U.S. Supreme Court, Otis Bowen v. American Hospital Association, et al., 106 S. Ct. 2101 No 84–15–9, June 9, 1986.
Wikler D. Ethical considerations in randomized clinical trials. Seminars Oncol 1981: 437–441.

ELIZABETH M. SCHMIDT

Treatment Decisions for Premature and Disabled Newborns: Hard Cases Make Bad Law

Among the many difficult questions the American legal system has attempted to tackle in the last twenty years, one of the most perplexing is whether the decision to withhold or withdraw medical treatment from selected premature or disabled infants should ever be legal. To date, a handful of cases,[1] a federal statute,[2] several state statutes,[3] and regulations from the Department of Health and Human Services[4] have addressed the issue. Despite these attempts to achieve a just resolution, the law remains ambiguous, confusing, and even contradictory. The response to this confusion among legal commentators has been to promote further legislation.[5]

This paper maintains that legislation cannot resolve such a complex dilemma. Every legislative proposal, ranging from that which would outlaw most nontreatment decisions to that which would allow parents and medical personnel almost unrestricted discretion, has similar, inevitable flaws. First, these legislative proposals attempt to resolve a problem with undefined dimensions. Second, they attempt to resolve a problem so fraught with unresolved moral questions that their implementation will lead to social unrest. Third, the nature of this problem – its complexities, uncertainties, and changing nature – makes it a difficult one to fit within the goals of the American legislative system – clarity, consistency, and predictability. Unless and until consensus exists about the scope of the problem and its moral resolution, legislation will fail.

The American public needs time to define the scope of the infant nontreatment problem and to work toward building a consensus before legislative resolutions are written in stone.[6] In the meantime, the American judicial system can continue to resolve the occasional disputes that come before the courts, relying on general child neglect laws. Although judicial resolution of nontreatment decisions poses most of the difficulties described above, it has the advantage of dealing with the complexities of specific cases rather than trying to resolve a myriad of complex situations at once. If the courts are used sparingly, our society may have time to work out these difficult problems without the rancor and disregard for the law that would likely accompany premature legislation. While inconsistency and uncertainty will

F.K. Beller and R.F. Weir (eds.), The Beginning of Human Life, 383–398.

continue, they are a necessary price to pay while society works toward a consensus.[7]

DIFFICULTIES WITH LEGISLATION

Until the mid 1980s, the legal response to nontreatment decisions for premature and disabled newborns came in the form of occasional litigation. The cases were inconsistent, sometimes ordering treatment for infants in which the medical prognosis was dismal,[8] and other times allowing parents not to treat infants when the problem was relatively minor.[9] In the face of this inconsistency, legal commentators have called for legislation to clarify the law.

Legislation became a viable option after the 1982 Baby Doe case in Bloomington, Indiana. In that case a juvenile court determined that parents need not provide surgery for a child born with both Down syndrome and an esophageal fistula.[10] The child died. The case galvanized the Reagan administration right-to-life advocates and the disability lobbies, who worked together to produce two federal responses to the case. The first was to promulgate regulations interpreting § 504 of the Rehabilitation Act of 1973 as forbidding most nontreatment decisions because they discriminated against infants on the basis of their handicap.[11] These regulations faced widespread hostility, and in 1986 the United States Supreme Court invalidated their restrictive provisions.[12]

The second response, the Child Abuse Amendments of 1984,[13] ostensibly forbid the withholding of medically indicated treatment from infants facing life-threatening conditions. These amendments allow nontreatment decisions in only the most narrowly defined circumstances: when the infant is dying, irreversibly comatose, or in such a condition that treatment would be futile.[14] Despite the narrow language, this rule does not apply to parents, physicians, or hospitals. It merely requires states seeking federal child abuse funding to adopt procedures for responding to reports of medical neglect.[15]

The Child Abuse Amendments remain in effect today. They are widely criticized[16] and ignored, however.[17] This paper argues that such a response was inevitable – and that a similar response could be expected for any other legislative proposal, whatever its political thrust.

The Definition of a Complex Problem

Legislation is generally proposed and enacted as a response to a social problem. With respect to medical treatment decisions for infants, legislative proposals respond to two opposing perceptions of the same problem. The "conservative" response, the one that helped foster the 1984 Child Abuse Amendments, perceives a pattern of abuse that kills many innocent infants each year. The "liberal" response, which proposes wide discretion for the decisionmaker, perceives a pattern of overtreatment that subjects infants to a torturous existence as victims of medical technology. Compromise proposals try to protect against both types of abuse.

Statistics are not available to help us understand which point of view, if either, correctly perceives the problem. In fact, agreement does not exist on which statistics are relevant. Should one include statistics about every illness or condition that is potentially life-threatening, including the common cold? Should every decision about every possible treatment be included? If not, which conditions, illnesses, or decisions are relevant?

Even if agreement existed on the relevant statistics, gathering the data would be practically impossible, for this decision is a silent one. Decisions not to treat are often made surreptitiously, and those who decide to go ahead with treatment would probably not admit, even to themselves, that nontreatment was considered and rejected.[18] Although one could extrapolate statistics from the occasional article in medical journals describing the practice of one hospital, it is unreasonable to generalize from those anecdotal observations because practices vary so widely among hospitals and physicians.[19] One could also draw statistics from polls of doctors,[20] but, by their nature, the questions are vague and polls about beliefs do not necessarily explain actions. Statistics concerning serious medical problems of infants and the rate of death for those problems are available,[21] but they do not indicate whether a nontreatment decision contributed to the death.

Finally, even if the decisions could be defined and documented, disagreement would exist about which decisions were in fact abusive. The same decision could be either abusive or compassionate, depending on one's value system. The statistics documenting the extent of a problem invariably would reflect the personal values of the statistician.

Thus, both a definition of this complex problem and a documentation of its existence remain elusive. Without definition and documentation, legislation is premature. No one can know whether endangered infants are protected or whether families and hospitals are subjected to unnecessary regulation. Instituting legislation for this infant nontreatment problem could be like using a bomb to kill an ant. The solution creates a strong risk of overkill and an equal risk of missing the problem altogether.

Legislation as a Solution for Unresolved Moral Questions

Perhaps the only area of agreement in this controversial area is that no true agreement exists.[22] The beliefs of both academics and the general public cover a wide spectrum, from those who would regulate every decision to those who would give parents almost unrestricted discretion.[23] These beliefs reflect strongly held moral values. Unfortunately, our legal system is not equipped to resolve such difficult moral problems.

Most legislation either reflects widespread moral agreement or regulates activities that do not bring ethical questions into play. Such legislation is, for the most part, both enforceable and socially accepted. Attempts to regulate unresolved moral problems, however, generate civil disobedience and bitterness instead of ready enforcement and social acceptance.

The abortion issue is a prime example of the problems that accompany legal resolution of an unresolved moral problem. Antiabortion laws first appeared in the United States in the midnineteenth century, amidst widespread agreement that abortion was wrong.[24] Over the years, however, as values shifted, the law was increasingly ignored. In some instances, legislators changed the law in response to changing values,[25] but the 1973 Supreme Court decision legalizing abortion created a legal solution for the issue.[26] Despite the pronouncement from the highest court in the land (or perhaps because of it), the question has not begun to be resolved. After almost twenty years of rallies, sit-ins, lobbying, legislation, and litigation, including several Supreme Court cases,[27] nothing close to a consensus exists.

Infant nontreatment questions are analogous to the abortion question, and to another unresolved question, that of the right to die.[28] Like abortion, nontreatment decisions make us question the meaning of life and who should make decisions about life. The issue is actually more complicated than abortion, however, for a child has been born and attained the undeniable status of person,[29] but its problems are so severe that questions about its survival are asked. Like right-to-die decisions, these decisions make us question the meaning of death and which lives are worth living. Yet they are also more complex than most right-to-die decisions, for an infant can never make its own decision, nor has it lived long enough for a surrogate decisionmaker to know what would be best for this person. It is presumptuous to think that legislation can resolve the dilemma of infant nontreatment decisions when it has been unable to resolve the issues in these two unrelated, but less complicated areas.[30]

In years past, questions with high moral overtones, such as nontreatment decisions, would have been directed to the clergy and philosophers, not legislators and judges. As our society has become secularized, we increasingly have turned away from religion and toward the law to answer difficult questions. Yet the law is not equipped to answer such questions. Although it can regulate behavior when agreement exists over the correctness of that behavior, it cannot define the meaning of life. Without such a definition, any attempt to regulate behavior in this area will encounter widespread resistance. Restrictive regulation will be ignored, and nonrestrictive legislation will create an uproar among those who believe innocent babies are being murdered.[31] This moral ambivalence will also make the task of drafting adequate language for the statute especially difficult.

The Conflict between Legislative Goals and the Complexities of the Problem

Legislation proposed and enacted to resolve this difficult problem is invariably designed to clarify the confusion surrounding the problem, because clarity, predictability, and consistency are prime goals of the legal system. Unfortunately, this particular problem is so complex that it defies these legislative goals.[32] Confusion, inconsistency, and uncertainty will exist whatever solution is imposed.

Substantive Legislation

Line-drawing legislation. Most legislation either draws the line defining the point at which a decisionmaker should be allowed to make a nontreatment decision or provides a standard for determining when such a decision should be made. To a large extent, the Child Abuse Amendments of 1984 take the line-drawing approach. They allow nontreatment decisions in three narrow situations: when the infant is dying, when it is irreversibly comatose, or when the treatment would be futile.[33] The line could be drawn at different points.[34] For example, some doctors propose that infants below a certain birthweight need not receive aggressive treatment,[35] while others describe certain clinical criteria that determine the deciding point.[36]

This type of legislation appears to have several practical advantages for achieving the goals of the legal system. First, it provides objectivity, because it is based on medical diagnoses rather than on an individual decisionmaker's value system. Second, it provides for consistency, because similar cases are treated alike.[37] Thus, one should be able to predict the outcome for an individual case. Finally, if the legislation is drawn carefully, clarity should be achieved.

Unfortunately, the nontreatment decision is so complex that definitional legislation cannot be as clear as it would appear. Over three thousand types of birth defects exist.[38] They appear in varying combinations and with varying degrees of severity. Low birthweight infants without birth defects also face a host of complicated problems.[39] Diagnoses are rarely made with 100 percent clarity, and the prognosis at birth is often uncertain, because the efficacy of a treatment varies with each patient, and long-term studies do not exist to show the efficacy of newer treatments.[40] Erring on the side of treatment is not always the solution, however, because the treatment itself can cause terrible complications.[41] Furthermore, requiring such caution would force babies to endure experimental treatments.[42] This complexity is heightened by the fact that these decisions are not one-time decisions; rather, they are made continually as the infant responds to therapy or develops further complications.[43] Finally, medical progress is ongoing and quickly changing. The categories drawn today may be obsolete tomorrow.

In the face of this complexity, any attempt to draw a line appears simplistic and counterproductive. Like the baseball fanatic who claimed that all disputes at first base could be resolved by moving the base back a step,[44] those who define which illnesses and conditions are severe enough to allow nontreatment decisions only move the arguments to a different plane. The discussion shifts from searching for a solution to responding to a definition.[45] Invariably, the definition does not cover many of the difficult situations, its application to difficult situations is formidable, and even the most carefully drawn definitions will appear ambiguous.[46]

Legislation providing a standard for decisionmaking. If definitional legislation is too simplistic for this complex problem, then perhaps legislation that creates a method for analyzing the problem could provide the necessary flexibility. Three methods have been proposed: determining the quality of the infant's future life, determining the best interests of the infant, and respecting the privacy of the family. The quality-of-life standard allows a decisionmaker to make a nontreatment decision when the infant's quality of life is extremely poor.[47] The best-interest standard allows such a decision when nontreatment would be in the infant's best interests.[48] The privacy standard compares the interests of the state with those of the family to determine whether the state has a sufficient interest to interfere with parental decisionmaking.[49]

These standards have the advantage of providing enough flexibility to handle the complex cases that were neither foreseen nor defined by the legislature.[50] In the process, however, they forfeit other goals of legislation. They are vague and ambiguous. To a large extent, the determination of a child's quality of life or its best interests depends on the values of the decisionmaker. Thus, similar cases will not necessarily be treated alike, and the goals of clarity, precision, and consistency will not be met.

In order to eliminate some of this ambiguity, legislators could define the standards with more precision. The standard could attempt to define the point at which a decision would be unacceptable, or at least give stronger guidelines for measuring the traits described in the standard. Doing so, however, runs the risk of losing the advantages of a broad standard and creating the disadvantages of line-drawing legislation. Whatever one's views about the moral correctness of any of these standards, the practical reality is that the standards are meaningless unless they are defined so carefully that they could be classified as line-drawing legislation, with all its inherent difficulties.

Procedural Legislation

Whenever the legal system finds itself at a loss with regard to substantive standards, the tendency is to provide procedural protections.[51] Such a tendency has appeared with a vengeance in the dilemma surrounding non treatment decisions for premature and disabled newborns. The theory is that, although we cannot determine the exact point at which nontreatment decisions should be legal, we can at least make sure that the decision is made carefully. Procedural proposals include designating the parents as the decisionmakers,[52] requiring hospital ethics committees to review the decisions,[53] and asking the courts to oversee the decisions.[54]

Whatever its other limitations, the American legal system can usually ensure procedural protection. Procedures are appealing because they are easily enforceable, and they do not raise difficult moral questions. Moreover, when no moral consensus exists about the correctness of an action, the legislature is far more likely to succeed at determining *who* should decide what is moral than it is at deciding *what* is moral.

These procedural protections are not the panacea they appear to be, however, for procedural requirements have substantive ramifications even when designed to sidestep substantive issues. Complex procedural requirements will discourage nontreatment decisions, whereas broad discretion to the decision-maker will encourage such decisions. Similarly, several layers of procedural protection will postpone decisions that need to be made quickly, while streamlined procedures could give a distraught and uninformed person the power over life and death.

Using procedural requirements to substitute for substantive ones begs the question. A point exists somewhere at which nontreatment decisions are wrong and should be illegal. Certainly a child born with breathing difficulties that can be solved with a few hours on a ventilator must be treated. If the designated decisionmaker decides against treatment, our society would still want a court to overturn that decision. Thus, procedural requirements must be coupled with substantive ones in order to resolve this problem. We are only fooling ourselves if we try to do otherwise.

Conceptual Problems

Even if legislation with coherent standards and procedures could be enacted, definitions of every concept in the statute would be needed. Especially in an area with this much controversy, the definitions should be precise, because those who disagree with the statute will be searching for ambiguities. Yet with such a controversial problem, the legislators may need broad language in order to gain enough votes to pass the statute.

Whether the language is broad or concise, the concepts behind these decisions often defy definition and distinction. Commentators remark frequently about the difficulties in defining concepts like "ordinary" and "extraordinary" care,[55] or of distinguishing between the removal of a respirator and the removal of nutrition and hydration.[56] Even concepts like "irreversible coma," which seem designed to avoid ambiguity, have definitional problems.[57]

Occasionally, a concept that works well for one nontreatment decision is unworkable in other situations. The first set of regulations promulgated by the Reagan administration[58] were based on the concept of discrimination against the handicapped. Although the Supreme Court invalidated the mandatory sections of these regulations on procedural grounds,[59] their approach could appear again either in regulations or in other legislation. The theory behind these regulations was that discrimination occurs when a nontreatment decision is made for a disabled infant who would have received treatment if it had no disability. This concept works well for a Down syndrome child who has another life-threatening condition such as duodenal atresia, because a child with duodenal atresia and no mental retardation would receive treatment. The concept breaks down in more complicated cases, however. On the one hand, all decisions, even those not to treat anencephalic babies, are based on their handicap. On the other hand, discrimination does not occur unless a similar group of healthy infants is treated differently. Such a comparison is conceptually impossible when an infant has multiple life-threatening disabilities because a "healthy" infant would never need similar treatment.[60]

Such confusion about concepts and definitions in legislation regarding nontreatment decisions is not surprising. The precision necessary for making definitions is impossible to find when neither a definition of the scope of the problem nor agreement as to a moral framework for making the decision exists. The nontreatment dilemma is so new and so morally perplexing that a coherent language for resolving the problem has not yet appeared.[61]

Proposed Remedies

Finally, legislation should include effective remedies or sanctions to enforce its rules. Yet few proposed or enacted statutes dealing with this problem succeed in doing so. The Child Abuse Amendments of 1984 have no teeth. They do not declare abusive nontreatment decisions illegal; rather, they provide a small amount of federal money to states that have procedures for responding to reports of medical neglect.[62] Other proposed statutes fail to mention enforcement mechanisms, or they suggest injunctive relief.[63] This reluctance to provide enforcement mechanisms reflects our societal ambivalence about the problem. However certain those who want to make restrictive legislation are of their moral position, sympathy exists for the families who make the "wrong" decision.[64]

Learning to Live with Legal Uncertainty

A recognition that legislation cannot resolve the dilemma surrounding nontreatment decisions for premature and disabled newborns raises the question of whether the legal system should have any role in these decisions. After all, most of the conceptual and practical problems created by instituting legislation also occur if the problem has a judicial resolution. Courts are no better able to resolve unresolved moral questions than legislatures. Moreover, their standards for resolving the problem are necessarily as ambiguous as any a legislature would apply, for courts' standards are based on analogous situations or on more generalized statutes and are even less precise than standards based on one specific situation that is covered by legislation. Further, decisionmakers' fear of lawsuits often causes them to disregard the infants' interests and worry about their own legal liability.[65]

Yet a total absence of legal regulation would permit decisions that everyone would find abusive, such as the refusal to provide oxygen for an otherwise healthy infant with birth asphyxia. Consensus about correct and incorrect decision *does* exist at the edges. Even the staunchest conservatives recognize that situations exist in which nontreatment decisions are appropriate.[66] And even the most extreme liberals recognize that limitations on parental discretion should exist.[67] This consensus does not cover a wide enough ground to justify legislation, however. For example, a statute limited to legalizing nontreatment decisions for anencephalics and outlawing such decisions for infants who need only a blood transfusion would be useless, because it would give no guidance for most of the cases. The courts, on the other hand, can handle cases at these two extremes without dealing with the middle ground, because courts answer only the particular question asked of them.[68] Thus, the judicial system, if used sparingly, should and could serve the limited function of ratifying societal judgment where consensus does exist and helping to form public opinion in extraordinarily difficult cases.

The courts' function of dealing with particular cases instead of general situations is their prime advantage over legislation. They can deal with the complexities of each case and make decisions based on those factors. Their precedential effect is limited to closely analogous cases in that jurisdiction. Thus, they do not need to resolve the entire complex problem at once.

Courts dealing with nontreatment questions have traditionally relied on child neglect standards to form the basis of their decisions.[69] Although several commentators believe that our laws forbid all nontreatment decisions,[70] these laws actually provide enough flexibility to handle the difficult cases. Traditional child neglect laws, for example, typically require parents to provide their children with necessary medical care.[71] Medical care is almost always "necessary" if the child will die without it.[72] Thus, many nontreatment decisions constitute neglect. Parents need not, however, provide medical care that has no feasible benefits, or that has more risks than benefits.[73] Moreover, parents who choose to follow one of two acceptable medical treatments have not neglected their child.[74] Thus, traditional neglect standards have the flexibility to allow some nontreatment decisions, even if they lack the precision to tell us which ones.

Employing general neglect standards as a vehicle for nontreatment decisions has distinct advantages over legislation specifically addressed to nontreatment decisions. Not only does it allow individual decisions about each particular case, but it puts the decisions in a larger social context. Moreover, medical neglect questions do not often come before the courts,[75] a situation which can leave room for a nonlegal resolution of the problem. Unless the parties request a declaratory judgment, a medical neglect case comes to the court after someone involved in the decision has contacted the child protective service agency and after that agency decides to take action. If the system is working well, only the most difficult or egregious case will go to court. Even then, the case is unlikely to have the precedential effect of a published opinion because of the confidential nature of most judicial proceedings.

Such an approach, which downplays the importance of a legal resolution to this problem, can give our society room to resolve the problem without the constant fear of, and concern for, the law that can retard the building of a moral consensus and skew the decisions that are made. We need research on current practices, universal reporting of nontreatment decisions, education of medical and legal personnel as well as the general public, and continued discussion of the complexities, nuances, and changing nature of this dilemma.[76] Above all, we need a coherent and consistent language for discussion. Each of these steps must be undertaken and resolved before coherent legislation will appear. Attempts to resolve the problem through stopgap legislation and unnecessary litigation merely undermine this process. Decisions are forced underground so that research and reporting are hampered, and the shrill rhetoric increases so that any semblance of consistent language and coherent discussion disappears.

At some level, the legal system is necessary. It need not always be the first line of defense, however. In this era of legislation and litigation, we occasionally must pause and realize that the legal system cannot resolve every problem. Moreover, when we turn our focus to legal solutions, we may lose the opportunity to resolve the problems in nonlegal ways.

Considering the confusion and inconsistency surrounding the legal system's attempts to determine the legality of nontreatment decisions for premature and severely disabled newborns, demands for legislation to clarify the situation are not surprising. Those who make these demands, however, have not fully examined whether their solutions would improve the situation. In today's environment, legal solutions add to the confusion and inconsistency.

The infant nontreatment problem defies definition and categorization. Nothing close to a moral consensus exists as to what is the best solution on an ethical, much less a legal, basis. Substantive standards determining when and under what conditions parents and physicians should have the discretion to make nontreatment decisions are either too strict to handle complex cases or too ambiguous to provide any clarification. Procedural standards merely beg these substantive questions. Few, if any, of the concepts needed to enact legislation are capable of definition, and no one can agree on appropriate remedies, even if the legislation appears satisfactory. These difficulties with a legislative solution point to the futility and wasted resources of drafting legislation to "solve" this dilemma.

Judicial resolution of nontreatment cases still should be available for difficult or egregious cases. Inconsistency and confusion will continue to exist, however, because of the lack of both a moral consensus and a satisfactory standard. We must learn to live with uncertainty in our legal system just as we have learned to live with uncertainty in medicine. Both law and medicine have their limitations. Despite our discomfort with this unsettled state of affairs, we cannot legislate miracles.

NOTES

1. *In re* Guardianship of Barry, 445 So. 2d 365 (Fla. Dist. Ct. Appl. 1984); *In re* L.H.R., 321 S.E.2d 716 (Ga. 1984); *In re* Infant Doe, No. GU 8204-004A (Ind. Cir. Ct. Apr. 12, 1982), *reprinted in* U.S. Comm'n on Civil Rights, Medical Discrimination Against Children with Disabilities 389 (1989) (hereinafter U.S. Civil Rights Comm'n Report), *appeal denied sub nom.* State *ex rel.* Infant Doe v. Baker, No. 482S140 (Ind. Sup. Ct. May 28, 1982), *cert. denied*, 464 U.S. 961 (1983); *In re* P.V.W., 424 So. 2d 1015 (La. 1982); Maine Medical Ctr. v. Houle, No. 74-145 (Super. Ct. Me. Feb. 14, 1974), *reprinted in*2 Issues L. & Med. 237 (1986) (ordering treatment for infant born with multiple defects and a blockage of the esophagus); *In re* Steinhaus, No. J-86-92 (Minn. Juv. Ct. Sept. 11, 1986), *reprinted in* U.S. Civil Rights Comm'n Report, *supra*, at 493, *modified*, *In re* Steinhaus, No. J-86-92 (Minn. Juv. Ct. Oct. 13, 1986), *reprinted in* U.S. Civil Rights Comm'n Report, *supra*, at 511; Weber v. Stony Brook Hosp., 467 N.Y.S.2d 685 (N.Y. App. Div.) (permitting parents to choose conservative treatment for infant with spina bifida, microcephaly, and hydrocephalus), *aff'd*, 456 N.E.2d 1186 (N.Y.) (per curiam), *cert. denied*, 464 U.S. 1026 (1983); *In re* Cicero, 421 N.Y.S.2d 965 (N.Y. Sup. Ct. 1979).
2. Child Abuse Amendments of 1984, 42 U.S.C. §§ 5101–5106, 5111–5113, 5115, 10401–10412 (1988).
3. *See, e.g.*, Ariz. Rev. Stat. Ann. § 36-2281 (1986); Ind. Code § 31-6-4-3(7)(f) (Burns Supp. 1991); R.I. Gen. Laws § 40-11-3 (1990); 17 Minn. Stat. Ann. § 260.015 subd. 2a(5) (West Supp. 1992); Mont. Code Ann. § 41-3-102(5)(1991). Because the states are not required to follow the Child Abuse Amendments, individual states' reactions to this problem remain important, despite federal legislation.
4. 45 C.F.R. § 84.55 (1991); 45 C.F.R. § 1340 (1990). In Bowen v. American Hosp Ass'n, 476 U.S. 610 (1986), the Supreme Court enjoined enforcement of subsections (b)–(e) of 45 C.F.R. § 84.55 after concluding that they exceeded the agency's statutory authority.
5. *See, e.g.*, R. F. Weir, Selectuve Nontreatment of Handicapped Newborns: Moral Dilemmas in Neonatal Medicine 112 (1984); T. S. Ellis, III, *Letting defective babies die: who decides?* 7 Am JL Med 393 (1982); Nancy K. Rhoden, *Treatment dilemmas for imperiled newborns: why quality of life counts*, 58 S Cal L Rev 1283 (1985); John A. Robertson, *Involuntary euthanasia of defective newborns: a legal analysis*, 27 Stan L Rev; Steven R. Smith, *Disabled newborns and the federal child abuse amendments: tenuous protection*, 37 Hastings LJ 765: 819–21 (1986); *Developments in the Law – Medical Technology and the Law*, 103 Harv L Rev 1519, 1584–1614 (1990); Elizabeth S. MacMillan, Note, *Birth-Defective Infants: A Standard for Nontreatment Decisions*, 30 Stan L Rev (1978).
6. Some would say that the Child Abuse Amendments of 1984, 42 USC §§ 5101–5106, 5111–5113, 5115, 10401–10412, are already written in stone. They are more of a moral directive than an enforceable statute, however. The amendments do not declare nontreatment decisions illegal. They merely require states to have procedures for dealing with medical neglect in order to receive some federal funding. 42 USC § 5106a(b).
7. This position contradicts, in part, another article I have written about this topic. In MacMillan, *supra* note 5, I pointed out the flexibility of traditional homicide and medical neglect laws, arguing that using these laws, nontreatment decisions could be legal in some circumstances. Because of the uncertainty of these laws, I proposed legislation that would permit nontreatment decisions when the treatment was medically infeasible, i.e., when the infant would die, even with the treatment, within six months to a year or when the infant was irreversibly comatose. Several years later, the Child Abuse Amendments of 1984 adopted a similar proposal. These amendments and my personal experiences have convinced me that this proposal did not answer all the questions. This realization has led me to appreciate anew the flexibility of the medical neglect laws, and to accept that legal uncertainty is a fact of life in this area. Thus, my thinking has come full circle in the last 14 years.
8. *See, e.g.*, Maine Medical Ctr. v. Houle, No. 74-145 (Super. Ct. Me. Feb. 14, 1974), *reprinted in* 2 Issues L Med 237.

9. *See, e.g., In re* Infant Doe, No. GU 8204-004A ((Ind. Cir. Ct. Apr. 12, 1982) *reprinted in* U.S. Civil Rights Comm'n Report, *supra* note 1, at 389 (1989), *appeal denied sub nom.* State *ex rel.* Infant Doe v. Baker, No. 482S140 (Ind. Sup. Ct. May 28, 1982), *cert. denied*, 464 U.S. 961 (1983).
10. *Id.*
11. 45 C.F.R. § 84 (1991) (interpreting § 504 of the Rehabilitation Act of 1973, 29 U.S.C. § 794 (1988).
12. The Supreme Court enjoined enforcement of 45 C.F.R. § 84.55(b)–(e) in Bowen v. American Hosp. Ass'n, 476 U.S. 610 (1986).
13. 42 U.S.C. §§ 5101–5106, 5111–5113, 5515, 10401–10412 (1988).
14. 42 U.S.C. § 5106g(10) (1988); 45 C.F.R. § 1340.15(b)(2) (1991).
15. 42 U.S.C. § 5106c(a)–(e) (1988).
16. *See* Dixie Snow Huefner, *Severely Handicapped Infants with Life-Threatening Conditions: Federal Intrusions into the Decision Not to Treat*, 12 Am. J.L. & Med. 171 (1986); Stephen A. Newman, *Baby Doe, Congress and the States: Challenging the Federal Treatment Standard for Impaired Infants*, 15 Am. J.L. & Med. 1 (1989); Rhoden, *supra* note 5, at 1312–18; Smith, *supra* note 5; Developments in the Law, *supra* note 5, at 1591–93. *Cf.* Loretta M. Kopelman et al., *Neonatologists Judge the "Baby Doe" Regulations*, 318 New Eng. J. Med. 677 (1988) (reporting results of survey of members of American Academy of Pediatrics, 76 percent of whom believed HHS regulations were unnecessary).
17. See U.S. Civil Rights Comm'n Report, *supra* note 1, at 111–17, for a discussion of the way hospitals and state agencies have ignored the law. For evidence that state laws regulating infant nontreatment decisions are ignored, see Eric Feldman and Thomas H. Murray, *State Legislation and the Handicapped Newborn: A Moral and Political Dilemma*, 12 L. Med. & Health Care 156 (1984).
18. In this era of litigation and legislation, not publicizing a decision would be wise. Oklahoma Children's Memorial Hospital has found itself embroiled in a lawsuit, *see* Johnson v. Gross, 125 F.R.D. 169 (W.D. Okla. 1989) (denying plaintiffs' motion for class certification), because of an article in *Pediatrics* describing practices at that hospital, Richard H. Gross et al., *Early Management and Decision Making for the Treatment of Myelomeningocele*, 72 Pediatrics 450 (1983). The case is discussed in U.S. Civil Rights Comm'n Report, *supra* note 1, at 19–20, and in Martin H. Gerry, *The Civil Rights of Handicapped Infants: An Oklahoma "Experiment,"* 1 Issues L. 7 Med. 15, 29–66 (1985).
19. *See* Raymond S. Duff & A.G.M. Campbell, *Moral and Ethical Dilemmas in the Special Care Nursery*, 289 New Eng. J. Med. 890 (1973); Gross, *supra* note 18.
20. *See* David Todres et al. *Life-Saving Therapy for Newborns: A Questionnaire Survey in the State and Massachusetts*, 81 Pediatrics 643 (1988); Siperstein et al., *Medical Decisions and Prognostications of Pediatricians for Infants with Meningeomyelocele*, 113 Pediatrics 835 (1988) *discussed in* U.S. Civil Rights Comm'n Report, *supra* note 1, at 104–5.
21. *See* U.S. Civil Rights Comm'n Report, *supra* note 1, at 213. This lack of statistics has practical ramifications. Bowen v. American Hosp. Ass'n, 476 U.S. 610 (1986), invalidated the restrictive provisions of 45 C.F.R. § 84.55, in part because the Department of Health and Human Services had no evidence that hospitals or physicians made these infant nontreatment decisions. *Id.* at 631.
22. *See* Hastings Center Research Project on the Care of Imperiled Newborns, *Imperiled Newborns*, Hastings Center Rep., Dec. 1987, at 5, 5 [hereinafter Hastings Center Project]; Joseph Goldstein, *Not for the Law to Approve or Disapprove – A Comment on Professor Mnookin's Paper*, 1984 Ariz. St. L.J. 685, 686 (1984).
23. *Compare* C. Everett Koop, *Life and Death and the Handicapped Newborn*, 5 Issues L. & Med. 101 (1989) (advocating strict regulation of these decisions) *with* Joseph Goldstein et al., Before the Best Interests of the Child 91–95, 194 (1979) *and* Joseph Goldstein, *Medical Care for the Child at Risk: On State Supervision of Parental Autonomy*, 86 Yale L.J. 645, 651–61 (1977) (advocating wide discretion for the parents). *See also* Weir, *supra* note 5,

for a description of the various beliefs in law, medicine, and philosophy. The polls cited *supra* note 21 give an indication of the varying beliefs among medical personnel, and Newman, *supra* note 5, at 7–8, shows that the general public has diverse views.

24. For a history of abortion laws see Roe v. Wade, 410 U.S. 113, 129–47 (1973). *See also Survey of Abortion Law*, 1980 Ariz. St. L.J. 67, 73–125 [hereinafter *Survey*],
25. *Survey, supra* note 24, at 109–11.
26. *Roe*, 410 U.S. at 164–65, held that a woman's constitutional right to privacy gave her the right to choose abortion during the first two trimesters of pregnancy.
27. *See, e.g.*, Webster v. Reproductive Health Servs., 492 U.S. 490 (1989); Thornburgh v. American College of Obstetricians & Gynecologists, 476 U.S. 747 (1986); City of Akron v. Akron Ctr. for Reprod. Health, 462 U.S. 416 (1983). At the time of writing this article, the Supreme Court had granted certiorari in the case of Planned Parenthood of Southeastern Pa. v. Casey, 947 F.2d 682 (3d Cir. 1991). *See* 60 U.S.L.W. 3498 (U.S. Jan. 21, 1992). Whatever its conclusion, the abortion debate will not be resolved.
28. Cases dealing with right-to-die issues include Cruzan v. Director, Mo. Dep't of Health, 110 S. Ct. 2841 (1990); Bouvia v. Superior Ct., 225 Cal. Rptr. 297 (Cal. App. 1986); Brophy v. New England Sinai Hosp., 497 N.E.2d 626 (Mass. 1986); Superintendent of Belchertown State Sch. v. Saikewicz, 370 N.E.2d 417 (Mass. 1977); *In re* Conroy, 486 A.2d 1209 (N.J. 1985); *In re*Quinlan, 355 A.2d 647 (N.J.), *cert. denied*, 429 U.S. 922 (1976).
29. *See Roe*, 410 U.S. at 157. Some philosophers have questioned whether a newborn is a person. *See, e.g.*, Helga Kuhse & Peter Singer, Should the Baby Live? 118–29 (1985); Tooley, *Abortion and Infanticide*, 2 Phil. & Pub. Aff. 37 (1972), but the legal community accepts the assumption that an infant is a "person," no matter how premature or disabled. *See* authorities cited in notes 5 and 16, *supra.*
30. Arguably, the nontreatment issue is also analogous to the civil rights issue, because infants face discrimination based on their handicap. The original federal regulations concerning this problem, 45 C.F.R. § 84.55 (1991), were based on this analogy. This paper argues, however, that this analogy works only for a small minority of the cases. *See* notes 55–60 *infra* and accompanying text.
31. "Ethical rules prematurely imposed upon an unready public are often ignored or resisted and prove difficult to implement." Huefner, *supra* note 16, at 203.
32. *See Developments in the Law, supra* note 5, at 1592; David K. Stevenson et al., *The 'Baby Doe' Rule*, 255 JAMA 1909 (1986).
33. 42 U.S.C. § 5106c(a)–(e) (1988). The concepts of "dying," "irreversibly comatose," and "futile" could be categorized as standards for making a decision because, as definitions, they are somewhat ambiguous. Nevertheless, the legislative intent was to draw a line, to determine which conditions could permit nontreatment decisions, rather than to outline a decisionmaking process.

    Most legislation is a combination of the approaches described in this paper. For example, the Child Abuse Amendments of 1984 include the line-drawing standards of "dying," "chronically and irreversibly comatose," and "futile," the general decisionmaking standard of "the physician's reasonable medical judgment," and the procedural mechanism of hospital infant care review committees. *Id.* Separating the approaches for purposes of this paper helps to clarify the strengths and weaknesses of each approach.
34. For examples of proposals that attempt to draw such lines, see Ellis, *supra* note 5, at 418–19; Robertson, *supra* note 5, at 267; Macmillan, *supra* note 5, at 624.
35. Paul Ramsey, Ethics at the Edges of Life 264 (1978) (making the suggestion hypothetically only); Jean B. Walker et al., *Cost-Benefit Analysis of Neonatal Intensive Care for Infants Weighing Less than 1,000 Grams at Birth,* 74 Pediatrics 20 (1984).
36. J. Lorber, *Selective Nontreatment of Myelomeningocele: To Treat or Not to Treat,* 53 Pediatrics 307 (1974).
37. For descriptions of the advantages of this type of legislation, see Ramsey, *supra* note 35, at 204; WEIR, *supra* note 5, at 210–11; MacMillan, *supra* note 5, at 625–27.
38. Newman, *supra* note 16, at 43–44, citing March of Dimes Birth Defects Found., Annual

Report 4 (1986). For a detailed description of some of these conditions and anomalies, see Weir, *supra* note 5, at 38–49.

39. Jeff Lyon, Playing God in the Nursery 80–109 (1985); Weir, *supra* note 5, at 39–40.
40. Hastings Center Project, *supra* note 22, at 11; President's Comm'n for the Study of Ethical Problems in Medicine & Biomedical & Behavioral Research, Deciding to Forego Life-Sustaining Treatment 220 (1983) [hereinafter President's Comm'n Report]; Weir, *supra* note 5, at 225–34. *See also* U.S. Civil Rights Comm'n Report, *supra* note 1, at 36–40, for anecdotal evidence of incorrect diagnoses and prognoses.
41. President's Comm'n Report, *supra* note 40, at 200; Newman, *supra* note 16, at 7.
42. President's Comm'n Report, *supra* note 40, at 36.
43. For example, in the Baby Jane Doe case, Weber v. Stony Brook Hosp., 467 N.Y.S.2d 685 (N.Y. App. Div.) *aff'd*, 456 N.E.2d 1186 (N.Y.) (per curiam), *cert. denied*, 464 U.S. 1026 (1983), the infant contracted meningitis on the second day of the proceedings in the state supreme court, a development which changed the medical options for the infant. Daniel M. Fox, *Introduction to the Baby Jane Papers*, 11 J. Health Pol. Pol'y & L. 195, 196 (1986).
44. "[I]n my mind the best rejoinder to those who have trouble with line-drawing is the comment of John Lowenstein of the Baltimore Orioles: 'They should move first base back a step to eliminate all the close plays.'" Frederick Schauer, *Slippery Slopes*, 99 Harv. L. Rev. 361, 380 n.52 (1985).
45. Before the § 504 regulations and Child Abuse Amendments, most of the legal literature asked what the best response to this difficult problem should be. *See, e.g.*, Ellis, *supra* note 5; Robert H. Mnookin, *Two Puzzles*, 1984 Ariz. St. L.J. 667 (1984); Robertson, *supra* note 5; MacMillan, *supra* note 5. After that point, much of the literature has been in response to the legislation, so that the legislation seems to be framing the debate. *See, e.g.*, Huefner, *supra* note 16; Newman, *supra* note 16; Smith, *supra* note 5.
46. These difficulties were manifested in the only case to discuss the Child Abuse Amendments to date, *In re* Steinhaus, No. J-86-92 (Minn. Juv. Ct. Sept. 11, 1986), *reprinted in* U.S. Civil Rights Comm'n Report, *supra* note 1, at 493. In *Steinhaus* the child was diagnosed as being in a persistent vegetative state. The mother, the treating physician, and the hospital ethics committee agreed that aggressive medical care should be discontinued. Originally, the judge ordered treatment because "persistent vegetative state" was not the same as "irreversibly comatose," the category described in the Child Abuse Amendments. One month later the judge changed this order, after further testimony that the child was "irreversibly comatose." *In re* Steinhaus, No. J-86-92 (Minn. Juv. Ct. Oct. 13, 1986), *reprinted in* U.S. Civil Rights Comm'n Report, *supra* note 1, at 511. There was no indication that the child's condition had changed.
47. *See* Goldstein et al., *supra* note 23; Goldstein, *supra* note 23, at 651; McCormick, *To Save or Let Die: The Dilemma of Modern Medicine*, 229 J.A.M.A. 1972 (1974); Rhoden, *supra* note 5, at 1322–23. For criticisms of this standard, see U.S. Civil Rights Commission Report, *supra* note 1, at 46–47; MacMillan, *supra* note 5, at 620–23.
48. *See* Weber v. Stony Brook Hosp., 467 N.Y.S.2d 685 (N.Y. App. Div.) *aff d*, 456 N.E.2d 1186 (N.Y.) (per curiam), *cert. denied*, 464 U.S. 1026 (1983); Hastings Center Project, *supra* note 23, at 15; President's Comm'n Report, *supra* note 43, at 217; WEIR, *supra* note 5, at 194; Norman Fost, *Baby Doe Problems and Solutions*, 1984 ARIZ. ST. L.J. 637, 642; MacMillan, *supra* note 5, at 606–9. A variation on the "best interests" standards is the "benefit/burden" standard, which permits nontreatment decisions when the burden of the treatment outweights the benefits of the treatment. *See* Newman, *supra* note 16, at 39.
49. Gostin, *Editor's Introduction: Family Practice and Persistent Vegetative State*, 17 L. Med. & Health Care 295 (1989). The privacy standard usually appears in court cases, because the concept has been developed in constitutional cases. *See, e.g., In re* L.H.R., 321 S.E.2d 716 (Ga. 1984); *In re* P.V.W., 424 So. 2d 1015 (La. 1982); *In re* Quinlan, 355 A.2d 647 (N.J.), *cert. denied*, 429 U.S. 922 (1976). The President's Commission Report, while not using the word "privacy," in fact endorsed such an approach, for parents are to make the

decision in circumstances under which there is no true agreement. President's Comm'n Report, *supra* note 43, at 220–23.

50. Newman, *supra* note 16, at 45.
51. Carl E. Schneider, *Rights Discourse and Neonatal Euthanasia*, 76 CAL. L. REV. 151, 155 (1988).
52. *See* Goldstein et al., *supra* note 23, at 194; President's Comm'n Report, *supra* note 40, at 218, 223; Goldstein, *supra* note 23, at 651–52.
53. Both sets of regulations proposed by the Department of Health and Human Resources recommend that hospitals adopt ethics committees called "infant care review committees." *See 45 C.F.R. § 84.55 (1991);* id. § 1340 (1990). *See also* President's Comm'n Report, *supra* note 43, at 225–28.
54. See *Developments in the Law, supra* note 5, at 161; MacMillan, *supra* note 5, at 630–32.
55. Fost, *supra* note 48, at 639–40; Albert R. Jonsen, *Traditional Distinctions for Making Ethical Judgments*, 1984 Ariz. St. L.J. 661, 664.
56. Cruzan v. Director, Mo. Dep't of Health, 110 S. Ct. 2841 (1990); Hastings Center Project, *supra* note 22, at 22; Rhoden, supra note 5, at 1328.
57. The court in *In re* Steinhaus, No. J-86-92 (Minn. Juv. Ct. Sept. 11, 1986), *reprinted in* U.S. Civil Rights Comm'n Report, *supra* note 1, at 493, *modified*, *In re* Steinhaus, No. J-86-92 (Minn. Juv. Ct. Oct. 13, 1986), *reprinted in* U.S. Civil Rights Comm'n Report, *supra* note 1, at 511, faced the ambiguity in this word, when it had to determine whether "irreversibly comatose" encompassed the "persistent vegetative state." *See* note 46 *supra*.
58. 45 C.F.R. § 84.55 (1988).
59. Bowen v. American Hosp. Ass'n, 476 U.S. 610 (1986).
60. *See* United States v. University Hosp., 729 F.2d 144, 156–57 (2nd Cir. 1984); Rhoden, *supra* note 5, at 1300.
61. Ikuta, *Dying at the Right Time: A Critical Legal Studies Approach to Timing of Death Issues*, 5 Issues L. & Med. 3, 60 (1989).
62. 42 U.S.C. § 5106c(a)–(e) (1988).
63. Goldstein et al., *supra* note 23, at 194; Developments in the Law, *supra* note 5, at 1613.
64. *See id.* at 94–95. "Put somewhat more starkly, how can parents in such situations be judged to give the wrong answer when there is no way of knowing the right answer?"
65. John D. Lantos et al., *The Linares Affair*, 17 L. Med. & Health Care 308, 314 (1989); Phyllis Theroux, *Parents Face Agonizing Decision: Should Surgery Be Performed on Brain-Damaged Boy?, L.A. Times, Dec. 16, 1988, at 8.*
66. See, e.g., Dr. C. Everett Koop, *quoted in* President's Comm'n Report, *supra* note 40, at 219 n.81 ("I personally foresee no medical solution to a cephalodymus or an anencephalic child.")
67. Goldstein et al., *supra* note 23, at 96; Goldstein, *supra* note 23, at 651–52.
68. Karl Llewellyn, The Bramble Bush 42 (1960).
69. *See, e.g., In re* Hofbauer, 393 N.E.2D 1009 (N.Y. 1979); Weber v. Stony Brook Hosp., 467 N.Y.S.2d 685 (N.Y. App. Div.), *aff'd*, 456 N.E.2d 1186 (N.Y.) (per curiam), *cert denied*, 464 U.S. 1026 (1983); *In re* Cicero, 421 N.Y.S.2d 965 (N.Y. Sup. Ct. 1979).
70. Robert A. Burt, *Authorizing Death for Anomalous Newborns, in* Genetics and the Law 435 (Aubrey Milunsky & George J. Annas eds., 1976); Mnookin, *supra* note 45, at 669–71. Homicide laws are rarely, if ever, invoked, however. President's Comm'n Report, *supra* note 43, at 35. This author has maintained elsewhere that homicide laws, like child neglect laws, do not always outlaw these decisions. Like medical neglect laws, homicide laws have the flexibility to deal with this difficult situation. *See* MacMillan, *supra* note 5, at 614–18.
71. For a listing of state child neglect laws, see statutes cited *supra* note 3.
72. Custody of a Minor, 393 N.E.2d 836, 845 (Mass. 1979); Raleigh Fitkin-Paul Morgan Mem. Hosp. v. Anderson, 201 A.2d 537, 538 (N.J.) *cert. denied*, 377 U.S. 985 (1964).
73. *In re* Tuttendario, 21 Pa. D. 561 (1912); *In re* Hudson, 126 P.2d 765 (Wash. 1942).

74. Weber v. Stony Brook Hosp., 467 N.Y.S.2d 685 (N.Y. App. Div.), *aff'd*, 456 N.E.2d 1186 (N.Y.) (per curiam), *cert. denied*, 464 U.S. 1026 (1983).
75. The cases listed in note 1, *supra*, constitute an exhaustive list of the reported and reprinted cases dealing with this issue. A few other unreported cases have been described in the literature describing the infant nontreatment issues. *See* President's Comm'n Report, *supra* note 40, at 216 n.77; Lyon, *supra* note 39, at 190–92; Joyce Price, *Doctors Cleared in Spina Bifida Babies' Deaths*, Wash. Times, Feb. 6, 1990, at 45. Thus, despite the attention this infant nontreatment issue has received, it rarely reaches the courts.
76. Weir, *supra* note 5, at 139, suggests we take an ethical approach to this problem. The proposals from the Hastings Center, *supra* note 22, at 6, are also designed to foster "a useful and productive dialogue about the policies that can best serve the interests of infants with serious medical problems."

Index